Human Aging and
Chronic Disease

The Jones and Bartlett Series in Health Sciences

Biological Bases of Human Aging and Disease
Kart/Metress/Metress

Aquatics
Sova

Aquatic Student's Handbook
Sova

Basic Law for the Allied Health Professions
Cowdrey

Basic Nutrition: Self-Instructional Modules, Second Edition
Stanfield

The Biology of AIDS, Third Edition
Fan/Conner/Villarreal

The Birth Control Book
Belcastro

Children's Nutrition
Lifshitz

Contemporary Health Issues
Banister/Allen/Fadl/Bhakthan/Howard

Drugs and Society, Third Edition
Witters/Venturelli/Hanson

Essential Medical Terminology
Stanfield

First Aid and CPR
National Safety Council

First Aid and Emergency Care Workbook
Thygerson

Fitness and Health: Life-Style Strategies
Thygerson

Golf: Your Turn for Success
Fisher/Geertsen

Health and Wellness, Fourth Edition
Edlin/Golanty

Healthy People 2000
U.S. Department of Health and Human Services

Healthy People 2000-- Summary Report
U.S. Department of Health and Human Services

Human Anatomy and Physiology Coloring Workbook and Study Guide
Anderson

Interviewing and Helping Skills for Health Professionals
Cormier/Cormier/Weisser

Introduction to Human Disease, Third Edition
Crowley

Introduction to Human Immunology
Huffer/Kanapa/Stevenson

Introduction to the Health Professions
Stanfield

Medical Terminology (with Self-Instructional Modules)
Stanfield/Hui

The Nation's Health, Third Edition
Lee/Estes

Personal Health Choices
Smith/Smith

Principles and Issues in Nutrition
Hui

Sexuality Today
Nass/Fisher

Step Aerobics
Brown

Teaching Elementary Health Science, Third Edition
Bender/Sorochan

Weight Management the Fitness Way
Dusek

Weight Training for Strength and Fitness
Silvester

Writing a Successful Grant Application
Reif-Lehrer

Human Aging and Chronic Disease

Cary S. Kart, Ph.D.
Eileen K. Metress, Ph.D.
Seamus P. Metress, Ph.D.

University of Toledo

Jones and Bartlett Publishers

Boston   *London*

Editorial, Sales, and Customer Service Offices
Jones and Bartlett Publishers
20 Park Plaza
Boston, MA 02116

Jones and Bartlett Publishers International
P.O. Box 1498
London W6 7RS
England

Library of Congress Cataloging-in-Publication Data
Kart, Cary S. (Cary Steven), 1946–
    Human aging and chronic disease / Cary S. Kart, Eileen K. Metress,
Seamus P. Metress.
       p.   cm.
    Includes bibliographical references and indexes.
    ISBN 0-86720-315-3
    1. Aging. 2. Aged – Diseases. 3. Chronic diseases. I. Metress,
Eileen K. II. Metress, Seamus P. III. Title.
    [DNLM: 1. Aging. 2. Chronic Disease – in old age. WT 104 K18h]
QP86.K37 1992
612.6'7 – dc20
DNLM/DLC
for Library of Congress   91-46510
                                           CIP

ISBN 0-86720-315-3

Figures 5.1, 5.4, 9.1, 9.2, 9.3, 9.4, 9.5, 13.1, and 13.2 originally appeared in *Aging, Health, and Society* by Cary S. Kart, Eileen K. Metress, and Seamus P. Metress, copyright © 1988 Boston: Jones and Bartlett Publishers. Figures 6.1, 6.2, 7.1, 7.2, 7.3, 12.1, 12.2, 12.3, 12.4, and 12.5, which also appeared in *Aging, Health, and Society*, were adapted from *Basic Human Anatomy and Physiology* by P. Anderson, copyright © 1986 Boston: Jones and Bartlett Publishers.

Printed in the United States of America
96 95 94 93 92   10 9 8 7 6 5 4 3 2 1

Contents

Preface

Surveys of gerontology programs in institutions of higher education in the United States have identified four courses as most commonly offered. These include *Biology and Physiology of Aging, Psychology of Aging, Social Gerontology,* and *Sociology of Aging.* Some have suggested that these make up a core curriculum in gerontology. Whether this is so is not really at issue here. In our view, students of gerontology based in the social and behavioral sciences need to understand the biological and physiological parameters of aging. Absent this information, their speculations about the possibilities and the limits of aging and older people may be based on stereotype and misinformation about human aging and disease. On the other hand, students of gerontology based in the natural and medical sciences run the risk of "biologizing" aging and older people – that is, of defining aging as a biological and/or medical problem only and neglecting the effects of cultural, environmental, psychological, and social factors on the aging process and older people.

This book, *Human Aging and Chronic Disease,* is aimed at both these student populations. The book provides an introduction to the biology of human aging and chronic disease for undergraduates and beginning graduate students. Material is presented in a context that highlights the additional cultural, environmental, psychological, and social factors that have an impact on aging and older adults. Thus, this is a book on the biology of aging that does not "biologize" older people.

The book is presented in three parts. Part I introduces students to biology and the aging process. Four chapters are included: Chapter 1 discusses aging broadly in the context of issues of longevity and prolongevity; Chapter 2 offers current theoretical perspectives on the biology of aging; Chapter 3 presents population dynamics and demographic characteristics of the aged; and Chapter 4 describes cognitive aspects of aging and disease.

Part II surveys the biomedical changes associated with the various body systems as they age. Included are chapters on skin, the skeletal system, age-associated changes in vision and hearing, the nervous system, the gastrointestinal system, the cardiopulmonary system, and the urinary and endocrine systems. In addition, material on chronic disease and its relationships to human aging is presented where relevant in each chapter. Part II also contains chapters on nutrition and aging, and on the biocultural bases of geriatric nutrition.

Part III presents individual chapters on biosocial aspects of aging, including sexuality and aging; drugs and aging; and exercise, health, and aging. An epilogue on the dangers of biologizing aging concludes the main body of the text. A glossary and subject index are also provided.

Acknowledgments

Special acknowledgments go to our contributing authors, Patricia H. Andrews, Ph.D. (University of Iowa Medical School), John C. Cavanaugh, Ph.D. (Bowling Green State University), Gere B. Fulton, Ph.D., J.D. (University of Toledo), and Lisa C. McGuire, M.A. (Bowling Green State University). Their efforts strengthened the book and allowed us to include additional important material on the biocultural, biomedical, biopsychological, and biosocial aspects of aging. Special thanks also to Jim Keating, who made it easy to sign on with Jones and Bartlett, and Joe Burns, who ushered us through the editorial process. Judy Ashkenaz, of Total Concept Associates in Brattleboro, Vermont, has edited copy with a sensitive eye and hand, and supervised the production process. She deserves our thanks, as well.

The three of us have been working together at the University of Toledo on issues of health and aging since the fall quarter of 1974. With this text, our shared work has been published in three different decades. Although this work has been well received, we take greater pride in thinking about how many students we have had contact with over these years through this work. There is no reason, biological or otherwise, that this should not continue. In matters of the relationship between aging and scholarly productivity, we surmise that such productivity must continue or even increase with age!

C.S.K., E.K.M., and S.P.M.

Contributing Authors

Patricia H. Andrews, Ph.D.
University of Iowa Medical School

John C. Cavanaugh, Ph.D.
Bowling Green State University

Gere B. Fulton, Ph.D., J.D.
University of Toledo

Lisa C. McGuire, M.A.
Bowling Green State University

PART **I**

Biology and the Aging Process

1

CHAPTER **1**

Longevity and Prolongevity

Nestled in the mountains of Guangxi province in China, in the county of Bama, seems to be a real-life Shangri-La. With clean air and water, sufficient food, and cool temperatures, few ever leave the region and many report experiencing long life. According to a recent article in the *Wall Street Journal* (Ignatius, 1990), Chinese demographers confirm the fact that the people of Bama, though poor in the material trappings of contemporary life, show the highest concentration of hundred-year-olds on the earth. Better yet, "most have clear minds and are in good health" (p. 1). Ninety-year-olds are described as having the blood pressure of 40-year-olds, and 80-year-olds work in the fields planting and harvesting maize and rice.

Luo Mahzeng is said to be the oldest living inhabitant of the area at 130 years of age. Presumably born in the year Abe Lincoln was elected president of the United States and at a time when China was engaged in opium wars with England and France, Ms. Luo still cooks and does housework. While we can be skeptical about the age claims, local officials are not. They cite old birth records and census data as proof of the longevity of China's Bamans.

County elders offer diverse opinions about their longevity; some argue that what advice is given really reflects the entrepreneurial spirit of the people and is really for the export market. For example, some locals espouse a diet rich in wild grass, snakes, and lizards, as well as the bovine creature they call the Wild Yellow Cow of the Mountains (Ignatius, 1990). The Bama Food Drink Factory, a local brewery, is currently marketing a new wine with "life-prolonging properties." Based on tips provided by county elders, the wine, called the "Spirit of Longevity," is said to contain extract of red-spotted lizards, three kinds of poisonous snake, dog and deer penises, and a secret blend of wild grasses and herbs. The wine is said to "taste like death" and be "strong, smelly and bitter" (p. 11). According to Ignatius (1990, p. 11), "It has quite a kick, and Bamans can't get enough of it."

The desirability of a long life and of lengthening that life has been a prevalent theme throughout history (Gruman, 1966). The Bamans exemplify at least two of three different themes developed to represent the quest for the prolongation of life. The

3

antediluvian theme involves the belief that in the past people lived much longer, best exemplified in the Book of Genesis, which records the life spans of ten Hebrew patriarchs who lived before the Flood. Noah lived for 950 years, Methuselah for 969 years, Adam for 930 years, and so on. The *hyperborean* theme develops the idea that in some remote part of the world there are people who enjoy a remarkably long life. According to the traditions of ancient Greece, a people live *hyper Boreas* (beyond the north wind): "Their hair crowned with golden bay-leaves they hold glad revelry; and neither sickness nor baneful eld mingleth among the chosen people; but, aloof from toil and conflict, they dwell afar" (Pindar, in Gruman, 1966, p. 22).

Finally, the *fountain* theme is based on the idea that there is some unusual substance that has the property of greatly increasing the length of life (Gruman, 1966). The search for the "fountain of youth" in 1513 by Juan Ponce de Leon (who accidentally discovered Florida instead) is a good example of this rejuvenation theme. According to the earliest account of Ponce de Leon's adventure, published by a Spanish official in the New World in 1535, the explorer was "seeking that fountain of Biminie that the Indians had given to be understood would renovate or resprout and refresh the age and forces of he who drank or bathed himself in that fountain" (Lawson, 1946, in Gruman, 1966).

These themes remain current. Our fascination with reportedly long-lived peoples like the Abkhasians of the Georgian Republic of Russia and the Bamans of Guangxi province of China reflects a modern-day hyperborean theme. Similarly, any student of American billboard and television advertising will recognize the fountain theme. Skin creams, hair colorings, body soaps, foods, vitamins, and even Chinese wine are all depicted as unusual substances that we may use to remain eternally young.

The persistence of these themes suggests that throughout the history of the study of aging and up to the present it has been difficult to distinguish between myth and history, between magic and science. The development of the systematic study of aging can be seen in this light. It is an attempt to make clear distinctions between myth and history, magic and science.

The physician Alexander Leaf (1973) quotes Frederic Verzar, the Swiss gerontologist, as saying: "Old age is not an illness. It is a continuation of life with decreasing capacities for adaptation." Some students of aging would disagree. It has been a popular view that if old age is not an illness in and of itself, there is at least a strong relationship between biological aging and pathology. This view posits that biological deterioration creates a state of susceptibility to disease, and susceptibility to particular diseases leads to death.

One way out of this disagreement may be to distinguish between biological and pathological aging (Blumenthal, 1968). It may be difficult to say at what point in life a person is old, but it is clear that everyone becomes so. Everyone ages. Genetic and other prenatal influences set the stage for the aging sequence and factors in the postnatal environment (demographic, economic, psychological, and social) act to modify this sequence (Sobel, 1966; Wilson, 1974). The changes that accompany aging occur in different people at different chronological ages and progress at different rates. Changes in physical appearance are the most easily recognized; it is also well known that some physical capabilities diminish. These changes may be placed in the category of biological aging.

Disease is another matter. As individuals grow older, they are more likely to become afflicted with certain diseases—many of which prove fatal. Changes that occur as a result of disease processes may be categorized as pathological aging.

In this chapter we discuss recent progress in mortality and life expectancy among the elderly. Description of the results of biological aging—those important bodily changes that occur as age increases – are presented in Chapters 5 through 14. Current theories or explanations of biological aging are evaluated in Chapter 2. Disease processes related to pathological aging are also reserved for discussion in Chapters 5 through 14.

MORTALITY

Gerontologists use the term *senescence* to describe all postmaturational changes and the increasing vulnerability individuals face as a result of these changes. Senescence describes the group of effects that lead to a decreasing expectation of life with increasing age (Comfort, 1979). Strehler (1962) distinguishes senescence from other biological processes in four ways: (1) Its characteristics are universal; (2) the changes that constitute it come from within the individual; (3) the processes associated with senescence occur gradually; and (4) the changes that appear in senescence have a deleterious effect on the individual.

Is senescence a fundamental or inherent biological process? Comfort (1979) is doubtful. He believes that attempts to identify a single underlying property that explains all instances of senescent change are misplaced. Yet, there does appear to be some pattern to our increased vulnerability through the life course. Roughly speaking, it appears that the probability of dying doubles every eight years.

This phenomenon has been recognized since 1825 when Benjamin Gompertz observed that an exponential increase in death rate occurred between the ages of 10 and 60. After plotting age-specific death rates on a logarithmic scale and finding an increase that was nearly linear, Gompertz suggested that human mortality was governed by an equation with two terms. The first accounted for chance deaths that would occur at any age; the second, characteristic of the species, represented the exponential increase with time. These observa-tions, sometimes referred to as Gompertz's law, seem reasonably to describe mortality in many human societies (Fries and Crapo, 1981). However, while we can accept the principle that the probability of our dying increases with age, it is important to emphasize that the probabilities themselves differ for males and females, vary by race, and change through time.

During 1988 an estimated 2.2 million deaths occurred in the United States. The preliminary death rate for that year was 8.8 deaths per 1,000 population; the 1982 rate of 8.5 deaths per 1,000 population was the lowest annual rate ever recorded in this country. The majority of these deaths involved elderly people. About 1.5 million (or about 71 percent) of the deaths occurred among individuals who were 65 years of age of older.

The leading cause of death among the elderly is heart disease, which accounts for about 42 percent of all deaths in old age. Malignant neoplasms (cancer) account for another 21 percent of the deaths (23 percent for men, 18 percent for women); cerebrovascular diseases account for 9 percent of deaths among the elderly. Together, these three account for about 72 percent of all deaths of elderly people and over 50 percent of the deaths of those under 65 in the United States in 1988. Obviously, the high proportion of the deaths of elderly people due to these three causes is an expression of vulnerability to these afflictions which begins earlier in the life cycle.

Figure 1.1 shows the pattern of death rates for five leading causes of death among the elderly between 1950 and 1979. Death rates for the elderly have declined overall since 1950, although most of the decline has been since about 1970. The age-adjusted death rate for the population 65 years of age and over fell by 27 percent between 1950 and 1979, and the decline for females was twice as great as that for males. The death rate for elderly men was considerably higher than that of elderly women (almost 70 percent in 1975), though this

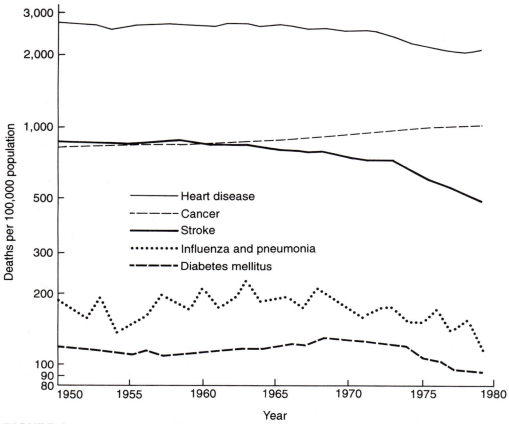

FIGURE 1.1 Age-adjusted death rates for persons 65 years of age and over, according to leading causes of death, United States, 1950–1979. (*Source:* National Center for Health Statistics; computed by the Division of Analysis from data compiled by the Division of Vital Statistics.)

Note: Causes of death are assigned according to the International List of Causes of Death. Because of the decennial revisions and changes in rules for cause-of-death selection, there may be some lack of comparability from one revision to the next. The beginning dates of the revisions are 1949, 1958, 1968, and 1979.

continues a long-term trend. The sex differential in death rates was 34 percent higher for elderly men in 1950; by 1986, elderly males aged 65 to 74 years had an overall death rate that was 77 percent above that for comparably aged females.

The death rates from heart disease have continued to decline between 1980 and 1986, although the pace of decline has been quicker for aged males than for aged females (12.6 percent versus 5.6 percent). The death rate for cancer, the second leading cause of death in 1979, has increased slowly over the years (13 percent in the 1950–1979 period). From 1980 to 1986, death rates from cancer for aged males have stayed about the same but have increased 8.3 percent for aged females. Sex differences are quite pronounced for cancer, especially lung cancer, for which male mortality is about four times greater than female mortality. However, since 1960, there have been large annual increases in lung cancer mortality for older women associated with cigarette smoking. The percentage change from 1960 to 1986 in mortality rates from lung cancer among women aged 65 to 74 is 480.2. This compares with a 22.1 percent increase in mortality rates from breast cancer for comparably aged women over the same time period. In 1986, for women aged 65 through 74 and for those aged 75 through 84, the death rate from lung cancer was higher than that from breast cancer (U.S. Bureau of the Census, 1990, Table 121).

Most elderly people die as a result of some long-standing chronic condition which is sometimes related to personal habits (e.g., smoking, drinking, poor eating habits) or environmental conditions (e.g., harsh work environments, air pollution) that go back many years. Prevention of illness and death from these conditions must begin before old age. Some deaths, such as those from accidents, have declined significantly. The death rate from accidents (and violence) for white males 65 years and over in 1986 was 28.4 percent lower than that in 1970; the comparable decline for aged white females during this period was 33.3 percent.

Sex Differentials in Mortality

As can be seen from Table 1.1, comparisons by race show that men have higher death rates than women in every age category. Some of this difference is almost certainly attributable to biological factors. For example, the larger proportion of males who die in infancy is apparently not explainable by any systematic variation in physical or social environmental factors. For most adults, however, it may be difficult to distinguish between biological

TABLE 1.1 Age-specific death rates, by race and sex, 1980

	Deaths per 1,000			
	White		Black	
Age	Male	Female	Male	Female
All ages	9.8	8.1	10.3	7.3
Age-adjusted	7.5	4.1	11.1	6.3
Under 1	12.3	9.6	25.9	21.2
1-4	0.7	0.5	1.1	0.8
5-9	0.3	0.2	0.5	0.3
10-14	0.4	0.2	0.5	0.3
15-19	1.4	0.5	1.4	0.5
20-24	1.9	0.6	2.9	0.9
25-29	1.7	0.6	3.7	1.3
30-34	1.7	0.7	4.6	1.7
35-39	2.1	1.1	5.9	2.5
40-44	3.2	1.7	8.1	4.1
45-49	5.2	2.8	12.0	6.3
50-54	8.7	4.5	17.6	9.1
55-59	13.8	7.0	24.6	13.1
60-64	21.4	10.8	33.8	18.6
65-69	33.1	16.4	44.8	25.4
70-74	50.2	25.9	60.5	37.6
75-79	74.7	41.9	80.9	52.4
80-84	112.7	72.4	115.5	80.3
85+	191.0	149.8	161.0	123.7

Source: National Center for Health Statistics, Advance Report of Final Mortality Statistics, 1980, *Monthly Vital Statistics Report,* vol. 32, no. 4 (1983), Tables 1 and 9.

and environmental contributors to death. Male-female differences in mortality may be due, in part, to sex differences in the use of physician services. Typically, women report using health services more frequently than men do. This may result in earlier and more effective treatment of their illnesses and may contribute to lower death rates relative to men (Marcus and Siegel, 1982). The childbearing experience of females and the overrepresentation of males in dangerous occupations are two additional factors that make it difficult to determine the relative effect on mortality of biological and environmental or sociocultural factors.

Francis Madigan (1957) attempted to differentiate between biological and environmental factors in mortality. His classic study compared the mortality experience of Catholic brothers and nuns who were members of teaching communities. Madigan argued that the life patterns of these two groups are quite similar, and that, over time, brothers and nuns are subjected to the same sociocultural stresses. Of particular importance here is the absence of sex-linked activities that are relevant to mortality – namely, childbearing for females and participation in dangerous occupations for males. Madigan found that the difference in death rates between brothers and nuns was greater than between males and females in the population as a whole and that this difference had been increasing during the decades under study. From this he argued that biological factors are more important than sociocultural ones. Further, he hypothesized that the death rate advantage enjoyed by women was bound up in their greater constitutional resistance to the degenerative diseases (Madigan, 1957).

Such a hypothesis is difficult to test empirically. Table 1.2 presents ratios of male to female death rates for the population 65 years of age and over, by age and race, from 1940 to 1980. In general, the table shows increasing male-female mortality differences throughout this period, although there

TABLE 1.2 Male-to-female death rate ratios among the elderly, by age and race, 1940–1980

Race and year	Death rate ratio, by age				
	65-69	70-74	75-79	80-84	85+
All Races					
1940	1.34	1.25	1.20	1.15	1.08
1950	1.58	1.40	1.29	1.21	1.13
1960	1.83	1.62	1.42	1.26	1.11
1970	2.02	1.82	1.61	1.41	1.15
1980	1.98	1.90	1.76	1.55	1.27
White					
1940	1.36	1.26	1.19	1.14	1.07
1950	1.62	1.42	1.29	1.20	1.12
1960	1.88	1.65	1.43	1.27	1.12
1970	2.10	1.86	1.62	1.42	1.16
1980	2.02	1.94	1.78	1.56	1.27
Other Races					
1940	1.20	1.20	1.28	1.33	1.25
1950	1.28	1.23	1.28	1.30	1.20
1960	1.47	1.37	1.30	1.30	1.18
1970	1.52	1.46	1.47	1.33	1.12
1980	1.74	1.58	1.53	1.45	1.32

Sources: Robert D. Grove and Alice M. Hertzel, *Vital Statistics Rates in the United States, 1940-1960* (Washington, DC: National Center for Health Statistics, 1968), Table 55; National Center for Health Statistics, *Vital Statistics of the United States, 1970,* vol. 2, *Mortality,* Part A (1974), Table 1-8; Advance Report of Final Mortality Statistics, 1980, *Monthly Vital Statistics Report,* vol. 32, no. 4 (1983), Table 1.

are still important differences in these ratios by age. Whereas among people aged 65 through 69 the male death rate is about twice that of females, the death rate of men in the 85 years and older group is still only 27 percent higher than that of women.

The general increase in mortality differences between the sexes very likely reflects a major shift in the cause pattern of mortality. During the twentieth century, the contribution of infectious and parasitic diseases and maternal mortality to overall mortality rates has diminished relative to that of the chronic degenerative diseases such as diseases of the heart, malignant neoplasms, and cerebrovascular diseases (Siegel, 1979). However, changes in recent decades in the male–female mortality ratio appear to be associated more with social and environmental factors than with biological ones. For example, according to Petersen (1975), the age-adjusted death rate from cancers was 65 percent higher for females than males in 1900, about equal between the sexes in 1947, and 20 percent higher for males by 1963. This figure remains about 21 percent higher for males in 1986. This changing pattern would seem to have more to do with technological advancements than with innate biological factors. The diagnosis and cure of those cancers most frequent among females, breast and uterine, has improved at a more rapid rate than that for the cancers most frequent among males, those of the lung and digestive system.

Can the pattern of increasing male-to-female death rate ratios among the elderly continue? Among those of all races and whites aged 65 through 69, ratios have actually fallen between 1970 and 1980. According to Zopf (1986), this deceleration suggests that the death rate differential between older men and women will not increase in the future as it has in the past. This is especially the case for the young-old, although increases in the mortality differential by sex are likely to continue for the old-old and for blacks.

Race Differentials in Mortality

The large racial differential in mortality rates does not often receive the attention it deserves because it is a hidden factor. If we return to Table 1.1 and look across the first row ("All Ages"), we observe that the death rate of black males is slightly higher than that of white males (10.3 versus 9.8), whereas the death rate for black females is slightly lower than that for white females (7.3 versus 8.1). Nevertheless, because of higher birth rates, blacks have a younger age structure, and this factor tends to mask true mortality. If we examine mortality across the second row ("Age-Adjusted") and in individual age groups, the full impact of race emerges. For example, infant mortality in the United States in 1980 was 121 percent higher among black than white females (21.2 versus 9.6) and 111 percent higher among black than white males (25.9 versus 12.3). Death rates among young adults 25 to 29 years of age are 118 percent greater for black males and 117 percent greater for black females. It is only at age 85 that the racial differential in death rates tends to disappear. According to the demographer Donald Bogue (1969, pp. 595–596), "Throughout almost all of the ages when great progress in death control has been accomplished, death rates for blacks are about double those of whites."

Although there has been some long-term progress in reducing the racial differential in mortality, this has slowed to a standstill recently. In 1970, the age-adjusted death rate for blacks was 53.6 percent higher than the comparable figure for whites. For 1987 this differential was 52.3 percent.

The race differential in mortality is greater for females than for males. As Table 1.1 shows, in 1980 black males had an age-adjusted death rate that was 48 percent higher than the rate for white males in 1980 (11.1 versus 7.5); this differential for females was 54 percent (6.3 versus 4.1). Also, the sex differential in mortality is smaller for blacks on a proportional basis than for the white population. Among whites, males have an age-adjusted death rate that is 83 percent higher than that among females; among blacks this difference is 76 percent. It appears that black women have not been able to achieve as large a share of the available advancements in death control as have black men (Bogue, 1969, pp. 596–597).

Two additional points should be stressed when dealing with racial differentials in mortality. First, there is no reason to believe that blacks in particular or nonwhites in general are biologically less fit than whites in their capacity to survive. What this point emphasizes is that racial differentials in mortality reflect unnecessarily high mortality among nonwhites. Second, other factors, not the least of which is socioeconomic status, confound mortality data. Kitagawa and Hauser (1973) have shown the age-adjusted mortality rates for Japanese-Americans to be about one-third the corresponding rates for whites and one-half as large as the rate for blacks. Their analysis of median family income among these groups suggests that socioeconomic status may account for a considerable proportion of the race differentials in mortality.

How does low socioeconomic status contribute to the higher mortality rates prevalent among blacks? Their lack of access to high quality medical care is one way. According to the U.S. Office of Health Resources Opportunity (1979), black people receive considerably fewer preventive health services, on the average, than do white people. Also, medical treatment of blacks is often delayed until the onset of later stages of disease (Gonnella, Louis, and McCord, 1976). A recent report in the *International Journal of Epidemiology* examined the number of Americans between the ages of 15 and 54 who died between 1980 and 1986 from a dozen disorders that normally are not lethal if treated early. Among the illnesses examined were appendicitis, pneumonia, gall bladder infection, asthma, influenza, and hernia. Eighty percent of

the more than 120,000 premature deaths were among blacks. According to one co-author, "If detected early and quality treatment is provided, nobody should be dying of these things. . . . Either [the patients] are not seeking the care or they are being blocked from the care" (*Toledo Blade*, 1990, p. 1).

Although we are unable to say precisely whether biological or social factors are more important contributors to mortality differentials among different population groups in our society, we recognize that aging, even biological aging, does not occur in a social vacuum. Age-adjusted death rates in our total population are, for example, only about one-third what they were at the beginning of this century. Additionally, even when considering those who as a group are already chronologically old, there has been a significant decline in death rates since 1960; for males aged 65 through 74 years, for example, the reduction from 1960 to 1988 is 27 percent; for comparably aged females, the reduction is 23 percent. These reductions in the death rates of our population reflect at least four factors, all of which involve attempts begun in the nineteenth century to increase control over the environment (Dorn, 1959): (1) increased food supply, (2) development of commerce and transportation, (3) changes in technology and industry, and (4) increased control over infectious disease.

LIFE EXPECTANCY

Progress in the reduction of mortality is also reflected in figures for average life expectancy at birth. Average life expectancy at birth, defined as the average number of years a person born today can expect to live under current mortality conditions, has shown great improvement since 1900. It rose from 49.2 years in 1900–1902 to 75.2 years in 1989 (Table 1.3). This change constitutes a 53

TABLE 1.3 Years of life expectancy at birth, by race and sex, 1900–1902 to 1989

Years	All groups	White		Other races	
		Male	Female	Male	Female
1900–1902	49.2	48.2	51.1	32.5	35.0
1909–1911[a]	51.6	50.3	53.7	34.2	37.7
1919–1921[a]	56.5	56.6	58.6	47.2	47.0
1929–1931	59.3	59.2	62.8	47.5	49.5
1939–1941	63.8	63.3	67.2	52.4	55.4
1949–1951	68.2	66.4	72.2	59.1	63.0
1959–1961	68.9	67.6	74.2	61.5	66.5
1969–1971	70.7	67.9	75.5	61.0	69.1
1980–1981	73.9	70.8	78.4	65.7	74.8
1989[b]	75.2	72.6	79.1	67.5	75.7

[a]Death registration states only.

[b]Data for 1989 are taken from Metropolitan Life Insurance Company, "Longevity Gains Continue," *Statistical Bulletin*, vol. 72, no. 3 (1991), pp. 19–26, Tables 1, 2.

Sources: National Center for Health Statistics, *Vital Statistics of the United States, 1978*, vol. 2, sec. 5, *Life Tables* (1980), Tables 5-A and 5-5; Annual Summary of Births, Deaths, Marriages, and Divorces: United States, 1981, *Monthly Vital Statistics Report*, vol. 30, no. 13 (1982), pp. 3–4, 15.

percent increase in life expectancy at birth, or an average annual gain of about 0.3 years in this period. Still, just as there are significant sex and racial differentials in mortality, there are similar differentials in life expectancy. As Table 1.3 shows us, the population group with the highest life expectancy at birth in 1989 is white female (79.1 years); nonwhite males have the lowest life expectancy (67.5 years). All groups have substantially increased life expectancies since 1900. Better sanitary conditions, the development of effective public health programs, and rises in the standard of living are three additional factors often cited with those listed above to explain increased life expectancy in this century.

Life expectancy at birth is a function of death rates at all ages. Thus, the statistic does not tell us at what specific ages improvement has occurred. We are particularly interested in judging progress in "survivorship" for those 65 and over. One technique for judging such progress is to look at actual survivorship rates. For example, in 1900–1902, 40.9 percent of all newborn babies could be expected to reach age 65; in 1986 the figure for females has more than doubled, to 84.6 percent. The proportion of persons surviving from age 65 to age 85 more than doubled between 1900 and 1984. In 1900–1902, 14.8 percent of those aged 65 could expect to survive to age 85; in 1984 this figure was 37.4 percent, although 46.1 percent of women aged 65 could expect to survive to age 85 (Metropolitan Life Insurance Company, 1985, 1987).

A second technique for measuring changes in survivorship involves looking at changes in age-specific life expectancy. Table 1.4 presents life expectancies at various elderly ages by sex and race in the United States for 1900–1902, 1980 and 1989. Overall, life expectancy at age 65 has moved ahead

TABLE 1.4 Years of life expectancy at various elderly ages, 1900–1902, 1980, and 1989

Year and age	White		Black	
	Male	Female	Male	Female
1900–1902[a]				
65	11.5	12.2	10.4	11.4
75	6.8	7.3	6.6	7.9
85	3.8	4.1	4.0	5.1
1980				
65	14.2	18.5	13.5	17.3
75	8.8	11.5	8.9	11.4
85	5.0	6.3	5.3	7.0
1989[b]				
65	15.2	18.9	13.8	17.4
75	9.3	11.8	8.9	11.4
85	5.2	6.5	5.7	6.8

[a]Death registration states only.

[b]Data for 1989 taken from Metropolitan Life Insurance Company, "Longevity Gains Continue," *Statistical Bulletin*, vol. 72, no. 3 (1991), p. 23, Table 2.

Sources: National Center for Health Statistics, *Vital Statistics of the United States*, vol. 2, sec. 5 (1978), *Life Tables* (1980), Table 5-4; Advance Report of Final Mortality Statistics, 1980, *Monthly Vital Statistics Report*, vol. 32, no. 4 (1983), Table 2.

somewhat more slowly than has life expectancy at birth since 1900. The increase of "expectation" values for those 65 and over between 1900–1902 and 1989 is in part a function of the relative lack of success the health sciences have had in reducing adult deaths caused by heart disease, cancer, and cerebrovascular diseases. In particular, as Table 1.4 shows, gains in life expectancies for aged males (white and blacks) have not kept pace with those for aged females. These have been the leading causes of death among persons 65 years and over since 1950. Although some modest progress in reducing death rates due to heart disease and cerebrovascular diseases has been made in the last forty years, the death rate from malignant neoplasms (cancer) has increased by about 13 percent since 1950.

PROLONGEVITY

Some information presented in this chapter may lead readers to believe that length of life has been increased and will continue to increase almost automatically as a by-product of technological and social changes. Whether or not this is really so is unclear and points up the necessity of distinguishing between the concepts *life expectancy* and *life span*. Life expectancy refers to the average length of life of persons, life span to the longevity of long-lived persons. Life span is the extreme limit of human longevity, the age beyond which no one can expect to live (Gruman, 1977, p. 7). Gerontologists estimate the life span at about 110 years; some have argued that it has not increased notably in the course of history. Is the human life span an absolute standard? Or can (should) we expect a significant extension of the length of life? Some have always shared the view that human life should be lengthened indefinitely. These are proponents of *prolongevity*, defined as the significant extension of the length of life by human action (Gruman, 1977,

p. 6). Others believe that new treatments and technology, as well as improved health habits, may continue to increase life expectancy but that human life span is unlikely to increase. In attempting to estimate the upper limits of human longevity, Olshansky and his colleagues (1990) suggest that it is highly unlikely that life expectancy at birth would exceed the age of 85. They argue that to achieve an average life expectancy at birth of 85 years in the U.S. population, mortality from all causes of death would need to decline at all ages by 55 percent and at ages 50 and over by 60 percent.

In addition to the Bamans of Guangxi province in China, prolongevitists point to the "long-lived" peoples in mountain regions of Ecuador (the Andean village of Vilacabamba), Pakistan (the Hunza people of Kashmir), and the Soviet Union (the Abkhasians in the Russian Caucasus) as examples of populations that have already extended the human life span (Leaf, 1973). Each of these groups purportedly shows a statistically higher proportion of centenarians in the population, with many individuals reaching 120, 130, or even 150 and 160 years. Unfortunately, there are many reasons for doubting the validity of these claims (Kyncharyants, 1974; Mazess and Forman, 1979; Medvedev, 1974, 1975). The Russian gerontologist Medvedev says that none of these cases of superlongevity is scientifically valid. He offers the following case as explanation of why many in the Caucasus claim superlongevity.

> The famous man from Yakutia, who was found during the 1959 census to be 130 years old, received especially great publicity because he lived in the place with the most terrible climate. . . . When . . . a picture of this outstanding man was published in the central government newspaper, *Isvestia,* the puzzle was quickly solved. A letter was received from a group of Ukrainian villagers who recognized this centenarian as a fellow villager who deserted from the army during the First World War and forged documents or used his father's. . . . It was found that this man was really only 78 years old. (Medvedev, 1974, p. 387)

There continues to be interest – even mass interest – in increasing human longevity. A good part of this interest originates in the antediluvian theme found in tradition and folklore – the notion that people lived much longer in the distant past. Noah, after all, supposedly lived to be 950 years old.

What are the prospects for continued reduction in death rates and life extension? As we have already shown, death rates have declined and are likely to continue to do so. However, some research suggests that there is little room for improvement, unless some significant breakthrough eliminates cardiovascular diseases. In any case, small improvement would seem to be attainable. According to Siegel (1975), if the lowest death rates for females in the countries of Europe are combined into a single table, the values for life expectancy at birth and at age 65 exceed those same values for the United States by 4.3 and 1.4 years, respectively. Table 1.5 shows average life expectancy at

birth, according to sex, for selected countries in the years 1979 to 1982. Although the United States has experienced gains in life expectancy during the twentieth century, it is clear that Canada, France, Netherlands, Sweden, Switzerland, Australia, and Japan have life expectancies at birth for both males and females that exceed those of the United States.

Most elderly people die as a result of some long-standing chronic condition which is sometimes related to personal habits (for example, smoking, drinking alcohol, poor eating habits) or environmental conditions (for example, harsh work environments, air pollution) that go back many years. Attempts to prevent illness and death from these conditions must begin before old age. But what if we could prevent death from these conditions? Table 1.6 gives a partial answer to this question, using life table data for 1969-1971. The elimination of all deaths in the United States caused by accidents, influenza and pneumonia, infective and parasitic diseases, diabetes mellitus, and tuberculosis would increase life expectancy at birth by 1.6 years and at age 65 by 0.6 years. Even the elimination of cancer as a cause of death would result in only a 2.5-year gain in life expectancy at birth and little more than half that (1.4 years) at age 65. This is because cancer affects individuals in all age groups. If the major

TABLE 1.5 Life expectancy at birth by sex, for selected countries

Country and year	Male	Female
North America		
Canada (1980-1982)	71.9	78.9
United States (1979-1981)	70.1	77.6
Europe		
Denmark (1980-1981)	71.1	77.2
Finland (1981)	69.5	77.8
France (1981)	70.4	78.5
Netherlands (1981)	72.7	79.3
Sweden (1981)	73.1	79.1
Switzerland (1981-1982)	72.7	79.6
United Kingdom: England and Wales (1980-1982)	71.1	77.1
Other areas		
Australia (1981)	71.4	78.4
Israel (1981)	72.7	75.9
Japan (1981)	73.8	79.1

Source: Adapted from Metropolitan Life Insurance Company, "Recent International Changes in Longevity," *Statistical Bulletin*, vol. 67, no. 1 (1986), pp. 16-21.

TABLE 1.6 Gain in life expectancy if various causes of death were eliminated

	Gain in years	
Various causes of death	At birth	At age 65
1. Major cardiovascular-renal diseases	11.8	11.4
2. Malignant neoplasms	2.5	1.4
3. Motor vehicle accidents	0.7	0.1
4. Influenza and pneumonia	0.5	0.2
5. Diabetes mellitus	0.2	0.2
6. Infective and parasitic diseases	0.2	0.1

Source: U.S. Public Health Service data of life tables by cause of death for 1969-1971, U.S. Bureau of the Census, Current Population Reports, Series P-23, No. 59, January 1978 (revised).

cardiovascular-renal diseases were eliminated, there would be a 11.8-year gain in life expectancy at birth, and even an 11.4-year gain in life expectancy at age 65. More recent work by Olshansky and his colleagues (1990) supports these data. These researchers estimate that if all mortality attributable to the combination of all circulatory diseases, diabetes, and cancer was eliminated, life expectancy at birth would increase by 15.8 years for females and 15.3 years for males. Such a decline would represent approximately 71 percent of all deaths in the United States in 1985. These diseases are not likely to be eliminated in the near future, although death rates as a result of them may be reduced.

Where there is substantial room for improvement in death rates and life expectancies in the United States is among men and nonwhites. As has already been pointed out, the death rate for aged men is considerably higher than the rate for aged women; and, controlling for sex, the death rates for elderly blacks are higher than those for their white counterparts.

Much more discussion of biogerontological research on prolongevity is needed. Improving death rates and life expectancies in the United States along the lines suggested herein would still not achieve an extension of the life span. On the other hand, if major advances in genetic engineering and/or new life-extending technologies are forthcoming as some believe (Olshansky et al., 1990), significant declines in mortality and extensions of longevity will likely follow. Should people live to be 120 or 130 years of age? When thinking about your answer, assume first that this would involve more than a simple increase in time at the end of life. Imagine that researchers could alter the rate of aging in such a way as to give extra years to all the healthy and productive stages of life. Under these conditions, extra years might be difficult to turn down. But what if a longer life meant a longer "old age," including greater frailty and worsening

health? Many of you, while thinking of answers to the question of whether we should extend the human life span, will think about pollution, overpopulation, dwindling energy resources, retirement policies, social security benefits, and the like. The list of negative implications is a long one and may simply reflect your negative characterization of old age. But if you think of old age in terms of the continuation of productive possibilities, then you may very well accept these extra years, however and whenever they come.

STUDY QUESTIONS

1. Describe the antediluvian, hyperborean, and fountain themes of aging. How are these themes reflected in modern society?
2. List the four classical hypotheses, identified by Comfort, that attempt to explain the mechanisms of aging.
3. Distinguish between biological aging and pathological aging. Define senescence. How can it be distinguished from other biological processes?
4. Taking biological and socioenvironmental factors into consideration, explain the impact of gender on mortality rates. What role do socioeconomic factors play in the racial differences in mortality rates observed in the United States today?
5. Define prolongevity. Distinguish between life expectancy and life span. Do the Abkhasians of the Russian Caucasus really live as long as they claim?
6. Explain:
   a. increased life expectancy at birth in this century
   b. the small increase in life expectancy from age 65 in this century
7. Compare the life expectancy at birth of people in the United States with that of citizens of other industrialized nations. Which groups in the United States would seem to show the greatest potential for improvement in the values of life expectancy and death rates? Why?
8. How much gain in life expectancy in the United States could be realized through the elimination of certain diseases? Where would the greatest gain come from?
9. Eliminating certain diseases, and thus extending life expectancy, would seem to be an inherently positive thing. Is the idea of extending the human life span equally as positive? Explain your answer.

BIBLIOGRAPHY

Blumenthal, H. T. 1968. Some biomedical aspects of aging. *Gerontologist*, 8: 3-5.

Bogue, D. J. 1969. *Principles of demography*. New York: Wiley.

Comfort, A. 1979. *The biology of senescence*, 3rd ed. New York: New American Library.

Dorn, H. 1959. Mortality. In Philip Hauser and Otis Duncan (Eds.), *The study of population*. Chicago: University of Chicago Press.

Fries, J. F., and Crapo, L. M. 1981. *Vitality and aging*. San Francisco: W. H. Freeman.

Gonnella, J. S., Louis, D. Z., and McCord, J. J. 1976. The staging concept: An approach to the assessment of outcome of ambulatory care. *Medical Care*, 14: 13-21.

Gruman, G. 1966. *A history of ideas about the prolongation of life*. Philadelphia: American Philosophical Society.

Gruman, G. 1977. *A history of ideas about the prolongation of life*. New York: Arno Press.

Ignatius, A. 1990. Secrets of Bama: In a corner of China, they live to be 100. *Wall Street Journal*, March 19, pp. 1, 11.

Kitagawa, E. M., and Hauser, P. M. 1973. *Differential mortality in the United States: A study in socioeconomic epidemiology*. Cambridge, MA: Harvard University Press.

Kyncharyants, V. 1974. Will the human life-span reach one hundred? *Gerontologist*, 14: 377-380.

Leaf, A. 1973. Getting old. *Scientific American*, 299(3): 44-52.

Madigan, F. C. 1957. Are sex mortality differentials biologically caused? *Milbank Memorial Fund Quarterly*, 35(2): 202-223.

Marcus, A. C., and Siegel, J. M. 1982. Sex differences in the use of physician services: A preliminary test of the fixed role hypothesis. *Journal of Health and Social Behavior*, 23: 186-196.

Mazess, R., and Forman, S. 1979. Longevity and age exaggeration in Vilacabamba, Ecuador. *Journal of Gerontology*, 34: 94-98.

Medvedev, Z. A. 1974. Caucasus and Altay longevity: A biological or social problem? *Gerontologist*, 14: 381-387.

Medvedev, Z. A. 1975. Aging and longevity: New approaches and new perspectives. *Gerontologist*, 15: 196-210.

Metropolitan Life Insurance Company. 1985. Slight gains in U.S. longevity. *Statistical Bulletin*, 66(3): 20-23.

Metropolitan Life Insurance Company. 1986. Recent international changes in longevity. *Statistical Bulletin* 67(1): 16-21.

Metropolitan Life Insurance Company. 1987. Trends in longevity after age 65. *Statistical Bulletin*, 68(1): 10-17.

Olshansky, S. J., Carnes, B. A., and Cassel, C. 1990. In search of Methuselah: Estimating the upper limits to human longevity. *Science*, 250(November 2): 634-640.

Petersen, W. 1975. *Population*, 3rd ed. New York: Macmillan.

Siegel, J. S. 1975. Some demographic aspects of aging in the United States. In A. Ostfeld and D. Gibson (Eds.), *Epidemiology of aging*. Bethesda, MD: National Institute of Health.

Siegel, J. S. 1979. *Prospective trends in the size and structure of the elderly population, impact of mortality trends, and some implications*. Current Population Reports, Special Studies Series P-23, No. 78. Washington, DC: U.S. Department of Commerce, Bureau of the Census.

Sobel, H. 1966. When does human aging start? *Gerontologist* 6: 17-22.

Strehler, B. 1962. *Time, cells and aging*. New York: Academic Press.

Toledo Blade. 1990. Report: Blacks die needlessly because of lack of routine care. *Toledo Blade*, November 29, p. 1, 6.

U.S. Bureau of the Census. 1990. *Statistical abstract of the United States: 1990*. Washington, DC: U.S. Government Printing Office.

U.S. Office of Health Resources Opportunity. 1979. *Health status of minorities and low-income groups*. DHEW Pub. No. (HRA) 79-627. Health Resources Administration. Washington, DC: U.S. Government Printing Office.

Wilson, D. L. 1974. The programmed theory of aging. In M. Rockstein (Ed.), *Theoretical aspects of aging*. New York: Academic Press.

Zopf, P. E., Jr. 1986. *America's older population*. Houston, TX: Cap and Gown Press.

CHAPTER 2

Biological Theories of Aging

Numerous theories have been proposed to explain why we age. No single one can definitively answer this age-old question. After all, aging is a complex phenomenon. Different explanations may be required for different aspects of the aging process; diverse phenomena may act together to account for biological aging. Although classification schemes vary, theories of biological aging can be described as focusing on one of two fundamental suppositions. One presupposes a genetic basis for the aging process; the other views senescence as a result of wear and tear. Attempts to explain the actual mechanism of biological aging have focused on (1) changes in the properties of replicating cells, (2) the loss of or injury to *postmitotic cells* (those that do not divide), and (3) primary changes in noncellular materials of the body. A fourth approach locates a mechanism of aging in a regulatory program of the body, such as the hormonal system or the immune system.

Biologic aging is viewed as a progressive decline in the ability to respond to the stresses of a dynamic environment. The decline in the ability to maintain *homeostasis* leads to functional impairment and, ultimately, death. Although it is difficult to distinguish between normal aging and disease, aging per se is usually distinguished by four criteria (Strehler, 1982). First, the aging process must be deleterious to the organism, reducing function. Second, it must be progressive, gradually occurring over time. Third, aging is intrinsic and, therefore, unrelated to modifiable environmental factors. Finally, it is universal, occurring in all members of the species.

Differentiating among normal aging, other superimposed changes, and disease is vital to understanding the aging process. The ultimate cause of the majority of deaths in older adults is the physiologic decline that increases the risk of disease. Mortality usually ensues when the ability to withstand the challenge of disease is overwhelmed. For instance, the increased risk of death from pneumonia among older persons is associated with age-related declines in the body's immune defense and reduced pulmonary reserve and function (Rothschild, 1984).

Unlocking the mystery of aging and extending the human life span has been the dream of many. Efforts at prolonging life have been in the written and oral records of societies dating back many thousands of years. Research in biogerontology continues. Yet, despite the fact that books on longevity and its promotion have appeared on bestseller lists in recent years, there are no magic potions to "cure" aging. Creams, vitamins, and nutrient supplements have been among the life-extending aids promoted. They represent the continuation of a "fountain" theme based on the idea that there is some unusual substance that has the property of retarding aging and greatly increasing the length of life. The search for the "fountain of youth" in 1513 by Juan Ponce de Leon (who accidentally discovered Florida instead) is a good example of this rejuvenation theme. The fountain theme still lives. In recent years, various so-called antiaging cures were highlighted in a congressional hearing on medical quackery (House Select Committee on Aging, 1984).

What follows in this chapter is an overview of some of the important research in the biology of aging. The goal of such research is not to grant immortality but to understand the aging process and, perhaps, improve the quality of life for the growing numbers of us who are being added to the ranks of the aged.

CELLULAR THEORIES OF AGING

In the early part of this century it was widely believed that cells in tissue culture could divide indefinitely. This belief was founded largely on the work of Alexis Carrel (1912) and his associates at Rockefeller University. Carrel kept a culture of chick heart cells continuously dividing for a period of 34 years until he retired and terminated the work. The period of cell division exceeded the life of a chicken and was considered evidence that tissue cells were potentially immortal. Carrel's work had a significant impact on the field of gerontology. During the first half of the twentieth century, aging was not considered a characteristic of cells (Cristofalo, 1985, 1990).

During the late 1950s and early 1960s, Leonard Hayflick and Paul Moorehead, then at the Wistar Institute, began studying the effects of cancer-causing viruses on normal cells in culture. In maintaining such cultures, they observed that cells undergo a limited number of divisions and then die. Across several experiments, Hayflick and Moorehead (1961) noted that human fetal fibroblastic cells (connective tissue cells) underwent an average of fifty divisions in vitro, with a range of 40 to 60, before losing the ability to replicate themselves. Others before them had noted the finite capacity for cell division. However, because of the esteem accorded Carrel's work, they had not had confidence in their own findings. Eventually, it was discovered that Carrel's cultures had been contaminated. During the maintenance of the growth medium, fresh chick cells had been added to the cultures.

The findings of Hayflick and Moorehead continue to be confirmed. Fries and Crapo (1981) report that in 1962 Hayflick froze several vials of embryo cells that had completed several divisions. Each year since that time, some vials have been thawed and cultured; they consistently go on to complete about 50 divisions.

The work of Hayflick and Moorehead proposed that senescence is a cellular as well as an organismic phenomenon. Aging, they held, is intrinsic to the cell and is not solely dependent on outside influences. Later, Hayflick (1965) reported that fibroblasts isolated from human adult tissue undergo a finite and predictable number of divisions. He noted that unless a cancerous transformation occurs (wherein unrestrained cell division occurs), senescence and cell death ultimately result.

Hayflick argued that (1) the limited replicative capacity of cultured normal human cells is an expression of programmed genetic events; and (2) the limit on normal cell division in vitro is a function of the age of the donor. It is now held that there is an inverse relationship between donor age and the replicative capacity of cultured cells (Martin, Sprague, and Epstein, 1970; Schneider and Mitusi, 1976). That is, the older the donor, the fewer the number of remaining cell divisions. Furthermore, the proliferative capacity of cells is directly related to the *maximum life span* of the species from which they are derived (Rohme, 1981).

As previously noted, cancer cells are capable of unlimited division. A famous line of human cancer cells referred to as HeLa (after Henrietta Lacks, the woman from whom they were taken in 1951) is still being cultured for use in standardized cancer cell studies (Gold, 1981). The continued study of cancer cells may yet reveal the attribute that limits the replicative capacity of normal cells.

Tissue culture studies have limitations, and it is almost certain that these experiments do not literally replicate the aging process. Although they may add to our knowledge of aging, they do not necessarily dictate that the human life span is limited by what happens to cultured cells (Cristofalo, 1985). That humans age simply because their cells have an intrinsically limited capacity to divide seems unlikely. Postmitotic cells, such as nerve and muscle cells, do not divide during adult life, yet they do show deterioration with age.

Researchers continue to suggest that aging may be genetically programmed into cells. Bernard Strehler hypothesized that programmed loss of genetic material could result in "aging." As Strehler (1973) notes, most cells possess hundreds of repetitions of DNA (the molecule of heredity) for the known genes they contain. Simply stated, the cell does not have to rely on a single copy of its genetic blueprint for any one trait. It has been found that as cells age a considerable number of repetitions are lost (Johnson, Crisp, and Strehler, 1972). This is especially the case for brain, heart, and skeletal muscle cells. Although these postmitotic cells do not divide, with age the blueprints dictating their

functional capacity might be affected. Strehler suspects that cells may be programmed, at a fixed point in life, to commence manufacturing a substance that inhibits protein synthesis within a cell.

An old school of thought maintains that aging is the result of genetic mutations. There are many variations of this theme. Orgel (1963, 1973) hypothesized that random errors or mutations progressively accumulated in transcriptions of DNA into RNA (ribonucleic acid, carrying instructions from DNA) or through errors in the translation of RNA into protein synthesis in the cell. Since the functional ability of a cell is dependent on the quality of protein production, random errors in synthesis could eventually impair function. Hence, *error catastrophe* results in cellular deterioration. Cristofalo (1972) asserts that cells with such serious errors would be limited in their capacity to influence survival. DNA is continuously repaired by enzymes that strike against faulty information. Current variations of error theories presuppose that the expression of mutations in protein synthesis may be influenced by errors in genes that are responsible for the repair capacity of the cell.

Another explanation of aging maintains that *free radicals*, produced in the course of normal cellular metabolism, cause an accumulation of cellular waste, and reduce cellular efficiency. Free radicals are atoms or molecular fragments formed as a by-product of cellular metabolism. They are numerous and, though short-lived, may serve as a source of cellular damage. Such damage could be reflected in the aging process.

It is speculated that the fatty "age pigment," *lipofuscin*, which accumulates to an appreciable extent in nerve, cardiac and skeletal muscle cells, may be an end product of cellular membrane damage caused by free radicals. It should be emphasized that current thinking holds that lipofuscin is, however, an indicator rather than a cause of aging.

In addition to being created as a part of normal metabolic/oxidative reactions, free radicals may also be produced by radiation. The classic work of Harman (1956) demonstrated that an excess of free radicals was produced in cells as a result of radiation exposure. Animals suffering radiation damage presented symptoms of aging and a decreased life expectancy.

Advocates of the free-radical theory of aging propose that certain chemicals, called *antioxidants*, combine with and "disarm" free radicals. A number of dietary antioxidants (a common one is BHT, the food preservative) have been administered to different organisms in an attempt to increase life expectancy. Length of life has been extended in numerous studies (Clapp, Satterfield, and Bowles, 1979; Comfort, Youhotsky-Gore, and Pathmanathan, 1971; Economos, Ballard, Miquel, Binnard, and Philpott, 1982; Harman, 1961; Munkres and Minssen, 1976; Oeriu and Vochitu, 1965). Harman reported that the inclusion of dietary antioxidants increased the average length of life of experimental animals by 15 to 30 percent. Animals receiving antioxidants showed lower weight, suggesting the possibility that dietary restriction may increase longevity and confound interpretation of such experiments. Another effect of adding antioxidants to the diet of experimental animals was a reduction in tumor production (Harman, 1968).

Vitamin and mineral supplements have been promoted with the hope of extending human life. Vitamins A, E, and C and the mineral selenium have antioxidant properties and deserve further study regarding possible antiaging and antineoplastic action. However, there is no current evidence to support such dietary supplementation among humans for the prevention of cancer or the extension of life (Ames, 1983; Schneider and Reed, 1985; Willet and MacMahon, 1984).

Higher organisms do possess sophisticated biochemical systems for scavenging free radicals. The enzyme *superoxide dismutase* is a part of such a system. This protective enzyme can rapidly destroy free radicals. A relationship has been noted between superoxide dismutase activity and life span in varying species and species strains (Bartosz, Leyko, and Fried, 1979; Cristofalo, 1990; Kellogg and Fridovich, 1976; Munkres, Rana, and Goldstein, 1984; Tolmasoff, Ono, and Cutler, 1980). It is possible that the regulation of superoxide dismutase is under the control of the same genes that dictate the life span of a particular species (Schneider and Reed, 1985). Superoxide dismutase tablets have been touted for their "antiaging" effect. However, there is no evidence that oral administration of the enzyme prolongs life. In fact, one report demonstrates that blood and tissue levels of this enzyme are not affected by its ingestion (Zidenburg-Cherr, Keen, Lonnerdal, and Hurley, 1983).

PHYSIOLOGIC THEORIES OF AGING

The above considered work is concerned with aging at the cellular or molecular level. It is quite a leap from studying the aging cell to studying aging of the organism. There are several physiologic theories that attempt to relate aging to the performance of the organism. Several of these theories deserve special mention.

One physiological theory of aging involves the body's system of immune defense. Normally, the immune system, through the action of special immune cells and the production of antibodies, protects us from material that the body regards as foreign, including cancer cells. With age, immune function declines. Also, increased levels of certain *autoantibodies* are found in the blood (Goidl, Thorbecke, and Weksler, 1980; Walford, 1982; Weksler, 1982). These are substances which are produced against host tissue. Normally, the body's immune defense distinguishes between host body cells (or self) and foreign substances subject to attack.

The significance of age-associated increases in autoantibodies is not well understood. They may contribute to inefficiencies in physiologic functioning. Why they are produced is also not known. Perhaps, once-normal body cells begin to appear different to the immune system. Their change in character may result from accumulated damage resulting from mutation or free-radical activity. If immune cells undergo similar changes, it might cause the production of aberrant antibodies. Also, body constituents may break down from disease or other damage and present themselves as "new" substances that the body's immune defense will not tolerate. Potentially, all of these factors might interact to produce *autoimmunity*.

One of the best documented age-related changes is the diminished functioning of the immune system (Walford, 1990). Indeed, it has been suggested that decreased immunocompetence (the decline in immune function) may have evolved as a protective mechanism against the ravages of autoimmunity (Schneider and Reed, 1985). A vigorous immune reaction might allow for an even greater production of autoantibodies.

A study of organismal aging dictates that attention be directed toward the immune system; the immune system is itself "organismal." It is in constant contact with virtually all body cells, tissues and organs. Kay and Baker (1979) and Kay and Makinodan (1982) point out that an alteration in the immune system could be expected to exert an effect on all other body systems. As immune competence decreases, the incidence of autoimmunity, infection and cancer increases (Good and Yunis, 1974; Gross, 1965; MacKay, 1972; MacKay, Whittington, and Mathews, 1977; Walford, 1990).

Immune function begins to decline shortly after puberty with the beginning atrophy and involution of the *thymus gland*. The thymus, located in the chest, is perhaps the structure most central to the aging of the immune system. Thymic hormone influences immune functioning. Its progressive, age-related loss is associated with declines in the reactivity of certain immune cells. The percentage of immature immune cells increases in association with the lack of thymic hormone. Other substances, termed *lymphokines*, are also important in activating and maintaining the immune response. One lymphokine, *interleukin-2* (IL-2), undergoes limited production with age (Thoman, 1985).

The immune status of a group of healthy *centenarians* (those having achieved 100 years of age) was studied by Thompson and his associates (1984). They selected such a study population because its members represented those who had withstood the high risk of cancer and various other disease for at least 100 years. Their immune status appeared similar to that of young-old individuals. Thymus-dependent functions were reduced in association with an apparent failure of certain immune cells to differentiate to functional maturity. The researchers noted that further work is needed questioning (1) when changes in immune cells of these centenarians commenced, (2) whether the changes represent irreversible programmed aging that began later in such a group, and (3) whether other factors are responsible for immune decline.

Collagen, an extracellular component of connective tissue, has also been implicated in age-related changes in physiological functions. Collagen, widely scattered throughout the body, is included in the skin, blood vessels, bone, cartilage, tendons and other body organs. With age, connective tissue shows a reduction in its elastic properties as well as an increase in *cross-linkages*. Cross-linkage is a process whereby proteins in the body (including collagen) bind to each other.

It has been postulated that the increased cross-linking of connective tissue (especially collagen) plays a significant role in impairing functional capacities. Accumulated cross-linkages could theoretically be responsible for the deterioration of various organs. For instance, less elastic blood vessels may have altered permeability, affecting nutrient transport and waste removal. Likewise, connective tissue changes in small vessels may lead to reduced elasticity and increased blood flow pressure leading to hypertension. Changes such as these could have far-reaching effects on all body organs. While it is true that cross-linking increases with age, few researchers presently view it as a major underlying cause of aging (Cristofalo, 1990).

Diabetics are susceptible to excessive cross-linking. They also undergo many complications, such as cataract formation and atherosclerosis, that are similar to age-related changes. Indeed, diabetes is often referred to as a model for studying the aging process. Elevated blood sugar levels promote cross-linkage formation (Cerami, 1985). At present it is believed that many of the long-term complications of diabetes are related to glucose-induced cross-linking, especially the cross-linking of collagen. Future work will likely provide greater insight into the possible role of glucose as a mediator of aging. Researchers at Rockefeller University are presently studying a drug that prevents blood sugar from promoting protein cross-linking. It is hoped that the drug can be used in the future treatment of diabetic complications. Perhaps its most provocative use in the distant future might be in the treatment of "aging" disorders in the nondiabetic (Wechsler, 1986).

Nathan Shock, noted gerontologist, has recently indicated that there is sufficient evidence to suggest that aging possibly emanates from impaired performance of endocrine and/or neural control mechanisms. Studies carried out by the National Institute of Health's Gerontology Research Center show that age-related declines in humans are greater for functions that require the coordinated activity of organ systems. Measurements of functions related to a single system, such as nerve conduction velocity, show considerably less age decrement than do functions that involve coordination between systems, such as maximum breathing capacity (which involves the nervous, respiratory, and muscular systems) (Kart, 1985).

STUDY QUESTIONS

1. What are two fundamental suppositions inherent in most theories of aging?
2. Identify four approaches that have been taken in attempting to explain the mechanisms of aging.
3. How is biological aging defined? Name four characteristics that are criteria of aging per se?
4. How did the work of Hayflick and Moorehead influence the field of gerontology? How did their conclusions differ from those of Carrel and his colleagues?
5. Note some of the work that has focused on aging at the cellular level. Which cellular theories suggest that aging may be genetically programmed into cells? Which cellular theories of aging appear to implicate diet or nutrition in the aging process?
6. Note some of the work that has focused on aging at the physiological level. What is the significance of age-related decline in the immune system? What is the cross-linkage theory of aging?

BIBLIOGRAPHY

Ames, B. 1983. Dietary carcinogens and anticarcinogens: Oxygen radicals and degenerative disease. *Science,* 221: 1256–1264.

Bartosz, G., Leyko, W., and Fried, R. 1979. Superoxide dismutase and life span of *Drosophila melanogaster. Experientia,* 35: 1193.

Carrel, A. 1912. On the permanent life of tissues. *Journal of Experimental Medicine,* 15: 516.

Cerami, A. 1985. Hypothesis: Glucose as a mediator of aging. *Journal of the American Geriatrics Society,* 33: 626–634.

Clapp, N., Satterfield, L., and Bowles, N. 1979. Effects of the antioxidant butylated hydroxytoluene (BHT) on mortality in BALB/c mice. *Journal of Gerontology,* 34: 497–501.

Comfort, A., Youhotsky-Gore, I., and Pathmanathan, K. 1971. Effect of ethoxyquin on the longevity of C3H mice. *Nature,* 229: 254–255.

Cristofalo, V. 1972. Animal cell cultures as a modal system for the study of aging. In B. Strehler (Ed.), *Advances in gerontological research* (pp. 45–79). New York: Academic Press.

Cristofalo, V. 1985. The destiny of cells: Mechanisms and implications of senescence. *The Gerontologist*, 25: 577–583.

Cristofalo, V. 1990. Biological mechanisms of aging: An overview. In W. Hazzard, R. Andres, E. Bierman, and J. Blass (Eds.), *Principles of geriatric medicine and gerontology* (pp. 3–14). New York: McGraw-Hill.

Economos, A., Ballard, R., Miquel, J., Binnard, R., and Philpott, D. 1982. Accelerated aging of fasted *Drosophila*: Preservation of physiological function and cellular fine structure by thiazolidine carboxylic acid (TCA). *Experimental Gerontology*, 17: 105–114.

Fries, J., and Crapo, L. 1981. *Vitality and aging*. San Francisco: W. H. Freeman.

Goidl, E., Thorbecke, G., and Weksler, M. 1980. Production of auto-anti-idiotypic antibody during the normal immune response: Changes in the auto-anti-idiotypic antibody response and idiotype repertoire associated with aging. *Proceedings of the National Academy of Science*, 77: 6788.

Gold, M. 1981. The cells that would not die. *Science 81*, 2: 28–35.

Good, R., and Yunis, E. 1974. Association of autoimmunity, immunodeficiency and aging in man, rabbits and mice. *Federation Proceedings,* 33: 2040–2050.

Gross, L. 1965. Immunologic defect in aged population and its relation to cancer. *Cancer*, 18: 201–204.

Harman, D. 1956. Aging: A theory based on free radical and radiation chemistry. *Journal of Gerontology*, 11: 298–300.

Harman, D. 1961. Prolongation of the normal lifespan and inhibition of spontaneous cancer by antioxidants. *Journal of Gerontology*, 16: 247–254.

Harman, D. 1968. Free radical theory of aging. *Journal of Gerontology*, 23: 476–482.

Hayflick, L. 1965. The limited in vitro lifetime of human diploid cell strains. *Experimental Cell Research*, 37: 614–636.

Hayflick, L., and Moorehead, M. 1961. The serial cultivation of human diploid cell strains. *Experimental Cell Research*, 25: 585–621.

House Select Committee on Aging, Subcommittee on Health and Long-Term Care. 1984. Anti-aging cures and quackery. In *Quackery: A $10 billion scandal*. Washington, DC: U.S. Government Printing Office.

Johnson, R., Crisp, C., and Strehler, B. 1972. Selective loss of ribosomal RNA genes during the aging of post-mitotic tissues. *Mechanisms of Aging and Development*, 1.

Kart, C. 1985. *The realities of aging*, 2nd ed. Boston: Allyn and Bacon.

Kay, M., and Baker, L. 1979. Cell changes associated with declining immune function: Physiology and cell biology of aging. In A. Cherkin, C. Finch, N. Kharasch, T. McKinodan, F. Scott, and B. Strehler (Eds.), *Aging* (Vol. 8). New York: Raven Press.

Kay, M., and Makinodan, T. 1982. The aging immune system. In A. Viidik, (Ed.), *Lectures on gerontology*, Volume I: On Biology of Aging, Part A. London: Academic Press.

Kellogg, E., and Fridovich, I. 1976. Superoxide dismutase in the rat and mouse as a function of age and longevity. *Journal of Gerontology*, 31: 405–408.

MacKay, I. 1972. Aging and immunological function in man. *Gerontologia*, 18: 285–304.

MacKay, I., Whittington, S., and Mathews, J. 1977. The immunoepidemiology of aging. In T. MaKinodan and E. Yunis (Eds.), *Immunity and aging* (pp. 35–49). New York: Plenum Press.

Martin, G., Sprague, C., and Epstein, C. 1970. Replicative lifespan of cultivated human cells: Effects of donor age, tissue and genotype. *Laboratory Investigation*, 23: 86–92.

Munkres, K., and Minssen, M. 1976. Aging of *Neurospora crassa* I: Evidence for the free radical theory of aging from studies of a natural-death mutant. *Mechanisms of Aging and Development*, 5: 79–98.

Munkres, K., Rana, R., and Goldstein, E. 1984. Genetically determined conidial longevity is positively correlated with superoxide dismutase, catalase, gluthathione peroxidase, cytochrome c peroxidase and ascorbate free radical reductase activities in *Neurospora crassa*. *Mechanisms of Aging and Development*, 24: 83–100.

Oeriu, S., and Vochitu, E. 1965. The effect of the administration of compounds which contain sulfhydryl groups on the survival of mice, rats and guinea pigs. *Journal of Gerontology*, 20: 417–419.

Orgel, L. 1963. The maintenance of the accuracy of protein synthesis and its relevance to aging. *Proceedings of the National Academy of Science*, 49: 517.

Orgel, L. 1973. The maintenance of the accuracy of protein synthesis and its relevance to aging. *Proceedings of the National Academy of Science*, 67: 1496.

Rohme, D. 1981. Evidence for a relationship between longevity of mammalian species and lifespans of normal fibroblasts in vitro and erythrocytes in vivo. *Proceedings of the National Academy of Science*, 78: 3584-3588.

Rothschild, H. 1984. The biology of aging. In H. Rothschild (Ed.), *Risk factors for senility*. New York: Oxford University Press.

Schneider, E., and Mitsui, Y. 1976. The relationship between in vitro cellular aging and in vivo human age. *Proceedings of the National Academy of Science*, 73: 3584-3588.

Schneider, E., and Reed, J. 1985. Life extension. *New England Journal of Medicine*, 312: 1159-1168.

Strehler, B. 1973. A new age for aging. *Natural History*, 2: 8-18, 82-85.

Strehler, B. 1982. Aging: Concepts and theories. In A. Viidik (Ed.), *Lectures on gerontology*. Volume I: On Biology of Aging, Part A (pp. 1-59). London: Academic Press.

Thoman, M. 1985. Role of interleukin-2 in the age-related impairment of immune function. *Journal of the American Geriatrics Society*, 33: 781-787.

Thompson, J., Wekstein, D., Rhoades, J., Kirkpatrick, C., Brown, S., Roszman, T., Straus, R., and Tietz, N. 1984. The immune status of healthy centenarians. *Journal of the American Geriatrics Society*, 32: 274-281.

Tolmasoff, J., Ono, T., and Cutler, R. 1980. Superoxide dismutase: Correlation with lifespan and specific metabolic rate in primate species. *Proceedings of the National Academy of Science*, 77: 2777-2781.

Walford, R. 1982. Studies in immunogerontology. *Journal of the American Geriatrics Society*, 30: 617.

Walford, R. 1990. The clinical promise of diet restriction. *Geriatrics*, 45(4): 81-83, 86-87.

Wechsler, R. 1986. Unshackled from diabetes. *Discover*, 7: 77-85.

Weksler, M. 1982. Age-associated changes in the immune response. *Journal of the American Geriatrics Society*, 30: 718.

Willet, W., and MacMahon, B. 1984. Diet and cancer — an overview. *New England Journal of Medicine*, 310: 633-638, 697-703.

Zidenberg-Cherr, S., Keen, C., Lonnerdal, B., and Hurley, L. 1983. Dietary superoxide dismutase does not affect tissue levels. *American Journal of Clinical Nutrition*, 37: 5-7.

CHAPTER 3

Population Aging and Health Status: The Aged Come of Age

There are now more than 30 million people aged 65 years and older in the United States. The growth in this group between 1980 and 1990 far outpaced the 10.5 percent growth in the U.S. population as a whole. Preliminary estimates from the 1990 Census show the number of persons 65 through 74 years of age to have risen by 20.6 percent among men and 15.9 percent among women between 1980 and 1990. If the U.S. population of those 65 years and over were all grouped together, they would make up the most populous state in the nation, exceeding the population of California. Actually, based on 1980 census data, there are more people aged 65 and older in the United States than the combined total resident populations of New England (Maine, New Hampshire, Vermont, Massachusetts, Rhode Island, and Connecticut) and the

Mountain States (Montana, Idaho, Wyoming, Colorado, New Mexico, Arizona, Utah, and Nevada).

Assessing the size and composition of the aged population in the United States requires an understanding of how this group is currently composed, how the elderly population has changed from the past, and how it may change in the future. Three population attributes, *fertility, mortality,* and *migration,* influence and are influenced by social and economic conditions. High birth rates in the first decades of the twentieth century have yielded large numbers of elderly 65 to 75 years later. Progress in public health and medicine has reduced the rates of illness and mortality, especially among infants and the young, allowing more of the population to live to be old. Immigration to the United States has also had an impact on the growth of the elderly population in recent years. Migrants who were young adults at the time of their immigration in the early decades of this century increased the numbers of persons in their respective age groups, leading to large numbers of older people decades later.

This chapter begins with a brief albeit systematic study of aged population trends and pheno.nena in the United States and concludes with an assessment of the health status of the older population. Much of the available data in the United States define the elderly as those 65 years of age and older. Although 65 + is an imprecise identifier of the older population, it is a useful designation for gerontologists and, for the most part, we follow it in this chapter. This definition, however, is not universal. We all may recognize the differences between 20-year-old persons and 40-year-olds, but we often overlook the same twenty-year difference between those who are 55 and those who are 75. Neugarten (1974) makes the distinction between the *young-old* (55 to 74 years of age) and the *old-old* (75 years of age and older). Recently, the National Institute on Aging has sought research proposals to study those individuals 85 years of age and older. This activity suggests the usefulness of further subdividing the old-old into those 75 to 84 years (*the elderly* and those 85 years and over (*the very-old*). The young-old are healthier, wealthier, and better educated than the old-old, and their family

and career experiences and expectations are quite different.

NUMBER AND PROPORTION OF THE ELDERLY

The elderly population of the United States has grown consistently since the turn of the century, when about 3.1 million men and women were aged 65 and over. The 1990 census is expected to show almost 31.8 million (see Table 3.1), a more than tenfold increase. This is much greater than the rate of increase for the total U.S. population, which is expected to increase about three times, from 76 to 250 million, in the same period.

As Table 3.1 shows, the absolute and proportional increases in the aged population are expected to continue into the twenty-first century, though at a slowed pace until the 2010–2020 decade. Between 1990 and 2000 the projected increase in the aged population is about 3.2 million, or a 10.2 percent decennial increase. This compares with the 6.1 million (23.7 percent) decennial increase projected between 1980 and 1990. This expected slowed growth rate in the elderly population is a reflection of the small cohorts caused by the low birth rate during the Great Depression and up

TABLE 3.1 Total aged population and percentage of total population that is aged, 1950–2020

	1950	1960	1970	1980	Projections			
					1990	2000	2010	2020
65 years and older (thousands)	12,397	16,675	20,087	25,708	31,799	35,036	39,269	51,386
Percentage of total population (%)	8.1	9.3	9.9	11.3	12.7	13.1	13.9	17.3
Increase in preceding decade (%)	–	34.5	20.5	28.0	23.7	10.2	12.1	30.9

Note: Based on Middle Series Census Bureau Projections. These projections are based on the following assumptions: (1) an average of 1.9 lifetime births per woman; (2) life expectancy in 2050 of 79.6; and (3) net immigration of 450,000.
Source: J. S. Siegel and M. Davidson, *Demographic and Socioeconomic Aspects of Aging in the United States,* Current Population Reports, Series P-23, No. 138 (Washington, DC: U.S. Department of Commerce, Bureau of the Census, 1984), Tables 2.1 and 2.5.

to World War II. The earliest of these small cohorts, born in 1929 or thereabout, reach age 65 during the last decade of this century. When the post-World War II babies reach age 65 shortly after the year 2010, the growth rate in the elderly population will again increase. Table 3.1 shows this; the projected increase in the elderly population between 2010 and 2020 is 30.9 percent. Later, this growth rate will most likely fall, reflecting a decline in birth rates that began in the 1960s.

AGING OF THE OLDER POPULATION

Not only has the older population of the United States grown in absolute size and proportion of the total population during this century, but it has also aged. Table 3.2 shows that the proportion of the aged who are 65 to 74 years of age has been getting smaller and will continue to do so until 2010; the proportion 75 or over has been getting larger, and this trend is also expected to continue. In 1900 the proportion of those 65 and over who were 75 or over was 29 percent. By the year 2000 this figure will be about 50 percent. By the year 2010, the aging trend of the population 65 years and over should reverse itself as larger cohorts born in the post-World War II period enter the younger seg-

ment (65 to 74 years) of the elderly population. The median age of the population is expected to rise to about 38 years by 2030. The aging of the older population expected to occur over the next two decades or so has important policy implications for local, state, and federal agencies. One example involves the likelihood of an increased need for extended care among the growing number of very old (Siegel and Davidson, 1984).

THE DEMOGRAPHIC TRANSITION

The pattern of an increasing number and proportion of elderly persons in the United States population is no real surprise to students of demography. In fact, it is predictable from a theory of population change used by many demographers to explain the growth in a society's population. This theory is concerned with the relationship between birth rates and death rates (as well as migration rates) and the resulting effects on the age composition of populations. The theory, which describes a three-stage process whereby a population moves from high fertility and high mortality to low fertility and low mortality, is often called the *demographic transition*.

The first stage of the demographic transition, characterized by high birth rates and high death

TABLE 3.2 Percentage distribution of the population 65 years and over, by age, 1950–2020

	1950	1960	1970	1980	1990	2000	2010	2020
65 years and over	100.0	100.0	100.0	100.0	100.0	100.0	100.0	100.0
65-69	40.7	37.7	35.0	34.2	31.5	26.0	29.8	32.3
70-74	27.8	28.6	27.2	26.6	25.3	24.5	21.9	25.6
75-79	17.4	18.5	19.2	18.7	19.6	20.7	17.1	17.0
80-84	9.3	9.6	11.5	11.6	12.8	14.2	13.9	10.8
85 and over	4.8	5.6	7.1	8.8	10.9	14.7	17.4	14.3

Note: Based on Middle Series Census Bureau Projections. See Table 3.1 for an explanation of assumptions.

Source: J. S. Siegel and M. Davidson, *Demographic and Socioeconomic Aspects of Aging in the United States,* Current Population Reports, Series P-23, No. 138 (Washington, DC: U.S. Department of Commerce, Bureau of the Census, 1984), Table 2.6.

rates, has been called the *high growth* potential stage because a decline in mortality, in the absence of other changes, implies very high rates of population growth (Matras, 1973, p. 25). Preindustrial societies are examples of populations in the first stage. Their death rates were very high. They were extremely vulnerable to crop failure and famine, possessed very limited environmental health controls, and had no health technologies to apply to the sick and disabled. Individuals in such societies usually had a short life expectancy, perhaps 35 or 40 years. Fertility was necessarily high as mortality took such a substantial toll. The continued existence of the society required these high birth rates.

The second stage, sometimes called the stage of *transitional growth*, is characterized by continued high birth rates but a declining mortality. In this second stage of demographic transition, the population grows very rapidly and also undergoes changes in age composition. Typically, the declining death rates are due to technological changes: increased food production, distribution, and availability; reduced vulnerability to crop failures and famine. The accompanying age composition changes usually involve some increased longevity but a marked increase in the proportion of the population that is young (resulting from a significant decline in infant and child mortality).

The third stage of demographic transition, characterized by low mortality and low or controlled fertility, is most often descriptive of modern Western societies. Populations experiencing this stage are capable of controlling birth rates so that very low or no population growth may eventually occur. No population has as yet shown the low fertility rates over a long time period expected in the third stage.

Some demographers believe that demographic transition theory is a useful tool only for analyzing population change in Western Europe and North America. William Petersen (1975), for example, argues that today's less-developed nations exhibit patterns of fertility, mortality, and migration that make them difficult to analyze in terms of a three-stage transition process. Typically, less modern societies interested in rapid development have imported Western health programs and medical technologies on a wholesale basis. This has resulted in significant "unnatural" declines in the death rates. Efforts to cut fertility have been less successful, with enormous population growth as a result. In eastern Europe, the state has intervened to try to achieve certain demographic goals. Such policies as family-size subsidies, state-controlled abortion centers, forced migration, and immigration or emigration restrictions may significantly affect population dynamics.

THE DEPENDENCY RATIO

The growth of the elderly population has led gerontologists to look to the demographic relationship between it and the rest of the population. To the degree that the old are to be supported by the society to which they have contributed, this relationship suggests the extent of social, economic, and political effort a society may be asked to make in support of its elderly.

One measure used to crudely summarize this relationship is known as the *dependency ratio*. Arithmetically, the ratio represents the number or proportion of individuals in the dependent segment of the population divided by the number or proportion of individuals in the supportive or working population. Although the dependent population has two components, the young and the old, students of gerontology have especially concerned themselves with the old-age dependency ratio. Definitions of *old* and *working* are "65 and over" and "18 to 64" years of age, respectively. Thus the old-age dependency ratio is, in simple demographic terms, 65+ / 18–64. This does not mean that *every* person aged 65 and over is dependent or that *every* person in the 18-to-64 range is working. However, we use these basic census categories to depict the relationship between these two segments of the society's population.

Table 3.3 shows old-age dependency ratios for the United States from 1970 to 2020. The ratio has increased in this century and is expected to continue to do so until the year 2020, when it is expected to increase dramatically. During the decade between 2010 and 2020, the baby boom children of the late 1940s and 1950s will begin reaching retirement age, thus increasing the numerator; and a lowered birth rate, such as now exists, means a relatively smaller work force population (18 to 64), reducing the denominator (Cutler and Harootyan, 1975). The projected old-age dependency ratio of 29 in 2020 indicates that every 29 individuals 65 years of age or over will hypothetically be supported by 100 working persons between the ages of 18 and 64. This constitutes a ratio of between 1 to 3 and 1 to 4. In 1930, this ratio was about 1 to 11.

Shifts in the old-age dependency ratio suggest that support of the aged will become increasingly problematic through the remainder of this century, into the twenty-first century, and especially serious after 2010. It would seem that unless future aged are better able to support themselves than are current cohorts of elderly, an increasing burden will fall on the working population, requiring government to play a larger part in providing health and other services to the aged.

Some would disagree, however. It may be argued that measuring the dependency burden of the elderly should not occur in a vacuum, and that the level of the child or "young-age" dependency ratio should be taken into account, since the share of society's support available for the elderly is affected by the level of young-age dependency (Siegel and Davidson, 1984). Table 3.3 also presents the young-age dependency ratios for the United States for 1970 and 1980 and projected through the year 2020. The child or young-age dependency ratio – the number of children under age 18 per 100 persons 18 to 64 years – is expected to decline from 61 in 1970 to 37 in 2020. This results from a continued expectation of reduced fertility and implies a generally decreasing burden on the working population.

The combination of old- and young-age dependency ratios, representing an overall dependency

TABLE 3.3 Old- and young-age dependency ratios, 1970–2020

Year	Ratio $= \dfrac{\text{Population 65 and over}}{\text{Population 18 to 64}} \times 100$	Ratio $= \dfrac{\text{Population under 18}}{\text{Population 18 to 64}} \times 100$	Total dependency burden
1970	18	61	78
1980	19	46	65
Projections			
1990	21	42	63
2000	21	41	62
2010	22	36	58
2020	29	37	66

Note: Based on Middle Series Census Bureau Projections. See Table 3.1 for an explanation of assumptions.

Source: J. S. Siegel and M. Davidson, *Demographic and Socioeconomic Aspects of Aging in the United States,* Current Population Reports, Series P-23, No. 138 (Washington, DC: U.S. Department of Commerce, Bureau of the Census, 1984), p. 113.

burden on the working-age population, declined sharply between 1970 and 1980 and is expected to be relatively stable through the year 2020. The total dependency burden in 2020, projected to be 66, is almost precisely the figure (65) used to describe the total burden in 1980.

Between 1980 and 2020, the projected share of the total dependency burden accounted for by those under 18 years of age declines from 71 percent to 56 percent. Presumably, this decline would permit the conversion of some funds and other support resources from use by children to use by the elderly. Support costs for the elderly are generally thought to be greater than for the young and historically more likely to become a public responsibility; in the United States, support for children tends to be a private family responsibility (Clark and Spengler, 1978). As a result, despite the expected shift in dependency burden between 1980 and 2020 from the young to the old, government may be expected to play a larger part in providing health and other support services to the aged.

SEX, RACE, AND ETHNIC COMPOSITION

Elderly women outnumber elderly men in virtually all settings within which aging takes place (Cowgill, 1972). This occurs despite the fact that the number of male births in a population always exceeds the number of female births (Matras, 1973, pp. 145-146). Typically, after the earliest ages, the male excess is reduced by higher male mortality; at the most advanced ages the number of females exceeds the number of males.

In the United States, the number of males for every 100 females – the *sex ratio* – in the over-65 population has been declining throughout this century. In 1900 the sex ratio was 102; by 1930 it had declined to 100.4. The sex ratio in these years, however, was still heavily influenced by the predominantly male immigration prior to World War I. As Table 3.4 shows, the 1980 sex ratio in the older population was 67.5 (it was 94.8 for the total population) and is projected to decline further until about

TABLE 3.4 Males per 100 females by age and race, 1950–2020

Age and race	1950	1960	1970	1980	1990	2000	2010	2020
					Projections			
All Races								
All ages	99.3	97.0	94.8	94.8	94.7	94.7	94.8	94.6
65 years and over	89.5	82.6	72.0	67.5	66.1	64.5	65.2	69.1
75 years and over	82.6	75.0	63.3	55.2	53.5	52.5	51.2	53.3
White								
All ages	99.6	98.1	96.3	95.2	95.4	95.5	95.5	95.4
65 years and over	89.1	82.0	71.3	67.2	66.4	65.3	66.4	70.7
75 years and over	81.9	74.2	62.6	54.5	53.3	52.8	52.0	54.4
Black								
All ages	96.5	93.8	91.8	89.6	90.7	91.2	91.7	92.1
65 years and over	95.8	86.5	76.3	68.0	61.7	56.1	54.5	58.2
75 years and over	93.2	82.6	70.5	60.0	53.0	47.9	43.7	43.7

Note: Based on Middle Series Census Bureau Projections. See Table 3.1 for an explanation of assumptions.
Source: J. S. Siegel and M. Davidson, *Demographic and Socioeconomic Aspects of Aging in the United States,* Current Population Reports, Series P-23, No. 138 (Washington, DC: U.S. Department of Commerce, Bureau of the Census, 1984), Table 3.1.

2010. Principally, we continue to explain the sex ratio of the aged population in terms of the higher mortality of males, particularly at the ages below 65. This higher mortality among males reduces the relative number of survivors at the older ages.

The female population 65 and over has been growing much more rapidly than the male population in this age stratum (Siegel, 1979, p. 34). Siegel notes that between 1960 and 1970 the female population 65 and over increased 28 percent, while the comparable male population increased by about 12 percent; between 1970 and 1980 the increase in the aged female population is about 25 percent, for the aged male population about 18 percent. This differential in growth rates added to the continued excess of males among the newborns, yields a proportion of those 65 and over among females that is considerably above that for males.

For 1980, aged females constituted about 13.0 percent of the total female population, and aged males constitute about 9.3 percent of the total male population. The sex ratio of the elderly population in 1980 corresponded to an excess of 5 million women, or about 19 percent of the total aged population. Twenty years earlier, in 1960, the excess was less than one million women (accounting for about 5 percent of the aged population). The latest Census Bureau estimates for the year 2000 project an excess of 7.6 million women, or about 20 percent of the total population 65 and over (Siegel and Davidson, 1984).

Because of enumeration problems, statistics on *minority elderly* should be viewed with some caution. Black elderly make up about 8.2 percent of the total elderly population, whereas 11.8 percent of the total United States population is black. In general, the United States black population is younger than the population of whites. The proportion of the black population that is 65 years of age and over is considerably smaller than that of the white population, for both males and females. Smaller proportions of blacks than whites survive to old age, although survival rates within old age are

quite similar across the races. Siegel and Davidson (1984) point out that according to *life tables* for 1978, 77 percent of whites survive from birth to age 65 as compared with 65 percent for blacks; for survival from age 65 to 85, the percentages converge to 34 and 31, respectively.

The key factor in the relative youthfulness of the black population is the higher fertility among blacks. On average, black women have 3.1 children, compared to the 2.2 recorded for white women. The median age of blacks is roughly 6 years less than that of whites. In 1988, for example, blacks had a median age of 27.5 years; the comparable figure for whites was 33.2 years.

Next to blacks, *Latinos* make up the largest minority in the United States, and this population is fast growing. In projections for 1990, Latinos constitute about 7.5 percent of the U.S. population, or over 19 million people. Officially, this population increased by 50 percent between 1970 and 1980, and is expected to increase another 35 percent between 1980–1990. The actual rate of growth has probably been higher as a result of illegal immigration. Some experts forecast that before the year 2000 Latinos will become the nation's largest minority group (Farley, 1982).

The Latino population is a heterogeneous group. About 60 percent are of Mexican origin. One in seven Latinos is of Puerto Rican background (14 percent); 6 percent are Cuban and 21 percent are of other Spanish heritage. The Latino population is an even younger population than blacks. High fertility and large family size, in addition to immigration of the young and repatriation of the middle-aged, contribute to the youthfulness of this group.

Many *ancestry groups* are represented within the United States population. Table 3.5 presents some data on single ancestry groups collected through the Ancestry and Language Survey conducted by the Census Bureau in late 1979. Though relatively small in numbers, those who identified themselves as singly of Russian ancestry had the largest propor-

TABLE 3.5 Percentage of the population 65 years and over, for specified ancestry groups, 1979 (single ancestry only)

Ancestry	Number, all ages (in thousands)	Percentage 65 years and over
German	17,160	14.8
English	11,501	17.9
Irish	9,760	16.3
Afro-American, African	15,057	7.3
Italian	6,110	16.3
Polish	3,498	19.2
Spanish (including Latin America)	9,762	4.6
Russian	1,496	27.4
French	3,047	13.1
All others	19,105	15.6
Total	96,496	13.6

Source: U.S. Bureau of the Census, Current Population Reports, Series P-23, No. 116, March 1982.

tion of elderly (27.4 percent), followed by the Polish (19.2 percent), English (17.9 percent), and Irish and Italian (16.3). The relative "agedness" of those of Russian and Polish ancestry results from the considerable migration to the United States that occurred early in this century, mostly before 1924. This explanation may similarly work for the Italians. English and Irish migration largely took place in the nineteenth century. Thus, the high proportion of elderly in these groups is likely a result of high fertility in the early years of the twentieth century and declining fertility in more recent years.

Migration has had great impact on the age distribution of the foreign-born population in the United States. Before World War I, immigration was relatively unrestricted. After the war, changes in policy brought a sharp curtailment to immigration. In 1970, a relatively high proportion of the elderly were themselves foreign-born – among those 65 years of age and older, 15.3 percent were born outside the United States. By 1979 this figure had dropped to 11.4 percent, and we can expect the proportion of the elderly population that is foreign-born to continue to decline. In 1979 only 7.7 percent of those aged 55 to 64 years and 5.1 percent of those aged 45 to 54 years were themselves foreign-born.

HEALTH STATUS

Human organs gradually diminish in function over time, although not at the same rate in every individual. By itself, this gradual diminishing of function is not a real threat to the health of most older people; diseases are another matter. Diseases represent the chief barriers to extended health and longevity. And, when they accompany normal changes associated with biological aging, maintaining health and securing appropriate health care become especially problematic for older people.

Efforts at maintaining health and functioning in old age include the formidable task of assessing health status. This assessment task is described as formidable for three related reasons (Kane and Kane, 1981). First, the elderly are often subject to multiple illnesses and, thus, to multiple diagnoses. Second, we have come to understand that the physical, mental, and social health of elderly individuals are closely interrelated; as a result, assessment must be multidimensional. Finally, measures of functioning that allow for assessment of an individual's ability to carry on independently, despite disease or disability, are probably the most useful indicators for practitioners.

The concept of physical health can be broken down into at least three subcategories: general physical health or the absence of illness; the ability to perform basic self-care activities including what are known as activities of daily living (ADLs); and the ability to perform more complex self-care activities that allow for greater independence including what are known as instrumental activities of daily living (IADLs). These subcategories are thought to reflect a hierarchical order in that each level generally requires a higher order of functioning than the preceding one.

Most health survey data show a pattern in which vigorous old age predominates (Gilford, 1988), but where there is a clear association of advancing age with poorer functioning (Manton, 1989). Manton (1989) suggests that function can be maintained well into advanced old age and that people vary greatly in the rate at which functional loss occurs. The potential for rehabilitation exists even where a decline in functioning is the result of a currently untreatable disease (Besdine, 1988). An active approach to preserving function with increasing age includes changing medical and institutional responses to disability and chronic disease among the elderly and altering negative attitudes about normal aging, even though these attitudes are accepted by many elderly themselves.

The great majority of older Americans live in the community and are cognitively intact and fully independent in their activities of daily living. Those that remain active may be individuals who exercise, eat nutritionally and have a positive psychological view of life. Manton (1989) presents data to support these findings. Still, most older Americans have had or currently have a serious illness. Today, chronic illnesses represent the key health problems affecting middle-aged and older adults. In fact, when compared with younger age groups, middle-aged and older adults show lower rates of acute conditions, including infective and parasitic conditions, respiratory conditions, conditions of the digestive system, and injuries (U.S. Bureau of the Census, 1985: Table 186).

Chronic conditions are long-lasting, and their progress generally causes irreversible pathology. Generally, the prevalence of chronic conditions among the elderly is higher than among younger persons. The reported prevalence rates among the elderly for heart conditions, hypertension, varicose veins, arthritis, diabetes, diseases of the urinary system, visual and hearing impairments, and deformities or orthopedic impairments show the most substantial differences when compared with the prevalence rates of chronic conditions among those in the younger age groups.

In the Supplement on Aging (SOA) to the 1984 National Health Interview Survey (NHIS), respondents aged 55 years and older were asked if they ever had one or more of a list of 13 illnesses, including osteoporosis, coronary heart disease, stroke, cancer, and Alzheimer's disease. About 4 in 10 (43.3 percent) reported never having had one of these illnesses, while 21.2 percent reported having two or more of these illnesses. Table 3.6 shows the number of illnesses by different demographic

TABLE 3.6 Number of illnesses and average number of bed days by selected characteristics

	Number of illnesses			Bed days	
	None	*1*	*2+*	*(1)*	*(2)*
Age					
55–64 years	53.2%	33.5%	13.2%	9.4	32.4
65–74	42.2	36.0	21.8	10.7	40.2
75–84	34.9	37.5	27.6	14.9	52.2
85+	30.7	34.3	34.9	20.9	67.8
Gender					
Male	47.5%	31.9%	20.5%	10.9	40.5
Female	40.2	38.2	21.6	12.4	43.4
Family income					
Under $15,000	38.0%	37.6%	24.5%	15.1	50.8
$15,000 or more	47.3	33.8	19.0	8.4	29.3
Race					
White	43.8%	34.8%	21.4%	11.4	39.9
Nonwhite	38.4	43.5	18.1	16.2	63.7
Residence					
Central city	42.7%	36.8%	20.5%	13.1	45.2
Suburban	46.2	34.1	19.8	10.6	38.1
Rural	40.7	36.2	23.1	12.0	44.3

(1) Average number of days per last 12 months, all cases.
(2) Average number of days per last 12 months, *excluding* all cases with zero days.

Source: 1984 Supplement on Aging, NHIS.

characteristics of the SOA respondents. Those aged 55 to 64 years are the only demographic group represented in the table that shows a majority (53.2 percent) of individuals never having one of these serious illnesses. Those aged 75 to 84 years are twice as likely as the youngest group (27.6 percent versus 13.2 percent) to have two or more of these illnesses; 34.9 percent of the old-old (those aged 85 years or more) report having two or more illnesses.

Modest differences in number of reported illnesses also exist by gender, family income, race, and residence. In general, females, those with incomes below $15,000, nonwhites, and rural residents reported the greatest number of illnesses.

Table 3.6 also shows the average number of days spent inactive in bed in the past 12 months as reported by SOA respondents. There seems to be a linear relationship between age and "bed days"; with age, the average number of bed days increases so that those 85 years and older spend twice as many days in bed as those aged 55 to 64 years. Females, those with lower income, nonwhites, and nonsuburbanites spend the most time, on average, inactive in bed.

Table 3.7 reports on the self-assessment of health status made by SOA respondents. About 70 percent of SOA respondents reported their health status in positive terms (excellent, very good, good). It is important to remember that a substantial correlation exists between subjective health status and measures of functional status in aged adults (Ferraro, 1980, 1985) and physical examinations or physician ratings (LaRue, Bank, Jarvik, and Hetland, 1979; Maddox and Douglas, 1973). Although almost three out of four (74.9 percent) persons aged 55 to 64 years assess their health in positive terms, less than two of three (63.6 percent) of those 85 years and older do similarly. Even among the very-old living in the community, however, only about one-third (36.4 percent) assess their health as fair or poor.

TABLE 3.7 Self-assessed health status by selected characteristics

| | Self-assessed health status | | | |
	Excellent or very good	Good	Fair	Poor
Age				
55-64 years	44.1%	30.8%	16.6%	8.4%
65-74	36.5	32.0	21.1	10.3
75-84	36.0	31.1	20.7	12.2
85+	35.0	28.6	23.2	13.2
Gender				
Male	39.4	30.3	19.1	11.2
Female	37.9	32.0	20.4	9.7
Family income				
Under $15,000	30.2	30.5	24.7	14.6
$15,000 or more	46.9	31.8	15.2	6.1
Race				
White	39.5	31.8	19.1	9.6
Nonwhite	28.7	25.6	27.1	18.5
Residence				
Central city	38.0	31.1	20.6	10.3
Suburban	42.0	32.3	17.5	8.2
Rural	35.3	30.3	21.7	12.7

Source: 1984 Supplement on Aging, NHIS.

There is variable correlation between other demographic measures and self-assessment of health among the aged. For example, less affluent elderly were almost twice as likely as were more affluent elderly (39.3 percent versus 21.3 percent) to assess their health as fair or poor. Whites are more likely than nonwhites to assess their health positively; 45.6 percent of nonwhites and 28.7 percent of whites assess their health as fair or poor. This differential is consistent with prior research (Schlesinger, 1987). Most nonwhites in the SOA are black (86 percent). Black/white differences in self-assessment of health status reflect real differences in health status and health service utilization (Gibson and Jackson, 1987). Geographic locale is also an important consideration. Elderly suburbanites have more positive assessments of their health than do elderly residents of central city and rural areas.

Gender differences in self-assessments of health status among the aged are quite modest. This is particularly interesting in light of the significant female advantage over males in mortality rates and life expectancy (Zopf, 1986).

Activities of Daily Living

Because general physical health measures have limits, especially for assessing the degree of independence and functioning an individual possesses even in the face of illness and impairment, and because self-ratings can be subject to variation over time and distortion based on psychological and/or environmental mechanisms, practitioners and researchers have sought to develop measures that reflect the practical aspects of physical functioning. Activities of daily living (ADL) scales have developed as the ultimate indicators of the elderly individual's capacity to deal with basic self-care.

With some variation across different instruments, items included to measure basic self-care of ADL activities include bathing, dressing, going to the bathroom, getting in or out of a bed or chair, walking, getting outside the house or apartment, and feeding. These are ordered in terms of decreasing dependency and are thought to form a Guttman scale (Katz, Ford, Moskowitz, Jackson, and Jaffee, 1963). That is, it is generally found that bathing is the least restrictive and most common problem and lack of the ability to feed oneself is indicative of the most severe restriction of function; difficulty in feeding oneself is highly associated with the presence of other problems and is the least common ADL difficulty. Kane and Kane (1981) point out that the actual choice of ADL scale may influence results, with different indicators being more or less sensitive to change in physical functioning over time.

Table 3.8 shows the proportions of those in the SOA reporting limitations in ADLs by age, gender, family income, race and residence. The oldest-old,

women, those elderly with family income under $15,000, nonwhites, and those residing in rural areas report the most limitations in ADLs. Age and income differences seem the strongest explainers of variation in ADL score. Almost 90 percent (88.2 percent) of those 55 through 64 years of age compared to about one-half (50.5 percent) of those 85 years and over report no limitations in ADLs; more than one-third (36.8 percent) of the oldest-old report two or more limitations in activities of daily living. SOA respondents with family income under $15,000 were about twice as likely as more well-to-do respondents (those with income greater than $15,000) to report limitations in ADLs (25.5 percent versus 13.1 percent).

Instrumental Activities of Daily Living

The concept of instrumental activities of daily living (IADLs) is both inclusive of the personal self-care reflected in the ADL measures and more complex. For example, going shopping, a commonly used IADL indicator, requires being able to get out of bed, dress, walk, and leave the house. Because the IADL tasks are more complicated and multifaceted, functional decrements are expected to show up first in the IADL items, and more older people are expected to report limitations in carrying out these instrumental activities than is the case for the more basic activities of daily living. This expectation is supported by the data in Table 3.8. In every case, except that of males, a greater proportion of SOA respondents report limitations with instrumental activities of daily living than is the case for the basic ADLs.

IADLs included in the SOA were preparing meals, shopping, managing money, using the telephone, doing light housework, and doing heavy housework. Although the general pattern shown for the IADLs in Table 3.8 is quite similar to that reported on for the ADLs, some differences are

TABLE 3.8 Percentage with limitations in activities of daily living (ADLs) and instrumental activities of daily living (IADLs) by selected characteristics

	ADL[a] Number of activities				IADL[b] Number of activities			
	One	Two or three	Four or more	Total	One	Two or three	Four or more	Total
Age								
55-64 years	5.4%	3.9%	2.5%	11.8%	9.8%	2.5%	1.6%	13.9%
65-74	7.9	5.6	3.7	17.2	13.0	4.2	3.3	20.5
75-84	11.1	9.1	7.3	27.5	15.9	9.0	7.6	32.5
85+	12.7	17.2	19.6	49.5	14.9	14.2	30.6	59.7
Gender								
Male	7.6	4.8	3.8	16.2	7.5	2.5	3.5	13.5
Female	8.5	7.6	5.7	21.8	16.0	6.8	5.7	28.5
Family income								
Under $15,000	10.7	8.7	6.1	25.5	16.5	7.6	5.6	29.7
$15,000 or more	5.6	4.0	3.5	13.1	9.3	2.7	3.6	15.6
Race								
White	8.0	6.3	4.7	19.0	12.5	4.9	4.6	22.0
Nonwhite	9.6	7.8	7.1	24.5	15.5	7.7	7.1	30.3
Residence								
Central city	8.5	7.1	5.1	20.7	12.7	6.6	4.6	23.9
Suburban	7.1	5.1	4.7	16.9	11.3	3.8	4.9	20.0
Rural	9.0	7.4	5.1	21.5	14.3	5.4	4.9	24.6

[a]ADLs include bathing, dressing, going to the bathroom, getting in/out of a bed or chair, walking, getting outside the apartment or house, feeding.

[b]IADLs include preparing meals, shopping, managing money, using the telephone, doing light housework, and doing heavy housework.

Source: 1984 Supplement on Aging, NHIS.

noteworthy. First, a significant majority of the oldest-old (59.7 percent) report one or more limitations in the IADLs, with almost one-third (30.6 percent) of this age group indicating four or more limitations. This suggests that many of the oldest-old are housebound, in need of major assistance at home, and perhaps at risk for institutionalization.

Second, female SOA respondents are more than twice as likely as males to be reporting IADL limitations (28.5 percent versus 13.5 percent). This is consistent with the earlier stated findings that women were more likely than men to have ever had one or more illnesses and to have more physi-

cian visits. Nathanson (1975) offers three categories of explanation for why women report more illness and limitation and use more medical service than do men:

1. It is culturally more acceptable for women to be ill.
2. Women's social roles are more compatible with reports of illness and use of medical services than is the case for men.
3. Women's social roles are, in fact, more stressful than those of men; consequently, they have more real illness and need more assistance and care.

The merits of these explanations continue to be debated (e.g., Verbrugge and Madans, 1985).

Kane and Kane (1981) suggest that, because of the complexity and multifacetedness of IADLs, how respondents report on the individual items may be biased by variations in motivation, mood, and overall emotional health. For instance, a depressed older person might be more likely to neglect IADL activities such as managing money or doing the housework than basic aspects of personal self-care such as dressing or using the toilet.

It can also be argued that social structural and/or environmental factors contribute to IADL limitations. A widower or widow who never performed certain IADL tasks when his or her spouse was alive and fit may report limitations because he or she never learned the skills, not because of an inability to perform the function. Also, an older woman may report limitations in shopping because markets are scarce in her inner-city neighborhood and she lacks transportation to area stores. As Lawton and Nahemow (1973) reported in the early 1970s, when the "fit" between an individual's competence and the environment in which the individual resides is good, adaptation is positive. This may be the case for the great majority of older people. When environmental demands are too great, adaptation is poor and the outcome (including self-care capacity) is likely to be negative.

MENTAL HEALTH

Estimates vary as to the proportion of the elderly population with mental health problems. According to Pfeiffer (1977), approximately 15 percent of the elderly population in the United States suffer from significant, substantial, or moderate psychopathological conditions. Gurland and Toner (1982) argue that 15 percent may represent only that proportion of the elderly with clinically significant depression. Roybal (1984) states that as many as 25 percent of the elderly have significant mental health problems. Presumably this percentage includes both long-term care facility and community residents.

Blazer (1980) reports that the rate of severe impairment of subjects in various studies ranges from 4 to 18 percent of community-dwelling elders and 32 to 47 percent of those elderly persons residing in long-term care institutions. Among the specified diagnoses, organic brain syndromes, depressive disorders, schizophrenia, and alcohol disorders account for high rates of patient care episodes in outpatient psychiatric services for old people in the United States. The same list obtains for inpatient facilities. Over 600,000 nursing home residents in the United States in 1973–1974 were diagnosed as senile. More recently, 15 to 70 percent of those found in various sorts of long-term care institutions showed symptoms of dementia (Blazer, 1980).

Figures on the mental health status of the elderly must be viewed with some caution. The epidemiology of psychopathological conditions is beset by conceptual and methodological difficulties. Even under careful conditions of assessment, diagnosing schizophrenia or depression is often difficult. Different doctors, using different definitions and criteria, and varying widely in their competence as well as in their understanding of aging processes, should make us suspicious of the adequacy of their diagnoses. For example, there has been a tendency to overestimate the incidence of dementia among the old, while underestimating that of depression. The symptoms of these disorders are similar, and correct diagnosis can also be confounded by attitudes toward the elderly (Butler and Lewis, 1982; Eisdorfer and Cohen, 1982). In addition, as Libow (1973) reminds us, much of the early mental change shown by elderly persons can be explained by changes in the environment.

A National Institute of Mental Health study of healthy male volunteers, whose average age was

70 at the start of the study and who were followed for 11 years, found a strong relationship between survival and the organization of a subject's behavior (Bartko and Patterson, 1971). The greater the complexity and variability of a day's behavior, the greater the likelihood of survival.

Sampling error also contributes to the generation of inaccurate estimates of the incidence of mental health problems among the aged. If samples are drawn from lists of present users of mental health services, then older people will be underrepresented. According to Kermis (1986), because older people do not use mental health services, the belief is that they do not need them. If samples are drawn from a community at large, older people with mental health problems are also underrepresented because many of them reside in groups or institutional settings (Kermis, 1986).

Despite the conceptual and methodological difficulties involved in determining the degree and extent to which psychopathological conditions are distributed among the elderly, it is clear that some older people do have mental health problems. These problems are often categorized according to the degree of actual impairment in brain functioning.

Depression, although it appears to be the most common of the functional psychiatric disorders in the later years, is not often recognized in older people (Kermis, 1986). Depression can vary in duration and degree; it may be triggered by loss of a loved one or by the onset of a physical disease. A depressed individual may show any combination of psychological and physiological manifestations. Core symptoms include abject and painful sadness, generalized withdrawal of interest and inhibition of activity, pervasive pessimism, decreased self-esteem, and poor self-prognosis (American Psychological Association, 1980). Kermis (1986) lists some atypical clinical features that further confuse diagnosis, including pseudodementia (apathy and slowness of cognition resembling dementia) and somatic complaints without obvious mood changes.

Depression in older persons is a treatable syndrome. If untreated it may become chronic and lead to social dysfunction, drug use, and/or physical morbidity (Gurland and Toner, 1982). Drug therapies are popular. Other treatment modalities are available, although, as Butler and Lewis (1982) indicate, many professionals view the elderly as "poor candidates" for the psychotherapies.

Suicidal thoughts often accompany depression. Gardner, Bahn and Mack (1964) found in their research that the majority of older persons committing suicide have been depressed. According to the U.S. Center for Health Statistics, the suicide rate among the elderly in 1986 was 68 percent higher than that among the total population. This statistic may present a conservative picture. Many doctors do not report suicides because they think it stigmatizes the surviving family members; family members themselves often hide or destroy suicide notes – usually unnecessarily – to try to ensure payments by life insurance companies.

Table 3.9 presents suicide rates by sex, race, and age group for 1986. Aged white males show the highest suicide rate of any group. Their rate is almost 3 times that of aged black males, about 6 times that of aged white females, and about 20 times that of aged black females. Aged females in the United States have among the lowest suicide rates in the world. Aged American males fall in the middle of the range represented by selected countries. Male elderly have higher suicide rates in Austria, Denmark, France, West Germany, and Japan; countries in which the elderly have lower suicide rates than is the case in the United States include England and Wales, Australia, Canada, Italy, and Poland, among others (U.S. Bureau of the Census, 1986, Table 1443).

Two additional common functional psychiatric disorders in the later years are paranoia and hypo-

TABLE 3.9 Suicide rates by sex, race, and age groups, 1986

	Male		Female	
	White	Black	White	Black
All ages	22.3	11.1	5.9	2.3
10-14 years	2.4	1.5	.7	.4
15-19	18.2	7.1	4.1	2.1
20-24	28.4	16.0	5.3	2.4
25-34	26.4	21.3	6.2	3.8
35-44	23.9	17.5	8.3	2.8
45-54	26.3	12.8	9.6	3.2
55-64	28.7	9.9	9.0	4.2
65 and over	45.6	16.2	7.5	2.4

Source: U.S Bureau of the Census (1990), Table 125.

chondriasis. *Paranoia* is a delusional state that is usually persecutory in nature. It often involves attributing motivations to other people that they simply do not have. Paranoia is more common in individuals suffering from sensory deficits such as hearing loss (Post, 1980). Some paranoia may be "caused" by changes in life situation, such as relocation or other stresses. Kermis (1986) describes a 72-year-old woman hospitalized while recovering from major heart surgery. She had a persistent delusion that CIA agents were spying on her. She recorded these occurrences and reported them to the staff, who discovered that her "CIA visits" corresponded to security guards' checks of the floor.

Characteristically, the initial premise of the paranoid is irrational, although the rest of the delusional system often follows logically. Kermis (1986) notes that if the paranoid's basic premise is accepted, the rest of the delusion often makes sense. Most paranoids have a fairly focused problem and are not impaired in their daily functioning. If the disorder remains chronic, however, social and marital function may be negatively affected (American Psychiatric Association, 1987).

Hypochondriasis is an overconcern for one's health, usually accompanied by delusions about physical dysfunction and/or disease. The conventional wisdom is that hypochondriacs displace their psychological distress onto the body. A number of observers have emphasized the utility of the condition – after all, it is far more acceptable in this society to be physically ill than it is to be emotionally or mentally disabled (Pfeiffer and Busse, 1973). Hypochondriacs will diligently seek medical help, yet treatment of the disorder is difficult because they are not predisposed to psychological explanations of their condition.

The 1987 revised edition of the *Diagnostic and Statistical Manual of Mental Disorders* (DSM-III-R) of the American Psychiatric Association (APA) makes the distinction between *organic mental syndromes* (OMS) and *organic mental disorders* (OMD). "Organic mental syndrome" is used to refer to a group of psychological or behavioral signs and symptoms without reference to etiology; "organic mental disorder" designates a particular OMS in which the etiology is known or presumed (APA, 1987). OMS can be grouped into six categories: (1) Delirium and Dementia, in which cognitive impairment is global; (2) Amnestic Syndrome and Organic Hallucinosis, in which there is selective cognitive impairment; (3) Organic Delusional Syndrome, Organic Mood Syndrome, and Organic Anxiety Syndrome, with features resembling schizophrenia, mood, and anxiety disorders, respectively; (4) Organic Personality Syndrome, where personality is affected; (5) Intoxication and Withdrawal, associated with the ingestion of or reduction in use of a psychoactive substance; and (6) Organic Mental Syndrome Not Otherwise Specified, which is a residual category.

According to the DSM-III-R (APA, 1987, p. 98), the most common forms of OMS are delirium, dementia, intoxication, and withdrawal. These syndromes display great variability in the same individuals over time as well as across different individuals, and may be present in the same individual simultaneously. Dementia is most common in the elderly and most often takes the form of Primary Degenerative Dementia of the Alzheimer's Type.

In the DSM-III-R, Primary Degenerative Dementia of the Alzheimer Type is identified as an organic mental disorder arising in the senium and presenium. What this means is that the disease is believed to be a physical disorder, and that it is subtyped according to age of onset. Senile onset (after age 65) is much more common than presenile onset, with few cases developing before the age of 50. Between 2 and 4 percent of the entire population over the age of 65 may have this dementia, with the proportion increasing in those over 75 years of age. The disorder is slightly more common in females than in males, and in rare cases is thought to be inherited as a dominant trait. Down syndrome is a predisposing factor to Alzheimer's disease.

Dementia of the Alzheimer's type has an insidious onset and a gradually progressive course (APA, 1987). It brings a multifaceted loss of intellectual abilities, including memory, judgment, and abstract thought, as well as changes in personality and behavior. Initially, the Alzheimer's victim experiences minor symptoms that may be attributed to stress or physical illness. With time, however, the person becomes more forgetful. Things get misplaced, routine chores take longer, and already answered questions are repeated. As the disease progresses, memory loss as well as confusion, irritability, restlessness, and agitation are likely to appear. Judgment, concentration, orientation, writing, reading, speech, motor behavior, and naming of objects may also be affected. Even when a loving and supportive family is available, the Alzheimer's victim may ultimately require institutional care (U.S. Department of Health and Human Services [USDHHS], 1984). Additional material on Alzheimer's disease is presented in Chapter 4, "Cogni-

tive Aspects of Aging," and Chapter 8, "The Nervous System."

At the present time, there is no cure for Alzheimer's disease. What are the possible causes of this debilitating disease? Since the 1970s, research scientists have been studying the evidence of a significant and progressive decrease in the activity of the enzyme choline acetyltransferase (ChAT) in the brain tissue of Alzheimer's patients. ChAT is an important ingredient in neurotransmissions involved with learning and memory. There appears to be a link between changes in this neurochemical activity and changes in cognition and the physical appearance of the brains of Alzheimer's patients (USDHHS, 1984). Additional research is needed to determine whether accumulations of trace metals in the brain (such as aluminum) are a primary cause of Alzheimer's disease or if other factors like slow-acting transmissible viruses might combine with environmental factors to trigger the onset of the disease (USDHHS, 1984).

Some scientists see an inherited predisposition or genetic marker to Alzheimer's disease. Zubenko and his colleagues at the University of Pittsburgh have discovered an abnormality in the blood that may predict the later onset of Alzheimer's. This abnormality was found in blood platelets, particles vital to the process of blood clotting. The blood platelets of Alzheimer's patients show less rigidity in their structural membranes, although this abnormality does not impair blood platelet functioning. Such an alteration would not likely have any direct causal effect bearing on Alzheimer's, but scientists speculate that the gene that does cause this change may have different, as yet unidentified, effects on brain cells (Schmeck, 1987). The platelet abnormality was not found in people with depression or mania, conditions sometimes confused with Alzheimer's disease. Interestingly, when the platelet was found in an Alzheimer's patient, it was 3.5 to 11 times more likely to appear in close relatives of the patient than in the general population at large. Family studies have already found that first-degree relatives of Alzheimer's patients are at a significantly higher lifetime risk of developing dementia, especially if the affected family member is a parent and if onset occurs before age 70 (Schmeck, 1987).

Do social or psychological experiences contribute to the cause or development of Alzheimer's disease? Too little research has been aimed at this question. For the most part, social and behavioral scientists have focused on the development of diagnostic tests, the changes in language use that result from brain dysfunction, and the need for special support for the families of disease victims (USDHHS, 1984).

The descriptions of the organic mental syndromes and disorders presented in DSM-III-R are clear and straightforward and give the impression that their recognition and diagnosis are equally so. However, there is some reliable evidence to demonstrate that these disorders are overdiagnosed (Clark, 1980; Fox, Topel, and Huckman, 1975; Glassman, 1980; Kaercher, 1980; Marsden and Harrison, 1972; Seltzer and Sherwin, 1978; Wells, 1978). For example, Duckworth and Ross (1975) compared psychiatric diagnoses given to patients over age 65 in Toronto, New York, and London. They found that organic brain disorders were diagnosed with more than 50 percent greater frequency in New York than in either Toronto or London. Though variation in patient populations may account for some of this difference, Wells (1978) suggests that in Toronto and London a greater emphasis is placed on recognizing functional disorders in the aged, and thus elderly patients are more likely to be labeled correctly.

Libow (1973) has used the term *pseudosenility* to refer to conditions that may manifest themselves as senility and thus cause misdiagnosis or mislabeling of OMS or OMD. Causes of pseudosenility include drug interactions, malnutrition, and fever.

When these conditions are treated, the senility often goes away. Although admittedly there are no definitive studies identifying the frequency of pseudosenility, a task force sponsored by the National Institute on Aging (NIA) suggests that 10 to 20 percent of all older people diagnosed with mental impairments have these reversible conditions (NIA, 1980).

The importance of OMS and OMD, in both numerical and personal terms, is being recognized increasingly. This recognition is reflected in gerontological and popular literature that points out that many curable physical and psychological disorders in the elderly produce intellectual impairments that may be difficult to distinguish from OMS or OMD. More important, this growing body of literature states clearly, if not emphatically, that normal aging does not include the symptoms of OMS or OMD; these are diseases, not inevitable accompaniments of aging.

IS THERE COMPRESSION OF MORBIDITY?

What if the time spent in chronic mental or physical illness and/or with functional limitations in the ADLs or IADLs before death could be reduced from current levels? Presumably, this would mean more years of a higher quality old age, even in an absence of further improvements in life expectancy. Fries (1980, 1987) has argued that this "compression of morbidity" may already be occurring. According to Fries (1987), a compression of morbidity may be considered to occur if the length of time between onset of disease and death is shortened.

This compression of morbidity hypothesis has generated some considerable debate in the gerontological literature. Some have argued that there simply is no evidence to support it. Kaplan (1991), employing data over the last 25 years from the Alameda County, California, studies of two cohorts of adults living in the community, points out that while there have been significant declines in age-specific mortality rates, these declines have been accompanied by an increase in the age-specific prevalence of chronic conditions and symptoms. From Kaplan's view, the overall picture is one of increased survival accompanied by increased morbidity and disability.

Olshansky and his colleagues (1991) also suggest the possibility of an expansion of morbidity through two hypothetical mechanisms. First, medical technology may continue to improve survival from disabling conditions associated with fatal diseases, but the progress of the diseases themselves may remain unchanged. Second, as mortality from fatal diseases in older ages is reduced, the morbidity and disability resulting from nonfatal diseases could continue unabated. Thus, the trade-off becomes reduced mortality in middle and older ages for a redistribution of causes of disability and an expansion of morbidity (Olshansky, Rudberg, Carnes, Cassel, and Brody, 1991). Much work remains to determine whether reductions in risk factors such as smoking and improvements in medical treatments lead to a compression of morbidity or whether causes of disability are redistributed with a resulting "longer life with worsening health."

STUDY QUESTIONS

1. Discuss the roles fertility, mortality, and migration have played in the growth of the aged population in the United States during the twentieth century.
2. What is a dependency ratio? How is the "mix" of old-age and young-age dependency ratios expected to change in the future and what is the significance of this change?
3. Define sex ratio. Applying the concept to the elderly population, how has the sex ratio changed since the beginning of the twentieth century? Why has it changed?
4. Why is recognition of minority elderly issues likely to increase in the future? Why may the importance of ancestry groups diminish among the elderly in this same future?
5. What does the concept of physical health encompass? Distinguish between the absence of illness, basic self-care activities and more complex indicators of functioning.
6. What is the relationship between sociodemographic characteristics of the elderly such as age, sex, race, family income, and residence and self-assessment of health, ADLs, and IADLs?
7. Identify and describe common functional psychiatric disorders in the later years. How do suicide rates vary by sex and race among the elderly?
8. Distinguish between organic brain syndrome and organic mental disorder. What are the diagnostic problems in determining the prevalence rate of these and other mental disorders afflicting the elderly?
9. What is Alzheimer's disease? Describe its symptoms. What do we know about the causes and cures for the disease?

BIBLIOGRAPHY

American Psychiatric Association. 1987. *Diagnostic and statistical manual of mental disorders*, 3rd ed., revised. Washington, DC: American Psychiatric Association.

Bartko, J., and Patterson, R. 1971. Survival among healthy old men: A multivariate analysis. In S. Granick and R. Patterson (Eds.), *Human aging II: An 11-year follow-up*. Washington, DC: U.S. Government Printing Office.

Besdine, R. 1988. Dementia and delirium. In J. W. Rowe and J. W. Besdine (Eds.), *Geriatric medicine*. Boston: Little, Brown.

Blazer, D. 1980. The epidemiology of mental illness in late life. In E. Busse and D. Blazer (Eds.), *Handbook of geriatric psychiatry*. New York: Van Nostrand Reinhold.

Butler, R., and Lewis, M. 1982. *Aging and mental health* (2nd edition). St. Louis: C. V. Mosby.

Clark, M. 1980. The scourge of senility. *Newsweek*, September 15, pp. 85-86.

Clark, R. L., and Spengler, J. J. 1978. Changing dependency and dependency costs: The implications of future dependency ratios and their composition. In B. Herzog (Ed.), *Aging and income: Programs and prospects for the elderly.* New York: Human Sciences Press.

Cowgill, D. 1972. A theory of aging in cross-cultural perspective. In D. Cowgill and L. Holmes (Eds.), *Aging and modernization.* New York: Appleton-Century-Crofts.

Cutler, N., and Harootyan, R. 1975. Demography of the aged. In D. Woodruff and J. Birren (Eds.), *Aging: Scientific perspectives and social issues.* New York: Van Nostrand.

Duckworth, G. S., and Ross, H. 1975. Diagnostic differences in psychogeriatric patients in Toronto, New York and London, England. *Canadian Medical Association Journal,* 112: 847–851.

Eisdorfer, C., and Cohen, D. 1982. *Mental health care of the aging: A multidisciplinary curriculum for professional training.* New York: Springer.

Farley, J. E. 1982. *Majority-minority relations.* Englewood Cliffs, NJ: Prentice-Hall.

Ferraro, K. F. 1980. Self-ratings of health among the old and old-old. *Journal of Health and Social Behavior,* 21: 377–383.

Ferraro, K. F. 1985. The effect of widowhood on the health status of older persons. *International Journal of Aging and Human Development,* 21: 9–25.

Fox, J. H., Topel, J. L., and Huckman, M. S. 1975. Dementia in the elderly – a search for treatable illnesses. *Journal of Gerontology,* 10: 557–574.

Fries, J. F. 1980. Aging, natural death and the compression of morbidity. *New England Journal of Medicine,* 303: 130–135.

Fries, J. F. 1987. An introduction to the compression of morbidity. *Gerontologica Perspecta,* 1: 5–7.

Gardner, E., Bahn, A., and Mack, M. 1964. Suicide and psychiatric care in the aging. *Archives of General Psychiatry,* 10: 547–553.

Gibson, R., and Jackson, J. 1987. The health, physical functioning, and informal supports of the black elderly. *Milbank Memorial Fund Quarterly,* 65 (Suppl.): 421–454.

Gilford, D. M. (Ed.). 1988. *The aging population in the twenty-first century.* Washington, DC: National Academy Press.

Glassman, M. 1980. Misdiagnosis of senile dementia: Denial of care to the elderly. *Social Work,* 25: 288–292.

Gurland, B. J., and Toner, J. A. 1982. Depression in the elderly: A review of recently published studies. In C. Eisdorfer (Ed.), *Annual review of geriatrics and gerontology.* New York: Springer.

Kaercher, D. 1980. Senility: A misdiagnosis. *Better Homes and Gardens,* November, pp. 27–32, 34–37.

Kane, R. A., and Kane, R. L. 1981. *Assessing the elderly: A practical guide to measurement.* Lexington, MA: D. C. Heath.

Kaplan, G. A. 1991. Epidemiologic observations on the compression of morbidity: Evidence from the Alameda County study. *Journal of Aging and Health,* 3(2): 155–171.

Katz, S., Ford, A., Moskowitz, R., Jackson, B., and Jaffee, M. 1963. Studies of illness in the aged. The index of ADL: A standardized measure of biological and psychosocial function. *Journal of the American Medical Association,* 185: 914–919.

Kermis, M. D. 1986. *Mental health in late life: The adaptive process.* Boston: Jones and Bartlett.

LaRue, A., Bank, L., Jarvik, L., and Hetland, M. 1979. Health in old age: How do physicians' ratings and self-ratings compare? *Journal of Gerontology,* 8: 108–115.

Lawton, M., and Nahemow, L. 1973. Ecology and the aging process. In Eisdorfer, C., and Lawton, M. P. (Eds.), *Psychology of adult development and aging.* Washington, DC: American Psychological Association.

Libow, L. 1973. Pseudo-senility: Acute and reversible organic brain syndrome. *Journal of the American Geriatrics Society,* 21: 112–120.

Maddox, G., and Douglas E. 1973. Self-assessment of health, a longitudinal study of elderly subjects. *Journal of Health and Social Behavior,* 14: 87–92.

Manton, K. 1989. Epidemiological, demographic, and social correlates of disability among the elderly. *The Milbank Quarterly,* 67: 13–57.

Marsden, C. D., and Harrison, M. J. G. 1972. Outcome of investigation of patients with presenile dementia. *British Medical Journal,* 2: 249–252.

Matras, J. 1973. *Populations and societies.* Englewood Cliffs, NJ: Prentice-Hall.

Nathanson, C. 1975. Illness and the feminine role: A theoretical review. *Social Science and Medicine,* 9: 57–62.

National Institute on Aging. 1980. Treatment possibilities for mental impairment in the elderly. *Journal of the American Medical Association,* 244: 259–263.

Neugarten, B. 1974. Age groups in American society and the rise of the young-old. *Annals of the American Academy,* September, pp. 187–198.

Olshansky, S. J., Rudberg, M. A., Carnes, B. A.,

Cassel, C. K., and Brody, J. A. 1991. Trading off longer life for worsening health: The expansion of morbidity hypothesis. *Journal of Aging and Health*, 3(2): 194–216.

Petersen, W. 1975. *Population*, 3rd ed. New York: Macmillan.

Pfeiffer, E. 1977. Psychopathy and social pathology. In J. Birren and K. Schaie (Eds.), *Handbook of the psychology of aging*. New York: Van Nostrand Reinhold.

Pfeiffer, E., and Busse, E. 1973. Mental disorders in later life: Affective disorder, paranoid, neurotic and situational reactions. In E. Busse and E. Pfeiffer (Eds.), *Mental illness in later life*. Washington, DC: American Psychiatric Association.

Post, F. 1980. Paranoid, schizophrenia-like and schizophrenia states in the aged. In J. E. Birren and R. B. Sloane (Eds.), *Handbook of mental health and aging*. Englewood Cliffs, NJ: Prentice-Hall.

Roybal, E. R. 1984. Federal involvement in mental health care for the aged. *American Psychologist*, 39: 163–166.

Schlesinger, M. 1987. Paying the price: Medical care, minorities, and the newly competitive health care system. *Milbank Memorial Fund Quarterly*, 65 (Suppl.): 270–296.

Schmeck, H. M. 1987. Blood abnormality may predict the onset of Alzheimer's disease. *New York Times*, October 29, p. 12.

Seltzer, B., and Sherwin, I. 1978. Organic brain syndromes: An empirical study and critical review. *American Journal of Psychiatry*, 135: 13–21.

Siegel, J. S. 1979. *Perspective trends in the size and structure of the elderly population, impact of mortality trends and some implications*. Current Population Reports, Special Studies Series P-23, No. 78. Washington, DC: U.S. Department of Commerce, Bureau of the Census.

Siegel, J. S., and Davidson, M. 1984. *Demographic and socioeconomic aspects of aging in the United States*. Current Population Reports, Special Studies Series P-23, No. 138. Washington, DC: U.S. Department of Commerce, Bureau of the Census.

U.S. Bureau of the Census. 1985. *Statistical abstract of the United States, 1986*. Washington, DC: U.S. Government Printing Office.

U.S. Bureau of the Census. 1986. *Statistical abstract of the United States, 1987*. Washington, DC: U.S. Government Printing Office.

U.S. Bureau of the Census. 1990. *Statistical abstract of the United States, 1990*. Washington, DC: U.S. Government Printing Office.

U.S. Department of Health and Human Services. 1984. *Progress report on Alzheimer's disease*, Vol. II. National Institutes of Health Publication No. 84-2500. Washington, DC: U.S. Government Printing Office.

Verbrugge, L., and Madans, J. 1985. Social roles and health trends of American women. *Milbank Memorial Fund Quarterly*, 63(4): 691–735.

Wells, C. E. 1978. Chronic brain disease: An overview. *American Journal of Psychiatry*, 135: 1–12.

Zopf, P. E. 1986. *America's older population*. Houston, TX: Cap and Gown Press.

CHAPTER 4

Cognitive Aspects of Aging and Disease

Lisa C. McGuire, M.A., and John C. Cavanaugh, Ph.D.

Many adults simply assume that cognitive deterioration is a normal part of the aging process. This assumption creates undue fear and concern, because cognition defines human functioning. Cognition includes aspects of the self that are taken for granted by many young people but valued by society: intelligence, memory, and personality. Cognitive impairments are feared aspects of growing old and lie at the heart of stereotypes about aging.

In this chapter, we will separate the myths of cognitive aging from the facts. First, we consider adult intelligence from two different theoretical perspectives. Second, we examine how memory changes with age. Third, we identify issues of health, lifestyle, and cognitive impairment, along with the relationship of these factors to adult cognitive development. Finally, we focus on cognitive aspects of personality.

INTELLECTUAL DEVELOPMENT

Adult intelligence has been studied from two major theoretical perspectives. The *cognitive stage theories* approach is more concerned with the thought processes underlying performance than with test performance per se. The *psychometric approach* views intelligence in terms of performance on standardized intelligence tests, largely ignoring underlying thought processes. We begin with the cognitive stage theories approach.

Cognitive Stage Theories of Intellectual Development

The cognitive stage theory approach is not concerned with whether a particular answer is right or wrong; what is important, however, is how the answer is obtained. Piaget's theory (and its extensions) provides a useful example of this approach.

Piaget's theory. According to Piaget (1970), intelligence is adaptation through action, creating the very ways in which we think. He believed that the development of intelligence involves the evolution of increasingly complex cognitive structures, which serve to define each of the stages in cognitive development.

For Piaget, thought is governed by the principles of adaptation and organization. *Adaptation* is the process of adjusting to the environment, and occurs through two processes: assimilation and accommodation. *Assimilation* is the process by which we make sense out of incoming information by fitting it into our existing base of knowledge (e.g., if the only word we have for four-legged animals is *cat,* we would think that a dog is called a cat, too). *Accommodation* involves changing one's knowledge to make it a better approximation of the real world (e.g., learning that some animals with four legs are dogs and others are cats).

The principle of *organization* refers to how people's thinking is put together. The organization of thought is reflected in cognitive structures that change over the life-span. These structures determine how we think; changes in cognitive structures yield fundamental changes in how we think. Piaget's research led him to conclude that there were four structures, underlying four stages, involved in cognitive development: sensorimotor, preoperational, concrete operational, and formal operational.

Intelligence during the *sensorimotor* period is reflected in actions; all knowledge is gained through the use of sensory and motor skills. A major accomplishment of this stage is object concept, in which the infant realizes the object still exists when it is out of view. The *preoperational* period is characterized by egocentric thought. Children in this stage believe that everyone (including inanimate objects) experiences the world exactly as they do. Although basic reasoning techniques are used by preoperational children, they are not based on formal logic principles.

Logical reasoning emerges in the *concrete operational* period. Children in this stage are able to classify objects according to logical principles, mentally reverse actions, recognize that a change in one dimension of an object may be compensated for by a change in another dimension, and understand transitivity (if A > B, and B > C, then A > C). Problem solving remains concrete; children have the ability to understand abstract concepts only in concrete terms. Finally, the *formal operational* period represents adult thought and is characterized by: (a) solving problems in a very systematic and step-by-step method, using hypothesis testing until the solution is confirmed or rejected; (b) thinking within one perspective at a time; (c) arriving at one unambiguous solution to a problem; and (d) thinking in an unconstrained manner that can be applied to real or imaginary situations.

Developmental trends in Piagetian thought. Much of the research on the course of Piagetian thought across adulthood has produced confusing results. Still, some general conclusions can be drawn; those from research on formal operations are especially relevant here. For example, there is little agreement on how many American adults achieve formal operations because formal operational thought may be used only in specialized situations.

Results from several studies show that older adults do not perform as well as younger adults on formal operational tasks (Clayton and Overton,

1973). Chandler (1980) indicates that the age difference in performance may not be related to ability differences, but may be due to lack of interest on the part of older adults in doing tasks that are perceived as abstract or as childish.

Postformal thought. Some researchers interpret age differences in formal operational abilities as indicative of another, qualitatively different style of thinking termed postformal thought, which is a step beyond Piaget's formal operations (Cavanaugh, Kramer, Sinnott, Camp, and Markley, 1985). *Postformal thought* is characterized by an increased tolerance of ambiguity, acceptance of more than one correct answer to problems, and the realization that reality constraints are important.

Perry (1970) found that young adults relied less on the expertise of authorities to determine what was right and wrong than did adolescents. During young adulthood, thinking evolves to reflect increased cognitive flexibility. Blanchard-Fields (1986) reports that nearly all adults can recognize a conflict between two opposing viewpoints and decide which position to adopt. Importantly, such a decision is made because adults believe it to be more valid for the context, not because it is viewed as absolutely right or wrong (Labouvie-Vief and Lawrence, 1985). This research is just beginning to focus on older adults; qualitative characteristics of their thinking remain to be discovered.

Psychometric Intelligence

The psychometric approach defines intellectual functioning in terms of the interrelationships of a person's scores on intelligence tests designed to measure intellectual abilities. The goal of the psychometric approach is to describe the structure of intelligence of the organization of these interrelationships (Sternberg, 1985). As shown in Figure 4.1, the structure of intelligence may be represented as a hierarchy, consisting of a general intelligence factor (e.g., Spearman's *g*), third-order factors, second-order factors, primary factors, individual tests, and test items (Cunningham, 1987). Most research on adult development has focused on primary and secondary factors.

When examining developmental characteristics of psychometric intelligence, special consideration must be given to the research design (Schaie and Hertzog, 1985). There are three primary designs: cross-sectional, longitudinal, and sequential. Cross-sectional designs include different groups of subjects of different ages. The results yield information about age differences but do not provide information about age change because age and cohort are confounded. Longitudinal designs involve following the same subjects over time, thereby producing information about continuity and change for a particular group (birth cohort) of people. Problems with longitudinal studies include subject attrition, lack of generalizability to other cohorts, and changing theories and measures. The best alternative is a sequential design, which combines longitudinal and cross-sectional designs. Sequential designs allow examination of both age differences and age changes in order to tease out cohort effects.

Primary mental abilities. Thurstone (1938) examined interrelationships among performances on intelligence tests and identified *seven primary mental abilities* (PMAs): number, word fluency, verbal meaning, associative memory, reasoning, spatial orientation, and perceptual speed. Thurstone considered PMAs to be the foundation of human intelligence.

In 1956, Schaie began one of the most comprehensive longitudinal and cohort-sequential studies of intelligence across adulthood, with a primary focus on five PMAs: number, word fluency, verbal meaning, inductive reasoning, and space. The first cross-sectional study revealed age differences in all five PMAs beginning by age 60. Performance levels

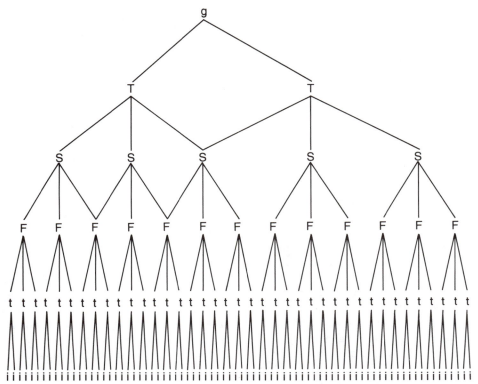

FIGURE 4.1 A hierarchical structure of ability factors: i, items or questions; t, individual tests; F, primary ability factors; S, second-order factors; T, third-order factors; g, general factor. (*Source:* "Intellectual Abilities and Age" by W. R. Cunningham, in K. W. Schaie (Ed.), *Annual Review of Gerontology and Geriatrics*, vol. 7, p. 119. Copyright © 1987 Springer Publishing Company, Inc., New York 10012. Used by permission.)

on tasks of verbal meaning, word fluency, and number did not peak until ages 46 to 50, while reasoning and spatial tests peaked in the 20s (Schaie, 1965). By the 1970 data collection, it became clear that cohort effects heavily influence adult intellectual development. A cohort-sequential analysis revealed longitudinal decrements for word fluency before age 60 but increases in verbal meaning until age 39. Schaie and Hertzog (1983) compared two independent 14-year longitudinal sequences (1956, 1963, and 1970; 1963, 1970, and 1977) after three waves of testing. These analyses

showed that there are some decrements in PMAs during the decade of the fifties that impair functioning only slightly. However, the decline in all PMAs after age 60 produces noticeable impairments in functioning.

Secondary mental abilities. Factor analyses of PMAs led to the discovery of six second-order mental abilities (SMAs), which are broadranging skills each containing several PMAs as their components (Horn, 1982). Two SMAs have received the most attention: fluid intelligence and crystallized intelligence. *Fluid intelligence* is a person's innate information-processing skills, independent of acquired experience and formal education, such as reasoning and problem solving. *Crystallized intelligence* represents intelligence as cultural knowledge acquired through experience and formal education, such as vocabulary and concept formation. Crystallized and fluid intelligence include the basic abilities traditionally associated

with human intelligence – verbal comprehension, reasoning, integration, and concept formation. Consequently, standardized intelligence test batteries typically measure both crystallized and fluid intelligence.

As depicted in Figure 4.2, fluid and crystallized intelligence develop differently across adulthood. Fluid intelligence declines as a person ages as a result of what some researchers believe to be physi-

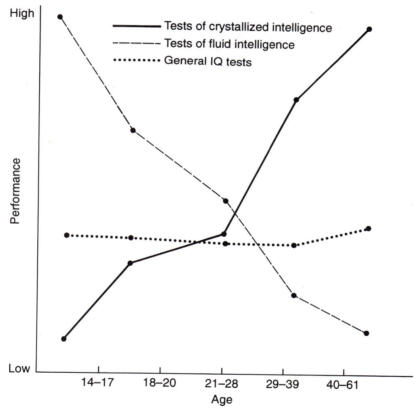

FIGURE 4.2 Performances on tests used to define fluid, crystallized, and general intelligence, as a function of age. (*Source:* "Organization of Data on Life-Span Development of Human Abilities" by J. L. Horn, 1970, in L. R. Goulet and P. B. Baltes (Eds.), *Life-Span Developmental Psychology: Research and Theory*, p. 463. New York: Academic Press. Reprinted by permission.)

ological processes such as neuronal fallout. In contrast, crystallized intelligence shows little decline with age, and may even increase with continued learning (Horn, 1982). This helps explain why older adults have problems performing and learning new tasks (fluid intelligence), but experience few problems with familiar tasks (crystallized intelligence). Horn (1970) reports that these changes in second-order abilities are not reflected in composite IQ, which tends to be constant over much of adulthood.

Moderating variables. An important aspect in interpreting changes in psychometric intelligence with age concerns personal and contextual variables that aid in explaining individual differences. *Cohort effects,* the most important of these, are specific environmental events and circumstances that produce marked developmental differences that are experienced by most members of a particular generation. One example of a cohort effect is growing up during the Depression; young people living during this period had very different experiences than young people living during the Vietnam Era. Cohort effects may give the appearance of age-related change when the change is actually a product of these generational differences. Other factors besides cohort effects that are important when interpreting results using psychometric measures of intelligence include: educational level (higher education correlates with less decline); occupation (jobs with high cognitive demands correlate with better performance on tests); and task relevancy (performance is better when tasks are familiar).

Denney's model of unexercised and optimally exercised abilities. Denney (1982) incorporates many ideas from the psychometric approach in her model of intellectual development. This model specifically demonstrates how different types of ability develop differently, and how experiential factors influence these processes.

Denney postulates two types of developmental functions. The first function, termed *untrained ability,* refers to the ability a normal healthy adult would exhibit without practice or training. Fluid intelligence is an example of an untrained ability, since it does not depend on experience and is unlikely to be formally trained (Horn, 1982). *Optimally exercised ability,* the second function, refers to the ability a normal healthy adult would demonstrate under the best conditions of training or practice. Crystallized intelligence is an example of an optimally exercised ability, in that the skills are used daily.

Denney argues that the developmental course of both abilities is the same. They tend to increase until late adolescence or early adulthood and slowly decline thereafter. At all age levels there is a difference in favor of optimally exercised ability, with the difference being less in early childhood and in old age. When this ability deviates from the norm, gains can be seen after training programs.

Denney's model seems to predict the results reported in several studies of psychometrically measured intelligence (Labouvie-Vief and Lawrence, 1985) and the reported differential effects of training with age (Willis, Blieszner, and Baltes, 1981). Denney forces us to rethink what we mean by declines in abilities measured by psychometric intelligence tests. Are the age differences in performance due to age-related changes, or to the lack of practice? Additional research is needed to answer that question.

EXPERTISE AND WISDOM

Although long associated with old age, expertise and wisdom are relatively new and emerging research topics in adult cognitive development. *Expertise* is the development of knowledge in a specific domain (Hoyer, 1984). Expertise consists of declarative knowledge (knowing what to do) and procedural knowledge (knowing how to do it). Both increase with practice and experience. The game of chess is a good example of a domain in which someone might exhibit expertise. Knowing which pieces move in what ways is declarative knowledge, and knowing the strategies that typically lead to victory is procedural knowledge.

Research on expertise demonstrates that healthy older adults, in supportive environments, have the capacity to maintain high levels of functioning in select areas, usually in their areas of specialization (Dixon, Kramer, and Baltes, 1985). The most important aspect of research on expertise is the idea that knowing a great deal about something may help compensate for declines in other cognitive processes (Salthouse, 1984).

Many societies view older people as wise. Kekes (1983) defines *wisdom* as a kind of interpretive knowledge that combines breadth and depth. The wise person is one who understands the significance of what is commonly known. Dittmann-Kohli and Baltes (1990) offer several signs that can be used to identify and assess wisdom: (1) expertise in the pragmatic aspects of daily living; (2) understanding of the significance of content domain; (3) breadth of ability to define and solve problems; (4) recognition of the complexity, difficulty, and uncertainty in problems; and (5) good, practical judgment. Approaching wisdom as reflecting expertise in living necessarily implies that it takes years of life experience to become wise. Thus, living into old age may be the only way to achieve wisdom.

REACTION TIME AND ATTENTION

Reaction time is a measure of how rapidly a person can respond to a stimulus, such as how quickly one presses the brake of a car to avoid hitting a kitten. Successful performance on reaction time tasks involves many factors, including sensation, perception, attention, short-term memory, intelligence,

decision making, and personality. In performing a reaction time task, people must perceive that an event has occurred, decide what to do about the event, and carry out the decision (Welford, 1977). Poor performance can be the result of a breakdown in any step in the process.

Researchers investigate how well adults of different ages perform on three types of reaction time tasks. Simple reaction time involves responding to one stimulus – for example, pressing a button as fast as possible when a light comes on. Simple reaction time is composed of decision time (the time from the onset of the stimulus until the response is initiated) and motor time (the time needed to complete the physical part of the response). The most noticeable age difference is in the decision time component (Salthouse, 1985). In choice reaction time tasks, people are presented with more than one stimulus and required to respond differently to each. Performance of older adults is much worse than that of younger adults on these tasks (Fozard, Thomas, and Waugh, 1976). The most difficult reaction time task is one involving complex reaction time, which requires making many decisions about when and how to respond (e.g., driving a car). Cerella, Poon, and Williams (1980) report that age differences on complex reaction time tasks increase as the task becomes more difficult. That is, older adults are at a disadvantage in situations demanding rapid responding, especially when the decision to be made is complex and difficult.

Because the speed of responding clearly decreases with age, many researchers have been interested in seeing if it could be improved through practice. Although older adults' performance improves, practice alone rarely eliminates age differences. It appears that some response slowing is an inevitable part of growing old (Spirduso and MacRae, 1990).

Two types of attention have been examined in aging research. Sustained attention refers to the ability to maintain vigilance over time. Evidence concerning age differences is sparse and conflicting

(McDowd and Birren, 1990). Selective attention is a person's ability to filter out relevant from irrelevant information. Most of the selective attention research requires participants either to screen out competing information or to perform two tasks simultaneously. Findings indicate decrements in an older adult's ability to perform such tasks (Madden, 1986).

MEMORY

Research on memory and aging focuses mainly on three aspects. *Primary memory* is a short-lived, limited-capacity store in which information is still "in mind" while it is being used (Poon, 1985). An example of primary memory is remembering the phone number you looked up long enough to make the call. Although primary memory is a temporary, small-capacity store, there are relatively few changes in it with age (Poon, 1985).

Secondary memory represents the ability to remember more extensive amounts of information over relatively longer periods of time. Everyday life is filled with examples: remembering class or work schedules, summarizing a book or movie, performing on an exam. Because of its ubiquitous use, secondary memory has been the focus of more research than any other aspect of memory (Poon, 1985).

Secondary memory is studied primarily by having people learn lists of items and then either recall or recognize the items. Recall is obtained by asking a person to remember as much of the to-be-learned material as possible without cues being provided. Recognition is tested by asking the person to pick out the items that were learned from a longer list that includes both target and distractor items.

As shown in Figure 4.3, older adults perform worse than younger adults on tests of recall or word lists, but these differences become smaller or are sometimes eliminated on recognition tasks (Poon,

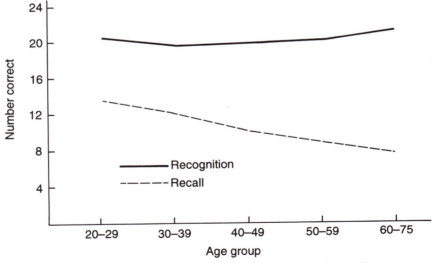

FIGURE 4.3 Recall and recognition scores, as a function of age. (*Source:* "Memory Storage and Aging" by D. Schonfield and B. A. Robertson, 1966, *Canadian Journal of Psychology,* vol. 20, pp. 228–236. Copyright 1966. Canadian Psychological Association. Reprinted with permission.)

1985). Older adults also tend to be less efficient at using strategies spontaneously, such as elaborating or putting items into categories to make information easier to learn. When older adults are instructed to use organizational strategies, however, they not only do so but also show a significant improvement in performance (Smith, 1980).

Several researchers have used prose passages rather than word lists to test secondary memory. In general, the results indicate that younger adults are clearly superior to older adults at remembering the details from text. However, age differences are less clear for remembering the gist of stories; this ability appears to be related to several personal variables such as education and verbal ability (Hultsch and Dixon, 1990).

Information in very-long-term storage is contained in *tertiary memory*. Such information includes facts learned earlier in life, the meanings of words, life experiences, and the like. Very little research is done on tertiary memory, for two main reasons. First, it is difficult to design a task measuring tertiary memory so that we know how to interpret performance. Second, if a person does not remember a fact from the past, it may be due either to an inability to retrieve the information or to a failure to have initially learned the information. Tertiary memory is sometimes tested with questionnaires asking about events of public knowledge available to everyone, such as the Challenger disaster. With this approach, few age differences are found in tertiary memory. This is not surprising, because tertiary memory is very similar to crystallized intelligence, described earlier, which shows little decrement with age.

Memory in everyday life. Surprisingly, only recently has there been substantial interest in examining age differences in the uses of memory in everyday life (West, 1986). Several aspects of everyday memory have been examined: spatial memory, memory for activities, autobiographical memory, and prospective memory.

Practical spatial memory involves remembering the location of objects; remembering landmarks; remembering routes through cities, countrysides, or buildings; and mentally rotating locations (Kirasic and Allen, 1985). Memory for object location generally shows age differences between young and older adults. In recalling the location of landmarks, older adults may be more likely to use experiential or personal relevance as a way to remember location, whereas young adults may be more likely to use spatial information. No age differences are found for route learning (Sinnott, 1984; Ohta, 1981).

When people are required to combine spatial and temporal (time-dated) information so that they can recognize a location when viewing it from a different perspective, young adults outperform older adults on unfamiliar locations. However, the age differences disappear when the locations used are familiar (Kirasic, 1980; Kirasic and Allen, 1985).

Memory for activities in everyday life involves the intentional, effortful retrieval of information learned incidentally or automatically. An example would be remembering whether you locked your door when you left home this morning. It turns out that whether actions are actually performed by the participant or are merely watched affects how many activities will be remembered correctly. Bäckman (1985) and Cohen and Faulkner (1989) both found that performed actions were remembered more accurately than activities that had only been watched. Cohen and Faulkner indicate that older adults are more likely to say that they actually performed tasks that they in reality only observed. In situations where accuracy is crucial, such as reporting activities to a physician or to a police officer, older adults may be more likely to confuse what they saw and what they did. Additionally, the type of task performed may affect the probability that it will later be remembered. For instance, Kausler and Hakami (1983) note that older adults remember problem-solving tasks better than perceptual-motor tasks, generic memory tasks, and list-learning tasks.

Older adults are consistently superior on prospective memory, that is, remembering to perform an action (Meacham, 1982). For example, when younger and older adults were asked to make a phone call on either a fixed or a variable schedule, older adults were consistently better at remembering to do so (Moscovitz, 1982; Poon and Schaffer, 1982; West, 1984). The difference was due to the fact that older adults wrote down the number and message to be given, whereas younger adults merely relied on their internal remembering strategies.

There is a natural tendency to compare performance on everyday memory tasks with performance on more traditional list-learning tasks, but this must be done with caution. Overall, age decrements in performance are less prevalent on everyday-memory tasks than on laboratory list-learning tasks (West, 1986). Older adults consistently perform better when they are confronted with information that is familiar, perhaps because this factor enhances their motivation to perform the task (Perlmutter, 1989).

Self-evaluation of memory abilities.

The knowledge that certain person or task factors make a memory task easier or harder is called *metamemory* (Cavanaugh and Perlmutter, 1982). In other words, metamemory is an awareness of the memory system and how it works. Older adults generally report more memory problems and have more negative views of current memory function than young adults (Cavanaugh and Poon, 1989; Dixon and Hultsch, 1983; Zelinski, Gilewski, and Thompson, 1980). In contrast to young adults, older adults report less knowledge about the internal workings of memory and its capacity, view memory as less stable, expect that memory will deteriorate with age, and perceive that they have less control over memory (Cavanaugh and Poon, 1989; Chaffin and Herrmann, 1983; Dixon and Hultsch, 1983; Zelinski et al., 1980).

The belief in inevitable age-related decline is not thought to involve all aspects of memory equally. In particular, memory capacity is viewed as declining more rapidly than use of memory strategies (Dixon and Hultsch, 1983), and name retrieval is particularly problematic (Cavanaugh, Grady, and Perlmutter, 1983). In contrast, remembering errands, appointments, and places appears to remain unchanged (Cavanaugh et al., 1983).

TRAINING COGNITIVE SKILLS

Older adults do not perform as well on tests of some primary abilities or on tests of secondary memory as do younger adults. Consequently, several attempts at training both primary abilities and memory strategies have been made.

Training Primary Mental Abilities

Pennsylvania State University's Adult Development and Enrichment Project (ADEPT) was a comprehensive training program involving a series of longitudinal studies (Baltes and Willis, 1982). Project ADEPT involved training people in how to take tests as well as in each primary ability being tested. Training on figural relations, for example, involved practice with paper-and-pencil tests, feedback from the experimenter, group discussion, and review of the kinds of problems involving figural-relations ability.

The ability-specific training resulted in improvements in primary abilities, but the degree to which gains were maintained and transferred varied. These findings are represented in Figure 4.4. Interestingly, the size of Baltes and Willis's improvements in fluid abilities were roughly equivalent to the average 21 year longitudinal decline in these abilities reported by Schaie (1983). The implications are that what appear to be normative declines in primary mental abilities may be slowed or reversed by specific training on those abilities.

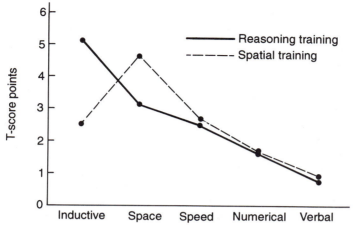

FIGURE 4.4 Gains in *T*-score points, resulting from training for inductive reasoning or spatial orientation, on inductive reasoning (Inductive), spatial orientation (Space), perceptual speed (Speed), numerical abilities (Numerical), and verbal abilities (Verbal). (*Source:* "Training the Elderly on the Ability Factors of Spatial Orientation and Inductive Reasoning" by S. L. Willis and K. W. Schaie, 1986, *Psychology and Aging,* vol. 1, pp. 239–247, Figure 1, p. 245. Copyright © 1986 by the American Psychological Association. Reprinted by permission.

Schaie and Willis (1986) extended the findings from Project ADEPT. They found that the cognitive-training techniques could reverse decline that had been documented reliably over a 14-year period. Moreover, the training procedures also enhanced the performance of many older people who had remained stable. This demonstrates that training is not only effective in raising the performance levels of decliners, but can even improve functioning in nondecliners beyond their initial levels. Schaie and Willis caution, however, that cognitive training techniques appeared to be ability-specific.

Hayslip (1986) compared inductive-reasoning training and anxiety reduction training. He found that both training groups improved their performance, and that the induction-training group had the highest level one month after training. However, there was little evidence of generalized train-

ing effects to other primary mental abilities. He concluded that at least part of the increased level of performance was due to a reduction in people's level of anxiety in taking tests of intellectual ability.

The results from Project ADEPT, and the data from Schaie and Willis's and Hayslip's research suggest that declines in fluid abilities are normative, but that these declines may be somewhat reversible with appropriate training.

Memory Skills Training

The idea that memory can be improved through acquiring skills has a long historical tradition (Yates, 1966). Harris (1984) lists four major methods of improving memory: internal strategies (e.g., forming an image of the information to be remembered in one's mind), repetitive practice (e.g., rehearsing the information over and over), physical treatment (e.g., medications), and external aids (e.g., writing the information to be remembered on a notepad).

Most research on memory training concerns internal strategies (Bellezza, 1981), which supply meaning and help to organize incoming information (Morris, 1979). Examples of internal strategies include the method of loci (remembering items by mentally placing them in locations in a familiar environment), mental retracing (thinking about all the places you may have left your keys), turning letters into numbers, and forming acronyms out of initial letters (e.g., NATO). Most memory courses train people to become efficient at using an internal strategy. Older adults have been successfully trained to use the method of loci as a way to help remember items to be purchased in the grocery store (Anschutz, Camp, Markley, and Kramer, 1985). Overall research indicates that training on most internal strategies improves memory significantly. Most of these training programs have rarely been assessed over long intervals, so the degree of improvement after the course ends and how long this improvement lasts are largely unknown. One exception was a three-year follow-up to the grocery shopping study which found that, even though loci were available, older adults had abandoned use of the strategy (Anschutz, Camp, Markley, and Kramer, 1987).

Repetitive practice, based on the analogy of memory as a mental muscle, is another approach to memory training. Exercising memory on one type of task strengthens it, setting the stage for better memory on a variety of other tasks (Harris and Sunderland, 1981). Exercising memory may have important benefits for a person during the rehabilitation process. First, the person knows that something is being done about his or her memory problems. Second, there is evidence from animal research (Wall, 1975) and human research (Black, Markowitz, and Cianci, 1975) suggesting that early intervention with physical exercise promotes recovery after damage to the motor cortex. Harris and Sunderland (1981) suggest that the same benefit might occur if memory practice begins at the first signs of loss.

External memory aids, such as diaries, address books, calendars, and notebooks, are devices commonly used to support memory in everyday situations (Cavanaugh et al., 1983). Some external memory aids, such as address books, are designed for storage of information, whereas others, such as a reminder list, serve as cues for action (Perlmutter et al., 1987). Advocating the use of external aids in memory rehabilitation is becoming increasingly popular. Consequently, internal memory aids should be used as much as possible, since they strengthen memory ability more than external aids do.

Our review of cognitive training programs indicates success in the short run. As yet, we do not know whether these gains will last. It is also important to note when designing training programs that people will not all benefit equally That is, substantial individual differences in the degree of improvement will occur.

HEALTH EFFECTS ON COGNITION

A person's health can affect his or her cognitive abilities. Health and life-style issues can directly affect cognitive abilities in the aging adult. The good news is that many of these can be controlled. In this section, we will consider health and life-style issues and their relationship to cognition and the dementias.

Health and Life-Style Issues

Health and life-style factors are important influences on cognitive functioning across adulthood. Overall, this is good news, as we do have considerable control over our life-style. There are exceptions to this, such as Alzheimer's disease and other hereditary forms of dementia. In this section, we will consider areas where we can and cannot influence the health-cognitive connection.

Cardiovascular studies.   The connection between disease and intelligence is controversial. Early data (e.g., Wilkie and Eisdorfer, 1971) indicate that significant intellectual decline was associated with hypertension. However, much of this early work is difficult to interpret because of the presence of diseases other than hypertension alone. More recent research, in which the effects of hypertension have been isolated, shows essentially no change in intellectual functioning due to this disease (Elias, Elias, and Elias, 1990). Because all of the research examining the effects of hypertension includes people on antihypertensive medication, we still need additional research to disentangle the drug-disease confound.

Exercise.   Aerobic exercise is claimed to improve cognitive performance; most of the research in this area, however, has focused on gains in reaction time. Several studies of both simple and choice reaction times indicate significant improvements in performance in older adults as a function of sustained exercise (Baylor and Spirduso, 1988). In other words, older adults who exercised regularly had significantly faster reaction times than sedentary older adults. Blumenthal and Madden (1988) demonstrate that exercise appears to increase the encoding and response processes for older adults. It is important to note that exercise does not have equivalent effects on all people. Even though it will improve reaction time in most people, the extent of the increase due to exercise is uncertain.

Nutrition.   Nutrition is an area often overlooked as the cause of memory failures (Perlmutter et al., 1987). Unfortunately, little is known about the specific nutrient deficiencies associated with memory impairment. The available evidence links thiamine deficiency to memory problems in general (Cherkin, 1984), and implicates niacin and B_{12} deficiencies in diseases having memory failure as a major symptom (Rosenthal and Goodwin, 1985).

Drugs.   Many drugs have been associated with memory problems. The most widely known of these is alcohol, the abuse of which over a long period of time, coupled with vitamin deficiencies, can create severe memory loss. Memory performance has also been found to be impaired by sedatives and tranquilizers (Block, DeVoe, Stanley, Stanley, and Pomara, 1985).

Dementia

Dementia refers to a family of diseases that have similar symptoms, all characterized by cognitive and behavioral deficits involving permanent brain damage. Some dementias can be treated effectively, and a few can be reversed. Stages in the course of dementia are described in Table 4.1.

It is important to realize that many diseases cause the problems outlined in stages 1 and 2. In fact, less than 10 percent of those individuals at stage 2 will develop more serious cognitive impairments within several years of clinical evaluation (Reisberg, Ferris, de Leon, and Crook, 1982). Cognitive deficits similar to those characteristics of stage 3 possibly indicate the presence of serious declines characteristic of Alzheimer's disease and related disorders.

Treatable conditions.   Some dementias, as well as some other conditions, can be treated effectively, and a few can even be reversed. The distinction between reversible and irreversible conditions has profound implications for the patient. Reversible dementias, delirium, and pseudodementia stem from treatable causes. Reversible

TABLE 4.1 Stages of dementia as measured by the global deterioration scale with corresponding clinical phases and characteristics

GDS stage	Clinical phase	Clinical characteristics
1. No cognitive decline	Normal	No subjective complaints of memory deficit. No memory deficit evident on clinical interview.
2. Very mild cognitive decline	Forgetfulness	Subjective complaints of memory deficit, most frequently in the following areas: (a) forgetting where one has placed familiar objects and (b) forgetting names one formerly knew well. No objective evidence of memory deficit on clinical interview. No objective deficits in employment or social situations. Appropriate concern with respect to symptomatology.
3. Mild cognitive decline	Early confusional	Earliest clear-cut deficits. Manifestations in more than one of the following areas: (a) patient may have gotten lost when traveling to an unfamiliar location; (b) co-workers become aware of patient's relatively poor performance; (c) word- and name-finding deficits become evident to intimates; (d) patient may read a passage or a book and retain relatively little material; (e) patient may demonstrate decreased facility in remembering names upon introduction to new people; (f) patient may have lost or misplaced an object of value; (g) concentration deficit may be evident on clinical testing.
		Objective evidence of memory deficit obtained only with an intensive interview conducted by a trained geriatric psychiatrist. Decreased performance in demanding employment and social settings. Denial begins to become manifest in patient. Mild to moderate anxiety accompanies symptoms.
4. Moderate cognitive decline	Late confusional	Clear-cut deficit on careful interview. Deficit manifest in the following areas: (a) decreased knowledge of current and recent events; (b) may exhibit some deficit in memory of one's personal history; (c) concentration deficit elicited on serial subtractions; (d) decreased ability to travel, handle finances, etc.
		Frequently no deficit in following areas: (a) orientation to time and person; (b) recognition of familiar persons and faces; (c) ability to travel to familiar locations.
		Inability to perform complex tasks. Denial is dominant defense mechanism. Flattening of affect and withdrawal from challenging situations occur.
5. Moderately severe cognitive decline	Early dementia	Patient can no longer survive without some assistance. Patients are unable during interview to recall a major relevant aspect of current lives, such as their address or telephone number of many years, the names of close members of their family (such as grandchildren), the name of the high school or college from which they graduated.
		Frequently some disorientation of time (date, day of week, season, etc.) or to place. An educated person may have difficulty counting back from 40 by 4's or from 20 by 2's.
		Persons at this stage retain knowledge of many major facts regarding themselves and others. They invariably know their own names and generally know their spouse's and children's names. They require no assistance with toileting or eating but may have some difficulty choosing

TABLE 4.1 *Continued*

GDS Stage	Clinical Phase	Clinical Characteristics
		the proper clothing to wear and may occasionally clothe themselves improperly (e.g., put shoes on the wrong feet, etc.).
6. Severe cognitive decline	Middle dementia	May occasionally forget the name of the spouse on whom they are entirely dependent for survival. Will be largely unaware of all recent events and experiences in their lives. Retain some knowledge of their past lives, but this is very sketchy. Generally unaware of their surroundings, the year, the season, etc. May have difficulty counting from 10, both backward and, sometimes, forward. Will require some assistance with activities of daily living; e.g., may become incontinent, will require travel assistance but occasionally will display ability to travel to familiar locations. Diurnal rhythm frequently disturbed. Almost always recall their own name. Frequently continue to be able to distinguish familiar from unfamiliar persons in their environment.
		Personality and emotional changes occur. These are quite variable and include: (a) delusional behavior (e.g., patients may accuse their spouse of being an imposter; may talk to imaginary figures in the environment or to their own reflection in the mirror); (b) obsessive symptoms (e.g., person may continually repeat simple cleaning activities); (c) anxiety symptoms, agitation, and even previously nonexistent violent behavior may occur; (d) cognitive abulia (i.e., loss of will power because an individual cannot carry a thought long enough to determine a purposeful course of action).
7. Very severe cognitive decline	Late dementia	All verbal abilities are lost. Frequently there is no speech at all—only grunting. Incontinent of urine; requires assistance toileting and feeding. Loses basic psychomotor skills (e.g., ability to walk). The brain appears to no longer be able to tell the body what to do. Generalized and cortical neurological signs and symptoms are frequently present.

Source: "The Global Deterioration Scale for Assessment of Primary Degenerative Dementia" by B. Reisberg, S. H. Ferris, M. J. de Leon, and T. Cook, *American Journal of Psychiatry,* vol. 139, pp. 1136-1139, 1982. Copyright © 1982, the American Psychiatric Association. Reprinted by permission.

dementias are disorders characterized by cognitive difficulties that can be fully reversed with treatment. Pseudodementia, which some view as related to depression, responds to treatment. However, the patient does not experience a complete turnaround; instead, remnants of cognitive impairment will remain. Delirium is characterized by impaired awareness of self and surroundings, attention deficits, possible memory impairment, tendencies toward hallucinations and delusions, disorientation, changes in alertness, disturbed sleep patterns, and rapid changes in symptoms and their severity (Lipowski, 1980). The underlying factor is a disruption of cerebral metabolism, which becomes more common with age. The National Institute of Aging (1980) emphasizes that almost any internal disturbance can lead to cognitive symptoms in older adults. Common causes include the toxic effects of medications or drug interactions, infections, electrolyte imbalances, malnutrition, and potassium deficits. Symptoms may also appear following surgery, fractures, head injuries, changes in the environment, and/or the death of a close relative.

Alzheimer's disease.   *Alzheimer's disease* is the most common form of progressive, degenerative dementia, possibly accounting for as many as 70 percent of all dementia cases (Davies, 1988). The major cognitive symptoms are: gradual declines in memory, learning, attention, and judgment; disorientation in time and space; difficulties in word finding and communication. Additionally, there are declines in personal hygiene and self-care skills, inappropriate social behavior, and changes in personality (Crystal, 1988; Davies, 1988).

In the beginning, these symptoms tend to be vague and mimic other psychological problems, such as depression or stress reactions. Unlike the case of these other disorders, however, in Alzheimer's disease the symptoms gradually worsen. A person who was previously outgoing is now quiet and withdrawn; a gentle person is now hostile and aggressive. Emotional problems, including depression, paranoia, and agitation, become increasingly apparent.

As the disease progresses, the person becomes incontinent and increasingly dependent on others for care, eventually becoming incapable of performing simple tasks such as eating or dressing. The rate of deterioration in Alzheimer's disease is highly variable from one person to the next, with the progression usually being faster when the onset occurs earlier in life (Bondareff, 1983).

Other types of dementia.   There are other progressive and degenerative dementias besides Alzheimer's disease. Multi-infarct dementia, caused by disruptions of blood flow in the brain (strokes), has a sudden onset with a stepwise progression. Affected abilities experience sharp declines with stepwise improvements finally reaching a plateau. The symptom pattern is highly variable, especially early in the disease.

Parkinson's disease is characterized by motor problems: very slow walking, stiffness, difficulty getting in and out of chairs, and a slow tremor.

These behavioral symptoms are caused by a deterioration of neurons in the midbrain that produce the neurotransmitter dopamine (Lieberman, 1974). Approximately 30 to 50 percent of Parkinson's disease patients will develop dementia (Boller, 1980).

Pick's disease is a very rare form of dementia that is hard to discriminate from Alzheimer's disease. It is characterized by little memory impairment in the early stages. There are, however, marked behavior changes, such as social inappropriateness, loss of modesty, and uninhibited sexual behavior (Lishman, 1978).

Huntington's disease usually manifests itself through prominent psychiatric disturbances, such as hallucinations, paranoia, depression, and clear personality changes (Berkow, 1987). Cognitive impairments do not appear until late in the disease, and the onset of symptoms is gradual, similar to the progression of Alzheimer's disease.

Diagnosis and treatment.   At present, the only way to diagnose Alzheimer's disease is by brain autopsy. However, some other forms of dementia, such as multi-infarct, can be diagnosed through brain imaging techniques. Some, such as Huntington's disease, can be identified through genetic tests even before symptoms emerge. With careful screening, even Alzheimer's disease can be diagnosed prior to autopsy; however, the early diagnosis relies on an extensive battery of tests.

Complete diagnostic examinations for dementia consist of thorough medical work-ups, blood tests, brain imaging, and neuropsychological tests. Neuropsychological tests consist of intelligence, memory, and language tests that help clinicians identify the specific cognitive problems being experienced. Table 4.2 summarizes the criteria for the diagnosis of probable Alzheimer's disease.

Unfortunately, there are no effective treatments for the irreversible forms of dementia (e.g., Alzheimer's disease). Although research is continuing

TABLE 4.2 Criteria for the diagnosis of probable Alzheimer's disease

1. Criteria for clinical diagnosis of *probable* Alzheimer's disease include:
   (a) Dementia established by clinical examination and documented by the Mini Mental State Test, Blessed Dementia Scale, or some similar examination and confirmed by neuropsychological tests
   (b) Deficits in two or more areas of cognition
   (c) Progressive worsening of memory and other cognitive functions
   (d) No disturbance of consciousness
   (e) Onset between ages 40 and 90, most often after age 65
   (f) Absence of systemic disorders or other brain diseases that in and of themselves could account for progressive deficits in memory and cognition
2. Diagnosis of probable Alzheimer's disease is supported by:
   (a) Progressive deterioration of specific cognitive functions, such as language (aphasia), motor skills (apraxia), and perception (agnosia)
   (b) Impaired activities of daily living and altered patterns of behavior
   (c) Family history of similar disorders, particularly if confirmed neuropathologically
   (d) Laboratory results of normal lumbar puncture as evaluated by standard techniques; normal pattern or nonspecific changes in EEG, such as increased slow-wave activity; and evidence of cerebral atrophy on CT with progression documented by serial observation
3. Other clinical features consistent with diagnosis of probable Alzheimer's disease, after exclusion of causes of dementia other than Alzheimer's disease, include:
   (a) Plateaus in the course of progression of illness
   (b) Associated symptoms of depression; insomnia; incontinence; delusions; illusions; hallucinations; catastrophic verbal, emotional, or physical outbursts; sexual disorders; and weight loss

   (c) Other neurological abnormalities in some patients, especially with more advanced disease and including motor signs, such as increased muscle tone, myoclonus, or gait disorder
   (d) Seizures in advanced disease
   (e) CT normal for age
4. Features that make the diagnosis of probable Alzheimer's disease uncertain or unlikely include:
   (a) Sudden, apoplectic onset
   (b) Focal neurological findings such as hemiparesis, sensory loss, visual field deficits, and uncoordination early in the course of the illness
   (c) Seizures or gait disturbance at onset or very early in the course of the illness
5. Clinical diagnosis of probable Alzheimer's disease:
   (a) May be made on the basis of dementia syndrome, in the absence of other neurological, psychiatric, or systemic disorders sufficient to cause dementia and in the presence of variations in onset, in presentation, or in the clinical course.
   (b) May be made in the presence of a second systemic or brain disorder sufficient to produce dementia, which is not considered to be the cause of dementia.
   (c) Should be used in research studies when single, gradually progressive severe cognitive deficit is identified in the absence of other identifiable cause.
6. Criteria for diagnosis of definite Alzheimer's disease are:
   (a) Clinical criteria for probable Alzheimer's disease
   (b) Histopathological evidence obtained from biopsy or autopsy
7. Classification of Alzheimer's disease for research purposes should specify features that may differentiate subtypes of the disorder, such as:
   (a) Familial occurrence
   (b) Onset before age 65
   (c) Presence of trisomy-21
   (d) Coexistence of other relevant conditions, such as Parkinson's disease

Source: National Institute of Neurological, Communication Disorders and Stroke (undated).

on a wide range of drugs, none has proved effective to date (Thal, 1988).

The Sick Role and Perception of Symptoms

A final interface between health and cognition relates to how adults deal with being ill. As you know from your own experience, being ill typically brings

out a different set of behaviors in a person. Some people are better patients than others, and some cope better with their symptoms. These behaviors, sometimes referred to as the *sick role*, and perceptions of one's symptoms are both important in understanding the elderly patient.

Although the sick role has been examined in many ways, surprisingly little research has focused on the elderly (Coe, 1981). In short, the concept of the sick role means that people with illnesses adopt one set of expected behaviors, while those caring for them (e.g., physicians) adopt a different set. Four areas may be especially important in considering the sick role and the elderly. Status differences between elderly patients and health care professionals may be especially large because of the elderly's lack of familiarity with modern high-technology diagnostic procedures. Second, many elderly persons maintain beliefs incompatible with modern approaches to disease; consequently, they may be unwilling to comply with complex medical treatment regimens. Third, many elderly accept medical information uncritically and may be offended when physicians do not involve themselves personally in the process of care. Finally, despite its advances, modern medicine is still incapable of effectively treating most chronic diseases of the type commonly experienced by older adults.

Simply attributing the physical experiences one has to illness may not be easy for older adults. As Kart (1981) among others has noted, many age-related changes in sensory perception may make it difficult for an older person to know that he or she is actually ill. Additionally, the symptom patterns themselves change with the age of the patient. Another complicating factor is that many older adults may inaccurately ascribe their discomfort to age as a result of incorrect stereotypes of their own aging process. Thus, rather than seeking medical advice, a person may simply dismiss symptoms as a sign of getting old. Finally, the cognitive changes discussed earlier may also reduce an older person's awareness of illness symptoms.

In sum, beliefs and stereotypes of aging and the normative changes in sensory and cognitive systems influence the older person's awareness and interpretation of symptoms of physical illness. Sensitivity to these issues is needed in working with older adults in health care settings.

COGNITIVE PERSONALITY THEORIES

Cognitive theories of personality development are based on the individual's conception of how his or her life should proceed. How people perceive themselves is more important for personality development than is the objective assessment of the self. Personality development in adulthood is related to a person's awareness of changes in personal appearance, behavior, and the reactions of others, together with an appreciation of the increasing closeness of death.

The work of two major cognitive personality theorists will be examined. Hans Thomae developed a cognitive theory of personality based on his longitudinal research in Germany. Susan Krauss Whitbourne researched people's own conceptions of the life course and how they differ from age norms and the expectations for society as a whole.

Thomae's Cognitive Theory of Personality

Thomae's (1980) cognitive theory of personality can also be viewed as a cognitive theory of aging. He offers three postulates that explain personality development, especially when adjusting to one's own aging. First, it is the perception of change, not objective change, that is related to behavioral change. Personality change is more or less likely depending on whether the individual perceives the change as normative. For example, the death of a spouse will probably elicit different reactions in widows in their twenties and their seventies. A widow 70 years old will experience less change, because this event was "on time" for her cohort. The 20-year-old widow will probably experience more changes because this event is "off time" unless she perceives it as a normative occurrence. Second, people perceive and evaluate any change in their life situation in terms of their dominant concerns and expectations at that time. People have different motives and concerns at different stages of life, leading them to perceive situations differently. Finally, the adjustment to aging is determined by the balance between people's cognitive and motivational structures.

Personality changes during adulthood cannot be reduced either to a "happens–does not happen" dichotomy or to a simple examination of scores on a personality test. Instead, personality change (and the need for it) is in the eye of the beholder. Each of us has the potential to change, but whether it happens depends on our desire for change. Unless people's perceptions of themselves and of the situation require change, overall personality stability will be the most likely result.

Whitbourne's Life Story Approach

According to Whitbourne (1987), people build their own conceptions of how their lives should proceed. The result of this is a *life-span construct,* which is the person's unified sense of the past, the present, and the future.

A person's life-span construct is influenced by many factors, such as identity, values, and social context. The life-span construct has two components that determine how it is manifested. First, the *scenario* is the component consisting of the person's expectations about the future. The scenario translates aspects of our identity that are important at a particular point in future plans. In other words, a scenario is the game plan of how we expect and want our lives to be in the future. *Life story* is the second component of the life-span construct. The life story is a personal narrative history that organizes past events into a coherent sequence, giving them meaning and continuity. This becomes our autobiography, which is told to others when they

ask about our past. The life story eventually becomes overrehearsed and stylized. Like autobiographical memory, our life story gets distorted with time and retelling (Neisser and Winograd, 1988). Life story distortions are actually ways of coping, which allow the person to feel that he or she was "on time" rather than "off time" in past events in the scenario. Many people feel better about their plans and goals, and are less likely to feel a sense of failure, as a result of life story distortions.

More research is needed in this area, but cognitive theories have much to offer the study of adult personality development. Converging evidence suggests that adults experience both stability and change, and the extent of each may be within their control. Adults' personalities appear to remain stable unless they perceive a need for change. Future research is likely to integrate the theoretical framework of cognitive theories with the research methods used in studying ego development and traits, which might provide an explanation for conflicting adults.

SUMMARY

Intellectual changes with age are considered from Piagetian and psychometric perspectives. Developmental changes in Piagetian thinking are apparent in formal operations, but some believe that adults' thinking represents a stage beyond formal thought. Performance on psychometric tests of intelligence shows declines on some primary abilities. Fluid intelligence tends to decline while crystallized intelligence does not. Cohort effects and experience are important moderating variables.

Older adults have the capacity to develop expertise. Wisdom is also associated with old age. Reaction time declines are a normal part of aging, but are somewhat sensitive to practice. Secondary memory functioning declines, as does the use of internal strategies. Memory functioning in everyday life shows less decline. Beliefs about one's own memory is an important influence on performance. Both fluid intelligence and memory ability are trainable.

Health and life-style are important factors in cognitive functioning. Although the effects of hypertension are unclear, exercise, diet, and drugs influence performance. Alzheimer's disease is a form of progressive dementia that is untreatable. Diagnosis is difficult; the only sure way is through autopsy. Older adults' stereotypes about health care and their own aging affect their perceptions of disease and symptoms.

Cognitive theories of personality emphasize the active role people have in determining their own life course. Change is possible, but largely to the extent one thinks it is necessary.

STUDY QUESTIONS

1. Distinguish between two major theoretical approaches used to study adult intelligence: the cognitive stage theories approach and the psychometric approach.
2. Which approach is represented by Piaget's theory? Identify processes of adaptation, assimilation, and accommodation. How is thought differentially characterized in the sensorimotor, preoperational, concrete operational, and formal operational periods?
3. How does research design affect the examination of developmental characteristics of psychometric intelligence? Distinguish among cross-sectional, longitudinal, and sequential designs.
4. Identify the following: primary mental abilities, secondary mental abilities, fluid intelligence, crystallized intelligence, untrained ability, and optimally trained ability.
5. Distinguish *expertise* from *wisdom*. Give examples.
6. Identify some factors that may explain age differences in reaction time. Do these factors operate similarly across different reaction time tasks?
7. Distinguish among primary, secondary, and tertiary memory. Identify several aspects of everyday memory and what we know about age differences in the uses of memory in everyday life.
8. What do we know about the training of cognitive skills in older adults? Where is training most effective? Least effective?
9. How do health and life-style issues affect cognitive abilities in the aging adult? In particular, distinguish Alzheimer's disease from other dementias and diseases.
10. Distinguish Thomae's and Whitbourne's approaches to a cognitive theory of personality development.

BIBLIOGRAPHY

Anschutz, L., Camp, C. J., Markley, R. P., and Kramer, J. J. 1985. Maintenance and generalization of mnemonics for grocery shopping by older adults. *Experimental Aging Research,* 11: 157–160.

Anschutz, L., Camp, C. J., Markley, R. P., and Kramer, J. J. 1987. Remembering mnemonics: A three-year follow-up on the effect of mnemonic training in elderly adults. *Experimental Aging Research,* 13: 141–143.

Bäckman, L. 1985. Further evidence for the lack of adult age differences on free recall of subject performed tasks: The importance of motor action. *Human Learning,* 4: 79–87.

Baltes, P. B., and Willis, S. L. 1982. Enhancement (plasticity) of intellectual functioning: Penn State's Adult Development and Enrichment Project (ADEPT). In F. I. M. Craik and S. Trehub (Eds.), *Aging and cognitive processes* (pp. 353–389). New York: Plenum.

Baylor, A. M., and Spirduso, W. W. 1988. Systemic aerobic exercise and components of reaction time in older women. *Journal of Gerontology,* 43: P121–P126.

Bellezza, F. S. 1981. Mnemonic devices: Classification characteristics, and criteria. *Review of Education Research,* 51: 247–275.

Berkow, R. (Ed.). 1987. *The Merck manual of diagnosis and therapy,* 15th ed. Rahway, NJ: Merck, Sharp, & Dohme Research Laboratories.

Black, P., Markowitz, R. S., and Cianci, S. 1975. Recovery of motor function after lesions in motor cortex of monkey. In R. Porter and D. W. Fitzsimmons (Eds.), *Outcome of severe damage to the central nervous system* (pp. 65–70). Amsterdam: Elsevier.

Blanchard-Fields, F. 1986. Reasoning on social dilemmas varying in emotional saliency: An adult developmental study. *Psychology and Aging, 1:* 325-333.

Block, R., DeVoe, M., Stanley, B., Stanley, M., and Pomara, N. 1985. Memory performance in individuals with primary degenerative dementia: Its similarity to diazepam-induced impairments. *Experimental Aging Research,* 11: 151-155.

Blumenthal, J. A., and Madden, D. 1988. Effects of aerobic exercise training, age, and physical fitness on memory-search performance. *Psychology and Aging,* 3, 280-285.

Boller, F. 1980. Mental status of patients with Parkinson disease. *Journal of Clinical Neuropsychology,* 2: 157-172.

Bondareff, W. 1983. Age and Alzheimer's disease. *Lancet,* 1: 1447.

Cavanaugh, J. C., Grady, J. G., and Perlmutter, M. 1983. Forgetting and use of memory aids in 20 to 70 year olds' everyday life. *International Journal of Aging and Human Development,* 17: 113-122.

Cavanaugh, J. C., Kramer, D. A., Sinnott, J. D., Camp, C. J., and Markley, R. P. 1985. On missing links and such: Interfaces between cognitive research and everyday problem solving. *Human Development,* 28: 146-168.

Cavanaugh, J. C., and Perlmutter, M. 1982. Metamemory: A critical examination. *Child Development,* 53: 11-28.

Cavanaugh, J. C., and Poon, L. W. 1989. Metamemorial predictors of memory performance in young and old adults. *Psychology and Aging,* 4(3): 365-368.

Cerella, J., Poon, L. W., and Williams, D. M. 1980. Age and the complexity hypothesis. In L. W. Poon (Ed.), *Aging in the 1980s.* Washington, DC: American Psychological Association.

Chaffin, R., and Herrmann, D. J. 1983. Self reports of memory abilities by old and young adults. *Human Learning,* 2: 17-28.

Chandler, M. J. 1980. Life-span intervention as a symptom of conversion hysteria. In R. R. Turner and W. Reese (Eds.), *Life-span developmental psychology: Intervention* (pp. 79-91). New York: Academic Press.

Cherkin, A. 1984. Effects of nutritional status on memory function. In H. J. Armbrecht, J. M. Prendergast, and R. M. Coe (Eds.), *Nutritional intervention in the aging process* (pp. 229-249). New York: Springer-Verlag.

Clayton, V. P., and Overton, W. F. 1973. *The role of formal operational thought in the aging process.* Paper presented at the meeting of the Gerontological Society of America, Miami, November.

Coe, R. M. 1981. The sick role revisited. In M. R. Haug (Ed.), *Elderly patients and their doctors* (pp. 22-33). New York: Springer.

Cohen, G., and Faulkner, D. 1989. The effects of aging on perceived and generated memories. In L. W. Poon, D. C. Rubin, and B. Wilson (Eds.), *Everyday cognition in adulthood and late life.* New York: Cambridge University Press.

Crystal, H. A. 1988. The diagnosis of Alzheimer's disease and other dementing disorders. In M. D. Aronson (Ed.), *Understanding Alzheimer's disease* (pp. 15-33). New York: Scribner's.

Cunningham, W. R. 1987. Intellectual abilities and age. In K. W. Schaie (Ed.), *Annual review of gerontology and geriatrics* (Vol. 7) (pp. 117-134). New York: Springer.

Davies, P. 1988. Alzheimer's disease and related disorders: An overview. In M. D. Aronson (Ed.), *Understanding Alzheimer's disease* (pp. 3-14). New York: Scribner's.

Denney, N. W. 1982. Aging and cognitive changes. In B. B. Wolman (Ed.), *Handbook of developmental psychology* (pp. 807-827). Englewood Cliffs, NJ: Prentice-Hall.

Dittmann-Kohli, F., and Baltes, P. B. 1990. Toward a neofunctionalist conception of adult intellectual development: Wisdom as a prototypical case of intellectual growth. In C. Alexander and E. Langer (Eds.), *Beyond formal operations: Alternative endpoints to human development.* New York: Oxford University Press.

Dixon, R. A., and Hultsch, D. F. 1983. Structure and development of metamemory in adulthood. *Journal of Gerontology,* 38: 682-688.

Dixon, R. A., Kramer, D. A., and Baltes, P. B. 1985. Intelligence: A life-span developmental perspective. In B. B. Wolman (Ed.), *Handbook of developmental psychology* (pp. 301-350). New York: Wiley.

Elias, M. F., Elias, J. W., and Elias, P. K. 1990. Biological and health influences on behavior. In J. E. Birren and K. W. Schaie (Eds.), *Handbook of the psychology of aging,* 3rd ed. (pp. 79-102). San Diego, CA: Academic Press.

Fozard, J. L., Thomas, J. C., and Waugh, N. C. 1976. Effects of age and frequency of stimulus repetitions on two-choice reaction time. *Journal of Gerontology,* 31: 556-563.

Harris, J. E. (1984). Methods of improving memory. In B. Wilson and N. Moffat (Eds.), *Clinical management of memory problems* (pp. 46-62). Rockville, MD: Aspen.

Harris, J. E., and Sunderland, A. (1981). A brief survey of the management of memory disorder in rehabilitation units in Britain. *International Rehabilitation Medicine,* 3: 206-209.

Hayslip, B., Jr. 1986. *Alternative mechanisms for improvements in fluid ability in the aged.* Paper presented at the meeting of the American Psychological Association, Washington, D.C., August.

Horn, J. L. 1970. Organization of data on life-span development of human abilities. In L. R. Goulet and P. B. Baltes (Eds.), *Life-span development psychology* (pp. 423-466). New York: Academic Press.

Horn, J. L. 1982. The aging of human abilities. In B. B. Wolman (Ed.), *Handbook of developmental psychology* (pp. 847-870). Englewood Cliffs, NJ: Prentice-Hall.

Hoyer, W. J. 1984. Aging and the development of expert cognition. In T. M. Schlecter and M. P. Toglia (Eds.), *New directions in cognitive science* (pp. 69-87). Norwood, NJ: Ablex.

Hultsch, D. F., and Dixon, R. A. 1990. Learning and memory in aging. In J. E. Birren and K. W. Schaie (Eds.), *Handbook of the psychology of aging,* 3rd ed. (pp. 258-274). San Diego, CA: Academic Press.

Kart, C. 1981. Experiencing symptoms: Attribution and misattribution of illness among the aged. In M. R. Haug (Ed.), *Elderly patients and their doctors* (pp. 70-78). New York: Springer.

Kausler, D. H., and Hakami, M. K. 1983. Memory for activities: Adult age differences and intentionality. *Developmental Psychology,* 19: 889-894.

Kekes, J. 1983. Wisdom. *American Philosophical Quarterly,* 20: 277-286.

Kirasic, K. C. 1980. *Spatial problem solving in elderly adults: A hometown advantage.* Paper presented at the meeting of the Gerontological Society of America, San Diego, November.

Kirasic, K. C., and Allen, G. L. 1985. Aging, spatial performance, and spatial competence. In N. Charness (Ed.), *Aging and human performance* (pp. 191-223). Chichester, England: Wiley.

Labouvie-Vief, G., and Lawrence R. 1985. Object

knowledge, personal knowledge, and process of equilibration in adult cognition. *Human Development,* 28: 25-39.

Lieberman, A. 1974. Parkinson's disease: A clinical review. *American Journal of Medical Science,* 267: 66-80.

Lipowski, Z. J. 1980. *Delirium.* Springfield, IL: Charles C Thomas.

Lishman, W. A. 1978. *Organic psychiatry: The psychological consequences of cerebral disorder.* Oxford, England: Blackwell Scientific.

Madden, D. J. 1986. Adult age differences in the attentional capacity demands of visual search. *Cognitive Development,* 1: 335-363.

McDowd, J. M., and Birren, J. E. 1990. Aging and attentional processes. In J. E. Birren and K. W. Schaie (Eds.), *Handbook of the psychology of aging,* 3rd ed. (pp. 222-233). San Diego, CA: Academic Press.

Meacham, J. A. 1982. A note on remembering to execute planned actions. *Journal of Applied Developmental Psychology,* 3: 121-133.

Morris, P. E. 1979. Strategies for learning and recall. In M. M. Gruneberg and P. E. Morris (Eds.), *Applied problems in memory* (pp. 25-57). London: Academic Press.

Moscovitz, M. C. 1982. A neuropsychological approach to perception and memory in normal and pathological aging. In F. I. M. Craik and S. Trehub (Eds.), *Aging and cognitive processes* (pp. 55-78). New York: Plenum.

National Institute of Aging. 1980. Senility reconsidered. *JAMA,* 244: 259-263.

Neisser, U., and Winograd, E. (Eds.). 1988. *Remembering reconsidered.* New York: Cambridge University Press.

Ohta, R. J. 1981. Spatial problem-solving: The response selection tendencies of young and elderly adults. *Experimental Aging Research,* 7: 81-84.

Perlmuter, L. C. 1989. Motivation. In L. W. Poon, D. C. Rubin, and B. Wilson (Eds.), *Everyday cognition in adulthood and late life.* Cambridge: Cambridge University Press.

Perlmutter, M., Adams, C., Berry, J., Kaplan, M., Person, D., and Verdonik, F. 1987. Aging and memory. In K. W. Schaie (Ed.), *Annual review of gerontology and geriatric* (Vol. 7) (pp. 57-92). New York: Springer.

Perry, W. I. 1970. *Forms of intellectual and ethical devel-*

opment in the college years. New York: Holt, Rinehart & Winston.

Piaget, J. 1970. Piaget's theory. In P. H. Mussen (Ed.), *Carmichael's manual of child psychology,* 3rd ed. (Vol. 1) (pp. 703–732). New York: Wiley.

Poon, L. W. 1985. Differences in human memory with aging: Nature, causes, and clinical implications. In J. E. Birren and K. W. Schaie (Eds.), *Handbook of the psychology of aging,* 2nd ed. (pp. 427–462). New York: Academic Press.

Poon, L. W., and Schaffer, G. 1982. *Prospective memory in young and elderly adults.* Paper presented at the meeting of the American Psychological Association, Washington, D.C.

Reisberg, B., Ferris, S. H., de Leon, M. J., and Crook, T. 1982. The Global Deterioration Scale for assessment of primary degenerative dementia. *American Journal of Psychiatry,* 139: 1136–1139.

Rosenthal, M. J., and Goodwin, J. S. 1985. Cognitive effects of nutritional deficiency. In H. H. Draper (Ed.), *Advances in nutritional research* (Vol. 7) (pp. 71–100). New York: Plenum.

Salthouse, T. A. 1984. Effects of age and skill in typing. *Journal of Experimental Psychology: General,* 113: 345–371.

Salthouse, T. A. 1985. Speed of behavior and its implication for cognition. In J. E. Birren and K. W. Schaie (Eds.), *Handbook of the psychology of aging,* 2nd ed. (pp. 400–426). New York: Academic Press.

Schaie, K. W. 1965. A general model for the study of developmental change. *Psychological Bulletin,* 64: 92–107.

Schaie, K. W. 1983. The Seattle longitudinal study: A twenty-one year exploration of psychometric intelligence in adulthood. In K. W. Schaie (Ed.), *Longitudinal studies of adult psychological development* (pp. 64–155). New York: Guilford.

Schaie, K. W., and Hertzog, C. 1983. Fourteen-year cohort-sequential studies of adult intelligence. *Developmental Psychology,* 19: 531–543.

Schaie, K. W., and Hertzog, C. 1985. Measurement in the psychology of adulthood and aging. In J. E. Birren and K. W. Schaie (Eds.), *Handbook of the psychology of aging,* 2nd ed. (pp. 61–92). New York: Academic Press.

Schaie, K. W., and Willis, S. L. 1986. Can decline in adult intellectual functioning be reversed? *Developmental Psychology,* 22: 223–232.

Sinnott, J. D. 1984. *Everyday memory and solution of everyday problems.* Paper presented at the meeting of the American Psychological Association, Toronto.

Smith, E. L. 1980. The role of exercise in the prevention of bone involution. In R. Chernoff and C. A. Lipschitz (Eds.), *Health promotion and disease prevention in the elderly* (pp. 89–96).

Spirduso, W. W., and MacRae, P. G. 1990. Motor performance and aging. In J. E. Birren and K. W. Schaie (Eds.), *Handbook of the psychology of aging,* 3rd ed. (pp. 183–200). San Diego, CA: Academic Press.

Sternberg, R. J. 1985. *Beyond IQ: A triarchic theory of human intelligence.* Cambridge: Cambridge University Press.

Thal, L. J. 1988. Treatment strategies. In M. K. Aronson (Ed.), *Understanding Alzheimer's disease* (pp. 50–66). New York: Scribner's.

Thomae, H. 1980. Personality and adjustment to aging. In J. E. Birren and R. B. Sloane (Eds.), *Handbook of mental health and aging* (pp. 285–301). Englewood Cliffs, NJ: Prentice-Hall.

Thurstone, L. L. 1938. *Primary mental abilities.* Chicago: University of Chicago Press.

Wall, P. D. 1975. Signs of plasticity and reconnection in spinal cord damage. In R. Porter and D. W. Fitzsimmons (Eds.), *Outcome of severe damage to the central nervous system* (pp. 35–54). Amsterdam: Elsevier.

Welford, A. R. 1977. Motor performance. In J. E. Birren and K. W. Schaie (Eds.), *Handbook of the psychology of aging,* 2nd ed. (pp. 61–92). New York: Academic Press.

West, R. L. 1984. *An analysis of prospective everyday memory.* Paper presented at the meeting of the American Psychological Association, Toronto.

West, R. L. 1986. Everyday memory and aging. *Developmental Neuropsychology,* 2: 323–344.

Whitbourne, S. K. 1987. Personality development in adulthood and old age: Relationships among identity style, health, and well-being. In K. W. Schaie (Ed.), *Annual review of gerontology and geriatrics* (Vol. 7) (pp. 189–216). New York: Springer.

Wilkie, F., and Eisdorfer, C. 1971. Intelligence and blood-pressure in the aged. *Science,* 172: 959.

Willis, S. L., Blieszner, R., and Baltes, P. B. 1981. Intellectual training research in aging: Modification of performance on the fluid ability of figural relations. *Journal of Educational Psychology,* 73: 41–50.

Yates, F. A. 1966. *The art of memory*. Middlesex, England: Penguin.

Zelinski, E. M., Gilewski, M. J., and Thompson, L. W. 1980. Do laboratory tasks relate to self-assessment of memory ability in the young and old? In L. W. Poon, J. L. Fozard, L. S. Cermak, D. Arenberg, and L. W. Thompson (Eds.), *New directions in memory and aging* (pp. 519–544). Hillsdale, NJ: Erlbaum.

CHAPTER 5

The Aging Skin

The skin is a marvelous organ whose elegant simplicity belies its structural and functional complexity. The skin's diverse, specialized cells and zones protect the trillions of cells within the body against physical and chemical injury, solar radiation, pathogenic microbes, and excessive temperature changes. As a sensory device the skin affords an evaluation of our physical surroundings and the satisfaction of a loving touch. Through paling and blushing, and the movement of its underlying musculature, the skin also provides an expression of human emotion.

Lifelong service to its owner subjects the skin to repeated insults. As a buffer zone between humans and their environment it undergoes frequent and cumulative injury. The face as a vehicle of emotion becomes etched with lines typical of its expression. In general, the skin becomes unevenly pigmented, dry, wrinkled, and loose. The hair grows thin and becomes less dense; nails, especially those on the feet, thicken. By displaying its own time-imposed changes, this outermost organ and its appendages have also come to serve as a classic index of age.

GENERAL CHANGES

Epidermal-Dermal Border

The largest and most thinly spread human organ consists of an outer avascular zone, the *epidermis*, and an underlying area of vasculated connective tissue, the *dermis* (see Figure 5.1). With age, the *basal membrane*, the normally undulated border between these two major skin regions, flattens, reducing their surface contact. Consequently, the nutrient transfer and waste clearance provided the epidermis through diffusion from dermal capillary beds below is reduced.

Additionally, the flattening of the epidermal-dermal junction makes older skin more susceptible to shearing force injury. The epidermis more easily

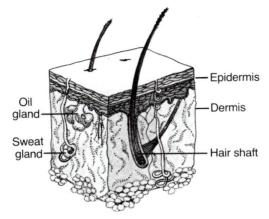

FIGURE 5.1 Skin cross-section

separates from the dermis, resulting in tearing or blistering of the skin. Bumping into something, wearing shoes that rub, or briskly removing a Band-Aid can cause such injury in the elderly.

Epidermis

The epidermis, thanks to the living and dead cells that make it up, provides the body with a protective shield against an array of potentially hazardous and irritating substances. The majority of epidermal cells are *keratinocytes.* They produce the protein *keratin* and proceed through successive stages within the epidermis. At their earliest stage they are *basal cells.* Basal cells rest at the deepest level of the epidermis and are the only keratinocytes to divide. As cell division in this lower area continues, cells are pushed upward toward the body surface at a steady rate. As they move further away from the dermal blood supply, keratinocytes lose their ability to reproduce and their cytoplasm is replaced with keratin. Eventually, they move to the body surface where (as portrayed in Figure 5.2) they form a protective layer of entirely dead cells that are continu-

ously flaked off into the environment. The outer layer of cells consists mainly of keratin, which is largely responsible for the skin's ability to keep various microbes and chemicals from penetrating. At the same time keratin helps maintain the moisture of underlying tissues.

Thus, the epidermis consists of several layers of thin, flat, scalelike cells that form a tissue called *stratified squamous* (scaled or platelike) *epithelium.* Epidermal tissue is constantly being replaced throughout life as living cells in successive stages move toward the outer body surface, losing their ability to divide and maintain themselves along the way. Normally, epidermal cell formation and death occur at a steady rate, except during wound healing, when production must temporarily exceed cell death, or when a cancerous transformation causes them to proliferate uncontrollably.

There is an age-related decrease in epidermal turnover rate, especially after age 50. Hence, older skin becomes more susceptible to chemical irritants. Chemical substances, including topical medications, remain longer. Likewise, epidermal wound healing takes longer in the elderly. These functional changes are related not only to epidermal turnover but to reduced tissue perfusion from the dermis as well. Insulting substances can accumulate, and less of the body's protective components are delivered.

Despite these changes, the essential barrier function of aged skin seems to be preserved. Epidermal thickness and diffusional resistance to water vapor do not significantly decline with age (Balin, 1990a). Irritating substances may remain on the skin longer for aforementioned reasons, but apparently not because of any significant change in the permeability of older skin.

In aged skin, epidermal cells become rather disorganized in their arrangement and tend to clump together. These changes are related to the breakdown in the normal rate of epidermal turnover and to diminished cellular cohesion. Consequently,

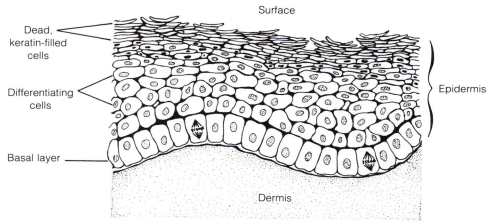

FIGURE 5.2 Drawing of animal epidermis. Cells in the basal layer reproduce and provide cells to the layer of differentiating cells. The differentiating cells become filled with keratin and form the outer layer of tough, flattened cells at the surface that slough off. (*Source:* David M. Prescott, *Cells: Principles of Molecular Structure and Function,* p. 203, © 1988 Boston: Jones and Bartlett Publishers.)

older skin takes on a rougher, sometimes scaly, appearance.

Melanocytes. Pigment-producing cells known as *melanocytes* are scattered within the epidermis. *Melanin,* the pigment that they manufacture, is responsible for an individual's skin color and for the degree of protection offered against the sun's ultraviolet rays. There is some decline in the number of melanocytes with age. More importantly, they become less functional (Gilchrest, 1982). Less effective pigment protection is afforded the elderly, increasing their risk of sun-induced skin cancer. Variations in activity of aging melanocytes account for the blotchy pigmentation seen in older skin, especially in sun-exposed areas.

Graying of the hair is due to a total loss of melanocyte function in the hair bulbs. Losses here occur earlier than in the skin, probably because of the tremendous demands the rate of hair growth places upon them. The scattered graying of individual hairs reflects the variation associated with the aging process.

Langerhans' cells. Langerhans' cells represent another major cell type found in the epidermis. They play a role in activating an immune response in the skin. With age, the number of Langerhans' cells decreases by approximately 50 percent (Silverberg and Silverberg, 1989). Their numbers are further reduced in sun-damaged skin. Their reduction may partially explain the decreased immune responsiveness of older skin and its decreased potential for sensitization to allergic substances. Additionally, increased susceptibility to skin tumors may occur because of impaired tissue rejection (Kripke, 1986; Richey, Richey, and Fenske, 1988; Balin, 1990a).

Dermis

The dermis contains blood vessels, nerves, sweat and oil-secreting glands, hair follicles, several cell types, and various proteins including collagen and elastin. Although the dermis is thicker than the epidermis, dermal thickness decreases progressively with age (Kurban and Bhawan, 1990). Its thinning accounts for the almost transparent character of older skin. Thinner skin is more susceptible to sun damage and trauma. Additionally, the dermis undergoes a decline in both its vasculature and the number of its cells and sweat glands, as well as changes in collagen and elastin.

The decline in dermal vasculature is far-reaching. It results in the pallor of older skin, a decreased inflammatory response, decreased clearance of foreign materials (and a prolongation of contact dermatitis), delayed wound healing, decreased sweating, and compromised thermoregulation.

Changes in sweat production, along with decreased dermal vascularity and a loss of *subcutaneous fat,* weaken thermoregulation in the older adult. Sweat production and blood flow work together to guard against excessive internal temperature. If the internal temperature increases, even slightly, the brain is stimulated to send impulses that will dilate the small blood vessels of the dermis and activate sweat production. As the sweat evaporates, it cools the surface temperature of the skin and the dermal blood flow. Cooled blood then flows to the rest of the body. In cases where the internal temperature drops, the brain sends impulses constricting dermal vessels. Reduced blood flow to the skin follows, allowing the body to remain warmer. Subcutaneous fat insulates the body; as it is lost, greater amounts of body heat escape.

Compromised thermoregulation makes the older person more susceptible to *hyperthermia* (heat exhaustion) and *hypothermia* (reduced body temperature). Elderly persons should avoid hot, stuffy rooms; excessive sun exposure on warm days; and overexertion. Likewise, care should be taken to avoid excessive chilling. Older persons often complain of being cold when others around them are comfortable. Warm clothing and well-heated houses provide more than comfort, as hypothermia can be life-threatening. Public policy programs at the state and local level that provide temporary cool shelter during times of intense heat and economic assistance with meeting fuel bills during winter months have been motivated not only out of financial concerns but by physical needs of the elderly as well (see Tables 5.1 and 5.2).

Certainly, wrinkling is the most obvious age-associated skin change. Wrinkling, which begins early and continues throughout life, is influenced by several factors, including the breakdown of collagen and elastin fibers in the dermis. These substances are important in maintaining skin quality and elasticity. They allow the skin to return to its original firmness and shape after being stretched. Collagen fibers decrease in number and become cross-linked. Smooth elastin fibers get coarse and less resilient. Consequently, the skin becomes lined and furrowed, and tends to sag. These changes are more pronounced where the skin is exposed to sunlight. Solar radiation damages collagen and elastin.

Loss of subcutaneous fat and the repetitive nature of facial expression also contribute to wrinkled, sagging skin. The human face, because of its musculature, is capable of tremendous movement and range of expression. Indeed, facial expressions represent an extremely important component of human communication. Smiles, laughter, frowns, disappointment, and anger are all recorded. The hand of time captures the lines typical of our expressions. Lines begin to form in areas of greatest movement; they proliferate and become deeper as the years pass. By the age of 40, most of us bear the lines typical of our expressions.

TABLE 5.1 The elderly and hypothermia

Who's at Risk?

1. The sick
2. The frail
3. The very old
4. The poor who can't afford enough heat
5. Those who live alone

Signs of Possible Hypothermia

Muscles: The muscles are often unusually stiff, particularly in the neck, arms, and legs. This stiffness may be accompanied by a fine trembling, perhaps limited to one side of the body or to one arm or leg.

Shivering: Shivering is a sign that the body is having trouble keeping warm. The shivering response is frequently diminished or absent in older adults, and the fact that an older person is not shivering in a cool or cold environment does not guarantee that the person is not cold.

Face: The face is frequently puffy or swollen, and this can be an important sign, especially when found in combination with cold skin and signs of confusion.

Coordination: The person often has difficulty walking and has problems with balance. Look for poor coordination and jerky movements.

Breathing and Heart Rate: Both are slowed at low body temperatures and may be very difficult to detect in severe hypothermia.

Skin: The skin is cool or cold. Pay special attention to the stomach, lower back, arms, legs, hands, and feet. The skin color is usually very pale, but it may also have large, irregular blue or pink spots.

Consciousness: As the body cools, consciousness is depressed. Some hypothermia victims will still be conscious when their body temperatures are as low as 80 degrees. Remember, though, that "consciousness" and "mental clarity" are two different things. A person can be "conscious and reactive" and yet still be in a confused, disoriented, and hypothermic state, so the level of consciousness is not always a reliable indicator of the victim's condition.

Confusion: One of the first changes brought on by hypothermia is a growing mental confusion, which becomes progressively worse as body temperature falls. Logical thinking becomes impossible and the person may become completely disoriented. Memory is affected and familiar things are forgotten.

Attitude: Apathy is common. Often the person doesn't care what happens and will do nothing to help reduce the danger; he or she may behave strangely, or become irritable, hostile, mean, and aggressive.

Note: Keep in mind that these signs do not necessarily mean a person is suffering from hypothermia; they are listed to alert you to the possibility.

What to Do

Until help arrives:

- Be careful in handling the person. Failure to do so can cause sudden death because the heart is weak when the body is cold.
- Insulate the victim with available coverings such as blankets, towels, pillows, scarves, or newspapers.

Some Things Can Worsen the Condition

- Do not attempt to rewarm the victim at home. Hot baths, electric blankets, and hot water bottles can be dangerous.
- Do not give the victim any food or drink.
- If the victim is unconscious, do not raise the feet. This will cause cold blood from the legs to flow into the body "core" and further depress the blood temperature.

How to Avoid Harm

1. Wear warm clothing. Wear several loose layers instead of tight clothing. A hat and scarf can reduce significant heat loss through the head and neck. Stay dry. Moisture can reduce or destroy the insulating value of clothing. Water conducts body heat over 25 times faster than air.
2. Use extra blankets. Hypothermia can develop during sleep.
3. Eat nutritious foods and exercise moderately; proper diet and physical conditioning help protect against abnormal cold and heat.
4. Get proper rest; fatigue makes one more vulnerable to subnormal cold and heat.
5. Drink adequate amounts of liquids, such as water. Limit alcohol intake because alcohol speeds up body heat loss.
6. For those who live alone, arrange for a daily check-in call.

Source: Adapted from V. Knauer, *Special Report on Cold Stress (Hypothermia) and Heat Stress* (Washington, DC: U.S. Office of Consumer Affairs, 1987).

TABLE 5.2 The elderly and hyperthermia

Signs of Possible Heat Stress

- Dizziness
- Rapid heart beat
- Diarrhea
- Nausea
- Cramps
- Throbbing headache
- Dry skin (no sweating)
- Chest pain
- Great weakness
- Mental changes
- Breathing problems
- Vomiting

Note: These symptoms can also signal other major problems, such as heart failure.

Special Precautions

- Curtail physical activity during extremely hot weather. Activity adds heart strain.
- Avoid hot foods and heavy meals. They add to body heat.
- Watch salt intake. Check with a physician before increasing the amount of salt or potassium in the diet. Don't take salt tablets without a doctor's permission.

- Avoid alcohol. It acts as a diuretic, resulting in fast water loss. In addition, alcohol can promote a sense of well-being, making one less aware of the danger signs of heat stress.
- For those who live alone, arrange for a regular check-in call.
- Take the heat seriously, pay attention to danger signs, and call a doctor at the first sign of trouble.

To Avoid Heat Stress

1. Keep air as cool as possible. Air-conditioned environments can provide life-saving relief. Fans can draw cool air into a home at night or help circulate indoor air during the day. Air movement reduces heat stress by removing extra body heat.
2. Cool baths or showers provide relief from the heat because water removes extra body heat 25 times faster than cool air. Placing ice bags or wet towels on the body is also helpful.
3. Wear loose-fitting, light-colored clothing in hot weather.
4. Hot weather increases the body's need for water. Do not wait until you are thirsty to have a drink. For those with a medical condition or a problem with water balance, check with a physician for advice on how much water to drink.

Source: Adapted from V. Knauer, *Special Report on Cold Stress (Hypothermia) and Heat Stress* (Washington, DC: U.S. Office of Consumer Affairs, 1987).

Although nerve endings in the skin are not greatly affected anatomically with age, some changes in nerve tissue occur, decreasing one's sensation of pressure and light touch. Pain perception and pain reaction threshold are somewhat reduced, predisposing the elderly to burns. The ability to sense danger tactilely and respond accordingly is reduced (Balin, 1990a; Richey, Richey, and Fenske, 1988; Winkleman, 1965).

Skin Appendages

Eccrine sweat glands become smaller, less numerous, and less active with age, decreasing the sweating response to dry heat. *Sebaceous glands,* more commonly referred to as oil-secreting glands,

increase in size while their numbers remain fairly constant. Nevertheless, their *sebum* (oil) output is reduced.

The rate of scalp and facial hair growth declines with age and hair shaft diameter is reduced. Hair distribution becomes less dense as the number of hair follicles declines. Atrophy of hair bulbs and sweat glands may be related to reduced blood flow.

Fingernails and toenails become brittle and less translucent, and develop longitudinal ridges. Toenails tend to become thickened and eventually deformed as a result of repeated microtrauma, circulatory impairment, and associated faulty nutrition of the tissues. Debris may build up beneath the toenail, causing pressure and discomfort. It may also provide a site for bacterial and fungal infection. Corns and callouses form as a result of rubbing and weight-bearing pressure. With these conditions the epidermis thickens, reflecting an increased number of cells stimulated by friction.

Subcutaneous Tissue

The subcutaneous tissue is located beneath the dermis. It contains fat cells, which insulate against heat loss, serve as a calorie storage depot, and protect against blunt and pressure-related injury. Age-related changes in the amount and distribution of subcutaneous tissue increase the risk of hypothermia and blunt and pressure-related trauma. Despite a general atrophy of subcutaneous tissue, it is increased around the abdomen and thighs (Kligman, Grove, and Balin, 1985), even in those who have not increased their caloric intake.

In addition to fat cells, this tissue contains blood vessels, nerves, and the ends of some sweat glands and hair follicles.

AGE-ASSOCIATED SKIN CONDITIONS

Xerosis

Older skin has a tendency to become dry and scaly. Known technically as *xerosis,* dry skin is the most common skin disorder in the elderly (Fitzpatrick, 1989). Reduced cohesion and clumping of outer epidermal cells contributes to the rough skin texture. Decreased water content of epidermal cells, along with decreased eccrine sweat and sebum production, make for a less well hydrated epidermis. Decreased perspiration may lead to the inefficient distribution of sebum, resulting in accelerated evaporation of skin moisture.

Roughened fine scales are characteristic of xerosis. They may be generalized in distribution but tend to be most pronounced on the lower legs. The degree of xerosis is influenced by various factors. It is generally most prevalent and severe during the winter months, when low humidity, central heating, and drying winds hasten the evaporation of moisture from the skin.

Xerosis can be relieved by the application of moisturizers and emollients. Superfatted soaps may be beneficial in maintaining moisture as soap itself can be drying. If bath oil is used, it should be applied to the body after a bath; it can form a slippery coating on the tub, posing a special danger for the elderly. Protective clothing should be worn during winter months to shield the skin from drying winds.

Pruritus

Pruritus, the technical term for itching, is a frequent symptom in older persons. It is commonly associated with xerosis. However, it should not be routinely dismissed as being due to "dry skin." Prolonged and generalized itching can be a warning sign of internal disease such as diabetes, renal failure, or malignancy. Contact dermatitis and drug reactions can also lead to pruritus.

Benign and Malignant Skin Tumors

Cutaneous tumors can originate from various cell types in the skin. Many are benign, some malignant. A few years ago one researcher offered an interesting suggestion regarding the frequent occurrence of benign proliferative growths in the elderly. He speculated that, perhaps, an age-related inability to regulate skin cell growth is a more striking characteristic than the decline in skin cell turnover rate (Gilchrist, 1982). Among the many such growths are seborrheic keratosis, cherry hemangiomas, lentigo senilis, sebaceous hyperplasia, actinic keratosis, and lentigo maligna. Only seborrheic and actinic keratoses will be reviewed here.

Seborrheic keratosis. Seborrheic keratosis is the most common benign skin growth affecting the older adult. It is derived from immature epidermal keratinocytes, but the cause of their appearance is unknown. A small, demarcated yellow-brown growth that appears glued to the skin, it is barely elevated and covered with a greasy, textured scale. Lesions most commonly appear on the trunk, face, scalp, and upper extremities.

These lesions are not considered premalignant but may be removed for cosmetic purposes because they can be unsightly and bothersome. They may be subjected to frequent trauma by a belt, bra strap, or comb. In such cases their removal can make life more comfortable and decrease the chance of infecting an open sore that could result.

Actinic keratosis. Actinic keratosis is a localized thickening of skin which most often occurs on sun-exposed areas of the body, especially the face, back of the hands, and forearms, but also on the neck, ears, and bald scalp. Initially, the thickening is a well-defined, tan or reddish-colored, slightly raised, sandpaper-like patch. When peeled off, the scaly surface soon reappears. An actinic keratosis is considered to be a premalignant growth that can develop into a skin cancer known as *squamous cell carcinoma*. After removal of an actinic keratosis, future prolonged exposure to sunlight should be avoided and sunscreens used to protect against harmful solar rays.

Excessive exposure to the sun's ultraviolet rays is a significant risk factor for all major forms of *skin cancer*. Epidermal cells and melanocytes can be transformed into perpetually dividing units by the sun's damaging rays. Skin cancer is the most common form of human cancer. It is most prevalent on exposed parts of the skin and in people who spend considerable time in the sun, whether as part of their job or as dedicated sun bathers.

Tanning is a protective mechanism wherein me-lanocytes, stimulated by the sun's rays, produce melanin and disperse it to epidermal cells. Pigment actually enters epidermal cells, absorbing solar rays and reducing penetration of the cell nuclei where damage to DNA can occur. Individuals of all races will undergo a deeper pigmentation as a result of prolonged exposure to sunlight. Skin cancer is most common among those who are fair-complexioned. The disease has been relatively unimportant among blacks, whose melanocytes synthesize greater amounts of protective pigment.

The word *cancer* is extremely frightening to most people. Its diagnosis can have a tremendous psychological impact. Skin cancer, however, is not usually life-threatening, and this fact should be communicated to persons displaying cancerous skin changes. The devastating effects of cancer are largely due to its ability to metastasize. Fortunately, the most frequently occurring forms of skin cancer rarely spread.

Lesions and their surgical removal can be somewhat disfiguring, particularly since they often appear in the facial or head area. Scars become less obvious with time. It should be acknowledged that concerns about appearance are not limited to the young. Anxiety about appearance should not be disregarded because of one's age.

Basal cell carcinoma. Basal cell carcinoma is the most frequent form of skin cancer. It develops from the basal layer of cells within epidermis. It usually appears as a small, translucent pearly nodule on sun-exposed areas of skin—especially the head, face and neck. Lesions are slow-growing and with time may be locally invasive, extending down into the dermis. Ulceration frequently occurs, with a crust forming on the surface. Fortunately, this most frequent form of skin cancer rarely spreads. Treatment is important because the condition can be highly destructive, with major disfigurement and/or infection resulting. With prompt attention, the cure of basal cell carcinoma is almost assured.

Squamous cell carcinoma. Squamous cell carcinoma arises from epidermal cells and can appear anywhere on the skin. It usually occurs in areas of sun-damaged skin, areas exposed to certain established environmental carcinogens or areas of previous injury such as a scar from a burn. The lesions frequently appear as firm, slightly red or pearly nodules. As previously noted actinic keratosis may evolve into a squamous cell carcinoma. When the latter occurs, it rarely metastasizes. The incidence of spread varies with the affected area. Because basal and squamous cell carcinomas are slow-growing and rarely metastasize, they are usually treated by removing the growth.

Malignant melanoma. Malignant melanoma is the most dangerous form of skin cancer. It springs from the uncontrolled growth of pigment producing cells in the epidermis and is noted for its metastasizing ability. Malignant melanoma generally begins as a small mole-like growth. It changes color, enlarges, and bleeds easily from minor trauma. Lesions may include flat or slightly raised areas with irregular margins expressing obvious pigmentation. Melanomas are generally deeply pigmented, ranging from shades of brown, black, blue, and even red. There are four forms of melanoma which vary in their specific appearance, general location, rate of growth, and prognosis.

Early diagnosis and treatment is critical for malignant melanoma. Metastasis can affect virtually every body organ. Treatment involves the removal of the growth along with surrounding tissue in an attempt to ensure that only normal, healthy cells remain behind. Chemotherapy may be recommended.

Skin cancer prevention. In an attempt to prevent skin cancer, it is best to avoid prolonged exposure to sunlight, especially during the time when ultraviolet rays are the strongest – from mid-morning to midafternoon. Protective clothing and sunscreens with a high sun protective factor (SPF 15 or higher) should be worn. These block the damaging ultraviolet rays that can strike the DNA of epidermal cells, causing its abnormal synthesis. Its transformation is a necessary step in tumor formation. Tanning salons and sun lamps should also be avoided (see Tables 5.3 and 5.4 and Figure 5.3).

The diagnosis of skin cancer has increased over the past several years, alarmingly so for malignant melanoma. Between the beginning and end of the previous decade, the number of newly reported melanoma cases increased over 90 percent. Once rare in persons under 40 years of age, it is now increasingly diagnosed among those in their twenties. Annually, it claims 6,000 lives.

The depletion of the earth's protective ozone layer, unprecedented leisure time/outdoor activities, and population growth in the Sunbelt areas have been cited as contributing factors (Sweet, 1989).

Preventive skin care should start at an early age. Individuals who have suffered a blistering sunburn at any time in their lives are at greater risk of developing melanoma. The 10- or 20-year-old with sun-damaged skin today may develop skin cancer in years to come as a result. Avoidance of the midday sun and the use of protective clothing and sunscreens is appropriate for children as well as adults. The more frequent incidence of skin cancer among the elderly is related to, among other things, the cumulative sun exposure they have experienced over a lifetime.

Age-related changes might cause a sense of complacency in the older adult regarding his or her current ability to tolerate sun exposure. Typical early warning signs of sun damage may be blunted. For example, reddened skin signaling too much expo-

---

TABLE 5.3 Tanning and sunlamps

1. What is "tanning"?

Tanning is your body's response that occurs when your skin is exposed to ultraviolet (UV) radiation, as from the sun. Just how much you tan depends a great deal on your own skin's natural ability to tan. If you naturally have a dark complexion, for example, you may tan more easily than a light-skinned person, who may burn rather than tan.

In the tanning process, changes other than skin color occur beneath the surface of the skin. Over the years, these changes may lead to a wrinkled, leathery appearance called "premature skin aging" and to skin cancer. Each time your skin is forced to darken itself, your chances of developing skin cancer in later life are increased. Other factors, including your skin's sensitivy to UV radiation, also affect your chances of developing skin cancer. It is true that a tan blocks out some radiation in attempting to protect the skin from further injury, but it is *inadequate protection* against skin cancer and premature skin aging.

2. Is tanning by sunlamps different from tanning by the sun?

Yes. To explain the difference, you need to have some understanding of ultraviolet radiation, found naturally in sunlight, which can cause you to tan or burn. There are two types of UV radiation that you are exposed to – ultraviolet A (UVA) and ultraviolet B (UVB). UVA radiation is 1,000 times less effective in causing burns than UVB. UVA radiation penetrates skin more deeply and causes you to tan or burn much more slowly. A small amount of UVB radiation can cause skin damage.

Most sunlamps give off either mostly UVA or UVB radiation. Some of the newer so-called UVA sunlamps give off as much as *10 times more UVA* than you receive from the sun and from the older UVB sunlamps. Because the amount of UVB radiation (the quick-burning rays) in these newer models may be less than what you get from the sun or older UVB sunlamps, users sometimes believe that UVA sunlamps are safe to use.

3. Is exposure from UVA sunlamps safe?

While skin and eye burns are less likely to occur with UVA exposure than with sunlight and UVB sunlamps, recent animal studies indicate that UVA radiation in high doses may increase your chances of developing skin cancer and may cause premature skin aging. That's not all. Other recent animal studies also suggest that you may be more likely to get skin cancer if you tan in the sun and with sunlamps than if you are exposed to the sun only.

People who suffer from cold sores may find that, with increased exposure to UV radiation, sores break out more often. People with certain genetic abnormalities (albinos, for example) are especially sensitive to UV radiation, as are those with certain diseases such as lupus erythematosus and acne rosacea.

4. Doesn't a tan, especially a dark tan, protect the skin from further UV damage?

A UVA tan offers some protection against further UV damage – about the same as a Sun Protection Factor (SPF) of 2 or 3. Even with a dark tan, UV damage continues to accumulate.

5. Would a sunscreen help protect my skin while tanning indoors?

Using a sunscreen while tanning by sunlamps requires longer tanning sessions. Therefore, sunscreens are not recommended except to protect parts of your body you don't want to tan (your lips, for example); for this purpose, use a sunscreen with an SPF of 15 or higher. For blocking larger parts of your body (your face, for example), use a dry fabric covering with a tight weave, in addition to a sunscreen, for maximum protection. Remember that sunscreens do not prevent UVA allergic-type reactions for people who are photosensitive.

6. Who is at highest risk for damage from UV radiation?

Generally speaking, individuals who have red or blond hair and blue eyes, are fair-skinned, have freckles and sunburn easily are at highest risk for skin damage. One rule to remember: If you burn and don't tan in sunlight, you probably will burn and won't tan using sunlamps.

Those with Type I skin should never expose themselves to sunlamp radiation.

Source: Adapted from U.S. Department of Health and Human Services, Public Health Service, Food and Drug Administration, HHS Publication No. (FDA) 87-8270.

---

sure may be reduced or absent due to a diminished inflammatory response.

The need to guard against the sun's harmful rays continues into old age. The older adult has reduced melanocyte function, reduced ability to repair DNA damage, and reduced immune protection. Langerhans' cells, already diminished in number in the elderly, are further compromised by excessive ul-

TABLE 5.4 Skin type and tanning: Which skin type are you?

Skin type	Sunburn and tanning history with skin type example
I	Always burns; never tans ("Celtic")
II	Burns easily; tans minimally
III	Burns moderately; tans gradually to light brown (average Caucasians)
IV	Burns minimally; always tans well to moderately brown (olive skin)
V	Rarely burns; tans profusely to dark (brown skin)
VI	Never burns; deeply pigmented; insensitve (black skin)

Source: U.S. Department of Health and Human Services, Public Health Service, Food and Drug Administration, HHS Publication No. (FDA) 87-8270.

traviolet light. The result is a decreased immunity to tumor cell growth (Richey, Richey, and Fenske, 1988).

Secondary Skin Cancer

Primary malignancies elsewhere in the body can spread to the skin, resulting in secondary skin cancer. Dispersal occurs by way of the lymph or blood vessels or through the direct expansion of an underlying tumor, although the latter is not considered a true metastasis. Metastatic skin lesions most commonly occur in persons between 50 and 70 years of age. Any new growth characterized as diffuse nodules, slightly marginated plaques, or purplish hemorrhagic nodules should be investigated. Lesions tend to appear in groups because the density of the dermis serves to restrict the infiltration and growth of large single tumors.

Metastatic skin lesions may appear before or after the primary cancer has been recognized. Less than one percent of all internal malignancies present themselves as pure skin metastases. Tumors with the greatest tendency to do so include those of the kidney, lung, ovary, and pancreas. However, cancer of the breast and oral cavity often spread by direct extension to overlying skin, most often after the primary site is recognized (White, 1985). Hence, secondary skin cancer may be the first indication of an internal malignancy in an otherwise asymptomatic individual. It may also be a sign that treatment of a known tumor was not successful in eradicating all malignant cells.

Pressure Sores

Several years ago an issue of *Medical World News* reported the case of an 85-year-old woman who attempted suicide by taking an overdose of sleeping pills. The major consequence of her unsuccessful act was the development of pressure sores over the heels of both feet. Having swallowed the pills, she had crawled into bed where she remained flat on her back in a comatose state for six hours. During that time the pressure exerted on the woman's heels had denied them an adequate supply of blood. As a result, tissue in those areas died.

Not all pressure sores have so dramatic an onset. Lesions caused by unrelieved pressure to an area can occur in individuals who are debilitated in any number of ways, usually as a result of illness or injury. Victims may have altered mental status, are frequently incontinent, and are uniformly unable to walk without assistance; often they are bed- or wheelchair-bound. Immobility is the most important risk factor. Elderly patients are at special risk. Two-thirds of all inpatients in geriatric wards or nursing homes demonstrate one or more conditions that increase their susceptibility to the development of these lesions (Seiler and Stahelin, 1985).

The persistence of localized pressure is inversely related to an individual's ability to move. Normally, during sleep a person will change positions and restore circulation to a localized pressure spot. How-

Type of Radiation	Skin Cancer	Skin Burns	Eye Burns	Photosensitity	Cataracts	Premature Skin Aging	Reduced Immunity	Blood Vessel Damage
UVA	possible	●	●	●	●	possible	possible	●
UVB	●	●	●	probable	●	●	●	●

Skin Cancer

The risk of skin cancer increases each time your skin is exposed to UV radiation. Although most cases of skin cancers are treatable through surgical or chemical removal, they can cause serious medical problems if not treated in the early growth stage. Another concern is that the number of skin cancers is on the rise.

Burns

Skin burns, more quickly caused by UVB than UVA radiation, can range from a slight redness of the skin to painful blisters. Severe eye burns, causing a sandy or gritty sensation (photokeratitis) or pink eyes (conjunctivitis), may occur within hours of sunlamp exposure if the eyes are not protected by special goggles that fit snugly around the eyes.

Photosensitivity

Certain chemicals in foods, medicines, and cosmetics you use may cause you to be extra sensitive to UV radiation. This is called "photosensitivity." Your body may react as if you had an allergic reaction. Symptoms are severe skin burn, itching and scaly skin, and rash.

Some common photosensitizing products are limes, celery, and some deodorant soaps, shampoos, and makeup. Some of the photosensitizing medicines are birth control pills, antibiotics, anticonvulsants, high blood pressure medications, diuretics, antihistamines, tranquilizers, and oral diabetes medications.

Cataracts

This condition is a "clouding" in the lens of the eyes that usually develops later in life and may lead to blindness. The risk of cataracts can be increased by both UVA and UVB radiation exposure to the unprotected eye. Wearing goggles that screen UV radiation can prevent this.

Premature Skin Aging

One of the most noticeable signs of repeated UV exposure over the years is premature skin aging, appearing much earlier in life than you may expect. According to some skin specialists, skin that has a dry, wrinkled, leathery appearance early in middle age can result from UV exposure that took place *before the age of 20.*

Blood Vessel Damage and Reduced Immunity

UVA and UVB radiation also can damage the blood vessels in a sublayer of your skin. UVA affects the immune system (the body's natural ability to fight infections). In some cases, it may be harmful. UVB suppresses some immune responses.

FIGURE 5.3 Hazards of UV radiation. (*Source:* Adapted from U.S. Department of Health and Human Services, Public Health Service, Food and Drug Administration, HHS Publication No. (FDA) 87-8270.)

ever, an individual who is heavily sedated, severely confused, or immobilized will either not experience or not react to signs of unrelieved pressure.

Pressure sores are often called *decubitus ulcers* or bed sores, both of which are misnomers. The former term comes from the Latin *decub,* meaning "a lying down." Confinement to bed is not the only way in which they develop. A large percentage results from unrelieved pressure exerted in a sitting position, often while in a wheelchair.

Certain areas of the body are more likely to be involved than others, as illustrated in Figure 5.4. Areas where little tissue exists between bone and skin are most subject to deprived blood flow in the face of unrelieved pressure. The vast majority of pressure sores are located in the lower part of the body. The following areas represent the most common sites of sore formation:

1. For a recumbent patient – the shoulder, lower back, and heels

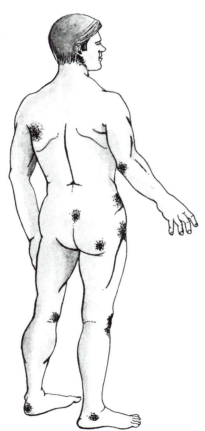

FIGURE 5.4 Common sites of pressure sore formation

2. For a patient lying on his or her abdomen – the knee, shin, and pelvis
3. For a patient lying on his or her side – the hip
4. For a sitting patient – the buttocks

Four factors have been implicated in the development of pressure sores: pressure, shearing force, friction, and moisture (Allman, 1989, 1990; Witkowski and Parish, 1982). Pressure induces blood loss in the affected area. Shearing force reduces the amount of pressure required to pinch off blood vessels. Such a force is exerted when one is seated and slides toward the floor or when the head of the bed is elevated and one slides toward the foot of the bed. Friction can cause epidermal blisters. It may be generated by sliding an individual across a bed. Moisture can increase friction and lead to epidermal injury. Thus, the incontinent or unattended immobilized patient is at further risk of damage.

Pressure and shearing forces tend to cause injury in deeper tissues with the damage spreading to the skin's surface. Animal studies have demonstrated that muscle and subcutaneous tissue are more susceptible to pressure-induced damage than is the epidermis (Daniel, Priest, and Wheatley, 1981). Friction and moisture seem to be more importantly related to the breakdown of superficial skin (Allman, 1989, 1990).

Various physical characteristics of the elderly contribute to the development of pressure sores. First, loose, lax skin can fold over compressing dermal blood vessels and superficial capillaries, compromising blood flow. Second, reduced subcutaneous fat may result in greater pressure over bony prominences. Third, blood flow to the skin may already be reduced by the presence of disorders common in advanced age, such as atherosclerosis or congestive heart failure.

In some instances, pressure sores are shallow, not involving full skin thickness. In such superficial cases, if the pressure source is eliminated, healing may occur relatively quickly. The deeper the sore penetrates, the slower the healing process and the more dismal the prognosis. Deep ulceration can occur suddenly. A reddened area of skin may erupt into a profound lesion without any warning. Underlying fat, muscle, and bone may be involved. Subsequent infection of the open wounds can be very serious. Microorganisms can be carried through the circulation to involve one or more organ systems. Multiple and often life-threatening complications can accompany pressure sores.

Treatment of pressure sores is costly in every way. For the patient, severe pain and discomfort must be borne. Furthermore, he or she may be stigmatized by the nature of deep ulcerations. Such lesions give off an offensive odor and are typically filled with the debris of dead tissue.

Healing can take weeks to months. Care provided during this time is costly. Special materials to clean and dress the wound properly, long-term antibiotic therapy to counteract infection, and procedures to remove dead tissue chemically or surgically must be employed. Special attention to nutrition is necessary to aid the body's defenses and the healing of the wound. Nursing staff and time involved in attending to these measures must also be considered. Perhaps for no other condition is the adage "An ounce of prevention is worth a pound of cure" so appropriate.

Frequent repositioning of immobilized persons at two-hour intervals has been the major recommended preventive strategy. In actuality, the frequency of repositioning necessary to prevent pressure-related injury is dependent on the overall risk status of the patient and on whether or not pressure-relieving support surfaces are used (Allman, 1990).

Older patients should be evaluated for their risk of developing a pressure sore. Nutritional status, overall physical condition, degree of mobility, activity patterns, level of consciousness (including medication status), and ability to control bowel or bladder should be considered in a care plan aimed at the prevention of this unnecessary and potentially devastating problem. Prevention may be difficult in high-risk groups such as the immobile and bedridden, but it is not as difficult as treatment and cure.

Herpes Zoster

Herpes zoster, commonly known as shingles, is characterized by localized skin eruption and pain. Its incidence increases with age and is dependent on a previous chicken pox infection. After recovery from chicken pox, the causative virus remains dormant, usually for years. As antibody levels wane with time, the virus is reactivated, spreading down nerve fibers to invade the skin. Reactivation of the virus results in herpes zoster.

Before it was known that one virus was the cause of two clinically distinct diseases, chicken pox was said to be the result of a varicella virus infection, and shingles was linked with herpes zoster virus. After Weller and Coons (1954) established that these "two" agents were really one, the virus was renamed varicella-zoster virus (VZV). It is now also referred to as Herpesvirus varicella.

The mechanism of reactivation is not understood. It appears that the virus, harbored within spinal nerve fibers, is reactivated when the host's immunologic capabilities can no longer contain its replicative efforts. Zoster can be elicited in response to other trigger factors associated with an altered immune response, including cancer (especially lymphoma), the use of drugs that suppress the immune response, and X-ray therapy.

Symptom onset can be sudden, ranging from localized tingling, itching, and burning, to pain. Eventually, an eruption appears along those areas of affected skin. Sometimes pain is present several days before skin lesions erupt. The localized pain of the preeruptive phase may be so intense that it is confused with gallstones, appendicitis, heart attack, pleurisy, or acute glaucoma, depending on the skin field supplied by affected nerve roots (Harnisch, 1984).

A complication of special importance to the elderly is *post-herpetic neuralgia* (Balin, 1990b). It involves persistent pain for one month or more after the rash has healed. In some cases the pain lasts for more than a year. This situation can be very frustrating for the victim of herpes zoster, who may need caring, sensitive reassurance that the pain will eventually disappear.

There has been speculation about the risk of cancer after herpes zoster because of the associated immune decline. One study (Ragozzino, Melton, Kurland, Chur, and Perry, 1982) followed 590 patients diagnosed with zoster and concluded that cancer risk was not significant for these patients. However, herpes zoster may be a problem for the immune-depressed cancer patient.

PHOTOAGING

Some of the time-imposed changes that take place in the skin are intrinsic; that is, they are natural and inevitable. One of the most fundamental changes that skin cells undergo as a result of genetically programmed senescence is their reduced proliferative capacity. The decreased turnover of cells within the epidermis is natural, intrinsic, and inevitable. Such is the case even if the rate of turnover can be altered.

Most of the visible changes of older skin are extrinsic, reflecting the cumulative insult of environmental damage. Most of these changes are due to photoaging – a series of chemical events activated by exposure to sunlight. Some intrinsic and photoaged skin changes overlap, but they are more conspicuous and severe in photoaged skin (Silverberg and Silverberg, 1989).

Sunlight-induced skin enemies include a roughened skin surface, mottled or irregular pigmentation, fine lines and wrinkles, deep furrows and sagging, numerous benign skin growths, the premalignant actinic keratoses, and various skin cancers.

Wrinkle creams and so-called miracle cures for aged skin are often purchased in the hope of eliminating or reducing the ravages of time. In fact, the many skin creams on the market seem to have no durable effect on the skin.

Topical tretinoin, or Retin-A, used since 1971 as a treatment for severe acne, is being studied for its effects on photoaged skin. It belongs to a group of vitamin A-related compounds known as retinoids, noted for their antioxidant properties. They have varied biologic effects. Among these are gene regulation, collagen synthesis, antineoplastic activity, and promotion of wound healing. Studies on Retin-A may provide further information about aging skin. However, the best prevention against the skin's many sun-induced changes is avoidance of excessive exposure to ultraviolet light (including exposure via sunlamps and tanning booths), the wearing of protective clothing, and the use of suncreams with a high protective factor.

VITAMIN D SYNTHESIS

Vitamin D is a unique nutrient because it can be manufactured by the body, whereas all others must be consumed in the diet. Its production is dependent on a series of chemical events that include the skin. A chemical produced by the liver is delivered to the skin where ultraviolet rays from the sun convert it into a precursor of active vitamin D. With age the skin becomes less responsive to the ultraviolet conversion (MacLaughlin and Holick, 1985). This situation leads to decreased vitamin D production and may occasionally result in vitamin D deficiency (Silverberg and Silverberg, 1989). Such a deficiency can contribute to skeletal conditions important in the elderly, including osteoporosis.

STUDY QUESTIONS

1. Differentiate the epidermis from the dermis. What types of age-related changes in structure and function take place in these two areas of skin?
2. Describe xerosis and senile pruritus. What factors are associated with the development and alleviation of these conditions?
3. Differentiate seborrheic keratosis from actinic keratosis.
4. How are exposure to sunlight and melanocyte activity related to skin cancer? Identify and differentiate the three major forms of skin cancer. Of what significance is secondary skin cancer to the older adult?
5. What are pressure sores? Identify some factors related to their development and prevention. What are some consequences of the development of pressure sores?
6. What is herpes zoster? How is it related to chicken pox?
7. Identify and explain the significance of photoaging.
8. How is the human skin related to vitamin D production and osteoporosis?

BIBLIOGRAPHY

Allman, R. 1989. Pressure ulcers among the elderly. *New England Journal of Medicine,* 320: 850-853.

Allman, R. 1990. Pressure ulcers. In W. Hazzard, R. Andres, E. Bierman, and J. Blass (Eds.), *Principles of geriatric medicine and gerontology.* New York: McGraw-Hill.

Balin, A. 1990a. Aging of human skin. In W. Hazzard, R. Andres, E. Bierman, and J. Blass (Eds.), *Principles of geriatric medicine and gerontology.* New York: McGraw-Hill.

Balin, A. 1990b. Herpes zoster. In W. Hazzard, R. Andres, E. Bierman, and J. Blass (Eds.), *Principles of geriatric medicine and gerontology.* New York: McGraw-Hill.

Daniel, R. K., Priest, D. L., and Wheatley, D. C. 1981. Etiologic factors in pressure sores: An experience model. *Archives of Physical Medicine and Rehabilitation,* 62(10): 492-498.

Fitzpatrick, J. 1989. Common inflammatory skin diseases of the elderly. *Geriatrics,* 44: 40-46.

Gilchrest, B. 1982. Skin. In J. Rowe and R. Besdine (Eds.), *Health and disease in old age.* Boston: Little, Brown.

Harnisch, J. 1984. Zoster in the elderly: Clinical, immunologic and therapeutic considerations. *Journal of the American Geriatrics Society,* 32: 789-793.

Kligman, A., Grove, G., and Balin, A. 1985. Aging of human skin. In C. Finch and E. Schneider (Eds.), *Handbook of the biology of aging.* New York: Van Nostrand Reinhold.

Kripke, M. 1986. Immunology and photocarcinogenesis. *Journal of American Academy of Dermatology,* 14: 149-155.

Kurban, R., and Bhawan, J. 1990. Histologic changes in skin associated with aging. *Journal of Dermatologic Surgery and Oncology,* 16: 908-914.

MacLaughlin, J., and Holick, M. 1985. Aging decreases the capacity of human skin to produce vitamin D3. *Journal of Clinical Investigation,* 76: 1536.

Ragozzino, M., Melton, J., Kurland, L., Chur, P., and Perry, H. 1982. Risk of cancer after herpes zoster: A population-based study. *New England Journal of Medicine,* 307: 393-396.

Richey, M., Richey, H., and Fenske, N. 1988. Aging-related skin changes: Development and clinical meaning. *Geriatrics,* 43: 49-64.

Seiler, W., and Stahelin, H. 1985. Decubitus ulcers: Preventive techniques for the elderly patient. *Geriatrics,* 40: 53-60.

Silverberg, N., and Silverberg, L. 1989. Aging and the skin. *Postgraduate Medicine,* 86: 131-144.

Sweet, C. 1989. "Healthy tan" — a fast-fading myth. *FDA Consumer,* 23: 11-13.

Weller, T., and Coons, A. 1954. Fluorescent antibody studies with agents of varicella and herpes zoster propagated in vitro. *Proceedings, Society of Experimental Biology and Medicine,* 86: 789.

White, J. 1985. Evaluating cancer metastatic to the skin. *Geriatrics,* 40: 67-73.

Winkleman, R. 1965. Nerve changes in aging skin. In W. Montagna (Ed.), *Advances in biology of skin* (Vol. 6). Oxford: Pergamon Press.

Witkowski, J. A., and Parish, L. C. 1982. Histopathology of the decubitus ulcer. *Journal of the American Academy of Dermatology,* 6(6): 1014-1021.

CHAPTER **6**

The Aging Skeletal System

Together our bones and muscles protect vital organs, give stability to the body, preserve its shape, and allow the freedom of movement and locomotion. Additionally, the skeletal system acts as a metabolic reservoir. Through the continuing process of bone remodeling, calcium enters and leaves the bones. Most of us take these provisions of the skeletomuscular system very much for granted.

Joint changes along with diminished bone and muscle mass can give way to increased fractures and falls, stooped posture and shortened stature, loss of muscle power, misshapen joints, pain, stiffness, and limited mobility. Arthritis and allied bone and muscular conditions are among the most common of all disorders affecting people over 65 years of age. In fact, joint and muscular aches, pains, and stiffness are often expected in old age. Frequently, all such symptoms are lumped together as discomforts of arthritis or "rheumatism." Such a practice can be dangerous. For instance, pain associated with bone cancer or another disease may be dismissed and needed medical attention delayed. Chronic, recurrent muscular and bone pain is not natural. In response to such symptoms, people of all ages should seek prompt medical attention.

Skeletomuscular changes are significant in that they can greatly alter an individual's life-style by making activities of daily living more difficult. Even though certain changes occur, they need not be inevitably disabling if proper diagnosis and treatment are given. Age-related changes and/or disease states of the skeletomuscular system rarely serve to directly shorten the life span. Nevertheless, if one is immobilized or bedridden as a result of pain, stiffness, or a fall or fracture, complications can lead to death.

A recognition of potential problems should not be used to paint a dismal picture for older people. Although the prevalence and disabling effects of certain skeletomuscular conditions increase with age, most older persons are not severely limited by changes or disease within this system. For certain disorders, an increasing emphasis is being placed on prevention. Primary prevention of arthritis may not be possible, but secondary and tertiary steps may be taken to retard serious effects and to increase the potential for independent living. It may be possible to prevent, or at least delay, the serious effects of bone loss by attention to modifiable lifestyle factors. This chapter will focus on selected skeletomuscular conditions that may be encountered by the older adult, including several forms of arthritis, osteoporosis, and Paget's disease.

ARTHRITIS

Arthritis is a major source of discomfort and disability for many older persons. It is one of the oldest known diseases. The cartoon image of a Neanderthal as a stooped brute with a bent-knee gait represents a caricature of an arthritic relative who lived over 40,000 years ago. The condition is still very much with us; it represents the number one crippler across all ages in the United States.

Arthritis is a generic term that literally means inflammation of a joint. There are over a hundred different kinds of arthritis; each is not necessarily accompanied by inflammation. However, all forms of arthritis do signify some type of joint involvement central to their definition.

The numerous types of arthritis vary in their causes, symptoms, and degree of joint inflammation and damage. Some forms of arthritis may first present themselves in middle or old age. Others may have developed decades earlier. *Osteoarthritis, rheumatoid arthritis,* and *gout* will be discussed here as conditions affecting the older adult.

To comprehend what arthritis is and the changes that accompany it, it is useful to understand the anatomy of joints or articulations. Where bones come together there exist articulating surfaces so that various body movements may be accomplished. The adjacent ends of bones are covered with *articular cartilage* and are encircled by a strong *fibrous articular capsule.* The *synovial membrane* lines the capsule and produces a lubricant for smooth articulation (Figure 6.1). The articular cartilage and synovial fluid allow for smooth, lubricated movement. The joint capsule and associated

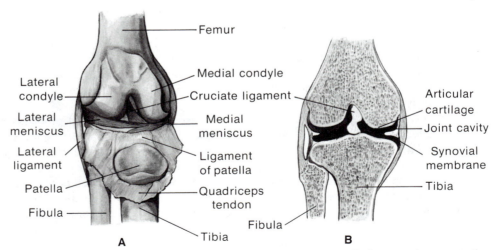

FIGURE 6.1 Knee joint. (A) Dissected from the front, with patella hanging down onto the tibia. (B) Section of the knee, revealing the joint cavity.

tendons and ligaments play an important part in lending stability to the joint.

Osteoarthritis

Osteoarthritis (OA), the most common joint disease, is usually encountered in persons older than 50 years. It is a defect of articular cartilage that is characterized by the gradual loss of this cushioning substance. Osteoarthritis is also referred to as *degenerative joint disease,* and it used to be assumed that such deterioration resulted from the mechanical wear and tear of aging. Simply stated, it was held that the use of a joint over the years eventually eroded the articular surface and led to possible joint failure. Today, this explanation is considered simplistic and inexact. Certain joints that receive considerable use, such as the knee, are frequently involved; others subject to the lifelong stress of frequent movement, such as the knuckles and ankles, are rarely involved. Although joint failure is poorly understood, when it occurs it appears to be the culmination of numerous pathologic events. A complex interplay of factors, such as biochemical, hereditary, inflammatory, and mechanical ele-

ments, possibly influence the degree and rate of cartilage thinning (Ettinger and Davis, 1990; Kaye, 1984).

As cartilage is lost, the resultant exposure of rough underlying bone ends can cause pain and joint stiffness. Bony growths or spurs known as *osteophytes* may appear at the articular margin or at sites of ligament/tendon attachment, producing a characteristic "lipping." These bony spurs account for much of the associated joint enlargement. As the condition continues, low-grade inflammation of the synovial membrane develops. Thus, inflammation is a secondary effect rather than the initial lesion of OA. Inflammation is often mild and unnoticed – in contrast to the inflammation of rheumatoid arthritis, the archetypal inflammatory joint disease (Altman, 1990; Altman and Gray, 1985).

In time, the joint capsule may become thickened, leading to restricted movement. Long-standing OA can result in joint instability and deformity. Occasionally, osteophytes may grow from both bone ends, causing the joint to meet and fuse. The joint then becomes locked and incapable of movement (Figure 6.2).

Degeneration that occurs in the absence of a known cause is referred to as *primary* or *idiopathic*

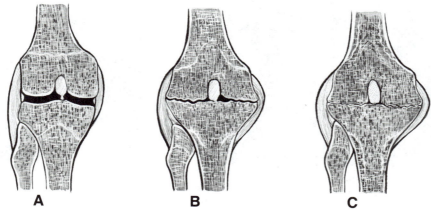

FIGURE 6.2 Osteoarthritis: Degeneration developing from A, normal, to C, fusion. Note the increased joint width after fusion.

OA. Secondary OA occurs in conjunction with previous joint damage or disease. For instance, joint injury resulting from an accident or infection may lead to OA. The effect of running on joint degeneration is a present-day concern. Some studies indicate that running does not necessarily predispose to OA (Lane, Bloch, Jones, Marshall, Wood, and Fries, 1986; Panush, et al., 1986). However, it is postulated that running can accelerate OA in joints with preexisting articular cartilage damage (Pascale and Grana, 1989).

Weight-bearing joints, including the lumbar spine, knees and hips, are commonly affected by osteoarthritis (Brandt and Fife, 1983; Moskowitz, 1987). Weight bearing, however, does not necessarily indicate risk of OA. The condition is often asymmetric, with one knee or hip showing damage. Likewise, the ankle, subject to such lifelong, weight-bearing stress, is rarely affected by primary disease. The cervical spine, *metatarsophalangeal joint* of the great toe (foot/toe), first *carpometacarpal joint* (wrist/hand), and distal and proximal *interphalangeal joints* (fingers) may also be affected. The familiar nodules known as *Heberden's nodes* may appear on the last joints of the fingers. *Bouchard's nodes* are the same phenomenon at the proximalinterphalangeal joints (Figure 6.3). Such cartilaginous/bony enlargements are seen in women more often than in men. Though disfiguring, they usually develop gradually, causing little pain. They are occasionally accompanied by swelling, pain, and a burning or tingling sensation at the end of the fingers. With or without pain, they make the execution of fine motor tasks more difficult.

Primary OA rarely involves the wrist or knuckles, which are the joints stressed by frequent, repetitive movement. Likewise, the elbow and shoulder are rarely involved except as a result of previous trauma. Thus, it is suggested that factors other than and in addition to simple weight bearing and joint use are involved in the development of disease.

A premature form of primary OA may sometimes result from a genetic defect in a joint-cushioning protein. This inherited form of disease may

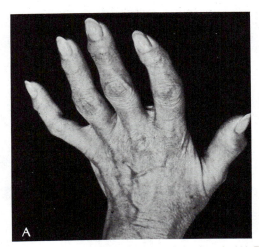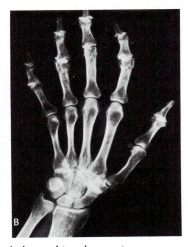

FIGURE 6.3 Osteoarthritis of the hand. (A) Proximal interphalangeal involvement (Bouchard's nodes), along with some distal interphalangeal involvement (Heberden's nodes). (B) X-ray of the same hand. (*Source: Arthritis*, 8th edition, by J. L. Hollander. Copyright © 1976 by Lea & Febiger, Publishers. Reprinted by permission.)

strike in the second or third decade, leaving its victim with painful and limited joint movement by middle age. Knees, hips, fingers, and elbows may be involved.

Osteoarthritis does not cause symptoms prior to radiographic change, although such change is not necessarily accompanied by symptoms. By the age of 75 years, 85 percent of individuals demonstrate radiographic evidence of OA in weight-bearing joints. Only 30 percent of these persons are symptomatic (Giansiracusa and Kantrowitz, 1982). It has been emphasized that OA is often overdiagnosed on the basis of radiographic evidence. Joint symptoms with X-ray changes may be due to conditions other than OA (Brandt and Fife, 1983; Ettinger and Davis, 1990). It is also possible for symptomatic OA to overlap with another disease, such as gout.

Symptomatic OA is generally characterized by pain with movement of the affected joint. As the condition progresses, pain may occur at rest as well. Pain is frequently poorly localized. For instance, hip movement may be associated with groin, thigh, buttocks, and lower back discomfort. Stiffness on awakening or movement may also be present. Known as *gelling or gel phenomenon,* the stiffness is of relatively short duration. It generally lasts less than 30 minutes, in contrast to that experienced by rheumatoid arthritis victims, among whom it may persist for several hours. Over time a progressive loss of range of motion occurs. The joint may become unstable and deformed.

There is no cure for osteoarthritis. Symptomatic relief includes rest balanced with exercise, physical therapy, moist heat, and drugs (analgesics and anti-inflammatory agents). Aspirin is one of several non-steroidal anti-inflammatory drugs that provide pain relief. It has been a mainstay of arthritis therapy. Although it is a highly *effective* product, certain side effects of long-term aspirin use must be noted. *Tinnitus* and hearing loss are eventually inescapable and may be cause for a switch in medication. Gastrointestinal irritation as a part of long-term therapy may be minimized by taking the drug with food or through the use of a buffered or enteric-coated product. Bleeding is yet another side effect to be considered. The individualized needs of a patient will dictate whether aspirin or another drug will be administered. The decision must weigh patient tolerance, cost, and the potential side effects posed by the given drug. Surgical intervention may be used to relieve pain and correct joint deformity.

Osteoarthritis patients need proper treatment and care. Like many victims of other forms of arthritis, they are easy prey for quackery. The Arthritis Foundation estimates that several hundred million dollars are spent annually on worthless gimmicks and so-called cure-alls. Medications, special devices, clinics, diets, and dietary supplements have been falsely presented as remedies for a disease that orthodox medicine cannot cure.

Rheumatoid Arthritis

Joint involvement in rheumatoid arthritis (RA) begins with an inflamed synovial membrane. The normally thin lining swells, thickens, and begins to override the articular cartilage. Eventually, the cartilage is softened as chemical reactions occur. Erosion of cartilage continues as fibrous connective tissue forms. In time, the joint can undergo extensive damage, with the capsule and ligaments inflamed, stretched, and destroyed. Tendons may drift out of their normal position, shorten, and produce deformity as the joint undergoes complete disorganization. Twisted, drawn fingers of the hand attacked by RA provide an example of joint distortion as a result of inflammation. Sometimes fibrous tissue formation can lead to joint fusion.

Rheumatoid arthritis is a chronic, systemic disease. It is not confined to joints; rather, it attacks connective tissue throughout the body. Symptoms of RA include general malaise, fatigue, weight loss, fever, anemia, and nodules that develop on soft tissues. The associated arthritis tends to be symmetrical and *polyarticular* (affecting multiple joints). Hands and feet are commonly affected. The knee, hip, ankle, shoulder, and elbow may also be involved. Red, swollen joints and gelling are characteristic of the disease.

The cause of RA is not fully known. It is recognized as an immunologic disturbance triggered by hereditary factors and, most probably, by exposure to a commonly encountered virus. A self-perpetuating inflammatory response ensues; if left unchecked, it can lead to joint destruction. Rheumatoid arthritis is an autoimmune disease wherein antibodies launch an attack detrimental to one's own tissues.

Diagnosis of rheumatoid arthritis is aided by a laboratory technique that demonstrates an *elevated* erythrocyte sedimentation rate, although a positive result can be indicative of disorders other than RA. Tests for *rheumatoid factor,* an abnormal antibody, are positive in 85 percent of RA patients. However, a positive rheumatoid factor test can indicate other disorders, such as systemic lupus erythematosis. Radiographs and synovial membrane tests, along with a symptomatic history, are also a part of diagnostic review.

There are many drugs available to treat RA, including aspirin and other nonsteroidal anti-inflammatory drugs (NSAIDS). Serious consideration must be given to the use of various other agents when the disease cannot be controlled by these measures. Additionally, balanced rest and exercise are important in the care of arthritis (Furst, 1990). Although rest is appropriate, prolonged rest can lead to stiffness, muscle weakness, and "frozen joints." Exercise does not mean strenuous activity or athletics; it refers to prescribed activities that put joints through their full range of motion. Rheumatoid arthritis is a progressive disease, but with early diagnosis and treatment the majority of persons can maintain good control of the disorder. Surgical techniques, though not routine, have been developed to remove damaged tissue and to correct deformity.

Rheumatoid arthritis presents itself most commonly between the ages of 20 and 60. Thus, the elderly RA patient has usually carried the disease into old age. In the older adult with advanced disease, other skeletomuscular problems may cause the disorder to worsen. The crippling effects of arthritis may become more pronounced with age. Progression of disease is characterized by periods of symptomatic exacerbation and subsidence known as flares and remissions.

It is not uncommon for elderly RA patients with long-standing disease to have few complaints of the pain and stiffness typically indicative of active inflammatory involvement. However, the chronic inflammatory process continues as does the risk of developing complications of RA (Csuka and Goodwin, 1990).

Approximately 10 percent of patients undergo disease onset after the age of 60 (Giansiracusa and Kantrowitz, 1982). Sometimes the pattern of late-onset disease differs from that seen in younger patients. Some reports have noted men equally affected as women, which is a deviation from the normal profile of occurrence. Also, a high frequency of remission has been observed within the first year (Ehrlich, Katz, and Cohen, 1970; Giansiracusa and Kantrowitz, 1982).

Gout

Gout is a metabolic disease that causes an acutely painful form of arthritis. It is frequently due to an inherited defect in *purine* metabolism, which results in excess blood levels of *uric acid*. Proteins in the body break down into purines. Uric acid is an end product of purine metabolism that is normally excreted through the kidneys. Heightened levels of the substance are caused by its increased production or faulty elimination.

Uric acid excesses can precipitate out to the joints to form sharp crystals, thus initiating an attack of gouty arthritis. This acute condition is characterized by sudden intermittent episodes of joint inflammation. The affected joint is painful, hot, swollen, and tender. Crystal deposits may develop in almost any part of the body, but in the vast majority of cases the great toe is the initial site of attack.

Gout episodes generally subside after a few days. Symptoms usually begin to manifest themselves between the ages of 40 and 55 years and tend to become more apparent with advancing age. As the condition progresses, discomfort can become more prolonged. Anti-inflammatory drugs are called for during the acute stages of gout so that joint symptoms may be relieved. Drugs that lower blood levels of uric acid are used between attacks and aid in preventing recurrences.

Since gout represents disordered purine metabolism, foods high in purines should be restricted. Such foods include gravy, broth, bouillon, consommé, meat (particularly organ meat), anchovies, mackerel, herring, sardines, scallops, mussels, and sweetbreads. Alcoholic beverages should also be avoided. A restricted purine diet does not guarantee decreased uric acid blood levels because purines can be manufactured by the body from simple metabolites. Hence, uric acid levels can increase even though outside purine sources are controlled by dietary restriction.

Some general dietary recommendations are in order for gout sufferers. Fats, protein, and carbohydrates are all necessary in a balanced diet. Excessive amounts of fat should be avoided because they can serve to prevent uric acid excretion. Protein intake should not be excessive. A substantial proportion of calories should be derived from carbohydrates because of their association with increased uric acid elimination. During acute stages of gout, purine intake should be severely restricted. Fluid consumption can aid in the elimination of uric acid. Those with gout should never go on a rapid weight loss diet. Fasting may cause precipitation of uric acid. It is important that weight loss be gradual and

that a weight loss diet not be initiated during an acute attack of gout.

Gouty arthritis does not always arise from an inherited defect in purine metabolism. Secondary gout may be associated with a number of causes. Diuretic medications given to lower blood pressure and rid the body of excess fluid may be related to a gout attack. Secondary gout may also develop in association with other drugs, as well as in certain medical conditions such as leukemia or cirrhosis (Kaye, 1984).

OSTEOPOROSIS

The majority of the more than 20 million cases of osteoporosis in the United States occur in women. This condition, wherein bone loss is accelerated to a symptomatic level, is the major cause of skeletal fractures in postmenopausal women and older persons in general. Women are more prone to the disease than men because they have less bone mass to begin with and because changes that take place during menopause lower calcium and estrogen levels, thereby accelerating loss of bone tissue.

Bone loss occurs in all people as they age, regardless of gender, race, ethnic group, or physical condition. Such normal age-associated loss of bone is termed *senile osteopenia*. For many persons adult bone loss continues to be asymptomatic. When it advances to the pathologic state known as osteoporosis, the structural integrity of bone tissue is so compromised that bones are more susceptible to fracture even after minimal trauma (Boskey, 1990). Osteoporosis can result in diminished height, stooped posture, pain, and tooth loss.

Certain nonmodifiable factors have been identified that increase the risk of osteoporosis. They include sex, race, heredity, and body frame. As noted earlier, women are at higher risk than men. Although men can develop osteoporosis, they do so in smaller numbers and generally at a later age. White and Asian women are at higher risk than black women, who tend to have greater bone density. A family history of osteoporosis also increases the risk of the disorder, as does a slight frame. Thin, small-boned women are more susceptible than are large-framed women. Although these factors cannot be controlled, there are modifiable life-style factors that may influence the integrity of bone and the bone-thinning process. Proper nutrition and regular exercise are among the life-style factors that will be presented in this chapter. However, a basic understanding of bone as living tissue is important to a full appreciation of preventive strategies in the development of osteoporosis.

Bone is dynamic tissue that is in a constant state of change. It consists of calcium and phosphorus in a protein matrix. Various other materials such as fluoride and magnesium lend support to the calcium and phosphorus crystals. Calcium is critical to the structural integrity of bone. Approximately 99 percent of the body's calcium is stored in bones (and teeth), giving them strength and rigidity. In turn, the skeleton serves as a "calcium bank" for the body.

Calcium concentrations in serum and body fluids must be maintained to allow for various vital activities, including blood clotting, enzyme activation and inhibition, muscle contraction, nerve conduction, and regulation of heartbeat. If serum calcium levels are not adequate, hormones assist in releasing calcium from bone, making it available for such functions. If calcium levels rise above normal, another hormone shuts down its release. Calcium is also added to skeletal tissue. Thus, bones are constantly being broken down and reformed. The turnover of bone is a lifelong process known as remodeling. During bone resorption, parathyroid hormone (PTH) stimulates bone-destroying cells called osteoclasts to release calcium from skeletal tissue. Bone formation, wherein calcium enters the skeleton, is mediated by bone-forming osteoblasts.

The rates of bone resorption and formation vary over the life cycle. During adolescence, when bones are growing and height is increasing, formation exceeds resorption. After growth is completed, bones continue to add mass. They reach their maximum strength and density sometime during early to middle adulthood, depending on the bone. For instance, vertebrae peak in strength and density during the mid-twenties, whereas the long bones of the arms and legs do so at about age 40 (Peck, 1985). During this time period, formation and resorption equal one another. After a plateau is reached, the rate of bone resorption exceeds that of formation, initiating a period of progressive bone loss. Thus, from middle adulthood on, bones begin a gradual and silent decline in mass and strength. If bone volume reaches a low enough level, osteoporosis is the end result.

Although all bones lose mass with age, some are more critically affected than others. This situation exists because of the distribution of two basic types of bone. Located within skeletal tissue is porous, trabecular bone. Although hard, it looks like a sponge or honeycomb in cross-section. Cortical bone, in contrast, surrounds it (being located on the outside) and is very dense and solid. Trabecular bone loss begins at an earlier age, resulting in a relative increase in the ratio of cortical to trabecular bone. During the teen years, the ratio is 55:45. By age 85 it is approximately 70:30 (Giansiracusa and Kantrowitz, 1982). Those bones with the greatest amount of trabecular area will thus undergo a greater decline of their mass. Indeed, the vertebrae, wrist, and hips, all high in trabecular bone, are the most common fracture sites.

Vertebral and wrist fractures are seen predominantly in women 10 to 15 years after menopause. They are associated with Type I osteoporosis, which is attributed to trabecular as opposed to cortical bone loss (Riggs and Melton, 1983). Their occurrence is a function not only of the trabecular area involved, but is related to the postmenopausal drop in estrogen levels as well. Estrogen deficiency makes bone more sensitive to PTH, which stimulates bone resorption (Hedayati and Zuzga, 1988; Slovik, Adams, Neer, Holick, and Potts, 1981). It is also believed to lead to reduced intestinal absorption of calcium (Aloia, Cohn, Vaswani, Yeh, Yuen, and Ellis, 1985). Estrogen loss is an established risk factor for osteoporosis (Chestnut, 1990; Ettinger, 1988; Meema, Bunkler, and Meema, 1975; Nordin et al., 1981). The maintenance of testosterone levels in men appears to exert somewhat of a protective effect on bone mass (Orimo and Shiraki, 1979; Horsman, Marshall, Nordin, Crilly, and Simpson, 1981).

Because vertebrae are comprised largely of trabecular bone, osteoporosis typically occurs first in the spine. Vertebral compression or *crush fractures* can occur spontaneously or from the stress of activities such as bending or lifting. Compressed vertebrae may lead to a loss of height and curvature of the thoracic spine (commonly known as *dowager's hump*). Both of these changes are irreversible. In severe cases of *dorsal kyphosis,* the lower ribs may come to rest on the *iliac crests* of the pelvis. A horizontal band of thickened skin across the abdominal area may result, as well as intestinal distention and constipation. Chest wall mechanics may also be impaired, affecting respiratory ventilation.

Osteoporosis is a common cause of backache in elderly women. It can range from mild to severe and can be localized or radiated toward the abdomen and into the pelvis or legs. Coughing, sneezing, and straining at the stool may exacerbate the problem. Vertebral osteoporosis is frequently episodic. One or more crush fractures may produce severe pain that can last for several weeks. For some, backache may become chronic; for others it disappears. Recurrent incidents of vertebral compression fractures result in progressive loss of height and increasing deformity.

Wrist fractures called *Colles fractures* often result from minimal trauma in the osteoporotic individual.

They typically involve the distal radius and usually occur when the arm is extended to break a fall. They are the least severe fracture associated with osteoporosis, but may represent a warning of significant bone loss.

Bone loss in the jaw can contribute to tooth loss. It can also make it difficult to construct and maintain well-fitting dentures (Renner, Boucher, and Kaufman, 1984).

Hip fracture is the greatest hazard associated with osteoporosis. It occurs later in life, usually in one's seventies or eighties, when a significant amount of cortical bone has been lost. Because of the loss of cortical bone, it is regarded as *Type II osteoporosis.* Hip fractures are a significant cause of morbidity and mortality, costing more than $7 billion annually (Cummings, Black and Rubin, 1985; Cummings, Rubin, and Black, 1990; Kelsey and Hoffman, 1987). Hip fracture carries a 25 percent chance of long-term institutionalization. Fatal complications such as pneumonia and pulmonary embolism generally result from imposed immobility. Twelve to 20 percent of elderly hip fracture victims die within six months (Cummings and Black, 1986; Magaziner, Smonsick, Kashner, Hebel, and Kenzera, 1989; Mossey, Mutran, Knott, and Craik, 1989).

Both elderly men and women are affected by Type II osteoporosis. It is suspected that 33 percent of women and half as many men in the older age group sustain hip fractures (Owen, Melton, Gallagher, and Riggs, 1980). Type II osteoporosis is a function of cumulative loss of bone and age-related impaired calcium absorption. That twice as many females suffer hip fractures as men has been related to their greater longevity as well as to initially lower peak bone mass.

It is estimated that the total number of hip fractures among older adults will increase from the 238,000 recorded in 1986 (U.S. Department of Health and Human Services, 1986) to 347,000 by the year 2020 and to 512,000 by 2040 (Cummings, Rubin, and Black, 1990). This projected increase is related to the growing number of elderly people in the United States and will be linked to a concomitant rise in disability, avoidable mortality, and medical costs.

There are certain basic differences between the pattern of fractures in the young and the old. In young adults it takes a considerable amount of force to break a bone. Among the elderly, however, a fracture can result from minor trauma, even bearing weight. For instance, it is likely that many of the falls and associated hip fractures of old age actually represent an osteoporotic femoral neck that broke under the stress of weight bearing, resulting in a fall. Another difference in fracture pattern involves location. The shaft of a long bone is a common fracture site among the young, whereas a site adjacent to a joint is more typically involved in the older adult. The number of hip (actually femoral neck) and distal radius fractures stands testimony to this fact. Finally, the fracture rate among young adults is higher for men, a situation largely related to occupational factors and potential accident situations. There is an emphasis today on prevention of osteoporosis. Ideally, such measures should start as early as possible. Maximizing bone construction during adolescence and early adulthood gives one a greater calcium reserve to carry into old age. The more calcium deposited in the "bone bank" when one is young, the more there will be to draw upon later. Prevention is not a goal reserved for the young; it is a lifelong aim. Although osteoporosis is an irreversible and progressive disease, there are measures that may slow further loss of bone tissue even in the osteoporotic patient. A consideration of preventive and treatment modalities is in order.

Diet is one of the major modifiable life-style factors which may affect progression of bone loss. The established RDA for calcium is 800 mg. Many consider the present RDA too low to maintain calcium balance, especially in postmenopausal women (Avioli, 1984; Heaney, Gallagher, Johnston, Neer, Parfitt, and Whedon, 1982; National

Institutes of Health, 1984). A calcium intake of 1,000 mg/day has been suggested for premenopausal and estrogen-treated women and 1,500 mg/day for postmenopausal women not on *estrogen-replacement therapy*. A National Institute of Health (NIH) panel submitted that such recommended intakes might serve to prevent fractures or to reduce their incidence after menopause (National Institutes of Health, 1984). Twenty-five percent of American women consume less than 300 mg per day, with the median calcium intake for females approximating 500 to 700 mg.

It must be underscored, however, that some researchers are now questioning whether dietary calcium in adulthood plays a role in osteoporosis prevention (Kolata, 1986). One study involving 107 women ranging in age from 23 to 88 years found no correlation between calcium intake and bone loss (Riggs and Melton, 1986). The women who were studied for an average of four years had a wide range of calcium intake (from 269 to 2,000 mg/day), with each subject's intake being relatively steady throughout the period of investigation. When women consuming more than 1,400 mg/day were compared with those whose intake was less than 500 mg, the rate of bone loss was found to be essentially the same.

Various researchers are quoted from a 1986 meeting of the American Society for Bone and Mineral Research to question the 1984 dietary recommendations of the NIH panel on osteoporosis (Kolata, 1986). Some maintain that the advice was based on tenuous evidence. Due to uncertainties regarding the long-term efficacy of calcium in preventing osteoporosis, a number of researchers would not advise calcium supplementation. Riggs cautions that, despite the "enormous media hype," the answers are not yet certain regarding osteoporosis prevention. Although he does not recommend calcium pills, Riggs does advise patients to consume 1,000 mg/day from dietary sources (Riggs et al., 1982; Riggs and Melton, 1983).

The best sources of calcium are dairy products. Because of concern about excessive calories, fat, and cholesterol consumption, low-fat dairy products are recommended. Sometimes, either *weight-watching* or *lactose intolerance* causes avoidance of dairy products. Leafy green vegetables such as collard, turnip, and mustard greens and broccoli are also good calcium sources. Some green vegetables such as spinach contain *oxalates,* which bind the calcium they contain, preventing its absorption. Sardines and salmon provide calcium if the bones are consumed. Legumes also are a source of calcium.

Various other dietary factors have been associated with calcium levels. High-protein/meat diets have been said to enhance bone loss and increase urinary calcium excretion. At present, there are conflicting data on this matter (Hedayati and Zuzga, 1988; Margen, Chu, Kaufmann, and Calloway, 1974; Spencer, Kramer, DeBartolo, Norris, and Osis, 1983; Spencer and Kramer, 1986; Wachman and Bernstein, 1968). Soft drink consumption and related high dietary phosphorus instigated concern that calcium absorption might be impaired, but this belief has been questioned (Allen, 194). There is speculation that a high-calcium, high-phosphorus diet may help to prevent bone loss (Liebman, 1985). Data also suggest that bone loss might be increased by "heavy" caffeine consumption.

Alcoholics frequently show evidence of bone loss, probably due to impaired calcium absorption (Allen, 1984; Hedayati and Zuzga, 1988) and intestinal and liver problems (Baran, Teitelbaum, and Bergefeld, 1980). Likewise, heavy drinkers frequently have poor diets and do not consume much calcium. Alcohol intake is recognized as a risk factor for osteoporosis; among males it increases the risk by 2.4 (Seeman, Melton, O'Fallon, and Riggs, 1983).

A decreased ability to absorb calcium occurs in both men and women during their sixties. Among women, an especially acute drop occurs at menopause. Most elderly women excrete approximately 60 mg more per day of calcium than they eat (Allen, 1984).

Vitamin D is also important in preventing osteoporosis because it is a major regulator of calcium absorption in the intestine. Vitamin D levels are dependent on dietary intake and on exposure to sunlight, which initiates synthesis of a form of vitamin D in the skin.

Concern about osteoporosis has focused much attention on the use of calcium supplements. Although many forms of calcium are available, calcium carbonate tablets are most frequently recommended. They contain a higher percentage of elemental calcium than other compounds, so fewer tablets are needed. Supplements containing dolomite or bone meal should be avoided because they may contain toxic contaminants, including lead. As previously indicated, various researchers would not recommend supplementation because long-term safety and efficacy are not known at present.

Supplements are available with added vitamin D. For older women, who tend to get less exposure to sunlight (and who are less efficient at endogenously manufacturing vitamin D), this addition may be very appropriate. Younger women, however, may be getting enough in their diet and via sunlight. Too much vitamin D can be toxic (Hausman, 1985; Resnick and Greenspan, 1989).

Daily calcium intake via diet and/or supplements should not exceed 1,500 mg per day. Calcium excesses can lead to soft tissue calcification. Individuals who are prone to or have a strong family history of kidney stones should take supplemental calcium only under the direction of a physician.

In conclusion, it must be underscored that there is debate on the effect of a high calcium intake during adulthood and calcium supplementation on estrogen-dependent bone loss. A perusal of the literature yields conflicting data (Burnell et al., 1986; Ettinger, 1988; Ettinger, Genant, and Cann, 1987;

Holbrook, Barrett-Connor, and Wingard, 1988; Horsman et al., 1977; Jensen, Christiansen, and Transbol, 1982; Matkovic, Kostial, Simonovic, Buzina, Broderac, and Nordin, 1979; Recker, Saville, and Heaney, 1977; Riggs, Seeman, Hodgson, Taves, and O'Fallen, 1982; Riis, Thomsen, and Christiansen, 1987; Smith, Reddan, and Smith, 1981). Calcium supplementation has not been conclusively demonstrated to have a beneficial effect on bone loss (Felicetta, 1989).

The role of physical activity in preventing bone loss has yet to be clearly defined. Research suggests that regular weight-bearing exercise in conjunction with the dietary aspects of bone maintenance is important in promoting bone formation and reducing skeletal losses in postmenopausal women as well (Nelson et al., 1991). Although definitive data do not exist to prove that exercise will prevent the disorder, it is known that a lack of physical activity hastens bone loss (Donaldson, Hulley, and Vogel, 1970; Mack, LaChance, and Vose, 1967; Rambaut, Dietlein, and Vogel, 1972; Smith, 1982). Inactivity resulting in bone loss may be induced by immobilization, loss of muscle function or the weightlessness demonstrated in space flight.

Regular exercise that works muscles against gravity, such as walking, seems to maintain and strengthen bone (Aloia, Cohn, Ostuni, Cane, and Ellis, 1978; Hedayati and Zuzga, 1988; Huddleston, Rockwell, Kulund, and Harrison, 1980; Sinaki, 1989). Muscular activity has been found to increase bone mass in elderly as well as young persons (Simkin, Ayalon, and Leichter, 1987; Smith, 1982; Smith, Reddan, and Smith, 1981). Aloia et al. (1978) reported that bone loss in younger women can be prevented by physical activity. It is possible that daily weight-bearing exercise may be the single most important external factor affecting bone formation.

Smoking is a risk factor for osteoporosis (Jensen, Christiansen, and Rodbro, 1985). Although the reason for this association is not known, it may be related to an earlier onset of menopause in women who smoke (Lindquist and Bengtsson, 1979; Lindquist, Bengtsson, and Hanson, 1979). Men who smoke are also at increased risk (Seeman et al., 1983). In one study it was found that 52 percent of osteoporotic smokers required dentures after age 50, compared to 26 percent for osteoporotic nonsmokers, and 8 percent for nonosteoporotic nonsmokers (Daniell, 1983).

A simple, low-cost test for osteoporosis is a present-day goal. Such a test would be helpful in detecting bone thinning before it had progressed to a clinically significant point. For many people the first sign of the silent loss of bone that has been taking place is a fracture. Sometimes osteoporosis is detected inadvertently by an X-ray taken for another problem. An X-ray can detect bone loss, but only after a significant amount of tissue is gone. There are various bone density tests for detecting the disorder. Because of cost and accessibility, however, they are not now routinely used.

Estrogen-replacement therapy (ERT) is the most significant form of treatment currently used to slow bone loss after menopause. Evidence indicates that fracture risk is significantly reduced with estrogen therapy (Ettinger, Genant, and Cann, 1987; Henneman and Wallach, 1957; Kiel, Felson, Anderson, Wilson, and Moskowitz, 1987; Nachtigall, Nachtigall, and Beckman, 1979; Weiss, Ure, Ballard, Williams, and Daling, 1980). Its use in those with low bone density and spinal compression fractures is questionable. Existing compromised bone mass is maintained along with, presumably, the future risk of fracture (Chestnut, 1990; Resnick and Greenspan, 1989). It is given shortly after menopause and seems to be most effective at reducing bone loss during the eight- to ten-year period following menopausal onset.

Not all women are candidates for ERT. It has been the subject of controversy and should be used with close medical supervision. Use of estrogen has been linked with endometrial cancer. The risk is reduced when estrogen is given in conjunction with the hormone progesterone (Judd, Cleary, Creasman, Figge, Kase, Rosenwaks, and Tagatz, 1981; Rubin et al., 1990; Weiss and Scyvetz, 1980). Though the findings are not conclusive, recent evidence suggests that estrogen usage may help protect postmenopausal women from coronary heart disease (Stampfer et al., 1991).

PAGET'S DISEASE

Paget's disease is a chronic, localized bone disease of unknown cause occurring primarily in geriatric patients. It begins slowly and may progress to cause skeletal deformity. This condition, first described and labeled *osteitis deforams* by Paget in 1877, affects approximately 3 percent of the population over 45 years of age. Men and women are equally affected.

Paget's disease is characterized by excessive bone resorption followed by accelerated formation of abnormal bone. A radiographic diagnosis is confirmed with the display of porotic areas of bone surrounded by areas of sclerosis and bone "repair." The sites most commonly affected are the vertebral column and sacrum, femur, skull, and pelvis. Single or multiple bone involvement may be expressed, the latter being most common.

STUDY QUESTIONS

1. How significant are skeletal changes among the elderly?
2. What is arthritis? How do various types of arthritis differ?
3. Briefly outline the anatomy of a joint.
4. Distinguish osteoarthritis from rheumatoid arthritis, including cause, changes, diagnosis, age of onset, degree of disfigurement, symptoms, and treatment.
5. What is gout? Note its cause, symptoms, and methods of treatment or management.
6. Differentiate senile osteopenia from osteoporosis.
7. With respect to osteoporosis, review:
   a. risk factors
   b. bone remodeling
   c. bones most critically affected
   d. Type I and Type II osteoporosis
   e. diagnosis
   f. treatment
8. Discuss how osteoporosis might be prevented.
9. Note three differences between the fracture pattern in the old and in the young.
10. What is Paget's disease?

BIBLIOGRAPHY

Allen, L. 1984. Calcium absorption and requirements during the life span. *Nutrition News,* 47: 1-3.

Aloia, J., Cohn, S., Ostuni, J., Cane, R., and Ellis, K. 1978. Prevention of involutional bone loss by exercise. *Annals of Internal Medicine,* 89: 356-358.

Aloia, J., Cohn, S., Vaswani, A., Yeh, J., Yuen, K., and Ellis, K. 1985. Risk factors for postmenopausal osteoporosis. *American Journal of Medicine,* 78: 95-100.

Altman, R. 1990. Osteoarthritis. *Postgraduate Medicine,* 87: 66-78.

Altman, R., and Gray, R. 1985. Inflammation in osteoarthritis. *Clinics in Rheumatic Diseases,* 11: 353-365.

Avioli, L. 1984. Calcium and osteoporosis. *Annual Review of Nutrition,* 4: 471-491.

Baran, D., Teitelbaum, S., and Bergefeld, M. 1980. Effect of alcohol ingestion on bone and mineral metabolism in rats. *American Journal of Physiology,* 238: E507.

Boskey, A. 1990. Bone mineral and matrix. Are they altered in osteoporosis? *Orthopedic Clinics of North America,* 21: 19.

Brandt, K., and Fife, R. 1983. The diagnosis of osteoarthritis. *Medical Student,* 9: 4-7.

Burnell, J., et al. 1986. The role of calcium deficiency in postmenopausal osteoporosis. *Calcified Tissue International,* 38: 187.

Chestnut, C., III. 1990. Osteoporosis. In W. Hazzard, R. Andres, E. Bierman, and J. Blass (Eds.), *Principles of geriatric medicine and gerontology.* New York: McGraw-Hill.

Csuka, M., and J. Goodwin. 1990. Rheumatoid arthritis. In W. Hazzard, R. Andres, E. Bierman, and J. Blass

(Eds.), *Principles of geriatric medicine and gerontology*. New York: McGraw-Hill.

Cummings, S., and Black, D. 1986. Should perimenopausal women be screened for osteoporosis? *Annals of Internal Medicine,* 104: 817-823.

Cummings, S., Black, D., and Rubin, S. 1985. Epidemiology of osteoporosis and osteoporotic fractures. *Epidemiology Review,* 7: 178-208.

Cummings, S., Rubin, S., and Black, D. 1990. The future of hip fractures in the United States. *Clinical Orthopedics and Related Research,* 252: 163-166.

Daniell, H. 1983. Postmenopausal tooth loss: Contributions to edentulism by osteoporosis and cigarette smoking. *Archives of Internal Medicine,* 143: 1678-1682.

Donaldson, C., Hulley, S., and Vogel, J. 1970. Effect of prolonged bed rest on bone mineral. *Metabolism,* 19: 1071-1084.

Ehrlich, G., Katz, W., and Cohen, S. 1970. Rheumatoid arthritis in the elderly. *Geriatrics,* 25: 103.

Ettinger, B. 1988. A practical guide to preventing osteoporosis. *Western Journal of Medicine,* 149: 691-695.

Ettinger, B., Genant, H., and Cann, C. 1987. Low-dosage estrogen combined with calcium prevents postmenopausal bone loss: Results of a three-year study. In D. Cohn, T. Martin, J. Meunier (Eds.), *Calcium regulation and bone metabolism: Basic and clinical aspects* (Vol. 9). Amsterdam: Elsevier.

Ettinger, W., and M. Davis. 1990. Osteoarthritis. In W. Hazzard, R. Andres, E. Bierman, and J. Blass (Eds.), *Principles of geriatric medicine and gerontology*. New York: McGraw-Hill.

Felicetta, J. 1989. Age-related changes in calcium metabolism. *Postgraduate Medicine,* 85: 85-94.

Furst, D. 1990. Rheumatoid arthritis: Practical use of medications. *Postgraduate Medicine,* 87: 79-92.

Giansiracusa, D., and Kantrowitz, F. 1982. Rheumatic disease. In J. Rowe and R. Besdine (Eds.), *Health and disease in old age* (pp. 267-296). Boston: Little, Brown.

Hausman, P. 1985. *The calcium bible*. New York: Warner Books.

Heaney, R., Gallagher, J., Johnston, C., Neer, R., Parfitt, A., and Whedon, G. 1982. Calcium nutrition and bone health in the elderly. *American Journal of Clinical Nutrition,* 36: 986-1013.

Hedayati, H., and Zuzga, J. 1988. Osteoporosis: Current review. *Journal of American Orthopedic Association,* 88: 1495-1508.

Henneman, P., and Wallach, S. 1957. A review of the prolonged use of estrogens and androgens in postmenopausal and senile osteoporosis. *Archives of Internal Medicine,* 100: 715.

Holbrook, T., Barrett-Connor, E., and Wingard, D. 1988. Dietary calcium and risk of hip fracture: Fourteen-year prospective population study. *Lancet,* 2: 1046.

Horsman, A., Gallagher, J. C., Simpson, M., and Nordin, B. E. C. 1977. Prospective trial of oestrogen and calcium in postmenopausal women. *British Medical Journal,* 2: 789-792.

Horsman, A., Marshall, D. H., Nordin, B. E., Crilly, R. G., and Simpson, M. 1981. The relation between bone loss and calcium balance in women. *Clinical Science,* 59: 137-142.

Huddleston, A., Rockwell, D., Kulund, D., and Harrison, B. 1980. Bone mass in lifetime tennis athletes. *Journal of the American Medical Association,* 244: 1107-1109.

Jensen, J., Christiansen, C., and Rodbro, P. 1985. Cigarette smoking, serum estrogens, and bone loss during hormone-replacement therapy early after menopause. *New England Journal of Medicine,* 313: 973-975.

Jensen, G., Christiansen, C., and Transbol, I. 1982. Treatment of postmenopausal osteoporosis: A controlled therapeutic trial comparing oestrogen/gestagen, 1, 25-dihydroxy-vitamin D3 and calcium. *Clinical Endocrinology,* 16: 515-524.

Judd, H., Cleary, R., Creasman, W., Figge, D., Kase, N., Rosenwaks, Z., and Tagatz, G. 1981. Estrogen replacement therapy. *Obstetrics and Gynecology,* 58: 267-275.

Kaye, R. 1984. A clinical perspective on rheumatoid arthritis, osteoarthritis and gout. *American Pharmacy,* N.S. 24(7): 474-477.

Kelsey, J., and Hoffman, S. 1987. Risk factors for hip fracture. *New England Journal of Medicine,* 316: 404.

Kiel, D., Felson, D. T., Anderson, J., Wilson, P., and Moskowitz, M. A. 1987. Hip fracture and the use of estrogens in postmenopausal women. *New England Journal of Medicine,* 317: 1169-1174.

Kolata, G. 1986. How important is dietary calcium in preventing osteoporosis? *Science,* 233: 519-520.

Lane, N., Bloch, D. A., Jones, H. H., Marshall, W. H., Jr., Wood, D. D., and Fries, J. F. 1986. Long distance running, bone density, and osteoarthritis.

Journal of the American Medical Association, 255: 1147-1151.

Liebman, B. 1985. Losers weepers: Is your body absorbing all the calcium you consume? *Nutrition Action,* 12: 9, 14.

Lindquist, O., and Bengtsson, C. 1979. The effect of smoking on menopausal age. *Maturitas,* 1: 141.

Lindquist, O., Bengtsson, C., and Hanson, T. 1979. Age at menopause and its relation to osteoporosis. *Maturitas,* 1: 175.

Mack, P., La Chance, P., and Vose, G. 1967. Bone demineralization of foot and hand of Gemini-Titan IV, V and VII astronauts during orbital flight. *American Journal of Roentgenology,* 100: 503-511.

Magaziner, J., Smonsick, E., Kashner, M., Hebel, J. R., and Kenzera, J. E. 1989. Survival experience of aged hip fracture patients. *American Journal of Public Health,* 79: 274-278.

Margen, S., Chu, J., Kaufmann, N., and Calloway, D. 1974. Studies in calcium metabolism: 1. The calciuretic effect of dietary protein. *American Journal of Clinical Nutrition,* 27: 584-589.

Matkovic, V., Kostial, K., Simonovic, I., Buzina, R., Broderac, A., and Nordin, B. E. C. 1979. Bone status and fracture rates in two regions of Yugoslavia. *American Journal of Clinical Nutrition,* 32: 540.

Meema, S., Bunkler, M., and Meema, H. 1975. Preventive effect of estrogen on postmenopausal bone loss. *Archives of Internal Medicine,* 135: 1436-1440.

Moskowitz, R. 1987. Primary osteoarthritis: Epidemiology, clinical aspects, and general management. *American Journal of Medicine,* 83: 5-10.

Mossey, J., Mutran, E., Knott, K., and Craik, R. 1989. Determinants of recovery 12 months after hip fracture: The importance of psychosocial factors. *American Journal of Public Health,* 79: 279-286.

Nachtigall, L., Nachtigall, R., and Beckman, E. 1979. Estrogen replacement therapy I: A ten-year prospective study in the relationship to osteoporosis. *Obstetrics and Gynecology,* 53: 277.

National Institutes of Health. 1984. *NIH consensus development conference statement on osteoporosis.* Bethesda, MD: National Institutes of Health.

Nelson, M., Fisher, E., Dilmanian, F., Dallal, G., and Evans, W. 1991. A 1-y walking program and increased dietary calcium in postmenopausal women: Effects on bone. *American Journal of Clinical Nutrition,* 53: 1304-1311.

Nordin, B., et al. 1981. Summation of risk factors in osteoporosis. In H. Deluca, H. Frost, W. Jee, C.

Johnston, and A. Parfitt (Eds.), *Osteoporosis: Recent advances in pathogenesis and treatment.* Baltimore, MD: University Park Press.

Orimo, H., and Shiraki, M. 1979. Role of calcium regulating hormones in the pathogenesis of senile osteoporosis. *Endocrinology Review,* 1: 1-6.

Owen, R., Melton, L., Gallagher, J., and Riggs, B. L. 1980. The national cost of acute care of hip fractures associated with osteoporosis. *Clinical Orthopedics Related Research,* 150: 172.

Panush, R. S., Schmidt, C., Caldwell, J. R., Edwards, N. L., Longley, S., Yonker, R., Webster, E., Stork, J., and Pettersson, H. 1986. Is running associated with degenerative joint disease? *Journal of the American Medical Association,* 255: 1152-1154.

Pascale, M., and Grana, W. 1989. Does running cause osteoarthritis? *The Physician and Sports Medicine,* 17: 1-6.

Peck, W. 1985. Brittle bones. *Nutrition Action,* 12: 4-8.

Rambaut, P., Dietlein, L., and Vogel, J. 1972. Comparative study of two direct methods of bone mineral measurement. *Aerospace Medicine,* 43: 646-650.

Recker, R., Saville, P., and Heaney, R. 1977. Effect of estrogens and calcium carbonate on bone loss in postmenopausal women. *Annals of Internal Medicine,* 87: 649-655.

Renner, R., Boucher, L., and Kaufman, H. 1984. Osteoporosis in postmenopausal women. *Journal of Prosthetic Dentistry,* 52: 581-588.

Resnick, N., and Greenspan, S. 1989. "Senile" osteoporosis reconsidered. *Journal of the American Medical Association,* 261: 1025-1029.

Riggs, B., Seeman, E., Hodgson, S. F., Taves, D. R., and O'Fallon, W. 1982. Effect of the fluoride/calcium regimen on vertebral fracture occurrence in postmenopausal osteoporosis: Comparison to conventional therapy. *New England Journal of Medicine,* 306: 446-450.

Riggs, B., and Melton, L. 1983. Evidence for two distinct syndromes of involutional osteoporosis. *American Journal of Medicine,* 75: 899-901.

Riggs, B., and Melton, L. 1986. Involutional osteoporosis. *New England Journal of Medicine,* 314: 1676.

Riis, B., Thomsen, K., and Christiansen, C. 1987. Does calcium supplementation prevent postmenopausal bone loss? *New England Journal of Medicine,* 316: 173-177.

Rubin, G., et al. 1990. Estrogen replacement therapy and the risk of endometrial cancer: Remaining controversies. *American Journal of Obstetrics and Gynecology,* 162: 148-154.

Seeman, E., Melton, L., O'Fallon, W., and Riggs, B. 1983. Risk factors for spinal osteoporosis in men. *American Journal of Medicine,* 75: 977-983.

Simkin, A., Ayalon, J., and Leichter, I. 1987. Increased trabecular bone density due to bone-loading exercises in postmenopausal osteoporosis women. *Calcified Tissue International,* 40: 59-63.

Sinaki, M. 1989. Exercise and osteoporosis. *Archives of Physical Medicine and Rehabilitation,* 70: 220-229.

Slovik, D., Adams, J., Neer, R., Holick, M., and Potts, J., Jr. 1981. Deficient production of 1,25-dihydroxy vitamin D in elderly osteoporotic patients. *New England Journal of Medicine,* 305: 372-374.

Smith, E. 1982. Exercise for prevention of osteoporosis: A review. *The Physician and Sports Medicine,* 10: 72-83.

Smith, E., Reddan, W., and Smith, P. 1981. Physical activity and calcium modalities for bone mineral increase in aged women. *Medicine and Science in Sports and Exercise,* 13: 60-64.

Spencer, H., and Kramer, L. 1986. Does a high protein (meat) intake affect calcium metabolism in men? *Food and Nutrition News,* 58: 11-13.

Spencer, H., Kramer, L., DeBartolo, M., Norris, C., and Osis, D. 1983. Further studies on the effect of a high protein diet as meat on calcium metabolism. *American Journal of Clinical Nutrition,* 37: 924-929.

Stampfer, M., Colditz, G., Willett, W., Manson, J., Rosner, B., Speizer, F., and Hennekens, C. 1991. Postmenopausal estrogen therapy and cardiovascular disease. *New England Journal of Medicine,* 325: 756-762.

U.S. Department of Health and Human Services. 1986. *National Hospital Discharge Survey.* Unpublished data.

Wachman, A., and Bernstein, D. 1968. Diet and osteoporosis. *Lancet,* 1: 958-959.

Weiss, N., and Scyvetz, T. 1980. Incidence of endometrial cancer in relation to the use of oral contraceptives. *New England Journal of Medicine,* 302: 551.

Weiss, N., Ure, C., Ballard, J., Williams, A., and Daling, J. 1980. Decreased risk of fractures of the hip and lower forearm with postmenopausal use of estrogen. *New England Journal of Medicine,* 303: 1193.

CHAPTER **7**

Age-Associated Changes in Vision and Hearing

The special senses provide a link with the outside world. They allow the individual to receive and interpret various stimuli, enhancing a person's interaction with the environment. Sensory changes that can influence one's perception of the world, response to stimuli, individual functioning, and activities do occur with age. It is also true that the perception of an individual by others may be influenced by sensory changes that he or she has undergone. The older person with impaired vision or hearing may be unfairly labeled as stubborn, eccentric, or "senile."

This chapter is concerned with age-associated changes in the special senses of vision and hearing. Implications of these changes will also be investigated. Changes in taste and smell are examined in Chapter 9.

GENERAL CHANGES: VISION

Many persons maintain near-normal sight well into old age. Nevertheless, the aged eye is subject to various changes and disabilities. *Presbyopia* is an age-associated change that occurs in the *lens* of the eye, leading to its relative inflexibility. Consequently, there is a reduced ability to focus on nearby objects and a tendency toward farsightedness. Presbyopia typically becomes noticeable during middle age, when glasses are necessary to do close work.

The lens of the eye also has a tendency to yellow with age. This change is significant because it results in difficulty discerning certain color intensities, especially the cool colors – blue, green, and violet. They tend to be filtered out and may be difficult to differentiate. Warm colors, including red, yellow, and orange, are generally more easily seen. This fact can be taken advantage of by marking objects such as steps and handrails with these latter colors, which tend to stand out.

Light adaptation and visual field changes also occur. The older eye's ability to adjust to abrupt differences in illumination is decreased. Both dark and light adaptation require greater time with age. The size of the visual field, the area that one can see while staring at a fixed point, is reduced. Thus, peripheral vision is reduced with advancing age.

Three disorders – *cataracts, glaucoma,* and age-related *macular degeneration* – represent the most common visual problems of the elderly. Each can be responsible for serious loss of vision. With proper recognition, attention, and treatment, these conditions need not spell disaster. Although irreparable damage associated with them cannot be re-

paired, further losses may be prevented and one's functional ability maintained or improved. In the diabetic, *diabetic retinopathy* may also be a significant cause of visual loss.

Presbyopia

Presbyopia is not a disease but a degenerative change that occurs in the aging eye. With this condition the lens (Figure 7.1) loses its ability to focus on near objects. *Visual accommodation* or focusing is normally permitted by the ability of the lens to change shape, thus accommodating for near and distant vision. Flexibility is afforded by its elastic nature. With aging, old lens fibers become compacted toward the center of the lens, reducing its elasticity. This factor, coupled with a weakening of eye muscles, does not allow the lens to contract to a suffi-

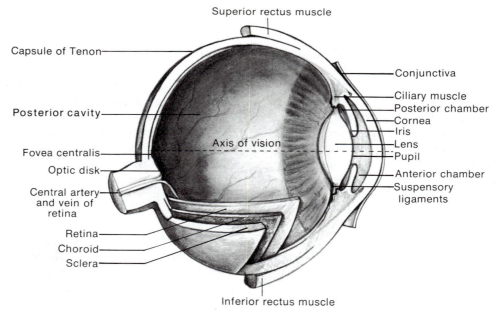

FIGURE 7.1 Structure of the eye, transverse section

ciently convex form that would allow near objects to be focused.

Changes in the lens lead to farsightedness. Thus, there is a marked tendency for older persons to hold things at a distance in order to see them. The newspaper may be held at arm's length because the print cannot be discriminated at closer range. Because of presbyopia, the majority of individuals need reading glasses or bifocals by the time they are in their forties or fifties. The glasses mechanically compensate for the loss of visual accommodation. Except for those persons who cannot afford to buy glasses, presbyopia does not pose any serious problems.

Reading glasses allow the individual to discern objects that are in the field of near vision. Bifocals may be needed depending on the individual's overall visual ability. Bifocals consist of two parts, one for near and one for distance vision. Adjusting vision from one area of the spectacle to another while viewing things at varying distances may not be easy. Adjustment problems may require patience on the part of the wearer.

Senile Cataracts

Cataracts are the most common disability of the aged eye. A cataract involves an opacity of the normally transparent lens. The opacity may be focal or diffuse and is accompanied by reduced visual acuity without pain or inflammation. The normally crystalline lens focuses incoming light onto the photoreceptors of the *retina* just as a camera's lens allows incoming light to be focused onto film. As the lens loses its transparency, there is interference with the passage of light. By definition, a cataract involves an associated reduction in vision.

There are various types of cataracts including congenital, genetic, metabolic, traumatic, toxic, and senile forms. Senile cataract, although the most common, is among the least understood. Its

diagnosis involves lens opacity in those over 45 years of age, after other causes of cataract have been eliminated.

There is a strong relationship between increasing age and the development of senile cataract. However, its formation appears to be a complex process, possibly affected by genetic and environmental factors as well. Further research is needed to determine what factors might be associated with an increased risk of its development. Present data suggest that geographic locale, familial factors, certain drugs, high blood pressure, and the existence of diabetes in those under 65 years of age warrant further study as possible risk factors. Exposure to various forms of radiation has also been implicated. Data indicate that the sun's ultraviolet light contributes to cataract formation (Straatsma, Foos, and Horwitz, 1985).

Depending on the degree of cataract development, an individual will suffer dimmed and blurred or misty vision. The person may need brighter light in which to read and may increasingly complain of glare. Objects may need to be held extremely close in order to be seen. As the cataract advances, useful sight is lost.

Treatment consists of surgical removal of the opaque lens. Surgery is indicated when vision loss interferes with the performance of activities (Straatsma et al., 1985). To compensate for the loss of the lens, eyeglasses, contact lenses, or intraocular lens implants are used. The latter consists of a plastic lens permanently implanted in the eye. It has become the most common means of compensating for the loss of the natural lens.

Glaucoma

Glaucoma is the second leading cause of blindness in adults in the United States and the first cause among blacks (Leske, 1983). It represents a group of diseases that, with few exceptions, result from an obstruction in the normal escape route of the nutrient fluid that bathes the anterior chamber of the eye (the space between the *cornea* and *iris* depicted in Figure 7.2). This clear fluid, known as *aqueous humor*, normally exits the anterior chamber into the *canal of Schlemm*, where it is eventually conducted through numerous small channels into the venous circulation. If the fluid is formed faster than it can be eliminated, an increase in eye pressure results. Pressure is transferred to the *optic nerve*, leading to its irreparable damage. If intraocular pressure continues to exceed the tolerance of the affected eye, total blindness can result.

Glaucoma can be primary or secondary in nature. *Primary glaucoma* is of unknown origin. It develops in the absence of previous eye disease or injury. It occurs most frequently in persons with a family history of the disease. It is suspected that there is a tendency to inherit those factors that might predispose one to the condition. *Secondary glaucoma* follows some eye disease or injury.

Primary disease may be designated as either *angle closure* or *open angle* glaucoma. Angle closure accounts for less than 5 percent of glaucoma cases

(Jindra, 1984). In order to understand this form of disease, it is necessary to review briefly the production of aqueous humor and how it makes its way to the anterior eye chamber.

Aqueous humor is produced in a structure that is just behind the root of the iris. From here it is secreted into a space bounded by the posterior surface of the iris and the anterior surface of the lens. The fluid circulates through the pupil into the anterior chamber. There is some resistance to the flow of aqueous humor into the anterior compartment. If an individual has a narrow anterior compartment, the resulting pressure can lead to the root of the iris closing off the exit of fluid in this area. Production of the fluid continues, intraocular pressure increases rather rapidly, and angle closure glaucoma develops.

Primary angle closure glaucoma is an acute glaucoma appearing suddenly and running a short course. Its victim suffers nausea, vomiting, eye pain, and redness along with clouded vision. Prompt medical attention is imperative if severe vision loss or blindness is to be prevented.

Ninety percent of all primary glaucoma is of the

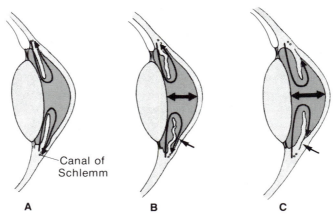

A   **B**   **C**

FIGURE 7.2 Glaucoma. (A) Normal aqueous humor drainage through the canal of Schlemm. (B) Open-angle glaucoma, showing a chronic condition treated by drugs. (C) Closed-angle glaucoma, requiring surgery (iridectomy) for correction.

open-angle type (Jindra, 1983; Leske and Rosenthal, 1979). With this form the outflow of aqueous humor is obstructed by degenerative changes in the channel that normally allows for its escape. This chronic type of glaucoma develops slowly and is often referred to as the "sneak thief of vision." The initial manifestations of the disease are so subtle that much damage may be done before medical attention is sought.

A gradual loss of *peripheral vision* is one of the earliest indications of glaucoma. This loss of side vision may cause its victim to bump into things or fail to see passing cars in the next highway lane. In time, so much within the normal range of vision becomes eliminated that the victim is said to suffer from "tunnel vision." If the condition is left untreated, those nerve centers allowing for central vision are also damaged and the individual loses all sight.

Persons over 40 years of age should have periodic eye examinations that include glaucoma testing. The irreparable damage it causes makes its prompt diagnosis and management imperative. There is no cure for glaucoma, but there are techniques for reducing the intraocular pressure or keeping it at a safe level. In severe cases surgery can be performed to provide a permanent filtration pathway for the aqueous humor. An opening for drainage can be made in the iris or the *sclera* (the outer white part of the eyeball). Such surgery is delicate and is often avoided for as long as possible. There are drugs and eye drops that serve to control indirectly the pressure within the eye.

In the past, glaucoma diagnosis was made on the basis of intraocular pressure alone. Such a practice is no longer valid given that optic nerve damage can occur at any pressure level. Ninety to 95 percent of persons with high pressure do not suffer optic nerve damage (Spaeth, 1984). They are considered at risk of a visual defect, but the risk is low and most never develop damage. Because prediction of defects in such persons is uncertain, some patients diagnosed on the basis of pressure level will be treated. Because optic nerve damage can occur at any pressure level, tests to measure vision field loss, not just intraocular pressure, are important.

Low-tension glaucoma exists when optic nerve damage occurs in the absence of elevated pressure. It is estimated that one-third to one-half of persons with glaucoma damage have eye pressure below the characteristic diagnostic level when first detected (Bengtsson, 1981; Leske, 1983). Some such cases will later manifest a pressure increase, but some will continue as low-tension glaucoma.

Despite the variation in pressure levels and optic nerve damage, lowering pressure via surgery or drugs remains the method of treatment. In the same way that glaucoma definitions have deemphasized specific numerical pressure values, treatment has concerned itself with lowering pressure to the point where nerve damage is halted. Rather than reducing intraocular pressure to a specific, universal numerical level, the goal is to lower it to a point tolerated by the affected eye.

Age-Related Macular Degeneration

Age-related macular degeneration (AMD), formerly known as senile macular degeneration, is the leading cause of legal blindness among older adults in the United States, but it remains a poorly understood disease. Damage is done to the *macula*, the key focusing area of the retina. As a result there is a decline in central visual acuity, making those tasks that are dependent on the discrimination of detail (such as driving or reading) difficult to impossible. Peripheral vision is retained.

For many with AMD, *central vision* is maintained for years. In such cases an individual is said to manifest "dry" or *atrophic* AMD, a slow version of the disorder. The majority of patients who are legally blind as a result of AMD have undergone a *neovascular* or *exudative* form of disease. In the latter condition, abnormal blood vessels form within the retina, with resultant hemorrhaging and destruction of vision (Ferris, Fine, and Hyman, 1984). Patients are at risk of continued development of new blood vessels in both the affected and the uninvolved fellow eye (Farber and Farber, 1990).

Increasing age has the strongest association with AMD of all risk factors examined to date. However, age is not a causal factor in AMD. Research suggests that it is familial/genetic and environmental factors active with the passage of time that make the condition "age-related." Evidence suggests that solar radiation is responsible for some of the deteriorative changes that lead to AMD (Young, 1988). Family history and blue or medium-pigmented eyes have been associated with an increased risk of AMD (Hyman, Lilienfeld, Ferris, and Fine, 1983; Young, 1988). Melanin helps to protect the eye against solar radiation damage.

It has been suggested that as our population continues to age, blindness as a result of macular disease will increase unless appropriate preventive and treatment modalities are introduced (Ferris, 1983). A type of laser therapy known as *argon laser photocoagulation* seeks to seal off or destroy the abnormally present blood vessels. It has been helpful for some patients with exudative AMD (Macular Photocoagulation Study Group, 1982). Perhaps, as treatment advances, cases of blindness associated with the disorder will be reduced. At present, not all persons with AMD are treatable.

Diabetic Retinopathy

Laser therapy is also proving beneficial in the treatment of diabetic retinopathy (Early Treatment Diabetic Retinopathy Study Research Group, 1985). This condition is a complication of diabetes that affects the capillaries and arterioles of the retina. A ballooning of these tiny vessels can eventually give way to hemorrhaging, neovascular growth, scarring, and blindness.

Vascular changes of diabetic retinopathy occur in and around the macula, leading to macular edema.

The retina swells, absorbing the fluid from leaking vessels. It eventually loses its shape so that the image it receives is distorted. A leading researcher at the National Eye Institute likened it to having wrinkled film in a camera (Ferris, 1985).

Severe eye disease increases with the duration of diabetes. The prevalence of diabetic retinopathy is 7 percent in those who have had diabetes for less than 10 years, whereas it is 63 percent in those who have had diabetes for over 15 years (Stefansson, 1990).

The Visually Impaired Older Adult

Over a lifetime an individual becomes dependent on vision for functioning in the surrounding world. For most persons, activities of daily living involve a dependence on visual acuity. Sewing on a button, setting the oven temperature, stirring the sauce, matching socks of the same color, balancing the checkbook, receiving a visitor at the front door – all are tasks that utilize eyesight.

Persons blind since birth have had a lifetime to adjust to living in a world that assumes everyone can see. Adjustment can be very difficult for those who suffer visual impairment after having been dependent on their sight. Family members, friends, and health care workers can help to make the adjustment less difficult. An understanding of the kind and amount of visual loss is imperative. Losses may be minor or severe. They may involve central vision, peripheral vision, or the entire visual field.

A thickened, yellowed lens may necessitate brighter light for performing tasks such as reading or sewing. For the cataract victim, light that is too bright can produce glare. It is important to determine the degree of illumination that is best for an individual.

One who has lost peripheral vision may see only a limited area in front of him or her. When talking with someone who has peripheral loss, be certain to position yourself in their visual field. If an object or task is being demonstrated, make certain this is done within the person's line of sight.

Vision loss can lead to problems in social interaction, especially if losses are undiagnosed or poorly understood. Family members may be suspicious of Aunt Mary's claims of poor vision when she is quite capable of detecting the spot directly left by someone cleaning the window. Although Aunt Mary's peripheral vision may have diminished, she still sees details within her central visual field!

Age-related changes necessitate a longer time for dark adaptation. Entering a dimly lit restaurant or theater can be made easier by allowing time for adjustment. Night lights can help to prevent accidents when rising from bed in the middle of the night to answer the telephone or go to the bathroom.

Coding schemes can be employed in the home setting to facilitate independent living. Fluorescent tape around electric outlets, light switches, thermostats, and keyholes can make chores easier. Coding can also make it easier to differentiate one bottle of pills from another. This goal might be achieved by taping different-colored pieces of paper to various medicine vials. For those not able to discriminate colors, other methods can be employed. The medicine with sandpaper glued to the cap can be identified as the pain reliever; the one with the felt cap might be the antihypertensive. Large-print instructions from the pharmacy can help the older person to comply with doctor's orders.

A person who has suddenly suffered visual losses may need extra care and patience. Such an individual may be understandably fearful and distrustful. Possible anxieties must be considered by relatives, friends, and health workers and demonstrated in their thoughtful actions. For example, announcing oneself when approaching the visually impaired can be helpful.

Special consideration should be given those who have age-related vision defect and are placed in an unfamiliar environment such as that of a hospital or nursing home. Call switches and items on a bedside table should be placed where they can be easily located. Caregivers may need to be especially sensitive and patient when teaching self-care tasks to the visually impaired. Such an individual may feel self-conscious, slow, and awkward. The task should not be rushed.

GENERAL CHANGES: HEARING

Impaired hearing is common among older persons. It is estimated that 30 to 60 percent of those over 65 and 90 percent of elderly nursing home residents suffer hearing loss (Libow and Sherman, 1981; Mader, 1984). Some loss is due to age-related physiological change in the auditory system, and some is due to disease and superimposed environmental insults. There is considerable variability in the gradual decline in hearing with advanced age.

There are three major types of hearing loss — conductive, sensorineural, and mixed. *Conductive* losses involve the outer and middle ear, whereas *sensorineural* losses involve the inner ear. An elderly person may manifest both conductive and sensorineural changes, resulting in a *mixed* loss.

Conductive Hearing Loss

Hearing loss can result from the interrupted conduction of sound waves. Normally these waves enter the external ear to be channeled to the *tympanic membrane* (ear drum) marking entry to the middle ear (Figure 7.3). Here vibrations are established and transmitted mechanically by a series of three delicate bones or *ossicles* (known as the malleus, incus, and stapes). Sound transmission defects involving any one of these structures can lead to hearing loss.

Fortunately, the most common cause of conductive impairment in the older adult is reversible. It

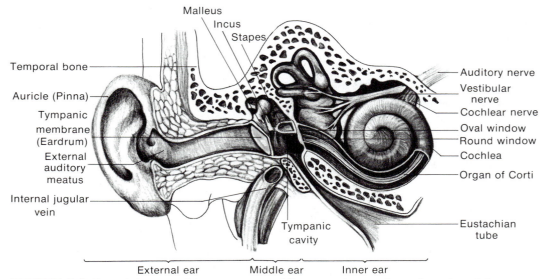

FIGURE 7.3 Frontal diagram of the outer ear, middle ear, and internal ear. A section of the cochlear duct has been cut away to show the position of the organ of Corti.

occurs when excessive ear wax or *cerumen* blocks the external ear canal. Older persons should be checked for a buildup of cerumen, which can be removed by irrigating the canal with a wax-dissolving solution.

Hardening of middle ear bone can also impede the transmission of sound waves. This condition, known as *otosclerosis,* actually begins during youth but may not become evident until later life. It represents the most frequent cause of conductive deafness in adults (Libow and Sherman, 1981). Although its cause is not fully understood, it can sometimes be corrected surgically and with a special hearing aid.

Paget's disease, a bone condition of unknown cause, may also cause conductive hearing loss due to closure of the external ear canal or ossicle involvement. *Otitis media,* a middle ear inflammation/infection, is not a major cause of hearing loss in the elderly.

Sensorineural Hearing Loss

Sensorineural hearing loss is related to disorders of the inner ear where conducted sound vibrations are transformed into electrical impulses by the *cochlea.* This auditory receptor organ has been dubbed the most complex mechanical apparatus in the human body (Hudspeth, 1985). A fluid-filled spiral cavity, the cochlea houses the *organ of Corti,* which possesses several rows of delicate, specialized *hair cells.* Sound waves transferred to the inner ear generate fluid movement in the cochlea and the undulation of hair cells. Hair cell stimulation produces nerve impulses that are carried by the auditory or *eighth cranial nerve* to the hearing center of the brain, where they are perceived as sound. Sensorineural hearing loss in older adults may be due to presbycusis, environmental/occupational noise, drug toxicity, or disease.

Presbycusis is the most common cause of bilateral, sensorineural hearing deficit in older adults (Olsen, 1984). It is related to permanent loss of the ability to detect high-frequency tones. It is due to various, yet poorly understood, senescent changes, which may include atrophy of the organ of Corti as well as hair cell decline. This type of loss is referred to as *sensory presbycusis.*

Presbycusis has been related to three other types of changes in the inner ear. Neural presbycusis involves a loss of cochlear neurons in the auditory pathways. Metabolic presbycusis results from the degeneration of the fibrous vascular tissue which lines the lateral wall of the cochlear duct, thought to secrete the cochlear fluid. Mechanical or conductive presbycusis is linked to degeneration of a segment of the cochlear wall, thus interfering with cochlear motion mechanics (Rees and Duckert, 1990).

All types of presbycusis influence the ability to hear high-pitched tones, while varying in their effects on other aspects of hearing. It is unlikely that only one form of presbycusic hearing loss occurs in a given individual.

At first, the loss of the ability to perceive higher frequencies does not involve normal speech patterns; as the condition progresses, conversation becomes affected. Because consonant sounds are in the higher frequencies and vowel sounds in the lower frequencies, speech discrimination will be poor. Speech can be heard but words cannot be detected. The victim may hear an unintelligible collection of vowel sounds. As the condition advances, middle and lower tones may also be lost.

There is variability in the progression of presbycusis, and it can coexist with other factors that impede hearing acuity. It is estimated that an infant is born with up to 20,000 hair cells in each ear. Over a lifetime, aging itself combined with exposure to loud noise, certain drugs, and disease can rob the cochlea of functioning hair cells. Dennis Drescher, an auditory biochemist at Wayne State University, quoted in *Science News,* estimates that if human

life expectancy could be greatly increased – say, to 140 years – it would probably mean living without hair cells (Franklin, 1984).

Noise-induced hearing loss, known as *acoustic trauma,* is recognized as the second most common cause of irreversible hearing decline in older persons (Darbyshire, 1984; Surjan, Devald, and Palfalvi, 1973). Exposure to excessive noise induces hair cell loss and sensorineural hearing deficit. The fact that older men have tended to exhibit slightly more hearing loss than older women may be related to workplace noise. Perhaps, as noise exposure becomes more uniform, we will see less of a gender-based difference in hearing decline.

Presbycusis and noise-induced loss are coexistent in many instances. Some studies have attempted to measure hearing loss in populations subjected to little noise pollution, in order to see if their profile of loss differs from that of the industrialized world. One study done several years ago reported little age-associated decline among a Sudanese tribe (Rosen, Bergman, and Plester, 1962), but this work has been criticized on methodological grounds (Mader, 1984). Distinguishing between normal, age-related, physiologic decline in hearing and that due to environmental or other secondary causes is an important area of gerontologic research.

Medications toxic to the ear can compromise hearing and are known as *ototoxic drugs.* Because elderly people often take several different drugs, their hearing should be monitored. Likewise, because elderly patients may already have some degree of hearing loss, known ototoxic drugs should be used with caution. It is sometimes possible to reverse the toxic effects of certain medications if early intervention takes place.

Underlying disease can sometimes result in sensorineural losses. Certain primary and metastatic tumors may result in unilateral hearing decline in the elderly. There is controversy regarding the association between atherosclerosis and hypertension and progressive hearing loss with age. The inner ear is dependent on a single end artery for its blood supply. Sudden and total deafness results if this artery is occluded (Libow and Sherman, 1981). Some type of auditory deficit occurs in 30 to 50 percent of persons with skull involvement in Paget's disease (Giansiracusa and Kantrowitz, 1982; Sparrow and Duvall, 1967). Associated conductive loss has been previously noted. When the temporal bone is affected, the cochlea (which rests within this bone) may be disrupted, causing a sensorineural hearing loss. Compression of the eighth cranial nerve is rare.

The Hearing-Impaired Older Adult

Hearing impairment can lead to social isolation, fear, frustration, embarrassment, low self-esteem, and anxiety for its elderly victim. A study of elderly men in a Veterans' Administration facility suggested that hearing impairment can have significant adverse effects on the quality of life (Mulrow, Aguilar, Endicott, et al., 1990). Depression has a twofold greater incidence in the hearing-impaired elderly (Herbst and Humphrey, 1980). It was demonstrated in a 1976 study that deafness may predispose to paranoid behavior (Cooper, Garside, and Kay, 1976), although no study has proved that hearing problems, in themselves, cause paranoia. Blindness in the elderly does not seem to be as importantly associated with paranoia (Charatan, 1984). Sensitivity to these possibilities is extremely important, as hearing-disabled individuals do not seem to be given the same consideration and understanding as those with other types of impairments (McCartney and Nadler, 1979).

An elderly individual with a permanent hearing loss should be evaluated for amplification via a hearing aid and have the benefit of aural rehabilitation. Of the approximately one million hearing aids sold in the United States in 1983, it is estimated that 56 percent were purchased by those age 65 and over (Cranmer, 1983; Mahon, 1983). About 500,000 hearing aids are sold annually to persons whose hearing deficit is at least partially attributed to presbycusis (Olsen, 1984).

Hearing aids are not a perfect substitute for normal hearing. They cannot restore the full frequency range of more severe losses. Sounds are made louder but not necessarily clearer. Hearing aids also pose adjustment problems. Many new users claim that the aids seem unnatural. For many persons who have insidiously lost their hearing over a long period of time, the new sounds delivered by the hearing aid are surely "unnatural" to them. Hearing aids amplify all sounds, not just those of speech. The new hearing aid user may have a difficult time divorcing restaurant noises, car horns, or television sounds from conversational patterns. Hearing aid users and their families need to be counseled appropriately.

There are various helpful principles and common courtesies for communicating with the hearing-impaired. In general, shouting should be avoided. It does nothing to aid in the delivery of lost frequencies and results in a booming and distortion of intelligible sounds. One should speak in a normal tone of voice, a little louder than usual, perhaps, but without shouting. Shouting often conveys a speaker's apparent annoyance and can lead to defensive or withdrawn behavior.

Additionally, a speaker should talk slowly. A message is much easier to understand if it is delivered at a slower pace. Besides, talking rapidly can create an impression of being in a hurry. This situation may cause the hard-of-hearing person to feel as if he or she is a burden and is taking too much of the speaker's time.

If a message is not understood the first time, finding other words to say the same things may also be helpful. It not only gives the hard-of-hearing person an additional set of sounds from which to understand a message, but it also gives more context from which meaning can be derived. Often, hearing one word can make the meaning of a whole sentence clear.

A speaker should also be aware of the powers of nonverbal communication. Facial expressions serve to convey moods, feelings, negatives, positives, excitement, and disapproval. They serve to enhance the comprehension of the spoken words and to make the hearing-impaired share in the lives of those around them.

With or without a hearing aid, lip reading can help with communication. A complicating factor is that some persons do not form words normally when speaking to the hard-of-hearing. Exaggeration can serve to confuse the lip reader. The speaker can help the lip reader by facing him or her, letting the light fall on the speaker's face, and not exaggerating lip movements. For some with impaired vision, the lip-reading task may be more difficult.

Patient compliance can be greatly affected by a person's hearing loss. Health care institutions are complex facilities. A stay in one of them brings an individual into contact with a number of workers, many of whom have directions to give and important information to impart. Unfortunately, such information may not be heard or understood by the patient who is hard of hearing.

Health workers may perceive a patient's limited reaction as apparent lack of interest. In the early stages of progressive hearing loss, an individual may appear preoccupied, inattentive, irritable, unsociable, and absent-minded (Voeks, Gallagher, Langer, and Drinka, 1990). If health workers did not know the person before admission to the health care facility, they may not be aware of the patient's hearing loss. Too often, confusion associated with hearing loss may be falsely attributed to "senility" in the older patient.

When planning for discharge from an institution, hearing loss must be acknowledged so that instructions about the use of mechanical devices or drug therapy are understood. Failure to hear such instructions may mean delayed recovery and even tragedy in the home situation. Written instructions can be provided the patient. Because the person may have also suffered visual losses, they should be written in large print. Also, a health worker or family member can ask the patient to repeat instructions to make certain that they were properly heard and understood.

Hearing aids are most useful when background noise is at a minimum, as in a quiet theater or lecture hall, or in private conversation in person or over the telephone. In noisy gatherings the wearer may be better assisted by switching off the aid. Individual adjustments, however, dictate the most appropriate behavior. Some persons, though initially annoyed by background noise, may learn to tune it out.

Problems associated with a new hearing aid may be caused by an improperly fitted earmold. In order to serve the wearer, the earmold must closely fit the anatomic structure of an individual's ear canal. Prolonged complaints about a hearing aid should be investigated. Difficulty may be due to more than just a long adjustment period. An earmold may not fit!

Only about 30 percent of the elderly who need hearing aids actually have them. This situation may be related to a number of factors. The older person may perceive that a hearing loss is an irreparable and normal part of getting old. Some researchers suggest that physicians, too, regard hearing loss as normal aging and intervention as futile (Humphrey, Herbst, and Faurqui, 1981). The individual may not want to admit that a hearing loss exists. Likewise, the hearing aid may be rejected for cosmetic purposes and because of the social stigma associated with it. Also, hearing aids are expensive. Neither routine hearing exams nor hearing aids are re-imbursed under Medicare. A recent study indicates that the potential need for hearing aids exceeds their actual use (Gates, Cooper, Kannel, and Miller, 1990).

As losses advance, hearing aid amplification may become less useful. *Cochlear implants* are being tested and refined in order to bypass the cochlea and its faulty hair cells so that the auditory nerve can be directly stimulated. A cochlear implant is an electronic device that utilizes electrodes that are microsurgically implanted into or near the cochlea to stimulate the nerve. They are intended for those with profound sensorineural hearing loss (Harrison, 1987).

SENSORY DEPRIVATION

The need for sensory stimulation cannot be over-emphasized. Vision and hearing represent two very important links with the outside world. If these links are broken and no effective steps to reinstate them are taken, an individual may retreat into his or her own world. A false label of senility may be given such victims.

The term *sensory deprivation,* denoting a lack of sensory stimulation, first came into use in the 1950s. During that time it was demonstrated that subjects reacted with increased suggestibility after a few days of visual, auditory, and tactile deprivation (Solomon, 1961). It is known that sensory deprivation results in impaired concentration, tension, anxiety, physical complaints, and hallucinations.

Sundowner syndrome refers to a behavioral pattern often exhibited at night when sensory stimulation is reduced. When the lights go out and quiet descends on the home or extended care facility, confusion and anxiety may lead to aggressive behavior. For one whose sensory contact is already compromised, further reductions can lead to confu-sion. A night light can help to reduce confusion (Charatan, 1984).

STUDY QUESTIONS

1. Note some general changes that take place within the aged eye and their significance.
2. What is presbyopia? Note its significance for the older adult.
3. What is a cataract? Are there any possible risk factors associated with its development? How is it treated?
4. What is glaucoma? Differentiate primary and secondary glaucoma; angle closure and open-angle glaucoma. What are the effects of glaucoma? How is it diagnosed and treated? Identify low-tension glaucoma.
5. Identify age-related macular degeneration and its various forms. What is its significance and potential for treatment?
6. What is diabetic retinopathy?
7. Briefly discuss some problems of and approaches to helping the visually impaired older adult.
8. Differentiate conductive from sensorineural hearing loss.
9. What is presbycusis and what is its significance for the older adult? Identify the following: acoustic trauma and ototoxic drugs.
10. Briefly discuss some problems of and approaches to helping the hearing-impaired older adult. What is a cochlear implant?
11. Identify sensory deprivation and sundowner syndrome.

BIBLIOGRAPHY

Bengtsson, B. 1981. The prevalence of glaucoma. *British Journal of Ophthalmology,* 65: 46-49.

Charatan, F. 1984. Mental stimulation and deprivation as risk factors in senility. In H. Rothschild (Ed.), *Risk factors for senility.* New York: Oxford University Press.

Cooper, A., Garside, R., and Kay, D. 1976. A comparison of deaf and non-deaf patients with paranoid and affective psychosis. *British Journal of Psychiatry,* 129: 532.

Cranmer, K. 1983. Hearing aid dispensing – 1983. *Hearing Instruments,* 34: 9-12.

Darbyshire, J. 1984. The hearing loss epidemic: A challenge to gerontology. *Research on Aging*, 6: 384–394.

Early Treatment Diabetic Retinopathy Study Research Group. 1985. Photocoagulation for diabetic macular edema: Early treatment diabetic retinopathy study report, No. 1. *Archives of Ophthalmology*, 103: 1796–1806.

Facer, G. 1985. Cochlear implant: Clinical status, 1985. *Mayo Clinic Proceedings*, 60: 137–138.

Farber, M., and Farber, A. 1990. Macular degeneration. *Postgraduate Medicine*, 88: 181–183.

Ferris, F., III. 1983. Senile macular degeneration: Review of epidemiologic features. *American Journal of Epidemiology*, 118: 132–151.

Ferris, F., III. 1985. New laser role for diabetes eyed. *Science News*, 128: 377.

Ferris, F., III, Fine, S., and Hyman, L. 1984. Age-related macular degeneration and blindness due to neovascular maculopathy. *Archives of Ophthalmology*, 102: 1640–1642.

Franklin, D. 1984. Crafting sound from silence. *Science News*, 126: 252–254.

Gates, G., Cooper, J., Kannel, W., and Miller, N. 1990. Hearing in the elderly: The Framingham cohort, 1983–1985. Part I. Basic audiometric test results. *Ear and Hearing*, 11: 247–256.

Giansiracusa, D., and Kantrowitz, F. 1982. Metabolic bone disease. In J. Rowe and R. Besdine (Eds.), *Health and disease in old age*. Boston: Little, Brown.

Harrison, R. 1987. Cochlear implants: A review of the principles and important physiological factors. *Journal of Otolaringology*, 16: 268–275.

Herbst, K., and Humphrey, C. 1980. Hearing impairment and mental state in the elderly living at home. *British Medical Journal*, 281: 903.

Hudspeth, A. 1985. The cellular basis of hearing: The biophysics of hair cells. *Science*, 230: 745–752.

Humphrey, C., Herbst, K., and Faurqui, S. 1981. Some characteristics of the hearing-impaired elderly who do not present themselves for rehabilitation. *British Journal of Audiology*, 15: 25–30.

Hyman, L., Lilienfeld, A., Ferris, F., III, and Fine, S. 1983. Senile macular degeneration: A case-control study. *American Journal of Epidemiology*, 118: 213–227.

Jindra, L. 1983. Open-angle glaucoma: Diagnosis and management. *Hospital Practice*, 18: 114c–114p.

Jindra, L. 1984. Closed-angle glaucoma: Diagnosis and management. *Hospital Practice*, 19: 114–119.

Leske, M. C. 1983. The epidemiology of open-angle glaucoma: A review. *American Journal of Epidemiology*, 118: 166–191.

Leske, M. C., and Rosenthal, J. 1979. Epidemiologic aspects of open-angle glaucoma. *American Journal of Epidemiology*, 109: 250–272.

Libow, L., and Sherman, F. 1981. *The core of geriatric medicine*. St. Louis: C. V. Mosby.

Macular Photocoagulation Study Group. 1982. Argon laser photocoagulation for senile macular degeneration. *Archives of Ophthalmology*, 100: 912–918.

Mader, S. 1984. Hearing impairment in elderly persons. *Journal of the American Geriatrics Society*, 32: 548–553.

Mahon, W. 1983. The million unit year: 1983 hearing aid sales and statistical summary. *Hearing Journal*, 1983: 9–16.

McCartney, J., and Nadler, G. 1979. How to help your patient cope with hearing loss. *Geriatrics*, 34: 69.

Mulrow, C., Aguilar, C., Endicott, J., et al. 1990. Association between hearing impairment and the quality of life in elderly individuals. *Journal of the American Geriatrics Society*, 38: 45–50.

Olsen, W. 1984. When hearing wanes, is amplification the answer? *Postgraduate Medicine*, 76: 189–198.

Rees, T., and Duckert, L. 1990. Auditory and vestibular dysfunction in aging. In W. Hazzard, R. Andres, E. Bierman, and J. Blass (Eds.), *Principles of geriatric medicine and gerontology*. New York: McGraw-Hill.

Rosen, S., Bergman, M., and Plester, D. 1962. Presbycusis study of a relatively noise free population in the Sudan. *Annals of Otolaryngology, Rhinology, and Laryngology*, 71: 727.

Solomon, P. 1961. *Sensory deprivation*. Cambridge, MA: Harvard University Press.

Spaeth, G. 1984. From eye pressure to nerve damage. *Science News*, 127: 351.

Sparrow, N., and Duvall, A., III. 1967. Hearing loss and Paget's disease. *Journal of Laryngology*, 81: 601.

Stefansson, E. 1990. The eye. In W. Hazzard, R. Andres, E. Bierman, and J. Blass (Eds.), *Principles of geriatric medicine and gerontology*. New York: McGraw-Hill.

Straatsma, B., Foos, R., and Horwitz, J. 1985. Aging-related cataract: Laboratory investigation and clinical management. *Annals of Internal Medicine*, 102: 82–92.

Surjan, L., Devald, J., and Palfalvi, J. 1973. Epidemiology of hearing loss. *Audiology,* 12: 396–410.

Voeks, S., Gallagher, C., Langer, E., and Drinka, P. 1990. Hearing loss in the nursing home: An institutional issue. *Journal of the American Geriatrics Society,* 38: 141–145.

Young, R. 1988. Solar radiation and age-related macular degeneration. *Survey of Ophthalmology,* 32: 252–269.

CHAPTER 8

The Nervous System

No single body system can operate alone. They are all interdependent, working together to maintain a stable environment. The nervous system provides coordination between the body's many systems. As conditions both inside and outside of the body fluctuate, the nervous system responds, allowing the body to adapt.

The nervous system receives, processes, and stores sensory information from within and from outside of the body. It allows action, generally by means of muscle contractions, in response to incoming sensory stimuli. Because it governs skeletal and smooth muscle contraction and relaxation, it ultimately controls body movements dependent on skeletal muscle and body organs, the walls of which are laden with smooth muscle.

A highly branched network of nerve cells extends throughout the body, eventually relaying information to and from its most complex organ – the brain. Some nerve cells are lost with age, although loss varies according to brain area. Losses may not always have direct functional correlates because of the nervous system's ability to compensate for them.

This chapter presents an overview of the aging nervous system before considering various specific, age-related disorders. Those disorders included are delirium and dementia, Parkinson's disease, and cerebrovascular accident. It should be underscored that in the last of these conditions, more commonly known as stroke, the primary lesion is vascular, not neurologic. It is considered here in that the resultant damage is to nervous tissue.

GENERAL CHANGES

Nerve cells are known as *neurons*. They represent the basic structural and functional unit of nervous tissue. Their specialized parts work to receive, conduct, and transmit nervous impulses. They consist of a cell body and two kinds of threadlike projections or nerve fibers called *dendrites* and *axons*. Dendrites receive information and conduct it to the cell body. From there it is relayed to the axon, where it is then transmitted to the next neuron.

Neurons do not physically touch each other. Indeed, there is a gap between them referred to as a *synapse*. Signals are sent from one neuron to another across this intervening space via chemicals called *neurotransmitters*. Groups of neurons and their respective synapses use the same kind of neurotransmitter and are thus referred to as *neurotransmission pathways*. For example, dopamine is a main neurotransmitter used in one such pathway controlling motor movements. Likewise, acetylcholine is employed in the pathway involving memory processing.

With age, various changes take place in nervous tissue. Nerve cell bodies accumulate the age pigment lipofuscin. Specific brain areas develop *neurofibrillary tangles* and *neuritic plaques*. The former are abnormal twisted masses of nerve filaments. The latter are degenerating or dying neurons that accumulate around a protein core. They are both present in the brains of normal elderly persons. However, larger numbers collect in the brains of those suffering from the severe mental deterioration associated with Alzheimer's disease (Blessed, Tomlinson, and Roth, 1968; Bondareff, 1985; Mayeux, 1990). It is worth noting that neurofibrillary tangles and senile plaques are also found in the brains of persons with Down's syndrome who are middleaged and beyond, in those with the dementia complex of Parkinson's disease, and in persons with the dementia associated with boxing (dementia pugilistica). Although their source is unknown, they may represent a nonspecific reaction to a variety of insults (Mayeux, 1990).

There is some significant age-related loss of neurons in specific areas of the brain. In that neurons do not regenerate, lost cells are not replaced. The rate, degree, and varied location of neuronal loss and its effect on function and behavior is the subject of ongoing research. However, it is known that neuronal declines do not always translate simply into an irreversible loss of function. The brain has a tremendous amount of reserve tissue. Additionally,

it has a dramatic ability to compensate for neuronal loss. Changes in the biochemistry and structure of the aging brain may not affect ordinary activities or performance until beyond age 75 (Poirier and Finch, 1990).

Dendritic structure changes with age. Scheibel (1982) noted a progressive loss of the normal dendritic branching and the eventual disappearance of dendrites with neuronal death. Although this phenomenon may occur in some neurons, it is not the case for all. It appears that in normal aging, some neurons die, thus losing dendrites, whereas others undergo dendritic growth until very late in life (Buell and Coleman, 1979). Dendritic growth has been proposed as a compensatory mechanism whereby neuronal pathways are maintained despite neuronal losses (Coleman and Flood, 1987). Thus, some neurons establish new synapses with more distant nerve cells to compensate for the degeneration of adjacent neurons.

Age-related declines in levels of various neurotransmitters have been noted (Drachman, Noffsinger, Sahakian, et al., 1980; McGreer and McGreer, 1976, 1980; Rogers and Bloom, 1985). Some of these changes may be associated with the altered synthesis of these nerve conducting chemicals. There may also be a reduction in the number of some receptor sites that are sensitive to the neurotransmitters.

With age, the rate of nerve conduction decreases; voluntary motor movements slow down; and the reflex time for skeletal muscle, peripheral nerves, and the spinal cord result in decreased agility and strength (Caplan, 1982).

CONFUSION

Confusion among elderly patients is frequently misunderstood and ill defined. A negative stereotype of aging in consort with a lack of information may lead some to view confusion or "senility" as an inevitable outcome of aging. Such is not the case. When severe confusion appears in an older person, it is related to an underlying physical or psychosocial dysfunction. Confusion may be acute and reversible when associated with illness, medications, or environmental changes. It may also be chronic and irreversible in conjunction with progressive disease. The appropriate diagnosis and management of elderly patients exhibiting confusion can critically influence their health and functional capacity (Kane, Ouslander, and Abrass, 1989). It can also influence whether they live or die.

Senility is a term with no specific clinical meaning. Older persons are often labeled senile because of sensory losses that impair their ability to perceive and interact appropriately within their environmental surroundings. They may also be called senile because they do not respond to a question in a manner or in a time frame deemed appropriate by an observer. Senility is a meaningless, subjective term that does not delineate any biologic or disease change in one's mental state.

Delirium

Delirium is an acute alteration in mental status, sometimes referred to as an acute confusional state. It has been termed many things, including acute confusion, acute organic brain syndrome, acute brain failure, metabolic encephalopathy, pseudosenility, and toxic psychosis. The *Diagnostic and Statistical Manual of Mental Disorders*, third edition, revised (DSM-III-R) (American Psychiatric Association, 1987), now offers consistent terminology and detailed diagnostic criteria in considering organic mental syndromes such as delirium and in assessing and monitoring a patient's level of cognitive functioning.

Symptoms of delirium include disordered cognitive function—that is, abnormal thinking, perception, and memory. Thinking does not proceed logically and sequentially. Disorientation to time is classically displayed. In more severe cases, disorientation to place and person may also be evident. Perceptual disturbances include hallucinations (whereby sensory experiences occur in the absence of external stimuli) and illusions (the misinterpretation of sensory stimuli). Recent memory is generally severely impaired. Remote memory may be unaffected.

Delirium is also marked by a reduced attention span, disturbed sleep-wake cycle, and abnormal psychomotor behavior. The latter feature may involve diminished or hyperactive movement, including unpredictable shifts from one to the other.

The onset of delirium is abrupt, usually developing over a period of a few hours to days (Tobias, Lippmann, Tully, et al., 1989). Symptom severity fluctuates throughout the day and symptoms tend to become worse at night. Symptoms are indicative of widespread derangement of cerebral metabolism.

Anyone can develop delirium, but the elderly are at special risk as a consequence of physical illness or drug intoxication (Lipowski, 1989). Such stressors tax the reduced capacity for homeostatic regulation brought about by aging. Drug intoxication is probably the most common cause of delirium in the older adult (Lipowski, 1990). Therapeutic doses of commonly prescribed drugs can induce the condition.

Other causes of delirium include dehydration and electrolyte imbalances, congestive heart failure, myocardial infarction, stroke, cancer, pneumonia, urinary tract infection, diabetes, and malnutrition. Alcoholism and withdrawal from sedative-hypnotic agents are other possible causes (Beresford, Blow, Brower, et al., 1988). Delirium is a complication in a variety of surgical procedures for elderly patients, including elective orthopedic surgery (Rogers, Liang, and Daltroy, 1989). Its frequency in patients suffering hip fractures approaches 50 percent (Berggren, Gustafson, Eriksson, et al., 1987). Delirium is not uncommon in hospitalized elderly (Francis, Martin, and Kapoor, 1990).

Multiple factors can work together to precipitate delirium in the elderly. Additionally, sensory deprivation and psychosocial stress such as that associated with bereavement or transplantation to a new environmental setting may facilitate its development and maintenance in one who is physically vulnerable to delirium (Lipowski, 1987).

The cognitive and attentional deterioration seen in delirium has been related to a general reduction in cerebral oxidative metabolism. Such diminished metabolism results in reduced production of cerebral neurotransmitters (brain chemicals), especially acetylcholine and epinephrine (Blass and Plum, 1983; Lipowski, 1983, 1990). Acetylcholine is necessary for normal information processing, attention, learning, and memory.

Delirium is of brief duration. It may last for hours, days, or weeks, but generally no more than one month. Recovery occurs if the underlying causal problem can be and is resolved. In some persons it is followed by dementia or death. It can be precipitated by potentially fatal, yet treatable conditions, such as dehydration. Failure to recognize such an underlying problem can result in death. Delirium may also develop at the terminal stage of a disease such as cancer, thus serving as a poor prognostic indicator.

In 1976 Hodkinson warned that the importance of acute mental confusion in the elderly could not be overemphasized. He noted it a common signal of the onset of physical illness in the older adult — more common, he said, than fever, pain, or tachycardia. Despite its prevalence and clinical significance, delirium is often misdiagnosed and overlooked by investigators. Lipowski (1990), a specialist in the study of acute confusional states, is encouraged by the recent introduction of uniform terminology and explicit diagnostic criteria for delir-

ium and expects these to aid in its diagnosis and research.

Dementia: Alzheimer's Disease

Dementia is generally defined as a clinical syndrome in an alert individual involving intellectual deterioration and memory loss of sufficient severity to interfere with daily living activities. It involves deficits in memory, abstract thinking, orientation, reasoning, and judgment. Various forms of dementia exist.

Alzheimer's disease (AD) is the most common form of dementia in the elderly. Although it was first described by Alois Alzheimer in 1907, the cause of this tragic, progressive, disabling disease remains unknown. In a medical journal of that year, Alzheimer outlined the five-year decline of a 51-year-old female patient with progressive dementia and the brain changes he found at autopsy. Eventually, the disease came to bear his name.

For many years the designation *Alzheimer's disease* was used only in reference to the presenile or early onset of dementia that met a given clinical and pathological definition. Onset of the dementia after age 65 was termed *senile dementia Alzheimer's type.* Now these two designations have been abolished. In recognition of the fact that the two conditions were really the same, Alzheimer's disease denotes a specific type of dementia regardless of age at onset.

Insidious and progressive memory loss is, perhaps, the most notorious symptom associated with AD. As the disease advances, victims demonstrate deteriorating motor skills, inappropriate behavior, and emotional instability. Patients become incontinent, mute, and unable to recognize family and friends. The majority develop seizures. With time, the AD patient needs total care and is bedridden. The most common cause of death is pneumonia.

AD is diagnosed in the living state by a thorough medical history, brain scans, laboratory tests, and a mental status exam. The purpose of these procedures is to rule out any other possible causes of the patient's behavioral and clinical symptoms (Kvale, 1986). Definitive diagnosis is made only by an examination of brain tissue at autopsy, as a brain biopsy is rarely done.

An autopsy is important because AD is characterized by various specific cerebral changes. These changes include a greater number and density of neurofibrillary tangles and neuritic plaques than are seen in nondemented, age-matched controls. These so-called hallmarks of the disease confirm the diagnosis. Although these changes were reported by Alzheimer in his 1907 article, the reasons that these changes develop and their relationship to the disease are still not understood.

The proportion of nondemented persons with neuritic plaques sharply rises during the seventh and eighth decades of life, with more than three-quarters of individuals affected by age 90. Nondemented persons over 50 will almost all express neurofibrillary tangles, which increase in number with the passing years (Tomlinson, 1982). It has, therefore, been speculated that AD represents an acceleration of normal aging. If this belief were true, then all persons would develop AD merely by living long enough. A review of the research to date indicates that AD is a specific disease process and is not characteristic of normal senescence (Martin, 1989).

Beta amyloid is a major constituent of the plaques seen in the brains of normal elderly persons. It is, however, abnormally abundant in the brains of Alzheimer's patients. Its role in AD has been the subject of speculation. Recent findings of researchers at Brigham and Women's Hospital in Boston may help to shed more light on amyloid accumulation. The protein was found in various non-neural tissues including skin, blood vessels, and intestinal tissue of AD patients. In a report on the finding in *Science News*, it was speculated that beta amyloid may carry future diagnostic and therapeutic possibilities. Likewise, further studies on its accumulation in the body may tell us more about its role in the disease process (Weiss, 1989).

In contrast to normal aging, continual dendritic growth is severely limited in AD (Buell and Coleman, 1981). Hence, the capacity to compensate for senescent changes such as neuronal loss may distinguish the AD-prone individual (Buell and Coleman, 1979). Neuronal loss in specific brain centers is a major feature of AD.

Although declines in various neurotransmitter and related enzyme levels occur with age, AD is characterized by a disproportionate decline in the cholinergic system (Francis, Palmer, Sims, et al., 1985). The cholinergic system and its neurons are the main transmission lines between brain areas responsible for higher cognitive functioning and memory. Choline acetyltransferase, an enzyme critical to acetylcholine synthesis, is greatly reduced in the AD patient.

Recent research has generated numerous causative possibilities for AD, including genetic, viral, immunologic, toxic, and other mechanisms. AD may be multifactoral. That is, it may result from the interplay of various factors.

Although in the majority of cases AD appears to occur sporadically, a positive family history increases the risk of developing the disease. The role of genetics is still not well understood. In some families the disease is transmitted as an autosomal dominant trait. In such a situation only one gene from one parent need be transmitted, making the risk of disease in such families nearly 50 percent. Early-onset AD, wherein the disorder is manifested in one's forties or fifties, appears to be more often associated with such a familial pedigree.

Establishing whether there are clear genetic and nongenetic subtypes of AD is difficult. It has been suggested that there may be a familial tendency to develop the disease at a particular age (Terry, 1978). If this is correct, then familial AD would be more likely detected in early-onset patterns. Those with a tendency to develop it later in life might not live long enough to do so (Martin, 1989). One group of researchers believes that familial-type AD has a wide range of onset within a family. In one-third of the familial cases they studied, the disease was not expressed until over age 70 (Fitch, Becker, and Heller, 1988).

It has also been theorized that a virus, especially a slow virus, might be related to the development of AD. A slow-acting virus has been identified in the cause of Creutzfeldt-Jakob disease, a rare disorder characterized by the rapid progression of dementia.

The immune system has also been implicated in AD. It is possible that an autoimmune reaction is triggered against a specific antigen in brain tissue. The response could be triggered by a protein in the brain or an infectious particle such as a virus. It has also been hypothesized that autoantibodies may damage the blood–brain barrier (the chemical barrier that keeps harmful substances out of the brain). Once damaged, toxins, viruses, or other injurious substances might gain access to normally protected brain tissue (Fillit, Kemeny, Luine, et al., 1987).

The finding of abnormally high concentrations of aluminum deposits in the brains of AD patients at autopsy has led to growing public concern that AD may be caused by this common element. Evidence linking aluminum with AD is meager and inconclusive. There is no experimental evidence that aluminum dissolved from cooking utensils causes dementia (Hughes, 1989).

There has been concern about aluminum in the water supply causing AD, especially since the publication of an article linking the two (Martyn, Barker, Osmond, et al., 1989). A survey of 88 county districts in England and Wales found that residents in areas with higher aluminum concentrations demonstrated a higher incidence of AD. However, the new evidence itself requires further study. There are questions about the accuracy of the AD diagnoses and the amount of aluminum ingested from the water supply (Hughes, 1989).

Various other areas of investigation regarding AD causation are underway, including possible inherited defects in the mitochondria (the cell's oxygen-dependent "energy factories"), neuron membrane defects, and protein deposits within the brain tissue.

Prevention and treatment of AD has been frustrated by the failure to identify a known cause of the disease. Treatment has been largely directed at the symptomatic relief of behavioral disturbances. Various pharmacologic agents are being used or studied in an attempt to intervene effectively in the disease process.

Multi-infarct Dementia

The second most common cause of dementia in the older adult is multi-infarct dementia (MID). It results from repeated damage to the brain due to inadequate blood flow. The resultant minor strokes produce few perceptible symptoms, save for diminished cognitive function and memory loss. As the underlying vascular problems increase, so too do deteriorated brain areas, or infarcts, and the seriousness of the mental decline. Hence, the condition is called multi-infarct dementia.

The onset of MID tends to be sudden rather than gradual as is characteristic of Alzheimer's disease. The functional decline follows an erratic, downward course. It is often referred to as a stepwise deterioration, indicating that the behavior worsens in a jerky, stepwise fashion.

Attention to modifiable risk factors of atherosclerosis and high blood pressure may carry the potential to reduce the future incidence of MID. This condition now represents 15 to 20 percent of all dementias affecting the elderly.

PARKINSON'S DISEASE

Parkinsonism or Parkinson's syndrome refers to a clinical condition characterized by muscular rigidity and a rhythmic tremor. The majority of cases are termed idiopathic Parkinson's disease, indicating that the condition has no recognizable cause. This type of parkinsonism represents a chronic, progressive condition of the central nervous system that occurs primarily in the elderly.

The onset of Parkinson's disease generally occurs between 50 and 65 years of age, during late middle age. Two other variants of the disorder have been recognized. The first, termed postencephalitic parkinsonism, was postulated to result from a type of encephalitis that peaked in occurrence from 1919 to the early 1930s (Poskanzer and Schwab, 1963). The second, drug-induced parkinsonism, is known to occur in some patients receiving large doses of certain drugs over time for the treatment of psychiatric disorders. The latter condition is often reversible if early diagnosis is followed by cessation of the drug therapy.

Symptoms of parkinsonism stem from a biochemical imbalance in the brain between the neurochemicals acetylcholine and dopamine. Normally, these neurotransmitters work to balance nervous excitation and inhibition, allowing for smooth motor function. This function is disrupted as dopamine-producing cells in the brain are lost, causing its deficiency. There is a direct relationship between the degree of dopamine deficiency and the severity of parkinsonism symptoms.

Muscular rigidity may involve one or both sides of the body and is responsible for decreased strength and speed of movement. Initiation of new movement is difficult. These symptoms can be very disabling. Postural problems lead to a forward-slanting, shuffling gait. The tremor, which occurs at rest, is called a rest tremor. It is an involuntary movement that can be socially embarrassing. Deliberate activity generally halts the tremor. The hands are frequently involved, producing what is referred to as a pill-rolling tremor. This rhythmic movement involves the thumb and first two fingers. Tremor may be worse when the individual is tired or emotionally distressed (Price and Wilson, 1986).

Approximately 15 percent of Parkinson's patients will exhibit essential tremor. Unlike the rest tremor typically associated with Parkinson's disease, essential tremor is intensified with action. It does not respond to antiparkinsonian drugs, but is often reduced with some other pharmacologic agents. The cause of essential tremor is unknown (Cote and Henly, 1990).

An expressionless, masklike face is also associated with the condition. The voice volume may be reduced and the speech pattern slow and monotonous. These features may give the illusion of reduced mental functioning or dementia in persons who have not undergone these latter changes. Handwriting deteriorates, becoming abnormally small and trailing off so that it cannot be deciphered. Many of these symptoms take a long time to develop.

Mental changes are not uncommon in Parkinson's patients. The prevalence of dementia is estimated at 15 percent according to Cote and Henly (1990). Others have reported it to be as high as 50 percent. However, patients in such studies have often been institutionalized, introducing a selection bias. Also, most patients are on medications that may influence their intellectual functioning. Criteria for identifying dementia vary in many studies. Diagnosed dementia in association with Parkinson's disease is 10 times more common than it is in age-matched controls (Fonda, 1985).

Medications that attempt to restore the balance in neurotransmission have been the mainstay therapy for Parkinson's disease. Various drugs are used, although the most effective therapy continues to be *levodopa* (L-dopa), a metabolic precursor of dopamine that converts to dopamine in the brain. Unfortunately, although L-dopa has done much to extend and maintain the functional capacity of the patient, its prolonged use may promote eventually disabling side effects (Greer, 1985). Some researchers, however, do not believe that the observed defect in voluntary movements is solely due to prolonged use of L-dopa (Ahlskog and Wilkinson, 1990). Drugs do not cure Parkinson's disease, which continues to progress despite their use.

Although it was first described by James Parkinson in 1917, the cause of the disease remains unknown. However, some important features of the disorder have been recognized. Dopamine deficiency has been correlated with a localized loss of cells in a part of the brain known as the *substantia nigra*. As dopamine-producing cells are lost in this area, so too is the ability to carry out purposeful, coordinated, and controlled movements. What remains elusive is why these cells are lost.

Recent investigations are leading some to theorize that Parkinson's disease may result from the combined effect of aging and environmental insult. With aging, cells in the substantia nigra are lost and dopamine levels decline. However, the majority of people who age do not develop Parkinson's disease. The 70 percent depletion in dopamine levels necessary for symptom onset does not occur as a result of aging. It may, however, be expressed among those who have suffered previous subclinical damage (Calne et al., 1985; Lewin, 1985a). Exposure to environmental toxins including certain pesticides, various industrial chemicals, or food ingredients might cause early, yet limited, destruction of dopamine-producing cells (Hertzman et al., 1990; Snyder and D'Amato, 1985; Tanner et al., 1987). Subsequent age-related losses then sufficiently compromise dopamine-producing capabilities to the extent that symptoms result.

Though controversial, this theory has been bolstered by studies linking a chemical by-product in synthetic heroin to the development of parkinsonian symptoms in humans and animals (Langston, Ballard, Tetrud, and Irwin, 1983; Lewin, 1985b). There is no recognized association between symptoms and narcotic use unless the drug is contaminated with a substance known as MPTP (N-methyl-4-phenyltetrahydropyridine). MPTP is actually converted to a *neurotoxin* (Langston, 1987). Animals and humans who have been exposed to the cell-damaging substance have demonstrated destruction of cells in the substantia nigra as well as symptoms of parkinsonism. Recent evidence suggests that synthetic heroin use can result in the losses of dopamine neurons in symptomless subjects as well (Calne et al., 1985). Young people using the drug for two years have begun to show symptoms of early parkinsonism. The chief of California's Division of Drug Programs in Sacramento reported that an epidemic of Parkinson's disease may be facing young adult synthetic heroin users (Bower, 1985).

On the basis of experimental work conducted during the late 1980s, it is speculated that drug treatment of neurodegenerative disorders such as Parkinson's disease and Alzheimer's disease may make striking advances. Drug therapy may be able to alter the underlying mechanism of neuronal destruction. Eldepryl, also known as selegiline, now used as adjuvant therapy in the treatment of some Parkinson's disease cases, may protect dopamine-producing neurons from toxic, destructive substances (Calesnick, 1990).

Surgical intervention in the treatment of Parkinson's disease has involved the implantation of tissue into the brains of patients. Adrenal gland tissue that produces dopamine-like hormones has been transplanted (Backlund, Granburg, and Hamberger, 1985; Madrazo, Drucker-Colin, and Diaz, 1987). Although some initial improvement was noted, caution has been expressed in the interpretation of the experimental procedure. Widespread use of the procedure is not considered warranted (Goetz, Olanow, and Koller, 1989). Donor tissue may consist of the patient's adrenal tissue, fetal tissue, or tissue culture. The procurement and use of fetal tissue has raised ethical and moral issues.

CEREBROVASCULAR DISEASE

Atherosclerotic changes in blood vessels that serve brain tissue can reduce its nourishment and result in the malfunction or death of brain cells. Impaired brain tissue circulation is known as *cerebrovascular disease*.

When a portion of the brain is completely denied blood, a *cerebrovascular accident* (CVA) or *stroke* results. The severity of a CVA is dependent on the particular area as well as the total amount of brain tissue involved. Thus, a stroke may affect such a small brain area that it goes unnoticed or such a large area that it causes severe damage or death. Cerebrovascular accident represents the third leading cause of death among the elderly in the United States.

There are a number of specific events that typically cause a CVA. *Cerebral thrombosis* is the main form of stroke among the elderly. It occurs when a blood clot or *thrombus* forms in an artery supplying the brain. Often the artery is damaged by atherosclerosis and the thrombus becomes lodged in the *narrowed channel*. A *cerebral embolism* may also be responsible for a CVA. In this instance, a clot called an *embolus* forms elsewhere and travels to obstruct a brain artery. Emboli arising from the heart are well-known causes of stroke.

A *cerebral hemorrhage* is another form of stroke wherein a blood vessel bursts, depriving an area of the brain of its blood supply. Accumulated blood from the rupture may put pressure on surrounding brain tissue, causing further serious damage. Cerebral hemorrhage is more likely to cause death than are the other forms of stroke. Victims usually go into a coma and die within a few days.

A small percentage of strokes occurs when a blood vessel on the brain's surface bleeds into the space between the brain and the skull. This situation is referred to as a subarachnoid hemorrhage.

Short-lived symptoms may precede a CVA. These episodic symptoms are known as little strokes or *transient ischemic attacks* (TIAs). Sudden motor weakness or numbness on one side of the body, speech disturbances, dimness or vision loss (especially in one eye), dizziness, and sudden falls are among the transitory symptoms that might be present. TIAs are warning signs of a possible impending stroke. They often precede a major stroke by days, weeks, or months. These transient ischemic attacks are sometimes labeled *carotid artery syndrome* in reference to a transient occlusion of the major arteries supplying the brain. Because a narrowed carotid artery may eventually be the focus of a complete occlusion, an operation known as an *endarterectomy* is sometimes performed to clear the inner lining of the artery.

When a stroke occurs, varying degrees of damage may result. *Hemiplegia* (paralysis of one side of the body), *hemiparesis* (weakness of one side of the body), *aphasia* (speech disorders), and sensory disturbances present special problems for the stroke victim. Rehabilitation efforts should begin immediately. Successful rehabilitation depends on the area and degree of brain damage, as well as the supportive attitude and encouragement of the rehabilitation team, family, and friends. Sudden neurologic and motor changes can greatly alter a person's perception of self and the world. They can cause a person to withdraw.

Brain damage affects opposite sides of the body. Right-brain damage may result in left-side hemiplegia or hemiparesis. It may be accompanied by memory deficits, spatial-perceptual deficits, and an impulsive behavioral style. Left-brain damage may cause right-side hemiplegia or hemiparesis as well as speech-language deficits, memory deficits, and a slow, cautious behavioral pattern. These noted deficits are typical for right-handed individuals. For left-handed persons the opposite may be true. Aphasia may denote impaired ability to comprehend or express language. In *receptive aphasia* a person has difficulty processing external stimuli. Because of damage within the speech center of the brain, the individual may not understand the spoken or written word. *Expressive aphasia* occurs when a person understands what is said but cannot form the words or gestures to respond to stimuli. A patient may also suffer from mixed aphasia, wherein both receptive and expressive deficits are present.

Tragically, aphasia may be incorrectly associated with mental deterioration. Tactless statements may be made in the presence of a person who can understand what is going on but who cannot respond appropriately. Likewise, the patient may be infantilized and treated as a child while being fully aware of the indignity of such treatment.

Patients should be encouraged to speak, and those around them should listen patiently. They should not be rushed or cut off in the middle of their attempts. Such behavior on the part of the listener can cause the person to feel awkward and self-conscious. The aphasic victim may thus become depressed and withdrawn.

Despite aphasic involvement, some persons may be able to repeat words or phrases that are a part of what is known as primitive or automatic language. For instance, they may be able to count, sing, or respond with "O.K." and "goodbye," while not being able to construct sentences or express original ideas. It is easier for the bilingual person to regain command of his or her native language. This factor should be kept in mind when working with such persons.

Stroke patients may also suffer from defective vision or blindness in one-half of their visual field. This condition is known as *hemianopia* or *hemianopsia*. In stroke patients, such visual losses are often compensated for by head turning. Those who work with or care for stroke victims should be aware

of such possible losses and attempt to aid patients in their compensation. For example, an individual with hemianopia may eat the food that appears on only half of the plate because the rest of it cannot be seen. Rotating the plate for such a person can be most helpful.

As a result of hemianopia, a stroke victim may not react to the appearance of someone in the doorway or may be startled as someone who has entered the room suddenly seems to come within view. This lack of awareness about a visitor's presence is related to the loss in visual field.

Care should be taken in positioning a hemianopic patient within a room. For example, a person who has lost the right field of vision should not be placed with his or her left side to a wall. That person would not be able to see what was taking place within the room itself, but would have a clear view of the wall!

It is imperative that paralyzed patients be turned regularly to prevent pressure sores, exercised to prevent joint contractures, and positioned so that they do not aspirate or choke on nasal-oral secretions. Rehabilitative efforts with them should likewise include understanding and patience. Useful gains may not be obvious for weeks or months after the initiation of a rehabilitative program.

Family members and health workers must be made aware that their attitudes toward the CVA victim and the recovery process can encourage the person to work harder or to give up. Short-term goals should be set, and small gains should be praised. Above all, dignity and independence must be respected. The patient must be allowed to do as much for himself or herself as is possible. A paternalistic or overly helpful attitude, though well intended, may slow recovery and make the patient feel helpless or useless. Gains in independent living can only enhance a person's sense of self-worth and dignity.

The majority of the approximately 300,000 persons who annually suffer their first stroke survive with residual neurologic deficits that can impair independence. For those with preexisting functional disability, stroke may impose additional impairment, which serves to increase the risk of institutionalization. Proper care of the elderly stroke victim demands functionally directed clinical examinations and ongoing periodic functional evaluation (Kelly and Winograd, 1985).

Treatment for stroke may involve drugs, surgery (carotid endarterectomy) and rehabilitation. Anticoagulants, including aspirin, may be employed in an attempt to prevent clot formation. Attention to various types of heart disease that might promote the formation of a "wandering" clot is also important. Diagnosis and treatment of TIAs may prevent a stroke.

A number of factors increase the risk of a CVA. In general, risk of stroke is greater in men and among blacks (Gillum, 1988). The high risk of stroke among blacks may be due to a greater prevalence of high blood pressure in this population. High blood pressure, especially diastolic hypertension (the lower number in a blood pressure reading), is one of the most significant risk factors for stroke. The incidence of CVA in those 65 to 74 years with diastolic pressure less than 90 Hg increases dramatically with incremental elevations in systolic blood pressure (the upper number in a blood pressure reading) (Borhani, 1986). Heart disease, leading to pumping failure or serving as a source of emboli, increases the risk of stroke. Risk is also greater among diabetic individuals. TIAs and previous strokes are major risk factors for stroke.

Although blood levels of lipoproteins are strongly related to coronary atherosclerosis, their relationship to cerebrovascular disease is less evident. Along with obesity and diet, elevated blood lipids and *hypercholesterolemia* are cited as less important risk factors for stroke than those cited in the previous paragraph (Power and Hachinski, 1990). However, in a literature review seeking a relationship between blood lipids, lipoprotein levels, and cerebrovascular atherosclerosis, it was concluded that such a relationship exists. It was found to be stronger in older than in younger individuals (Tell, Crouse, and Furberg, 1988). Further work is needed in this area.

STUDY QUESTIONS

1. Review the various specialized parts of a neuron and how nerve impulses are transmitted. Discuss various changes that take place in nervous tissue with age.
2. Briefly discuss the concept of senility among older adults.
3. What is delirium? Present an overview of this condition. What are some of its possible causes? How is delirium significant for the older patient?
4. Present an overview of Alzheimer's disease. Include how it is diagnosed, major brain changes associated with it, and possible causes.
5. What is multi-infarct dementia? How does it differ from Alzheimer's disease?
6. What is Parkinson's disease and what are some of its major symptoms? Why is it speculated that it may result from the combined effects of aging and environmental insult?
7. Note the various specific events that can cause a cerebrovascular accident or stroke. Which one is most common among the elderly?
8. What is the significance of a TIA? Note some of the possible consequences of a stroke. Identify various risk factors for cerebrovascular accident.

BIBLIOGRAPHY

Ahlskog, J., and Wilkinson, J. 1990. New concepts in the treatment of Parkinson's disease. *American Family Physician*, 41: 574–584.

Alzheimer, A. 1907. Uber eine eigenartige Erkangkung der Hirnrinde. *All Zeitshrift Psychiatry*, 64: 146.

American Psychiatric Association. 1987. *Diagnostic and statistical manual of mental disorders*, 3rd ed., revised. Washington, DC: Author.

Backlund, E., Granburg, P., and Hamberger, B. 1985. Transplantation of adrenal medullary tissue to striatum in parkinsonism: First clinical trials. *Journal of Neurosurgery*, 62: 169–173.

Beresford, T., Blow, F., Brower, K., et al. 1988. Alcoholism and aging in the general hospital. *Psychosomatics*, 29: 61–72.

Berggren, D., Gustafson, Y., Eriksson, B., et al. 1987. Postoperative confusion after anesthesia in elderly patients with femoral neck fractures. *Anethesia Anala*, 66: 497-504.

Blass, P., and Plum, F. 1983. Metabolic encephalopathies in older adults. In R. Katzman and R. Terry (Eds.), *The neurology of aging*. Philadelphia: F. A. Davis.

Blessed, G., Tomlinson, B., and Roth, M. 1968. The association between quantitative measures of dementia and of senile change in the cerebral gray matter of elderly subjects. *British Journal of Psychiatry*, 114: 797.

Bondareff, W. 1985. The neural basis of aging. In J. Birren and K. Schaie (Eds.), *Handbook of the psychology of aging*. New York: Van Nostrand Reinhold.

Borhani, N. 1986. Prevalence and prognostic significance of hypertension in the elderly. *Journal of the American Geriatrics Society*, 34(2): 112-114.

Bower, B. 1985. Tracking the roots of Parkinson's disease. *Science News*, 128: 212.

Buell, S., and Coleman, P. 1979. Dendritic growth in the aged human brain and failure of growth in senile dementia. *Science*, 206: 854-856.

Buell, S., and Coleman, P. 1981. Quantitative evidence for selective dendritic growth in normal human aging but not in senile dementia. *Brain Research*, 214: 23-41.

Calesnick, B. 1990. Selegiline for Parkinson's disease. *American Family Physician*, 41: 589-591.

Calne, D., Langston, J., Martin, W., Stoessl, A., Ruth, T., Adam, M., Pate, B., and Schulzer, M. 1985. Positron emission topography after MPTP: Observations relating to the cause of Parkinson's disease. *Nature*, 317: 246-248.

Caplan, L. 1982. Neurology. In J. Rowe and R. Besdine (Eds.), *Health and disease in old age*. Boston: Little, Brown.

Coleman, P., and Flood, D. 1987. Neuron numbers and dendritic extent in normal aging and Alzheimer's disease. *Neurobiology of Aging*, 8: 521.

Cote, L., and Henly, M. 1990. Parkinson's disease. In W. Hazzard, R. Andres, E. Bierman, and J. Blass (Eds.), *Principles of geriatric medicine and gerontology*. New York: McGraw-Hill.

Drachman, D., Noffsinger, D., Sahakian, B., Fleming, P., Noffsinger, D., and Kurdziel, S. 1980. Aging, memory and the cholinergic system: A study of dichotic listening. *Neurobiology of Aging*, 1: 39-43.

Fillit, H., Kemeny, E., Luine, V., et al. 1987. Antivascular antibodies in the sera of patients with senile dementia of the Alzheimer's type. *Journal of Gerontology*, 42: 180-184.

Fitch, N., Becker, R., and Heller, A. 1988. The inheritance of Alzheimer's disease: A new interpretation. *Annals of Neurology*, 23: 14-19.

Fonda, D. 1985. Parkinson's disease in the elderly: Psychiatric manifestations. *Geriatrics*, 40: 109-114.

Francis, J., Martin, D., and Kapoor, W. 1990. A prospective study of delirium in hospitalized elderly. *Journal of the American Medical Association*, 263: 1097-1101.

Francis, P., Palmer, A., Sims, N., Bower, D., Davison, A., Esiri, M., Neary, D. Swoden, J. and Wilcock, G. 1985. Neurochemical studies of early-onset Alzheimer's disease: Possible influence on treatment. *New England Journal of Medicine*, 313(1): 7-11.

Gillum, R. 1988. Stroke in blacks. *Stroke*, 19: 1-9.

Goetz, C., Olanow, W., and Koller, W. 1989. Multicenter study of autologous adrenal medullary transplantation to the corpus striatum in patients with advanced Parkinson's disease. *New England Journal of Medicine*, 320: 337.

Greer, M. 1985. Recent developments in the treatment of Parkinson's disease. *Geriatrics*, 140: 34-41.

Hertzman, C., et al. 1990. Parkinson's disease: A case-controlled study of occupational and environmental risk factors. *American Journal of Industrial Medicine*, 17: 349-355.

Hodkinson, H. 1976. *Common symptoms of disease in the elderly*. Oxford: Blackwell.

Hughes, T. 1989. Aluminum and the human brain. *The Practitioner*, 233: 920, 922-923.

Kane, R., Ouslander, J., and Abrass, I. 1989. *Essentials of clinical geriatrics*. New York: McGraw-Hill.

Kelly, J., and Winograd, C. 1985. A functional approach to stroke management in elderly patients. *Journal of the American Geriatrics Society*, 33(1): 48-60.

Kvale, J. 1986. Alzheimer's disease. *American Family Physician,* 34(1): 103-110.

Langston, J. 1987. MPTP: The promise of a new neurotoxin. In C. Marsden and S. Fahn (Eds.), *Movement disorders 2*. London: Butterworths.

Langston, J., Ballard, P., Tetrud, J., and Irwin, I. 1983. Chronic parkinsonism in humans due to a product of meperidine-analog synthesis. *Science*, 219: 970-980.

Lewin, R. 1985a. Clinical trial for Parkinson's disease. *Science*, 230: 527-528.

Lewin, R. 1985b. Parkinson's disease: An environmental cause? *Science*, 229: 257-258.

Lipowski, Z. 1983. Transient cognitive disorders (delirium, acute confusional states) in the elderly. *American Journal of Psychiatry*, 140: 1426-1436.

Lipowski, Z. 1987. Delirium (acute confusional states). *Journal of the American Medical Association*, 258: 1789-1792.

Lipowski, Z. 1989. Delirium in the elderly patient. *New England Journal of Medicine*, 320: 578-582.

Lipowski, Z. 1990. Delirium (acute confusional states). In W. Hazzard, R. Andres, E. Bierman, and J. Blass (Eds.), *Principles of geriatric medicine and gerontology*. New York: McGraw-Hill.

Madrazo, I., Drucker-Colin, R., and Diaz, V. 1987. Open microsurgical autograft of adrenal medulla to the right caudate nucleus in two patients with intractable Parkinson's disease. *New England Journal of Medicine*, 316: 831-834.

Martin, R. 1989. Update on dementia of the Alzheimer type. *Hospital and Community Psychiatry*, 40: 593-604.

Martyn, C., Barker, D., Osmond, C., et al. 1989. Geographical relation between Alzheimer's disease and the aluminum in drinking water. *Lancet*, 1: 59-62.

Mayeux, R. 1990. Alzheimer's disease. In W. Hazzard, R. Andres, E. Bierman, and J. Blass (Eds.), *Principles of geriatric medicine and gerontology*. New York: McGraw-Hill.

McGreer, E., and McGreer, P. 1976. Neurotransmitter metabolism and the aging brain. In R. Terry and S. Gershon (Eds.), *Neurobiology of aging*. New York: Raven.

McGreer, E., and McGreer, P. 1980. Aging and neurotransmitter systems. In M. Goldstein, D. Caine, A. Liegerman, and M. Thorner (Eds.), *Advances in biochemical psychopharmacology* (Vol. 23). New York: Raven.

Poirier, J., and Finch, C. 1990. Neurochemistry of the aging human brain. In W. Hazzard, R. Andres, E. Bierman, and J. Blass (Eds.), *Principles of geriatric medicine and gerontology*. New York: McGraw-Hill.

Poskanzer, D., and Schwab, R. 1963. Cohort analysis of Parkinson's syndrome: Evidence for a single etiology related to sub-clinical infection about 1920. *Journal of Chronic Disease*, 16: 961-973.

Power, C., and Hachinski, V. 1990. Stroke in the elderly. In W. Hazzard, R. Andres, E. Bierman, and J. Blass (Eds.), *Principles of geriatric medicine and gerontology*. New York: McGraw-Hill.

Price, S., and Wilson, L. 1986. *Pathophysiology*. New York: McGraw-Hill.

Rogers, J., and Bloom, F. 1985. Neurotransmitter metabolism and function in the aging central nervous system. In C. Finch and E. Schneider (Eds.), *Handbook of the biology of aging*. New York: Van Nostrand Reinhold.

Rogers, M., Liang, M., and Daltroy, L. 1989. Delirium after elective orthopedic surgery: Risk factors and natural history. *International Journal of Psychiatry in Medicine*, 19: 109-121.

Scheibel, A. 1982. Age-related changes in the human forebrain. *Neurosciences Research Progress Bulletin*, 20: 577-583.

Snyder, S., and D'Amato, R. 1985. Predicting Parkinson's disease. *Nature*, 317: 198-199.

Tanner, C., et al. 1987. Environmental factors in the etiology of Parkinson's disease. *Canadian Journal of Neurological Science*, 14: 419-423.

Tell, G., Crouse, J., and Furberg, C. 1988. Relation between blood lipids, lipoproteins, and cerebrovascular atherosclerosis: A review. *Stroke*, 19: 423-430.

Terry, R. 1978. Aging, senile dementia, and Alzheimer's disease. In R. Katzman and R. Terry (Eds.), *Alzheimer's disease: Senile dementia and related disorders*, Aging, Vol. 7. New York: Raven Press.

Tobias, C., Lippmann, S., Tully, E., et al. 1989. Delirium in the elderly. *Postgraduate Medicine*, 85: 117-130.

Tomlinson, B. 1982. Plaques, tangles, and Alzheimer's disease. *Psychological Medicine*, 12: 449-459.

Weiss, R. 1989. Alzheimer's protein not restricted to brain. *Science News*, 136: 197.

CHAPTER 9

The Aging Process and the Gastrointestinal System

The human gastrointestinal tract is the product of four million years of biocultural evolution. Our species evolved from primate ancestors who were primarily vegetarian but with the capability of omnivorous alimentation. The omnivorous nature of our species helped it expand and evolve to fit a wide variety of ecologic conditions. Judging from the development of a great variety of cultural traditions with dissimilar eating customs, it seems that our gastrointestinal system has served the species well.

All members of our species are subject to the aging process, which brings both general and specific changes in the gastrointestinal tract. These changes include *atrophy* of the secretion mechanisms, decreasing motility of the gut, loss of strength and tone of the muscular tissue and its supporting structures, changes in neurosensory feedback on such things as enzyme and hormone release, innervation of the tract, and diminished response to pain and internal sensations. Although the indisputable evidence for the relationship be-

tween these changes and aging is still not abundant, there is certainly enough circumstantial evidence to consider the possibilities. It remains for further research to determine the magnitude of the changes and identify the possible preventive, rehabilitative, and supportive measures to deal with them effectively. Holt (1983) recently commented that in the United States the major clinical digestive problems that affect the elderly are plagued by lack of research.

Gastrointestinal (GI) symptoms such as indigestion, heartburn, and epigastric discomfort increase with age, and the identification and evaluation of these symptoms are difficult. In geriatric clinics, about 18 percent of all patients have significant GI symptoms and mortality from GI diseases is second (20 percent) only to that from lung cancer (Levitan, 1989 a,b). Many symptoms are caused by normal functional changes in the tract, but with increasing age symptoms are often associated with serious pathologic conditions such as cancer. Gastrointestinal symptoms are a matter of great concern to many people. The threat or fear of cancer often associated with such symptoms can exert a great deal of psychological pressure on an individual. Stress of this type not only affects the mental health of the individual but can also affect other body systems, causing or complicating problems such as *hypertension* and chronic respiratory disease.

Health professionals who deal with gastrointestinal disorders of the aged must be flexible in their approach. Every disorder should be evaluated carefully before it is dismissed as simply a functional manifestation. If further evaluation indicates a functional disorder, an effort should be made to explain the nature of the problem to the patient in clear, concise, jargon-free terms. A sympathetic attitude and face-to-face discussion of the situation may sometimes do more for an individual than explicit medical intervention.

The signs and symptoms that individuals often associate with one part of the gastrointestinal tract may in reality be associated with another part of the tract. This is caused by the phenomenon of referral as well as by the fact that the organs are part of an integrated system and thus interrelated; for example, discomfort perceived as originating in one's stomach may actually be coming from lower in the gastrointestinal tract. With this in mind and for the sake of convenience, simplicity, and better organization, we will now embark on an organ-based survey of the gastrointestinal tract and its problems (Shamburek and Farrar, 1989; Rosenberg, Russell, and Bowman, 1989).

MOUTH

Many older people often have poor oral hygiene and seem to lose their sensitivity to irritations of the mouth. The former may be the result of the loss of a positive self-image, irregular visits to a dentist, or physical disabilities that hinder proper care of the mouth and teeth. Loss of sensitivity has serious implications for the health of elderly persons. Many irritations go unnoticed, and the widespread tendency to think that all sores are canker sores that will heal results in delay in checking sores that may be malignant.

Any sore that does not disappear within two weeks should be evaluated by a physician. Regular visits to a dentist interested in preventive dentistry would help in detection, but such regular dental visits, unfortunately, are often a luxury for those on limited income (neither Medicare nor Medicaid provides reimbursement for dental services to the elderly). Malignancies may occur where irritations are produced by broken and jagged teeth or around the periphery of an ill-fitting denture. Pain is usually not characteristic of the early stages of malignancy, but any slightly raised ulcers with raised edges that are painful to touch should be suspect. Treatment for a diagnosed malignancy will depend on the age and condition of the patient and on the nature and extent of the lesion.

Loss of taste is a common complaint among the elderly. This can be caused by atrophy of the taste buds, which comes with age, as well as by lesions of the facial nerve and the medulla, *thalamus,* and temporal lobe of the brain. Hughes (1969) has suggested that taste, smell, and hearing changes can be caused by cellular degeneration of the parietal lobe at the foot of the *postcentral gyrus.*

Some researchers have suggested that people have 70 percent fewer taste buds at age 70 than at age 30. Arey, Tremaine, and Monzingo (1935) observed an 80 percent reduction in taste function in a group of 74- to 80-year-olds. Schiffman and Pasternak (1979) report that the number of taste buds per papilla, the number of papillae, and the number of nerve endings for taste and smell all decrease with age. Rollin (1973) suggests that the number of taste bud nerve endings decreases with age, especially after age 60. However, this may be related to changes in the fifth and seventh cranial nerves (Harris, 1952). Bradley (1988) has recently reported that the number of taste buds varies from person to person but does not decline with age.

Changes in salivary flow, smoking, and diseases such as multiple sclerosis, cancer, diabetes mellitus, and hypertension all contribute to the alteration of taste and smell (Dye, 1984). Drugs taken to control diseases can also affect taste and smell (Schiffman, 1983). It has been suggested that zinc deficiency may contribute to reduced taste acuity. However, one double-blind study of institutionalized patients failed to produce any significant improvement after 95 days of zinc supplementation (Greger and Geissler, 1978). Henkin, Schechter, and Raff (1974) suggest that zinc is only one among many substances causing changes in taste acuity.

Age-related changes in the sense of smell may also contribute to the declining quality of *gustatory* sensation. Stevens, Bartoshuk, and Cain (1984) suggest that aging is associated with increased thresholds for taste and smell, but smell is more affected than taste. Stevens, Plantinga, and Cain (1982) note that older people (ages 65–83) rate odors as being only half as intense as do young adults (ages 18–25). The same researchers noted individual variation in some older subjects, although this may be related to interaction of the aging process with existent pathologic conditions. Changes in smell with age are less well documented than changes in taste, but because smell contributes to perception of taste, we need more basic research on smell in order to understand declining taste acuity more completely.

Of the four basic tastes, salty, bitter, and sour decline in sensitivity, but sweet taste does not appear to be affected by age (Bartoshuk and Weiffenbach, 1990). Balogh and Lelkes (1961) found that older adults were most sensitive to bitter tastes. Busse (1978) notes that the elderly frequently complain that food tastes bitter or sour. It is suspected that this may be due to age increases in the size and prominence of *papillae* sensitive to bitter tastes on the back of the tongue, along with a decrease in papillae on the anterior part of the tongue, which are sensitive to sweet and salty taste.

Thresholds for each taste are not as much affected as the ability to perceive subtle differences within each taste category. Reduced tactile thresholds in the oral mucosa and reduction in sensitivity of the olfactory nerves also affect taste perception. Changes in taste perception may lead to increased use of spices, seasonings, and flavoring by some older persons.

Loss of taste can affect appetite and thus indirectly affect nutritional status. Declining nutritional status can further affect ability to cope with certain stresses and situations that affect health status. Loss of taste, coupled with social-psychological changes often associated with aging, certainly does not help to stimulate a person to take the time to organize and prepare a meal, even if food is available. Still, for many elderly people there is nothing more enjoyable than preparing and eating a good meal.

Taste sensitivity and preference are affected greatly by lifelong consumption patterns. A study of laborers in India indicated that their ratings of the pleasantness of sour and bitter tastes differed significantly from those of Westerners (Moskowitz et al., 1975). The Indians repeatedly rated higher concentrations of quinine and citric acid as pleasant. The obvious explanation for this lies in the lifelong consumption of large amounts of sour foods by Indians. Mattes and Mela (1986) have considered the possibility that interpretation of taste studies may be influenced by dietary preferences rather than by sensory responses.

A number of noteworthy mucosal changes occur in the elderly. Sublingual spider nevi have been found in about half of some aged populations but are not associated with vitamin C deficiency, as suggested by some researchers (Exton-Smith and Scott, 1968). The appearance of the nevi is considered to be a normal aspect of the aging vascular system. *Leukoplakias,* which are small elevated white patches, were found in 21 percent of an elderly population; 12 percent of these were found to be premalignant (Bhaskar, 1968). Dryness of the mouth, a common complaint, may be caused in part by mouth breathing, thicker mucus, decreased production of saliva, and/or an earlier bout with dehydration. A dry mouth can lead to selection of self-lubricating foods such as custard and gelatin desserts, which may lack fiber or bulk and thus contribute to chronic constipation. Many drugs are known to affect the amount and consistency of saliva (Chauncey, Feldman, and Wayler, 1983). However, Baum (1989), in a longitudinal study among 208 subjects in Baltimore, found that saliva flow was not affected by age.

Dental changes such as missing teeth, attrition, weakening of tooth support, and poorly functioning dentures affect oral function and can lead to dietary and cosmetic changes. Functionally, teeth serve to masticate food and help initiate the process of digestion. They are important in proper speech because certain sounds involve the contact of the tongue and the teeth. Socially, teeth function to some degree as symbols of sexuality, and their loss does affect facial appearance. Yet, they are not really essential to survival of our species, since cultural innovations can carry out most of their functions.

About 50 percent of all Americans have lost a majority of their teeth by age 65, and about 75 percent are totally edentulous by age 75. This is the result of neglect by individuals and the dental profession. A number of factors lead people to neglect their teeth, including the expense of dental care, its low priority in the hierarchy of expenses, and the fact that little social stigma is attached to loss of teeth, especially in low socioeconomic brackets. Loss of teeth in itself generally does not pose a great health hazard. Finally, poor dental and nutrition education in the earlier years of the life cycle is associated with significant tooth loss in the later years.

Edentulousness is strongly correlated with low income and fewer than nine years of schooling, according to the National Center for Health Statistics. Surveys indicate, however, that edentulousness has decreased since 1960. During the decade between 1960 and 1970, the proportion of males in the 65-to-74 age group who were edentulous dropped from 45 to 43.6 percent; for females in the same age range the percentage who were edentulous dropped from 52.9 to 45 percent. These changes are more dramatic for aged black males, with a drop from 36 to 28 percent in ten years. Hatton and associates (1989) report that since the mid-1970s the number of people aged 65 and older who are edentulous has been surpassed by those who retain at least some teeth. It has been suggested that the greater availability and utilization of dental services may be responsible for these trends (Kiyak, 1984).

Given that half the population of the United States has or needs dentures by age 65 and about 75 percent of those over 65 have complete dentures, it should be apparent that denture problems are a major concern for the elderly. Well-fitting dentures probably do not exist; fit is a subjective category that depends largely on the individual's capacity to adapt to dentures. Many people get along well with dentures that are far from a perfect fit, whereas others with dentures that meet all the criteria for a physically good fit complain incessantly about their performance. It is easier to fit and satisfy a younger patient in her fifties or sixties than a very old patient. The geriatric dentist should be cautioned that in long-time denture wearers, radical changes should not be introduced just to fit the textbook theory.

Maxillary dentures are usually the best fitting and most functional. The broad-based structure of the maxilla allows for better construction and easier tolerance. The *mandible* has a number of characteristics that hinder the development of a truly effective plate. The mandible's narrow horseshoe shape is more difficult to fit. In addition, the greater mobility of the mandible causes the peripheral mucobuccal fold to be more active and thus have a tendency to dislodge the plate. The lower lip, tongue, and sublingual muscles may tend to dislodge the denture during speaking or swallowing. For these reasons, healthy mandibular teeth should be preserved as long as possible to act as anchors for partial dentures. Friedman (1968) has suggested that the cuspids are excellent as anchors because their long roots make them less susceptible to loss.

Full dentures tend to be a last resort after attempts with partial plates have failed. They are also used in cases of serious *periodontal disease* that necessitates complete removal of all teeth. About every five years dentures must be relined or replaced because of changes in the supportive tissues. After tooth loss there is a tendency for *resorption* of the alveolar bone forming the supporting ridges, leaving flat ridges that make stabilization of dentures inadequate.

Denture wearers ubiquitously complain of sore mouths, poor chewing capacity, and the constant fear of losing their teeth at embarrassing moments. Widely advertised dental adhesives are distasteful and generally short lived in effectiveness. The elderly denture wearer must be educated to realize that the devices are a compromise – a useful though inefficient substitute for lost teeth.

Dental Caries

Pathologic dental conditions in the aged present a somewhat different pattern than in younger groups. Dental caries, or tooth decay, is the greatest cause of tooth loss up to age 35, but subsequently periodontal disease becomes the greatest source of

tooth loss (Hatton, Gogan, and Hatton, 1989). Dental decay continues to occur in older people, however, and the effects of earlier dental caries persist in the form of missing teeth and the use of dental plates in later years. There is strong research and clinical evidence indicating increased rates of root caries in the elderly. For example, Baum (1981a, 1981b) found that persons over age 60 had four times more root caries than those under 40.

Three factors are present in caries production: (1) a more or less susceptible tooth, (2) bacterial plaque on the surface of the tooth, and (3) a dietary substrate such as carbohydrates. A variety of oral bacteria are capable of causing tooth decay, but the major culprit appears to be *Streptococcus mutans,* which readily ferments monosaccharides and disaccharides to lactic acid.

The process of tooth decay starts with the formation of a sticky, viscous film called *plaque* in which bacteria grow, multiply, metabolize food debris, and convert carbohydrates to organic acids. The plaque protects the decay bacteria from normal oral cleansing. Organic acids, such as lactic acid, make contact with the tooth enamel and demineralize tooth hydroxyapatite. This in turn allows the bacterial proteolysis of tooth collagen, creating cavities. The amount of decalcification and decay seems to be related to the length of time caries-causing bacteria are in contact with the tooth.

Sucrose is prominent in the decay process in three ways. It is easily converted by bacterial enzymes to dextrans and levans, which form the structural basis of plaque; in the plaque itself, it serves as a reserve food supply for bacteria, remaining available even after all traces of a meal have disappeared from the oral cavity; it is readily converted to lactic acid by bacterial action.

The role of saliva in the process of tooth decay is still unclear. It has been suggested that it helps clear food residues and neutralizes the acid medium essential for decay. Urea in the saliva may be converted to ammonia by *ureolytic* microbes in the plaque resulting in a higher pH. Others have suggested that saliva may serve as an ionic source of fluorine, calcium, and phosphorus, all of which are incorporated into the tooth surface structures.

It is difficult to determine the effects of specific nutrients on caries development. Tooth resistance is a developmental phenomenon, so an earlier nutrient imbalance may affect resistance to decay later in life. A number of nutrients have been implicated in the process of tooth decay, including protein, fat, phosphate, a variety of trace elements, and simple carbohydrates. Protein may protect against tooth decay by increasing the salivary *urea* and ammonia levels to neutralize the pH, promoting an immune response that may inhibit bacterial colonization and generally assuring the integrity of body tissues. Fat seems to have cariostatic effects such as increasing antimicrobial activity, reducing the time and quantity of food that is retained in teeth, increasing flow of saliva, and aiding in the production of a protective film on the teeth (DePaola and Alfano, 1977).

It is possible that phosphates cleanse the teeth and aid in remineralization of tooth surfaces. The calcium-to-phosphorus ratio may also be related to caries development. Mann (1962) found a calcium-phosphorus ratio of 0.55 to be associated with few or no caries. A number of other trace elements — molybdenum, strontium, vanadium, lithium, barium, and boron — are described as cariostatic, whereas lead and selenium have been associated with cariogenesis (Glass, 1973). The systematic effects of most of these trace elements on tooth resistance are still unclear.

Fluorine has been shown to influence caries development through a variety of mechanisms that are still not fully understood. Its ingestion during tooth development can reduce caries by 60 percent, and topical applications after eruption can lead to reductions of 20 percent (DePaola and Alfano, 1977). Stam and Banting (1980) found in-

creased rates of root caries with age, but the older residents of a nonfluoridated community had twice as many untreated and filled root surface lesions. In one way, fluorine appears to be related to the formation of a stabilized enamel, *apatite,* which resists dissolution by organic acids. In another way, fluorine's effects may be related to the promotion of recrystallization of carious teeth. Some fluorine ions seem to replace hydroxide ions in the apatite (fluoroxyapatite), forming an acid-insoluble matrix that is fixed for the life of the tooth. It may also affect the efficiency of plaque formation or the capacity of some microbes to break down sugars to acids.

Dietary supplements in the form of fluoride tablets are apparently not practical, as they are rapidly cleared from the body and it is hard to deliver the exact amounts needed physiologically. Fluorine added to salt at the level of 90 mg of fluorine per kilogram of salt can result in a 30 to 40 percent reduction in decay. At present, fluoride is added to water supplies throughout the United States and is most effective at levels of 0.7 to 1.2 parts per million (ppm) of drinking water. Levels of about 1.5 ppm can result in discolored or mottled teeth.

Although fluorine and phosphorus appear to be cariostatic, selenium, magnesium, calcium, lead, silicon, and platinum have been reported as caries-promoting. Also, deficiencies of vitamin C, zinc, and protein may increase the pathologic potential of oral bacteria by allowing easier penetration of the teeth by bacterial toxins.

Simple carbohydrates have been strongly implicated in the promotion of tooth decay. The form of the sugar and the length of retention in the mouth appear to be more important than the amount. The physical consistency of a food is related to retention and hence to cariogenic potential; solid foods are worse than liquids, and sticky foods such as caramel, sweet pastry, ice cream, and syrups are the most troublesome. The circumstances surrounding consumption also play an important role. For example, sugar at mealtime or with liquids is less cariogenic than it is between meals. It has also been suggested that sugary foods containing phosphates are less of a threat because of the cariostatic influence of phosphates.

General advice concerning diet and dental decay should include the elimination or reduced use of cariogenic foods, the addition of potentially caries-protective foods such as fats and proteins, and the inclusions of foods that require strong mastication.

Although caries constitute a less serious problem in later years, prevention of the condition should be a significant part of health maintenance among the aging. Previous caries experience determines the number and quality of teeth carried into old age, and the maintenance of healthy teeth should continue. The number and condition of the teeth affect the efficiency of the digestive process and can influence dietary intake. Also, the presence of healthy teeth is important for the anchorage of a partial dental plate, which is functionally preferable to a full plate.

Periodontal Disease

Periodontal disease is the leading cause of tooth loss after age 35. After reviewing data from two nationwide studies, Douglas, Gillings, Sollecito, and Gammon (1983) report that 58.9 percent of men aged 65 to 74 years and 43 percent of women in the same age group were affected by periodontal disease.

When only the gums and soft tissues are involved, the periodontal condition is referred to as *gingivitis*. When bone is also affected, it is called *periodontitis*. Systematic factors involving hormones and nutrition as well as plaque formation are important in the etiology of periodontal conditions (Bahn, 1970). The process of periodontal deterioration is initiated by bacterial action in the gingival crevices. It appears that older people develop a greater susceptibility to microbial plaque, with severe periodontal involvement (Holm-Pederson, Agerback, and Theilade, 1975). Plaque develops, causing one of the most concentrated bacterial populations known to affect human beings. The gum margins fall away from contact with the teeth, and the process invades the bone and eventually affects the periodontal ligament, which can lead to tooth loss. Chronic infection associated with this process can also lead to tooth loss.

Nutritional status affects an individual's susceptibility to periodontal disease. It may exert its influence by promoting an immune response, enhancing tissue integrity, and affecting the production of saliva and gingival fluid. Tough, fibrous foods may be effective in removing plaque. Tough foods also help minimize gland atrophy and encourage increased saliva flow with a higher protein content (Alfano, 1976), although there is little conclusive evidence at this time that saliva actively deters periodontal disease.

As in caries development, soft and sticky carbohydrate foods are an effective medium for bacterial growth, especially beneath the gum margin. Calculus or tartar, a hard deposit of calcium salts, mucin, and bacteria, is also associated with periodontal disease. The cause of tarter formation is obscure; it may simply be an advanced form of plaque. It appears that the massaging effect of rough food prevents its formation.

Lutwak (1976) has suggested that periodontal disease may be, in part, a form of nutritional osteoporosis, in which the dietary factor is a chronic dietary deficiency of calcium in association with an excess of dietary phosphorus. American diets are notably high in phosphorus because of the large amounts of meat, poultry, fish, milk, and flour consumed. Milk consumption has generally been declining in the American diet, and milk has often been replaced by soft drinks that are notably unbalanced in their calcium/phosphorus ratios. As evidence, Lutwak (1976) cites retrospective studies that link the appearance of vertebral osteoporosis and periodontal disease, and the severity of axial osteoporosis and edentulousness. Clinical evidence that calcium supplementation can do more than halt the progress of osteoporosis has not been produced; but, from a preventive point of view, a proper calcium/phosphorus ratio should be emphasized for dietary intake during the earlier adult decades.

ESOPHAGUS

We are generally taught that the esophagus is a part of the gastrointestinal tract that simply acts as a tube connecting the oral cavity with the stomach. Most people are barely aware of its existence and even less worried that it might malfunction. During the aging process, however, this part of the tract may become a great concern for many.

A number of symptoms associated with the esophagus become more common with advancing age (Sonies, Parent, Morrish, and Baum, 1988). Among these are difficulty in swallowing (dysphagia), substernal pain, heartburn, belching, and general epigastric discomfort. Any of these conditions can be a sign of great danger. Difficulty in swallowing can be related to stroke, Parkinson's disease, *diabetes mellitus*, pseudobulbar palsy, bronchial tumors, carcinoma of the esophagus, or, more often, the general loss of motility that comes with advancing age. Heartburn, belching, substernal pain, and epigastric discomfort can be related to aberrant peristalsis or defects in sphincter relaxation which in turn may be related to age changes in the nerve tissue that stimulates these actions.

Esophageal pain can be readily confused with cardiac-related pain. More often such pains are caused by gastric reflux, *esophagitis,* and/or diffuse muscular spasms of the sphincters. In general, esophageal pain can be distinguished from cardiac pain by its response to antacids and *anticholinergics*

and by its characteristic burning sensation rather than suffocating pressure. Esophageal pain is most often brought on in response to changes in posture (such as stooping, lying down, or straining) as well as through the ingestion of too much food. Much relief can be obtained by avoiding postural stresses and by eating smaller and more frequent meals. More recently, the role of hiatus hernia in reflux has been reevaluated by some researchers who feel that a competent lower esophageal sphincter is the most important antireflux barrier (Castell, 1975).

Hiatus hernia can lead to a number of esophageal symptoms or complicate other existing conditions. There are basically two types of hiatus hernia: the common sliding type (Figure 9.1) and the paraesophageal type. In the common sliding type, the junction of the esophagus and the cardiac portion of the stomach move above the normal position at the diaphragm and lead to gastric reflux. In the paraesophageal type, a portion of the cardiac end of the stomach herniates through the diaphragm hiatus alongside the esophagus.

Hiatus hernia appears to be increasing in incidence. The majority of affected individuals are over 50 years old, and women appear to be affected more than men. In an early study, Brick and Amory (1950) observed it in only 18 percent of their subjects below the age of 50 but in 28 percent of those over age 70. McGinty (1971) noted that hiatus hernia occurs in as many as 65 percent of those over 60 and most often in obese women; recently Levitan (1989a, 1989b) cites research that indicates 70 percent of patients over 65 exhibit hiatal hernia.

Hiatus hernia can occasionally lead to such complications as esophagitis and ulceration stricture of the esophagus; surgical correction is rarely recommended and usually has a slim chance of success. Medical management such as weight reduction, changes in the size and frequency of meals, medication, and sometimes sleeping with the head of the bed elevated six inches can bring relief.

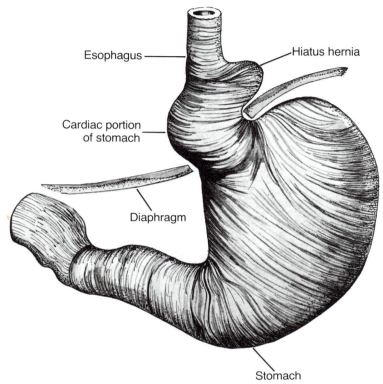

Esophagus

Hiatus hernia

Cardiac portion
of stomach

Diaphragm

Stomach

FIGURE 9.1 Hiatus hernia

Although most disorders of the esophagus are not terminal, there is a steady rise in the incidence of carcinoma of the esophagus with age (Langman, 1971). The average age at diagnosis is 60. *Squamous carcinoma* accounts for 5 to 7 percent of all forms of malignancy (McKeown, 1965) and about one in five of these cases occur in those over 70. Most tumors are located in the distal portion and are prevalent in men. The greater number of tumors in the distal portion may be a statistical artifact of the inclusion of cardioesophageal junction tumors in this category.

The carcinoma can be the cause of great suffering in an elderly patient. The two most common symptoms are chronic difficulty in swallowing and esophageal spasms of long duration. Excessive salivation, which is often related to an obstruction or irritation of the esophagus such as that produced by malignancy, may accompany these conditions. Thirst, hiccups, bleeding, and anemia are also common with these conditions. The causes of esophageal carcinoma are unclear, but some researchers have suggested relationships to smoking, alcoholism, *achalasia,* and dietary practices. Treatment with an esophagectomy has a mortality rate of 20 percent and a five-year survival rate of 5 percent. Many patients are not physically up to surgery anyway. In general most treatment is *palliative,* including radiation therapy, and the prognosis is grave.

STOMACH

Although little absorption of nutrients takes place in the stomach, the digestive process (except for the minor action of *ptyalin* in the mouth) starts in this organ. Basically, gastric juice contains *hydrochloric acid, pepsin, lipase,* and *mucin,* which initiates the digestion of proteins and some fats. It seems that a number of alterations of the stomach occur with advancing age, but researchers disagree on how much change occurs and the rate of such change. One thing on which most researchers agree is that hyperacidity becomes rare, but hypoacidity and *achlorhydria* increase in incidence.

According to Fikry and Aboul-Wafa (1965), atrophic changes in the gastric mucosa initially affects acidity and fat digestion; later, the production of *pepsinogen* needed in protein digestion is affected, and finally the production of mucin is affected. Mucin protects the stomach from its own juices. These changes are caused by the active role of the normal gastric mucosa in the production of stomach acid, lipase, pepsinogen, and mucin. Bertolini (1969) has suggested that the change from acid to alkaline pH affects the intestinal floral growth of older people. This can lead to some nutritional deficiencies because the intestinal flora are active in both the use and synthesis of essential nutrients. Russell (1986) feels that changes in gastric secretion of acid and pepsin could result in impaired digestion and/or absorption of iron, calcium, copper, zinc, folic acid, B_{12}, and protein.

The three most common categories of stomach disorder are *gastritis, peptic ulcer,* and *gastric carcinoma. Gastritis,* which can be acute, is usually caused by some type of injury to the gastric mucosa, such as that associated with drugs, alcohol, or some bacterial toxins. Chronic gastritis, on the other hand, can be of two types, chronic hypertrophic gastritis and chronic atrophic gastritis. The former is characterized by burning, gnawing pains, and indigestion and must be diagnosed by a gastro-scope because barium radiographs give the appearance of normality. There does not appear to be much of a change in the gastric acid, but the gastroscopic examination reveals prominent and inflamed *rugae.* Atrophic gastritis is used to categorize a wide variety of gastric inflammations with a range of symptoms from very vague epigastric discomfort to very painful acute flare-ups. Krasinski (1986) found the prevalence of atrophic gastritis in healthy Bostonians over age 60 to be 20 percent and in those over age 80 to be 40 percent; while Bird, Hall, and Schade (1977) found it in 68 percent of 657 consecutive elderly patients admitted to a geriatrics unit. The disorder is associated with reduced acid secretion, mucosal atrophy, chronic *pancreatitis,* and alcoholism. Russell (1986) speculates that the presence of atrophic gastritis could decrease the bioavailability of zinc and calcium associated with high-fiber diets. Dietary and medical management is the most common approach to these disorders.

Ulcers (Figure 9.2) do not change in old age, although the symptoms may be atypical. Many cases are asymptomatic. Weight loss, anemia, and painless vomiting (sometimes with blood) are common signs in the elderly, but perforation is rare and great pain may be absent. A number of peptic ulcers in the elderly probably represent chronic ulcers acquired in middle age, when they are far more prevalent. First-time cases are rare in old age, but the prognosis for recovery is good. Peptic ulcers at advanced ages have a poorer prognosis, with more than two out of three ulcer deaths being caused by peptic or gastric ulcers.

Deaths from peptic ulcers are increasing at a time when deaths from stomach cancer are decreasing. Because many of the aged take a great number of medications for multiple problems, drug-induced ulcers are not uncommon. Drugs can increase gastric secretions and lower the resistance of the gastric mucosa, thus leading to ulcer development. Aspirin, phenylbutazone, and corticosteroids are examples of drugs associated with ulcer development.

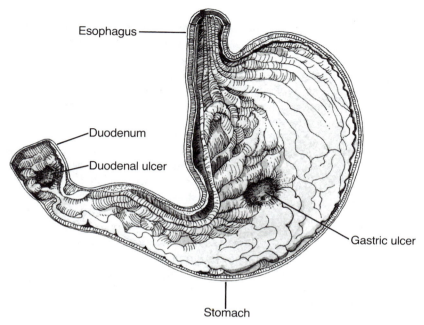

FIGURE 9.2 Gastric and duodenal ulcers

Preferred treatment for peptic ulcers should be conservative. Bed rest, an important part of ulcer therapy in younger patients, is not recommended for older people because some of the problems associated with immobilization (embolism, for example) are more serious than the ulcer. Ulcer diets have proved to be of little value in older people. Failure to heal within six weeks points toward a malignancy and possible surgery, although this is generally reserved for special cases such as pyloric obstruction. In England, McKeown (1965) observed that gastric ulcers make up 10 percent of all the ulcers in those over age 60; one-third of all ulcer deaths were in the 60-plus age group.

Recently, for unknown reasons, the incidence of stomach cancer has been declining, but it still remains a common tumor with an unfavorable prognosis. It is more common in men, people over 60 years of age, and those with type A blood. Stomach cancer reaches its peak incidence in the eighth and ninth decades of life. There are a few hints that it may be familial. Those with *pernicious anemia* and atrophy of gastric mucosa seem to have a higher probability of being affected. The most common sites are in the *pylorus* and *antrum,* but any portion of the organ can be affected.

Often symptoms are nonspecific and may involve weight loss, loss of appetite, malaise, and anemia, with some epigastric discomfort possible. This situation can lead to self-medication with antacids and thus delay diagnosis. The more classic signs of nausea, indigestion, difficulty in swallowing, bloody vomit, and tarry stools will manifest themselves in many cases. Differentiating gastric ulcers and carcinoma by symptoms is very difficult. The early symptoms and initial response to the treatment of symptoms are often similar, but persistent weight loss, bleeding, and anemia are suggestive of cancer. The size and location of lesions are poor indicators for differential diagnosis, but a lesion plus achlorhydria also suggests cancer.

Diagnosis can be best accomplished by gastroscopy because a cytologic sample can give an accuracy of 85 to 95 percent. Radical surgery is often contraindicated in the elderly because of its high risk. Those experiencing such surgery show a five-year survival rate of only 5 to 10 percent. Radiotherapy and chemotherapy are also of little help.

SMALL INTESTINE

Few changes occur in the small intestine, because cell renewal continues in this organ well into old age (Corazza, Frazzoni, Gatto, and Gasbarrini, 1986). Malignant tumors of the small intestine are rare, although changes in other organs such as the liver, gallbladder, pancreas, and kidney can alter the functioning of the small intestine. A great deal of medical information is lacking on the aging of the small intestine. Testing and research procedures are complex and make excessive demands on both the elderly patient and the researcher.

In the *duodenum* there are two major problems associated with old age, *diverticula* and peptic ulcers. Duodenal diverticula were thought to be rare, but Bockus (1966) estimates that 10 percent of those over 55 years of age have them and that they increase in number with age. Diverticula are highly associated with complications such as osteomalacia, iron deficiency anemia, and B_{12} and folate deficiency, as well as general intestinal malabsorption. Thus, in elderly persons, a vitamin deficiency or intestinal malabsorption might lead one to suspect duodenal diverticula as the basis. Surgery is rarely indicated. Patients seem to respond well to antibiotic therapy using septrin and lincomycin.

Duodenal ulcers are more frequent than gastric ulcers, and the risk is no greater in the elderly.

Symptoms may present themselves differently because of diminished pain sensation in the elderly; surgery is usually not recommended because of its high risk. Therapy includes antacids and often anticholinergics; both precipitate diarrhea, constipation, and urinary retention. A switch to a greater number of smaller meals (for example, six per day) of nonirritating foods will help keep the stomach from being empty and may act to neutralize stomach acid. Many researchers believe that the conventional bland diet does not promote ulcer healing and is too difficult for the patient to follow. The stress involved in trying to follow a special diet religiously may counteract any positive effects. A commonsense approach to diet that considers the individual patient's needs, abilities, and attitudes is important.

Upper gastrointestinal bleeding in the elderly should be evaluated to determine its origin. It can come from a variety of sources, such as peptic ulcers. Persons affected by cirrhosis will bleed not only from the varices but also from gastritis, ulcers, and gastric erosion, which is often associated with cirrhosis. The incidence of such bleeding ranges from about 15 to 40 percent of cases. Gastric erosion often produced by heavy aspirin use can lead to bleeding. *Ischemia, polyps, fibromas, lipomas,* and *lymphomas* can also lead to upper gastrointestinal bleeding.

Tarry blood in the stool indicates an upper gastrointestinal source, whereas bright red blood indicates a large bowel disorder. Sometimes a sluggish large bowel can lead to tarry stools, and a rapid transit time from the upper tract can result in bright red blood in the stool. Whatever the cause, bleeding from the upper tract should not be summarily dismissed by a simple diagnosis.

Malignant tumors of the small intestine are rare but are more frequent in men. They tend to affect the distal section more than the proximal. The appendix is the most common site, but it does not *metastasize* readily. The *ileum* is the next most common site, but tumors here are usually more malignant and frequently multiple.

Intestinal obstruction is one of the more common problems of the aging tract, usually falling into one of two classes, mechanical or paralytic. Table 9.1 compares the two conditions as to causes, symptoms, and diagnosis. Mechanical obstructions are usually treated by surgery and paralytic obstructions by medical treatment such as antibiotic therapy and fluid replacement.

Appendicitis in the aged has a higher mortality rate than in the rest of the population (7 percent versus 1 percent) and as high as 23 percent in those over 80 (Smithy, Wexner, and Dailey, 1986). This may be the result of a number of factors: (1) the misconception that appendicitis is rare in the elderly, (2) delayed diagnosis and treatment, (3) early perforation, (4) mildness of the symptoms, and (5) greater incidence of preexisting disease associated with it (Rossman, 1971).

TABLE 9.1 Obstructions of the small intestines

	Mechanical	Paralytic
Causes	Adhesions, volvulus, worms, diverticulitis, hernias, tumors, gallstones, fecoliths	Pneumonia, pancreatitis, biliary colic, ureteral calculus, myocardial infarction, septicemia, hematoma, hypopotassemia, thrombus of mesentery, peritonitis
Symptoms	Cramped severe pain, vomiting, distension, constipation, borborygmi present (gas)	Absent or mild pain, vomiting, distension, constipation, borborygmi absent (gas)
Diagnosis	Plain radiograph shows fluid levels in distended loops; barium enema shows obstruction	Plain radiograph same as mechanical; barium enema shows no point of obstruction

Source: Adapted from I. Rossman (Ed.), *Clinical Geriatrics* (Philadelphia: J. B. Lippincott, 1986).

Appendectomy appears desirable unless perforation with abscess has occurred; then drainage would be the wisest course, followed by surgery later on. There is a strong correlation between delay in presentation of symptoms and perforation. Decreased vascularity, thinning of the mucosa, fibrosis of the musculature, fatty infiltration of the wall, and luminal narrowing have been observed in the elderly appendix and may be related to the rapid progression of inflammation resulting in early perforation and abscess formations (Freund and Rubenstein, 1984). The incidence of perforation in the elderly ranges from 32 to 73 percent (Freund and Rubenstein, 1984). Nonoperative management, which might be necessary in some high-risk elderly, calls for bowel rest and antibiotic therapy followed by a carefully planned appendectomy at a later date.

A number of rare but serious conditions such as potassium deficiency, related to thiazide use by heart patients, and abdominal angina also occur in the small bowel. For a more complete description and inventory of these disorders, the reader is referred to more detailed texts in geriatric medicine and gastroenterology (e.g., Brocklehurst, 1973).

The small intestine is the most important portion of the gastrointestinal tract with respect to both digestion and absorption of food. It is supplied with enzymes from the pancreas, bile from the *hepatobiliary* system, and enzymes from its own intestinal mucosa. Its absorptive surface is increased many times by the fingerlike projections know as villi. Still, it is the portion of the gastrointestinal tract about which the least is known with respect to the effects of aging.

A number of age changes have been identified, but researchers are not in agreement about them. It appears that a decrease in the size and the permeability of the capillary bed is a very important change. At the same time, other changes diminish the elasticity of the blood vessels and the lungs. These changes have important implications for the effectiveness of nutrient absorption and the possibility of blood vessel blockage or obstruction. Delay in peripheral nerve transmission and vasomotor response is important, given that the operation of the gastrointestinal system is under neurohormonal control.

Beginning at about age 40, there is a diminution of pancreatic enzymes, which are secreted into the small intestine. Few hard data exist that indicate age-related changes in the intestinal glands. A change in the composition of the bacterial flora of the intestine has been documented. These changes in the ecology of the gut can be detrimental. Reduction of gastric acidity and enzymes can lead to rapid growth of organisms such as the streptococci at the expense of the normal organisms of the gut. The replacement of these normal organisms results in a loss of many of the vitamins they synthesize. The overgrowth of ecologically foreign organisms can lead to lowered resistance of the tract as well as to an irritated and inflamed mucosal lining.

Abnormal bacterial growth can bind vitamin B_{12} and affect its availability for the individual's use. Some bacteria deconjugate bile salts; this depletes the bile salt pool available for fat metabolism. By-products of deconjugation may actually be toxic to the gut as well as carcinogenic. Species belonging to Clostridia, Bacteroides, and Veillonella that are not usually found in the small bowel invade from the large bowel and may cause physical damage and create imbalances in the small intestine environment. Treatment in the short term usually involves antibiotic therapy plus the administration of vitamins. In chronic cases, intermittent antibiotic administration over a long period may be necessary.

In considering the changing absorptive characteristics of the small intestine, one must be aware that the situation in the bowel is complicated by changes occurring elsewhere in the gut. These interrelationships may alter any tests to determine functional changes. It appears that fat and carbohydrate absorption are somewhat curtailed but still remain adequate for normal nutrition. Protein absorption caused by slight enzymatic changes may be impaired to some small degree, especially in relation to changes in the initial stages of protein digestion. This may be related to the reduced *trypsin* activity of the pancreas.

Fat digestion can be impaired by associated hepatobiliary disease (Figure 9.3). After age 20 lipolytic activity seems to be reduced by 20 percent, but apparently without an appreciable effect on fat digestion. Becker, Meyer, and Necheles (1950) observed that aged individuals absorb a high-fat meal in about twice the time it takes for a young adult.

Malabsorption and maldigestion in elderly people are common, and thus it is impossible to deal individually with all the causes or factors that contribute to a *malabsorption* or *maldigestion syndrome*. Some of the conditions that can lead to malabsorption are (Balachi and Dobbins, 1974; Montgomery, Haboubi, Mike, Chester, and Asquith, 1986):

1. Surgical alterations such as esophagectomy, gastrectomy, and small bowel resections
2. Pancreatic insufficiency caused by pancreatitis or a tumor
3. Hepatobiliary insufficiency caused by such conditions as decreased bile acid synthesis, gallstones, and *hepatitis*

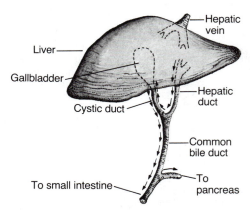

FIGURE 9.3 Hepatobiliary system

4. Stasis and bacterial overgrowth
5. Drug-induced changes caused by alcohol, *anticonvulsants,* cathartics, diuretics, colchicine, and antibiotics
6. Cardiovascular abnormalities such as congestive heart failure, constrictive pericarditis, arteriosclerosis, and intestinal angina
7. Radiation injury caused by accidental, occupational, or therapeutic exposures
8. Endocrinopathy such as diabetes, Addison's disease, and thyroid disease
9. Paget's disease
10. Collagen vascular disease
11. Amyloidosis
12. Celiac sprue
13. Neoplastic disease
14. Paraproteinemia such as *multiple myeloma*

Malabsorption syndromes are difficult to manage because the small bowel mucosa are diseased. The best syndromes are treated by parenteral administration of vitamins and minerals or the oral administration of pharmacologic doses rather than physiologic doses of these nutrients. Correction of the underlying cause should be the clinical goal, but often this is impossible (because its cause is not known) or impractical (because medical means are not available). Hence, in most cases of malabsorption, nutritional management is the only way of sustaining the patient. The plan for management must fit the individual case or circumstances.

GALLBLADDER

Gallbladder problems are a major source of concern and stress for many elderly people. The incidence of most gallbladder problems increases markedly after age 65. Changes in the ability to empty the gallbladder and in the physical composition of bile are the most consistent age-related changes. Bertolini (1969) found that bile tends to be thicker, richer in cholesterol, and reduced in volume in the elderly. Statistics indicate an increase in the incidence of *gallstones* with age. Glen (1981) reported that 25 to 30 percent of those aged 50 to 60, and 55 percent of those over 80 had gallstones, compared to only 10 percent of people younger than 30. Ponka, Welborn, and Brush (1963) found that 55 out of 200 aged patients with abdominal pain had gallstones. Stones are more common in elderly women than in men, but after age 70 sex differences are insignificant. Those with diabetes, on estrogen therapy, and with bile absorption problems have a high risk of developing gallstones.

Most cases of gallstones in the elderly appear to be asymptomatic. The most common manifestations are indigestion, nausea, vomiting, *fat intolerance, obstructive jaundice,* and episodes of *cholecystitis* (Harness, Strodel, and Talsma, 1986). The pain associated with gallstones is generally located in the upper right quadrant just below the rib cage, or in the right shoulder. The risk of obstruction of the common or cystic ducts is a real threat that can lead to inflammation, infection, and *stasis* proximal to the stone. This in turn can lead to complications such as pancreatitis, liver problems, and retrograde cholecystitis. The lack of bile in the small intestine can lead to deficiencies of the fat-soluble vitamins. As a precaution, vitamin K should be supplemented when preparing such persons for surgery.

The course of treatment for gallstones is at issue among surgeons. Some prefer to perform surgery in an effort to forestall complications, even if the person is asymptomatic (Margrotta, Horowitz, Willis, and Wallack, 1988). Surgery involves some added risks for the elderly: The mortality for those over 70 is 7 percent, compared to only 1 percent for those below age 60 (Hyams, 1973). However, emergency surgery has a higher mortality rate (11 percent) than elective surgery.

Stones in the common bile duct are increasingly prevalent among the elderly in the United States. If these are not removed, cholangitis or stricture may occur, with a mortality rate of 20 percent (Johnson and Hosking, 1987). Others believe that a more conservative approach with emphasis on medical management is the best course of action. This latter attitude is based on the increased risks of surgery, the fact that incidence of carcinoma of the gallbladder is low, the possibility that other diseases or conditions may be causing the symptoms, and the general mental stress imposed by surgery.

Medical treatment usually consists of a program of weight reduction, avoidance of fatty foods, and the use of antacids. Some studies have shown that diets high in wheat bran, guar gum, and pectin reduced the lithogenic index. Hospitalization is based on the severity of symptoms, the condition of the patient, and an assessment of the overall risks associated with ambulatory or home treatment. Of course, surgical removal (cholecystectomy) is generally supported in acute situations such as obstruction, *cholangitis,* and other possible life-threatening situations.

Carcinoma of the gallbladder is a very rare condition but occurs more often in women than men; it is three times more common in those over age 70. Its diagnosis is very difficult because it is often confused with liver carcinoma or mistaken as a manifestation of liver metastasis from more common cancer sites such as the stomach. It is often associated with chronic calculous cholecystitis. Treatment is not promising. Prognosis is very poor, with an average life expectancy of six months.

LIVER

The liver is the largest gland and one of the most important of the body's organs. It metabolizes and stores carbohydrates, fats, proteins, minerals, and vitamins and acts as a detoxifying and bactericidal agent. It also controls the production and secretion of bile. It does not decrease in size with age, and its percentage of body weight, 2.5 percent, remains the same until about age 70, when it starts to decline until it reaches about 1.6 percent of body weight by the tenth decade (Morgan and Feldman, 1967). Haberman (1962) estimated that three out of four aged persons have one or more functional abnormalities of the liver. However, Rosenberg, Russell, and Bowman (1989) found no age-related changes in liver functions in the normal elderly. They also note that age restrictions on liver transplants have been removed because older livers perform as well as younger livers.

There is little evidence for cell loss with age, so it is likely that liver abnormalities are caused by changes in cell function such as slight anatomic changes or the changing interaction between spatially related cells (Shock, 1964). Tauchi and Sato (1968) noted a reduction in the number of mitochondria in aging liver cells. This phenomenon is not accompanied by decline of liver function. It may be caused by the increased size of aging cells, which produce more enzyme, or by the oxidative capacity of older cells.

Certain enzymes capable of catabolizing protein increase production with age. This leads to a slightly reduced capability of the aging liver to synthesize protein. Thompson and Williams (1965) found linear decreased storage capacity with age, but the secretory transport maximum was not altered. Calloway and Merrill (1965) affirmed these observations in their research. It is possible that synthesis of certain enzyme systems can be maintained while general synthetic activity of the organ is decreasing. Despite obvious anatomic and physiologic changes, the functional capacity of the aged liver remains within the range of normal variation, but the elderly are common recipients of hepatotoxic drugs and combinations of chemical agents that could interfere with liver clearance.

Jaundice is a common manifestation of liver disease. It can be associated with cirrhosis, drug effects, and hepatitis. It appears that about half the cases of jaundice are caused by the benign disorders just mentioned, and the other half are caused by carcinoma of the pancreas or hepatobiliary tract. In cases of undetermined jaundice, one must go through a four- to six-week observation period to allow for subsidence, rather than performing surgery (Rossman, 1968).

Cirrhosis of the liver is the most serious or final stage of liver injury and degeneration. The liver is contracted and loses most of its ability to function, and once a fibrous connective tissue replaces the liver cells the condition is irreversible. Cirrhosis is the fifth most common cause of death in the United States today. It is positively associated with chronic alcoholism, which itself is an important disorder in the elderly (Scott and Mitchell, 1988).

The nature of the relationship between cirrhosis and alcoholism is still being debated. One current view holds that cirrhosis is a result of the interaction of chronic alcoholism and long-term nutritional deficiencies, from which most alcoholics suffer. Such deficiencies can lead to fatty liver and eventual fibrosis of the liver. The liver is more susceptible to damage from toxic agents and infectious organisms when there is a nutritional deficiency.

Diet is an important aspect in the treatment of cirrhosis. It seems that a diet high in calories from carbohydrates and proteins, with moderate amounts of fats and provisions of vitamins, is the best for maximum recovery. It allows for the repair of hepatic cells and supports hepatic function. Vitamin supplements and liver extract are often recommended. Protein should be rich in lipotrophic factors, which mobilize liver fat and thus act to prevent fatty infiltration and degeneration of the liver cells. Because the appetite is often poor, six to eight small meals a day would be most effective.

Viral hepatitis is an infectious disease of the liver that is becoming more common in older people, although it still is primarily a disease of the young. In the young it is usually a rather mild disease, but in the elderly it can be quite serious, resulting in a progressive liver disease such as cirrhosis. Complete bed rest is mandatory, with an accompanying diet high in carbohydrates and protein supplemented with B complex vitamins (Brewer's yeast) and vitamin K. Fat need not be restricted, as once thought, but alcohol is totally forbidden. Serum hepatitis is similar in causes and symptoms but is transferred by injection from a carrier to a victim. It is a more serious condition, but treatment is basically the same, with some persons requiring hospitalization. The elderly may contract serum hepatitis through transfusions and the use of poorly sterilized medical equipment and needles for drugs. It is more common in older men who take drugs or sell their blood for an alcohol stake.

PANCREAS

The pancreas is an important component of both the gastrointestinal and endocrine systems. It is under both hormonal and neurologic control and is thus subject to the effects of age changes in those systems. The specific changes in the pancreas are both enzymatic and structural. The organ pancreas exhibits an age-related reduction of the pancreatic proteolytic enzyme activity from age 40 onward. Trypsin is one of the most important proteolytic enzymes; it splits the larger protein molecules (polypeptides) into smaller ones (peptides), which the intestinal enzymes reduce further. Without trypsin, protein digestion could be seriously impaired, although the evidence for impairment is conflicting. Bartos and Groh (1969) stimulated the pancreas by single doses of *pancreozymins* and secretin and induced similar volumes of pancreatic juice in subjects of various ages. They also observed that with repeated stimulation, the volume of pancreatic juices decreases with increasing age. According to Gullo, Ventrucci, Naldoni, and Pezzilli (1986), the great reserve capacity of the secretory cells in the pancreas prevents the impairment of digestion.

Structurally, the major changes in the pancreas are reduced alveolar cell generation, *adipose* and *amyloid infiltration,* and the obstruction of the pancreatic ducts. These conditions are major causes of pancreatitis. However, Gullo and his associates examined pancreatic function in a population of 66 to 88 years old and found some minor changes but none that were clinically significant (Gullo et al., 1986).

The symptoms of pancreatic disease, except for acute pancreatitis, are vague. Pain is the most common symptom. However, Rittenbury (1961) observed that 12 percent of his patients over 60 did not exhibit pain. Acute pancreatitis can be confused with gallstones or other diseases of the hepatobiliary tract. Nausea and vomiting are usually associated with acute pancreatitis rather than with carcinoma. Loss of appetite, weight loss, general weakness, and epigastric pain radiating into the back and abdomen, as well as tenderness and rigidity of the abdomen, are usual symptoms of acute pancreatitis. Acute pancreatitis presents a picture of a critically ill patient who may be unconscious, hallucinating, severely disoriented, and/or in a state of severe pain. Immediate hospitalization and application of intensive care are required.

Chronic pancreatitis is associated with loss of appetite, loss of weight, general weakness, jaundice, and constipation, but less diarrhea than one finds in younger age groups. It can usually be managed at home with the use of anticholinergics and dietary restrictions. Patients may experience persistent pain that requires consideration and understanding.

Carcinoma of the pancreas has been a rare malignancy in those over 60, but it is more common in men. It is, however, increasing steadily and has become the fourth most common death-causing cancer in the United States. The sixth decade is the period of peak incidence, and the male/female ratio is 3:1. This cancer is very difficult to diagnose early and is often confused with either peptic ulcer, chronic pancreatitis, or liver disease. In 60 percent of the cases, it involves the head of the pancreas; it most often metastasizes to the liver, lungs, and bones. The general symptoms of loss of appetite, wasting weakness, and weight loss are similar to those of chronic pancreatitis, but in carcinoma there is epigastric pain that radiates to the back and is relieved by bending forward. Indigestion characterized by belching, heartburn, and nausea are common, along with constipation and diarrhea. Persistent painless development of obstructive jaundice usually is indicative of carcinoma.

Blood may be present in the stools, but anemia is rare. People with diabetes have a higher incidence of pancreatic carcinoma, and in possibly one-third of the cases it can result in diabetes because of the destruction of the *islets of Langerhans*. Diagnosis may involve the use of radioactive protoscan, pancreatic angiography, and serologic analysis of serum lipase, *amylase,* and alkaline phosphatase levels.

Emotional disturbances in the form of depression occur in about three out of four cases. Psychiatric and general supportive assistance are often necessary. Treatment is merely palliative to relieve pain and discomfort. The effectiveness of both surgery and chemotherapy is poor, and the prognosis is very poor.

LARGE INTESTINE

The picture of clinical problems in the large bowel is almost exclusive to the elderly. It also presents a complex of possibly interrelated syndromes that are amenable to the application of preventive medicine.

Little attention has been paid to age-related anatomic and physiologic changes in the large bowel. The anatomic changes that may be of significance are atrophy of the mucosa and of the connective tissue, morphologic abnormalities in cell structure, and arteriosclerosis that generally affects the celiac axis and *mesenteric* vessels. Physiologically, the large bowel is not a digestive organ but a storage organ for waste and a major site for water absorption.

Because of its transitory storage function, large bowel motility is important and has been the subject of much research. Studies have attempted to measure motility by the use of balloons and open-ended tubes inserted into the rectum, but measuring pressure is difficult because the colon itself is an open-ended tube. Also, the contraction and inflation of the lower bowel presents a different picture of intra-bowel pressure.

Measuring colonic activity is also problematic because colonic motility is unpredictable and shows significant variation over time within the individual. Motility increases during and after food intake, although this is not usually associated with propulsive activity unless the person is physically active (Holdstock, 1970). Diarrhea and some drugs can cause hypomotility; other drugs, such as morphine, can lead to hypermotility.

Duthie and Bennett (1963) investigated sensation in the anal canal and noted a mechanism for recognizing the bolus contained in the rectum by sphincter sensation. This produces the ability to distinguish between feces, fluid, and gas within the rectum, and it is possible that incontinent older people may have an impaired mechanism.

Some research has noted that bearing down and attempted forced defecation can diminish the tone of the external sphincter. Also, in straining, the anterior rectal wall tends to descend following the stool, and it is possible that this can lead to prolapse in those elderly people with a weak pelvic floor.

Constipation is said to be the most common gastrointestinal complaint of the elderly, with a slight predominance in women (Sonnenberg and Koch, 1989). There is no evidence that it is an inevitable outcome of aging. These worries are often symptomatic of a lack of other interests. Concern about constipation may also be a holdover from an era of medicine when irregularity was thought to carry the risk of autointoxication. Many of the elderly today

were raised during a time when a daily bowel movement was considered to be essential for good health. Perhaps this fixation on regularity will disappear as the younger generation becomes older, although the pharmaceutical and advertising industries keep the myth alive today. Of those elderly who claim to be constipated, 25 percent have normal transit time (Eastwood, 1972).

Careful evaluation of constipation in the elderly is important, because it is a possible symptom of underlying disease. The various causes of constipation are as follows:

1. Lesions of the gut (obstruction, idopathic megacolon, aganglionosis)
2. Neurologic trauma or damage
3. Metabolic causes (hypercalcemia, *porphyria*, drugs such as laxatives)
4. Endocrine system (*hypothyroidism*)
5. Psychological causes (depression, stress)
6. General immobility

Lack of exercise and/or unbalanced diet with respect to bulk may also be implicated in cases of constipation. A lifetime of environmental factors such as poor dietary fiber, neglect or high-motility periods, and chronic use of irritant laxatives interact to produce chronic constipation (Castle, 1989).

In treating constipation, an individual approach is most efficient. After the possibility of disease or obstruction has been ruled out, a therapeutic regimen consisting of dietary modification and increased physical activity should be worked out. Laxative dependence may be difficult to eliminate, but a compromise may be generated. Dietary changes are difficult to implement because long-standing food habits often hold great emotional significance. Changes in physical activity may be impossible in many cases. A number of studies indicate that eating wheat bran and other insoluble fibers will increase frequency of defecation and eliminate the need for laxatives (Hope and Down, 1986; Fischer, Adkins, Hall, Scaman, Hsi, and Marlett, 1985).

If fecal impactions are formed, manual removal may be necessary. Enemas may work, but care must be taken to avoid large volume because sudden distension of the colon could rupture it or an existent diverticula. There is also the possibility of inducing shock in an elderly person.

Fecal incontinence is another serious problem in some older persons. It is not a threat to survival but, rather, a challenge to self-image. An alert person can be thoroughly embarrassed and very depressed by the onset of this condition, which rivals urinary incontinence as one of the major problems in the care of the elderly. Fecal incontinence is less frequent than its urinary counterpart and more readily managed, but it is far more unpleasant for patients, medical staff, and the family. Studies in England point out that fecal incontinence is a major problem in long-term care patients. Watkins (1971), for instance, found an incidence of 60 percent in his study of geriatric wards, and Brocklehurst (1951) found 75 percent incontinent in a Glasgow long-term care facility.

The causes of fecal incontinence are diverse and include carcinoma of the colon or rectum, diverticular disease, ischemic colitis, protocolitis, diabetic neuropathy, and the side effects of drug use. Incontinence may also result from hemorrhoidal surgery, which disrupts the anal sphincter. Fecal impaction can be associated with a spurious diarrhea that can be carried around the impacted area. A variety of studies also point to a neurogenic basis for some cases of fecal incontinence in older persons.

Most fecal incontinence is preventable. The basic approach toward prevention involves treating the local causes of fecal impaction by treating the constipation. Treatment of neurogenic-based incontinence involves habit training similar to the potty training of a child. The induction of constipation followed by planned evacuation can make the process predictable and manageable, especially in an insti-

tutional setting. For management in the home, an enema followed by a bisacodyl suppository left in the rectum should complete the process within an hour and a half. By these means, the elderly person may be spared any embarrassment.

Carcinoma of the large bowel is the most common malignancy in those over 70 and second only to lung cancer as a killer among the cancers (McKeown, 1965). Late diagnosis remains a distressing problem despite the fact that over half the carcinomas are within range of the examining finger and about three-fourths are within range of the proctoscope. Five-year survival rates for early presymptomatic cases are 50 percent or higher, and the mortality rates associated with the surgery are low.

Cancer of the colon is more common in women, whereas rectal cancer is more common in men. The percentage involvement by site in the large bowel is shown in Table 9.2. The signs and symptoms vary with the section of the bowel affected. Any sign of change in bowel habits along with loss of appetite, weakness, weight loss, and anemia should be thoroughly investigated. Sometimes colon cancer can be confused with fecal impaction of the rectosigmoid presenting a hard mass, but a carcinoma is usually fixed (Figure 9.4). Treatment generally involves resection of the bowel, and it has the best prognosis of all gastrointestinal carcinomas.

Benign polyps of the bowel, familial polyposis coli, and ulcerative colitis are associated in half the

TABLE 9.2 Differential occurrence of bowel cancer

Rectum	55%
Sigmoid colon	16% to 20%
Right colon	15%
Left colon	10%
Transverse colon	5%

Note: Categories are not mutually exclusive.

Source: Based on information in I. Rossman (Ed.), *Clinical Geriatrics* (Philadelphia: J. B. Lippincott, 1986).

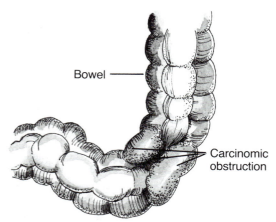

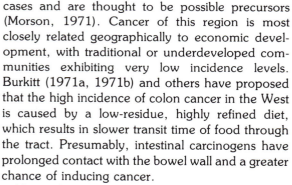

FIGURE 9.4 Carcinomic obstruction of the bowel

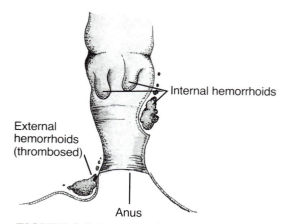

FIGURE 9.5 Internal and external hemorrhoids

cases and are thought to be possible precursors (Morson, 1971). Cancer of this region is most closely related geographically to economic development, with traditional or underdeveloped communities exhibiting very low incidence levels. Burkitt (1971a, 1971b) and others have proposed that the high incidence of colon cancer in the West is caused by a low-residue, highly refined diet, which results in slower transit time of food through the tract. Presumably, intestinal carcinogens have prolonged contact with the bowel wall and a greater chance of inducing cancer.

Hemorrhoids are present in most people over 50 years of age. They consist of ruptured blood vessels that are located around the anal sphincter (Figure 9.5). They can be either external or internal, and they can range from asymptomatic to very painful with bleeding that necessitates surgery. Some of the major causes in the elderly are constipation, prolonged use of cathartics or enemas, and straining at the stool. Dietary treatment can promote healing and make a bowel movement comfortable. In general, eight to ten glasses of water a day and a diet that is balanced but bulk-producing can reduce or prevent hemorrhoids. One should also avoid the

use of harsh laxatives and try to regularize the time of bowel movement each day. The increased incidence of hemorrhoids in the Western world has also been related to a low-fiber diet.

Polyps and benign tumors of the colon are often common in the rectosigmoid area. They can produce bleeding but probably do not cause cancer and are generally treated by simple excision. Familial *adenomatous coli polyps* have a high association with cancer and are treated by a complete colostomy. This is a hereditary disorder, and thus it would be wise to screen an afflicted person's relatives for the condition. Ulcerative colitis also has some pseudopolyps that have a very high carcinogenic potential. Ulcerative colitis exhibits a second peak in those over 60. In the elderly it makes a more rapid appearance, with less systemic involvement and smaller relapse rate.

Ischemic colitis is rarely diagnosed in the elderly, but ischemic bowel diseases are on the increase in this group. This type of colitis is usually the result of an occlusion of the mesenteric arteries because of arteriosclerosis, most often at the splenic flexure, which is the most critical point in the circulation of blood to the bowel. The most common symptoms are abdominal pain and loose stools with red blood or clots. The onset can be sudden and accompanied by intramural gas in the bowel, the result of a bacterial invasion of the bowel wall. Congestive heart failure seems to be an important precipitating factor. Any fear of eating in the elderly should merit consideration of this disorder. Treatment may involve surgical removal of the bowel, especially if stricture is present. The prognosis is poor after surgery, but most cases are transitory.

Diverticular disease of the colon tends to be a disease of the later decades of life, increasing from age 40 onward. By one estimate, these diseases occur in 18 percent of those aged 40 to 59, 19 percent of those 60 to 79 and 42 percent in those over 80 years of age (Minaker and Rowe, 1982). Thompson and Patel (1986) have recently suggested a rise from 5 percent in the fifth decade to 50 percent in the ninth decade. They appear to be increasing in incidence, especially in the industrial nations. Women are affected more often than men, and the overall number of diverticula increase with age. The most common site is the sigmoid colon. McKeown (1965) found the incidence with symptoms to be about 7 percent in those over 70, but symptoms can range from none at all to *peritonitis*. In the United States the risk of developing diverticulosis is 50 percent (Painter and Burkitt, 1985), whereas it is virtually unknown in the developing countries of Asia and Africa.

Diverticula are actually tiny herniations of the mucous and submucous layers through the muscle layer. They form a pocket or balloonlike structure that projects from the bowel about 1 to 2 cm. Fecal matter can collect at the opening of a diverticulum and form fecoliths; these ulcerate the mucosa and promote infection. The symptoms of diverticulitis are abdominal pain, diarrhea or constipation (or alternating bouts of each), and bleeding. Complications are rare, but on occasion diverticula can perforate and give rise to pericoloc abscess, *peritonitis*,

or *fistula* of the bladder, vagina, or other parts of the gut. These conditions call for immediate surgery.

In general, medical management consists of a high-residue diet and antibiotic therapy. The use of a high-residue diet is a complete therapeutic turnabout from the previous treatment, which called for a bland, low-residue diet. Painter and Burkitt (1971) showed that adding bran to the diet as a fiber supplement gave good results in treating diverticular disease. Eastwood, Smith, Brydon, and Pritchard (1978) showed that other types of fiber produced similar results.

In 1900 diverticular disease was practically unknown in the Western world. In the past 75 years it has become the most common affliction of the colon. It may affect over one-third of the population over the age of 50 in the industrial countries, but it is unknown or rare in most developing countries. Burkitt (1971a, 1971b) has proposed that diverticular disease, along with gallstones, hiatus hernia, adenomatous polyps of the large bowel, varicose veins, appendicitis, carcinoma of the large bowel, ischemic heart disease, and even obesity can be associated with a highly refined diet that is short of dietary fiber.

Indigenous African populations eating higher fiber diets have a rapid transit time for food passage through the gastrointestinal tract and large, soft stools. In the industrial societies this is not so; transit times are three to seven days, compared to a little over 30 hours in Africa, and stool weight averages 100 grams a day as compared to 300 grams in Africans. Burkitt believes that viscid feces are more difficult to propel, thus raising the pressure within the lumen of the intestine and, with it, forcing the pouches of the intestine out through weak spots in the muscle layer to form diverticula. At this point the weight of the evidence supports the Burkitt hypothesis, but fiber diets are not a miracle cure-all. It is most likely that diet is but *one* of a complex of factors that are involved in the causes of the disorders cited by Burkitt.

OVER-THE-COUNTER PREPARATIONS FOR GASTROINTESTINAL RELIEF

Because gastrointestinal disturbances are of great concern to many people, over-the-counter remedies are very popular. The remedies most often purchased generally deal with indigestion, constipation, diarrhea, and hemorrhoids. Some of these remedies are simply a waste of money, but the use or misuse of many of them can lead to serious health problems.

Antacids

Antacids are used to treat indigestion but are varied in composition and side effects. Sodium bicarbonate is a basic element in such products as Alka-Seltzer, Bromo-Seltzer, Brioschi, Eno, and Fizrin. Sodium bicarbonate is a patent antacid but the least desirable for regular use. The major problems associated with sodium bicarbonate use are alkalinization of the body fluids, which can lead to kidney stone formation, and recurrent urinary infections. Its use can result in diminished kidney function and can be harmful to those with hypertension or congestive heart failure.

Any antacid that contains more than 115 mg of sodium per maximum daily dose is unsuitable for those on a low-sodium diet. Because many people have undetected kidney and heart disease, people must consider the sodium content of any antacid. Kidney and heart disease tend to increase with age. No one over 60 should take more than 2,300 mg of sodium antacid tablets a day. For example, a heart patient on a 1,000- to 2,000-mg sodium diet could upset the dietary balance with a single dose of many of the sodium bicarbonate antacids. A single dose of Alka-Seltzer contains 1,040 mg of sodium, and a single dose of Bromo-Seltzer contains over 1,496 mg. Each can add significantly to a person's sodium intake if used regularly.

Alka-Seltzer also contains aspirin, which is a stomach irritant and problematic for an ulcer patient. Bromo-Seltzer contains phenacetin and caffeine. The former has been implicated in kidney disease, and the latter stimulates acid secretion in the stomach. These ingredients are unnecessary in antacids. Fizrin contains sodium carbonate, which is obsolete as an antacid and is a highly alkaline irritant that is possibly corrosive. Brioschi and Eno contain only sodium bicarbonate.

Another major group of antacids contains calcium carbonate as the major ingredient. Calcium carbonate is rapid-acting and has a high neutralizing capacity. Tums and Pepto Bismol tablets are the major brands of this type. Calcium carbonate antacids cause constipation and raise calcium levels to an undesirable state, which can lead to impaired kidney function and possibly kidney stones. It is recommended that the maximum dosage should be 8 grams per day for a maximum duration of two weeks. Tums, at 0.5 grams per tablet, could accomplish this with 16 tablets, and there are indications that some people approach this level of use. Calcium carbonates cause acid rebound, and as little as 0.5 grams can increase gastric acid production; thus, the remedy may be self-defeating.

Pepto Bismol tablets contain calcium carbonate plus glycocoll, whereas Pepto Bismol liquid contains no antacids, only bismuth subsalicylate. It can lead to blackened stools, which could possibly mask gastrointestinal symptoms of pathologic conditions.

Two of the safest antacids are aluminum hydroxide and magnesium hydroxide. Aluminum hydroxide has no dosage limits; it is slow in its action but generally gives prolonged relief. Some have suggested that it decreases phosphate absorption, thus helping kidney patients with high phosphate levels. Its major side effect is severe constipation. Amphogel is a well-known antacid of this type. Rolaids combines aluminum hydroxide with sodium bicarbonate, but the 53 mg per tablet of sodium is high for those on a low-sodium diet.

Magnesium hydroxide is appropriate except for those with chronic kidney disorders, who should take no more than three teaspoons or four tablets a day. Milk of magnesia is an example of this type; it is effective and safe but has a laxative effect.

An alternative approach has been to combine the aluminum and magnesium compounds into one type. This allows the constipating and laxative tendencies to cancel each other out, thus eliminating any side effects. Maalox and Digel use aluminum and magnesium hydroxide, but Digel also contains simethicone, which is an unproven gas-control agent. Gelusil contains aluminum hydroxide and another magnesium compound, magnesium trisilicate. Magnesium hydroxide is faster-acting and generally a little more effective than the trisilicate. Some remedies such as Mucotin and Magnatril contain all three compounds.

Constipation Remedies

Constipation remedies are also an important consideration, since the elderly purchase them in attempts to achieve regularity. It is estimated that 40 to 60 percent of the elderly use laxatives regularly. Advertising techniques tend to heavily exploit the elderly population with strong emotional pitches that are often family- or nostalgia-oriented. More than 700 over-the-counter constipation remedies exist – strong testimony to their marketability. Despite the advertising and testimonials, none are perfect or harmless. Laxatives are not different from cathartics, simply milder. There is a general belief among gastroenterologists that regular use of cathartics does more harm than good. In many cases they can be the cause rather than the cure of constipation. Laxatives can also decrease absorption of certain vitamins and possibly upset the body's electrolyte balances.

Diarrhea is another common occurrence in the elderly. It is generally self-limiting but can be a symptom of serious pathologic conditions. Most over-the-counter antidiarrheal agents are mixtures of kaolin and *pectin,* and their efficacy is questionable. There are prescription antidiarrheal drugs containing codeine, opium, and paregoric that are very effective and not habit-forming in the quantities prescribed.

Hemorrhoidal Remedies

Hemorrhoids are often the result of straining associated with constipation. Many preparations exist that purport to relieve pain and itching, shrink swollen tissues, and promote healing. There is much evidence that most of these products do not accomplish what is advertised. Hemorrhoid preparations come as suppositories or topical ointments. The suppositories usually contain mixtures of bismuth salts, topical anesthetics such as Benzocaine, vasoconstrictors such as ephedrine, and antiseptics. Ointments contain the same substances and might be more useful, since contact with the affected area is direct. The suppositories often move up the rectum after insertion, away from the problem area. More effective in treating hemorrhoid problems than any combination of pharmaceuticals would be hot sitz baths for 15 minutes three or four times a day and dietary changes to produce a softer, bulkier stool. The real dangers in using these self-treatment preparations is the delay in having the symptoms checked out by a physician for links with more serious conditions. Rectal problems of this sort can be associated with serious gastrointestinal disease higher in the tract or with minor bacterial or fungus infections around the anal opening.

Mouthwashes

In an effort to counteract bad breath, mouthwashes may be used frequently by the socially conscious older person. Most mouth odors originate not in the mouth but further down the gastrointestinal tract. Likewise, there is no evidence that mouthwashes do anything to eliminate such odors. At most, the effect is temporary or psychological because the individual perceives a fresher mouth. Mouthwashes can contribute to the drying of the mucous membranes or can aggravate preexisting inflammation or infection, since most of them contain alcohol. This effect can complicate the dry mouth complaints of the elderly, which are related to mouth breathing, decreased salivation, and a tendency toward dehydration.

STUDY QUESTIONS

1. What is the significance of gastrointestinal symptoms to the elderly?
2. Note some general changes that take place in the mouth and comment on the following:
   a. significance of sores in the mouth
   b. loss of taste and its influence on eating patterns
   c. changes in smell
   d. the loss of teeth and eating habits
   e. denture problems
3. What factors interact in the production of dental caries? How does the caries experience differ in the elderly? What is the possible role of nutrition in tooth decay?
4. What is the significance of periodontal disease to the elderly? Identify the factors that lead to the development of periodontal disease.
5. What are some esophageal symptoms that are significant for the aged? Identify hiatus hernia and its importance for the elderly.
6. What are the major age-related changes in the stomach? What are the major disorders of the stomach and their significance for the elderly? Identify the two major problems of the duodenum. Compare the incidence and significance of ulcers in the stomach and the duodenum.
7. Discuss the possible changes in the small intestine related to the digestion and absorption of food. What is the possible significance of changes in the ecology of the bacterial flora of the intestine? What are some of the conditions that can lead to malabsorption?
8. Why is the gallbladder a major source of concern for the elderly? Identify the changes in the liver with age. What are some of the major disorders of the liver that are important for the elderly?
9. Identify some age-related changes in the pancreas. What are some of the major disorders of the pancreas?
10. How does the large bowel present a clinical picture with a set of problems almost exclusive to the elderly? Identify some of the age-related changes in the large bowel. Discuss the origins and significance of constipation in the elderly. What is the importance of fecal incontinence?
11. In what ways may cancer of the colon, hemorrhoids, and diverticular disease be related to diet?
12. Discuss the problems associated with use of over-the-counter:
    a. antacids
    b. constipation remedies
    c. hemorrhoid remedies
    d. mouthwashes

BIBLIOGRAPHY

Alfans, M. C. 1976. Controversies, perspectives, and clinical implications of nutrition in periodontal disease. *Dental Clinics of North America*, 20(3): 519–548.

Arey, L. B., Tremaine, M. J., and Monzingo, F. L. 1935. The numerical and topographical relation of taste buds to human circumvallate papillae throughout the life span. *Anatomical Record*, 64: 9–25.

Bahn, A. N. 1970. Microbial potential in the etiology of periodontal disease. *Journal of Periodontology*, 41: 603–610.

Balachi, J. A., and Dobbins, W. V. 1974. Maldigestion and malabsorption: Making up for lost nutrients. *Geriatrics*, 29: 157–166.

Balogh, K., and Lelkes, K. 1961. The tongue in old age. *Gerontologica Clinica,* 3(Suppl.): 38-54.

Bartos, V., and Groh, J. 1969. The effect of repeated stimulation of the pancreas on the pancreatic secretion in young and old men. *Gerontologica Clinica,* 17: 56-62.

Bartoshuk, L. M., and Weiffenbach, J. M. 1990. Chemical senses and aging. In E. L. Schneider and J. W. Rowe (Eds.), *Handbook of the biology of aging* (pp. 429-443). San Diego: Academic Press.

Baum, B. J. 1981a. Characteristics of participants in the oral physiology component of the Baltimore longitudinal study of aging. *Community Dentistry Oral Epidemiology,* 9: 128-134.

Baum, B. J. 1981b. Evaluation of stimulated parotid saliva flow rate in different age groups. *Journal of Dental Research,* 60(7): 1291-1296.

Baum, B. J. 1989. Salivary gland fluid secretion during aging. *Journal of American Geriatric Society,* 37: 453-458.

Becker, G. H., Meyer, J., and Necheles, H. 1950. Fat absorption in young and old age. *Gastroenterology,* 14: 80-92.

Bertolini, A. M. 1969. *Gerontologic metabolism.* Springfield, IL: Charles C Thomas.

Bhaskar, S. N. 1968. Oral lesions in the aged population. *Geriatrics,* 38: 137-149.

Bird, T., Hall, M., and Schade, R. 1977. Gastric histology and its relation to anemia in the elderly. *Gerontology,* 23: 209-321.

Bockus, H. L. 1966. *Gastroenterology.* Philadelphia: W. B. Saunders.

Bradley, R. M. 1988. Effects of aging on the anatomy and neurophysiology of taste. *Gerodontics,* 4: 244-248.

Brick, I. B., and Amory, H. I. 1950. Incidence of hiatus hernia in patients without symptoms. *Archives of Surgery,* 60: 1045.

Brocklehurst, J. C. 1951. *Incontinence in old people.* Edinburgh: Churchill Livingstone.

Brocklehurst, J. C. (Ed.). 1973. *Textbook of geriatric medicine and gerontology.* Edinburgh: Churchill Livingston.

Burkitt, D. M. 1971a. Epidemiology of cancer of the colon and rectum. *Cancer,* 28: 3.

Burkitt, D. M. 1971b. Possible relationship between bowel cancer and dietary habits. *Proceedings Royal Society Medicine,* 64: 964.

Busse, E. W. 1978. How mind, body and environment influence nutrition in the elderly. *Postgraduate Medicine,* 63: 118-123.

Calloway, N. O., and Merrill, R. S. 1965. The aging adult liver. *Journal American Geriatrics Society,* 23: 594-598.

Castell, D. O. 1975. The lower esophageal sphincter: Physiologic and clinical aspects. *Annals Internal Medicine,* 83: 390-401.

Castle, S. 1989. Constipation: Endemic in the elderly? *Medical Clinics of North America,* 73(6): 1497-1509.

Chauncey, H. H., Feldman, R. S., and Wayler, S. H. 1983. Oral aspects of aging. *American Family Physician,* 28: 147-152.

Corazza, G. R., Frazzoni, M., Gatto, M. R. A., and Gasbarrini, G. 1986. Ageing and small bowel mucosa. *Gerontology,* 321: 60-65.

De Paola, D. P., and Alfano, M. C. 1977. Diet and oral health. *Nutrition Today,* 12(3): 6-11.

Douglas, C. W., Gillings, D., Sollecito, W., and Gammon, M. 1983. National trends in the prevalence and severity of periodontal diseases. *Journal of the American Dental Association.* 107: 403-412.

Duthie, H. L., and Bennett, R. C. 1963. The relation of sensation in the anal canal to the functional anal sphincter: A possible factor in anal incontinence. *Gut,* 4: 179-182.

Dye, C. 1984. Age related changes in taste and smell that affect nutritional adequacy. In H. J. Armbrecht, J. M. Prendergast, and R. M. Coe (Eds.), *Nutrition interventions in the aging process.* New York: Springer-Verlag.

Eastwood, H. D. H. 1972. Bowel transit studies in the elderly. *Gerontologica Clinica,* 14: 154-160.

Eastwood, H. D. H., Smith, A. N., Brydon, W. G., and Pritchard, J. 1978. Comparison of brain, ispaghula and lactulose on colon function in diverticular disease. *Gut,* 19: 1144-1149.

Exton-Smith, A. N., and Scott, D. L. (Eds.). 1968. *Vitamins in the elderly.* Bristol, England: John Wright & Sons.

Fikry, M. E., and Aboul-Wafa, M. H. 1965. Intestinal absorption in the old. *Gerontologica Clinica,* 7: 171-178.

Fischer, M., Adkins, W., Hall, L., Scaman, P., Hsi, S., and Marlett, J. 1985. The effects of dietary fibre in a liquid diet on bowel function of mentally retarded individuals. *Journal of Mental Deficiency Research,* 29: 373-381.

Freund, H. R., and Rubenstein, E. 1984. Appendicitis in the aged: Is it really different? *American Surgeon,* 50: 573-576.

Friedman, J. W. 1968. Dentistry in the geriatric patient. *Geriatrics,* 23: 98-107.

Glass, R. L. 1973. Prevalence of human dental caries and waterborne trace metals. *Archives of Oral Biology,* 18: 1099-1104.

Glen, F. 1981. Surgical management of acute cholecystitis in patients 65 years and older. *Annals of Surgery,* 193: 56-59.

Greger, J. L., and Geissler, A. H. 1978. Effect of zinc supplementation on the taste activity of the aged. *American Journal of Clinical Nutrition,* 31: 633-637.

Gullo, L., Ventrucci, M., Naldoni, P., and Pezzilli, R. 1986. Aging and exocrine pancreatic function. *Journal of the American Geriatrics Society,* 34: 790-792.

Haberman, J. L. 1962. Liver function studies in the aged: What are normal values? *Northwestern Medicine,* 61: 1038-1040.

Harness, J. K., Strodel, W. E., and Talsma, S. E. 1986. Symptomatic biliary tract disease in the elderly patient. *American Surgeon,* 52: 442-450.

Harris, W. 1952. Fifth and seventh cranial nerves in relation to the nervous mechanism of taste sensation: A new approach. *British Journal of Medicine,* 1: 831-836.

Hatton, E. R., Gogan, C. M., and Hatton, M. N. 1989. Common oral conditions in the elderly. *American Family Physician,* 40(5): 149-162.

Henkin, R. I., Schechter, P. J., and Raff, M. S. 1974. Zinc and taste activity. In W. J. Pories et al. (Eds.), *Clinical applications of zinc metabolism.* Springfield, IL: C. C. Thomas.

Holdstock, D. J. 1970. Propulsion in the human colon and its relationship to meals and somatic activity. *Gut,* 11: 91.

Holm-Pederson, P., Agerback, N. M., and Theilade, E. 1975. Experimental gingivitis in young and elderly individuals. *Journal of Clinical Periodontology,* 2: 14-24.

Holt, P. R. 1983. Digestive disease and aging: Past neglect and future promise. *Gastroenterology,* 85: 1434-1436.

Hope, A. K., and Down, E. C. 1986. Dietary fibre and fluid in the control of constipation in a nursing home population. *Medical Journal of Australia,* 144: 306-307.

Hughes, G. 1969. Changes in taste sensitivity with advancing age. *Gerontologica Clinica,* 11: 224.

Hyams, D. E. 1973. The liver and biliary system. In J. C. Brocklehurst (Ed.), *Textbook of geriatric medicine and gerontology.* Edinburgh: Churchill Livingstone.

Johnson, A. G., and Hosking, S. W. 1987. Appraisal of the management of bile duct stones. *British Journal of Surgery,* 74: 555-560.

Kiyak, H. A. 1984. Utilization of dental services by the elderly. *Gerodontology,* 3: 17-26.

Krasinski, S. D. 1986. Fundic atrophic gastritis in an elderly population. *Journal of the American Geriatrics Society,* 34: 800.

Langman, M. J. 1971. Epidemiology of cancer of esophagus and stomach. *British Journal of Surgery,* 58: 792-793.

Levitan, R. 1989a. G. I. problems in the elderly, Part I: Aging-related considerations. *Geratrics,* 44(9): 53-56.

Levitan, R. 1989b. GI problems in the elderly, Part II: Prevalent diseases and disorders. *Geriatrics,* 44(11): 80-86.

Lutwak, L. 1976. Periodontal disease. In M. Winick (Ed.), *Nutrition and aging.* New York: Wiley.

Mann, G. V. 1962. The health and nutrition states of Eskimos. *American Journal of Clinical Nutrition,* 11: 31-76.

Margrotta, S. J., Horowitz, J. R., Willis, I. H., and Wallack, M. K. 1988. Cholecystectomy in the elderly. *American Surgeon,* 150: 509-512.

Mattes, R. D., and Mela, D. J. 1986. Relationships between and among elected measures of sweet taste preference and dietary intake. *Chemical Sensitivity,* 11: 523-539.

McGinty, M. D. 1971. Hiatal hernia. *Hospital Medicine,* 7: 133-143.

McKeown, F. 1965. *Pathology of the aged.* London: Butterworths.

Minaker, K. L., and Rowe, J. W. 1982. Gastrointestinal system. In J. W. Rowe and R. W. Besdine (Eds.), *Health and disease in old age.* Boston: Little, Brown.

Montgomery, F. D., Haboubi, N., Mike, N., Chesner, I., and Asquith, P. 1986. Causes of malabsorption in the elderly. *Age and Aging,* 15: 235-240.

Morgan, Z., and Feldman, M. 1967. The liver, biliary tract and pancreas in the aged. *Journal of American Geriatrics,* 5: 59-69.

Morson, B. C. 1971. Precancerous conditions of the large bowel. *Proceedings of the Royal Society of Medicine,* 64: 959.

Moskowitz, H. R., et al. 1975. Cross-cultural differences in simple taste preferences. *Science,* 190: 1217-1218.

Painter, N. S., and Burkitt, D. P. 1971. Diverticular disease of the colon: A deficiency disease of Western civilization. *British Journal of Medicine,* 2: 450-454.

Painter, N. S., and Burkitt, D. P. 1985. Diverticular disease of the sigmoid colon: Twentieth century problem. *Clinics in Gastroenterology,* 4: 3-30.

Ponka, J. L., Welborn, J. K., and Brush, B. E. 1963. Acute abdominal pain in aged patients: An analysis of 200 cases. *Journal of the American Geriatrics Society,* 11: 993-1007.

Rittenbury, M. 1961. Pancreatitis in the elderly patient. *American Surgeon,* 27: 475-495.

Rollin, H. 1973. Elektrische geschmacksschwellen der zunge und des weichen gaumens. *Archiv fuer Klinische und Experimentelle Ohren-, Nasen-, und Kehlkopf Hilkunde,* 204: 81-88.

Rosenberg, I. H., Russell, R. M., and Bowman, B. B. 1989. Aging and the digestive system. In H. N. Munro and D. E. Danford (Eds.), *Nutrition, aging and the elderly.* New York: Plenum Press.

Rossman, I. (Ed.). 1971. *Clinical geriatrics.* Philadelphia: J. B. Lippincott.

Russell, R. M. 1986. Implications of gastric atrophy for vitamin and mineral nutrition. In M. L. Hutchinson and H. Munro (Eds.), *Nutrition and aging.* Orlando, FL: Academic Press.

Schiffman, S. S. 1983. Taste and smell in disease, Part I. *New England Journal of Medicine,* 308: 1275-1279.

Schiffman, S. S., and Pasternak, M. 1979. Decrease discrimination of food odors in the elderly. *Journal of Gerontology,* 34: 73-79.

Scott, R. B., and Mitchell, M. C. 1988. Aging, alcohol and the liver. *Journal of the American Geriatric Society,* 36: 255-265.

Shamburek, R. D., and Farrar, J. T. 1989. Disorders of the digestive system in the elderly. *New England Journal of Medicine,* 322: 438-443.

Shock, N. W. 1964. Intrinsic factors in aging. In P. F. Hansen (Ed.), *Age with a future.* Copenhagen: Munksgaard.

Smithy, W. B., Wexner, S. D., and Dailey, T. H. 1986. The diagnosis and treatment of appendicitis in the aged. *Diseases of the Colon and Rectum,* 29: 170-173.

Sonies, B. C., Parent, L. J., Morrish, K., and Baum, B. J. 1988. Durational aspects of the oral-pharyngeal phase of swallow in normal adults. *Dysphagia,* 3: 1-10.

Sonnenberg, A., and Koch, T. R. 1989. Physician visits in the U.S. for constipation 1958 to 1986. *Digestive Disease Science,* 34: 606-611.

Stam, J. W., and Banting, D. W. 1980. Comparison of root caries prevalence in adults with lifelong residence in fluoridated and non-fluoridated communities. Paper presented at the annual meeting of the International Association for Dental Research, Los Angeles.

Stevens, J. C., Bartoshuk, L. M., and Cain, W. S. 1984. Chemical senses and aging: Taste versus smell. *Chemical Senses,* 9: 167-179.

Stevens, J. C., Plantinga, A., and Cain, W. S. 1982. Reduction of odor and nasal pungency associated with aging. *Neurobiology of Aging,* 3: 125-132.

Tauchi, H., and Sato, T. 1968. Age change in size and number of mitochondria of human hepatic cells. *Journal of Gerontology,* 23: 454-461.

Thompson, E. N., and Williams, R. 1965. Effect of age on liver function with particular reference to bromusulphalein excretion. *Gut,* 6: 266-269.

Thompson, W. G., and Patel, D. F. 1986. Clinical picture of diverticular disease of the colon. *Clinical Gastroenterology,* 15: 903-916.

Watkins, J. S. 1971. Personal communication cited in Brocklehurst, J. C. The large bowel. In J. C. Brocklehurst (Ed.), *Textbook of geriatric medicine and gerontology.* Edinburgh: Churchill Livingstone.

CHAPTER 10

Nutrition and Aging

Human aging is a complex process caused by a number of mechanisms that operate simultaneously. Several of the major theories of biological aging include a nutritional component. In general, it appears that nutrition plays a dual role in the aging process. First, nutritional components are probably involved in the physiological and anatomical changes that cause cell destruction and limit cell regeneration. Second, diet plays an important part in the course of degenerative diseases that often accompany aging (Munro, 1989).

Diet plays a role in *protein synthesis* by supplying the nutrients necessary for normal enzyme activity and production. One theory of biological aging postulates that aging is caused by flaws in the mechanism of protein synthesis. For instance, alteration of enzymes may result in defects in one or more of the steps in protein synthesis. Such changes in the protein synthesis process could result in the synthesis of abnormal proteins.

The immunologic theory suggests that aging is caused by the gradual breakdown in the immunologic process in the body. Antibody synthesis may become defective and produce antibodies that attack the body itself. Antibodies are proteins and thus need amino acids for their synthesis; it is possible that dietary amounts of protein are required for normal antibody production.

Another theory proposes that molecular fragments called *free radicals* may react with *polyunsaturated fatty acids* in the cell membranes to form *peroxidation products*. These products may hinder the flow of nutrients in and out of the cell, thus leading to increased cell death. Vitamin E can play a leading role in protecting the excessive *oxidation* of cellular *lipids* through inhibition of the *peroxidation reaction*. Vitamin C may also be important because it acts as a synergist to vitamin E activity and as a trap for free radicals.

The etiology of many degenerative diseases includes a nutritional component. Adequate lifelong consumption of fluorine not only may help prevent caries in the young but also may be related to a decreased risk of osteoporosis. British researchers are convinced that adequate fiber in the diet can prevent diverticulosis, large bowel cancer, and a variety of other degenerative diseases. Excessive sodium intake is related to the course of congestive heart disease, hypertension, cirrhosis of the liver, and retention of fluids in body tissues. Arteriosclerosis seems to be related to intake of saturated fat and cholesterol. Many researchers now believe that refined sugars may be the major culprit in heart disease, in addition to playing a role in the development of dental caries and diabetes mellitus.

Little has been done in the past to research the possibility of using proper nutrition and diet supplementation to ward off the effects of the aging process. Despite the examples cited here, nutritional components in the diseases of the elderly have only recently begun to be studied. Unfortunately, at the same time that the scientific community has been underactive in the field of geriatric nutrition, many elderly persons have become converts to expensive food fads. In the face of inaction by the nutritional scientists, at least the food faddists give the elderly some hope in their battle against advancing age.

In this chapter, we describe the basic nutritional requirements of the elderly. Chapter 11 includes discussion of the social and cultural aspects of geriatric nutrition.

NUTRITIONAL NEEDS OF THE ELDERLY

There is no evidence that requirements for nutrients decrease with age. Suggested decreases in food quantity relative to metabolic changes and decreased activity mean that the quality of the food must be higher than at an earlier age. Recommended dietary allowances for the aged should not be followed rigidly but, rather, used as a guide for planning individual diets. Placing people into broad categories is always dangerous because it ignores *biochemical individuality*. This concept is most relevant for the elderly because so many have one or

more chronic disorders that interact with their nutritional status.

Nutrients are chemical constituents of food necessary for proper body functioning: to supply us with energy, aid in the growth and repair of body tissues, and help in the regulation of body processes. Some nutrients perform all three functions.

At present there are six major accepted categories of nutrients: carbohydrates, fat, protein, vitamins, minerals, and water. Although all types of dietary fiber (except lignin) are recognized as carbohydrates, fiber is not yet recognized as an essential nutrient. However, fiber should not be ignored in a consideration of the food constituents essential to proper body functioning. This nondigestible portion of plant food adds bulk to the diet and is important in maintaining intestinal motility. Some epidemiological data indicate that it may be an important variable in the prevention of such disorders as colon cancer and cardiovascular disease.

Although the categories of nutrients are well recognized, the specific amounts of each nutrient needed for optimal functioning is a matter of much controversy. Scientists debate among themselves about how much of a particular nutrient is needed on a daily basis to ensure the body's efficient performance. Perhaps part of the reason for confusion in this area is the fact that the field of nutritional science is relatively young. Nutrition did not become officially identified as a separate discipline of study until the founding of the American Institute of Nutrition in 1934. Atwater, Rose, Lusk, McCallum, and others pioneered the study of nutritional science, especially in the area of energy balance and vitamin deficiency. Since then, much more has been learned about animal nutrition than about human nutrition as research priorities have centered around such issues as the cost-benefit concerns of raising livestock for a profit. However, our knowledge is increasing and, it is hoped, will continue to do so as more research on human nutrition is undertaken.

DIETARY STANDARDS

Two kinds of "standards" are involved in a consideration of the nutritional requirements of the elderly (and everyone else, for that matter). Intake at levels of *minimal requirements* of certain nutrients prevent the development of overt symptoms of nutritional deficiency disease. *Optimal requirement* intake provides nutrients at levels that should assure the maintenance of optimal health in most individuals. For the most part, nutritional scientists agree on the minimal requirements, but the optimal requirements sometimes are subject to controversy. Much of this controversy surrounds the concept of *recommended dietary allowances* (RDAs), which originated as a result of human population surveys used to determine health status in relation to nutrient intake, controlled human feeding experiments, and animal studies on metabolism. The RDAs, as shown in Table 10.1, do not represent minimal or optimal requirements. They are intended as reference points for planning diets for all groups of people to provide the greatest health benefits. The RDAs are continually being researched, and revisions are made approximately every five years. Hegsted (1989) states that the current RDA in the United States contains a great deal of error and especially lacks sensitivity for the elderly.

Previously, it was believed that the nutritional requirements of the elderly were similar to those of other age groups. New data have helped change this belief (Ausman and Russell, 1990). For example, it is now clear that the progressive physical changes associated with aging can affect nutritional requirements. Changes in digestive functions, enzyme-producing organs, intestinal mucosa, and kidney functioning influence the speed and efficiency with which food is digested, nutrients are absorbed, and the residual matter is excreted (Brocklehurst, 1979). Age-related changes in blood vessels influence their ability to nourish body tissues at the levels they once did. Disease associated with

TABLE 10.1 Recommended dietary allowances (RDAs), 1980, for individuals aged 51 to 75

	Males	Females
Fat-soluble vitamins		
A	1,000 μg R.E.[a]	800 μg R.E.[a]
D cholecalciferal	5 μg	5 μg
E	10 T.E.[b]	8 T.E.[b]
K	70–140 μg	70–140 μg
Water-soluble vitamins		
C	60 mg	60 mg
Thiamin	1.2 mg	1.0 mg
Riboflavin	1.4 mg	1.2 mg
Niacin	16 mg	13 mg
B$_6$	2.2 mg	2.0 mg
Folic acid	400 μg	400 μg
B$_{12}$	3.0 μg	3.0 μg
Pantothenic acid	4–7 mg	4–7 mg
Biotin	100–200 μg	100–200 μg
Energy		
Age 51–75	2,400[c] Calories	1,800[d] Calories
Over 75	2,050[c] Calories	1,600[d] Calories
Protein	56 grams	44 grams

[a]R.E. = Retino equivalents.

[b]T.E. = Tocopherol equivalents.

[c]For men average height 70 inches, 154 pounds.

[d]For women average height 64 inches, 120 pounds.

Source: National Research Council, Food and Nutrition Board, *Recommended Dietary Allowances, Revised 1980* (Washington, DC: National Research Council, National Academy of Sciences, 1980).

age may also directly or indirectly modify nutrient needs. More research is needed in this area to provide a better understanding of how the progress of different diseases interacts with age-related changes to modify nutrient needs. It is already known that in many instances drugs used to treat disease can also affect nutritional status. However, all of these factors exhibit a great deal of variability in individuals of particular ages.

Social factors associated with aging may also affect the nutritional requirements of older people. For example, older persons may be more vulnerable to protein deficiency as sociocultural and physical stresses contribute to the excretion of nitrogen, an important constituent of protein. This deficiency may be exacerbated by low consumption of protein and the presence of absorption problems.

As we have already seen, assessing nutritional adequacy in the elderly is not a simple problem. Yet it is an essential stage in formulating sound ideas on the possibility of variable nutritional needs of the elderly. The major assessment problems for clinicians, planners, and researchers may be characterized as follows:

1. Many of the changes associated with the aging process often overlap or imitate the signs of a nutritional deficiency. For example, vascular "spiders" under the tongue are often noted as a sign of vitamin C deficiency, but in most cases they are simply a sign of increased capillary fragility associated with aging.
2. Some nutrient deficiencies have nonspecific symptoms, and some of these symptoms may be due to deficiency of one or more of several nutrients.
3. Chronic disease or other disorders may alter the nutritional requirements for an affected individual.
4. Diseases with a related nutritional component (such as osteoporosis or periodontal disease) may be associated with a poor dietary history. What we eat throughout life influences our nutritional status in later years.
5. The use of vitamin supplements is believed to be widespread among the elderly. Such usage might not be accounted for in surveys of dietary adequacy. It is possible for vitamin supplementation to upset dynamic balances among nutrients, thus altering the "normal" requirements of a given nutrient or nutrients (Garry, Goodwin, Hunt, Hooper, and Leonard, 1982).
6. The impact of age is variable among individuals – each individual is a unique sum of life experiences, diseases, and the aging process.

However, most changes are more marked and possibly more uniform after age 75. Nevertheless, the aged are far more heterogeneous as a group than are other population groups.

National surveys carried out in the last twenty years indicate that a substantial proportion of the U.S. aged population is nutritionally vulnerable. Many elderly people consume diets that are insufficient in calories and deficient in nutrients necessary for maintaining physical health and well-being. The low-income aged and those who are sick or disabled would seem to be particularly vulnerable. Although these surveys have generally excluded the institutionalized and do not evaluate the general health status of respondents, it is well known that disease weighs heavily on the maintenance of adequate nutritional status. The national surveys also show that many aged are consuming diets wholly inappropriate for complementing therapeutic regimens for managing acute or chronic diseases. Data from a wide array of local and regional studies (see Kart and Metress, 1984, for a review of some of these studies) further emphasize the complexity of factors that may interact to affect the food intake and nutritional status of the aged. These include socioeconomic considerations such as income and education, sex, living arrangements, and the availability of meal programs to supplement dietary intake.

Recognizing the nutritional vulnerability of the aged requires understanding the nutritional needs of older people. What are these nutritional needs?

CALORIES

Most nutritionists agree that there is a strong case for recommending a reduced intake of calories for the elderly. Calories represent measures of food energy and are derived from three nutrients: carbohydrates, fats, and protein. In general, the energy needs of the elderly decline as a result of reduction of activity and a slowing of the *basal metabolism rate* (BMR), although the former may decline more drastically than the latter. The BMR refers to the amount of energy that the lean body mass needs in order to carry out its basic functions. With age, there is a decline in the ratio of lean body mass to fat, which results in a lower BMR since the metabolic needs of fat tissue are less than those of lean. Even of those who exercise regularly, there is a decrease in the number of calories that need to be consumed.

According to the National Research Council (1980), the rate of reduction of caloric needs is individually variable but may approximate 5 percent per decade between ages 55 and 75, and 7 percent per decade after the age of 75. The amount of reduced energy needs also varies with an individual's size and level of physical activity. Zheng and Rosenberg (1989) report that there is a decline in need of 600 calories per day at age 80 compared to age 30, with a concomitant decline in physical activity equal to 400 calories per day. Disease and disability complicate the situation in two ways. They can contribute to inactivity and decreased energy needs, or they can lead to increased energy demands for the performance of certain tasks due to various kinds of increased stress and strain.

Reduced activity itself may be related to changes in motivational state, social conditions (e.g., the advent of retirement), or the presence of chronic disease. Activity is valuable for the health and well-being of the elderly individual for a variety of reasons (Rudman, 1989), including the following:

1. It requires energy expenditure, thus helping to maintain an energy balance and aiding in the avoidance of obesity.
2. It leads to greater activity and increases work capacity, both of which lead to greater consumption of calories. Failure to consume ade-

quate calories can contribute to fatigue and lassitude.
3. It prevents or slows *atrophy* associated with chronic disease and inactivity by maintaining good muscle tone.
4. It lowers blood sugar levels, often improving glucose tolerance and lowering insulin dosage level in diabetics.
5. It is stimulating and may serve to lift an individual's spirits.

Although caloric needs are reduced in later life, the need for specific nutrients does not decrease. Quantitative and qualitative variety must be included in the diet in order to provide the necessary amounts of all essential nutrients. However, it must be emphasized that adequate calorie consumption is necessary to allow for a sufficient intake of the essential nutrients. In 1989, Andres and Hallfrisch reported inadequacies in the diets of older people in folacin, vitamins D, B_6, B_{12}, zinc, magnesium, and calcium. They also proposed that the reason for much of the decline in intake was that the older people did not eat enough food to collect the proper amount of nutrients.

CARBOHYDRATE NEEDS

Carbohydrates constitute a major portion of most diets. Over the years, they have developed an undeserved reputation as the cause of weight gain. Certainly this energy-yielding nutrient can contribute to excess weight if it is part of an overall dietary plan that includes too many calories. For instance, many of the so-called snack and junk foods are high in calories, refined carbohydrates, and fats, and low in other nutrients. However, cookies, crackers, pastries, and doughnuts are not the only foods in the carbohydrate category. It is also represented by the complex carbohydrates found in fruits, vegetables, cereals, and breads – foods that are also rich in protective nutrients such as vitamins and minerals. Carbohydrates are the main sources of dietary fiber. It is recommended that the majority of calories consumed consist of complex carbohydrates in the form of the aforementioned foods. Foods high in refined sugars, though a source of pleasure to many, should be eaten in moderation to avoid unnecessary increments in energy intake. Such advice regarding carbohydrate consumption applies to persons of all ages.

PROTEIN NEEDS

Protein needs appear to be similar in both the young and the old. For older adults, however, important physical and social factors must be considered that may increase the likelihood of a marginal protein status. Poor chewing ability and the high cost of protein-rich foods can limit protein intake. Substituting dairy products or eggs for harder-to-chew meats may pose other difficulties. These products are expensive, and milk may not be tolerated because of a lactase deficiency or merely because the adult has not regularly included it in the diet since youth. Transporting heavy cartons of milk may also be difficult, especially for the socially isolated individual who has no assistance in shopping.

Some adults may be advised by a physician to curtail intake of red meat and unskimmed dairy products because of the high cholesterol and saturated fat content of these foods. Fish, poultry, and combinations of plant foods can supply the necessary protein in the diet. Animal products are known as complete proteins, which means that they supply all of the eight essential amino acids, or building blocks for protein. In general, plant foods contain smaller amounts of protein than animal products and, in most cases, are lower in one or more of the essential amino acids. Proteins that do not have the proper balance of essential amino acids are known as incomplete proteins. A better protein balance can be obtained by combining plant foods. For example, casseroles containing beans and rice are complete in their amino acid content and are an easy-to-chew and less expensive substitute for steak.

It has been noted that increased stress leads to higher rates of nitrogen excretion, which may result in a negative nitrogen balance (Young, Perera, Winterer, and Scrimshaw, 1976; Young, 1978). Because the elderly are potentially subject to multiple stress factors, including role changes, increased risk of illness, and multiple disease states, "normal" protein intake may be insufficient for optimal health. Decreased ability to absorb nutrients, related to age-induced changes in the digestive system, affects protein balance. At present evidence is inconclusive in support of the contention that the elderly have increased needs for the amino acids lysine and methionine (Young et al., 1976).

It has also been suggested that protein needs may be reduced in old age. Such suggestions are related to the observations that body protein mass declines with age (Forbes and Reina, 1970) and that the rate of protein synthesis decreases (Winterer, Steffer, Perera, Uauy, Scrimshaw, and Young, 1976). Declining renal function may also make it difficult to handle high concentrations of protein waste.

FAT NEEDS

Age does not alter an individual's need for fat. Fats should be limited to less than 25 to 30 percent of total caloric intake at all ages. Reducing fat consumption is an easy way to reduce the total intake of calories. Although the data are conflicting, the relation of fat consumption to cardiovascular disease must be considered in dietary planning even though there is no conclusive evidence to indicate that modifying fat intake in older persons will influence the risk of heart attack or stroke.

Restricting fat intake too drastically may interfere with absorption of fat-soluble vitamins. Besides serving as a carrier of certain vitamins and an essential fatty acid, linoleic acid, fats are important in the diet for flavor and satiety. A totally fat-free diet would be monotonous, tasteless, and counterproductive to good eating habits. Furthermore, we must consider that fat absorption often decreases as one ages, and that consequently absorption time is lengthened. This situation is related to several factors, including a decreased production of pancreatic lipase (a fat-splitting enzyme), gall bladder and liver disorders that decrease fat *emulsification,* and structural changes in the intestinal mucosa that interfere with fat absorption.

VITAMIN NEEDS

Nutrition-conscious people seem to show particular attentiveness to their vitamin intake. Table 10.2 describes the many dietary sources of essential vitamins. Many people, unsure of the state of their vitamin intake, seek insurance, or "super-effects," by turning to the use of vitamin supplements. The elderly are no exception to this practice. Although there is some evidence of vitamin deficiencies among the aged, there seems to be little justification for wholesale vitamin supplementation by older people. However, it might be useful to use supplements selectively with at-risk groups such as elderly men living alone, those with physical disorders or sensory impairment, and those suffering from depression, including the recently bereaved.

Vitamin supplementation is not without problems. Vitamin absorption or storage may be affected by organs that are no longer functioning optimally as a result of age-related changes in organ structure and function. A field study by Baker and his colleagues (Baker, Frank, and Jaslow, 1980) demonstrated that because of vitamin malabsorption in the elderly, intramuscular vitamin injections may be necessary to maintain adequate blood levels of certain vitamins. A few vitamins pose the threat of toxic effects in those engaged in overzealous consumption. Furthermore, vitamin supplementation can disturb the dynamic interrelationships among certain nutrients. With these points in mind, let us examine specific vitamin needs during the later years.

TABLE 10.2 Major dietary sources of essential vitamins

Fat-soluble vitamins	Foods
A	Milk, butter, cheese, liver, and fortified margarine (retinol) Green and yellow vegetables and fruits (carotene)
D	Cod liver oil, fortified milk and margarine, liver, fatty fish, eggs
E	Seeds; nuts; green, leafy vegetables; corn oil margarines; oils such as corn, safflower
K	Green, leafy vegetables; liver
Water-soluble vitamins	
Thiamin	Pork, organ meats, whole grains, legumes
Riboflavin	Milk, eggs, cheese, meats, green vegetables, legumes
Niacin	Liver, lean meats, whole grains, legumes
B_6	Whole grains, meat, vegetables, bananas, legumes
Pantothenic acid	Organ meats, eggs, legumes, whole grains
Folacin	Legumes, whole wheat, green vegetables
B_{12}[a]	Organ meats, muscle meats, eggs, shellfish, liver, dairy products
C	Citrus fruit; tomatoes; green peppers; cabbage; potatoes; other fruit (melon, strawberries); other dark green, leafy vegetables

[a]No known plant source.

Fat-Soluble Vitamins

The fat-soluble vitamins are A, D, E, and K. These vitamins are absorbed in the small intestine and carried by digested dietary fats. The body stores these vitamins mostly in the liver. Toxic symptoms can result from the storage of excess levels of vitamins A and D.

Vitamin A promotes healthy epithelial tissues, tooth growth and tooth enamel development in children, and the ability to see in dim light. It has also been shown to play a role in carbohydrate metabolism and may serve in an anti-infective capacity through its role in normal mucus formation. Healthy mucous membranes that are bathed in their secretions provide a more effective barrier to the invasion of various pathogenic microorganisms. Some investigators have also reported a correlation between a low intake of vitamin A and betacarotene and a susceptibility to chemical carcinogens affecting the respiratory system, colon, and urinary bladder (Wald, Idle, Boreham, and Bailey, 1980). Dietary vitamin A assessed by dietary green and yellow vegetable intake has been correlated with lower cancer rates (Colditz, Branch, and Lipnick, 1985). It is possible, however, that the high vegetable intake may correlate with decreased fat or protein intake.

Vitamin A deficiencies can result from poor intake, from poor intestinal absorption, or from diseases that affect the utilization of vitamin A. In the elderly, vitamin A deficiency is most likely to become a problem as a result of impaired absorption or disease rather than underconsumption. A variety of factors can lead to poor absorption, including a reduced availability of bile (important in the emulsification of fats), overuse of laxatives, antibiotic therapy, and cirrhosis of the liver. Increasing dysfunction of the gall bladder and liver are often associated with aging and can lead to reduced availability of bile because of physical obstruction and/or inadequate production by the liver. Low levels of bile disrupt fat digestion and absorption, and absorption of the fat-soluble vitamins. Laxative use, which is high in the elderly, may serve to flush this vitamin out of the body. Oil-based laxatives (such as mineral oil) act as carriers of vitamin A and are especially significant in the disruption of vitamin A absorption.

Antibiotic therapy may introduce disruptive ecological changes in the digestive tract and can result in altered absorption of nutrients. Cirrhosis of the liver, common in elderly alcoholics, affects the ability of the liver to metabolize and store vitamin A.

The primary function of vitamin D appears to be in aiding the absorption of calcium for maintenance of healthy bone tissue. It contributes to this function by increasing the absorption of calcium from the small intestine and increasing the rate of bone mineralization. Common factors associated with a deficiency of this nutrient in the elderly are malabsorption syndromes and limited exposure to the sun. Sunlight converts a biologically inactive substance in the skin, 7-dehydrocholesterol, to vitamin D. Available information on vitamin D metabolism and the elderly is limited. Osteomalacia, the adult counterpart of rickets, has been observed in elderly persons living alone. This condition is probably the result of a complex set of factors, including reduced outdoor activity (which reduces exposure to sunlight), malabsorption, declining renal function (which influences calcium resorption), and inadequate intake of vitamin D. A deficiency of vitamin D and calcium can be most severe in its effects on skeletal integrity.

Age-related changes associated with vitamin D metabolism have been proposed to account for the reported decrease in vitamin D metabolites in some elderly groups. It has been suggested that with increasing age the kidney makes insufficient quantities of the most active form of vitamin D. Further, there appears to be some evidence for age-related end organ resistance to vitamin D. It is also well known that after age 60 there is a significant progressive decrease in intestinal calcium absorption in humans (Welser, 1984).

Vitamin E has been championed by faddists as a panacea for a variety of ailments and conditions (Roberts, 1981). It is claimed to be a relevant factor in improving conditions ranging from heart disease to a poor-quality sex life. These alleged benefits have great appeal to many of the elderly. In fact, the *antioxidant* qualities of the vitamin are presumed by some to fight or retard the aging process itself (Roberts, 1981; Ledvina, 1985). Few of vitamin E's suggested benefits have been confirmed by well-controlled scientific research, although some evidence suggests a higher requirement for older populations (Machlin and Brin, 1980).

Vitamin E is necessary for the integrity of the red blood cell and for the proper metabolism of polyunsaturated fats. Its supplementation has improved a painful leg condition known as *claudication*. Deficiency of vitamin E has rarely been observed except in premature infants and has proven exceptionally hard to induce in control populations (Horwitt, 1976).

Vitamin K is essential for the formation of *prothrombin* in the liver and thus is necessary for proper blood clotting. Deficiency of this vitamin has never been reported in healthy adults. However, low levels of vitamin K may be related to bleeding tendencies often associated with biliary disease and surgery. Likewise, availability of this vitamin may be affected by antibiotic therapy that disrupts the vitamin K-producing intestinal flora and by diseases such as colitis that affect the absorptive mucosa of the small intestine.

Vitamin K deficiency is not a major problem among the elderly. However, blood levels of this vitamin should be checked and possibly supplemented because of its importance in proper blood clotting when preparing elderly persons for surgery. There is some evidence for an age-related change in vitamin K metabolism that decreases its effectiveness.

Water-Soluble Vitamins

The water-soluble vitamins include the B-complex vitamins and vitamin C. Sometimes termed labile, water-soluble vitamins taken in excess of daily need are excreted in the urine. They differ from the fat-soluble vitamins in that they normally do not accumulate in toxic quantities, although symptomatic changes have been observed in those taking megadoses of some B vitamins. Excessive amounts of water-soluble vitamins, however, may alter the dynamic balance among other nutrients or increase the need for some others. More studies are needed to determine the risk of kidney damage as a result of ingesting consistent excesses of the water-soluble vitamins. Many of these are subject to destruction as a result of food preparation and cooking practices, especially when large amounts of water are involved.

B-complex vitamins include thiamin (B_1), riboflavin (B_2), niacin, vitamin B_6 (pyridoxine), folacin (folic acid), vitamin B_{12}, biotin, and pantothenic acid. These vitamins differ chemically, but their functions are interrelated.

Thiamin has an important role in the process that changes glucose to energy. The need for thiamin varies directly with calorie intake. It functions as part of a *coenzyme* that is indispensable in carbohydrate metabolism, providing a supply of energy to the nerves and brain. Because of this relationship, thiamin deficiency usually involves neurological manifestations and mood changes. Thiamin also appears to be essential for fat and protein metabolism. Poorly balanced or highly refined diets, stress, alcoholism, and impaired intestinal absorption are most often the precipitating factors in thiamin deficiency. Alcoholics have low intake and decreased absorption, which put them at risk for deficiency.

Serum levels of thiamin are often reported to be low in surveys of older populations. Zheng and Rosenberg (1989) reported the incidence of biochemical deficiency of thiamin as ranging from 3 to

59 percent. Frequent use of diuretics can contribute to a deficiency as a result of increased excretion. The high-carbohydrate diets often consumed by elderly persons on marginal or fixed incomes can disturb the thiamin–carbohydrate balance, leading to a deficiency because of thiamin's role in the proper utilization of carbohydrates (Wilson, Fisher, and Fuqua, 1975; Brin and Bauernfeind, 1978). The elderly may need more thiamin than the young because of age-associated health conditions. Common among these conditions are elevated temperature, malignancy, *parenteral* administration of glucose without thiamin, *hemodialysis* (which removed thiamin), the stress of surgery, and alcoholism.

Whanger (1973) has suggested that thiamin may be inactivated in older people as a result of a lack of hydrochloric acid in gastric secretions and altered intestinal flora that binds ingested thiamin. Cheraskin, Ringsdorfer, and Hicks (1967) suggested a relationship between low thiamin intake and greater frequency of cardiovascular complaints in older people. Thiamin intake and status should be regularly monitored in the elderly.

Riboflavin is essential for normal tissue maintenance, tear production, and corneal integrity. It is also a constituent of enzymes important in energy metabolism. Deficiencies are often associated with high-carbohydrate diets lacking in animal protein, milk, and vegetables. Visual impairments, such as sensitivity to bright light, and skin problems, such as epithelial lesions, are common signs of a deficiency. Deficiencies of riboflavin have been reported with some regularity in the elderly, with incidence of low biochemical indices ranging from 2 to 24 percent (Zheng and Rosenberg, 1989). Some have suggested that it might be the most common subclinical deficiency among the elderly poor, whose diets are notoriously low in meats and vegetables (e.g., see Exton-Smith and Scott, 1968). In general, however, the clinical evidence for riboflavin is scant.

Niacin is a functional component of coenzymes that are essential for the release of energy from carbohydrates, fats, and proteins. It also plays a significant role in the synthesis of fats and protein by the body. Niacin can be *endogenously* manufactured rather inefficiently from the amino acid tryptophan (60 mg of tryptophan yields 1 mg of niacin). Niacin deficiency is associated with narrow, maize-dominated diets or highly refined diets limited in animal protein. Alcoholics, food faddists, and those with malabsorption problems may also suffer from niacin deficiency.

The deficiency is rarely reported among the elderly, with the exception of elderly alcoholics, but one reviewer found that over one-half of the studies show low niacin intake in over one-quarter of the elderly subjects (Fleming, 1982). Those on heavy aspirin therapy for conditions such as arthritis are at risk because aspirin may interfere with the passage of niacin from plasma to tissue. Some personality changes observed in the elderly and usually attributed to the aging process, such as mental confusion and depression, may be due to deficiency of niacin as well as other B-complex deficiencies (Exton-Smith and Scott, 1968).

The vitamin B_6 group includes three closely related components that serve as coenzymes for biological functions involving amino acid metabolism and protein synthesis. The B_6 group seems to be poorly absorbed by individuals with liver disease and is commonly deficient in persons with uremia and gastrointestinal disease. Because these conditions are often present in the elderly, these relationships bear watching. There are reports of high rates of biochemical B_6 deficiency in the elderly. This could be due to low dietary intakes or a change in B_6 metabolism with age that could result in higher B_6 requirements (Suter and Russell, 1989).

The drug dihydroxyphenylalanine (L-dopa), a neurotransmitter, is used in the treatment of Parkinson's disease. The B_6 vitamin, pyridoxine, enhances the conversion of L-dopa to *dopamine*. Because dopamine cannot cross the blood–brain barrier, conversion may result in a nullification of the therapeutic effects of the drug. Therefore, persons on L-dopa drug therapy should avoid taking vitamin supplements containing vitamin B_6.

Folic acid (or folacin) is important in the metabolism of a number of amino and nucleic acids, and especially in hemoglobin synthesis. This vitamin's activities are interrelated with those of vitamin B_{12}. Folacin intake is frequently reported as low among the elderly, especially the poor or sick. It may be the most common deficiency in the older adult (Girdwood, Thompson, and Williamson, 1967). Herbert (1967) suggests that it is the most common overall nutritional deficiency. But reports of folic acid depletion are variable, ranging from 2 to 3 percent in the Hanes II survey in 1976–1980 up to 60 percent in a group of deprived urban black elderly (Sandstead, 1987). A number of conditions often associated with old age affect folic acid availability. Stomach and small intestine surgery are associated with decreased absorption of the vitamin. However, this may be compensated for by synthesis of folic acid as a result of increased intestinal bacterial activity (Russell, Krasinski, Samloff, Jacob, Hartz, and Brovender, 1986). Leukemia, Hodgkin's disease, Crohn's disease, collagen disease, tuberculosis, and malignancies appear to increase the demand for folacin (Exton-Smith, 1978).

Anticonvulsant drugs frequently used by the elderly are antagonistic to folacin. Research indicates that possibly 90 percent of all alcoholics are deficient in folic acid (Leevy and Kurnan, 1975; Halsted, 1980). This deficiency may be the result of liver damage or damage to the intestinal mucosa. Folacin is vital to the production of red blood cells; in the absence of proper levels, *macrocytic anemia* occurs, a condition in which the red blood cells are larger and fewer in number than normal. Organic brain syndrome (OBS) has also been associated with low folacin intake (Batata, Spray, Bolton, Higgins, and Woolner, 1967). However, the nature of the relationship between the two is not clear. It is not known if the disorder leads to decreased dietary

intake and a consequent folacin deficiency or if such a deficiency results in the impaired mental ability associated with OBS (Sneath, Chanarin, Hodkinson, McPherson, and Reynolds, 1973).

Vitamin B_{12} is a compound that contains cobalt as a central part of its organic molecule. The exact functions of this vitamin are not completely understood. It appears to be necessary for cellular formation and functioning, especially in the bone marrow and digestive tract, and to maintain the integrity of the nervous system. It is chemically interrelated with the vitamin folacin, is stored in the liver, and is absorbed very slowly from the small intestine. Marcus and associates (1987), in a study among elderly people in New York City, identified 26 out of 378 subjects as having low B_{12} levels. It was further determined that the cause of the deficiency was generally lack of transcobalamin, a blood protein responsible for transport of B_{12}.

An intrinsic factor produced by the stomach is necessary for B_{12} absorption. If absorption does not take place, *pernicious anemia* results, with its concomitant production of characteristically large, immature red blood cells. Like folacin, vitamin B_{12} is needed for the maturation of red blood cells. When it is unavailable, these cells are pale, irregular in shape, and reduced in number. Vitamin B_{12} absorption seems to decrease with age. This may result from a decrease in the *intrinsic factor* produced by the gastric mucosa. Antibodies against the gastric mucosa have been found in the blood of some patients, suggesting an autoimmune condition that may be responsible for disruption of the absorption of this particular vitamin (Davidson, Passmore, Brock, and Truswell, 1975). Changes in gastric acidity, a malabsorption syndrome associated with partial or total removal of the stomach or ileum, and the taking of certain drugs can also interfere with the uptake of vitamin B_{12}. Deficiencies of this vitamin in the elderly are rarely due to low dietary intake. When B_{12} cannot be properly absorbed, it may be administered by injection.

A B_{12} deficiency may be associated with a folacin deficiency. In fact, suspected folacin problems should not be treated without first investigating vitamin B_{12} status. Folacin therapy can mask the earliest symptoms of B_{12} deficiency, delaying detection until irreparable nerve damage has been done. There is a possibility that some elderly persons labeled "senile" or arteriosclerotic may have a B_{12} deficiency and suffer consequent alterations in brain functioning. McRae and Freedman (1989) suggest that vitamin B_{12} deficiency should be managed aggressively because the resulting neurological and psychiatric disorders – confusion, disorientation, and memory loss – could eventually lead to dementia. Fleck (1976) reported that some elderly persons who demonstrated these conditions improved after vitamin B_{12} was administered.

Pantothenic acid, as a component of coenzyme A, is necessary to change fats and sugar into energy and is needed for the formation of adrenal and other hormones that also change proteins to fat and sugar. Some investigators (for example, Baker, Frank, Thind, Jaslow, and Louria, 1968) have suggested that it plays an undetermined role in *hypoglycemia*. The vitamin is widely distributed in foods, and no deficiency has been reported in human beings. Thus, the elderly do not appear to suffer any special risks of a deficiency.

Vitamin C (ascorbic acid) is the only water-soluble vitamin that is not part of the B-complex group. Most species of animals are able to synthesize it from simple sugars, but humans and our primate relations must include an external source of vitamin C in our diet. Although vitamin C was the first vitamin synthesized in the laboratory, we still know very little about its specific chemical activity. Recently, vitamin C has been promoted as a cure or preventive for a wide range of conditions, from the common cold to cancer. These claims have not been confirmed by carefully controlled scientific studies.

Vitamin C plays an important role in cellular metabolism, but the mechanisms involved are poorly understood. Its most important function is in the formation and maintenance of collagen, which forms the organic matrix of the connective tissue found in skin, bones, teeth, and muscle. The vitamin also plays an important role in wound healing and promotes elasticity and strength of capillary walls. Garry and Hunt (1986) have observed that elderly subjects with low plasma levels of ascorbic acid have impaired cognitive functioning.

Vitamin C is important in folic acid metabolism as part of the reaction that converts folic acid to its active form, folinic acid. It also prevents the oxidation of folates, assuring their physiological activity. Vitamin C plays an important part in the absorption of iron from the intestine by reducing ferric iron to the more efficiently absorbed ferrous iron. Its role as an antioxidant, in the utilization of vitamin B_{12}, and in the body's *detoxification process* is not yet fully understood. The possible role of vitamin C in cholesterol metabolism and atherosclerosis must be investigated as well. Its role in the prevention of cancer has recently been challenged by a well-designed, carefully controlled double-blind study by Creagen and his associates (1979). These researchers found that the administration of 10 grams of vitamin C a day to cancer patients did not improve immune response or survival time.

The use of vitamin C to prevent the common cold has been the subject of controversy among researchers. Anderson, Reid, and Beaton (1972), in a very well known and carefully conducted double-blind study, concluded that vitamin C reduced the severity and frequency of colds. They cautioned, however, that the observed reduction might be due to a pharmacological rather than a nutritional effect. To some researchers, it appears that vitamin C reduces the symptoms of a cold by an *antihistamine effect*, while at the same time leaving an individual's ability to transmit the disease unaffected. Contradictory studies in this area necessitate more research and possibly better criteria for determining the presence or absence of "colds."

The role of vitamin C in the aging process may involve its relationship with vitamin E. It has been suggested that vitamin C synergistically aids vitamin E in *antiperoxidative* activities (Weg, 1978). At present there is little evidence to support this hypothesis. *Megadoses* of vitamin C may simply be a waste of money unless one is biochemically deficient in this vitamin. Toxicity from larger doses of vitamin C has not been a major problem, but side effects such as urinary tract stones (Stein, Hasan, and Fox, 1976) inactivation of vitamin B_{12} (Herbert and Jacobs, 1974), and dependency deficiency have been reported (Rhead and Schrauger, 1971).

Vitamin C intake has been reported to be low in elderly populations, especially among those who live alone or who have disabilities that hinder shopping. Low serum ascorbic acid levels are not a normal accompaniment of biological aging, and the fact that older persons respond to supplementation seems to support this observation. The multiple stresses associated with aging, as well as some drugs, may depress vitamin C levels (Baker, 1967). Vitamin C is readily destroyed in food preparation and cooking, and thus a marginal diet leaves little room for error. There is no reason to recommend an increase in vitamin C intake for the average older adult, unless future research supports higher RDAs of this vitamin for all age groups. Such an increase has been suggested by Linus Pauling and his supporters but rejected by most orthodox nutritionists. Among the elderly poor, ascorbic acid status is either prevalent or infrequent, depending on which study one reads. This situation may be the result of disagreements over both desirable levels of intake and the interpretation of laboratory evidence (Sandstead, 1987).

MINERALS

Minerals are homogeneous inorganic substances that are necessary for the proper functioning of the body. Some minerals are referred to as *macronutrients* because they are needed in relatively large amounts (over 100 mg per day). Others, needed in very small amounts, are termed *micronutrients*. Table 10.3 contains the 1980 RDAs and major dietary sources for minerals. The amount of a particular mineral needed in the body is not necessarily related to its relative biological importance. Each of these essential nutrients serves the body in one or more of five different ways: (1) as a structural component of the skeleton; (2) in the maintenance and regulation of the body's *colloidal systems;* (3) in the maintenance of the *acid–base equilibrium;* (4) as a component or activator of enzyme systems; and (5) as a component or activator in other biological units or systems. Minerals are often interrelated in function, and thus a deficiency of one may affect the functioning of others. For example, copper is necessary for the proper utilization of iron.

The degree of solubility of a mineral is generally related to its use in the body. Insoluble minerals are found in the teeth, bones, nails, and hair, whereas the more reactive minerals, such as the *electrolytes,* are found in the blood.

Inefficient mineral absorption occurs easily. A number of dietary, morphological, and physiological factors add to decreased absorption. The following factors have a tendency to reduce absorption:

1. Chemical compounds, such as *phytic acid* and *oxalic acid* found in some foods (for example, spinach and oatmeal), combine with some nutrients such as calcium and iron to form insoluble compounds which are excreted.
2. High-cellulose diets reduce the availability of absorption time by inducing hypermotility.
3. Laxatives and diarrhea can also produce hypermotility.
4. A deficiency or excess of one nutrient can reduce the absorption of another.
5. Hypogastric activity due to antacid use or old age can reduce the solubility of all minerals.

In the elderly, mineral malnutrition may be related to the decreased absorptive ability that comes

TABLE 10.3 RDAs and major dietary sources for minerals

	Males	Females
Macronutrients:		
Calcium (Ca)	800 mg	800 mg
Magnesium (Mg)	305 mg	300 mg
Sodium (Na)[a]	1,100-3,300 mg	1,100-3,300 mg
Potassium (K)[a]	1,875-5,625 mg	1,875-5,625 mg
Phosphorus (P)	800 mg	800 mg
Chlorine (Cl)[a]	1,700-5,100 mg	1,700-5,100 mg
Sulfur (S)	No RDAs at this time	
Micronutrients (trace elements):		
Manganese (Mn)[a]	2.5-5 mg	2.5-5 mg
Iron (Fe)	10 mg	10 mg
Copper (Cu)	2-3 mg	2-3 mg
Iodine (I)	150 μg	150 μg
Zinc (Zn)	15 mg	15 mg
Fluorine (F)[a]	1.5-4 mg	1.5-4 mg
Molybdenum (Mo)[a]	0.15-0.5 mg	0.15-0.5 mg
Selenium (Se)[a]	0.05-0.2 mg	0.05-0.2 mg
Chromium (Cr)[a]	0.05-0.2 mg	0.05-0.2 mg
Vanadium (V)		
Cobalt (Co)		
Tin (Sn)	No RDAs at this time	
Nickel (Ni)		
Silicon (Sl)		

Minerals	Foods
Ca	Milk; cheese; dark green, leafy vegetables; legumes
P	Milk, cheese, meat, poultry, grains
K	Fruits, meat, milk, potato
Cl	Salt
Na	Salt, meat, cheese, processed food
Mg	Whole grains; green, leafy vegetables
Fe	Eggs; meat; legumes; green, leafy vegetables
F	Drinking water, tea, seafood
Zn	Meat, shellfish, nuts
Cu	Meats, drinking water
I	Iodized salt, marine products
Mn	Legumes, cereals, nuts
Mo	Legumes, meats
Cr	Vegetables, whole grains

[a]Less information is available so the ranges are less precise and not as well graded by age.

Source: National Research Council, Food and Nutrition Board, *Recommended Dietary Allowances, Revised 1980* (Washington, DC: National Research Council, National Academy of Sciences, 1980).

with age, to marginal diets, and to the effects of stress and immobilization in mineral balance. The major minerals that may be of significance to the elderly will be surveyed next.

Calcium

Calcium is necessary for the proper mineralization of bone. It is important in the growth and maintenance of the skeleton and also plays an important role in blood clotting, cell wall permeability, muscle contractability, neuromuscular transmission, and cardiac function. The function of calcium is closely related to that of phosphorus and vitamin D. The ratio of calcium to phosphorus in the diet, which should be 1:1 and certainly no greater than 1:2, is crucial in determining the balance of calcium metabolism. If the phosphorus levels become too high, calcium is withdrawn from the bones to restore a proper equilibrium. Over the long term, this process can result in a gradual reduction of bone density.

Vitamin D aids calcium metabolism by enhancing transport of the mineral across the intestinal wall. Deficiency of this vitamin can result in disturbances of calcium metabolism known as rickets in the young and osteomalacia in the older adult. The body may be able to adapt to low intake of calcium without immediate ill effects, but there is evidence that long-term low intake is undesirable because the amount of bone present in old age may be directly related to the integrity of the skeletal mass of maturity (Garn, 1975). Chronic nutritional imbalance during the twenties and thirties may affect the health of the skeleton in old age.

When a deficiency of calcium occurs, it is often accompanied by overly sensitive motor nerves, loss of muscle tone, and occasional decalcification of the bones. *Osteoporosis*, a decrease in total bone mass, is common in the elderly, especially females. Its cause has been attributed to the aging process, changes in hormone balance, long-term dietary practices, and physical inactivity. Some researchers believe that the condition does not respond to calcium supplements (e.g., Garn, 1975). However, calcium supplementation may still prove helpful in preventing further progression of the condition and bone resorption (Albanese, 1979). Calcium supplements should be taken with meals because the lower acidity of the aging stomach will prevent their absorption when taken alone. A full stomach, however, will produce more acid. Poor calcium intake may also be a significant factor in the origin and progression of periodontal disease; some evidence has suggested that periodontal disease can be reversed by adequate calcium intake (Lutwak, 1976).

There is no direct evidence of a necessity for increased calcium intake among healthy elderly persons. However, calcium intake can become deficient or imbalanced in older people as a result of chronic illness, malabsorption syndrome, increased lactase deficiency, and economic limitations. Chronic illness and malabsorption reduce the bioavailability of the mineral. Long-term use of antacids containing aluminum can upset the calcium/phosphorus balance by hindering absorption of calcium due to stomach acid buffering. The stress associated with both chronic illness and diminished psychosocial status can lead to increased calcium excretion as well as decreased appetite (Albanese, 1979; Watkin, 1979). McGandy, Russell, and Jartz (1986) report that 20 percent of men and 38 percent of women consume less than two-thirds of the RDA for calcium.

Phosphorus

Phosphorus is important in bone formation, metabolism, and the transport of fatty acids. Phosphorus intake is frequently excessive among Americans who consume large quantities of meat and carbonated soft drinks while reducing their intake of dairy products. Excessive levels of phosphates in the blood pose a threat to those elderly persons experiencing decreased renal function. Phosphate levels can be controlled by a diet high in carbohydrates and low in protein and phosphorus, or by use of an *aluminum hydroxide gel* to bind phosphorus in foods and the intestinal fluid (Watkin, 1979).

Magnesium

Magnesium plays an important part in cell respiration and in the metabolism of fats, proteins, and carbohydrates. It is involved in bone and tooth formation, muscle and nerve irritability, delay in the formation of *fibrin* (necessary in blood clotting), and prevention of kidney stone formation.

Magnesium may lower cholesterol and retard lipid deposition in the aorta. A deficiency of magnesium is rare. Calcium/magnesium ratios may be more significant than the total level of magnesium. Reduced serum calcium levels are often present with magnesium depletion. Several complicating conditions common in the elderly can contribute to the production of a deficiency characterized by depression, muscular weakness, and convulsions (Shils, 1969). These conditions include chronic alcoholism, acute or chronic renal disease with defective renal tubular reabsorption, excessive use of diuretics, impaired gastrointestinal absorption, the use of certain antibiotics, and excessive use of enemas.

Potassium

Potassium is necessary for the maintenance of the body's acid–base and water balances as well as for proper neuromuscular function. It also plays a significant role in blood pressure regulation, and potassium loading appears to reduce blood pressure in hypertensives (Tammen, 1983). Potassium deficiency can be a significant problem for the elderly. It is characterized by muscular weakness, disorientation, depression, and irritability. This deficiency becomes more common with age, especially among those on diuretics or those with prolonged diarrhea. Low potassium levels have been correlated with muscular weakness, and some researchers suggest potassium supplementation as a course of treatment (MacLeod, Judge, and Caird, 1975; MacLeod, 1975). Reestablishing a balance by dietary means can be difficult because of the frequently noted reluctance of the elderly to eat citrus fruits and milk. Bananas and apple juice seem to be more readily accepted and are good sources of potassium.

Sodium

Sodium, like potassium, is essential for water balance, acid-base equilibrium, and proper nerve function. A dietary deficiency of sodium is virtually unheard of in healthy adults. It can result from sodium-restricted diets or diuretic therapy. A sodium deficiency can cause muscle cramps, mental apathy, and reduced appetite. For most Americans, a deficiency of sodium is of less concern than is excess sodium intake.

Iron

Iron is needed for the formation of hemoglobin, and a deficiency of this mineral produces anemia. Iron deficiency anemia can cause fatigue, weakness, and listlessness, which if present add to the variety of factors reducing the quality of life for many of the elderly. To maintain an iron balance, an individual must absorb at least 1 mg of iron per day to compensate for daily losses of iron in the shedding of cells even though the body recycles much of the heme from these shed cells. Anemia per se is not a satisfactory criterion for determining the incidence of iron deficiency in the elderly. Other indices of iron status must be used because factors such as folic acid, B_{12}, copper, and vitamin C can contribute to anemia.

Iron is converted to a form that is more absorbable by the activity of hydrochloric acid in the stomach. Many older individuals have reduced secretion of hydrochloric acid and, as a consequence, reduced availability of dietary iron. Elderly people suffering from ulcers, malignancies, and hemorrhoids lose blood into the intestine and may develop an iron deficiency. Furthermore, many elderly people take aspirin or phenylbutazone, which may cause internal blood loss.

Iron deficiency is difficult to treat by increased iron intake alone. Only an average of 10 percent of dietary iron is absorbed, and the absorptive potential varies from food to food. Meat consumption generally enhances iron absorption. Vitamin C and copper are necessary for the proper utilization of iron. Supplementation with ferrous iron may be necessary to meet the suggested daily intake of 10 mg. For the elderly on a low income, the daily intake of iron may be rather low given the expense of meats. In addition, fruits, which are a vital source of vitamin C, may similarly be avoided because of their high cost.

Zinc

Zinc is a component of several enzyme systems. It plays an important role in the synthesis of proteins and nucleic acids and is involved in insulin production. Deficiency in adults can result in poor appetite, an impaired ability for wound healing, and a diminished sense of taste and smell (Freedman and Biank, 1988). Marginal zinc deficiency can be a problem in the elderly.

A number of conditions not uncommon in the elderly, such as cirrhosis, kidney disease, malabsorption syndrome, malignancy, and alcoholism, can promote a zinc deficiency. Some studies have suggested that healing and taste acuity improved after zinc supplementation, although significant change has been difficult to demonstrate (Nordstrom, 1982). Since a relationship exists between zinc/copper ratios and *hypercholesteremia,* zinc supplementation must include a careful consideration of copper intake as well. It would, therefore, be wise for individuals of any age to avoid megadoses of zinc.

Iodine

Iodine is essential for proper thyroid function. Deficiencies do not appear to be a significant nutritional problem in the elderly. However, if an individual must go on a salt-free diet, alternative sources of iodine might be necessary. Many researchers believe that the use of iodine in food processing has greatly increased the amounts supplied in diets in the United States (Mertz, 1981).

Fluorine

Fluorine has been linked to the prevention and treatment of osteoporosis (Nordstrom, 1982). Its preventive role is probably established in early adulthood. Fluorine salts used in the treatment of osteoporosis can approach toxic levels, and their administration should therefore be carefully monitored.

Chromium

Chromium may be linked to adult-onset diabetes and cardiovascular disease, two of the leading causes of ill health in the elderly. Chromium is essential for the maintenance of normal *glucose tolerance* (Gurson, 1977). It may function as an *insulin cofactor* that serves to potentiate insulin by binding it to the cell membranes (Mertz, 1967, 1981). Chromium levels in the blood decline with age along with glucose tolerance. Some researchers have reported that chromium supplements for adult-onset diabetes improve glucose tolerance (Levine, Streetan, and Doisy, 1968), but in general such studies have yielded mixed results (Freedman and Blank, 1988). Chromium may also be involved in controlling the level of blood lipids and the rate that lipid deposits accumulate in the aorta (Nordstrom, 1982). Chromium supplements have been used successfully in older people to treat hypercholesteremia (Schroeder, 1976). Borel and Anderson (1984) report that marginal chromium deficiency is widespread.

Selenium

Selenium is utilized by enzyme systems essential to the integrity of cell membranes. Selenium and selenium-containing amino acids may aid in preserving the stability of the membranes of such subcellular structures as the mitochondria, microsomes, and lysosomes. Selenium appears to inhibit peroxidation, which can result in cell damage. It is possible that it works with vitamin E or at least serves to spare vitamin E in its antioxidant capacity (Li and Vallee, 1973). Thus, a potential relationship between selenium and biological aging exists (Harman, 1986).

Table 10.4 summarizes the possible functions of eight additional trace mineral nutrients that are sig-

TABLE 10.4   Additional essential minerals

Mineral	Function
Copper	Enzyme component Essential for iron metabolism
Manganese	Energy use (thiamine utilization) Exotropic actions
Cobalt	Constituent of vitamin B_{12} (dietary sources may be unnecessary since B_{12} is an essential nutrient)
Vanadium	Mineralization of teeth and bones Inhibition of a cholesterol synthesis May also have a toxic effect
Nickel	Health of epithelial tissue
Molybdenum	Prevent dental cavities Iron metabolism
Sulfur	Part of cell protein, cartilage and tendons Detoxification process Constituent of many proteins via S-containing amino acids
Chlorine	Acid–base balance Formation of gastric juice

nificant in the overall consideration of an individual's nutritional requirements.

WATER

Water is one of the most significant components of a balanced diet at any age, although the elderly can be particularly vulnerable to water balance disturbances. All metabolic reactions require water, and sometimes even small changes in water balance can lead to metabolic irregularities. Water is essential in a number of physiological functions. It aids the processes of swallowing, digestion, and transport of ingested food, and is an important medium for waste elimination. It also functions in the regulation of body temperature through sweating and may aid in reducing the osmotic load on the kidney. In some geographic areas characterized by hard water, it can contribute to mineral nutrition by adding zinc, fluorine, and copper to the diet.

Dehydration is a not-infrequent occurrence in some elderly people. The condition may result from a disease and may be exacerbated by minimal water intake. Dehydration can affect both fluid and electrolyte balance. The relationship of water to constipation and urinary problems was discussed in Chapter 9.

Symptoms of water imbalance that are simply accepted as characteristic of old age can sometimes be controlled by carefully monitoring water intake. Water imbalances may result in such symptoms as apathy, body weakness, depression, mental confusion, and difficulty in swallowing. In order to maintain a proper balance of body fluid, water intake should be of sufficient quantity to produce a quart or more of urine per day. Nutritionists and physicians suggest the equivalent of approximately six to seven glasses of water a day to ensure a proper water balance.

NUTRITION AND DRUGS

Nutrients and drugs interact in two major ways. First, drugs may have an effect on nutrient absorption and metabolism. For example, certain antibiotics lead to malabsorption of nutrients and a decrease in appetite. Second, the nutritional and health status of the host may affect drug metabolism. An example is the relationship between adequate protein intake and the potentiation of L-dopa in Parkinson's disease. These two kinds of interactions must be viewed against the declining ability of the aging organism to deal with the effects of some drug therapies.

Pharmacokinetics and pharmacodynamics provide specific information that is useful when considering interactions between nutrients and drugs.

Pharmacokinetics concerns itself with how much, how long, when, how, if, and where a drug will be absorbed, transported, used, metabolized, and excreted (Poe and Holloway, 1980). *Pharmacodynamics* is the study of the biochemical and physiological effects of drugs and their mechanisms of action (Comfort, 1977). The study of pharmacokinetics and pharmacodynamics indicates that changes in drug utilization occur as a result of age-dependent factors (Roe, 1989).

Cardiovascular output decreases as one ages and thus can affect the distribution of pharmacological agents throughout the body. Gastrointestinal changes can reduce the absorption of drugs, and altered renal capacity affects the excretion of drugs. These observations necessitate the consideration of altered dosages and alternative drug choices, as well as efforts to reduce multiple drug usage.

Roe (1976) has reviewed the evidence for the production of nutritional deficiencies during prolonged drug therapy. Elderly individuals and their health care providers should be aware of the negative effects of uncompensated drug therapy and the impact of certain foods on the effectiveness of certain drugs. It should be remembered that the elderly, compared to the general population, take more drugs and are more likely to take multiple drugs and to be chronic users of drugs (Lamy, 1980, 1981). They are therefore especially susceptible to drug–nutrient interactions. The problems, prospects, and theoretical models of drug–nutrient interaction are complex and varied. An outline of the most important drug–nutrient interactions affecting the elderly is presented in Table 10.5. Additional material on drugs and the elderly is presented in Chapter 15.

TABLE 10.5 Drug–nutrient interactions to be aware of in elderly persons

Drug	Nutritional effects
Alcohol	Can lead to deficiencies in all nutrients, especially B vitamins. Can replace eating.
Aminopterin Methotrexate (used to treat leukemia)	Inhibits folate utilizations. However, if folate is supplemented, drug may not be as effective.
Antacids	Magnesium salts can cause diarrhea, limiting absorption of all nutrients. Protein absorption may be adversely affected when stomach acidity is reduced. Aluminum hydroxide binds phosphates.
Antibiotics	1. Tetracycline can bind iron, magnesium and calcium salts. 2. Many antibiotics are antagonistic to folic acid and can result in deficiencies of other nutrients. 3. Can lead to malabsorption. 4. Neomycin binds bile acids and affects fat-soluble vitamin absorption. 5. Neomycin causes intestinal structural changes that result in malabsorption of N, Na, K, Ca, lactose.
Anticoagulants	Can cause vitamin K deficiency.
Anticonvulsants	Primadone, phenobarbitol induce folate defiency and vitamin D deficiency.
Antidepressants	Some cause accelerated breakdown of vitamin D. If the monamine oxidase (MAO) inhibitor-type is used, patients become intolerant to foods containing tyramine, such as aged cheese, red wine, beer, dry salami, and chocolate. These foods can precipate hypertensive crisis when MAO inhibitors are being used.

continued

TABLE 10.5 *Continued*

Drug	Nutritional effects
Aspirin and other anti-inflammatory drugs	1. Many cause gastrointestinal bleeding; arthritic patients who ingest large quantities may develop iron deficiency anemia secondary to blood loss. 2. Aspirin usage can affect folic acid status. 3. Aspirin and indomethacin can increase need for vitamin C by impairing its effectiveness.
Barbiturates	1. Some cause breakdown of vitamin D. 2. Excessive sedation of nursing home patients for behavior control can result in missed meals. 3. Folic acid is malabsorbed.
Cathartics	Reduce intestinal transit time necessary for proper absorption of some nutrients.
Cholesterol-lowering drugs such as chlofibrate	Any drug-altering blood lipids can affect absorption of fat-soluble vitamins. Vitamin K deficiencies can be produced.
Colchicine, used in gout	Causes malabsorption of fat, carotene, sodium, potassium, vitamin B_{12}, folic acid, and lactose
Diuretics	Most diuretics cause potassium to be lost in urine. Blood levels of potassium must be monitored, since mental confusion can result from low levels of potassium. Dietary sources of potassium should be consumed. (Magnesium may be deficient in long-term diuretics.)
Glucocorticoids, used in allergy and collagen disease	Impair calcium transport across mucosa.
Hormones	1. ACTH and cortisone therapy increases excretion of sodium, potassium, and calcium, and may contribute to the development of diabetes, hypertension, obesity, and water retention. Calcium and potassium supplements may be needed, as well as special diet prescriptions if hypertension and diabetes develop. 2. Calcitonin treatment: Decreases serum calcium levels as calcium is deposited into bone. Tetany may develop without oral calcium supplements. 3. Estrogen therapy: Over an extended period, may result in deficiences of folic acid and vitamin B_6. Patient should not receive folic acid supplements until vitamin B_{12} status is confirmed to be satisfactory. 4. Hormone therapy can cause peptic ulcers, which require dietary management. 5. Prednisone causes malabsorption of calcium.
Isoniazid (INH) (a drug used to treat tuberculosis)	Causes B_6 deficiency in some persons because it is an antagonist to the vitamin.
Laxatives	Harsh laxatives may cause diarrhealike effects: Food passes through the GI tract too fast to be absorbed. Mineral oil absorbs vitamins A and D, preventing them from being absorbed.
Licorice candy	Limits potassium absorption.
Metformin and Phenformin Hypoglycemic agents used in diabetics	Competitively inhibit vitamin B_{12} absorption.
Para-amino salicylic acid, used to treat tuberculosis	Can cause malabsorption of fat and folic acid; blocks absorption of vitamin B_{12}.
Potassium chloride, used to replenish potassium lost due to diuretic use	Depresses absorption of vitamin B_{12}.

STUDY QUESTIONS

1. Differentiate between minimal and optimal nutritional requirements and indicate how they are related to the RDA concept.
2. In what ways can physical activity contribute to nutritional balance in elderly individuals?
3. What are the major problems associated with carbohydrate, protein, and fat consumption among the elderly?
4. Discuss the pros and cons of vitamin supplementation for the elderly.
5. Identify the role and indicate some of the major problems among the elderly with regard to:
   a. Fat-soluble vitamins
   b. B-complex vitamins
   c. Vitamin C
6. What are the major functions of the essential mineral nutrients? Differentiate between macronutrients and micronutrients. Why is the absorption of most minerals inefficient? Is this particularly significant for the elderly?
7. Identify the role and indicate the most significant problems among the elderly with regard to:

calcium	zinc	potassium	selenium
phosphorus	iodine	chromium	iron
magnesium	fluorine	sodium	

8. Discuss the role of water in the physiological functions of the elderly. What major problems are associated with water imbalance among the aged?
9. Differentiate between pharmacokinetics and pharmacodynamics. What age-dependent factors influence drug use? Identify several drug-nutrient interactions to which health care professionals need to be sensitive in working with the elderly.

BIBLIOGRAPHY

Albanese, A. A. 1979. Calcium nutrition in the elderly. *Nutrition and the M.D.*, 5(12): 1-2.

Anderson, T. W., Reid, D. B., and Beaton, G. H. 1972. Vitamin C and the common cold: A double blind trial. *Canadian Medical Association Journal*, 107: 503-508.

Andres, R., and Hallfrisch, A. 1989. Nutrient intake recommendations needed for the older American. *Journal of the American Dietetic Association*, 9(12): 1739-1741.

Ausman, L. M., and Russell, R. M. 1990. Nutrition and aging. In E. L. Schneider and J. W. Rowe (Eds.), *Handbook of the biology of aging* (pp. 384-406). San Diego: Academic Press.

Baker, E. M. 1967. Vitamin C requirements and stress. *American Journal of Clinical Nutrition*, 20: 583-590.

Baker, H., Frank, O., and Jaslow, S. P. 1980. Oral versus intramuscular vitamin supplementation for hypovitaminosis in the elderly. *Journal of the American Geriatrics Society*, 28(1): 42-45.

Baker, H., Frank, O., Thind, J. S., Jaslow, S. P., and Louria, D. B. 1968. *Clinical vitaminology: Methods and interpretation*. New York: Wiley.

Batata, M., Spray, G. H., Bolton, F. G., Higgins, G., and Woolner, L. 1967. Blood and bone marrow changes in elderly patients with special reference to folic acid, vitamin B_{12}, iron and ascorbic acid. *British Medical Journal*, 2: 667-669.

Borel, J. S., and Anderson, R. A. 1984. Chromium. In E. Frieden (Ed.), *Biochemistry of essential ultratrace elements* (pp. 175-199). New York: Plenum Press.

Brin, M., and Bauernfeind, J. C. 1978. Vitamin needs of the elderly. *Postgraduate Medicine*, 63(3): 155-163.

Brocklehurst, J. C. (Ed.). 1979. *Textbook of geriatric medicine and gerontology*. Edinburgh: Churchill and Livingstone.

Cheraskin, E., Ringsdorfer, W. M., and Hicks, B. S. 1967. Thiamin-carbohydrate consumption and cardiovascular complaints. *Internationale Zeitschrift fur Vitaminforschung*, 37: 449-455.

Colditz, G. A., Branch, L. G., and Lipnick, R. J. 1985. Increased green and yellow vegetable intake and lowered cancer deaths in an elderly population. *American Journal of Clinical Nutrition*, 41: 32-36.

Comfort, A. 1977. Geriatrics: A British view. *New England Journal of Medicine*, 297: 624.

Creagen, E. T., Moertel, C. G., O'Fallon, J. R., Schutt, A. J., O'Connell, M. J., Rubin, J., and Frytak, S. 1979. Failure of dose vitamin C therapy to benefit patients with advanced cancer. *New England Journal of Medicine*, 301: 687-690.

Davidson, S., Passmore, R., Brock, J. F., and Truswell, A. S. 1975. *Human nutrition and dietetics*. London: Churchill and Livingstone.

Exton-Smith, A. N. 1978. A long and healthy life. *Physiotherapy*, 64(12): 352-357.

Exton-Smith, A. N., and Scott, D. L. 1968. *Vitamins in the elderly*. Bristol: John Wright and Sons.

Fleck, H. 1976. *Introduction to nutrition*. New York: Macmillan.

Fleming, B. B. 1982. The vitamin status and requirements of the elderly. In G. B. Moment (Ed.), *Nutritional approaches to aging* (pp. 84-117). Boca Raton, FL: CRC Press.

Forbes, G. B., and Reina, J. C. 1970. Adult lean body mass declines with age: Some longitudinal observations. *Metabolism*, 19(9): 653-663.

Freedman, M. L., and Blank, A. J. 1988. Controversies and questions in geriatric nutrition. *Journal of Geriatric Drug Therapy*, 2(4): 5-30.

Garn, S. 1975. Bone loss and aging. In R. Goldman and M. Rockstein (Eds.), *The psychology and pathology of human aging*. New York: Academic Press.

Garry, P. J., Goodwin, J. S., Hunt, W. C., Hooper, E. M., and Leonard, A. G. 1982. Nutritional status in a healthy elderly population: Dietary and supplementary intakes. *American Journal of Clinical Nutrition*, 36: 319-331.

Garry, P. J., and Hunt, W. C. 1986. Biochemical assessment of vitamin status in the elderly. In M. L. Hutchinson and H. Munro (Eds.), *Nutrition and aging* (pp. 117-137). Orlando, FL: Academic Press.

Girdwood, R. H., Thompson, A. D., and Williamson, J. 1967. Folate status in the elderly. *British Medical Journal*, 2: 670-672.

Gurson, C. T. 1977. The metabolic significance of diet. In H. H. Draper (Ed.), *Advances in nutrition research*. New York: Plenum.

Halsted, C. H. 1980. Folate deficiency in alcoholism. *American Journal of Clinical Nutrition*, 33: 2736-2740.

Harman, D. L. 1986. Free radical theory of aging. In J. E. Johnson (Ed.), *Free radicals, aging and degenerative diseases* (pp. 3-50). New York: Alan R. Liss.

Hegsted, D. 1989. Recommended dietary intake of elderly subjects. *American Journal of Clinical Nutrition*, 50: 1190-1194 (Suppl.).

Herbert, V. 1967. Biochemical and hematologic lesions in folic acid deficiency. *American Journal of Clinical Nutrition*, 20: 562-672.

Herbert, V., and Jacobs, E. 1974. Destruction of vitamin B_{12} by ascorbic acid. *Journal of the American Medical Association*, 230: 241-242.

Horwitt, M. K. 1976. Vitamin E: A re-examination. *American Journal of Clinical Nutrition*, 29: 569-578.

Kart, C. S., and Metress, S. P. 1984. *Nutrition, the aged, and society*. Englewood Cliffs, NJ: Prentice-Hall.

Lamy, P. P. 1980. Drug interactions and the elderly – a new perspective. *Drug Intelligence and Clinical Pharmacy*, 14: 513-515.

Lamy, P. P. 1981. Nutrition and the elderly. *Drug Intelligence and Clinical Pharmacy*, 15: 887-891.

Ledvina, M. 1985. Vitamin E in the aged. In R. R. Watson (Ed.), *Handbook of nutrition in the aged* (pp. 89-109). Boca Raton, FL: CRC Press.

Leevy, C. M., and Kurnan, T. 1975. Nutritional factors and liver disease. *Modern Trends in Gastroenterology*, 5: 250-261.

Levine, R. H., Streetan, D. P., and Doisy, R. 1968. Effects of oral chromium supplementation on the glucose tolerance of elderly human subjects. *Metabolism*, 17(2): 114-125.

Li, T. K., and Vallee, B. 1973. Biochemical and nutritional role of trace elements. In R. S. Goodhart and M. E. Shils (Eds.), *Modern nutrition in health and disease*, pp. 408-441. Philadelphia: Lea & Febiger.

Lutwak, L. 1976. Periodontal disease. In M. Winick (Ed.), *Nutrition and aging* (pp. 145-153). New York: Wiley.

Machlin, L. J., and Brin, M. 1980. Vitamin E. In R. B. Altin-Slater and D. Kritchevsky (Eds.), *Nutrition and the adult micronutrients* (pp. 245-266). New York: Plenum Press.

MacLeod, C. C., Judge, T. G., and Caird, F. I. 1975. Nutrition of the elderly at home, III: Intakes of minerals. *Age and Aging*, 4(1): 49-57.

MacLeod, S. M. 1975. The rational use of potassium supplements. *Postgraduate Medicine*, 57(2): 123-128.

Mareus, N., et al. 1987. Low serum B_{12} levels in a hematologically normal elderly subpopulation. *Journal of the American Geriatrics Society*, 35(7): 635-638.

McGandy, R. B., Russell, R. M., and Jartz, S. C. 1986. Nutritional survey of healthy non-institutionalized elderly. *Nutritional Research*, 6: 785-798.

McRae, T. D., and Freedman, M. L. 1989. Why vitamin B_{12} deficiency should be managed aggressively. *Geriatrics*, 44(11): 70-79.

Mertz, W. 1967. The biological role of chromium. *Federation Proceedings*, 26: 186-193.

Mertz, W. 1981. The essential trace elements. *Science*, 213: 1332-1338.

Munro, H. N. 1989. The challenges of research into nutrition and aging. In H. N. Munro and D. E. Danford

(Eds.), *Nutrition, aging and the elderly* (pp. 1-24). New York: Plenum Press.

National Research Council, Food and Nutrition Board. 1980. *Recommended dietary allowances*, revised. Washington, DC: National Academy of Sciences.

Nordstrom, J. W. 1982. Trace mineral nutrition in the elderly. *American Journal of Clinical Nutrition*, 36: 788-795.

Poe, W. D., and Holloway, D. A. 1980. *Drugs and the aged*. New York: McGraw-Hill.

Rhead, W. J., and Schrauger, G. N. 1971. Risks of long-term ascorbic acid overdosage. *Nutrition Reviews*, 29: 262-263.

Roberts, H. J. 1981. Perspectives on vitamin E as therapy. *Journal of the American Medical Association*, 240(2): 129-131.

Roe, D. 1976. *Drug-induced nutritional deficiencies*. Westport, CT: Avi Publishing Company.

Roe, D. 1989. Drug-nutrient interactions in the elderly. In H. N. Munro and D. E. Danford (Eds.), *Nutrition, aging and the elderly* (pp. 363-384). New York: Plenum Press.

Rudman, D. 1989. Nutrition, fitness and the elderly. *American Journal of Clinical Nutrition*, 49: 1090-1098.

Russell, R. M., Krasinski, S. D., Samloff, I. M., Jacob, R. H., Hartz, S. C., and Brovender, S. R. 1986. Folic acid malabsorption in atrophic gastritis: Compensation by bacterial folate synthesis. *Gastroenterology*, 9(6): 1476-1482.

Sandstead, H. H. 1987. Nutrition in the elderly. *Gerodontics*, 3: 3-13.

Schroeder, H. A. 1976. Nutrition. In E. V. Cowdry and F. U. Steinberg (Eds.), *The care of the geriatric patient*. St. Louis: C. V. Mosby.

Shils, M. E. 1969. Experimental production of magnesium deficiency in man. *Annals of the New York Academy of Science*, 162(2): 847-855.

Sneath, P., Chanarin, I., Hodkinson, H. M., McPherson, C. K., and Reynolds, E. H. 1973. Folate status on a geriatric population and its relationship to dementia. *Age and Aging*, 2: 177-182.

Stein, H. B., Hasan, A., and Fox, I. H. 1976. Ascorbic acid-induced uricosuria: A consequence of megavitamin therapy. *Annals of Internal Medicine*, 84: 385-388.

Suter, P. M., and Russell, R. M. 1989. Vitamin nutrition and requirements. In H. N. Munro and D. E. Danford (Eds.), *Nutrition, aging and the elderly* (pp. 245-292). New York: Plenum Press.

Tammen, R. L. 1983. Effects of potassium on blood pressure control. *Annals of Internal Medicine*, 96: 773-780.

Wald, N., Idle, M., Boreham, J., and Bailey, A. 1980. Low serum vitamin A and subsequent risk of cancer. *Lancet*, 2: 813.

Watkin, D. M. 1979. Nutrition, health and aging. In M. Rechcigl (Ed.), *Nutrition and the world food problem*. Basel, Switzerland: S. Karger.

Weg, R. 1978. *Nutrition and later years*. Los Angeles: University of Southern California Press.

Welser, M. M. 1984. Calcium. In N. W. Solomens and I. H. Rosenberg (Eds.), *Absorption and malabsorption of mineral constituents* (pp. 15-68). New York: Alan R. Liss.

Whanger, A. D. 1973. Vitamins and vigor at sixty-five plus. *Postgraduate Medicine*, 53(2): 167-172.

Wilson, E. D., Fisher, K. H., and Fuqua, M. E. 1975. *Principles of human nutrition*. New York: Wiley.

Winterer, J. C., Steffer, W. P., Perera, W. D., Uauy, R., Scrimshaw, N. S., and Young, V. R. 1976. Whole body protein turnover in aging man. *Experimental Gerontology*, 11: 78-87.

Young, V. R., Perera, W. D., Winterer, J. C., and Scrimshaw, N. S. 1976. Protein and amino acid requirements of the elderly. In M. Winick (Ed.), *Nutrition and aging*. New York: Wiley.

Young, V. R., Perera, W. D., Winterer, J. C., and Scrimshaw, N. S. 1978. Diet and nutrient needs in old age. In J. A. Behnke, C. E. Finch, and G. B. Moment (Eds.), *Biology of aging*. New York: Plenum Press.

Zheng, J. J., and Rosenberg, I. H. 1989. What is the nutritional status of the elderly? *Geriatrics*, 44(6): 57-64.

CHAPTER 11

The Biocultural Basis of Geriatric Nutrition

Aging is a *biocultural* process. Biology determines the potential duration of life, the relative length of the various phases of the life cycle, the physical signs associated with aging, and the nature and development of chronic and degenerative disease. Culture enables us to extend life expectancy through the development and application of science and technology. Culture also defines the stages of the life cycle and the ways in which people make the transition from one phase to another. Cultural stresses may even hasten the aging process.

There are two general but complementary approaches to a discussion of the biocultural basis of geriatric nutrition. The first involves the influence of nutrition on the biological aging process itself and its effect on the development of degenerative diseases that often accompany aging. A second approach, emphasized in this chapter, examines the factors that influence the eating patterns of the elderly.

SOCIOCULTURAL FUNCTIONS OF FOOD

Food is necessary for an organism to survive and prosper physiologically. In humans, food and eating behavior are embedded in a *sociocultural matrix*. In addition to biological nourishment, food serves many socially and culturally significant functions. These include the development of interpersonal relationships as well as feelings of security. Depending on the culture in question, food may also serve to express status, religious or ethnic identity, and feelings of pleasure and creativity.

Food influences behavior through *enculturation,* the process by which new generations come to adopt traditional ways of thinking and behaving (Harris, 1985). The process is based largely on the control that older generations exert over younger ones in terms of rewards and punishments. According to psychoanalyst Erik Erikson (1968), the first sustained human contact is the mother-infant relationship in which the infant learns to trust the mother as a function of the interaction associated with the feeding process. For older children, rewards and punishments may also involve food; for example, dessert may be offered or withheld in an attempt to influence behavior. Among adults, certain types of food are used to gain social and economic advancement, to show conformity or rebelliousness, and to recognize important achievements. In our society, births, confirmations and bar mitzvahs, weddings, and even death may be "celebrated" with food.

Food is used to initiate and maintain a variety of interpersonal relationships. In most cultures, in fact, food is one of the most important means of fostering social relationships. Individuals can be held together or set apart by food and eating behaviors and relationships. Examples of this include coffee breaks and "brown bag" lunch groups at work or school, and community groups that share food and eat together at church or other gathering places. Generally, people share meals with friends, not strangers, although sitting down together for a meal is often symbolic of a truce between antagonists.

Food is important in the expression of group identity or solidarity. The former Catholic custom of abstaining from meat on Friday served as a group identification for those who adhered to it in the face of societal pressure to ignore church doctrine. Religious or supernatural ideologies often influence, even dictate, eating patterns. Eating or not eating certain foods or combinations of foods can demonstrate one's faith or serve as a protective device. Specific foods may serve as commemorative symbols recalling significant past events (for example, Easter or Passover). Among Eastern Orthodox Christians, lentil soup with vinegar is often served on Good Friday. The lentils are symbolic of the tears of the Virgin Mary, and the vinegar reminds the faithful of how Christ on the cross was given vinegar instead of water to drink.

Ethnic and racial identity can be reaffirmed by the use of traditional foods. The popularity of "soul foods" (for example, collard greens and chitlins) among northern blacks is viewed by some as a return to cultural roots. The Black Muslim views this phenomenon quite differently and rejects "soul food" as symbolic of slavery, poverty, and degradation.

People also eat for sensory pleasure. Taste, texture, appearance, novelty, and other organoleptic qualities may be the major reasons for eating or not eating certain foods. In the absence of other kinds of gratifications, special or forbidden foods may gratify those who are generally deprived in other ways.

Finally, food may serve to express an individual's creativity. The preparation of good or exotic food may be an individual's only recognized achievement. In such a case, food is a very important source of attention, status, and personal worth. Some individuals may exhibit creativity in food preparation in addition to other accomplishments. Such creativity may simply add to or enhance the individual's own perception of personal worth or may increase his or her status in the eyes of others.

FACTORS AFFECTING NUTRITIONAL STATUS

The factors that affect the nutritional status of the elderly can be divided into two broad groups: (1) those that result from metabolic and physiological changes associated with aging and (2) those that affect the amount and type of food eaten. The latter group includes sociocultural factors, which are probably the most important influences on eating habits at any age. It also includes biological factors that can affect food selection and intake.

Effects on Metabolism and Physiology

It is generally recognized that caloric needs often decrease after age 55 (Winick, 1980). This results from decreased basal metabolism and a diminished activity pattern that is generally associated with aging. The slowing of basal metabolism is probably due to a loss of cell and tissue mass. Diminished activity may be a result of limitations brought on by chronic disease, lack of interest, or social isolation, among many other reasons.

The ability of the human body to respond to chemical imbalances is lessened with age. For example, after ingesting a dose of sodium bicarbonate (baking soda), the body takes eight times longer at age 70 than it would at age 30 to reestablish normal sodium levels in the blood. There is some evidence of an age-associated decrease in the size and permeability of the capillary bed of the small intestine, as well as a possible change in the permeability of the blood vessels as a result of collagenous changes. These alterations may diminish the capacity of blood vessels to take up and distribute nutrients (Exton-Smith, 1972).

Changes in digestive secretions may affect the digestion and absorption of food. The salivary glands begin to deteriorate at around age 60. This factor together with certain others, such as "mouth-breathing," tends to dry the mouth, possibly forcing the selection of soft, self-lubricating foods. This in turn reduces the range of choice among foods and can result in a fiber-deficient diet that leads to or aggravates chronic lower bowel problems such as constipation (Niessen, 1984). The secretion of the intrinsic factor of the gastric mucosa decreases, which may be related to an age-associated decrease

in the production of hydrochloric acid. This is significant because decreased intrinsic factor lowers the absorption of vitamin B_{12}, and reduced acidity affects iron and calcium absorption (Winick, 1980). A diminution of secreted pancreatic enzymes begins at about age 40, but there is little hard data to indicate that age-related changes occur in the enzymes of the intestinal mucosa.

Age-related changes in the composition of the bacterial flora of the intestine have been documented. These changes can be detrimental and are probably related to reduced gastric acidity or to enzymatic action that allows the rapid growth of other organisms, such as streptococci, at the expense of the normal flora. This condition can result in the loss of nutrients synthesized by the displaced organisms as well as lowered resistance of the tract to disease. It also results in an irritated and inflamed mucosal lining.

Abnormal bacterial growth in the intestine can bind vitamin B_{12} and affect its availability for the body's use. Fat metabolism can be affected by bile salt depletion resulting from *bacterial deconjugation* of bile salts. Furthermore, some of the by-products of deconjugation may be toxic and/or carcinogenic to the gut. Occasionally, bacterial groups such as *Clostridia, Bacteroides,* and *Veillonella* invade the small intestine from the large intestine, causing physical damage and upsetting environmental balances. This condition may necessitate short-term antibiotic therapy in conjunction with the administration of vitamins. In rare cases, when chronic conditions develop, intermittent long-term antibiotic therapy may be necessary.

Disorders of the hepatobiliary tract can also lead to fat maldigestion, which in turn can affect the body's utilization of the fat-soluble vitamins A, D, E, and K. There is some evidence of a 20 percent reduction in lipolytic activity in the elderly, but this has no appreciable affect on fat digestion. Becker, Meyer, and Necheles (1950) observed that it took aged individuals about twice the time required by younger people to absorb a high-fat meal.

Maldigestion and *malabsorption* are common conditions in the elderly, and the causal factors are numerous. These conditions, perhaps especially malabsorption, are responsible for many of the nutrient imbalances observed in the elderly. Balachi and Dobbins (1974) note some of the conditions that can lead to malabsorption:

1. Surgical alterations (e.g., esophagectomy, gastrectomy, and small bowel resections)
2. Pancreatic insufficiency caused by inflammation or tumor
3. Hepatobiliary insufficiency caused by such conditions as gallstones and hepatitis
4. Stasis and bacterial overgrowth
5. Drug-induced changes caused by alcohol, anticonvulsants, cathartics, diuretics, and antibiotics
6. Cardiovascular abnormalities such as congestive heart failure, constrictive pericarditis, arteriosclerosis, and abdominal angina
7. Radiation injury caused by accidental, occupational, or therapeutic exposures
8. Endocrinopathy such as diabetes, Addison's disease, and thyroid disease
9. Paget's disease
10. Collagen vascular disease
11. Amyloidosis
12. Celiac disease, sprue
13. Neoplastic disease
14. Paraproteinemia such as multiple myeloma

Malabsorption syndromes are difficult to manage when the small bowel mucosa are diseased. These syndromes can best be treated by parenteral administration of vitamins and minerals or oral administration of pharmacologic rather than physiologic doses of these nutrients. Correction of the underlying condition should be the clinical goal, although this may be impossible in many cases either because the cause of malabsorption is not known or because the medical means to correct it are not available. In most cases of malabsorption, nutritional management is the only way to sustain the patient. Any plan for its management must fit the individual case or circumstances.

Large bowel problems are common concerns for many of the elderly. In particular, constipation or the fear of constipation has long been a concern for many older people. Even the casual observer might note the frequency with which advertising campaigns for laxatives are directed toward the elderly. Judging from the popularity of books on high-fiber diets (e.g., Fredericks, 1976; Reuben, 1976; Galton, 1976; Westland, 1982; Adams and Murray, 1986), there is an increasing interest in the use of such diets. Recommendations for the use of high-fiber diets seem to be related to an effort to prevent bowel cancer as well as a variety of other conditions, including hemorrhoids, diverticulosis, and diabetes. The clinical and epidemiological evidence supporting the widespread health benefits of a high-fiber diet is controversial and incomplete (Kelsay, 1978). Despite these inconclusive findings, a great number of people have embarked on preventive health programs based on increasing the amount of fiber in the diet.

Little evidence exists to suggest that significant amounts of essential nutrients are absorbed by the large intestine, but large intestine distress, real or imagined, can greatly affect the variety and nature of individual dietary choice, thus creating problems of nutrient imbalance. Many of these problems seem to be readily amenable to treatment if techniques of preventive medicine are used. Diet plays a significant role in preventive medicine, although dietary changes may be difficult to implement because of long-standing habits. But the most efficient approach to most functional bowel problems is a therapeutic regimen consisting of dietary modification and increased physical activity.

Factors Governing Food Intake

Those who work with the elderly often come to realize that metabolic and physiological barriers to proper nutrition may be minor compared to those factors that actually regulate food intake. Factors governing food intake determine the quantity, quality, and combinations of foods eaten, and are intricately interwoven into the fabric of the elderly person's social life. Again, food can be as important among the elderly for social and psychological reasons as it is for physiological well-being.

Biophysical and sociocultural variables affect food intake. The interaction of these variables results in a systematic process that affects both the biological and sociocultural environment of an individual in the aging process. Such adaptation is truly biocultural in nature.

Biophysical changes that affect dietary intake include loss of teeth, reduced fine motor coordination, diminished vision, reduced sense of taste and smell, physical discomfort associated with eating, chronic disease, and decreased physical activity. These changes affect the efficiency of the alimentary tract and can alter dietary choice and are sometimes associated with changes in self-image as well as problems of isolation and depression. It is extremely important to remember that not all of these conditions are natural and inevitable outcomes of the aging process. Many can be corrected or alleviated.

Loss of teeth or the existence of denture problems can lead to dietary modifications that emphasize foods that are softer and easier to chew (Geissler and Bates, 1984). This can lead to reduced dietary bulk in the diet, further complicating lower bowel conditions. McGandy (1986) found that among elderly males, denture wearers had diets of lower quality. Chewing problems of a mechanical nature are real for many of the elderly. Some studies have noted decreased efficiency in mastication with the successive loss of teeth. For example,

the loss of a first molar can reduce efficiency on one side by as much as 33 percent (Neumann, 1970; Yurkstas, 1954).

A denture wearer must chew food four times as long to reach the same level of mastication as a person with natural teeth. Half the population of the United States is in need of dentures by age 65, and about two-thirds are totally edentulous by age 75 (Busse, 1978). Well-fitting dentures do not exist; "fit" is a relatively subjective phenomenon that often depends on the adaptive qualities of the individual involved. It is easier to fit and satisfy younger old people in their fifties or sixties than the "old-old," for whom shrinkage of the gums and palate complicate the problems of fit.

Maxillary dentures usually fit better than *mandibular dentures* because of the broad-based structure of the maxilla. The greater mobility of the mandible and the tendency for the muscles and tongue to dislodge the denture during speech and swallowing make a comfortable fit in this area less likely. Public dislodgement of dentures can be embarrassing for sensitive individuals. Fear of such embarrassment can result in the rejection of certain foods to the detriment of the nutritional status of the individual.

The loss of neuromuscular coordination is a biophysical problem associated with aging (Kohrs, Czajka-Narins, and Nordstrom, 1990). This condition can be further complicated by deteriorating vision, Parkinson's disease, stroke, or chronic arthritis. Fine motor coordination declines with age, but the existence of a chronic disease such as arthritis may greatly magnify the functional significance of any changes. Neuromuscular problems may lead to an inability to handle certain utensils, appliances, or foods. For those living alone, this inability can lead to the inefficient use of food resources. In the presence of others, both at home and in public, it is a source of embarrassment that can lead to a diminished use of important foods.

The psychological effects of these reduced capacities and the situations they may precipitate can further diminish self-image and affect the social functions of eating. The percentage of individuals who have difficulty preparing meals increases from 3.5 percent for those 65 to 69 years to 26.1 percent for those over 85 years (Dawson, Hendershot, and Fulton, 1987). The same study recorded percentages of 1.9 and 37 with regard to difficulty in shopping. People who work with the elderly must be aware of these possibilities and try to suggest alternatives to ensure adequate nutrition while preserving personal dignity.

A declining number of taste buds as well as neurological problems can affect appetite. At age 70 a person has only 30 percent of the number of taste buds present at age 30 (Arey, 1935). Loss of taste is a common complaint among the elderly (Schiffman and Covey, 1984). The ability to distinguish salty, bitter, and sour tastes declines with age, but the recognition of sweetness does not appear to be affected (Bartoshuk and Weiffenbach, 1990). Apparently, thresholds for each taste are less affected than the ability to perceive subtle differences within each taste category (Schiffman and Covey, 1984). This may be problematic taken in combination with sociocultural factors that tend to suppress appetite.

A diminished sense of taste can lead to overseasoning of foods with consequent irritation of sensitive parts of the digestive tract. In the case of salt, overuse can contribute to hypertension, heart disease, and kidney malfunction. The role of changes in taste and smell in the dietary pattern of the elderly is probably individually variable. Food preference, however, involves not only taste and smell but also food temperature, consistency, texture, and appearance (Holt, Kohrs, and Nordstrom, 1987). Murphy (1985) feels that odor and cognitive characteristics are important determinants of taste recognition in the elderly.

Interpretation of taste studies is difficult because, according to Mattes (1986), there are three principal measures of taste: threshold sensitivity; super threshold sensitivity (taste-level discrimination); and individual preferences for certain tastes. Further, Mattes and Mela (1986) argue that measure of taste preference may be related to dietary practices more than to sensitivity responses.

Most gastrointestinal discomfort associated with food ingestion is psychologically based, although biophysical causes such as hiatus hernia do exist. Useful research on the effect of particular foods on the digestive tract is scarce. In a study of a meals-on-wheels program, Zimmerman and Krondl (1986) found that 40 percent of their subjects reported one or more food intolerances. Elderly individuals should be encouraged to avoid any foods that seem to induce symptoms such as heartburn and distension. Care must be taken to replace the nutritional contribution of the eliminated foods with alternative foods that are sources of the lost nutrients. Replacement is vital if an eliminated food was a key dietary source of essential nutrients. For example, if citrus fruit juice is eliminated from the diet, care must be taken to assure proper vitamin C intake through consumption of alternative sources such as tomatoes and potatoes.

Chronic diseases also may necessitate modified diets. Chronic illness affects motivation and can deplete the energy needed to perform certain daily routines. Chronic disease can also affect the physical process of shopping for food, preparing it and even eating it. As described earlier, the percentage of individuals having difficulty shopping increases almost twenty times (1.9 percent versus 37.0 percent) from those aged 65 to 69 to those aged 85 years; for preparing meals, this increase is more than seven times (3.5 percent versus 26.1 percent) (Dawson et al., 1987). Modified diets are often expensive and can be difficult to follow, especially if the person does not fully understand the necessity or the directions. Unfortunately, nutritional counseling is rarely available when this situation arises.

Elderly individuals can and must be made to realize the nature of their dietary problems. They should be educated to understand fully the regimen prescribed and the consequences of not following it. An adequate counseling program does more than provide information on special diets. Diets should be devised to allow individual choice – monotony can destroy even the most well conceived diet.

Changes in the level of physical activity are also related to nutritional status. Exercise is needed to aid in the metabolism of foods. It is useful in relieving tension and maintaining mental well-being and is necessary to maintain the strength and vigor to undertake everyday tasks. Lack of energy for shopping or meal preparation can lead to an undesirable emphasis on easily prepared, high-carbohydrate refined foods, such as bread, jelly, jam, or ready-to-eat cereals and cakes. Many of these foods have an extremely high sugar content. Mental stress from depression (and related inactivity) can lead to a further reduction in physical activity and consequently decrease energy and motivation below the levels necessary to shop for and prepare food.

The sociocultural factors that affect food intake are more varied and have a greater impact on nutrients than the biophysical factors discussed earlier. Each elderly person is the product of years of experience in a sociocultural setting modified only by individual perception and choice. Dietary habits and ideas are likewise long-standing and difficult to change. People often seem arbitrarily to prefer or reject certain foods in the face of direct evidence that such foods are good or bad for them.

The tendency to establish an attachment to certain foods may represent an individual's desire for security at a time in life when, as a result of changing roles and status, his or her level of insecurity is quite high. Dietary habits are often associated with memories of youth, pleasant and unpleasant, and in this context take on increased significance. The elimination of preferred foods or the addition of objectionable ones should not be attempted unless there is a definite threat to health. The psychological stress of such impositions can negatively affect the value originally associated with the dietary change.

Income is a primary factor in determining diet at all ages. Many gerontologists believe that the major problems of geriatric nutrition are a function not of age but, rather, of the socioeconomic status (SES) of the aged. A summary of the findings of recent national nutrition surveys would suggest they are right. Retirement income, in comparison with preretirement earnings, is reduced for the great majority of older people. Poverty is a fact of life for many of the elderly, especially the nonwhite aged. Housing, health care, transportation, and other expenses compete with food for available money. Figure 11.1 shows the percentage distribution of average expenditures for families whose head-of-household is under 65 years of age, as well as for families whose head-of-household is older than 65. When compared with younger families, aged families spend a greater proportion of their income on food, housing, and health care. Calasanti and Hendricks (1986) have termed the SES factor "access to opportunity."

Many elderly shoppers cannot buy food using the criteria of past eating habits or optimal nutrition because they lack purchasing power. They may develop a tendency to purchase cheaper foods that are high in refined carbohydrates, such as bread and cereals, rather than buying more expensive protective foods such as meat, fruit, and vegetables. It is not the carbohydrates per se that are bad but, rather, the lack of dietary variety fostered by such purchasing patterns that often leads to reduced dietary quality and risk of malnutrition. In Massachusetts, McGandy (1986) found significant decreases in nutrient intake with low income status. In a study of a congregate meals program, Vanzandt and Fox (1986) found that 30 percent of their subjects felt that "expenses" were the most important food and dietary problem.

The elderly, like the poor in general, are often forced to shop at more expensive stores because of

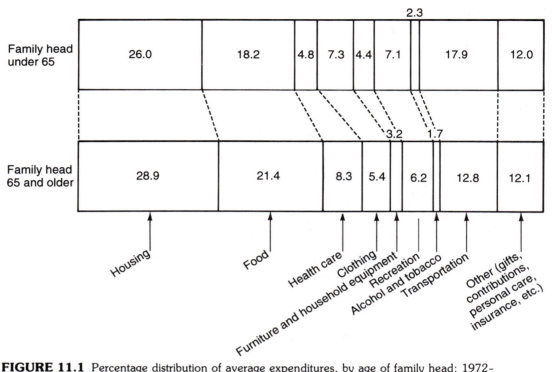

FIGURE 11.1 Percentage distribution of average expenditures, by age of family head: 1972–1973. (*Source:* Herman B. Brotman, "The Aging of America: A Demographic Profile," in *The Economics of Aging, A National Journal Issues Book* (Washington, DC: U.S. Government Research Corporation, 1978), p. 38.)

the absence of chain stores in local neighborhoods or lack of transportation to volume-sale stores with lower prices. Alternatively, the need to obtain credit to purchase food between retirement checks may arise. This necessitates the use of "Ma and Pa" grocery stores that give credit but must charge higher prices and carry a smaller variety of products than chain stores.

The elderly are often unable to take advantage of sales or quantity discounts because they lack proper storage facilities such as refrigeration and pest-free cupboards. Many people take for granted conveniences not always available to the poor or elderly. If money is not available for food at the time of the

month when sales occur, the advertised bargains are unobtainable. Food activist groups have observed the deliberate price inflation of food products by food retailers at the time of the month when welfare and social security checks arrive. The poor certainly do pay more (Caplovitz, 1967), and a significant proportion of the elderly are poor or at risk for poverty.

Marketing techniques aimed at higher profits such as end-of-aisle displays and multiple-item pricing affect both young and old. But many elderly people have less margin for error in budgeting their limited funds. Modern marketing procedures are geared toward younger consumers with families.

The elderly, especially those who live alone or have storage problems, need smaller quantities of food. But small quantities are often unavailable or, if available, are relatively more expensive than the same foods bought in larger amounts. The current trend toward prepackaging perishables also creates problems for the elderly. The quantities prepackaged are aimed at families, not single consumers. This orientation makes it necessary for the elderly shopper to ask for less, which is often embarrassing and necessitates repackaging of the product. Furthermore, opening food packages may pose a challenge, even for the young. Elderly individuals with failing vision, waning strength, and declining fine coordination may be frustrated by modern packaging materials.

As we have emphasized, eating is a social-psychological activity (Pike, 1968), part of the complex arrangements of interpersonal interactions. As such, it has significant social and psychological impacts on the elderly. For the elderly, food can be a great comforter during times of loss, such as the death of a spouse or companion or the loss of social involvements. Losses force the rearrangement of the individual's world and upset balances. However, reestablishment of the old balance or creation of a new one may be difficult. Foods associated with significant events and periods in the lives of old people and their loved ones may be helpful to individuals who must readjust their world.

Dietary stress can follow the loss of a spouse. Although widowers remarry at a substantially higher rate than widows, those who do not remarry may have special difficulty in adjusting. Widowers are often unable to take care of their own basic needs, especially if they have been married since youth and were socialized to depend heavily on their wives. For this reason, some of the worst nutritional problems are found among elderly widowers.

Widows are often able to continue to perform the domestic tasks that they have performed throughout their lives, but they may find themselves in financial distress. If her spouse functioned as the money manager throughout the marriage, a new widow may be unable to cope with even simple household management problems. Even for women prepared to handle these aspects of a spouse's death, the going may be difficult. Loss of companionship can seriously affect an individual's motivation to shop, cook, eat, remain active, or even go on living.

Loss of companionship may also reduce physical activity or social participation that previously diverted attention from many of the problems associated with old age. Emotional stress and depression are often associated with changing roles, isolation, chronic disease and disabilities, financial stress, and simply the fear of getting old. Depression is found in 8 to 15 percent of those over 65 living in the community and in 50 percent of those 65 or older living in nursing homes (Garetz, 1976). It may be associated with both over- and undernutrition, either of which can lead to disability or death.

Emotional stress can cause a loss of appetite and the development of negative protein, calcium, and magnesium balances because of increased excretion often associated with stress (Altschule, 1978; Scrimshaw, 1964). Stress can also lead to compulsive eating and the onset of obesity, which may further complicate health problems associated with old age. The elderly person who feels rejected or neglected by his or her family and friends may use eating as an attention-getting device. Other people may not listen to frequent complaints about arthritis, but if a person is not eating or is eating too much, friends and relatives generally worry and pay more attention.

Isolation can affect motivation to eat, shop, prepare meals, and maintain social relationships. Many people can adjust to isolation if it is self-imposed, and some may even prefer it. Even when it is not self-imposed, many people handle isolation well if there is some hope of an eventual positive change in the situation. But few persons can manage involuntarily imposed isolation that leaves them with no hope in sight.

Phillips (1957) has studied the relationship between losses, role changes, and adjustment to old age. His study of almost 1,000 aged individuals 60 and over – the retired compared to the employed, the widowed compared to the married – showed significantly more maladjustment among retirees, widows, and those with role losses. Maladjustment was measured by self-reports on the amount of time spent daydreaming about the past, thinking about death, and being absent-minded. Phillips argued that individuals who spend considerable time in such activities have difficulty in fulfilling their needs, including the need for appropriate caloric intake and dietary balance. Interestingly, Phillips employed a research variable he referred to as "identification as old." The item is a measure of self-image and simply asks, "How do you think of yourself as far as age goes – middle-aged, elderly or old?" He found that individuals who perceive themselves as elderly or old are significantly more maladjusted than those who perceive themselves as middle-aged. In addition, age identification appears to *reverse* the relationship between role loss and maladjustment. Thus, for example, those who are employed but identify themselves as old are more likely to be maladjusted than those who are retired but identify with middle age. How and why it is that some elderly individuals, even those who have suffered a role loss and are widowed, identify with middle age is still open to empirical investigation.

Finally, a number of basic logistical problems affect the ability of the elderly to get enough to eat. Lack of adequate cooking facilities may be a problem for those living in low-cost housing such as rented rooms or single-room-occupancy hotels. The use of cooking facilities may be discouraged by the presence of appliances or utensils that are old or dangerous. Pots with loose or absent handles and dull can openers can cause painful burns or cuts for an elderly person with poor vision or coordination problems. One solution to such minor environmental threats is avoidance, although losing the option to use such devices may seriously limit the range of possibilities for meal preparation and nutritional intake. Seasonal limitations of mobility, especially in the north, may also affect intake of perishable items that must be purchased frequently. Kim and Caldwell (1986) found that more persons had inadequate intake of energy, vitamin A, and calcium during the winter.

FOOD FADDISM

The dangers of *food faddism* are a subject that nutrition educators tend to overstate or exaggerate. The large majority of people who engage in food faddism – patronizing health food stores or stocking up on megavitamins – do not threaten their health but simply pay more for what they eat (Metress, 1980). Read and Graney (1982) note that in one study the cost of supplements came to as much as 20 percent of a monthly income of $300. It is often alleged that the elderly are particularly susceptible to the promises of food faddism (Davis and Davis, 1981). Although no scientific attempt has been made to ascertain whether the effects of food fads are positive or negative, most standard sources simply assume a negative impact. Recently, however, a study of nearly 3,200 elderly participants in a health screening program revealed that 46 percent of women and 34 percent of the men regularly used vitamin supplements (Hale, Stewart, and Cerda, 1982). Sheehan, Read, and DeLatte (1987) studied 600 elderly in seven western states and found that 60 percent used dietary supplements.

If the elderly are more susceptible to food faddism, what are the possible reasons and consequences for health? The attitude of organized medicine toward aging and geriatric problems may play an important role in the popularity of geriatric food faddism. With minor exceptions, modern medicine, which still emphasizes acute, curative care, has shown little interest in geriatric medicine. For many physicians, the problems of elderly patients are seen in terms of a negative prognosis. In this regard, physicians may mirror the values of our society as a whole with regard to aging.

Given this situation, it is not surprising that many elderly people turn to food fads. The fad gives the individual what at least appears to be some authoritative sanction for hopes that are often false. The individual can feel, at least, that he or she is actively doing something about his or her condition, and not just passively allowing it to deteriorate.

Poor nutrition education during the younger years also affects an individual's ability to evaluate nutritional claims. Without accurate knowledge, the consumer of any age is easy prey for flashy, manipulative advertising pitches by both food faddists and corporate producers. According to Gussow (1978), the deficiencies in current nutrition education in the United States are due to poorly trained health educators, government neglect, and corporate control. We have been socialized to "a quick-fix mentality" (Metress, 1980). Americans seem to be constantly searching for simplistic technological solutions to societal problems of all types. Socially and psychologically, food fads are an example of a falsely simplistic solution to fears and doubts about health and aging.

Many basic nutrition textbooks refer to the harmful effects of food faddism on the health of the elderly (for example, *hypervitaminoses*). Is there really a threat, and, if so, is it of minor or major proportions? Certainly, a variety of harmful effects can occur. These include vitamin toxicity, complication of existing health conditions, delay in seeking needed treatment, undue expense, unbalanced

diets, and simply disappointment. But what are the realities of these threats to the well-being of the elderly?

Toxicity due to superintake of some nutrient is a common charge of critics of food faddism. A review of the literature, however, discloses no quantitative and little anecdotal evidence of toxicity from food fads among the elderly. Actually, the two best known threats of hypervitaminosis involve the fat-soluble vitamins A and D. Given the fat malabsorption problems often associated with the aging gut, it seems unlikely that enough of either of these vitamins would be absorbed to lead to hypervitaminosis in most cases (Metress, 1980). However, the threat of complications in existing conditions is real. Occasionally, radical diets aggravate a pathological state such as constipation or diabetes, or can cause gallbladder trouble. Most people have some awareness of the limitations imposed by their known medical problems. Undiagnosed threats could pose a problem for the fad eater, but the necessary coincidence of pathology and fad is probably rare.

Self-treatment with fad diets could mean delay in securing necessary medical treatment, perhaps the most serious consequence of all self-care strategies. Most serious disorders, however, are of such a nature as to cause alarm in a person despite attempts to deal with it through self-care. The undue expense of adherence to self-treatment regimens has been advanced as another negative effect, especially for those on marginal incomes. The costs of a food fad may indeed divert needed money elsewhere – this would seem to be a real concern (Hale et al., 1982).

The threat that unbalanced fad diets might lead to covert or even overt malnutrition would not seem to be a significant concern except for those on an extreme dietary regimen. To date, there is no evidence that elderly people suffer from such dietary deficiencies as a result of this factor. Finally, the disappointment that false hope brings is more often short-lived than not and is certainly of no great long-term psychological significance for most people. The concept and consequence of false hopes are relative to a particular situation. In certain circumstances a false hope may lead to better adjustment to a condition for which little can be done anyway.

Are there benefits in the practice of food fads? If so, do they outweigh the possible threats? This is a difficult question to answer empirically. Some food fads may actually have beneficial effects or at least lead to better eating habits. With regard to the recent revival of interest in fiber as an important constituent of the diet, it should be recalled that for years this nutrient was also promoted by food faddists.

Participation in faddism may result in a psychological lift related to the feeling that at least one is doing something about the "miseries" of old age. This kind of psychological uplift may motivate some people to resume activities that were given up or curtailed. Increased participation can lead in turn to a renewed interest in life and to the development of a more positive attitude toward the aged.

STUDY QUESTIONS

1. Why is aging considered a biocultural process? What is the role of nutrition in this process?
2. What are the two general but complementary approaches to the discussion of the biocultural basis of geriatric nutrition?
3. What are the major sociocultural functions of food?
4. Discuss the effects of age-related changes in metabolism and physiology on the nutrition of the elderly. Identify the major age-related biophysical changes that affect the intake of food among the elderly.
5. Identify the major sociopsychological and socioeconomic changes that affect nutritional intake in the elderly.
6. Discuss the possible impact of food faddism on the elderly.
7. What are some of the major problems associated with nutrition education that can affect efforts to communicate with the aged consumer?

BIBLIOGRAPHY

Adams, R., and Murray, F. 1986. *A healthier you with a high-fiber diet.* Atlanta, GA: Communications Channel.

Altschule, M. 1978. *Nutritional factors in general medicine.* Springfield, IL: Charles C Thomas.

Arey, L. B. 1935. The numerical and topographical relation of taste buds to human circumvallate papillas throughout the life span. *Anatomical Records,* 64: 9-25.

Balachi, J. A., and Dobbins, W. V. 1974. Maldigestion and malabsorption: Making up for lost nutrients. *Geriatrics,* 29: 157-160.

Bartoshuk, L. M., and Weiffenbach, J. M. 1990. Chemical senses and aging. In E. C. Schneider and J. W. Rowe (Eds.), *Handbook of the biology of aging* (pp. 429-443). San Diego: Academic Press.

Becker, G. H., Meyer, J., and Necheles, H. 1950. Fat absorption in young and old age. *Gastroenterology,* 14: 80-92.

Brotman, H. B. 1978. The aging of America: A demographic profile. In *The economics of aging: A National Journal issues book.* Washington, DC: Government Research Corporation.

Busse, E. W. 1978. How mind and body and environment influence nutrition in the elderly. *Postgraduate Medicine,* 63: 118-125.

Calasanti, T. M., and Hendricks, J. 1986. A sociological perspective on nutrition research among the elderly. *Gerontologist,* 26: 232-239.

Caplovitz, D. 1967. *The poor pay more: Consumer practices of low-income families.* New York: Free Press.

Davis, A. K., and Davis, R. I. 1981. Food facts, fads, fallacies and folklore of the elderly. In J. Hsu and R. L. Davis (Eds.), *Handbook of geriatric nutrition.* Park Ridge, NJ: Noyes.

Dawson, D., Hendershot, G., and Fulton, J. 1987. *Aging in the eighties: Functional limitations of individuals 65 and over.* Department of Health and Human Services Publication No. PHS-87-1250. Hyattsville, MD: U.S. Public Health Service.

Erikson, E. 1968. *Identity, youth and crises.* New York: W. W. Norton.

Exton-Smith, A. N. 1972. Psychological aspects of aging: Relationship to nutrition. *American Journal of Clinical Nutrition* 25(8): 853-859.

Exton-Smith, A. N. 1978. Nutrition in the elderly. In J. W. T. Dickerson and H. Lee (Eds.), *Nutrition in the clinical management of disease.* Chicago: Year Book Medical Publishers.

Fredericks, C. 1976. *Carlton Fredericks' high-fiber way to total health.* New York: Pocket Books.

Galton, L. 1976. *The truth about fiber in your food.* New York: Crown Books.

Garetz, F. K. 1976. Breaking the dangerous cycle of depression and faulty nutrition. *Geriatrics,* 31(6): 73-75.

Geissler, C. A., and Bates, J. F. 1984. The nutritional effects of tooth loss. *American Journal of Clinical Nutrition,* 39: 478-489.

Gussow, J. D. 1978. *Thinking about nutrition education: Or why it's harder to teach eating than reading.* Paper presented at AAAS meeting, Houston, Texas.

Hale, W. E., Stewart, R. G., and Cerda, J. J. 1982. Use of nutritional supplements in an ambulatory population. *Journal of the American Geriatric Society,* 30: 401-409.

Harris, M. 1985. *Culture, people, nature: An introduction to general anthropology.* New York: Thomas Y. Crowell.

Holt, V., Kohrs, M. B., and Nordstrom, J. W. 1987. Food preferences of older adults. *Journal of Nutrition for the Elderly,* 6: 47-55.

Kelsay, J. L. 1978. A review of research on effects of fiber intake in man. *American Journal of Clinical Nutrition,* 1: 142-159.

Kim, S. K., and Caldwell, N. R. 1986. Dietary status of elderly persons living in an urban community during winter and summer seasons. *Journal of Nutrition for the Elderly,* 5: 5-21.

King, J., Cohenour, S. H., Corruccini, C. G., and Schneeman, P. S. 1978. Evaluation and modification of the basic four food guide. *Journal of Nutrition Education,* 10(1): 27-29.

Kohrs, M. B., Czajka-Narins, D. M., and Nordstrom, J. W. 1990. Factors affecting nutrition status of the elderly. In H. N. Munro and D. E. Danford (Eds.), *Nutrition, aging and the elderly* (pp. 305-333). New York: Plenum Press.

Mattes, R. D. 1986. Effects of health disorders and poor nutritional status on gustatory functions. *Journal of Sensory Studies,* 1: 275-290.

Mattes, R. D., and Mela, D. J. 1986. Relationship between and among selected measures of sweet taste preference in dietary intake. *Chemical Sensation,* 11: 523-539.

McGandy, R. B. 1986. Nutritional status survey of healthy non-institutionalized elderly. *Nutritional Research,* 6: 785-798.

Metress, S. P. 1980. Food fads and the elderly. *Journal of Nursing Care,* 13: 10-13, 24.

Murphy, C. 1985. Cognitive and chemosensory influences on age related changes in the ability to identify blended foods. *Journal of Gerontology,* 40: 42-52.

National Research Council, Food and Nutrition Board. 1980. *Recommended dietary allowances,* revised. Washington, DC: National Research Council-National Academy of Sciences.

Neumann, G. 1970. *Lectures in bioanthropology.* Bloomington: Indiana University Press.

Niessen, L. C. 1984. Oral changes in the elderly: Their relationship to nutrition. *Postgraduate Medicine,* 75(5): 231-251.

Phillips, B. 1957. A role theory approach to adjustment in old age. *American Sociological Review,* 32: 212-217.

Pike, M. 1968. *Food and society.* London: John Murray.

Read, M., and Graney, A. S. 1982. Food supplement usage by the elderly. *Journal of the American Dietetic Association,* 80: 150-153.

Reuben, D. 1976. *The save-your-life-diet.* New York: Ballantine.

Schiffman, S. S., and Covey, E. 1984. Changes in taste and smell with age-nutritional aspects. In D. Harman and R. Alfin-Slater (Eds.), *Nutrition and gerontology* (pp. 43-64). New York: Raven Press.

Scrimshaw, N. 1964. Ecological factors in nutritional disease. *American Journal of Clinical Nutrition,* 14: 114-122.

Sheehan, E. T., Read, M., and DeLatte, A. C. 1987. Vitamin and food supplement practices of the elderly in seven western states. *Federation Proceedings,* 46: 3405-3411.

Vanzandt, S., and Fox, A. 1986. Nutritional impact of congregate meal programs. *Journal of Nutrition for the Elderly,* 5: 31-43.

Westland, P. 1982. *High-fiber cookbook: A positive health guide.* New York: Arco.

Winick, M. 1980. *Nutrition in health and disease.* New York: Wiley.

Yurkstas, A. A. 1954. The effect of missing teeth on masticatory performance and efficiency. *Journal of Prosthetic Dentistry,* 4: 120-126.

Zimmerman, S. A., and Krondl, M. M. 1986. Perceived intolerance of vegetables among the elderly. *Journal of the American Dietetic Association,* 86: 1047-1051.

CHAPTER 12

The Cardiopulmonary System

Age-related changes in the heart and blood vessels are critical to the entire aging process. Although current knowledge does not allow us to specify the rank order of the effect of various systems on senescent decline, the cardiovascular system has been targeted as deserving of considerable attention in any evaluation of such decline (Eisenberg, 1984).

It is well known that cardiovascular disease has tremendous impact on individual survival. It is a major contributor to morbidity and mortality in the elderly. Heart attack, high blood pressure, congestive heart failure, and stroke afflict millions of Americans. The chances of experiencing any of these conditions increase with age. Heart disease is the leading cause of death among older adults. Heart disease, stroke, and related disorders kill almost as many Americans as all other causes of death combined (American Heart Association, 1990). The most important underlying factor associated with the incidence of these disorders is *atherosclerosis* — a condition characterized by a buildup of fatty deposits within the arterial wall.

Attempts are being made to reduce the risk of heart disease and stroke. The United States and a few other countries have witnessed a downward trend in cardiovascular mortality (Feinleib, 1983a; Havlik and Feinleib, 1979; Pyorala, Salonen, and Valkonen, 1985). The decline started in the United States in or around 1970 and has been impressive for both coronary heart disease and stroke (Feinleib, 1983a; Gordon and Thom, 1975; Pyorala, Epstein, and Kornitzer, 1985; Walker, 1974). It is estimated that during a ten-year period, 300,000 persons aged 35 to 64 were saved as a result of a reduction in coronary heart disease (Feinleib, 1983a). The reason for the decline in mortality is not fully understood. It is believed that both primary and secondary prevention have contributed to this decline.

This chapter will review the aging cardiovascular system. It will examine coronary heart disease, high blood pressure, and congestive heart failure. Stroke is included in Chapter 8. Additionally, this chapter will briefly consider pulmonary heart disease (*cor pulmonale*), most commonly caused by chronic obstructive pulmonary disease (COPD).

The prevalence of COPD increases with age. Cigarette smoking is the single most important factor in the development of obstructive pulmonary disease and lung cancer. Both of these pulmonary diseases will be reviewed, as well as upper and lower respiratory infections that are significant for older adults.

GENERAL CHANGES

Present knowledge of the heart and disease in old age does not always make it possible to distinguish between intrinsic age-related changes and those in-duced by either deconditioning or disease (Kitzman and Edwards, 1990). The normal adult human heart is the size of a clenched fist. It is a masterpiece of technology. This muscular mass, referred to as the *myocardium,* beats 100,000 times a day, resting only between beats; with age, it tends to enlarge.

Moderate cardiac enlargement may result from increased blood pressure (Lakatta and Gerstenblith, 1990) and peripheral vascular resistance, which places a greater workload on the heart. It may also be related to the loss of elasticity of the aorta (Figure 12.1). This large artery, which receives blood freshly pumped from the left ventricular chamber and whose branches ultimately carry blood to all parts of the body, stiffens and dilates with age. Hence, a greater workload is placed on the heart as it pumps against the resistance of an inelastic aorta.

Heart weight has been shown to increase by 1 to 1.5 grams per year between the ages of 30 and 90 years. This increased weight has been attributed to

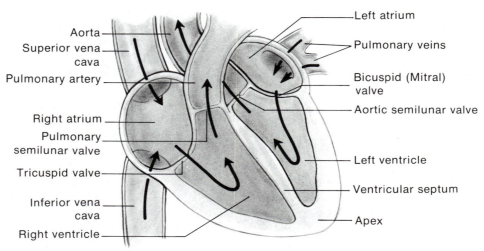

FIGURE 12.1 Diagram of the heart. Arrows indicate direction of blood flow.

increased ventricular wall thickness. The latter seems to be an adaptive mechanism in response to the increased myocardial workload cited previously (Gerstenblith, Fredrikson, Yin, Fortuin, Lakatta, and Weisteldt, 1977; Linzback and Akuamoa-Boateng, 1973; Morley and Reese, 1989).

Although it can be retarded by physical conditioning, there is a recognized decline in cardiac output with age. This decline cannot be totally explained by a sedentary life-style; it is observed among the physically conditioned as well. However, the Baltimore Longitudinal Study on Aging, which contained a highly screened population of healthy subjects, found no change in cardiac output with aging (Rodeheffer, Gerstenblith, Becker, Fleg, Weisfeldt, and Lakatta, 1984). A slight decrease in heart rate was observed, but it was offset by a slight increase in left ventricular output.

Changes in cardiac output need not be significant as long as the older individual is not in a stressful situation. During the stress of exercise the younger person's heart beats faster and undergoes an increase in the strength of muscular contractions. The heart's ability to respond to stress does decline with age.

The amount of oxygen that can be delivered to and used by muscles, known as maximum oxygen consumption, progressively declines with age. The age-related decline appears to be secondary either to a diminished muscular capacity to utilize oxygen or a failure to increase the volume of blood diverted to muscles (Morley and Reese, 1989). Some of the decline is modifiable with physical conditioning, smoking cessation, and weight reduction.

Generally, the anatomic and physiologic changes that take place in the aging heart allow it to function adequately if the coronary artery system is not greatly damaged. Because coronary artery disease is such a prevalent condition among older Americans, however, it is very difficult to determine to what extent the heart ages independently of the disease.

CORONARY ARTERY DISEASE

Coronary artery disease increases in incidence with age and is the major cause of heart disease and death in older Americans. It occurs when arteries supplying heart tissue become narrowed, reducing blood flow to the heart. Tissue that is denied an adequate blood flow is called *ischemic*. Hence, coronary artery disease is also known as *ischemic heart disease* as well as coronary heart disease (CHD).

Factors responsible for the narrowed and constricted arteries are not fully understood. What is known is that an overwhelming number of persons develop a condition known as *atherosclerosis*. In this condition, the large arteries in particular undergo a narrowing of their *lumen* due to the buildup of *atherosclerotic plaque*. Plaque contains various substances including cholesterol crystals, calcium salts, and connective tissue. As plaque formation advances, a blood clot is likely to form, increasing the risk of blocking an already narrowed artery.

Plaque formation is a gradual process localized within the *intima*, the innermost layer of the arterial wall (Figure 12.2). Lesions of atherosclerotic development, known as *atheromas,* develop progressively and are categorized as *fatty streaks, fibrous plaques,* and *complicated lesions* (Ross, 1983, 1986).

Autopsy data indicate that fatty streaks, the earliest detectable lesions, begin very early in life. They form when white blood cells become laden with fats and collect beneath the tissue lining the insides of arteries. Initially they are relatively harmless and clinically insignificant, but they may progress into the raised lesions of artery-narrowing plaque, which can eventually lead to heart attack. Detection of these early lesions can be traced to now-classic autopsy studies reported in the 1950s. Moon (1957) examined the coronary arteries of subjects ranging from fetuses to young adults. He noted what he interpreted as beginning atheromas in infants as young as three to four months of age. Only

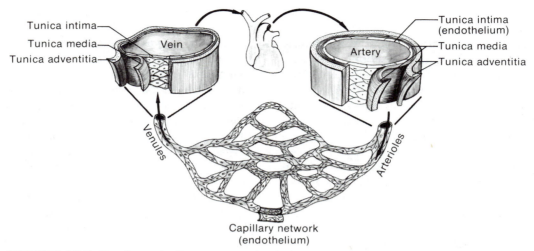

FIGURE 12.2 Blood vessels. Diagrammatic sketch showing the single-cell endothelium of all the vessels and the layered muscular coats of arteries and veins.

the fetal tissue displayed no evidence of fatty streaks or incipient plaque formation. Studies by Holman, McGill, Strong, and Geer (1958) revealed evidence of fatty streaks in the aorta by 3 years of age.

Studies of U.S. soldiers killed in Korea and Vietnam demonstrated that by young adulthood the more advanced lesions of fibrous plaque could be present on the walls of coronary arteries. Fibrous plaque is composed of a cap of fibrous connective tissue overlaying the fat-engorged regions of arterial wall. Extensive plaque formation was demonstrated in 77.3 percent of the 200 postmortem examinations of Korean War casualties, although the mean age of those examined was only 22.1 years (Enos, Holmes, and Beyer, 1953, 1955).

As fibrous plaques progress, they occupy more of the arterial channel. Ultimately, arterial blood flow is compromised. The fibrous plaque often evolves into a complicated lesion characterized by calcification, hemorrhaging, ulceration, release of debris, thrombus formation (a blood clot), and occlusive disease (see Figure 12.3).

Although the clinical consequences of the athero-sclerotic process typically appear in adulthood and often among the elderly, it is now clearly recognized that the process begins in childhood. Data from observations on large numbers of children in the Bogalusa Heart Study, the Muscatine Study, and the Lipid Research Clinic Program trace the early natural history of coronary heart disease and underscore the need to begin its prevention in the adult early in life (Berenson, Srinivasan, Hunter, et al., 1989).

Although the mechanism behind atherosclerotic development is the subject of much study, a leading theory regarding its initiation is the *response to injury hypothesis* (Ross, 1986; Ross and Glomset, 1973). This theory poses that damage is done to the inner lining of the arterial wall, exposing it to blood flow. *Platelets,* carried in the blood, can thus adhere to the exposed area and release growth-promoting substances that stimulate smooth muscle cell division. These cells, normally located in the middle layer of the arterial wall (*media*), proliferate and migrate into the intima, where they fill with lipids. The normally smooth arterial margin swells,

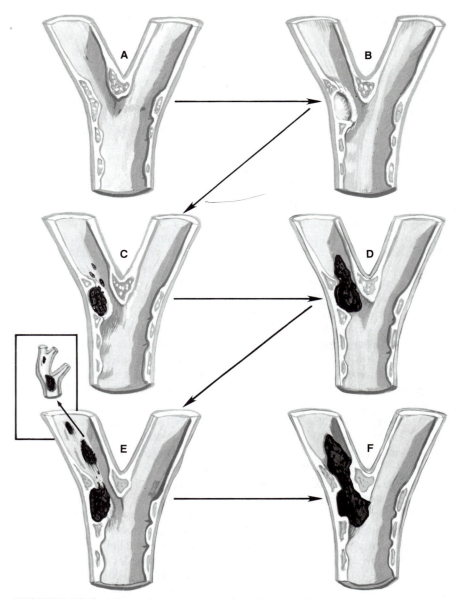

FIGURE 12.3 Atherosclerosis with resultant thrombus formation.
(A) Atherosclerotic plaque at arterial bifurcation. (B) Loss of intimal continuity
(ulcer formation). (C) Aggregation of platelets and fibrin on roughened surface;
fibrinoplatelet emboli may occur. (D) Thrombus formation superimposed.
(E) Embolization of contents of plaque (cholesterol and/or calcium) and fragments
of organized thrombus; occlusion of blood vessels distally in arterial tree.
(F) Thrombus causes total arterial occlusion.

becoming bumpy and irregular, narrowing the passageway. It is speculated that arterial injury could be triggered by numerous chemical and mechanical factors including cholesterol, cigarette smoke, hormones, and high blood pressure. The possible role of viruses in the development of arterial injury and smooth muscle cell proliferation is also being studied (Melnick, Adam, and DeBakey, 1990).

Arterial injury allows platelet-derived growth factor (PDGF), along with other plasma components including lipids and insulin, to interact with arterial tissue. These substances may alter arterial metabolism, stimulating both medial smooth muscle cell migration and division. Theoretically, if exposure to the damaging and growth-promoting substances is repetitive, lesion formation would progress.

An accelerated and premature atherosclerotic process is responsible for significant morbidity and mortality in patients undergoing heart *transplantation, coronary bypass surgery,* and balloon angioplasty (Barnhart, Pascoe, Mills, et al., 1987; Fuster and Chesebro, 1986; McBride, Lange, and Hillis, 1988). The latter is an invasive blood vessel-opening procedure. It involves running a catheter into a partially blocked artery and temporarily inflating a very small balloon to compress the arterial plaque. The mechanisms outlined in the response to injury hypothesis seem pertinent to the accelerated atherosclerosis following the inadvertent vascular injury associated with these medical treatments (Ip, Fuster, Badimon, et al., 1990).

Another major theory regarding atherosclerotic development is the *monoclonal hypothesis.* It holds that plaques are essentially benign tumors that arise from single smooth muscle cells. A monoclonal origin for atheromas does not negate the response to injury hypothesis. It maintains that at least some atherosclerosis is characterized by a "cancerlike" event whereby single smooth muscle cells are transformed to proliferate. The role of serum cholesterol in this transformation is unknown.

Over the years plaque formation slowly and silently progresses. As reduced blood flow becomes significant, the syndrome of *angina pectoris* may be present. Angina is a recurring, dull pain emanating from behind the breastbone. It may be varyingly reported as burning, heaviness, tightness, pressure, severe pain, or squeezing in the chest. Pain may also be reported in the left arm, shoulder, neck, jaw, and side of the face. It happens when the blood supply to the heart muscle is inadequate and may be triggered by physical activity or emotional upset. Symptoms are transitory, usually lasting for a few minutes. If an older person's activity is limited by other chronic conditions or life-style, he or she may not exercise enough to bring about or be aware of anginal symptoms (Gerstenblith and Lakatta, 1990).

Coronary artery disease and prolonged ischemia of heart muscle can lead to a heart attack. Such an event may occur because normal cardiac contractions are interrupted, resulting in a *cardiac arrest.* It may also occur because the reduced blood supply to the heart causes the *death of heart tissue.* This situation is termed a *myocardial infarction.* The extent of involved heart tissue determines the severity of the episode. If only a small portion of heart muscle is affected, cardiac reserves allow the work of the heart to be continued.

A heart attack in an older adult with coronary artery disease may be triggered by varying mechanisms. A coronary artery may be suddenly blocked as a result of a blood clot formed on the outer face of an ulcerated atheromatous *plaque.* This is referred to as a *coronary thrombosis.* Less frequently, the blockage may result from the contents of the atheroma (atheromatous debris) spilling out into the arterial channel. Hemorrhaging near the arterial plaque, further obstructing the opening, and arterial spasm are two other mechanisms that might cause a heart attack. Finally, the sudden increased oxygen needs of the heart precipitated by strenuous activity such as snow-shoveling can induce severe ischemia and heart attack.

Sometimes an individual's pattern of *collateral circulation* will be life-saving. This pattern describes a system of smaller blood vessels that compensate for a main vessel blockage by supplying blood to the critical area. If it were not for these collateral vessels, death from heart attack would occur much earlier and much more frequently than it does at present.

With age there may be insufficient cardiac reserve to withstand the attack. Mortality associated with myocardial infarction for persons over 70 years of age is twice that of those under age 70. It should be emphasized that the effect of age itself is not known. Prognosis probably rests with the severity and duration of disease. Left ventricular dysfunction and multivessel coronary artery disease are the two most powerful predictors of poor prognosis following a heart attack. They are more likely to be present in the elderly (Morley and Reese, 1989).

It is generally recognized that symptom presentation for myocardial infarction among the elderly may be atypical and variable. Chest pain, though still common (Konu, 1977; MacDonald, Baillie, and Williams, 1983; Tinker, 1981; Williams, Begg, Semple, and McGuinness, 1976), becomes a less frequent complaint with advancing age (Bayer, Chadha, Farag, and Pathy, 1986; MacDonald, 1984; Morley and Reese, 1989). In extreme old age, shortness of breath or acute confusion may be a more prominent symptom. One study concludes that in patients over 85 years of age atypical symptom presentation becomes the rule (Bayer et al., 1986). *Silent heart attack* may occur (Bayless, 1985; Marchand, 1955), where pain and discomfort are absent. In some cases, however, myocardial infarctions have been inappropriately described as "silent" (because of the absence of chest pain) in the presentation of other symptoms such as shortness of breath and/or acute confusion.

The reason for the possible absence of pain during myocardial infarction is not known. It is speculated that the silence of the episode may be due to an age-associated diminished sensitivity to ischemic pain. Desensitivity, confusion, and failure to note such an event may also result from reduced blood flow to the brain which is secondary to the related reduction in cardiac output.

Intermittent claudication is often a signal of widespread atherosclerotic involvement and a forerunner of impending heart attack (Kannel and McGee, 1985). It is characterized by pain as well as fatigue and weakness in legs affected by occlusive disease, generally referred to as *peripheral vascular disease*. The pain of peripheral vascular disease usually begins in the toes and may gradually involve the entire lower leg. Changes characteristic of poor nourishment of the lower limbs include thinning of skin, hair loss, and toenail thickening. Ischemia may also result in decreased muscle mass contributing to limb weakness (Adelman, 1982). Gangrene and amputation may result, although the risk is low. This serious complication occurs predominantly among advanced diabetics who continue to smoke. Peripheral vascular disease is not an inevitable consequence of aging and should yield to the same preventive measures as cardiovascular disease.

Prevention of morbidity and mortality associated with the atherosclerotic process must take into account certain important risk factors. Cigarette smoking, high blood pressure, elevated serum cholesterol levels, and diabetes are recognized as major risk factors that are subject to modification. Obesity, sedentary life-style, and excessive stress are also contributing factors. Heredity, gender (male), race (black), and age are major risk factors that cannot be changed. The more risk factors present, however, the greater the chance of serious atherosclerotic lesions. Attention should be given to those factors an individual can control as well as those modifiable through physician care.

Cigarette smokers have twice the rate of heart attack of nonsmokers, and severity of risk is related to the number of cigarettes smoked per day. Smoking is the most powerful risk factor for peripheral vascular disease and the most prevalent risk factor for sudden death resulting from a heart attack. The American Heart Association (1990) reports that smokers experience two to four times the risk of sudden death (within an hour) after a heart attack compared with nonsmokers. Sixty-two percent of women dying suddenly from coronary heart disease have been identified as heavy smokers, defined as smoking more than 20 cigarettes per day (Spain, Siegel, and Bradess, 1973).

Smoking cessation can reduce the risk of heart attack even among long-time smokers. Ten years after quitting, those who smoked a pack a day or less demonstrate a risk of death from coronary disease that is almost the same as if they had never smoked. In general, persons who quit smoking reduce their risk to half that of those who continue to smoke (American Heart Association, 1990; Gordon, Kannel, and McGee, 1974). One study suggests that women who stop smoking before the onset of heart attack experience no excess risk when compared with lifelong abstainers (Willet, 1981).

Long-term inhalation of cigarette smoke may result in repetitive injury to arterial tissue, accelerating the atherosclerotic process (Bierman, 1990). Research suggests that smoking may affect the arterial lining, platelet adhesion, heart rhythm, oxygen utilization and transport, heart rate and blood pressure, and blood cholesterol levels (American Heart Association, 1980). Smoking is significant as an independent factor but is especially harmful when other risk factors are present.

High blood pressure adds to the workload of the heart and is associated with an increased risk of CHD mortality. Proper diet, exercise, and medication are a part of blood pressure control.

Serum cholesterol level is consistently correlated with CHD risk. Studies relate the regular intake of large amounts of saturated fat and cholesterol as contributory to elevated blood lipid levels. The American Heart Association has recommended a prudent diet in which 30 to 35 percent of total caloric intake is derived from fats; less than one-third of these calories should be derived from *saturated fats,* and up to 10 percent can come from *polyunsaturated fats* and oils. To make up for lost calories via fat restriction, *complex carbohydrate* consumption should be increased to allow for 50 percent of energy intake. Practically applied, these recommendations call for an increased intake of fruits, vegetables, legumes, and whole grains; a reduced intake of high-fat red meat, pork, and organ meat; and the use of unsaturated and polyunsaturated vegetable oils and margarine for table spreads, salad dressings, cooking, and food preparation. Vegetarians in the United States demonstrate below-average blood lipid levels and a lower incidence of CHD (Taylor, 1976).

Cholesterol is produced by the body and is also ingested in foods. It is insoluble in aqueous solution. Therefore, it is transported in the bloodstream attached to fat and protein complexes known as *lipoproteins.* There are four major groups of lipoproteins (chylomicrons, very-low-density lipoproteins, low-density lipoproteins, and high-density lipoproteins) designated on the basis of their density. Density is said to increase as the proportion of protein increases in the lipoprotein complex.

Approximately 80 percent of circulating cholesterol is carried in the form of *low-density lipoprotein* (LDL). LDLs transport cholesterol from the bloodstream to cells. They have been termed "bad" cholesterol because excess levels, rejected by the cells, are deposited to help trigger the formation of plaque. An excess of cholesterol carried by LDLs is associated with an increased risk of coronary heart disease. Conversely, increased concentrations of *high-density lipoproteins* (HDLs) seem to protect against coronary heart disease. HDLs have been termed "biological vacuum cleaners." They help to clear excess cholesterol from the blood, facilitating its eventual transport to the liver, where it is broken down and excreted.

As noted earlier, dietary fat, particularly saturated fat, and cholesterol are proposed to be the major dietary factors influencing blood lipid levels. HDL levels are also influenced by exercise, cigarette smoking, gender, and age (Khan and Manejwala, 1981). Women usually have higher levels of HDL than men. Generally, among adults, the LDL:HDL ratio increases with age (Gordon, Casteli, Hjortland, Kannel, and Dawber, 1977). Research is needed on age-related aspects of cholesterol metabolism in humans.

Most cases of diabetes occur during middle age and among people who are overweight. Diabetes significantly increases the risk of heart attack. Control of elevated blood sugar levels alone does not seem to reduce atherosclerotic involvement characteristic of the large blood vessels in the diabetic. Attention to the various modifiable risk factors associated with CHD is imperative.

Obesity is related to CHD through its influence on serum cholesterol, high blood pressure, and the development of adult-onset diabetes. Weight loss should be achieved by a proper diet and exercise. A program of regular physical activity should be encouraged as part of one's CHD prevention program.

Exercise that may protect against disease or improve survival following a heart attack includes walking, running, cycling, and swimming. Such activities should be engaged in for 15 to 30 minutes every other day. With regular exercise of this nature, the functional capacity of the cardiovascular system is increased and the myocardial oxygen demand decreased for any given level of physical activity. Data from the 1988 Behavioral Risk Factor Surveillance System (BRFSS) indicate that sedentary life-style is the most prevalent modifiable risk factor for coronary heart disease (Centers for Disease Control, 1990).

Atherosclerosis is one form of *arteriosclerosis*. The latter is a generic term referring to the loss of elasticity or hardening of the arteries. It can occur secondary to a disease state and as a result of aging. Unfortunately, these two terms are often used interchangeably, causing confusion regarding their distinction. Several years ago Kohn (1977, p. 297) put the distinction in perspective by stating:

> It would be more useful to restrict the term arteriosclerosis to its original and literal meaning – hardening of the arteries – and to consider the other varieties of vascular changes as separate entities. While loss of distensibility is a general aging phenomenon, occurring in all populations and possibly developing at comparable rates, degree of atherosclerosis in individuals and populations is variable.

Age-related change in the arterial wall does not simply in itself lead to atherosclerosis. It is probably the case that intrinsic aging and environmental factors operate over time in conjunction with genetic factors to cause the "age-related" condition. Coronary heart disease is recognized to begin in childhood. In an attempt to encourage the adoption of healthy life-styles, cardiovascular health education for schoolchildren is important (Berenson, Srinivasan, Hunter, et al., 1989).

HIGH BLOOD PRESSURE

Blood pressure represents the force exerted by blood flowing against vessel walls and created by the pumping action of the heart. High blood pressure, also known as hypertension, is dangerous because it indicates reduced blood flow to vital organs and increases the risk of heart attack, heart failure, stroke, and renal failure. Kidney damage may be a cause of high blood pressure, but more often the kidney is the victim of high blood pressure. Hypertension associated with inelastic and occluded renal arteries leads to ischemic renal tissue. Poorly nourished kidneys cannot remove sufficient fluid from blood for urine output. Hence, a vicious cycle begins. The fluid volume of the blood increases, as does blood pressure and the workload placed upon the heart.

Blood pressure readings are represented by two numbers as designated in Figure 12.4. The first is *systolic pressure*. It measures the force exerted when the heart beats, sending blood into the arteries. The second is *diastolic pressure;* it measures the pressure in the arteries while the heart is resting between beats. The risk of cardiovascular morbidity and mortality rises in a continuous fashion as either systolic or diastolic pressure increases, making the establishment of an absolute threshold level for hypertension difficult (Applegate, 1990).

Among the elderly, high blood pressure is generally categorized as either *isolated systolic hypertension* (ISH) or *combined systolic-diastolic hypertension* (SDH). ISH exists when a systolic pressure level of 160 mm Hg or above occurs in the presence of a diastolic pressure of less than 90 mm Hg (Borhani, 1986; Hulley, Feigal, Ireland, Kuller, and Smith, 1986). SDH occurs when systolic pressure is greater than 140 to 160 mm Hg and diastolic is equal to or exceeds 90 mm Hg.

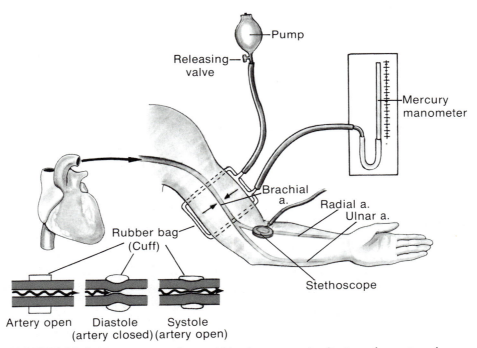

FIGURE 12.4 Measurement of arterial blood pressure. Application of an external pressure closes the brachial artery. As the external pressure is decreased, the manometer registers the first passage of blood through the constriction (systole). As the external pressure decreases further, the pulsation diminishes and disappears (diastole).

ISH accounts for much of the increased prevalence of reported high blood pressure in the elderly (Drizd, Dannenberg, and Engel, 1986). It is partially associated with rigidity of the aorta and a loss of arterial elasticity (Gifford, 1986), which forces the heart to work harder to sustain normal blood flow. Elevated systolic pressure is recognized as the single greatest risk factor for increased cardiovascular disease among the elderly (Applegate, 1990; Kannel and Gordon, 1978). The impact of systolic blood pressure on mortality is independent of the corresponding level of diastolic pressure.

Diastolic pressure is less likely than systolic pressure to increase during old age (Gifford, 1986). It tends to peak during the mid-fifties in men and the early sixties in women. Elevated diastolic pressure is a prevalent condition and a strong risk factor for cardiovascular disease. According to data from the Framingham study, however, it is somewhat more predictive of coronary heart disease in those under age 45. Its predictive power decreases somewhat with age, whereas that of systolic pressures increases (Kannel, Gordon, and Schwartz, 1971). For those over age 60, systolic pressure is more predictive of coronary heart disease.

Various medications are available to treat high blood pressure. Diuretics rid the body of excess fluid and sodium. Vasodilators widen constricted or narrowed blood vessels. Other drugs attempt to prevent vascular constriction.

Although specific causes of high blood pressure are usually unknown, a number of predisposing factors have been identified. Black Americans are more likely to develop high blood pressure than white Americans. Obesity and elevated blood lipids are also implicated, as is excessive alcohol consumption (Potter and Beevers, 1984; West, Maxwell, and Nobel, 1984). Deficiency of potassium, calcium, and magnesium may also contribute to hypertension (Kannel, 1986; Karanja and McCarron, 1986; Khaw and Thom, 1982; McCarron, Morris, Henry, and Stanton, 1984; McCarron and Morris,

1985). Weight reduction with or without sodium restriction has been associated with lowering blood pressure (Koolen and Van Brummelen, 1984; Maxwell, Kushiro, and Dornfeld, 1984). Strong evidence exists that a reduced salt intake can lower high blood pressure among humans (MacGregor, et al., 1982). There is less scientifically firm evidence that low salt intake can prevent the condition. Vegetarian diets have also been linked with lower blood pressure (Ophir, Peer, and Gilad, 1983). Definitive causal factors for hypertension in the elderly, including how such factors may differ from those in younger patients, are not understood at present (Applegate, 1990). Ninety percent of the high blood pressure cases in the general population are of unknown cause and are categorized as *essential, idiopathic,* or *primary hypertension.* In 10 percent of the cases an underlying problem such as previous kidney disease, congenital aortal defect, or endocrine disorder is responsible. When high blood pressure is related to such a definable cause, it is referred to as *secondary hypertension.* Secondary forms of hypertension are not common in the elderly. They are suspected, however, in older patients resistant to treatment and in those with diastolic pressures in excess of 115 mm Hg (Kane, Ouslander, and Abrass, 1989).

An age-related increase in blood pressure is not uncommon in Western societies; indeed, it has often come to be expected with advancing years. Hypertension should not be regarded as a benign aspect of the aging process (Borhani, 1986). Its presence is a serious risk factor in the elderly. Neither should it be viewed as an inevitable consequence of aging. Data from the Framingham study indicate that an age-related increase in blood pressure does not occur in all persons (Kannel and Gordon, 1978). Likewise, average blood pressure does not tend to rise with age among those living in less-developed countries. These populations have a significantly lower incidence of hypertension and coronary heart disease. They also have low-sodium/

potassium-rich diets, have higher levels of physical activity, and do not show the age-associated weight gain so common in Western nations (Page and Friedlander, 1986). Life-style factors may contribute more to hypertension and coronary heart disease in industrialized societies than does aging.

CONGESTIVE HEART FAILURE

Congestive heart failure is a state of circulatory congestion produced by the impaired pumping performance of the heart. It generally involves left heart failure and enlargement of the left ventricle known as *left ventricular hypertrophy*. It is associated with atherosclerosis, myocardial infarction, high blood pressure, and/or impaired renal blood flow. Such conditions put additional strain on the heart, forcing it to work harder. Heart enlargement occurs as cardiac tissue responds to increased pumping demands. Overextended cardiac muscle fibers become greatly weakened with time. Right heart failure as well as failure of both sides of the heart can also occur.

Because the heart cannot pump efficiently, blood collects in tissues, producing symptoms. *Edema* (swelling) of the legs and ankles is common. When fluid backs up in the lungs, shortness of breath is the result. Congestive heart failure can be treated with drugs, diet, and rest. If an underlying cause of congestive heart failure is recognized (such as high blood pressure) then that problem must be treated.

Congestive heart failure increases with age. Three-quarters of all ambulatory patients with the condition are over 60 years old (Lakatta and Gerstenblith, 1982). Although presentation occurs in an older person with superimposed disease(s), most cases respond to treatment.

Autopsy data reveal that older patients with congestive heart failure show underlying disease processes similar to those found in middle-aged persons (Dock, 1972). However, diagnosis of heart failure in the elderly may sometimes be more difficult to establish. For example, edema may be due to poor venous drainage. Likewise, older patients with other physical limitations may not be able to tax themselves sufficiently to produce heart failure symptoms that are not present at rest (Gerstenblith and Lakatta, 1990).

PULMONARY HEART DISEASE

There is a very precarious relationship between the heart and lungs. In fact, the cardiovascular and respiratory systems could be said to operate as a unit. Damage or disease in one of these organ systems is often secondarily reflected in the other. In pulmonary heart disease the right side of the heart enlarges in response to certain lung changes. This condition is known as *right ventricular hypertrophy* or *cor pulmonale*. Delicate capillary beds within the air sacs of the lungs allow for the gaseous exchange of carbon dioxide and oxygen. If a significant number of these beds become destroyed as a result of obstructive lung disease, blood begins to back up between the lungs and the right side of the heart from which it has been pumped. In an attempt to compensate for undue strain, the right side of the heart enlarges. Right-side heart failure can eventually result.

Symptoms associated with pulmonary heart disease are those of a respiratory and circulatory nature and include cough, shortness of breath, bluish skin as a result of a reduced oxygen supply, edema, chest pain, and substernal discomfort. Treatment and management of pulmonary heart disease is closely associated with the treatment and management of the lung disorders that give rise to the condition.

THE PULMONARY SYSTEM

A number of aging changes collectively exert an effect on the respiratory system. These changes, which serve to reduce maximum breathing capacity, are significant in that they cause fatigue in an elderly person more easily than in a younger person. However, these changes are not sufficient to cause apparent symptoms at a resting state. In the absence of disease they do not significantly affect the life-style of an older individual. The efficiency of the respiratory system declines with age as evidenced by *weakened intercostal muscles,* decreased elasticity of the thoracic cage and chest wall, less efficient emptying of the lungs, and increased rigidity of internal lung structures (Ostrow, 1984; Piscopo, 1981; Tockman, 1990).

Respiratory diseases are more prevalent in older individuals than in the general population. The threat of serious respiratory infection increases with age, as does the threat of chronic obstructive pulmonary disease and lung cancer. The threat of respiratory infection is partially related to age-associated reductions in host resistance to infectious microorganisms. Likewise, the ability of the lungs to clear infectious and environmental insults is reduced with age (Tockman, 1990). However, obstructive pulmonary conditions and lung cancer do not increase in incidence because of inherent aging factors. Environmental conditions such as exposure to cigarette smoke and polluted air play an important role in their development.

RESPIRATORY INFECTION

Pneumonia and respiratory infections are among the leading causes of death among the elderly. Pneumonia in the elderly may not present the typical symptoms of cough, sputum production, or fever. Sometimes older patients will demonstrate unique symptoms (Esposito, 1989), including confusion, loss of appetite, weakness, or a fall (Yoshikawa, Norman, and Grahn, 1985). Thus, the appearance of such nonspecific symptoms should not be dismissed. Bacterial pneumonia among the aged is related to a more diverse array of microorganisms than those associated with lower respiratory disease in younger adults (Andrew, Chandrasekeren, and McSwiggan, 1984; Verghese and Berk, 1983; Yoshikawa, Norman, and Grahn, 1985).

Pneumococcal infections, especially pneumococcal pneumonia, are a major cause of morbidity and mortality among the American elderly (Fedson, 1985; Goodman, Manton, and Nolan, 1982). The pneumococcal vaccine has been recommended for adults over 65 years as protection against pneumococcal pneumonia (Centers for Disease Control, 1984). The vaccine is in widespread use, although it may not be as effective among elderly persons (Kane, Ouslander, and Abrass, 1989; Shapiro and Clemens, 1984). There is conflict regarding clinical trials of the vaccine's ability to reduce the incidence or severity of pneumococcal infection (Forrester, Jahnigen, and LaForce, 1987; Sims, Steinman, and McConville, 1988; Simberkeff, Cross, and Al-Ibrahim, 1986). Immunization against pneumococcal pneumonia is considered a safeguard for the institutionalized elderly population.

The threat of aspiration pneumonia increases with age. This condition develops as a result of sucking various foreign materials, including gastric contents, into the lung tissue. Although everyone is at risk of having an accident of this nature, a number of conditions predispose older persons (Bartlett, 1990). They may be confined to bed, suffering from esophageal disorders, neurologic disease, or diminished levels of consciousness. As Zavala (1977, p. 46) notes:

In extended care facilities and hospitals, aspiration occurs all too frequently when a well-meaning attendant attempts to force-feed elderly stroke victims or . . . debilitated patients in an attempt to "put meat on their bones."

The seriousness of the episode depends on the amount and the kind of material aspirated. The incident may result in serious lesions, minor irritation, debilitating pulmonary disease, or suffocation. Those who work with older persons should be aware of the risk and take care not to rush them in swallowing medications or food.

Influenza is a major cause of respiratory disease for older adults (Setia, Serventi, and Lorenz, 1985). The Advisory Committee on Immunization Practices of the Centers for Disease Control recommends annual vaccination, especially for elderly nursing home residents (Centers for Disease Control, 1985, 1987). Influenza also contributes to the increased incidence and heightened mortality of pneumonia in the elderly (Bartlett, 1990). Hospitalization and mortality rates for pneumonia are correlated with seasonal and annual incidence of influenza (Glezen, Decker, and Perrotta, 1987). Superimposed pneumonia may be a serious complication of influenza.

Tuberculosis remains an important health problem among the elderly. It has been referred to as the most easily treated serious infectious disease likely to occur among older adults (Stead and Dutt, 1990). Its significance in the elderly is related to its natural history and to special medical conditions of aged persons. Initial exposure to *Mycobacterium tuberculosis*, the agent that causes the disease, may produce inactive infection (no discernible symptoms or mild illness) and long-lasting immunity. The bacteria generally remain dormant for many years but are capable of reactivating as immune defenses against them are reduced in old age. Tuberculosis in the elderly is often of this reactivation type.

Besides having lived through a time period when the chance of exposure to *M. tuberculosis* was high, the elderly are also subject to special conditions that serve to increase the likelihood of reduced defenses and reactivation such as impaired cell-mediated immunity, malnutrition, alcoholism, and various superimposed diseases. The determining factors and reactivation process are, however, poorly understood.

Tuberculosis has resulted in severe outbreaks in nursing homes where both reactivation and primary-contact type disease may occur (Lewis, 1988; Narain, Lofgren, and Warren, 1985; Stead, 1981; Stead and Dutt, 1990; Stead, Lofgren, and Warren, 1985). Approximately 20 to 30 percent of nursing home admissions show evidence of tuberculosis exposure (most likely from an old infection) by testing positive to a tuberculin skin test. About 3 percent of such patients will develop active tuberculosis within the nursing home. Other patients who fail to respond to a tuberculin test are susceptible to infection if exposed to someone with active infection (Stead, 1989).

Primary infection in a nonimmune nursing home patient may progress to serious disease and death. Tuberculosis often remains undetected, simulating bacterial pneumonia, the cause of which may not be pursued in the elderly. In an interview, William Stead, a recognized tuberculosis expert, stated that many older persons with tuberculosis go to their grave undiagnosed, often leaving behind several newly infected persons (cited in Lewis, 1988, p. 12).

A tuberculosis patient may appear to be failing in health, with loss of appetite and resultant weight loss. A chronic cough, the most common symptom, may be attributed to a cold, influenza, or bronchitis.

Elderly nursing home residents are at greater risk for tuberculosis than elderly persons living in the community. Stead urges that a sputum sample for

TB testing be submitted whenever a nursing home resident is treated for pneumonia or bronchitis. Prompt diagnosis and proper drug treatment are of overwhelming importance in recovery. Likewise, transmission is best halted by early detection and treatment. With effective therapy, patients are generally considered noninfectious within 10 to 14 days (Stead and Dutt, 1990).

Reinfection with tuberculosis can happen among older persons whose initial infection occurred so many years ago that the microorganisms have been completely eliminated from the body and the immune memory lost. Most of today's elderly were previously exposed to or infected with the causative bacteria and at one time tested tuberculin-positive. However, the majority of elderly persons test tuberculin-negative (Stead and Dutt, 1990).

It is important that nursing home residents be tested for tuberculosis upon admission to the facility. The American Geriatrics Society recommends two-step tuberculin testing whereby a resident is tested upon admission and again one to two weeks later (Finucane, 1988). Because of the "booster phenomenon," an initial negative test may be followed by a positive reaction when the test is given again in a week or two.

Employees can also transmit infection, emphasizing the significance of preemployment and annual tuberculosis screening for workers. Also important is work restriction for employees who are ill (Crossley, Irvine, Kaszar, and Loewenson, 1985; Lewis, 1988; Smith, 1985).

CHRONIC OBSTRUCTIVE PULMONARY DISEASE

Chronic obstructive pulmonary disease (COPD) includes *chronic bronchitis* and *emphysema*. Chronic bronchitis is defined on the basis of clinical symptoms and their duration. It is manifested as a chronic cough and sputum production for a minimum of three consecutive months over at least two consecutive years. Its prevalence increases with advancing age. Cigarette smoking is the single most important risk factor in the development of the condition. Atmospheric/industrial pollution is an additional but less significant risk factor.

Respiratory airways contain mucus-producing cells. Their secretions normally serve to trap various foreign invaders. Hairlike projections called *cilia* use whiplike motions to propel mucus toward the mouth where it is either expectorated or swallowed. Chronic irritation overwhelms the anatomic defenses of the respiratory tract. Cilia become paralyzed and eventually disappear. Mucus-producing cells enlarge. Hypersecretion of mucus along with mucosal swelling allows mucus plugs to become trapped in the airways. Oxygen intake is reduced. With widespread obstruction, carbon dioxide is retained. Eventually, greater demand is placed on the heart.

As the condition continues, air becomes trapped beyond the mucus plugs and in time causes the *alveoli* of the lungs to remain inflated. Normally, the elastic alveoli inflate as they receive inhaled air. Oxygen thus comes into contact with the capillaries of the delicate walls of the air sacs. During the process of exhaling, stale air is removed from the air sacs, allowing space for a fresh supply of oxygen to make its way once again to lung tissue. When air sacs remain inflated by trapped air, the amount of space provided for gaseous exchange is reduced. Air sac walls may eventually rupture, irreversibly reducing the total amount of respiratory surface space.

When the air sacs become overinflated, the walls stretched and torn, and capillary beds destroyed, emphysema has made its appearance (Figure 12.5). The term *emphysema* actually refers to these anatomic changes. Shortness of breath be-

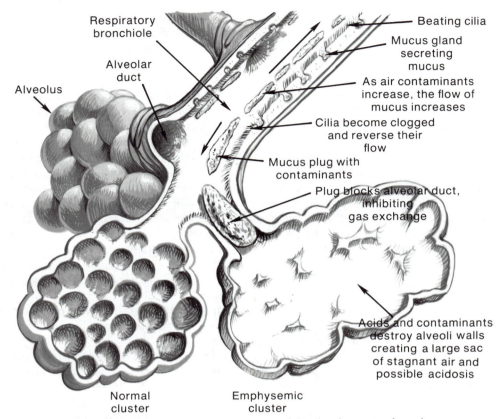

FIGURE 12.5 Diagrammatic representation of the development of emphysema.

comes pronounced, and exhalation becomes prolonged and difficult.

Chronic obstructive lung disease develops slowly and insidiously. As symptoms begin to unfold, they may be considered a part of old age. It should be emphasized that chronic cough, expectoration, and shortness of breath do not represent signs of aging. Persons displaying these symptoms must be urged to seek the care of a physician.

Depending on the degree of damage suffered, persons will be more or less limited in their activ-

ities. When symptoms first appear, the individual may experience fatigue after climbing stairs or walking. As the disease progresses, exhaustion may result from something as simple as buttoning a shirt. Shortness of breath, the chief symptom of emphysema, initially presents itself on exertion; eventually, it is present even at rest.

Most persons dying from emphysema actually succumb to heart disease. The changes in the lungs lead to cor pulmonale and can result in congestive heart failure. Respiratory infections also become a special risk for these persons. The disease changes make them more susceptible to infection and complicate their recuperation.

LUNG CANCER

Diseases related to cigarette smoking may be referred to as the United States' most preventable health problems. Such is the case for lung cancer, which is principally a disease of older persons who have smoked cigarettes (Tockman and Ball, 1990). Lung cancer risk increases with the intensity and duration of cigarette smoking, the depth of inhalation, and the tar and nicotine content of the cigarettes. Lung cancer risk decreases with smoking cessation. The reduced risk will approach that of a nonsmoker 10 to 15 years after smoking has ceased (Doll and Peto, 1976).

STUDY QUESTIONS

1. How significant is cardiovascular disease among the elderly? Note some general changes that occur in the aging heart and its function.
2. Define the following terms: coronary artery disease; ischemic; ischemic heart disease; atherosclerosis; atherosclerotic plaque; intima.
3. Identify the various lesions of atherosclerotic development and note their significance.
4. Briefly explain the response to injury hypothesis; the monoclonal hypothesis.
5. Identify and note the significance of: angina pectoris; cardiac arrest; myocardial infarction; coronary thrombosis; collateral circulation; silent heart attack; intermittent claudication; peripheral vascular disease.
6. Note the various mechanisms by which a heart attack can be triggered.
7. Identify and discuss risk factors associated with atherosclerosis and heart attack.
8. Differentiate: atherosclerosis from arteriosclerosis; essential or primary hypertension from secondary hypertension; systolic from diastolic blood pressure.
9. How is high blood pressure generally defined? Note the two categories important among the elderly. What are some risk factors related to high blood pressure?
10. What is congestive heart failure? How is it related to left ventricular hypertrophy and edema?
11. Discuss right ventricular hypertrophy or cor pulmonale.
12. How significant are pneumonia and respiratory infections, in general, for the older adult? Explain.
13. What is chronic obstructive pulmonary disease? Differentiate chronic bronchitis from emphysema.

BIBLIOGRAPHY

Adelman, B. 1982. Peripheral vascular disease. In J. Rowe and R. Besdine (Eds.), *Health and disease in old age*. Boston: Little, Brown.

American Heart Association. 1980. *Risk factors and coronary heart disease: A statement for physicians*. Dallas, TX: National Office.

American Heart Association. 1990. *Heart facts – 1990*. Dallas, TX: National Center.

Andrew, J., Chandrasekeren, P., and McSwiggan, D. 1984. Lower respiratory infections in an acute geriatric male ward: A one-year prospective surveillance. *Gerontology*, 30: 290.

Applegate, W. 1990. Hypertension. In W. Hazzard, R. Andres, E. Bierman, and J. Blass (Eds.), *Principles of geriatric medicine and gerontology*. New York: McGraw-Hill.

Barnhart, G., Pascoe, E., Mills, S., et al. 1987. Accelerated coronary arteriosclerosis in cardiac transplant patients. *Transplant Reviews, 1*: 31-46.

Bartlett, J. 1990. Pneumonia. In W. Hazzard, R. Andres, E. Bierman, and J. Blass (Eds.), *Principles of geriatric medicine and gerontology*. New York: McGraw-Hill.

Bayer, A., Chadha, J., Farag, R., and Pathy, M. 1986. Changing presentation of myocardial infarction with increasing old age. *Journal of the American Geriatrics Society, 34*: 263-266.

Bayless, R. 1985. The silent coronary. *British Medical Journal, 290*: 1093.

Berenson, G., Srinivasan, S., Hunter, S., et al. 1989.

Risk factors in early life as predictors of adult heart disease: The Bogalusa Heart Study. *American Journal of the Medical Sciences,* 296: 141-151.

Bierman, E. 1990. Aging and atherosclerosis. In W. Hazzard, R. Andres, E. Bierman, and J. Blass (Eds.), *Principles of geriatric medicine and gerontology.* New York: McGraw-Hill.

Borhani, N. 1986. Prevalence and prognostic significance of hypertension in the elderly. *Journal of the American Geriatrics Society,* 34: 112-114.

Centers for Disease Control. 1984. Pneumococcal polysaccaride vaccine usage in the United States. *Morbidity and Mortality Weekly Report,* 33: 273-281.

Centers for Disease Control. 1985. Prevention and control of influenza. *Morbidity and Mortality Weekly Report,* 34: 261-275

Centers for Disease Control. 1987. Prevention and control of influenza. *Annals of Internal Medicine,* 107: 521.

Centers for Disease Control. 1990. Coronary heart disease attributable to sedentary lifestyle – Selected states, 1988. *Morbidity and Mortality Weekly Report,* 39: 541-544.

Crossley, K., Irvine, P., Kaszar, D., and Loewenson, R. 1985. Infection control practices in Minnesota nursing homes. *Journal of the American Medical Association,* 254: 2918-2921.

Dock, W. 1972. Cardiomyopathies of the senescent and senile. *Cardiovascular Clinics,* 4: 362.

Doll, R., and Peto, R. 1976. Mortality in relation to smoking: Twenty years observation on male British doctors. *British Medical Journal,* 2: 1525-1536.

Drizd, T., Dannenberg, A., and Engel, A. 1986. *Blood pressure levels in persons 18-74 years of age in 1976-1980 and trends in blood pressure from 1960-1980 in the United States.* Vital Health Statistics, No. 11. Washington, DC: U.S. Government Printing Office.

Eisenberg, S. 1984. Cardiovascular changes as risk factor for senility. In H. Rothschild and C. Chapman (Eds.), *Risk factors for senility.* New York: Oxford University Press.

Enos, W., Holmes, R., and Beyer, J. 1953. Coronary disease among United States soldiers killed in action in Korea. *Journal of the American Medical Association,* 152: 1090-1093.

Enos, W., Holmes, R., and Beyer, J. 1955. Pathogenesis of coronary disease in American soldiers killed in Korea. *Journal of the American Medical Association,* 158: 912.

Esposito, A. L. 1989. Pneumococcal pneumonia with abdominal pain. *Hospital Practice,* 24: 61-67, 70-72.

Fedson, D. 1985. Improving the use of pneumococcal vaccine through a strategy of hospital-based immunization: A review of its rationale and implications. *Journal of the American Geriatrics Society,* 33: 142-150.

Feinleib, M. 1983a. The magnitude and nature of the decline in coronary heart disease mortality. In *The decline in coronary heart disease mortality – The role of cholesterol change?* Proceedings of the College of Physicians and Surgeons of Columbia University, Anaheim, California, November, pp. 5-9.

Feinleib, M. 1983b. Risk assessment, environmental factors and coronary heart disease. *Journal of the American College of Toxicology,* 2: 91-104.

Finucane, T. 1988. The American Geriatrics Society statement on two-step PPD testing for nursing home patients on admission. *Journal of the American Geriatrics Society,* 36: 77-78.

Forrester, H. L., Jahnigen, D. W., and LaForce, F. M. 1987. Inefficacy of pneumococcal vaccine in a high-risk population. *American Journal of Medicine,* 83(3): 425-430.

Fuster, V., and Chesebro, J. 1986. Role of platelets and platelet inhibitors in aortocoronary artery vein-graft disease. *Circulation,* 73: 227-232.

Gerstenblith, G., Fredrikson, J., Yin, F., Fortiun, N., Lakatta, E., and Weisteldt, M. 1977. Echocardiographic assessment of a normal adult aging population. *Circulation,* 56: 273-278.

Gerstenblith, G., and Lakatta, E. 1990. Disorders of the heart. In W. Hazzard, R. Andres, E. Bierman, and J. Blass (Eds.), *Principles of geriatric medicine and gerontology.* New York: McGraw-Hill.

Gifford, R. 1986. Management of isolated systolic hypertension in the elderly. *Journal of the American Geriatrics Society,* 34: 106-111.

Glezen, W., Decker, M., and Perrotta, D. 1987. Survey of underlying conditions of persons hospitalized with acute respiratory disease during influenza epidemics in Houston, 1978-1981. *American Review of Respiratory Disease,* 136: 550.

Goodman, R., Manton, K., and Nolan, T. 1982. Mortality data analysis using a multiple-cause approach. *Journal of the American Medical Association,* 247: 293.

Gordon, T., Casteli, W., Hjortland, M., Kannel, W., and Dawber, T. 1977. High density lipoprotein as a protective factor against coronary heart disease: The Framingham Study. *American Journal of Medicine,* 62: 707-714.

Gordon, T., Kannel, W., and McGee, D. 1974. Death and coronary attacks in men after giving up cigarette smoking. *Lancet,* 2: 1348.

Gordon, T., and Thom, T. 1975. The recent decrease in CHD mortality. *Preventive Medicine,* 4: 115-125.

Havlik, R., and Feinleib, M. 1979. *Proceedings of the conference on the decline in coronary heart disease mortality.* National Institutes of Health, Publication No. 79-1610. U.S. Department of Health, Education and Welfare, Public Health Service.

Holman, R., McGill, H. C., Jr., Strong, J. P., and Geer, J. C. 1958. The natural history of atherosclerosis: Early aortic lesions as seen in New Orleans in the middle of the 20th century. *American Journal of Pathology,* 34: 209.

Hulley, S., Feigal, D., Ireland, C., Kuller, L., and Smith, W. 1986. Systolic hypertension in the elderly program (SHEP): The first three months. *Journal of the American Geriatrics Society,* 34: 101-105.

Ip, H., Fuster, V., Badimon, L., et al. 1990. Syndromes of accelerated atherosclerosis: Role of vascular injury and smooth muscle cell proliferation. *Journal of the American College of Cardiologists,* 15: 1667-1687.

Kane, R., Ouslander, J., and Abrass, I. 1989. *Essentials of clinical geriatrics.* New York: McGraw-Hill.

Kannel, W. 1986. Nutritional contributors to cardiovascular disease in the elderly. *Journal of the American Medical Association,* 34: 27-36.

Kannel, W., and Gordon, T. 1978. Evaluation of cardiovascular risk in the elderly. *Bulletin of the New York Academy of Medicine,* 54: 573.

Kannel, W., Gordon, T., and Schwartz, M. 1971. Systolic vs. diastolic blood pressure and risk of coronary heart disease. *American Journal of Cardiology,* 27: 335.

Kannel, W., and McGee, D. 1985. Update on some epidemiologic features of intermittent claudication: The Framingham Study. *Journal of the American Geriatrics Society,* 33: 13-18.

Karanja, N., and McCarron, D. 1986. Calcium and hypertension. *Annual Review of Nutrition,* 6: 475-494.

Khan, M., and Manejwala, A. 1981. Cholesterol metabolism and atherosclerosis in aging. In J. Hsu and R. Davis (Eds.), *Handbook of geriatric nutrition.* Park Ridge, NJ: Noyes Publications.

Khaw, K., and Thom, S. 1982. Randomized double-blind cross-overtrial of potassium on blood pressure in normal subjects. *Lancet,* 2: 1127-1129.

Kitzman, B. W., and Edwards, W. D. 1990. Age related changes in the anatomy of a normal heart. *Journal of Gerontology,* 45(2): M33-39.

Kohn, R. 1977. Heart and cardiovascular system. In C. Finch and L. Hayflick (Eds.), *Handbook of the biology of aging.* New York: Van Nostrand Reinhold.

Konu, V. 1977. Myocardial infarction in the elderly. *Acta Medica Scandinavica,* 604(Suppl.): 9.

Koolen, M., and Van Brummelen, P. 1984. Sodium sensitivity in essential hypertension: Role of the renin-angiotensin-aldosterone system and predictive value of an intravenous frusemide test. *Journal of Hypertension,* 2: 55-59.

Lakatta, E., and Gerstenblith, G. 1982. Cardiovascular system. In J. Rowe and R. Besdine (Eds.), *Health and disease in old age.* Boston: Little, Brown.

Lakatta, E., and Gerstenblith, G. 1990. Alterations in circulatory function. In W. Hazzard, R. Andres, E. Bierman, and J. Blass (Eds.), *Principles of geriatric medicine and gerontology.* New York: McGraw-Hill.

Lewis, L. 1988. Infectious diseases in the nursing home. *Long-Term Care Currents,* 11: 7-12.

Linzback, A., and Akuamoa-Boatang, E. 1973. The alterations of the aging human heart: I. Heart weight with progressing age. *Klinica Wochenschrift,* 51: 156-159.

MacDonald, J. 1984. Presentation of acute myocardial infarction in the elderly – a review. *Age and Aging,* 13: 196.

MacDonald, J., Baillie, J., and Williams, B. 1983. Coronary care in the elderly. *Age and Aging,* 12: 12.

MacGregor, G., Best, F. E., Cam, J. M., Markandu, N. D., Elder, D. M., Sagnella, G. A., and Squires, M. 1982. Double-blind randomized cross-over trial of moderate sodium restriction in essential hypertension. *Lancet,* 1: 351-354.

Marchand, W. 1955. Occurrence of painless myocardial infarction in psychotic patients. *New England Journal of Medicine,* 253: 51.

Maxwell, M., Kushiro, T., and Dornfeld, L. 1984. Blood pressure changes in obese hypertensive subjects during rapid loss: Comparison of restricted versus unchanged salt intake. *Archives of Internal Medicine,* 1144: xx.

McBride, W., Lange, R., and Hillis, D. 1988. Restenosis after successful coronary angioplasty: Pathophysiology and prevention. *New England Journal of Medicine,* 318: 1734-1737.

McCarron, D. A., Morris, C. D., Henry, H. J., and Stanton, J. L. 1984. Blood pressure and nutrient intake in the U.S. *Science,* 224: 1392-1398.

McCarron, C. A., and Morris, C. D. 1985. Blood pressure response to oral calcium in persons with mild to moderate hypertension: A randomized, double-blind, placebo-controlled, crossover trial. *Annals of Internal Medicine,* 103(6): 825-831.

Melnick, J., Adam, E., and DeBakey, M. 1990. Possible role of cytomegalovirus in atherogenesis. *Journal of the American Medical Association,* 263: 2204-2207.

Moon, H. 1957. Coronary arteries in fetuses, infants and juveniles. *Circulation,* 15: 366.

Morley, J., and Reese, S. 1989. Clinical implications of the aging heart. *American Journal of Medicine,* 86: 77-86.

Narain, J., Lofgren, E., and Warren, E. 1985. Epidemic tuberculosis in a nursing home: A retrospective cohort study. *Journal of the American Geriatrics Society,* 33: 258-263.

Office of Technology Assessment. 1979. *A review of selected federal vaccine and immunization policies.* Washington, DC: U.S. Government Printing Office.

Ophir, O., Peer, G., and Gilad, J. 1983. Low blood pressure in vegetarians: The possible role of potassium. *American Journal of Clinical Nutrition,* 37: 755.

Ostrow, A. 1984. *Physical activity and the older adult.* Princeton, NJ: Princeton Book Company.

Page, L., and Friedlander, J. 1986. Blood pressure, age and cultural change. In M. Horan, G. Steinberg, J. Dunber, and E. Hadley (Eds.), *Blood pressure regulation and aging: Proceedings from an NIH symposium.* New York: Biomedical Information Corporation.

Piscopo, J. 1981. Aging and human performance. In E. Burke (Ed.), *Exercise, science, and fitness.* Ithaca, NY: Movement Publications.

Potter, J., and Beevers, D. 1984. Pressor effect of alcohol in hypertension. *Lancet,* 1: 119-122.

Pyorala, K., Epstein, F., and Kornitzer, M. 1985. Changing trends in coronary heart disease mortality: Possible explanations. *Cardiology,* 72: 5-10.

Pyorala, K., Salonen, J., and Valkonen, T. 1985. Trends in coronary heart disease: Mortality and morbidity and related factors in Finland. *Cardiology,* 72: 35-51.

Rodeheffer, J., Gerstenblith, G., Becker, L., Fleg, J., Weisfeldt, M., and Lakatta, E. 1984. Exercise cardiac output is maintained in healthy human subjects: Cardiac dilution and increased stroke volume compensated for in diminished heart rate. *Circulation,* 69: 203-212.

Ross, R. 1983. Recent progress in understanding atherosclerosis. *Journal of the American Geriatrics Society,* 31: 231-235.

Ross, R. 1986. The pathogenesis of atherosclerosis. *New England Journal of Medicine,* 314: 488-500.

Ross, R., and Glomset, J. 1973. Atherosclerosis and the arterial smooth muscle cell. *Science,* 180: 1332.

Setia, U., Serventi, I., and Lorenz, P. 1985. Factors affecting the use of influenza vaccine in the institutionalized elderly. *Journal of the American Geriatrics Society,* 33: 856-858.

Shapiro, E., and Clemens, J. 1984. A controlled evaluation of the protective efficacy of pneumococcal vaccine for patients at high risk of serious pneumococcal infections. *Annals of Internal Medicine,* 101: 325-330.

Simberkeff, M. S., Cross, A. P., and Al-Ibrahim, M. 1986. Efficacy of pneumococcal vaccine in high risk patients: Results of a Veterans Administration cooperative study. *New England Journal of Medicine,* 315(21): 1318-1327.

Sims, R. V., Steinman, W. C., and McConville, J. H. 1988. The clinical effectiveness of pneumococcal vaccine in the elderly. *Annals of Internal Medicine,* 108(5): 653-657.

Smith, P. 1985. Infection control in nursing homes. *Journal of the American Medical Association,* 254: 2951-2952.

Spain, D., Siegel, H., and Bradess, V. 1973. Women smokers and sudden death: The relationship of cigarette smoking to coronary heart disease. *Journal of the American Medical Association,* 224: 1005-1007.

Stead, W. 1981. Tuberculosis among elderly persons: An outbreak in a nursing home. *Annals of Internal Medicine,* 94: 606.

Stead, W. 1989. Tuberculosis among the elderly: Forgotten but not gone. *Health Letter,* 5: 7-9.

Stead, W., and Dutt, A. 1990. Tuberculosis: A special problem in the elderly. In W. Hazzard, R. Andres, E. Bierman, and J. Blass (Eds.), *Principles of geriatric medicine and gerontology.* New York: McGraw-Hill.

Stead, W., Lofgren, J., and Warren, E. 1985. Tuberculosis as an epidemic and nosocomial infection among the elderly in nursing homes. *New England Journal of Medicine* 312: 1483-1487.

Taylor, C. 1976. Serum cholesterol levels of seventh-day adventists. *Paroi Arterielle/Arterial Wall,* 3: 175.

Tinker, G. 1981. Clinical presentation of myocardial infarction in the elderly. *Age and Aging,* 10: 237.

Tockman, M. 1990. Aging of the respiratory system. In W. Hazzard, R. Andres, E. Bierman, and J. Blass (Eds.), *Principles of geriatric medicine and gerontology.* New York: McGraw-Hill.

Tockman, M., and Ball, W., Jr. 1990. Lung cancer. In W. Hazzard, R. Andres, E. Bierman, and J. Blass (Eds.), *Principles of geriatric medicine and gerontology.* New York: McGraw-Hill.

Verghese, A., and Berk, S. 1983. Bacterial pneumonia in the elderly. *Medicine,* 62: 271.

Walker, W. 1974. Coronary mortality: What is going on? *Journal of the American Geriatrics Society,* 227: 1045-1046.

West, L., Maxwell, D., and Nobel, E. 1984. Alcoholism. *Annals of Internal Medicine,* 100: 405.

Willet, W. 1981. Cigarette smoking and non-fatal myocardial infarction in women. *American Journal of Epidemiology,* 113: 575-582.

Williams, B., Begg, T., Semple, T., and McGuinness, J. B. 1976. The elderly in a coronary unit. *British Medical Journal,* 2: 451-453.

Yoshikawa, T., Norman, D., and Grahn, D. 1985. Infections in the aging population. *Journal of the American Geriatrics Society,* 33: 496-503.

Zavala, D. 1977. The threat of aspiration pneumonia in the aged. *Geriatrics,* 32: 47-51.

CHAPTER **13**

Disorders of the Urinary System

Urinary disorders are significant causes of death and morbidity in the elderly. Only 3 percent of the elderly have histologically normal kidneys. Total renal function in an elderly individual may only be 50 percent of that of the young adult (Anderson and Williams, 1983). Urinary incontinence is a major problem in old age, and urinary tract infections are also a common complaint. Renal complications accompany a variety of pathologic conditions that are common among the elderly. Prostate disease, a major etiologic factor in many bladder disorders, is a disease category most often associated with death. Given this kind of pattern, it is no wonder that impairment of the functional efficiency of the urinary tract is a matter of great practical concern for the elderly and those who care for them.

SYMPTOMS OF URINARY TRACT DISTURBANCE

A number of common symptoms of urinary tract dysfunction are important in a consideration of the aging urinary tract. Although not diseases themselves, they are often indicative of existent disease or malfunction. These symptoms are polyuria, nocturia, frequency of urination, urinary retention, blood in the urine, urinary incontinence, and uremia.

Polyuria

Polyuria is a condition characterized by increased amounts of urine being excreted (a daily urine volume greater than 2,500 ml). Its cause can be excess intake of fluids such as coffee, tea, or beer, use of diuretic substances such as acetazolamide (Diamox) for glaucoma, and altered renal function. Disorders such as *diabetes insipidus, diabetes mellitus,* and *hypocalcemia* are associated with increased excretion of urine. Diabetes insipidus is rare in the elderly, but diabetes mellitus and hypocalcemia are not uncommon. Polyuria can be a feature of early renal failure. It is important for individuals with polyuria to compensate for the fluid loss by increasing intake to prevent dehydration.

Nocturia

Nocturia is the need to get up to urinate during the night. It is estimated that almost two-thirds of the elderly population awaken to urinate two or more times a night. This condition can be simply related to too much fluid intake during the late evening; reduced fluid intake before bedtime can afford some relief from this condition, as can urinating before going to bed. However, nocturia can also be related to urinary infections such as cystitis and pyelonephritis, prostatic hypertrophy, certain medications, and uninhibited neurogenic bladder. It may be a reflection of early renal disease, but it is commonly associated with cardiac and hepatic failures. Frequent nighttime urination in the absence of high fluid intake should be the cause for some concern.

Increased Frequency of Urination

Under normal conditions a person passes urine four to six times a day, for a total of about 700 to 2,000 ml a day. The person with urinary frequency will pass urine every hour or two during the day and possibly three to four times a night. The most common cause of increased urination is infection of the bladder, kidneys, or prostate. The condition also can be caused by polyuria, anxiety, a small bladder, and/or irritative or obstructive lesions. Prostate hypertrophy and urinary infection can be differentiated by other symptoms, the latter usually being associated with scalding or burning dysuria, whereas the former is more commonly associated with hesitation, a poor stream, and dribbling. The frequency of urination accompanying diabetes mellitus can be identified by its association with an excessive thirst, hunger, weight loss, and often a family history of diabetes.

Dysuria

Dysuria is a condition that varies in symptoms from a slight burning on urination to severe pain in the urethra and bladder neck. It is usually associated with increased frequency of urination and often related to urinary infection, most commonly due to bacteria. It is also associated with prostatic enlargement, bladder stones, urethritis, and senile vaginitis. Persistent symptoms in the absence of infection require careful examination of the bladder and urethra.

Retention of Urine

Inability to urinate in old men most often is associated with prostate enlargement (Figure 13.1). It may come without warning or be associated with other illnesses such as a cold or influenza. There may not be any pain even when the condition is acute, but restlessness or confusion can develop. Large doses of medications for colds, ulcers, or diarrhea; tranquilizers; and anticholinergics may cause urinary retention. Other causes include nervous disease or urinary tract obstruction. Frequent voiding of very small units of urine can really be considered urinary retention. In women, fecal impaction and urethral stricture are among the most common causes of retention. Lesions of the frontal

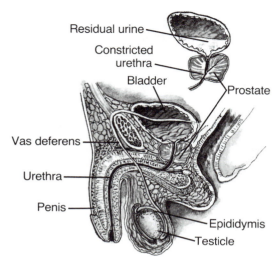

Residual urine

Constricted urethra

Bladder

Prostate

Vas deferens

Urethra

Penis

Epididymis

Testicle

FIGURE 13.1 Prostate-urethra relationship

cortex of the brain and degenerative changes of the bladder are causes of urine retention as well.

Hematuria

Blood in the urine may be detected by *urinalysis* and in some cases by a red to brown discoloration of the urine, depending on the amount of blood and the acidity of the urine. Slight hematuria may cause no discoloration and may only be detected by chemical and/or microscopic examination. Bloody urine associated with pain is most often caused by an infection or the presence of a stone. Bloody urine in the absence of pain may be the first sign of cancer of the bladder or kidney. Thus, it is very important that hematuria be evaluated for its cause; this is usually done through pyelography and cystoscopy. When such an examination is to be done, detailed discussion between patient and physician should reduce the trauma of the event. *Hematuria* is also associated with renal embolism, subacute bacterial endocarditis, diseases with abnormal bleeding tendencies such as thrombocytopenia, acute nephritis, and trauma such as catheter accidents or misuse.

Uremia

The accumulation of toxic materials in the blood is an important condition associated with a number of renal disorders. Hodkinson (1981) identifies three types of uremia. Prerenal *uremia* is caused by a fall in renal blood flow. This leads to a decline in the glomerular filtration rate, nitrogen retention in the glomerular filtration rate, and nitrogen retention in the blood stream. The chief causes of prerenal uremia are dehydration from vomiting, diarrhea, the use of diuretics, and/or not drinking enough water. Cardiac output failure associated with hemorrhages, shock, acute myocardial infarction, and heart failure may also be causative factors. Prompt recognition is important, because the condition is reversible if discovered early enough.

Postrenal uremia is a result of an obstruction of the urinary outflow from the kidneys with the development of a back-pressure effect. It is reversible, but sustained pressure can lead to irreversible damage. The major associated causes of obstruction are prostate problems and carcinoma of the bladder (which obstruct the bladder outlet and/or the ureters). It is less prevalent than prerenal uremia.

Renal uremia results from disease of the kidney. It is a progressive condition and in many cases irreversible. Uremia is not specific to any disease; it is a general result of renal failure and is due to a variety of causes. Early symptoms include fatigue, lack of vigor, weakness, weight loss, and lack of mental alertness, which may develop gradually over a period of weeks or even years. Some neuromuscular manifestations such as muscle cramps, twitches, and convulsions may occur along with gastrointestinal symptoms such as nausea, vomiting, diarrhea, and loss of appetite. Malnutrition will sometimes develop, and hypertension and heart failure are common. Untreated uremia will undoubtedly result in death. The prognosis for uremic patients is generally good for those in whom the precipitating factors (such as urinary obstructions) can be identified and treated. On the other hand, patients in whom the cause of uremia is unknown or the result of a multitude of physiologic insults to the kidneys over a long period of time have a very poor prognosis.

AGE CHANGES IN THE TRACT

Bladder and Urethra

The bladder of an elderly person has a capacity of less than half (250 ml) that of a young adult (600 ml) (Diokno, 1980) and often contains as much as 100 ml of *residual urine* (Figure 13.2). The onset of the desire to urinate is delayed in older persons. Normally, the *micturition reflex* is activated when the bladder is half full, but in the elderly it often does not occur until the bladder is near capacity. The origin of this alteration of the micturition reflex is unclear, but it may be related to age changes in the frontal area of the cerebral cortex, or to damage associated with a cerebral infarction or tumor. The reduced bladder capacity coupled with a delayed micturition reflex can lead to problems of frequent urination and extreme urgency on urination. These conditions, even if they do not render one incontinent, are annoying to the older person. They often make the individual feel useless, so it is helpful if the physician explains the changes in an effort to negate these feelings. Even normal elderly patients have a greater frequency of urinary symptoms. Diokno, Brown, and Brock (1986) found urgency, frequency, slow stream, and trouble in voiding among 10 to 40 percent of older people with incontinence.

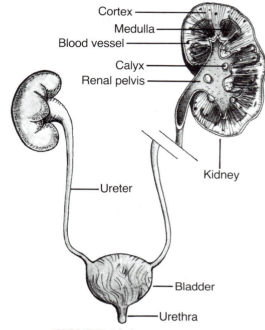

FIGURE 13.2 Urinary system

The bladder outlet in aged women exhibits a high incidence of funneling, which may be the result of deterioration of the pelvic diaphragm. The *pelvic diaphragm* is a muscular mass that helps to maintain the tone of the bladder and contributes to proper closure of the bladder outlet. If the pelvic diaphragm is weak, it can contribute to imperfect closure of the bladder and leakage known as *stress incontinence*. Stress incontinence results when there is a sudden rise in intravesical pressure, as occurs in coughing or sneezing. Surveys indicate that stress incontinence can occur at any age. Muscular strengthening and retraining under the supervision of a physiotherapist can afford relief in many cases. Incontinent women often exhibit a mucosal prolapse of the external urethra. At this time the specific causes and significance of prolapse of the urethra are uncertain. It does not appear to be related to parity or urinary infections.

Bladder diverticula are common (25 to 30 percent) in elderly men and undoubtedly are related to bladder obstruction with raised pressures and hypertrophy of the bladder muscle (trabeculation). Bladder diverticula are rare in women but are sometimes found in women with bladder problems of neurologic origin. The importance of bladder diverticula in the development of bladder disorders is still unclear.

Urinary Incontinence

Urinary incontinence is a major urinary tract problem of the elderly, especially the institutionalized elderly. It was estimated in 1987 that the United States spent $10.3 billion on incontinence (Pannill, 1989). Surveys indicate that institutionalized persons have a greater incontinence rate than those living in the community. This difference in rates is probably due to the fact that a large number of those institutionalized are in fact there because of incontinence. If one uses only severe incontinence as a category, the problem tends to become more prevalent with advancing age, peaking in the eighties (Yeates, 1976). The prevalence of urinary incontinence varies from 14 to 51 percent of older community-living adults, but ranges from 35 percent in acute care institutions to 55 percent of the permanently institutionalized adults (Pannill, 1989).

Urinary incontinence can be defined as the involuntary passing of urine in an undesirable place or situation (Yeates, 1976). Undesirability of place, however, may reflect personal or community norms. The condition is complicated and poorly understood. It is a matter of great concern for the elderly individual, family members, age mates, and the geriatric personnel caring for the individual. Many times families give up trying to care for elderly members if they become incontinent. Shuttleworth (1970) estimated that more than 20 percent of the admissions to geriatric units are prompted by inability to deal with incontinence. Incontinent patients greatly increase the work load in geriatric units and can seriously test the morale of many geriatric staffs. Patients also feel depressed, helpless, and useless. Group therapy with the family and the patient should be encouraged to help mutual understanding and improve communication on both sides. Possibly, feelings of shame on the part of the patient can be reduced and hostility from the family mitigated.

Incontinence may lead to admission refusal by a residential home. It can also make one an unwelcome member of any social group or club. Ory and associates (1986) found that incontinence causes significant social isolation and interferes with daily living activities in 25 to 50 percent of those affected. Psychologically, incontinence can lead to depression, insecurity, and apathy. The psychologic effects on an individual are devastating and necessitate supportive care by a geriatric staff. The nurse or family member should retain a positive approach at all times. If the staff or family does everything for the patient, dependency will develop. Continence should be expected and the incontinent patient made to feel that continence and independence will return. If the staff has minimal expectations, the patient's performance will likely be correspondingly low.

The true prevalence of incontinence among the elderly is difficult to determine because of problems in defining the category and the self-reports characteristic of many health inventories. Only skillful questioning may allow for the identification of an incontinent person. The words *urinary incontinence* mean different things to different researchers; thus, surveys are not universally comparable.

A number of factors have been studied in relation to incontinence. Among these are sex, age, infection, physical activity, disease of the central nervous system, and the ability to care for oneself. A number of researchers have found little difference between the sexes, although Brocklehurst and his associates (1951; Brocklehurst, Dillane, and Griffiths, 1968) found incontinence in twice as many women as men. He suggests that this difference might be related to the greater prevalence of dementia in women. Age differences seem unimportant, and most researchers believe that infection does not play a significant role.

Herzog, Diokno, and Fritz (1990), in a two-year study of urinary incontinence in noninstitutionalized elderly in Washtenaw County, Michigan, confirmed Brocklehurst's identification of sex differentials. This study revealed self-reported rates of 37.7 percent for females and 18.9 percent for males, whereas one year later the same individuals reported 20 percent for females and 10 percent for males. The study also indicated that females develop more stable incontinence with lower remission rates. An epidemiological survey by Diokno, Brown, and Brock (1986) also confirmed the male–female differentials, with females exhibiting a prevalence of 37.7 percent compared to 18.9 percent for males.

Females have also been found to exhibit a higher rate of stress incontinence than males. This is possibly related to the strains of childbirth leading to weakness in the bladder outlet and pelvic musculofascial attachments. Some observers have also suggested that consistent failure to heed the normal urge to urinate when younger may lead to problems in old age. Because of social convention and anatomy, women may be more often forced to defer urination. Women also exhibit a greater prevalence of the mixed type of incontinence than men, who have a greater prevalence of the urge type of incontinence, especially given that prostatism can lead to an unstable bladder and/or incomplete emptying of the bladder.

Incontinence is less common in those who are physically active. It is also not as common in those who are still able to dress, walk, and feed themselves. However, studies of those elderly persons confined to bed indicate that 25 percent are incontinent. Diseases of the central nervous system (such as stroke, upper motor neuron lesions, and organic brain syndrome) are the most important predisposing factors. Prostatic hypertrophy and senile vaginitis may also be associated with incontinence. According to Brocklehurst (1963), age-related urinary incontinence is usually the result of the interaction of predisposing and precipitating factors. The sequence of events is schematically outlined after Brocklehurst in Table 13.1.

The International Continence Society Standardization Committee formulated definitions for four types of urinary incontinence (Bates, Bradley, Glen, and Griffith, 1979). The four definitions are as follows:

1. Stress incontinence is characterized by urine leakage during exercise, coughing, sneezing, or laughing.
2. Urge incontinence is defined as voluntary urinary loss immediately preceded by a desire to void.
3. Reflex incontinence is defined as the sudden loss of large volumes of urine without any sensation of urgency or bladder distension.
4. Overflow incontinence is manifested as frequent or continuous loss of small amounts of urine together with a distended bladder.

An additional three types of incontinence are mentioned in the literature:

1. Mixed incontinence due to a combination of urge and stress
2. Functional incontinence referring to urine loss associated with mobility restrictions, cognitive impairment, and environmental barriers without pathology of the lower urinary tract

TABLE 13.1 Urinary incontinence

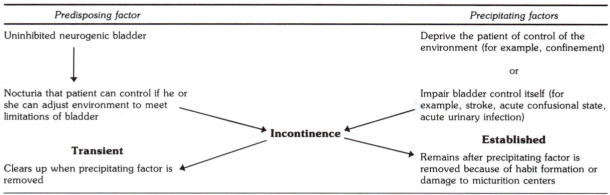

Predisposing factor	Precipitating factors

Uninhibited neurogenic bladder

Nocturia that patient can control if he or she can adjust environment to meet limitations of bladder

Transient

Clears up when precipitating factor is removed

Incontinence

Deprive the patient of control of the environment (for example, confinement)

or

Impair bladder control itself (for example, stroke, acute confusional state, acute urinary infection)

Established

Remains after precipitating factor is removed because of habit formation or damage to micturition centers

Source: Information used for this table can be found in J. C. Brocklehurst, "The Aetiology of Urinary Incontinence in the Elderly," in *Conference on Medical and Surgical Aspects of Aging: Current Achievements in Geriatrics* (London: Anderson & Isaacs, 1963).

3. Iatrogenic incontinence including physician-induced urine loss, often in relation to medications (Herzog, Diokno, and Fritz, 1989)

Knowledge and awareness of such variations will be important in systematizing an approach to an individual patient's problem.

Psychological factors such as regression, feelings of helplessness, dependency, attention seeking, insecurity, rebellion, sensory deprivation, and disturbed conditioned reflexes can all contribute to the development of incontinence. Continence depends on alertness; oversedation, drowsiness, stupor, or coma can disrupt continence. Poor motivation also plays an important role. Confused, depressed, demoralized patients whose lifelong routine has been seriously disrupted may also deliberately violate social conventions regarding urination. Loss of home, youth, and social life can cause individuals to give up and lose their psychological ability to cope.

Psychiatric problems such as dementia, schizophrenia, neuroconfusional states, and psychotic depression also contribute to incontinence. Although neurologically caused incontinence may be uncommon, diseases such as multiple sclerosis, spinal cord lesions, acute spinal cord compression, vascular stroke, and Parkinson's disease may also be associated with incontinence.

From the foregoing catalog of possible causative factors, it should be evident that no single approach to treatment is possible but that treatment and control must be individualized. Treatment of incontinence is complex and often time-consuming. At the most basic level, treatment should attempt to remove or overcome the precipitating factors. Reeducation in bladder function is important. Special exercise can diminish frequency of urination and nocturia (Shepherd, 1980). This involves a positive attitude by the staff and the patient. Drug therapy can take several courses, including the pharmacologic blockage of the bladder reflex; the regulation of diuresis with powerful diuretics; the use of hormones such as estrogen to affect the trigone of the bladder, to increase capacity; or the use of a variety of drugs to reduce bladder overactivity.

Physical therapy may help to restore muscles that play a part in incontinence or enable one to retain muscles to perform their basic functions. Occupational therapy can distract the patient's attention from the condition and promote the general physical and mental well-being of the patient, possibly overcoming psychologic causes of incontinence.

Some groups of patients will never regain continence. For these patients, one must consider the *catheter* and external appliances to control the condition. Catheters have been criticized because of the risk of infection. This risk, however, is often associated with the techniques of the caregivers who are emptying the appliance. The apparatus can become clogged by deposited sediments (sanding), especially from dehydrated patients who excrete concentrated urine or residual urine. The apparatus can also get kinked, thus interrupting flow. To avoid this, a careful record of output should be kept and recorded at about two-hour intervals. Older patients, especially those in a confused state of mind, will often pull out their catheters.

The indwelling catheter should not cause pain. Sometimes the bladder neck is constricted and the catheter is too large. If a patient complains of pain, assessment by a professional should be made. Placement in a room or ward with persons having similar problems can often help the patient to accept and deal with the problem more effectively. Social activity can divert the patient's attention from the catheter. Today, the risk of infection has been considerably reduced by the advent of disposable plastic catheters. Despite the problems associated with catheters, they will probably remain an important method of dealing with incontinence.

The use of absorbent products is one of the most common methods for managing incontinence both in the community and in institutions (Starer and Libow, 1985; Mitteness, 1987). One problem with external appliances involves separating patients from their urine and keeping them warm and comfortable. Consideration of social and ego needs is also important. The devices should not be degrading or socially offensive The control of odors and stains is aesthetically and psychosocially important. Until recently, most external devices have been devised with staff convenience and routine in mind, rather than the patient's condition and therapy.

The absorbent pants conduct fluid outward through a pad in the genital area external to the body of the pant. As long as this pad remains unsaturated, the patient will be warm and dry. Trials in England indicate not only that the pant works in practice but that patients previously considered hopeless have learned to become continent or have reduced their incontinence. The garment is intended for self-use and is psychologically and socially satisfying to most patients (Willington, 1973). This type of development clearly caters to the patient's recovery or successful adaptation rather than to the logistical needs of the staff or institution. However, geriatricians caution that the absorbent pants should be used only as a last resort (Starer and Libow, 1985) because premature use could discourage attempts to correct the condition. Judging by their popularity, however, it does seem that the incontinent are choosing the absorbent pants as the first intervention (Herzog, Diokno, and Fritz, 1989).

Prevention of incontinence was rarely considered in the past. Isaacs (1976) suggests a number of strategies that can be taken to intervene at various points of vulnerability: strengthening weakened sphincter and muscles by exercises, faradism, the use of surgery and external devices, taming the detrusor muscle mass, regulating fluid intake, or blocking hyperactivity with drugs. The signal to urinate can be amplified by diuretic drugs or by higher fluid intake; activity programs can be used to sublimate bladder anxieties. Finally, the hospital or institutional environment can be adapted to promote human dignity by allowing free and ready access to lavatory facilities and by encouraging the staff to become aware of opportunistic micturition.

The careful recording of incontinence helps to determine the extent of the individual's problem. The regimen of record keeping can serve to direct the staff's attention to the patient at regular intervals, and to establish routines for getting the patient to the lavatory to empty the bladder. The staff can also reinforce the patient by maintaining a positive attitude that will foster self-esteem and independence.

Much management of urinary incontinence is self-devised. Many people try to deal with this problem by heightened awareness of toilet locations, frequent toileting, and the use of absorbent pads. Many incontinent persons have not consulted a physician. This is unfortunate, because surgical corrections, drug therapy, and behavioral modifications are now promising approaches to incontinence. Urinary incontinence is treatable but must be identified promptly and dealt with professionally.

Urinary Tract Infections

Urinary infections have been studied in three types of elderly population: those in private homes, in extended-care facilities, and in hospitals. Urinary tract infections account for 30 to 50 percent of all cases of bacteremia and sepsis in the elderly regardless of the setting (McCue, 1987). The highest incidence occurs in hospitals, and the lowest is found among those living in private households. Rates for hospitalized patients were found to be 32 to 33 percent (Brocklehurst, Dillane, and Griffiths, 1968; Gibson and Pritchard, 1965; Walkey, 1967). Dontas, Papanayiotou, and Marketos (1966) observed a rate of 25 percent in nursing homes, and Sourander (1966) and Brocklehurst (1963) found a rate of 20 percent among those in private households. Women over 65 living at home had an incidence of 20 percent, whereas men had low rates through the sixth decade and showed a gradual rise to 20 percent from the seventh decade on (Brocklehurst et al., 1968). It is possible that the increase among men is related to prostate surgery, because some researchers believe that prostate fluid may have *bactericidal* or *bacteriostatic* properties.

Urinary infections are generally accompanied by burning sensations, painful urination, increased nocturnal frequency, precipitancy, suprapubic tenderness, flank pain, and sometimes fever. A urinary infection may present only fever or clinical deterioration such as confusion in the elderly and worsening glucose control in the diabetic. Infection is not related to incontinence, the other common urinary disorder of the elderly. The most common pathogen is the bacterium *E. coli*. Two categories of urinary infection have been identified, acute and chronic. The acute type, associated with precipitancy and incontinence, seems to localize in the lower urinary tract and usually clears up if treated properly with antibiotics. The chronic type does not respond well to treatment. It is often associated with some kind of obstruction and affects both the kidney and the lower urinary tract.

Bacteriuria is common in the elderly, and there is some debate about whether to treat it if it is asymptomatic, which is most often the case. Active cystitis may be encouraged by various neurogenic or mechanical factors that lead to urinary retention, and is often associated with such conditions as benign prostatitis, diverticula of the bladder, bladder stones, arteriosclerosis of the bladder, and irritable bladder of senile dementia. *Cystitis* is common in women with a congenitally short urethra. Finally, clinical instrumentation for diagnostic or therapeutic purposes induces a surprising number of infections.

The differential prevalence among women of urinary infections could be related to a number of factors, such as the tendency toward having a short urethra in close proximity to the rectal opening, dilation and slowed peristalsis of the urethra in pregnancy, urethral compression by an enlarging uterus in pregnancy, and the absence of prostatic fluid with its *bacteriostatic* qualities. Sociocultural factors such as the nature of sexual activity, personal hygiene practices, socioeconomic status, and analgesic abuse may affect the incidence of urinary infections. Metabolic disturbances such as diabetes, stones, and gout appear to lower the system's resistance to infection.

Treatment of urinary infections should start with a thorough diagnosis to avoid unnecessary therapy and expense, allow the correct choice of drugs, and assure the success of aggressive therapy. Adequate antimicrobial treatment is necessary to ensure that infection is eradicated and to prevent its possible spread to other areas. Usually 10 to 14 days of drug therapy is recommended. The patient must be adequately instructed with respect to the importance of carrying out the prescribed therapy and not discontinuing it after early relief from symptoms. Therapeutic regimes are varied ranging from antibiotic therapy to the use of ascorbic acid tablets.

Another aspect of infective care is high fluid intake. High fluid intake helps relieve symptoms by diluting the urine, increasing urine flow for a flushing effect, preventing dehydration because of fever or polyuria, and acidifying the urine. However, large amounts of fluid may lower the concentration of antibacterial drugs below their level of effectiveness and render the antimicrobial therapy useless. Patients should be cautioned about the use of folk medicine approaches that might interfere with the orthodox medical treatment for urinary tract infections.

Recurrent or stubborn infections should be checked for association with obstructions, metabolic disturbances, or structural abnormalities. In some chronic patients the medical goal may be bacterial control because full eradication is difficult and might require aggressive means that could lead to other problems.

Prostate Gland

The prostate gland is often implicated in a variety of disorders of the urinary tract. Two groups of changes in the gland have been identified by Moore (1952). Presenile changes occur between ages 40 and 60 and are characterized by irregular changes in the smooth muscle fibers and prostate tissue. Senile changes occur between ages 60 and 80 and develop more slowly and diffusely, exhibiting less variation from one part of the gland to another.

Prostate problems are a major concern to many elderly men, but many do not report their symptoms until a late stage (Anderson and Williams, 1983). There are three major causes of prostate troubles: *vesical* contracture of the neck, *nodular (benign) hyperplasia,* and carcinoma. Vesicular neck obstruction is usually characterized by slight urination hesitancy in early stages and in its later stages by nocturia. Slowing of the urinary system and/or complete retention are usually indicative of some lesion of the bladder neck. Some precipitating factors have been identified as acute illness, exposure to cold, and excessive alcohol intake.

Nodular or benign hyperplasia is very common from age 50 on, with individuals in their sixties showing high rates of incidence (Birkhoff, 1983). Most corrective operative procedures are carried out on individuals in these age cohorts. Hyperplasia is also an important cause of death. McKeown (1965) found that 8 percent of her patients exhibiting hyperplasia died from it or its complications. Men in their seventies and eighties show a decline in problems, and the gland is characterized by nodules within it. It is possible that an endocrine connection exists, because nodules do not develop unless the testes are operating. The inner and outer areas may be affected by different hormones. The symptoms associated with benign hyperplasia are increased frequency of urination, poor stream formation, dribbling, nocturia, and retention with overflow. Occasionally hematuria results because of the rupture of veins in the prostate. Treatment can include prostatic removal. The most common type of surgery, retropubic prostatectomy, has a high level of safety.

Carcinoma of the prostate is the most frequent malignancy of old men (Hodkinson, 1981); all older men should have regular physical examinations to monitor the condition of the prostate. Carcinoma is rare before age 50 but is present in possibly 95 percent of men in their eighth decade (Anderson and Williams, 1983). It may produce little or no obstruction, but when it does the condition may be too far along to treat successfully. It commonly spreads to the pelvis and lumbar spine, where it is usually associated with great pain. Prostate removal does not rule out the development of cancer in the area. In those over 70, surgery is rarely recommended because the individual's life expectancy is relatively unaffected by the condition. At advanced ages individuals often die of other causes before the carcinoma takes its toll. However, Klein (1979) reports 42,000 new cases a year in the United States, with 17,000 deaths. Overall it is the second most common malignancy in American men and the third most common cause of cancer deaths in men over age 55 (Brendler, 1990). Table 13.2 summarizes the developmental aspects of prostate carcinoma along with possible therapeutic approaches.

Many men are concerned about the effects of prostatic surgery or therapy on their sexual potency or masculinity. Some time should be devoted to explaining to the patient the real and imagined side effects associated with treatment of prostate dis-

ease. Possible adverse side effects of the treatment should be weighed against the effects of nontreatment. In some cases the patient may choose nontreatment rather than risk a change in his real or perceived male image.

CHANGES AND DISEASES IN THE AGING KIDNEY

The aging kidney appears macroscopically normal in 50 percent of cases, but histologically only 3 percent are without some abnormality. Renal function declines with age, leading to decreases in glomerular filtration rate, effective plasma flow, and tubular absorption and excretion. There appears to be a decrease in average renal function with age that accelerates with advancing age (Lindeman, 1985). It has been suggested that this decline is related to loss of nephrons (Anderson and Brenner, 1986). At age 70 one has half to one-third fewer nephrons than at age 30 (McKeown, 1965), and after age 40 there is an increasing inability to replace injured renal cells. With increasing age the kidneys themselves are found to be smaller, 250 grams at age 40 but 200 grams at 80 years of age (Epstein, 1985; McLachlin, 1987), and the nephrons themselves are smaller in size and fewer in number.

The total number of glomeruli falls by 30 to 40 percent by age 70, and the surface area decreases progressively after age 40 (McLachlin, 1987). By age 80 the number of nonfunctioning glomeruli rises to 10 to 30 percent (McLachlin, 1987). Within the functioning glomeruli, other changes occur, such as basal membrane thickening and decreased size and numbers of tufts. At the same time the number and length of proximal tubules decrease and tubal diverticula, the possible progenitors of cysts, become common in the distal nephron. A number of vascular changes have also been identified that may affect blood flow (Brown, 1986).

TABLE 13.2 Developmental stages of prostate carcinoma

Stages	Treatment
1. Not suspected clinically Not palpable Discovered incidentally (as by surgery)	No treatment; careful observation
2. Hard and irregular but not too large Palpable prostatic nodules Confined to prostate	Radical prostatectomy if young enough and healthy
3. Obvious spread to adjacent pelvic tissues with fixation	Radiation therapy
4. Distant metastases	Hormonal treatment Radiation of painful metastatic sites

Source: Information used for this table can be found in W. F. Whitmore, "Symposium on Hormones and Cancer Therapy: Hormone Therapy in Prostatic Cancer," *American Journal of Medicine,* 1956, vol. 21, p. 697.

Despite these dramatic changes, loss of renal tissue is probably secondary in importance to the structural vascular changes that occur with age. The arterial tree atrophies, and a thickening of the intima layer of the small arteries develops. This is caused by a proliferation of elastic tissue, which decreases the functional efficiency of the system. The large arteries often develop intimal hyperplastic layers many times complicated by arteriosclerosis. Williams and Harrison (1937) observed that narrowing of the large arteries is usually due to aging, whereas the smaller arteries are influenced by both age and hypertension. Anatomic narrowing of the blood vessels and persistent vasoconstriction have a tendency to reduce flow through the system. It is estimated that the total renal blood flow declines 10 percent per decade after age 20 (Epstein, 1985). The renal blood flow of an octogenerian averages only 300 ml/minute, compared to 600 ml/minute in the young adult (Beck and Burkhart, 1990).

It appears, then, that vascular changes may be more significant in declining renal efficiency than renal tissue loss. Still, vascular changes may have secondary effects contributing to the loss of nephrons. This is very significant when the kidney is seriously malfunctioning or when severe atherosclerosis is superimposed on the aging process. In the absence of diagnosed renal insufficiency, however, the age-related changes are significant enough to require drug dosage adjustments (Epstein, 1985; McLachlin, 1987).

Pyelonephritis

Pyelonephritis, an inflammation of a part of the kidney, is the most common kidney disease at any age. Changes in the kidney that are the result of previous inflammations and past infections complicate this condition. This disease is more prevalent with advancing age, with the eighties being the period of highest prevalence. More than two-thirds of the observed cases are in those over 60 years of age. McKeown (1965), in observing a sample of 70-year-olds, found an incidence of 16 to 20 percent. One autopsy study (Gleckman, 1982) of patients aged 50 through 101 reported a 20 percent prevalence rate for acute pyelonephritis. The condition is prevalent much earlier in women. For organizational purposes we will now consider acute and chronic pyelonephritis as separate problems of the elderly.

Acute Pyelonephritis

Acute pyelonephritis is associated with bacterial infections such as E. coli, staphylococci, streptococci, and Proteus, with E. coli being responsible in the majority of cases. There is some dispute about whether the pathway taken by the infecting microorganisms is through the bloodstream or by the ascension of the urinary tract. This condition is often associated with obstructions in the lower tract. The kidneys are often swollen and soft and generally unequal in size. A variety of forms of stasis related to prostate problems, calculi, neurologic disease, circulatory disorders, prolonged recumbency, and tumors are all associated with acute pyelonephritis (Gleckman, 1982). It is twice as frequent in diabetics, possibly because sugar in the urine may favor bacterial growth and because of the greater frequency of catheterization among diabetics. In younger age groups, acute pyelonephritis is associated with or contributes to complications of hypertension.

Any form of urinary instrumentation carries with it the risk of infection. Indwelling catheters result in infections in about 90 percent of cases, although these may take a long time to develop. Cystitis associated with infections can result in a vesicoureteral reflux that can lead to pyelonephritis. Instrumentation apparently can either introduce bacteria to the tract, or the mechanical pressure associated with instrumentation can induce transient bacteremia. It is also possible that infection can be carried by the blood from another infective locus in the body.

In old age acute pyelonephritis can often lead to death through a combination of infection with uremia. In an old-age series, McKeown (1965) found 5 percent mortality from acute pyelonephritis; half of these deaths were the result of complications of prostatic disease. In the other half, death was associated with carcinoma, renal or vesical calculi, or cerebral vascular accidents. Brocklehurst (1973) found a 20 percent prevalence rate in a series of autopsied patients.

Chronic Pyelonephritis

Chronic pyelonephritis is, in most cases, the result of recurrent inflammatory episodes of the kidney. It is often, as its name implies, a progressive inflammatory process. It is probably caused by hypersensitivity to drugs and/or chemicals and is an increasingly common cause of acute renal failure. It is also more common and more refractory to treatment than acute pyelonephritis, which responds to antibiotics. By the time it is detected in its chronic phase, its cause is obscure. Some experimental evidence indicates that intrarenal scars of treated pyelonephritis may render the kidney more susceptible to reinfection. McKeown (1965) noted its occurrence in 11 percent of an old-age series and observed a slightly higher incidence in men with prostatic disease. Its prevalence increases with age, but overdiagnosis in autopsy must be considered a possibility. It is not often fatal, although occasionally it precipitates hypertensive heart failure or uremia.

In chronic pyelonephritis the kidney is generally reduced in size and presents a deformed outline. The scars are U-shaped as opposed to the V-shaped scars associated with vascular lesions. It is difficult to differentiate the scars of pyelonephritis from vascular scarring (which itself may predispose the kidney to local pyelonephritis infections). Both types of lesions occur together but are etiologically independent of each other. In the case of scarring, whatever the cause, damage to kidney tissues and blood vessels occurs and leads to reduced functional efficiency. Therapeutic measures for treatment and management of these infections have been mentioned in the section on general urinary infections. Again, precautions are necessary in approaching infections of the urinary tract. Pyelonephritis-associated infections will be more difficult to treat than those in the lower tract.

Renal Calculi

Renal calculi (kidney stones) are clinically more common in the years 30 to 60. On autopsy they tend to be high in the 50- to 70-year-old group (McKeown, 1965). Vesical calculi start in middle age and increase until old age. More prevalent in men, they are often complications of urinary tract obstructions related to infection and prostate enlargement. Most calculi are asymptomatic, and new ones are rare in old age. Over three-quarters of all stones are passed spontaneously without medical assistance. People rarely die from them, but they are not as readily passed by older people and can present dangerous obstructions that should be diagnosed and treated. The causes of their formation are still rather obscure, and several theories exist. It has been noted that sterile urine usually is associated with stones composed of uric acid and oxalate, whereas infective urine is most often associated with the more common stones of phosphate and carbonate composition. It has been suggested that a large daily fluid intake of more than two liters might significantly reduce the incidence of stone formation.

Glomerulonephritis

Inflammation of the glomeruli in both the acute and chronic forms is known as *glomerulonephritis*. Both conditions are generally rare in old age and are uncommon as causes of renal failure (Abrass, 1985). Few patients with chronic nephritis would survive beyond 70. The pathologic condition is the same at any age, but when present in the elderly it may be complicated by arteriosclerosis, hypertension, and pyelonephritis. Acute glomerulonephritis may be so mild that it is asymptomatic, but in other cases it may proceed rapidly to uremia and death. It often presents itself nonspecifically with nausea, malaise, arthralgias, and a tendency toward pulmonary infection (Morrin, Hinglais, and Nabaira, 1978). In a majority of cases it has its origin in an untreated streptococcal infection of the respiratory system. It is probable that the renal damage is caused by an autoimmune response in the kidney of susceptible individuals. This response may promote a lingering inflammation after the infecting microbe is eradicated.

Treatment is based on responding to the individual symptoms of renal failure. Penicillin treatment for 10 days may be prescribed to eradicate the causative agent. Once the inflammation is established, it can continue even without the presence of the streptococcus organism. Complete and usually uneventful recovery occurs in 95 percent of children. Adults have a more difficult time because coexistent conditions may lead to complications. Up to 50 percent of adults may show signs of the disease for over a year, although complete healing usually occurs within six months.

Chronic glomerulonephritis occurs when the acute phase lasts beyond a year, although it may occur in patients with no evidence of an acute phase. After this time period it is unlikely that the condition will ever heal completely. A variable period of time may pass during which the only symptoms are proteinuria and abnormal urinary sediment. This is called the latent phase. Eventually, most patients will develop progressive renal failure with uremia and death. The psychologic aspects of patient care are extremely important in chronic glomerulonephritis. The patient must understand the variable nature of an ultimately grave prognosis. Many patients are able to continue to work almost until the time of death.

Treatment involves medication to relieve symptoms or associated problems such as congestive heart failure. There is no evidence that restricted activity or bed rest is particularly beneficial. Some dietary modifications of salt and protein intake are often necessary. In general, the best approach is to allow the patient to determine his or her own physical limitations.

Nephrotic Syndrome

Nephrotic syndrome is associated with two primary features: great amounts of protein in the urine and lowered levels of blood protein. *Proteinuria* may exceed 3 to 4 g per 24 hours and is ultimately responsible for most of the clinical manifestations of the disease (Finkelstein and Hayslett, 1976). The other features associated with nephrotic syndrome are edema, hypercholesterolemia, and fat in the urine. The causes of nephrotic syndrome are unknown in a majority of the cases. It is associated with two major groups of diseases. Primary renal diseases such as chronic glomerulonephritis, lipoid nephrosis, proliferative glomerulonephritis, and membranous *nephropathy* account for over 95 percent of the cases in children, but systemic diseases are more often indicated in the elderly. Systemic diseases such as malignancies, polyarteritis, lupus erythematosis, amyloidosis, syphilis, malaria, renal vein thrombosis, and especially diabetes mellitus account for most cases in older people (Schreiber, 1984).

The basic mechanism involved is the enhancement of glomerular permeability, letting higher-molecular-weight material (protein) pass through into the urine. The nephrotic syndrome has been identified traditionally as a relatively common problem in the elderly. Fawcett, Hon, and Jones (1971) found that one in four cases occurs in adults over age 60. However, the exact incidence and prevalence rates for nephrotic syndrome in the elderly are unknown because of the frequency of its misdiagnosis. The prognosis in adults does become poorer with advancing age, and those afflicted will probably die from uremia. Temporary remission may occur.

Treatment for nephrotic syndrome involves supportive treatment to relieve or control symptoms, because in most cases the disease process involved cannot be controlled. Corticosteroids often cause a remission in a small minority of adults, but they are much more effective in children. It is not known for sure how corticosteroids prevent the inevitable progression toward uremia, and steroid therapy is very controversial. Restriction of sodium intake is suggested to control edema, because the capacity to excrete sodium is reduced in nephrotic syndrome. Diuretics can be used if sodium continues to accumulate, but they should be started at low doses to avoid depletion of intravascular volume. Elderly patients do not tolerate such sudden shifts because of waning homeostatic function; they may go into shock. A high-protein diet of at least 90 to 100 grams a day should help control proteinuria and avoid possible undernutrition associated with the loss of protein.

Nephrosclerosis

Nephrosclerosis, a hardening and thickening of the kidney tissues, is due to the development of thickened and hardened arteriolar walls in most people affected by high blood pressure. There is no known cure, but antihypertensives used to lower the blood pressure can sometimes slow or stop the development of this condition. Before nephrosclerosis becomes medically important, a person so affected often dies from cardiac or cerebral complications. Death when associated with nephrosclerosis is most often due to uremia.

Diabetic Kidney Problems

Nephrosclerosis, nodular glomerulosclerosis (Kimmelstiel-Wilson lesion), pyelonephritis, and nephrotic syndrome are all common in diabetics. Renal disease is the most common cause of death in diabetics when the disease is of over 20 years' duration. Management of renal disease in diabetics presents many problems because of the need to treat and control diabetic changes and the renal disease symptoms concurrently. Much of the treatment involves a symptomatic approach: Renal dialysis and transplants are risky even in young diabetics. Because of individual variability, however, each case should be evaluated to determine appropriate treatment.

TUMORS OF THE TRACT

Tumors are relatively rare in the kidney, accounting for only 1 to 2 percent of all malignancies. Renal tumors are infrequent in the elderly and very rarely metastasize. Urethral tumors are also rare and difficult to diagnose, and they usually are inoperable by the time they are discovered. An intermittent small urine stream, along with blood in the urine, may suggest a tumor. Bladder tumors decrease in incidence from a peak in the sixties. Bladder cancer is usually contained within the organ and is thus operable. However, 80 percent of all masses are cysts.

A FINAL WORD ON URINARY DISORDERS

In the control of urinary disorders in the elderly, several diagnostic examinations are very important. The evaluation of urinary tract dysfunction should consist of the following steps: routine urinalysis, digital examination of the prostate, estimation of residual urine by catheterization, and finally urography and cystography. The latter tests should not be applied routinely because they involve substantial risk and discomfort. Urinary symptoms in any age group should be investigated promptly and thoroughly. Treatment should be prompt, as exact as possible, and as aggressive as warranted in order to prevent further or future damage to the urinary tract.

The urinary tract is a complex and poorly understood organ system. The more intricate aspects of its functioning are just beginning to be delineated. Recent advances in dialysis and kidney transplants have increased medical ability to deal with some of the more threatening problems, although these avenues are expensive and rare in their utilization, especially with respect to the elderly. Many people believe that transplantations and dialysis should not be considered for the very old. It would seem that the best approach to the problems of the urinary tract in old age is to encourage adequate care in the younger years.

STUDY QUESTIONS

1. What are the general symptoms of urinary tract disturbance and their significance?
2. What are the significant changes that take place in the bladder and urethra with age?
3. What are the causes of incontinence? How prevalent is urinary incontinence in the elderly? What are some of the possible methods of treatment or management of urinary incontinence?
4. What is the prevalence of urinary tract infections in the elderly? What are some of the symptoms of tract infection?
5. Identify some factors that might help to precipitate urinary tract infections. Why do women have a higher prevalence of tract infections? Why is it important to treat such infections?
6. Identify the major changes associated with aging in the prostate gland. What is the prevalence and significance of prostate cancer in older men?
7. Identify some of the major age-related changes in the kidney.

8. Identify and note the significance of:
    a. pyelonephritis
    b. renal calculi
    c. glomerulonephritis
    d. nephrotic syndrome
    e. nephrosclerosis
    f. diabetic kidney
9. Why are urinary problems of special sociopsychological significance to elderly populations?
10. How can prompt identification and explanation of urinary symptoms by health workers serve the mental health and well-being of an affected individual?

BIBLIOGRAPHY

Abrass, C. W. 1985. Glomerulonephritis in the elderly. *American Journal of Nephrology,* 5: 409–419.

Anderson, F., and Williams, B. 1983. *Practical management of the elderly,* 4th ed. London: Blackwell Scientific Publications.

Anderson, S., and Brenner, B. M. 1986. Effects of aging on the renal glomerulus. *American Journal of Medicine,* 80: 435–440.

Bates, P., Bradley, W. E., Glen, E., and Griffith, D. 1979. The standardization of terminology of lower urinary tract function. *Journal of Urology,* 121: 551–554.

Beck, L. H., and Burkhart, J. M. 1990. Aging changes in renal function. In W. R. Hazzard (Ed.), *Principles of geriatric medicine and gerontology* (pp. 555–581). New York: McGraw-Hill.

Birkhoff, J. D. 1983. Natural history of benign prostatic hyperplasia. In F. Hinman (Ed.), *Benign prostatic hyperplasia.* New York: Springer Verlag.

Brendler, C. B. 1990. Disorders of the prostate. In W. R. Hazzard (Ed.), *Principles of geriatric medicine and gerontology* (pp. 582–591). New York: McGraw-Hill.

Brocklehurst, J. C. 1951. *Incontinence in old people.* Edinburgh: Churchill-Livingstone.

Brocklehurst, J. C. 1963. The aetiology of urinary incontinence in the elderly. In *Conference on medical and surgical aspects of aging: Current achievements in geriatrics.* London: Anderson & Isaacs.

Brocklehurst, J. C. 1973. *Textbook of geriatric medicine and gerontology.* Edinburgh: Churchill-Livingstone.

Brocklehurst, J. C., Dillane, J. B., and Griffiths, L. 1968. The prevalence and symptomology of urinary infection in an aged population. *Gerontologica Clinica,* 10: 242.

Brown, W. 1986. Aging and the kidney. *Archives of Internal Medicine,* 146: 1790-1796.

Diokno, A. C. 1980. Late genitourinary tract complications associated with severe pelvic injury. *Surgery, Gynecology and Obstetrics,* 150(2): 150-154.

Diokno, A. C., Brown, M. B., and Brock, B. M. 1986. Prevalence of urinary incontinence and other urological symptoms in the non-institutionalized elderly. *Journal of Urology,* 136: 1022-1025.

Dontas, A. S., Papanayiotou, P., and Marketos, S. 1966. Bacteriuria in old age. *Lancet,* 2: 305.

Epstein, M. 1985. Aging and the kidney: Clinical implications. *American Family Practice,* 31(4): 123-137.

Fawcett, I. W. P., Hon, H., and Jones, H. F. 1971. Nephrotic syndrome in the elderly. *British Medical Journal,* 2: 387-390.

Finkelstein, F. O., and Hayslett, J. P. 1976. Nephrotic syndrome: Etiology, diagnosis, and treatment. *Geriatrics,* 31(8): 39-52.

Gibson, I. I. J., and Pritchard, J. G. 1965. Screening investigations in the elderly. *Gerontologica Clinica,* 7: 330.

Gleckman, R. 1982. Acute pyelonephritis in the elderly. *Southern Medical Journal,* 75: 551-555.

Herzog, A. R., Diokno, A. C., and Fritz, N. 1989. Urinary incontinence: Medical and psychosocial aspects. *Annual Review of Gerontology and Geriatrics,* 9: 74-119.

Herzog, A. R., Diokno, A. C., and Fritz, N. 1990. Two year incidence, remission and change patterns of urinary incontinence in non-institutionalized older adults. *Journal of Gerontology,* 45(2): 67-74.

Hodkinson, H. M. 1981. *An outline of geriatrics,* 2nd ed. New York: Academic Press.

Isaacs, S. 1976. The preservation of continence. In F. L. Willington (Ed.), *Incontinence in the elderly.* New York: Academic Press.

Klein, L. A. 1979. Prostatic carcinoma. *New England Journal of Medicine,* 300: 824-833.

Lindeman, R. D. 1985. Longitudinal studies on the rate of decline in renal function with age. *Journal of the American Geriatric Society,* 33: 278-284.

McCue, J. D. 1987. Gram-negative bacillary bacteremias in the elderly, incidence, etiology and mortality. *Journal of the American Geriatrics Society,* 35: 213-216.

McKeown, F. 1965. *Pathology of the aged.* London: Butterworths.

McLachlin, M. 1987. Anatomic, structural and vascular changes in the aging kidney. In J. F. Nunez and J. F. Cameron (Eds.), *Renal function and disease in the elderly* (pp. 3-26). London: Butterworths.

Mitteness, L. S. 1987. The management of urinary incontinence by community living elderly. *The Gerontologist,* 27: 185-193.

Moore, R. A. 1952. Male secondary sexual organs. In A. L. Lansing (Ed.), *Cowdry's problems of aging,* 3rd ed. Baltimore: Williams and Wilkins.

Morrin, P. A., Hinglais, N., and Nabaira, B. 1978. Rapidly progressive glomerulonephritis. *American Journal of Medicine,* 65: 446-456.

Ory, M. G., Wyman, J. F., and Yu, L. 1986. Psychosocial factors in urinary incontinence. *Clinical Geriatric Medicine,* 2: 657-672.

Pannill, F. C., III. 1989. Practical management of urinary incontinence. *Medical Clinics of North America,* 73(6): 1423-1440.

Schreiber, M. J. 1984. The natural history of atherosclerotic and fibrous renal artery disease. *Urology Clinics of North America,* 11: 383-390.

Shepherd, A. M. 1980. Re-education of the muscles of the pelvic floor. In D. Mandelstam (Ed.), *Incontinence and its management.* London: Croom-Helm.

Shuttleworth, K. E. 1970. Incontinence. *British Medical Journal,* 4: 727-729.

Sourander, L. B. 1966. Urinary tract infection in the aged: An epidemiological study. *Annals of Internal Medicine, Fenniae Suppl.,* 55: 45.

Starer, P., and Libow, L. S. 1985. Obscuring urinary incontinence: Diapering of the elderly. *Journal of the American Geriatrics Society,* 33: 842-846.

Walkey, F. A. 1967. Incidence of urinary infection in the elderly. *Scottish Medical Journal,* 12: 411.

Whitmore, W. F. 1956. Symposium on hormones and cancer therapy: Hormone therapy in prostatic cancer. *American Journal of Medicine,* 21: 697.

Williams, M. E., and Pannill, F. C., III. 1982. Urinary incontinence in the elderly: Physiology, pathophysiology, diagnosis and treatment. *Annals of Internal Medicine,* 97: 895-907.

Williams, R. H., and Harrison, T. R. 1937. A study of renal arteries in relation to age and hypertension. *American Heart Journal,* 14: 645-658.

Willington, F. L. 1973. The marsupial principle in the management of urinary incontinence. *British Medical Journal,* 3: 626-628.

Yeates, W. K. 1976. Normal and abnormal bladder function in incontinence of urine. In F. L. Willington (Ed.), *Incontinence in the elderly.* New York: Academic Press.

CHAPTER **14**

The Endocrine System
and Age

The endocrine system exhibits a variety of changes with aging, and many researchers look to this system with the hope of finding the key to the aging process. Some researchers have suggested that changes in the pituitary, thyroid, or adrenal glands may be related to the onset of senescence. As far back as 1889, Brown-Sequard in France suggested that some of the functional changes associated with aging could be reversed or prevented by hormone extracts or cell suspensions. Throughout the twentieth century a number of researchers have subscribed to *rejuvenation* procedures based on hormone replacement therapy (Hull, 1984). Little evidence from clinical observation or empirical research supports this kind of hypothesis. At this time there is a paucity of research data available on the significance of the biochemical and anatomic changes that occur in the endocrine glands with advancing age. Histologic changes do occur, but none are unique, and we are unsure how they are related to function.

Disorders of the endocrine system are not frequent in old age, and when they do occur, most often they are related to pathologic changes rather than age. In fact, most endocrine disorders exhibit their highest incidence in early and middle adulthood. Diabetes and thyroid disorders are the most important endocrine problems of the elderly that have a significant effect on health and function.

Because of the integrated nature of the endocrine system, in which each gland can affect the others as well as the central nervous system, it is difficult to isolate the factors that cause deviation in endocrine function. There seems to be a wide margin of compensation that buffers the system in the face of age-related atrophy of organs. Multiple health problems and the many drugs taken by the elderly also complicate diagnosis, treatment, and research efforts with respect to the endocrines. Conflicting results make cross-checking, patience, and aggressive diagnostic procedures important el-

237

ements in the identification of an endocrine problem in the older person.

THYROID GLAND

With aging, the thyroid decreases in mass relative to a person's body weight, but related functional changes are difficult to substantiate. *Nodularity* increases with age, and it is estimated that after the eighth decade the incidence of nodularity is 100 percent. Much of this is micronodularity, and there are no good statistics on the incidence of palpable nodules in the elderly (Gilbert, 1981). Aging is also associated with an increase in *interfollicular* fibrous tissue (Gambert and Tsitouras, 1985). At the beginning of the twentieth century, the elderly were observed to have a lower basal metabolism rate (BMR) than young persons, leading to the idea that hypothyroidism was associated with aging. However, Tzankoff and Norris (1977), using a healthy, upper-middle-class population from Baltimore, showed that the decline in BMR with age was due to an age-related decline in lean muscle mass, not an aging thyroid. No evidence exists in humans that thyroid hormone activity is altered by the aging process (Gregerman, 1990).

Thyrotoxicosis

Hyperthyroidism was once thought to be rare in elderly populations, but better diagnosis, more widespread testing, and greater clinical awareness in combination with greater longevity has changed this view. It is estimated that 25 to 30 percent of all *thyrotoxicosis* occurs in those over 65 (Gilbert, 1981). The disease apparently is often unnoticed because its symptoms may be atypical, not conforming to the textbook picture. As many as 25 percent of the cases in the elderly will present atypical symptoms.

The primary symptoms are cardiac failure, atrial fibrillation, tachycardia, angina pectoris, congestive heart failure, increased body temperature, higher blood pressure, and apathy. The disorder is often accompanied by a weight loss of as much as 20 pounds, along with depression and mental confusion. The muscle-weakening tremors and fatigue that often occur are ignored because they tend to be so common in the elderly. *Exophthalmia,* so characteristic of younger age groups, and raised basal metabolism are often not present. The palpably enlarged thyroid mass (*Grave's disease*) of younger ages is not found in up to 20 percent of elderly thyroid patients (Ingbar, 1978), and in 10 to 15 percent no thyroid enlargement can be discerned by either scanning or sonography (Gregerman, 1990). However, multinodular goiter (*Plummer's disease*) accounts for as many as three-quarters of the goiter cases among the elderly.

Hyperkinesis is not as common as it is in the young, and anorexia is more common than increased appetite. Increased carbohydrate intake often associated with hyperthyroidism can lead to the development of *hyperglycemia* or loss of sugar control in a diabetic person. In fact, hyperglycemic irregularities may be the first clue to hyperthyroidism in the elderly. Heat intolerance with continuous perspiration is often reported in the elderly. A prevalence rate of 25 to 70 percent for heat intolerance in the elderly has been reported (Gregerman, 1990).

The nature of the condition puts great stress on the heart; thus, cardiac symptoms and complications increase with the duration of illness and age. These complications often result in death, and preexisting heart disease results in a poor prognosis for those with thyrotoxicosis.

Thyrotoxicosis often can be managed by drug treatment alone, but *radioiodine* therapy may be necessary. Radioiodine therapy is most commonly used in the elderly because there is no need to worry about genetic effects or the induction of hypothyroidism as in younger groups. But radioiodine therapy in the elderly may necessitate larger doses because delays are not as acceptable in the elderly. Hyperthyroidism in the elderly does require lifetime follow-up. Surgery is used only in unusual situations, where a question of malignancy exists or in large obstructive goiters. In some situations a variety of antithyroid drugs may prove useful.

Hypothyroidism or Myxedema

Myxedema or extreme hypothyroidism is purported to be a much less frequent thyroid disorder than thyrotoxicosis, but many studies indicate that it is commonly encountered at advanced ages. It is caused by a deficiency of thyroid hormone due to (1) Hashimoto's disease, (2) iodine deficiency, (3) hypothalamic or pituitary insufficiency, (4) surgical or chemical ablation of the thyroid as in treatment of Grave's disease, and/or (5) autoimmune thyroiditis. After diabetes, it is the most common endocrine disorder of the elderly. A recent study of patients over age 60 screened for the thyroid disease on admission to the hospital revealed a surprising 12 percent rate of hypothyroid disease (Livingston, 1987). Women have a five times greater incidence than men (Jeffreys, 1972). Obvious cases of hypothyroidism are generally recognized, but it has been suggested that less overt cases go unnoticed because the signs are generally attributed to normal aging. The symptoms are basically the same in both the elderly and the young and include puffy face, weakness, cold intolerance, croaky voice, thickened tongue, mental and physical sluggishness, perceptual deafness, and constipation. Signs related to hair loss and skin changes are not too useful in the aged, but vague musculoskeletal symptoms such as stiffness and aching may be important. The mental changes are so important among the elderly that often the condition is confused with dementia or psychosis. Diagnosis in the elderly is difficult, however, and only about one-third of the cases present the "classic" symptoms (Livingston, 1987).

The full picture of myxedema develops only after a long period of hypothyroidism and thus is often overlooked clinically in its earlier stage. Because hypothyroidism is often ignored or overlooked in the elderly, however, true myxedema is more likely to occur than in younger populations. If adequately treated before related damage is done, the condition can be compatible with long life expectancy. However, severe changes are often accompanied by ischemic heart disease with its possibility of myocardial infarction; also, the associated dementia may not be totally reversible.

Treatment usually involves lifelong hormone replacement therapy. L-thyroxine is the simplest, safest drug of choice. Its dosage must be carefully monitored for individual variability and especially in cases with coexistent ischemic heart disease. The initial dosages should be small and gradually increased to a maintenance level of 0.2 to 0.3 mg a day. Sawin and colleagues (Sawin, Herman, Molitch, London, and Kramer, 1983) have recently demonstrated that the required dose of thyroxine for those 60 years of age is considerably less than for younger groups. An electrocardiogram should be a requirement before initiating treatment, because thyroid treatment can precipitate a myocardial infarction in those with ischemic heart disease.

Thyroid Cancer

Thyroid cancer is infrequent, causing only 0.5 percent of all cancer deaths with the peak between 40 and 60 years of age. Thyroid cancers are even less frequent with increasing age. Those that do occur may be more aggressive and carry a poor prognosis. Anaplastic carcinomas account for less than 10 percent of all thyroid malignancies and are rare malignancies at all ages. However, 50 percent of these carcinomas occur in those over 60 years of age, and they are almost uniformly fatal within six months (Gilbert, 1981). Voice changes related to nodular presence deserve careful evaluation (Rowe and Besdine, 1982).

DIABETES AND THE ISLET OF LANGERHANS

Diabetes is an ancient disease. It was first described in the Egyptian Ebeas papyrus in 1500 B.C. It is a true disease of civilization: Prevalence rates increase with urbanization, sedentary life-styles, modern work patterns, and the dietary changes associated with modern life. As early as diabetes was recognized, it was not until 1788 that Rollo proposed a sound dietary approach to the treatment of diabetes.

Diabetes is the fifth most prominent cause of disease-related death in the United States. It is estimated that over 10 million people in the United State are affected by diabetes, and its prevalence appears to be increasing for all sex and age groups at an annual rate of 6 percent. A 1977 estimate by the federal government suggests that this condition costs about $6 billion annually in the form of medical expenses and lost productivity. A similar study in 1985 estimated $6 to $8 billion for direct costs and an equal amount for disability or premature death (U.S. Department of Health and Human Services, 1985). In terms of individual affliction, diabetes can lead to blindness, kidney failure, stroke, and gangrene in the extremities. Coronary heart disease, due to blood vessel degeneration, is twice as likely in victims of diabetes as in their unafflicted counterparts.

As a result of increasing life expectancy and effective management of the disease, diabetics generally live long lives. In fact, there is a growing number of older diabetics. Besides those who have had the disease since youth, older diabetics include those who have developed it in late middle age and those who first manifest it in later life. This last group often experience the mildest course of pathology and are easiest to manage.

However, many cases of diabetes go unnoticed, so the exact incidence among the elderly is unknown, although there appears to be a steady increase in its incidence from childhood to old age. It is estimated that 2 million Americans over age 65 are diabetic and that possibly an additional 2 million remain undiagnosed (Bennett, 1984). The rate peaks between the ages of 65 and 75 at 64.4 per 1,000 tested, and at age 75 drops to 57.9 per 1,000 people tested. It is estimated that 20 percent of all diabetics are 60 years or over and that 5 percent of the entire population over 65 are diabetic (U.S. Public Health Service, 1978). It is estimated that 1 out of 4 people over 85 years of age are diabetic (Bennett, 1984). The number of known diabetics in the United States over age 65 has doubled in the last twenty years (Bennett, 1984). Older men are now exhibiting a higher prevalence of diabetes than older women (Palumbo, Elveback, Chu, Connally, and Kurland, 1976), in contrast to a decade ago when women had appreciably higher rates (U.S. Public Health Service, 1977). This change could be due to several factors: (1) more men being diagnosed today, (2) lowered mortality of men with diabetes, and/or (3) increased incidence of diabetes in males resulting from life-style factors.

Diabetes is not a single disease entity. At least two major categories of the condition are recognized: Type I, known as *idiopathic insulin-dependent diabetes* (or juvenile diabetes), and Type II, *idiopathic insulin-independent diabetes* (adult-onset). There is little evidence to suggest a nutritional component in the etiology of Type I, which is probably associated with an immunological disturbance possibly influenced by heredity or a viral infection. Type I, though primarily associated with children, has been known to develop occasionally at other ages. Type II, the most common kind of diabetes, usually occurs after age 40 and is associated with obesity and possibly enkephalin sensitivity (Baird, 1981). Ketoacidosis does not develop in these patients, but they may need insulin to control symptomatic hyperglycemia. However, some diabetes develops in association with other conditions such as pancreatic disease, Cushing's syndrome, acromegaly drug damage, and insulin receptor abnormalities.

The true incidence of diabetes in the elderly is unknown. The condition is easily missed because of several factors. First, the classical symptoms of thirst, increased urination, severe wasting or weakness, and elevated fasting blood glucose are rarely present. Second, hyperglycemia can occur without glycosuria. Finally, the condition's symptoms may be confused with those of other conditions common among the elderly, such as congestive heart failure, uremia, and cholecystitis.

Overdiagnosis of diabetes may occur if the diagnostician uses only the standard tests because glucose tolerance normally decreases with age, thus affecting norm interpretations. There is also much disagreement on the efficacy of diagnostic criteria that can be applied to older persons.

The detection of diabetes in older persons is usually incidental to such things as hospitalization, eye examinations, testing for other disorders, and complications from other diseases. Blurred distance vision because of refractory changes produced by hyperglycemia is common in the elderly. *Pruritus vulvae* is a common symptom among elderly women. In screening procedures the most sensitive test is a blood glucose test two hours after a high-carbohydrate meal (100 g). If further testing is required, a glucose tolerance test is in order but this test is worthless if not done properly. According to Moss (1976), the following procedural points are important to ensure the validity of a glucose tolerance test:

1. Use a high-carbohydrate diet (300 g) for 3 days.
2. Do not perform the test under the stress of infection, surgery, or emotional upset.
3. Suspend all medications that could affect the test results:
   a. Cortisone, estrogens, and nicotinic acid raise blood glucose.
   b. Aspirin, antihistamines, and antidepressants lower blood glucose.
4. Adjust the amount of glucose used for individual body weight and age.

Many cases of diabetes in the elderly are associated with being overweight. In fact, some researchers believe that diabetes is the only significant pathologic condition related to overweight (Mann, 1971). The mortality rates for those who are over age 60 and diabetic are higher than for the general population, but only modestly so (Bennett, 1984). The onset of diabetes in the elderly is occasionally associated with the use of corticosteroids, thiazide diuretics, and pancreatic disease. Often cases of secondary diabetes occur in which there is direct damage to the pancreas. This diabetic pattern, like juvenile diabetes, is quite unstable and difficult to control.

There are three major clinical complications of diabetes; (1) accelerated atherosclerosis of large vessels, (2) microvascular disease of the capillary basement membranes in the kidney and retina, and (3) neuropathy with peripheral sensorimotor defects and autonomic nervous system dysfunction. These complications cause most of the death and disability associated with diabetes (Green, 1986).

The long-term complications of diabetes are numerous (see Table 14.1). Such complications as hypertension, coronary artery disease, cerebrovascular disease, peripheral vascular disease, retinopathy, glaucoma, neuropathies, and a variety of renal disorders are important to consider when planning for the management of diabetes. Vascular disease is responsible for about 75 percent of the

TABLE 14.1 Diabetes and increases in age-related complications

Renal disease	25 ×
Blindness	25 ×
Gangrene	20 ×
Vascular insufficiency	20 ×
Hypertension	3 ×
Myocardial infarction	25 ×
Stroke	2 ×

deaths from diabetes (Hirohata, 1967). Atherosclerosis progresses twice as fast in diabetics, and coronary heart disease is twice as common in diabetic men and five times as common in diabetic women. The characteristic pain of myocardial infarction is less severe in diabetics, and the mortality rate after heart attacks is higher. Age-specific mortality rates are consistently higher in diabetics from the complications of atherosclerosis, especially stroke and myocardial infarction (Pyorala, 1987).

Peripheral vascular disease is an important complication of diabetes and can be associated with the development of gangrene. Amputation of the feet is 50 times more common in diabetic men and 80 times more common in diabetic women than in the normal population. The threat of eventual amputation can be a very stressful situation for the elderly diabetic who already fears confinement for other reasons.

Neuropathies associated with diabetes are varied, but the most common manifestations are associated with the lower extremities. Symptoms can vary from numbness, tingling, and nocturnal burning to loss of the Achilles reflexes and loss of the ability to sense vibrations with the feet. These problems can be greatly improved by control of diabetes. Because there is little or no feeling present in the lower extremities, one must avoid extremes of heat and cold, and traumatizing situations such as tight shoes. Ulcerations can readily become infected, with most serious results.

The upper extremities are also affected but not as frequently and with milder manifestations. Autonomic nervous system neuropathies can lead to impotence, urinary bladder distension, gastric dilation, and orthostatic hypotension. The latter condition should alert diabetics about the need to get out of a bed carefully in order to avoid a possible damaging fall.

Renal disorders are common in diabetics. In many diabetics renal lesions appear within ten years of onset of the disease. Pyelonephritis is common in the elderly. Progressive renal failure may result in heart failure, hypertension, uremic acidosis, and eventually death. Low-salt and low-protein diets are prescribed in the latter stages of renal disease. There is no specific treatment for diabetic renal disease, and little evidence thus far supports the advantages of diabetic control in delaying the progression of nephropathy. A variety of factors such as infection and loss of sodium-retaining capabilities disturb renal function. The prognosis for a diabetic with renal problems is indeed grave.

Ocular disorders are frequent in older persons. The three most common disorders are cataract, retinopathy, and glaucoma. *Diabetic retinopathy* is the leading cause of blindness among persons subject to chronic disease. The prevalence in the United States is 16/100,000. Diabetics have a 13 times greater chance of becoming blind than nondiabetics. Even among those who are not totally blind, varying degrees of impaired vision are common in older diabetics. Retinopathy can be slowed by blood glucose control, glaucoma responds to pressure-reducing drugs, and cataracts can be removed surgically. All diabetics should be examined by an ophthalmologist yearly, and those showing proliferative changes even more often.

Skin problems are also associated with diabetes, in whom skin lesions are probably associated with small blood vessel diseases in the skin structures. Skin infections are common, especially *moniliasis*. Care must be taken to keep skin lesions clean and free of infection. Warm, soapy water for cleansing and the application of antibiotics such as neomycin have proved helpful.

Diet and Diabetes

A simple cause-and-effect relationship between diet and diabetes does not exist, but the American Diabetes Association (1974) suggests that improved nutrition could reduce the incidence of diabetes in the United States by 30 percent. Most researchers would probably agree that obesity is the one proven diabetogenic factor. In fact, some researchers believe that diabetes is the only significant pathological condition related to being overweight (Mann, 1971). Diabetes is rare in societies where obesity is uncommon. In the United States, approximately 75 percent of those with adult-onset diabetes are obese, and obese people are three times more likely to manifest diabetes than those of normal weight.

Baird (1981) found the incidence of obesity to be higher among diabetics in all social classes and in both sexes. She could not find any significant difference in the quality of food consumed by her general samples of obese and nonobese subjects. Those with diabetes, however, ate significantly more food than nondiabetics did. It also is significant that weight loss does reverse some of the metabolic disturbances of diabetes. In an early piece of research, Newburgh and Conn (1939) showed that weight loss corrected abnormal glucose tolerance in 90 percent of a middle-aged population.

The search for qualitative nutritional factors that promote diabetogenesis is controversial and plagued with contradictory results. Nutritional factors could be involved relative to damage to the pancreas, impaired glucose tolerance, and impaired function of the beta cells. Little experimental data is available to provide strong support for a nutritional basis for any of these mechanisms.

Epidemiological studies correlating diabetes with dietary variations are abundant, but the evidence presented is generally inconclusive for establishing cause and effect. Noting the fall in diabetic mortality during wartime, Himsworth (1949) proposed that a high-fat diet was diabetogenic, given that fat consumption dropped noticeably during wartime food shortages. But he failed to consider that sucrose consumption also dropped abruptly and significantly at this time. Other data available at the time would have pointed out, also, that although Eskimos have a diet very high in animal fat, this population exhibits a very low incidence of diabetes.

A number of researchers have sought a correlation between a high incidence of diabetes and consumption of sucrose, or refined sugar. Cohen (1961) noted that Yemenite Jews emigrating to Israel had a low incidence of diabetes. However, after a period of years in Israel and adoption of a typical Israeli diet in which 20 to 25 percent of the total calories came from sucrose, prevalence rates increased to approximately those of Western countries. Campbell (1963) arrived at conclusions similar to Cohen's while studying Asians and Africans in and around Durban, South Africa. Cleave and Campbell (1966) also found diabetes to be related to the increased use of refined sugar in the Natal area of India. Yudkin (1969) demonstrated a significant correlation between the amount of sugar consumed and mortality from diabetes in 22 countries.

A number of other epidemiologists found little data in their studies to support a sucrose–diabetes relationship. Baird (1972), in Scotland, found no relationship between sugar consumption and diabetes, and similar studies in England came to the same conclusion. Poon-King, Henry, and Rampersad (1968) studied five geographical districts in Trinidad and found the incidence of diabetes lowest in districts with highest per capita consumption of sugar. In the South Pacific, Prior (1974) found variations in diabetes not accounted for by dietary consumption of sugar and suggested that other environmental factors as yet unidentified might be more important. Is it possible that some individuals, or even populations, may have a genetically based sensitivity to sucrose? If so, it might be possible to prevent diabetes in such populations by having them avoid high levels of sucrose stimulation (Cleave and Campbell, 1966).

Trowell (1975) and others have suggested a link between fiber-depleted diets and a high incidence of diabetes. He noted that mortality from diabetes fell in Britain during the world wars, when a coarser, less refined flour was consumed. The same research (Trowell, 1978) suggested that the incorporation of fiber into the diet may lower blood insulin and blood glucose levels. Miranda and Horowitz (1978) support this contention. The specific effects of selected components of the dietary fiber complex are also being investigated in relation to lowering the incidence of diabetes. It must be remembered that when dietary fiber is increased, the protein, fat, vitamin, and/or mineral content of the diet may be altered as well, and these factors must be considered in any explanation of observed effects. Some investigators have suggested a strong genetic component among various ethnic groups, especially blacks, American Indians, and Mexicans.

In a study among Mexican Americans in Starr County, Texas, Harris, Ferrell, and Barton (1983) found that 14.5 percent of those between age 65 and 74 had diabetes, compared to an age-equivalent population of Anglos in Rancho Bernardino, California, that exhibited a rate of 5.9 percent (Barrett-Connor, 1980). Gardner, Stern, and Haffner (1984) suggested that the higher prevalence of diabetes in Mexican-Americans may be a result of Amerindian admixture (Knowler, Bennett, Hamman, and Miller, 1978).

A study by Gardner, Stern, and Haffner (1984) tends to support the Indian admixture hypothesis. These investigators found that even when controls for increased obesity were taken into account, Mexican-Americans showed a two to four times greater incidence of diabetes than Anglos. This excess appears to be proportional to the amount of Amerindian admixture in the Mexican-American population. It would appear that ethnic or racial studies of genetic propensity for the development of adult-onset diabetes could be useful in the early identification of individuals at risk. This kind of information could also be useful in health promotion or health counseling programs that emphasize a preventive approach to diabetes.

Treatment and Management

Mild, late-onset diabetes can often be controlled by dietary restriction of carbohydrates to around 100 g per day. Some cases will require oral drug treatment with the sulfonylureas such as tolbutamide (Orinase), chlorpropamide (Diabinase), acetohexamide (Dymelor), and tolazamide (Tolinase). Oral treatment should be used only in persons whose diet has failed to control hyperglycemia. The oral treatment may not be sufficient to control diabetes under conditions of severe stress, such as surgery or systemic infections. These drugs are not recommended for people with severe liver or kidney disease. The most common side effects of oral drugs are rashes, flushing, headaches, nausea, gastrointestinal distress, tachycardia, hypoglycemia, and hyponatremia.

Severe cases of diabetes require insulin injections, although the procedures are essentially the same for any age group; older people may have trouble administering insulin because of poor eyesight and diminished fine motor coordination. Home glucose monitoring may be a chore under these conditions. It should also be noted that urine glucose monitoring is inadequate because of age changes in glucose excretion. Home health service visits may be required to keep severe diabetics in the community and out of major medical trouble.

Diabetic coma and insulin shock are two important acute complications of diabetic management. *Diabetic acidosis* (coma) is the result of impaired glucose utilization that leads to high blood sugar. This is followed by increased utilization of fats, which produces an excess of *ketones,* causing ketosis. The diabetic may rapidly dehydrate, suffering circulatory collapse, rapid deep breathing, dulling of the senses, and finally coma. This is a grave emergency, often requiring hospitalization. Insulin must be supplied and the water and electrolyte balance restored. This condition may be precipitated by infections, injuries, stress, or negligence in insulin therapy.

A variant form of diabetic coma is *hyperosmotic nonketotic coma.* It is a relatively frequent occurrence in the elderly, and mortality is very high, often as a result of thrombic incidents. It occurs most frequently in those over age 50 with mild or undiagnosed diabetes. Almost one-half of patients developing this kind of coma die. Treatment must include massive amounts of intravenous fluids to replace the substantial losses of water and insulin. In both forms of diabetic coma, potassium deficiency must be remedied by potassium supplements after the patient's condition has been stabilized. Even with adequate treatment, the mortality rate remains 40 to 70 percent (Arieff and Carroll, 1972).

Insulin shock or acute hypoglycemia can occur in connection with an overdose of insulin or oral hypoglycemics that lowers the blood glucose level below normal. It can also be precipitated by taking insulin or the oral drugs but neglecting to eat, and it can be caused by unusual exercise. Early symptoms are perspiration, pallor, numbness, tremors, confusion, gait instability, convulsions, and loss of consciousness. It must be recognized quickly because cerebral damage, myocardial infarction, and death are possible complications.

Diabetics should carry a source of glucose at all times to counter the onset of this state. Orange juice, carbonated beverages, candy, and other sources of sugar may be used in this situation. The diabetic should pay careful attention to insulin dose, avoid omitting meals and drinking alcohol, and carefully monitor urine glucose levels. In a person who is unable to swallow, forced feeding should be avoided; an injection of 1 mg of glucagon will sufficiently raise the blood sugar. All individuals working with or related to diabetics should be aware of the distinction between diabetic coma and insulin shock. Mistaken action could result in death (Table 14.2). In diabetic coma the patient will exhibit the

TABLE 14.2 Differentiating ketosis and insulin shock

Ketosis	Insulin shock
Dry skin and tongue	Moist skin and tongue, sweating
Low blood pressure	Normal or raised blood pressure
Hyperventilation	Shallow or normal breathing
Diminished reflexes	Brisk reflexes
Plantar responses: usually flexion	Plantar responses: usually extension
Ketonuria	No ketonuria
Glycosuria	No glycosuria
Hyperglycemia	Hypoglycemia
Reduced plasma bicarbonate	Normal plasma bicarbonate
Several days of poor health common	Onset sudden, usually good health prior to attack
Recent infection or digestive disturbance common	Skipping a meal or unusual overexertion common

odor of acetone on the breath and have sugar and acetone in the urine, but in insulin shock these characteristics are absent.

In the past, two methods were used in the care of older diabetics. One stressed strict and rigorous diet control; the other allowed more freedom in selecting a diet and used insulin to control hyperglycemia. In the late 1950s the introduction of the oral hyperglycemic tablet led to the neglect of dietary therapy and promoted an overdependence on medication. The negative impact of this abuse has yet to be determined.

A balanced diet is the key to the management of diabetes. Remember that the lifelong food habits of an individual will be difficult to change. The less the diet is manipulated and modified to achieve balance, the greater the probability of adherence to the diet. A number of principles are important:

1. A diet should be compatible with an individual's economic and social background.
2. A diet should be compatible with an individual's activity profile.
3. A diet should be made up of readily available, commonly used foods.
4. A diet should plan three well-balanced, regularly spaced meals with small, nutritious snacks in between.
5. Foods high in pure sugar should be eliminated.
6. A diet should contain a balance of carbohydrate, protein, and fat, at approximately the following levels: 55 percent to 60 percent complex carbohydrate, 10 percent to 20 percent protein, and 30 percent fat.
7. Adequate salt intake must be assured, and potassium should be watched; chromium supplements might be helpful to those who do not respond well to insulin.
8. A broad-spectrum multivitamin supplement might be helpful, since excretion of water-soluble vitamins is often excessive.
9. Large, heavy meals should be avoided, particularly before retiring for the night.
10. Midmorning and midafternoon snacks are a must for those taking insulin.

Recent dietary recommendations suggest lower amounts of fat, saturated fat, and cholesterol, and higher amounts of complex carbohydrates than are typical of the North American diet. However, Gerald Reaven of Stanford University's School of Medicine has recently issued some cautions about high-carbohydrate, low-fat diets because very low fat diets can promote heart disease. A panel of the National Institute of Health recently suggested as a precaution that any diabetic who goes on a high-carbohydrate diet should be tested to prevent adverse effects of blood-lipid ratios (Kolata, 1987).

Exercise and Diabetes

Exercise promotes increased insulin secretion and better utilization of glucose by the body. The principal problem is that the elderly are less active because of declining physical status and/or lack of motivation. An exercise program should be related to an individual's functional capacity and need not be rigorous. Mild exercise performed in several sessions can be effective. Elderly persons should be encouraged to walk daily because recent research indicates that the effects of exercise on diabetics are short-lived, disappearing in 72 hours (Kolata, 1987). Asking another person to take part in an exercise program can make it more interesting and more likely to be continued. The social aspect of the walk can satisfy certain interpersonal needs for the older person while at the same time answering some of the need for physical activity.

Exercise can be an effective adjunct to diet therapy because it enhances weight loss by utilization of ingested calories and may improve one's sense of well-being even when dieting. It may enhance compliance because the increased energy expended may lessen dietary restrictions. Most overweight elderly diabetics do not need insulin because a program of diet and physical activity can improve insulin sensitivity and lower blood glucose. Once sufficient weight is lost, however, a weight-maintaining diet should be initiated.

Problems in Patient Education

Patient education is a part of complete diabetic therapy. The diabetic has a lifelong condition that he or she must learn to control and live with. If the diabetic is in possession of accurate, up-to-date medical information, the incidence of complications and hospital admissions can be reduced. People working with the elderly should be able to convey and clarify practical information about diabetic management.

The diabetic must become a careful observer of his or her own physical condition. Daily examination of the body, especially the feet, is a must. Each body part should be checked for any change in appearance such as swelling, redness, numbness, and bleeding. Changes in vision, coordination, and ability to walk should be noted. Changes of this sort should be reported to a health care practitioner. The diabetic should avoid tight clothing or shoes and the use of any external medicine or application not recommended by a health care practitioner.

Reduced blood supply and lessened peripheral nerve sensation make foot problems more serious in diabetics. Shoes that are too tight or poorly shaped can cause unnoticed trauma that might ulcerate, become infected, and lead to loss of one's foot or leg. The purchase of well-fitting shoes is important. It has been suggested that this be done in the evening or late afternoon to allow for expansion of the feet. Sores, cracks, and other injuries should receive prompt attention to avoid complications. Usually, bed rest is needed to promote healing. Thick, tough toenails must be trimmed regularly but can present a problem that may require podiatric care.

According to Duncan (1976), 7 percent of diabetics are blind, and many more have partially impaired vision. This means that they will have total or partial problems in seeing syringe calibrations, traumatized body parts, and toenails. Depending on the circumstances, a home visitor may be required for maintenance care. Premeasured syringes, Braille devices, and magnifying glasses are helpful in many instances.

The diabetic patient living at home should also be cognizant of environmental hazards that may lead to injury. Trauma from slippery floors, steep stairs, and poorly lit areas is common. Care must be taken to eliminate or modify such hazards. Steep stairs should be replaced and slippery, bare wood floors carpeted. The diabetic at home should have easy access to a supply of quick sugar, glucagon, and insulin. Relatives or people living with or visiting known diabetics should know the location of such supplies and be able to use them in emergencies.

With proper management, diabetics can live long, useful lives. They need not be embarrassed by overprotective family and friends concerned over the presence of sweets and sources of trauma. Diabetics need not be subjected to harassment by insurance companies who cancel their health insurance and double their life insurance premiums. Employers need not feel that diabetics must be specially treated or eliminated. The diabetic is a person with a highly manageable pathologic condition; he or she is not an invalid or handicapped individual.

PARATHYROID

The parathyroid gland's importance in the regulation of calcium metabolism (and thus of skeletal integrity) makes it of some interest to those who study aging. *Radioimmune assays* indicate an 80 percent increase in the circulation level of parathormone elements between age 30 and 80. More sensitive tests that detect only the intact hormone reveal a 30 percent increase over the same period (Rowe and Besdine, 1982). This condition is possibly due to "mild hyperparathyroidism" associated with the age-related decrease in intestinal calcium absorption (Bullamore, Wilkinson, Gallagher, and Nordin, 1970). Such a decrease results in lower levels of ionized calcium in the blood, leading to parathormone release.

Hyperparathyroidism in the elderly differs from the condition in young age groups in that it is associated with alterations in mental status. It is possible that even mild alterations in serum calcium can result in significant alterations of mental status especially in those with preexisting mild central nervous system disease. It is therefore probable that the hypercalcemia associated with hyperparathyroidism is an important treatable cause of mental failure in the elderly (Mannix, 1980). Parathyroid surgery can produce dramatic results, and the elderly seem to tolerate it well, with the exception of those with severe heart or respiration problems (Mannix, 1980). These patients can often be managed by more conservative drug therapy. The possible relationship of the parathyroid to some cases of osteoporosis is also of interest to those studying the aging process.

In people over 60 years of age, the incidence rate for women is 2 cases per 1,000 women and in men 1 case per 1,000 men. Most of these cases are asymptomatic, but the condition does occur with increasing frequency in the elderly (Heath, Hodgson, and Kennedy, 1980).

POSTERIOR PITUITARY GLAND

One of the most serious and least recognized electrolyte disorders of the elderly is the tendency toward water intoxication (hyponatremia). This condition can be associated with oversecretion of *antidiuretic hormone* (ADH). In the absence of renal failure the condition can be relatively easily di-

agnosed clinically. The elderly appear prone to the development of ADH-induced water intoxication in a variety of stress states such as viral illness, after anesthesia and surgery, during some kind of drug therapy, and in concert with a variety of pulmonary and central nervous system disorders (Rowe and Besdine, 1982).

The symptoms of *hyponatremia* are anorexia, confusion, depression, lethargy, and weakness. In more severe cases seizure and stupor may be present. Given the nature of these symptoms and their nonspecificity, it might be valuable to check for this syndrome in those elderly persons who exhibit them after being recently subjected to great stress.

DISORDERS OF THE ADRENAL GLANDS

There is no evidence that older people are particularly prone to the development of relatively rare disorders of the adrenals such as overproduction and underproduction of steroids, or adrenal neoplasms. Nevertheless, it is important to keep the adrenals in mind when evaluating elderly patients because many problems observed in the elderly could be related to adrenal disorders. This is especially true when more common causes have been ruled out. It has been recognized recently that benign neoplasms are increasingly common, but these appear to present no threat to the individual. Unless specific clinical indications are present, such findings probably merit no further action.

STUDY QUESTIONS

1. Why is a consideration of the endocrine system significant for the study of aging?
2. How does the thyroid gland change with age?
3. What is the significance of thyrotoxicosis in the aged? How does the symptomatology of thyrotoxicosis differ in the elderly from that of earlier years?

4. How is thyrotoxicosis managed in the elderly? What is the importance of hypothyroidism among the elderly? Why do many cases go unnoticed?

5. What are the symptoms of hypothyroidism? Do the symptoms exhibit age-related differences?

6. What is the significance of diabetes as a health problem for the elderly? Why are we seeing a higher prevalence of diabetes in older men in recent years? Why is the true incidence of diabetes in the elderly unknown?

7. Differentiate insulin-dependent and insulin-independent diabetes? Identify the problems associated with the diagnosis of diabetes in the elderly.

8. Identify the major long-term complications of diabetes and their significance. What is the possible association of diabetes with diet? What do cross-cultural studies indicate about the possible causes of diabetes?

9. What are the major methods for controlling late-onset diabetes? Differentiate insulin shock and diabetic coma. How is each condition dealt with therapeutically? What are some major principles of diet management that are of importance to diabetics?

10. What is the role of exercise in diabetic management? Identify the major patient education problems associated with diabetic management in the elderly. What are some of the social-psychological aspects of living with diabetes?

11. What is the possible significance of hyperparathyroidism among the elderly?

12. How may pituitary disorders be of significance to the elderly?

BIBLIOGRAPHY

American Diabetes Association. 1974. *Annual report.* New York: Author.

Arieff, A. L., and Carroll, H. J. 1972. Non-ketotic hyperosmolar coma with hyperglycemia. *Medicine,* 51: 73–94.

Baird, J. D. 1972. Diet and the development of clinical diabetes. *Acta Latina,* 19: 621–637.

Baird, J. D. 1981. Diet and the development of clinical diabetes in man. *Proceedings of the Nutritional Society,* 40: 213–217.

Barrett-Connor, E. 1980. The prevalence of diabetes mellitus in an adult community as determined by history or fasting hyperglycemia. *American Journal of Epidemiology,* 111: 705–712.

Bennett, P. H. 1984. Diabetes in the elderly: Diagnosis and epidemiology. *Geriatrics,* 36(5): 37–41.

Bullamore, J. R., Wilkinson, R., Gallagher, J. C., and Nordin, B. E. C. 1970. Effect of age on calcium absorption. *Lancet,* 2: 535–540.

Campbell, C. D. 1963. Diabetes in Asians and Africans in and around Durban. *South African Medical Journal,* 37: 1195–1208.

Cleave, T. L., and Campbell, C. D. 1966. *Diabetes, coronary thrombosis and the saccharine disease.* Bristol: J. D. Wright.

Cohen, A. M. 1961. Prevalence of diabetes among different ethnic Jewish groups. *Metabolism,* 10: 50–58.

Duncan, T. G. 1976. Teaching common sense health habits to diabetic patients. *Geriatrics,* 31(10): 93–96.

Gambert, S. R., and Tsitouras, P. D. 1985. Effect of age on thyroid hormone physiology and function. *Journal of the American Geriatrics Society,* 33(5): 360–365.

Gardner, L. I., Stern, M. P., and Haffner, S. P. 1984. Prevalence of diabetes in Mexican-Americans: Relationship to the percent of gene pool derived from American Indians. *Diabetes,* 33: 86–92.

Gilbert, P. D. 1981. Thyroid function and disease. In L. S. Lebow and F. T. Sherman (Eds.), *The core of geriatric medicine* (pp. 246–274). St. Louis: C. V. Mosby.

Green, D. R. 1986. Acute and chronic complications of diabetes mellitus in older patients. *American Journal of Medicine,* 80(Suppl.): 39–50.

Gregerman, R. I. 1990. Thyroid diseases. In W. R. Hagg, R. Andres, E. L. Bierman, and J. P. Bless (Eds.), *Principles of geriatric medicine and gerontology* (pp. 719–738). New York: McGraw-Hill.

Harris, C. L., Ferrell, R. E., and Barton, J. S. A. 1983. Diabetes among Mexican-Americans in Starr County, Texas. *American Journal of Epidemiology,* 118: 659–672.

Heath, H., Hodgson, S. F., and Kennedy, M. A. 1980. Primary hyperparathyroidism: Incidence, mobility and potential impact in a community. *New England Journal of Medicine,* 302: 189–193.

Himsworth, H. P. 1949. The syndrome of diabetes and its causes. *Lancet,* 1: 465–472.

Hirohata, T. 1967. The natural history of diabetes I mortality. *Diabetes,* 16: 878–881.

Hull, D. A. 1984. *The biomedical basis of gerontology.* London: Wright and Sons.

Jeffreys, P. 1972. The prevalence of thyroid disease in

patients admitted to a geriatric department. *Age and Aging,* 1: 33-40.

Ingbar, S. H. 1978. The influence of aging on human thyroid economy. *Geriatric Endocrinology,* 5: 13-17.

Knowler, W. C., Bennett, P. H., Hamman, R. F., and Miller, M. 1978. Diabetes incidence and prevalence in Pima Indians: A nineteenfold greater incidence than in Rochester, Minnesota. *American Journal of Epidemiology,* 108: 497-505.

Kolata, G. 1987. Diabetics should lose weight and avoid diet fads. *Science,* 235: 163-164.

Livingston, E. H. 1987. Prevalence of thyroid disease and abnormal thyroid tests in older hospitalized and ambulatory persons. *Journal of the American Geriatrics Society,* 35: 109-115.

Mannix, H. 1980. Hyperparathyroidism in the elderly. *American Journal of Surgery,* 64: 729-731.

Mann, G. V. 1971. The obesity spook. *American Journal of Public Health,* 61: 1491-1498.

Miranda, P. M., and Horowitz, D. L. 1978. High-fiber diets in the treatment of diabetes mellitus. *Annals of Internal Medicine,* 88: 482-486.

Moss, J. M. 1976. Pitfalls to avoid in diagnosing diabetes in the elderly. *Geriatrics,* 31(10): 52-55.

Newburgh, L. H., and Conn, J. W. 1939. A new interpretation of hyperglycemia in obese middle-aged persons. *Journal of the American Medical Association,* 112: 7-11.

Palumbo, P. J., Elveback, L. R., Chu, C. P., Connally, D. C., and Kurland, L. T. 1976. Diabetes mellitus: Incidence, prevalence, survivorship and causes of death in Rochester, Minnesota, 1945-1970. *Diabetes,* 25: 566-573.

Poon-King, T., Henry, M. V., and Rampersad, F. 1968. The prevalence and natural history of diabetes in Trinidad. *Lancet,* 1: 155-160.

Prior, I. A. M. 1974. Diabetes in the South Pacific. In S. S. Hildebrand (Ed.), *Is the risk of becoming a diabetic affected by sugar consumption?* (pp. 4-13). Bethesda, MD: International Sugar Foundation.

Pyorala, K. 1987. Diabetes and atherosclerosis: An epidemiological view. *Diabetes and Metabolism Review,* 3(2): 463-470.

Rowe, J. W., and Besdine, R. W. 1982. Endocrine and metabolic systems. In J. W. Rowe and R. W. Besdine (Eds.), *Health and disease in old age* (pp. 137-156). Boston: Little, Brown.

Sawin, C. T., Herman, T., MoLitch, M. E., London, M. H., and Kramer, S. M. 1983. Aging and the thyroid: Decreased requirement for thyroid hormone in old hypothyroid patients. *American Journal of Medicine,* 75: 206-209.

Trowell, H. C. 1975. Dietary-fiber hypothesis of the etiology of diabetes mellitus. *Diabetes,* 24: 762-765.

Trowell, H. C. 1978. Diabetes mellitus and dietary fiber of starchy foods. *American Journal of Clinical Nutrition,* 31: 553-557.

Tzankoff, S. R., and Norris, A. H. 1977. Effect of muscle mass decrease in age-related BMR changes. *Journal of Applied Physiology,* 3: 1001-1009.

U.S. Department of Health and Human Services, National Institutes of Health. 1985. *Diabetes in America.* Bethesda, MD: Department of Health and Human Services, National Diabetes Data Group.

U.S. Public Health Services. 1978. *Diabetes data.* Bethesda, MD: U.S. Department of Health, Education and Welfare.

Yudkin, J. M. 1969. Dietary fat and dietary sugar in relation to ischemic heart disease and diabetes. *Lancet,* 2: 4-5.

PART **III**

Biosocial Aspects of Aging

CHAPTER **15**

Sexuality and Aging

Gere B. Fulton, Ph.D., J.D.

The very thought of combining the words *sexuality* and *aging* in the same sentence may be a bit much for some readers. After all, we live in a society that extols the virtues of youth. The elderly are often relegated to an early obsolescence, and expressions of sexuality other than tenderly holding hands while strolling beneath a setting sun are regarded as inappropriate behavior. The poet Robert Browning wrote, "Grow old along with me! The best is yet to be, the last of life for which the first was made . . ." Could he have possibly been thinking about sex too, or everything but sex, as he penned those words? And can we compare Browning's words to contemporary satire of the accompaniments of aging, including male concerns about the loss of virility and female concerns about the loss of fertility and desirability? Which of these visions of sexuality and aging are we to embrace: an aging process in which love and sex mature and blossom,

or one in which the passion of sexuality that flamed in youth is little more than a flickering ember in the elderly?

Several years ago I was asked to make a presentation on "Sexuality and Aging" at a seminar for geriatric workers. Because men and women often bring different perspectives to the topic of sexuality, I invited a female colleague with whom I had often worked to join me in speaking to the group. In planning the presentation, we were initially unsure about whether it would be better to treat the topic in a "scientific" way, by citing all the appropriate research, or perhaps to personalize the issues. We wondered whether our efforts would be most productive if we focused on facts or feelings, empiricism or experiences. The former was certainly safer. Dealing with things that tend to make people uncomfortable is much easier when we can keep them at arm's length.

We decided to combine an "intellectual" approach to sexuality and aging with an "experiential" component. This approach involved introducing the topic with a traditional lecture format, followed by a film featuring an elderly couple and showing a sexual relationship. The film, though sexually explicit, was made to portray the playfulness, joyfulness, and mutual enjoyment of the couple, not just the genital aspects of the relationship. The film had been widely used in similar programs for members of the helping professions – medicine, social work, counseling, and even theology – and was always a very useful discussion-starter. Still, every group is different, and we did not know what effect it would have on this group. Although the group seemed comfortable with the lecture portion of our presentation, things changed when we showed the film.

Along about the time the couple in the film, a pot-bellied old man and his clearly postmenopausal partner, took off their clothes, even in the semi-darkened auditorium it was evident that several people were heading, quickly, for the doors. When I realized what was happening, I followed, attempting to talk with them. One or two, willing to talk back, expressed their anger at being subjected to such pornography. I tried to explain to them that the film was not shown to offend them and, moreover, that the film was clearly not pornographic. (The market for a porno film featuring a couple like this is all but nonexistent!) Several people accepted my explanation and returned to the auditorium. The exodus had been a small one.

After the film ended, we asked for comments. Although most of the group said nothing, it was clear that the film had had a significant effect. There was a lot of chatter and nervous laughter in the auditorium. After this subsided, we had an opportunity to talk with the group about our reasons for showing the film and, especially, the reactions the film had provoked.

Several days later I received a letter from a woman who had attended the seminar. She was angry for not responding at the time of the film by expressing feelings on behalf of "herself and others." "How," she asked, "is the nun sitting next to me to know that the film was not about love, but about heat?" The letter continued:

> The sex act is a small part of that time span, why are you so hung up on the genitalia? I'm sorry for you. Life has so much beauty and *love*, caring and sharing, that you cannot see, feel, know the richness of living fully because you seem to be stuck at the genital stage. How sad for the lives you influence to think that sex is all there is . . .

I decided to respond and told this letter-writer that I was sorry for *her* discomfort in sitting next to a nun (toward whom she had obviously reacted in a stereotypical fashion), but I also chided her for her assumption that this nun was neither mature nor intelligent enough to differentiate for *herself* love from "heat" as cleverly and unerringly as the writer had. I tried to explain that rather than being "hung up on the genitalia," we were just attempting to authenticate the genital expression of our sexuality in a society that has systematically attempted to deny the legitimacy of such expression.

So much for risk taking. All of us, but perhaps especially those who work with the elderly, would seem to have a good deal to learn about sexuality and aging. Nursing home personnel, in particular, seem to have been indoctrinated with the attitude that expressions of sexuality are inappropriate among their elderly residents. Sexual activity is typical regarded as "a problem," even when it occurs between husband and wife.

Paula Wringer, a nurse who consults with several nursing homes, relates the following story:

> A woman "about 80 or so" came up to her and said she had a problem that she hoped Wringer could help her with. She said she had a boyfriend; and the last time they were together in her room, a couple of the staff

came in and started laughing. "All we were doing was sitting close and holding hands" she told me, "and they thought it was funny." And then she began to cry. She was so upset by that. She felt further dehumanized. She said, "I'm here and I can't get out. I want to be with this man, and I don't want to be laughed at." Wringer then made arrangements for the couple to have two evenings a week to themselves, with no disturbances. (Smith, 1988)

It seems quite common to regard sexuality in later life as amusing or even repugnant. Young people are as uncomfortable with the sexuality of their parents as the parents are with the sexuality of their adolescent children. Pocs and his colleagues (Pocs, Godow, Tolone, and Walsh, 1977) reported that a majority of the 646 college students they surveyed believed that their parents (1) never had intercourse before they were married, (2) never had oral–genital sex, and (3) had intercourse once a month or less. About one-fourth of the students, both men and women, believed their parents never had intercourse or had it less than once a year!

It is evident that some students felt it was wrong even to think about their parents' sexuality. Six percent refused to answer most of the items that dealt with premarital petting; premarital, marital, and extramarital intercourse; and oral–genital sex. Nearly 20 percent ignored the questions about past and present parental masturbation. A few students expressed their feelings about the survey more bluntly: "This questionnaire stinks." "Whoever thinks about their parents' sexual relations, except perverts?"

Thinking about their parents engaging in sexual behavior was obviously problematic for many college students. What might their response have been had the survey focused on the sexuality of their grandparents? It is only too obvious that most of these students (and we, too) have been raised in a society that still retains certain Victorian standards regarding sexual expression by older people.

There is some evidence that these repressive attitudes are becoming less common. In some cases the attitudes of staff who work with the institutionalized elderly may be more supportive concerning sexual expression of nursing home residents than those of the elderly themselves. The explanation for this may lie partially in the interplay of factors such as illness, dependency, and isolation that lead the elderly to view themselves as unattractive and sexless. An alternative explanation might be that staff attitudes may be little more than an expression of the fashionable response and quite unrelated to their own behavior. One researcher (Kaas, 1978) has called for observational studies to determine if staff members do indeed behave consistently with the way they respond in surveys. Other researchers of sexuality in nursing homes have concluded that:

To be old is to be sexually oppressed. The old values inhibit, then the younger generations disapprove, and finally society sets up many formal barriers to accessibility of sexual partners. Sexual behavior for the aged, though not physiologically impossible nor affectionately dismissible, is culturally and psychologically restricted. The news should be spread around that sexuality for the aged is a good thing, for those who want it. (Wasow and Loeb, 1979, p. 79)

SEXUAL ACTIVITY AND THE AGED

Sexuality for the aged is a good thing for those who want it. Just how many of the elderly want to continue to engage in sexual behavior? Kinsey and his colleagues (Kinsey, Pomeroy, and Martin, 1948, 1953) found that both male and female sexual activity declined with age, although the pattern of decline was less dramatic among the females. Male sexual activity began a steady decline after reaching a peak in the late teenage years or early twenties;

female sexual activity was likely to peak later and decline less noticeably with aging.

Pfeiffer and his colleagues (Pfeiffer, Verwoerdt, and Wang, 1968, 1969a) came to a somewhat different conclusion concerning the differential effects of aging on the sexual attitudes and appetites of men and women. They reported that among their subjects over the age of 60, men were far more likely than women to report both interest in and current participation in sexual intercourse. Among the subjects who had stopped having intercourse, women were more likely to attribute the cause to factors beyond their control; men who had ceased this form of sexual activity were more likely to attribute the cause to themselves. In decreasing order of importance, women cited death of their spouse, husband's illness, and divorce or separation. A large number indicated that impotence or loss of interest in sex by the male heralded the end of their sexual activity.

Men were less likely to accept celibacy as the inevitable outcome of the loss of a spouse. The most frequently cited reason for not engaging in sexual intercourse among older men was impotency (50 percent); smaller percentages identified either illness or a loss of sexual interest. Nearly two-thirds of the women between the ages of 61 and 71 in this study were not participating in coitus, whereas nearly three-quarters of the comparably aged men were. One-third of the women stated that they had "no interest in sex"; only 6 percent of the males responded similarly. It is possible that because most women are married to men older than themselves, their lower levels of sexual activity may be a reflection of the lower sexual activity of an older male spouse (Diokno, Brown, and Herzog, 1990).

The difference between the findings of Kinsey and associates and those of Pfeiffer and his co-workers may be the result of several factors, including data collection techniques, the characteristics of the samples, and differences in the time periods in which the data were collected.

SEXUAL ATTITUDES OF THE AGED

Much remains to be learned about sexuality and aging. Wasow and Loeb (1979, p. 73) have noted that "when we focus on elderly persons confined to nursing homes, the literature dealing directly with sexuality is almost nonexistent." Research in the area of sexuality, let alone geriatric sexuality, is not "politically" proper, and recruitment of subjects can be difficult. Pfeiffer (1969) has noted that relatives, too, can be a problem, especially when they insist that participants withdraw from "such foolishness."

Even among the noninstitutionalized elderly, the environment is likely to play a substantial role in regard to their feelings about sexuality. Weinstein and Rosen (1988) reported that middle-income adults residing in age-segregated retirement communities exhibited significantly more sexual interest, sexual activities, and liberal sexual attitudes than did middle-income adults residing in age-integrated mainstream communities.

Our understanding of sexuality and aging has been furthered by several studies. In the first of these, Starr and Weiner (1981) collected data from 800 subjects between the ages of 60 and 91. Participation in the study was requested from those who attended a series of presentations on "Love, Intimacy, and Sex in the Later Years." The sample included only relatively healthy men and women who were living independently.

The picture that emerges from this study of the elderly is of a zest for life, including sex. Their findings, which the authors identify as "surprising," reveal:

1. A strong continuing interest in sex
2. The belief that sex is important for physical and mental well-being
3. The perception of most of the respondents that sex is as good now as when they were younger
4. That for a large number, both male and female, sex is better in the later years

5. That orgasm is considered an essential part of the sexual experience
6. That most of the women are orgasmic and always have been
7. That the orgasm for many is stronger now than when younger
8. That masturbation is an acceptable outlet for sexual needs
9. That for the majority, living together without marriage is acceptable
10. That an overwhelming number of respondents, including widows, widowers, divorcees and singles, are sexually active
11. That most are satisfied with their sex lives
12. That many vary their sexual practices to achieve satisfaction
13. That for some older people, oral sex is considered the most exciting sexual experience
14. That respondents typically show little embarrassment or anxiety about sex
15. That most enjoy nudity with their partners
16. That the ideal or fantasized lover for most, particularly women, is close to their own age
17. That most see their sex lives remaining pretty much the same as they grow even older

The authors hasten to add, however, that this was not the case for all the elderly they interviewed.

> Some, who had cast themselves in society's mold of the older person, were living in a wasteland that senselessly denied them pleasure and fulfillment. And it was they, we felt, who could perhaps most benefit from what we were learning. (Starr and Weiner, 1981, p. 7)

Consumer's Union, the organization that sponsors the magazine *Consumer Reports*, published the results of their study of "Love, Sex, and Aging" (Brecher, 1984). Responding to an announcement in the November 1977 issue of the magazine, more than 5,000 men and women, aged 50 and over, requested more than 10,000 questionnaires. Al-

though the questionnaire was long, usable responses included 1,844 from women and 2,402 from men. Brecher and his colleagues (1984, p. 15) acknowledge that there is a bias in the sample:

> It is limited to those particular readers of *Consumer Reports* who filled out and returned the November 1977 coupon – and to their relatives and friends. It is also limited to those, who, having received the questionnaire in the fall of 1978, answered the questions and mailed back their answers during the next few months. It is probable that sexually inactive women and men were less likely than the sexually active to mail back their questionnaires – though some did. No doubt those with little interest in sex, or with a dislike of sex, were also less likely to mail back the questionnaires – but some did.

The findings clearly cannot be extrapolated to the total U.S. population over 50, but they may apply to other groups that resemble the sample: those with higher-than-average socioeconomic status (as reflected by income and education), better-than-average health (as with the Starr-Weiner sample referred to earlier), greater interest in sex, and so on. This is clearly the largest study of sexuality and aging undertaken to date; for that reason alone, the findings are compelling.

Some of the comparative generalizations that emerge are:

1. The sexual aspect of marriage is more important for the husbands than for the wives.
2. Unmarried women and men who remain sexually active after age 50 (either with a partner or through masturbation) report higher levels of life enjoyment than those who do not engage in sex.
3. More husbands than wives have engaged in extramarital sex since age 50.
4. More men than women have engaged in homosexual activities since age 50. More women

than men, however, have felt sexually attracted to a person of their own sex since 50.

5. Fewer women and men in their eighties are sexually active than are younger women and men; but some women and men in their eighties continue to engage in and enjoy a wide range of sexual activities.

6. Relatively few men engage in sex with prostitutes after age 50. Some of those who do, however, report that their encounters with prostitutes contribute substantially to their enjoyment of life.

7. Postmenopausal women taking estrogen are more active sexually than postmenopausal women not taking estrogen.

In a study of nearly 2,000 men and women over age 60, living in an age-integrated community setting, Diokno and others (1990) found that 74 percent of the married men and 56 percent of the married women were sexually active; among the unmarried the percentages fell to 31 and 5, respectively. They estimated that slightly more than one-third (35.3 percent) of the married men in their sample had impaired erectile ability (*erectile impotency*).

The picture that emerges from these studies is that sexuality, in both men and women, endures a great deal better than many other functional systems. In the absence of disease, sexual desire and capacity are lifelong. Even when intercourse fails as a result of infirmity, need for other aspects of the sexual relationship persists, such as closeness, touching, caressing, sensuality, and being valued. This is contrary both to folklore and to the preconceptions of some hospital and nursing home administrators. It is even contrary to the beliefs of many of the elderly themselves. Many of the elderly have been, to use Alex Comfort's terminology, "hocussed out" of continuing sexual activity by a society that disallows it for the old, exactly as they have

been "hocussed out" of so many other valuable activities of which they are fully capable (e.g., useful work or social involvement).

Still, as evidenced by the previously cited research, "hocussing" has not been totally successful. Many older people have simply gone on having sex without talking about it, unabashed by the accepted and destructive social image of the "dirty old man" and the asexual, undesirable older woman. Older people have not been asked about their sexual experiences because many physicians and researchers "knew" that they had none, and they were assumed to have none because few thought to ask. For some elderly, the fantasy of the celibate senior that they held when they were younger became a blueprint for their own aging, what Comfort refers to as a "classical case of bewitchment by expectation" (Comfort, 1976).

According to Thienhaus (1988, p. 63), the issue of sexual activity among the elderly may be summarized as " 'some do, some don't, and there is nothing wrong with either.' Whether they do it or not depends primarily on availability of partners, the degree of sexual activity earlier in life, and the interference of medical illness." And, one might add, on societal conditioning and institutionally imposed barriers as well (Bretschneider and McCoy, 1988).

AGE-RELATED CHANGES IN SEXUAL FUNCTION

There are, to be sure, changes in sexual function that are related to the aging process. Often these changes are not understood and, consequently, are experienced with greater anxiety. Perhaps they are best appreciated when viewed in the context of the sexual response cycle, as first proposed by Masters and Johnson (1966).

Masters and Johnson arbitrarily divided the sexual response cycle into four phases: (1) excitement, (2) plateau, (3) orgasm, and (4) resolution. These phases are characterized in the sexually responsive female as follows:

Excitement

In the sexually aroused female there is an engorgement of blood in all distensible body parts, including the breasts, the labia, and the clitoris. This vasocongestive response is diminished in the postmenopausal female. The diminution seems linked to estrogen deficiency and may not be experienced among women on estrogen-replacement therapy (ERT). Myotonia, or generalized muscle tension, decreases with age. The onset of vaginal lubrication, which may occur in younger women within seconds, may occur more slowly with the aging female.

Plateau

Perhaps the most noticeable change that occurs during this phase of the sexual response cycle is a swelling in the outer or distal one-third of the vagina. This swelling narrows the introitus and increases the traction on the penis during coital thrusting. Masters and Johnson labeled this phenomenon the orgasmic platform. Although the intensity of the vasocongestion is somewhat reduced, the aged female develops an orgasmic platform much as her younger counterpart.

The "ballooning" of the inner two-thirds of the vagina, labeled the "testing" phenomenon by Masters and Johnson, and the accompanying elevation of the uterus, may also be diminished by hormonal alterations associated with menopause. This loss of vaginal elasticity, along with the lessened lubrication, may be a source of discomfort during coital thrusting. There is the increased probability that sudden penile penetration or intercourse of long duration may create small fissures in the lining of the vagina. These changes, too, are less likely to be seen among women who receive exogenous estrogen. Water-soluble lubricants are also helpful in compensating for vaginal dryness.

Orgasm

The orgasmic phase is marked by contractions of the uterus, the paravaginal musculature, and the muscles of the pelvic floor, including the rectal sphincter. Both the number and the intensity of these contractions may be reduced in the postmenopausal female. This is experienced as a change in the character of the orgasm. Masters and Johnson (1982, p. 53) indicate that "although these involuntary physiologic alterations may be experienced, the subjectively appreciated levels of sensual pleasure derived from coital connection usually continue unabated."

Much less frequently encountered by the aging female, though associated with the aging process, are painful uterine spasms during orgasm. This problem, too, is prevented or abated by estrogen-replacement therapy.

Resolution

During resolution the expanded inner two-thirds of the vagina shrinks back to a collapsed, unstimulated state with marked rapidity. This rapid vaginal collapse in older women, as opposed to younger women, may be the result of the increased rigidity and lack of elasticity in the senescent vaginal barrel.

ADDITIONAL AGE-RELATED SEXUAL CHANGES

Females

Some additional general changes in the aging female were also noted by Masters and Johnson (1966). After the ovaries reduce or cease estrogen production, the walls of the vagina begin to involute. They become very thin; lose the rough, corrugated appearance of the younger women's vagina; and change in color from a reddish purple to a light pink. There is a shortening in vaginal length and a reduction in width that, in association with the loss of expansive ability described previously, may make comfortable accommodation of the erect penis difficult. The resulting dyspareunia (pain with intercourse) may trigger the onset of vaginismus (involuntary contractions of the muscles surrounding the outer portion of the vagina) as a self-protective response to painful stimuli. Vaginismus should be suspected where there is a history of painful coitus or following a long period of incontinence in the aging female. The diagnosis can be made clinically by a pelvic examination. Masters and Johnson (1982, p. 53) indicate that it is "probably the most frequently missed diagnosis in the field of gynecology." Once identified, it can be readily reversed with relaxation and muscle-retraining exercises.

Also linked to diminished lubrication is a burning on urination in the hours subsequent to intercourse. This discomfort develops as a result of coital thrusting that has caused mechanical irritation of the bladder and urethra. Symptoms of dysuria (pain with urination) and dyspareunia may last for 24 to 36 hours after intercourse.

Males

The changes in the aging male are not quite as detailed as those in the female and, consequently, do not lend themselves as nicely to explanation within each phase of the sexual response cycle. As the male ages, the major differences in sexual response relate to the duration of each of the phases in the cycle. The older man is slower to obtain an erection, and the erect penis is likely to be less firm than during the younger years. This results in a change in the angle between the erect penis and the abdominal wall. Whereas in a young man the angle approximates 45 degrees; in the elderly man the same angle may be 90 degrees or more (Thienhaus, 1988, p. 63). He is also less likely to experience an erection as a result of purely psychic stimuli, requiring instead, more direct stimulation either by himself or his partner. Along with this comes an occasional reduction in or loss of ejaculatory demand.

Although the male continues to have a high level of interest in the sensual pleasure associated with coitus, the subjectively experienced demand to ejaculate may be reduced. Alex Comfort has described this reduced demand to ejaculate in the older male as follows: "It takes him a little longer to get an erection, but he can hold it just as well as he's got it, and he can have an awful lot more sex per orgasm" (Easton, 1977). In view of the fact that loss of ejaculatory control – premature ejaculation – is the most commonly experienced sexual dysfunction among young men, it would seem that this phase of sexual functioning, rather than deteriorating, improves considerably with age.

The aging male, with the sensation of ejaculatory imperativeness, has the psychosexual demand to ejaculate but may be subject to a loss of or inefficiency in neurophysiological control of the process. Ejaculation, which is a two-stage process in the younger male, is reduced to one stage in the older male. There is also a lessening of expulsive force propelling the seminal fluid. It has been suggested that these two factors may combine to make coitus a less pleasurable physiological experience for him as compared to his younger days. Penile detumescence occurs immediately after ejaculation, and the refractory period may last for a number of days, depending on the individual.

There is no question that the human male's sexual responsiveness wanes with age. Not only does his coital activity typically decrease, but the incidence of masturbation and nocturnal emission also declines with advancing years. Compared to changes in other areas such as vital capacity, muscular strength, and flexibility, however, sexual changes are functionally minimal. Sexuality, in both sexes, endures a great deal better than many other functional systems.

The reasonably healthy aging male does not lose his facility for erection at any time; this is demonstrated by the occurrence of morning erections in men who think they are impotent. There is no physiological reason that an older man cannot achieve an erection for purposes of intercourse if he experiences erections during sleep or in the mornings. Any male, not just the elderly, might do well to take advantage of well-established circadian and seasonal variations in serum testosterone, a significant factor in regard to both libido and erection. Serum testosterone levels tend to peak in the early morning hours, fall slowly during the day, and then begin to rise again at midnight (Morely et al., 1987). In addition to this hormonal advantage, morning sex may also be enhanced by a rested body and a relaxed attitude.

If the aging male avoids talking himself out of effective sexual functioning by worrying about the physiological factors in his sexual response cycle, if his peers do not destroy his sexual confidence, and if he and his partner maintain a reasonably good state of health, he certainly can and should continue unencumbered sexual functioning late in life.

Unfortunately, however, aging is often accompanied by the onset of other health problems, many of which have a concomitant effect on sexual function. Consequently, the incidence of sexual dysfunction, among males especially, tends to increase with age. Morely and his associates (1987) estimate that one in three males over age 40 seeking general medical care will have some difficulty in obtaining erections adequate for intercourse.

Although a common cause of *erectile dysfunction* among older men – as is true for younger men – is performance anxiety, other causes are alcohol use, the effects of medication, vascular disease, endocrine dysfunction, diabetes, and obesity. Arthritis and other conditions that may impair mobility and/or cause discomfort are also linked to a decrease in sexual function. It has been suggested that psychogenic causes are more likely to occupy a primary role in sexual dysfunction among the young, whereas organic problems become etiologically more important with aging (Morely et al., 1987). All sexual dysfunction, however, regardless of age, is likely to involve multiple factors. Attempts to identify a single cause are likely to be unsuccessful.

Alcohol, which can interfere with erection in men of all ages, seems to inhibit sexual response in much smaller doses with the elderly. Erectile dysfunction is seen as both an acute and a chronic effect of alcohol consumption, especially in cases of drug dependency or abusive drinking. Chronic patterns of abusive drinking can produce hypogonadism, the most common endocrine cause of sexual dysfunction. Altered body and facial hair and small, soft testicles on physical examination suggest hypogonadism, which could be confirmed by measurement of circulating serum testosterone levels (Morely et al., 1987). Others drugs – both prescribed and over-the-counter varieties – may also be implicated in erectile failure. Prominent among these are the antianxiety and antihypertensive medications.

It has been suggested that medications are the most frequent cause of impaired erectile response in the medical outpatient population (Morely et al., 1987). Among the groups of drugs so linked, the antihypertensive agents are the most common causes of dysfunction. Some studies report that as many as 40 percent of patients treated for hypertension complain of erectile impairment. Morely and his associates state that "there appears to be *no* class of antihypertensive medication without effects on sexual function" (1987, p. 1018). Significantly, the development of sexual dysfunction associated with the use of a particular medication is a major cause of noncompliance.

Vascular disease is another common cause of erectile dysfunction. Impaired blood flow through the peripheral vessels severely reduces filling of the erectile tissues in the penis. Moreover, reduced penile blood pressures were found, in one sample of patients with erectile dysfunction, to be highly correlated with occurrence of a major vascular event within two to three years. It therefore behooves the clinician to include questions about sexual function, and especially about erectile impairment, in their general evaluation of men seen in their office (Diokno et al., 1990).

There have been reports that urinary incontinence and interrupted urinary stream are highly correlated with erectile dysfunction. Significantly, in patients with hypogonadism, the administration of testosterone, either orally or by intramuscular injection (or in the future by transscrotal patches), may produce a rapid growth of prostatic tissue which, in turn, may interfere with urination.

Obesity may also interfere with sexual functioning. It is often reported as aesthetically displeasing to a partner and may also detract from one's self-image. Diabetes probably interferes with potency in several ways; whether due to diabetic neuropathy or to some specific effect of hyperglycemia on the complicated hydraulics of the penis, the effect on sexual function is well recognized. Morely and his associates (1987) have estimated that up to 20 percent of elderly males with impaired erectile function have diabetes. Given the widely publicized findings about the effect of diabetes on sexual function, however, it is difficult to isolate the organic from the psychological causes. Given the fact that diabetes produces vascular atherosclerosis, neuropathy, and concomitant medical and psychological therapies, the cause of erectile impairment in these patients is clearly multifactorial.

The interaction of psychological factors with organic conditions is particularly intriguing and frustrating. Problems with sexual function often result from psychological misconceptions, as in this example:

> For instance, an older man who had a recent coronary occlusion may be left with the advice that "it's all right to resume sex" and at the same time be cautioned to watch out for signs of recurring angina. The patient is likely, then, to be focusing on prodromal warning symptoms while engaging in sexual activity. The watch for such prodromes will obviously interfere with the "letting go" that is a prerequisite for successful sexual performance. (Thienhaus, 1988, p. 65)

Medications may also produce a seemingly paradoxical effect on sexual function. Antidepressant medication that makes the patient feel like having sex again may well cause anorgasmia. Referring to this phenomenon as "Murphy's Law of Psychopharmacology," Theinhaus (1988) notes that this is true not only with tricyclic antidepressants, but for antiparkinsonian and antipsychotic medications as well. Both may have anticholinergic effects that impair erection. Thioridazine, an antipsychotic often prescribed for older patients, may also cause retrograde ejaculation, although this side effect is more often seen in younger patients.

Nutritional deficiencies, especially zinc, may also impair sexual response. Interestingly, Diokno and associates (1990) found that daily consumption of at least one cup of coffee a day correlated with a higher proportion of elderly women being sexually active, whereas non-use of coffee correlated with an increased prevalence of erectile failure in men. They offer the following explanation:

> Caffeine in coffee belongs to the family of the methylxanthines, a potent central nervous system stimulant and smooth-muscle relaxant. It is known to enhance response to sensory stimulation and hasten response to normal reflexes because of its direct action on the nervous tissue. However, besides possible physiological mechanisms, it is possible that specific health conditions that affect potency and sexual activity may also preclude use of coffee. (p. 200)

Members of both sexes may find it difficult to resume sexual functioning following extended periods of abstinence. This problem is often described in women and men, respectively, as the widow's and the widower's syndromes. Upon attempting a resumption of sexual activity, depending on the person's age and the duration of sexual continence, the combination of heightened anxiety and lack of sexual activity may commonly result in failure. This seems to be a classic case of "use it or lose it."

Despite the physiological changes associated with menopause, if the opportunity for regular coital expression is present or if there is opportunity for regular sexual activity, it will have a significant influence on the sexual performance of the aged female. In Masters and Johnson's (1966) study of the geriatric response cycle, some women over 60 were repeatedly observed to expand and lubricate the vagina effectively even with thinning vaginal walls and shrinking labia. The past history of these women revealed that they had maintained regular intercourse, once or twice a week, for their entire adult lives. It would seem that both the male and the female, in the absence of physical or mental infirmity, are capable of sexual performance throughout their lives.

AGING, SEX, AND SOCIETY

Victorian influence on our society has for years decreed that the aged possess little or no socially acceptable sexuality. What our prejudiced culture regards as virility at 25 becomes lechery at 65. Such attitudes are unfair. They create guilt, misunderstanding, and undeserved condemnation. Whereas many of the taboos concerning sexuality for adults, and even adolescents, have been reexamined and discarded, the taboos against sex in old age have been more durable.

The reasons for these attitudes are many. Traditionally, sexuality has been equated with youth and beauty. What is so often forgotten is that we are sexual beings all of our lives; we are libidinous from birth to death. Perhaps it is the loss of procreative ability and the fading of *conventional* sex appeal that stigmatize the desires and behavior of the aged.

Older people themselves may have many negative attitudes toward sexuality in the aged. They may suppress their sexual desires, regarding them as unnatural. This may be traced, in part, to the difficulties children have in imagining their parents or grandparents making love or even having sexual desires. They tend to reject sexuality for their elders and often discourage remarriage. As children, they were cautioned about sex and taught to regard it as dirty; when they became parents, they reversed the process and condemned sex in their elders. What must be remembered, however, is that we all have the same need for intimacy and touch, regardless of age. Sex is often viewed, moreover, as an affirmation of life and a denial of death. Levitan (1973) has suggested that an active sex life may well be a significant deterrent to suicide. A sexual relationship in old age can be and often is a boost to the older person's psyche.

Physicians' attitudes toward sexuality among the aged are extremely important. Very often, their response to a geriatric patient's sexual problem is, "Well . . . what do you expect at your age?" Most older people respect the opinions of their doctors. When physicians give the impression that they deem sex unnecessary, something strictly for the young, they reinforce everything society has said about aged sexuality. Many times the physician has been poorly trained in the area of human sexuality, may have unresolved issues about his or her own sexuality, or may have difficulty in his or her own mind with the idea that older people have sexual needs.

Occasionally an older man will discontinue sexual relations within marriage. Masters and Johnson (1966) have suggested several reasons why this might occur. Monotony is probably the most constant factor in an aging male's loss of interest in sex with his spouse. He may simply be bored with his partner and thus may choose to abstain. Other variables include male concern with economic pursuits, which reduces the time and attention needed to maintain a good marriage and a happy sex life, as well as physical or mental infirmities and the fear of impotence.

There is every reason to believe, however, that maintained regularity of sexual expression, coupled with adequate physical well-being and a healthy mental orientation to the aging process, will combine to provide a sexually stimulating climate within a marriage. This climate will provide a capacity for sexual performance that frequently may extend to and beyond the eighth and ninth decades of life.

Sex can and does play an important part in the lives of the aged. The most important factors contributing to the variation in sexual behavior appear to be the past sexual experience, age, and sex of the individual. Income and social class are also involved. Continuity of life-style seems to be instrumental in the sexual behavior of the aged. Those for whom sex was important early in life are more likely to continue to be sexually active later in life; those for whom sex was of little importance early in life will be more likely to reach an early terminus of their sexual behavior in later life.

But what about the aged woman who is a widow? What opportunity does she have for sexual expression? Pfeiffer and colleagues (1969) suggest that much of the decline in sexual interest in aging females is not physiological but a protective mechanism. It may well be adaptive to inhibit sexual desire when little opportunity for sexual fulfillment exists. Christenson and Gagnon (1965) found that widowed female subjects masturbated twice as much as their married counterparts. They also discovered that one factor in maintaining postmarital sexual activity was the woman's ability to experience orgasm fairly regularly. Once the capacity for sexual response is discovered by the female, it is clear that she is more likely to continue to have coitus postmaritally (Christenson and Gagnon, 1965). This study did not take into account the difficulties some women may have in accepting masturbation and the dearth of available male sexual partners. As noted by Pfeiffer and colleagues (1968), many women find masturbation unfulfilling and are unwilling to engage in postmarital sexual behavior. There seems to be no easy answer to the problem that aged females experience in finding adequate sexual outlets.

SEX, AGE, AND THE HELPING PROFESSIONS

If there is to be any progress in the quest for acceptance of sexuality among the aged, the responsibility rests most heavily on those in the health and helping professions. Support and encouragement of sexual behavior should be given without embarrassment or evangelization. Sexuality in old age is a different, perhaps quieter, experience, but no less sexual and no less an experience than in youth.

In addition to establishing a climate in which the sexuality of the aged is acknowledged and valued, we need to address ourselves to four more specific concerns:

1. We need to ensure that sexual growth programs are available to habilitate and rehabilitate the sexually dysfunctional aged. In the case of the disabled, it has been traditional to suggest that reference to their sexual needs would embarrass them; in fact, however, when counseling and rehabilitation programs were offered they were enthusiastically embraced. It seems reasonable to suspect that the same would happen with the elderly (Comfort, 1974).

2. In old-age homes and mental institutions, a reexamination of policies that have led to the total segregation of the sexes and even the separation of husbands and wives should be undertaken, since such practices are now realized as contributing to failure in treatment. The institutionalized old should have the same right as the rest of us have to engage in or abstain from sexual activity without interference.

3. In the health field, proper attention must be given to training medical personnel to give equal attention to the sexual needs of the aged in all aspects of medical practice. Physicians must realize that a negative attitude on their part can very often pronounce a death sentence upon the sexual life of older patients. As with younger persons, sexual information should routinely be included when taking the histories of older persons, who must, in turn, be encouraged to bring their sex-related problems to their physicians for treatment.

4. For our youth-oriented culture as a whole, an end is needed to the concept that debilities come with age and to the belief that a person is "over the hill" at 60. There is one great problem with ageism. Think of the other prejudices: White racists do not turn black, and anti-Semites do not wake up to find they are Jewish. But we shall all, if we are lucky, get to be old.

Comfort (1974) has suggested that old people often stop having sex for the same reasons that they stop riding bicycles – general infirmity, thinking it looks ridiculous, or having no bicycle. Most people, however, can and should expect to have sex long after they no longer wish to ride bicycles. Such people may well require fewer tranquilizers and less institutionalization and may expect to live richer lives. Certainly there will be fewer "obstreperous malcontents" among the old whom the society has heretofore worked so industriously to desexualize.

STUDY QUESTIONS

1. Compare the findings of Kinsey and co-workers with those of Pfeiffer and associates regarding sexual activity and age.
2. On the basis of studies concerning sexual attitudes of the aged, what, in general, can be concluded about "geriatric sexuality"?
3. Review the four phases of the sexual response cycle in the female, including changes noted in postmenopausal women.
4. Identify some general changes in the aging female that may influence symptoms experienced with or as a result of sexual intercourse.
5. Present an overview of changes in the aging male that may influence sexual response.
6. Review some factors that contribute to sexual behavior of the aged.
7. Discuss the responsibilities of the health and helping professions regarding sexuality and the aged.

BIBLIOGRAPHY

Brecher, E. M. 1984. *Love, sex, and aging*. A Consumer's Union report. Boston: Little, Brown.

Bretschneider, J. G., and McCoy, N. L. 1988. Sexual interest and behavior in healthy 80- to 102-year-olds. *Archives of Sexual Behavior*, 17(2): 109-129.

Christenson, C. V., and Gagnon, J. 1965. Sexual behavior in a group of older women. *Journal of Gerontology*, 20(3): 351-356.

Comfort, A. 1974. Sexuality in old age. *Journal of the American Geriatrics Society*, 22(10): 440-442.

Comfort, A. 1976. *A good age*. New York: Crown.

Diokno, A. C., Brown, M. D., and Herzog, A. R. 1990. Sexual function in the elderly. *Archives of Internal Medicine*, 150: 197-200.

Easton, D. M. 1977. Alex Comfort speaks on sex and aging. *Resource guide*. San Francisco: Multi Media Resource Center.

Kaas, M. J. 1978. Sexual expression of the elderly in nursing homes. *Gerontologist*, 18(4): 372-378.

Kinsey, A. C., Pomeroy, W. B., and Martin, C. E. 1948. *Sexual behavior in the human male*. Philadelphia: Saunders.

Kinsey, A. C., Pomeroy, W. B., and Martin, C. E. 1953. *Sexual behavior in the human female*. Philadelphia: Saunders.

Levitan, D. 1973. The significance of sexuality as a deterrent to suicide among the aged. *Omega*, 4(2): 163-174.

Masters, W. H., and Johnson, V. E. 1966. *Human sexual response*. Boston: Little, Brown.

Masters, W. H., and Johnson, V. E. 1982. Sex and the aging process. *Medical Aspects of Human Sexuality*, 16(6): 40ff.

Morely, J. E., et al. 1987. UCLA geriatric grand rounds: Sexual dysfunction in the elderly male. *Journal of American Geriatrics Society*, 35: 1014-1022.

Pfeiffer, E. 1969. Geriatric sexual behavior. *Medical Aspects of Human Sexuality*, 3: 19ff.

Pfeiffer, E., Verwoerdt, A., and Wang, H. S. 1968. Sexual behavior in aged men and women. *Archives of General Psychiatry*, 19: 753-758.

Pfeiffer, E., Verwoerdt, A., and Wang, H. S. 1969. The natural history of sexual behavior in a biologically advantaged group of aged individuals. *Journal of Gerontology*, 24: 193-198.

Pocs, O., Godow, A., Tolone, W., and Walsh, R. H. 1977. Is there sex after 40? *Psychology Today*, 6: 54-58.

Smith, D. 1988. Intimacy and sex in the nursing home. *Purdue University Perspective*, 4(Fall).

Starr, B. D., and Weiner, M. B. 1981. *The Starr-Weiner report on sex and sexuality in the mature years*. New York: Stein and Day.

Thienhaus, O. J. 1988. Practical overview of sexual function and advancing age. *Geriatrics*, 43(8): 63-67.

Wasow, M., and Loeb, M. B. 1979. Sexuality in nursing homes. *Journal of the American Geriatrics Society*, 37(2): 73-79.

Weinstein, S., and Rosen, E. 1988. Senior adult sexuality in age-segregated and age-integrated communities. *International Journal of Aging and Human Development*, 27(4): 261-270.

CHAPTER **16**

Drugs and the Elderly

Patricia H. Andrews, Ph.D.

Older people often suffer from multiple chronic conditions (Kane, Ouslander, and Abrass, 1989). As a result, they consume a high proportion of all prescribed drugs, approximately 25 to 30 percent (Carty and Everitt, 1989; Quinn, Applegate, Roberts, Collins, and Vanderzwaag, 1983). In addition, many elderly people use nonprescription preparations and home remedies. Because elders demonstrate a preponderance of chronic illnesses, the duration of the drug therapy, whether it be prescription or nonprescription, is most often long-term. The need for long-term therapy coupled with age-related physiologic changes, disease characteristics, the potential for adverse drug reactions, and compliance problems may lead to drug-induced iatrogenesis, premature loss of independence, and a general decline in quality of life.

Drugs are viewed as a major component in the management of chronic diseases, often to the ex-clusion of nondrug alternatives (Lamy, 1984). The goal of drug therapy is to maintain or enhance health status (Patton, 1985). With this goal in mind, the chapter is organized to provide information pertinent to drug therapy in the elderly on the following topics: pharmacokinetics, pharmacodynamics, adverse drug reactions, drug interactions, compliance, and considerations for reasonable drug prescribing.

PHARMACOKINETICS

When considering drug therapy for elderly individuals, health care providers must be cognizant of possible physiologic differences that may affect a substance's activity in the body. *Pharmacokinetics* is the study of drug distribution after the medication has been ingested. It includes factors such as drug absorption, distribution of the drug into various body parts, metabolism or biotransformation of the drug, and elimination of the drug from the body (Simonson, 1984). Because the elderly provide a heterogeneous picture of physiologic function, some or all of these factors must be considered before engaging in a particular drug regimen.

Absorption

Absorption is defined as "the process by which a substance proceeds from the site of administration across biological membranes into general circulation" (Tsujimoto, Hashimoto, and Hoffman, 1989). The predominant administration route of medications is by mouth. Consequently, any disruption in the gastrointestinal (GI) tract can disturb absorption of medication.

There are several age-related changes that occur in the GI tract (see Chapter 9 for a more developed description of these changes). For example, the surface area of the GI tract decreases as a result of a decline in the number of cells that constitute its lining (Pucino, Beck, Seifert, Strommen, Sheldon, and Silbergleit, 1985). In addition, gastric acid production declines with age, causing a rise in the pH of the stomach, which may decrease the solubility of basic drugs (Lamy, 1980) or increase dissolution time for tablets or other solid drugs (Dawling and Crome, 1989). Decreased intestinal motility and increased gastric emptying time also exert an effect. They may influence the speed with which a drug takes effect or its chemical alteration in the gut (Dawling and Crome, 1989). Likewise, a decreased gastric blood flow may result in faulty or delayed absorption of a drug.

Despite the potential for all of these changes, absorption of drugs is not usually compromised in elderly individuals. Tregaskis and Stevenson (1990)

conjecture that various age-related GI tract changes may actually compensate for one another. For example, the decrease in gastric acid production may slow the dissolution of tablets, but the decrease in the rate of gastric emptying may counterbalance the slowed dissolution by keeping the drug in contact with the gastric mucosa for a longer duration. Similarly, the decreased absorptive surface may be compensated for by a decrease in intestinal motility, allowing more time for absorption.

Distribution

After a drug is absorbed in the gastrointestinal tract, it is distributed throughout the body in the blood. The aim is to transport a therapeutic dose to the target organ receptor sites. The volume of distribution, a measure of the concentration of a particular drug at the target receptor sites, is an index of how effectively a drug reaches its target organ (Cherry and Morton, 1989). Many age-related physiological changes can curtail the appropriate concentrations from being actualized.

Plasma protein binding. Serum albumin is a protein that binds to many drugs in the circulatory system (Kane et al., 1989; Lamy, 1980). The extent to which a drug binds to this protein affects its availability for distribution throughout the body. Only the free fraction or non-protein-bound portion of the drug is active. It is this portion that diffuses through the body to its target organ (Cherry and Morton, 1989). As the free fraction of the drug finishes its action and is excreted from the body, more of the protein-bound drug becomes detached from the circulating albumin. In this way a dynamic equilibrium is achieved whereby a desired therapeutic action is maintained over a period of time.

Aging is associated with a decrease in serum albumin production by the liver (O'Brien and Kursch,

1987). Decreased production may be even greater in seriously ill elderly persons (Kane et al., 1989) or those who are nutritionally compromised (O'Brien and Kursch, 1987). A decline in serum albumin results in higher free fraction drug levels. In practice this means more drug can be diffused to the target receptor sites with the potential for an intensified drug effect (Cherry and Morton, 1989; Patton, 1985). In addition, if more than one protein-bound drug is administered concurrently, competition for an already diminished number of protein binding sites may alter the therapeutic effect of one or more of the drugs (Pucino et al., 1985). For example, drugs having a higher affinity or attachment potential for protein may "fill" binding sites more quickly than drugs with a lesser affinity, thereby altering the free fraction of the latter substance and its therapeutic effect.

Body composition. Age-related changes in body composition may significantly affect the volume of drug distribution in the body (Buechler and Malloy, 1989; Dawling and Crome, 1989). With age the proportion of adipose tissue increases while total body water and lean tissue mass decrease. Although both sexes have a higher body fat ratio in old age, aging women exhibit a higher proportion of body fat than do aging men, which is consistent with lifelong trends (Lamy, 1980).

These changes in body composition may have a profound influence on the duration and intensity of a drug's effect (Buechler and Malloy, 1989). For instance, fat-soluble substances will be more widely distributed and stored in adipose tissue. This fact implies that the elderly may experience a prolonged and potentially enhanced pharmacologic effect from lipophilic drugs – those with an affinity for fat tissue. In contrast, water-soluble drugs will be less widely distributed throughout the body and more concentrated in the blood because of the decrease in body water content. Therefore, unpredicted high circulating drug levels can occur,

with consequent enhanced response and possible toxic effects.

Cardiac output. The apparent decline in cardiac output with age may affect tissue/organ perfusion. Consequently, there may be a delay in a drug's effective concentration at target organ receptor sites.

Decreased blood flow to the liver and the kidneys is of particular concern (Dawling and Crome, 1989). Because both of these organs play important roles in drug metabolism and elimination, a decrease in their perfusion may lead to higher blood concentrations of circulating drugs and, therefore, to drug toxicity.

Metabolism

The liver is responsible for the biotransformation or metabolism of drugs before they are excreted by the kidneys. A drug is metabolized by the liver into water-soluble components or metabolites that are more easily eliminated via the kidneys (Simonson, 1984). This metabolism is accomplished by two types of liver enzyme systems.

The liver undergoes several age-related changes that may affect its drug-metabolizing capabilities. These include a decline in size and blood flow as well as a reduction in certain of its enzymes (Buechler and Malloy, 1989; Woodhouse and James, 1990). In addition, nutritional deficiencies, which are common among the elderly, may contribute to decreased enzyme activity. These changes may influence a drug's blood concentration, increasing the risk of toxicity.

The reader must be cautioned that there is not yet any conclusive evidence that definitively demonstrates these age-related hepatic changes to contribute uniformly to depressed drug metabolism in the elderly. The effects of aging on drug metabolism are complex and not easily predicted (Kane et al., 1989). Determination of liver function must be assessed on an individual basis.

Excretion

Excretion or elimination is the process by which substances are expelled from the body. Renal excretion is the most important route in eliminating drugs and drug by-products (Meyer and Hirsch, 1990). Therefore, any perturbation in kidney function may place an individual at increased risk of drug toxicity and other adverse drug reactions.

There appear to be several age-related changes in the kidney that may depress its drug-elimination capabilities. Among these changes are reduced kidney size, glomerular filtration rate, ability to concentrate urine, conservation of sodium, and renal blood flow (Meyer and Hirsch, 1990; Pucino et al., 1985). Kidney function may be further diminished by conditions such as congestive heart failure, diabetes, and dehydration (Kane et al., 1989). Alterations in kidney function can cause an increased drug concentration in the blood, thereby prolonging the pharmacologic effect.

Deteriorated renal function may be the major contributor to altered drug effects with age. However, there is much variability in renal function among the elderly. Therefore, assessment of kidney function in each individual is imperative prior to the initiation of drug therapy in an elderly person. See Figure 16.1 on renal creatinine clearance assessment in the elderly.

PHARMACODYNAMICS

Swift (1990) defines *pharmacodynamics* as the study of the response (type, intensity and duration) of a given concentration of a drug at its target organ receptor sites (site of action). Elderly people are thought to be more sensitive to the pharmacologic response of drugs. However, drug response may be either enhanced or reduced in the elderly (Nolan and O'Malley, 1989; Pucino et al., 1985).

Because research on pharmacodynamic response is difficult to conduct, there has been relatively little data gathered on the effects of aging on pharmacodynamics (Nolan and O'Malley, 1989). It is difficult to separate response differences related to normal aging from those attributable to multiple disease conditions. Furthermore, response to drugs

---

Assessment of renal function is an important step in prudent drug therapy management among the elderly (Cherry and Morton, 1989). A common means of estimating the level of kidney function is to calculate the creatinine clearance rate from urine samples. Glomerular filtration rate may be determined as a function of creatinine clearance; that is, excretion of creatinine is directly proportional to glomerular filtration abilities.

Creatinine is a by-product of muscle breakdown, but muscle tissue is decreased with age, and less creatinine is produced in the aged body. If there is a concurrent decline in glomerular filtration rate,

however, the levels of creatinine may appear to be normal when in fact the levels are quite high for an elderly person. Put another way, creatinine is produced at a lower rate in elderly persons with reduced muscle mass, but reduced kidney filtration rates may not clear the creatinine efficiently. What seems to be a normal creatinine level is actually an excessive amount of creatinine that is not being eliminated by defective kidneys. Unless age-related adjustments are made in the creatinine clearance equation, it would appear that routine estimates of renal function in the elderly based solely on creatinine levels may be deceptive.

FIGURE 16.1   Renal creatinine clearance: An assessment tool for kidney function in the elderly

varies depending on which drug is studied and on the unique physiology of the individual; thus, generalizations are extremely difficult to make (Montamat, Cusack, and Vestal, 1989).

Altered age-related organ response may occur as a result of altered physiology, disease states, nutritional deficiencies, and/or other variables. For example, some elderly individuals experience an increased susceptibility to postural hypotension due to an age-related reduction in baroreceptor response and other factors. This means an elderly person's body may not be able to maintain the necessary blood pressure when standing up from a lying or sitting position. As a result, the person may experience dizziness or a fainting episode with possible injury. This impaired compensation for postural changes can be exacerbated by antihypertensive drug therapy (Swift, 1990). Likewise, age-associated declines in some of the neurochemicals in the central nervous system put some elderly persons at a higher risk for adverse reactions associated with central nervous system drugs (Nolan and O'Malley, 1989; Pucino et al., 1985).

Although there may be increased risks of tissue or organ sensitivity to drugs in the elderly, a caution must be appended to any blanket recommendation to reduce doses of all drugs prescribed to the elderly (Caird, 1985). There is much physiological heterogeneity among elderly people. Perhaps a better solution is to monitor plasma concentrations of various drugs closely and note any alteration in response. This approach can aid the clinician in discovering doses at which a desired effect is accomplished.

ADVERSE DRUG REACTIONS

An adverse drug reaction (ADR) is any undesirable or unintended effect of a drug (Mead, 1985). ADRs are estimated to occur two to three times more frequently in elderly persons than in the general popu-

lation (Wade and Bowling, 1986), with the highest incidence among those in their eighth and ninth decades. An estimated 3 to 10 percent of all hospital admissions of the elderly result from ADRs (Nolan and O'Malley, 1989). Furthermore, ADRs may play a significant role in altered functional abilities of the elderly (O'Brien and Kursch, 1987). Some may result in problems such as falls, delirium, or incontinence, which can threaten independence and diminish quality of life. In many instances ADRs can be anticipated and therefore prevented (Lamy, 1984).

Factors Contributing to ADRs in the Elderly

Various factors can predispose an elderly person to an increased frequency of adverse drug reactions. Some of these are as follows:

1. Certain classes of drugs are more likely to be associated with adverse drug reactions in the elderly (Kleinfeld and Corcoran, 1988). These include analgesics, antacids, anticoagulants, antihypertensives, antibiotics, arthritis drugs, cardiac drugs, central nervous system drugs, diuretics, and steroids. These drugs are commonly prescribed for elderly patients.

2. Age-related alterations in pharmacokinetics can occur, whereby a given drug dosage produces higher blood concentrations in elderly patients than in the young (Cadieux, 1989; Lamy, 1986).

3. Age-related alterations of homeostasis can lead to ADRs in the elderly person (Harper, Newton, & Walsh, 1989). In the absence of stress, most elderly people are able to maintain homeostatic function. However, when the body is faced with a stressor, such as the introduction of a new drug, the ability to return to the physiologic status quo may be diminished. For example, physiologic response necessary for adjustment of blood pressure in reac-

tion to postural changes may be diminished in an elderly person. This person may function at an acceptable level to avoid self-injury under normal circumstances, but if a blood pressure–lowering drug is introduced into the body, adverse drug effects may occur in the form of falls resulting in injury.

4. Gender differences occur in the manifestation of ADRs (Cadieux, 1989; Denham, 1990). More elderly women than elderly men experience ADRs in response to drug therapy. This may be due in part, to body composition differences and drug distribution trends. Women have a higher fat-to-lean tissue ratio than men throughout the life span. Therefore, lipophilic drugs may be stored for a longer duration, contributing to an increased incidence of ADRs in women. Furthermore, women on the average have a higher life expectancy than men and, therefore, may experience more severely diminished organ reserves and curtailed abilities to metabolize drugs. Finally, women throughout their life span generally seek health care more frequently than do men and may receive more medication for treatment, increasing their chance for drug interactions and ADRs.

5. Multiple disease increases the risk of developing an ADR (Denham, 1990; Harper et al., 1989). Certain illnesses have the potential to alter physiologic functions, which may subsequently affect pharmacologic effects in the body. For example, cirrhosis of the liver results in healthy hepatic tissue being replaced by nonfunctional scar tissue. This nonfunctioning tissue then contributes to reduced metabolism of drugs, thus increasing the risk of ADRs.

6. Polymedicine, also referred to as polypharmacy, is a common problem among the elderly that has been shown to contribute to an increased risk of ADRs (Denham, 1990; Lamy, 1980). The potential for an ADR is enhanced when one's physiologic response is altered by another drug.

7. Increased drug doses appear to be associated with an increased risk of an adverse drug reaction (Cadieux, 1989). In general, the longer a drug is used and the higher the dose, the greater the chance of developing some undesirable effect. Another issue related to dose is a drug's therapeutic range (Nolan and O'Malley, 1989). Drugs that have a narrow therapeutic range – that is, a narrow range of acceptable blood concentrations to effect the desired action without causing toxicity – are more likely to result in ADR development. Maintenance of restricted drug levels is difficult over time; therefore, frequent measures of blood concentrations must be recorded. Adjustment of drug doses helps to reduce the risk of ADRs. These drugs (e.g., anticoagulants, cardiac drugs, and insulin) are more frequently prescribed for elderly people than for the young (Montamat et al., 1989).

8. Those individuals with previous allergic reactions or other undesirable effects associated with drugs are more prone to experience these effects again (Cadieux, 1989; Denham, 1990).

Common Manifestations of Adverse Drug Reactions

The recognition of adverse drug reactions presents a considerable challenge to clinicians serving the elderly (Kleinfeld and Corcoran, 1988). Adverse drug reactions may present as symptoms mistakenly associated with the aging process or as an exacerbation of a preexisting disease condition. Furthermore, temporal associations between drug ingestion and the onset of symptoms may be clouded by a patient's inaccurate recall of the chronology of events. Finally, the presenting problem may be atypical of the drug being used.

Several intermediate effects may ultimately contribute to the final presenting symptom. This process of progressing to an atypical presenting symptom is known as the "cascade effect." An example presented by Harper and his colleagues (1989) features a diuretic that is a common drug used by elderly people. Diuretics, which are used to enhance the elimination of water and sodium from the body, can lead to dehydration and decreased potassium levels. Both of these conditions can cause hypotension and delirium, which may ultimately lead to the presenting symptom – a fall. Falls are not usually associated with the adverse effects of diuretics. Although the association between the cause and the effect is not always clear-cut, the cautious clinician will relentlessly investigate presenting symptoms of unknown origin and consider the possibility of an adverse drug reaction in any elderly patient.

Some more common ADRs and their causal agents are presented next.

Confusion. Confusion is a common adverse drug reaction in the elderly (Gordon and Preiksaitis, 1988). Most reversible dementia is caused by drug-induced reactions (Harper et al., 1989). Persons with preexisting cognitive impairment are more prone to develop drug-induced confusion. Confusion may be sloughed off as a normal symptom of aging.

Confusion, whether it be newly presented or an exacerbation of a preexisting problem, should be investigated as a possible drug-induced reaction. Some drugs found to be associated with confusion are antianxiety drugs, sedative-hypnotic agents, tricyclic antidepressants, antipsychotic drugs, drugs with anticholinergic properties such as antihistamines, antispasmodics, antidiarrheal agents, antiparkinson drugs, and antiarrhythmic drugs (Harper et al., 1989). All of these classes of drugs are commonly used by elderly people.

Depression. Depression is a common clinical disorder among the elderly (Harper et al., 1989). It

is also a diagnosis that is often missed because of the diffuse symptoms the elderly report – fatigue, loss of appetite, disturbance in sleep maintenance, and various vague physical complaints. These symptoms are often associated with a myriad of other physical problems experienced by the elderly.

There are a number of drugs that may cause depression (see Table 16.1). Drug history should be considered in evaluating possible causes of depression in the older patient. If drug-induced depression is discovered, the clinician must be mindful that a recurrence is possible with other drug therapies (Harper et al., 1989). Care must be exercised in selecting drugs with minimal potential for depressive reactions among elderly patients.

Falls. For the elderly, falls are a significant cause of hospitalization, permanent loss of mobility and independence, and mortality (Kane et al., 1989). Numerous conditions can result in falls among the elderly – impaired cognition, vision, proprioception, mobility, and physiologic adjustment to postural changes (Harper et al., 1989).

TABLE 16.1 Some drugs associated with drug-induced depression

Alcohol
Anticonvulsants
Antiparkinsonian agents
Antipsychotic drugs
Barbiturates
Benzodiazepines (minor tranquilizers)
Beta-adrenergic blockers and other selected antihypertensives
Corticosteriods
Digitalis-based drugs (cardiac drugs)
Nonsteroidal anti-inflammatory drugs
Thiazide diuretics

Source: Adapted from F. Pucino, C. L. Beck, R. L. Seifert, G. L. Strommen, P. A. Sheldon, and I. L. Silbergleit, "Pharmacogeriatrics," *Pharmacotherapy,* 1985, vol. 5, no. 6, p. 321.

However, drug intake is also a factor shown to be associated with increased risk of falls in the elderly. Elderly individuals who are predisposed to falls may be at exceptional risk while taking particular drugs or drug combinations. Drugs that act on the central nervous system are closely related to falls, as are any drugs that effect a hypotensive response in the elderly (Harper et al., 1989; Kane et al., 1989). As previously mentioned, through a series of steps diuretics may cause unsteadiness and falls in the elderly. Also, any drug that results in dizziness – for example, some antiarthritics, antihistamines, antianxiety agents, and alcohol – can cause a predisposed person to stumble and fall.

Gastrointestinal effects. Drug-associated alterations in gastrointestinal structure and function may occur (Pucino et al., 1985). Gastric bleeding resulting in chronic blood loss in the elderly can cause episodes of low hemoglobin count. This in turn can lead to symptoms of fatigue, lethargy, and shortness of breath. Some severe cases of low hemoglobin can actually end in cardiac problems and cognitive impairment as a result of a decrease in oxygen to the heart and brain. Anti-inflammatory drugs, particularly aspirin, are a noted cause of gastric bleeding in the elderly (Kane et al., 1989).

Functional problems associated with various drugs include nausea and vomiting associated with digoxin toxicity, bronchodilators, lithium, and aspirin (Pucino et al., 1985). In addition, some antacids (magnesium agents), antibiotics, and some antiarrhythmics cause diarrhea, and constipation is caused by narcotic analgesics, anticholinergic drugs, aluminum-containing antacids, and some antidepressants and antipsychotic drugs (Simonson, 1984). All of these adverse reactions must be considered before prescribing a specific drug regimen for an elderly person. Likewise, before any of these symptoms warrant treatment, all possible efforts should be made to rule out the possibility of drug-associated initiation.

Postural hypotension. Various diseases common to the elderly (cerebrovascular, cardiovascular, and Parkinson's disease) may pose challenges to blood pressure maintenance. Any additional source of perturbation to blood pressure control among the elderly may result in a drop in blood pressure and related dizziness and/or falls.

Hypotension is an adverse effect associated with a number of medications used by the elderly (Montamat et al., 1989). Antihypertensives, antipsychotics, antiparkinsonian agents, and vasodilators are some of the drugs that may cause a hypotensive reaction in the elderly. Clinicians have the responsibility to predict which of their patients may have a predisposition to detrimental hypotensive reaction to certain medications. Most likely the person who registers an orthostatic response or who is ingesting a number of drugs known to cause hypotension is a poor candidate for another drug that may contribute to further decreases in blood pressure, resulting in falls (Harper et al., 1989).

Sexual dysfunction. Iatrogenic sexual dysfunction may severely diminish the quality of life among elderly people. Because some elderly people may view their sexual activity as a private matter, this adverse reaction may often go unreported (Pucino et al., 1985; Simonson, 1984). Clinicians bear the responsibility of knowing which drugs may cause sexual dysfunction and of asking their patients if they have experienced any such problems. Antihypertensives and antipsychotics are two types of drugs that are known to have adverse effects on sexual function. The clinician should make every effort to advise alternative medications for individuals experiencing sexual dysfunction as a result of drug therapy.

Sensory Changes

Alterations in vision and hearing are often seen as concomitants of the aging process. As a consequence, adverse drug reactions manifested as declines or alterations in sight and hearing often go unreported by patients and unnoticed by clinicians. Commonly used classes of drugs such as cardiac agents, corticosteroids, some gastrointestinal agents, and antipsychotics may cause disturbances in vision (Pucino et al., 1985; Simonson, 1984). Some antiarthritics, antibiotics, and aspirin may cause ototoxic effects ranging from tinnitus to permanent hearing loss (Kane et al., 1989). In order to avoid these types of sensory declines, the clinician must assess the functional level of the eyes and ears prior to initiating drug therapy. Baseline sensory levels can help in the identification of adverse effects brought on by drugs.

Urinary incontinence. Incontinence in the elderly is often embarrassing to the person experiencing it and therefore may go unreported to the clinician. Some elderly persons are already predisposed to bouts of urinary incontinence due to physiologic changes, such as decreased bladder capacity or existing disease states that affect functional status – for example, strokes, dementing illnesses, or diabetes (Harper et al., 1989). Drugs that lead to urinary retention or overflow incontinence are often used by the elderly in their treatment regimens. Some drugs that can cause urinary incontinence in the elderly are diuretics, antihistimines, antidepressants, antipsychotics, muscle relaxants, and antihypertensives (Lamy, 1980; Simonson, 1984). According to Harper and her associates (1989), any drug that affects functional integrity among the elderly must be suspect in the causation of drug-induced incontinence. Therefore, it is important that clinicians assess baseline functional capacity to ensure that incontinence is not related to drug therapy. If incontinence occurs, other treatments must be explored.

DRUG INTERACTIONS

The effects of drugs in the body can be altered by the presence of other factors such as other drugs, disease states, and food or nutrients. Although the most commonly recognized interactions stem from multiple drug use, other problematic categories include drug-disease, drug-food, and drug-laboratory test interactions (Simonson, 1984). Lamy (1986) reports that elderly people are at a higher risk of experiencing drug interactions due to various factors – physiologic, pathophysiologic, and sociogenic or behavioral – associated with the aging process. For example, an elderly person may experience various age-related changes in organ systems that decrease homeostatic recovery. In addition, he or she may experience any number of pathologic conditions, superimposed on the declines in organ reserve, that require multiple drug therapies. Furthermore, he or she may be unable to comply with a complicated multidrug regimen. Adverse reactions may be viewed by the clinician as a new illness for which a new battery of drugs must be prescribed.

Drug-Drug Interactions

Drug-drug interactions occur when the introduction of two or more drugs into the body at approximately the same time causes an altered response to occur for one or both of the drugs (Ferrini and Ferrini, 1989). The types of interactions that may occur include synergism, potentiation, or antagonism (Lamy, 1980, 1986). Synergism is an infrequent type of drug interaction that occurs when the combined effect of two drugs is greater than the sum of their unique actions. Potentiation is an interaction in which combining two drugs results in a much greater response than could be predicted on the basis of pharmacologic studies. Antagonistic interactions occur when for some reason one drug diminishes or completely curtails the effect of another drug.

The elderly are at a greater risk for drug-drug interactions because of their increased consumption of multiple medications. To illustrate, there is a 5 percent risk of drug interaction in patients using two to three drugs, but a 50 percent interaction potential when five to eight drugs are used (Cadieux, 1989). In addition, elderly people tend to use drugs that are often implicated in drug interactions such as anticoagulants (to prevent blood clotting), hypoglycemics (to lower blood sugar levels), cardiac drugs, antihistamines, antidepressants, tranquilizers, analgesics (pain killers), and alcohol. See Table 16.2 for some examples of common drug-drug interactions in the elderly.

Lamy (1984) states there are several variables that heighten the risk of drug-drug interactions among the elderly. Those factors include the following:

1. Use of two or more drugs
2. Use of alcohol with drugs
3. Use of self-prescribed nonprescription drugs with prescription drugs
4. Involvement of more than one prescriber
5. Use of more than one pharmacy to purchase medications

Some authors believe that most drug-drug interactions could be avoided (Dawling and Crome,

TABLE 16.2 Sample of drug–drug interactions in the elderly

Drugs interacting	Effect
Antibiotics (tetracycline) with antacids or iron-containing agents	Reduced absorption of antibiotic
Anticoagulant (warfarin) with aspirin	Enhanced blood thinning
Antidepressant (tricyclic) with antihypertensive	Increased blood pressure lowering effect
Lithium with diuretics	Electrolyte imbalance
Diuretic (furosemide) with antibiotic (cephalosporin)	Kidney toxicity
Diuretic (furosemide) with aminoglycosides (antibiotics)	Toxicity to the ear
Cardiac agent (digoxin) with diuretic	Enhanced loss of potassium, irregular heart rate
Minor tranquilizer with alcohol	Reduced perception of environment (e.g., hypothermia, falls, etc.)

1989). The prescriber has an obligation to be aware of the drugs his or her patients are taking and of the potential interactions that may occur. By carefully selecting drugs and monitoring their effects, potential drug-drug interactions may be avoided. Prescribers may also avoid potential drug-drug interactions by employing nondrug therapy whenever possible and prescribing drug therapy more conservatively.

Drug-Disease Interactions

Drugs used to treat a specific disease in an elderly person may be contraindicated for one or more coexisting diseases (Hershey, 1988). The prescriber cannot address each condition as a separate entity; rather, the combined effects of drugs prescribed for all conditions must be considered. For instance, the individual who has diabetes and hypertension may have decreased glucose tolerance if certain diuretics are prescribed (Kane et al., 1989). There are numerous opportunities for drugs and diseases to interact in the elderly. See Table 16.3 for examples of such interactions. The point is that clinicians must know the health profile of their patients and prescribe accordingly.

Drug-Food Interactions

Foods have been implicated in altered drug actions in the elderly. Drug-nutrient interactions result from physical or biochemical relationships between drugs and nutrients (Roe, 1984). These interactions are of concern when they hamper the thera-

peutic effect of the drug in some way or result in a toxic effect. With this thought in mind, the prescriber and other health care professionals must consider the possibility of drug-food interactions when providing instruction about proper drug administration.

Absorption of certain drugs may be either enhanced or diminished as a consequence of simultaneous ingestion of a particular food (Roe, 1984). For example, acetaminophen is less well absorbed when taken with or shortly after foods high in carbohydrates (Bauwens and Clemmons, 1980). Likewise, absorption of tetracycline is curtailed when a person ingests foods or food supplements containing calcium, iron, or zinc (Simonson, 1984). These substances bind with tetracycline, thereby rendering it unavailable for absorption.

Other drugs may undergo enhanced absorption when taken with or shortly after certain foods. Griseofulvin, an antifungal drug, is absorbed more effectively when taken with or after eating fatty foods (Roe, 1984). This medication is often prescribed to combat fungal infections of the lower extremities in elderly persons who have a disease of the peripheral vascular system (Roe, 1984).

Increased incidence of toxic effects are also seen in food-drug interactions. For instance, one such well-publicized incident involves monoamine oxidase (MAO) inhibitors (Simonson, 1984). MAO inhibitors are prescribed for depression. A hypertensive crisis can occur when these drugs are taken with foods containing tyramine – aged cheeses, red wines, and chocolate, to name a few (Horwitz, Lovenby, Engelman, and Sjoerdsme, 1964). Because this toxic reaction can cause a debilitating stroke or even death, it is imperative that the clinician educate the patient in proper medication behavior.

A final thought regarding food effects on drug action is more general in nature with respect to drug metabolism and excretion. A lowered protein level

---

TABLE 16.3 Examples of potential drug–disease interactions

Drug	Disease/reaction
Beta blockers	Destabilization of controlled asthma in the elderly
Antipsychotics	Increased immobility in elderly Parkinson's disease patients
Diuretics	Worsening of malnutrition through loss of electrolytes
Psychotropics	Exacerbation of preexisting dementia
Narcotics	Exacerbation of constipation to severe fecal impactions
Aspirin	Exacerbation of existing gastrointestinal irritation

Source: Adapted from R. L. Kane, J. G. Ouslander, and I. B. Abrass, *Essentials of Clinical Geriatrics*, 2nd ed. (New York: McGraw-Hill, 1989).

in the diet may result in lowered drug metabolism. These changes in metabolic rate may alter a drug's therapeutic effect. In contrast, renal excretion of drugs is enhanced by a restriction in dietary protein when there is impaired kidney function (Roe, 1984). These factors must be considered when making recommendations on dietary instruction for a drug regimen. The implications are not always straightforward.

Drug-Diagnostic Test Interaction

Drugs may induce alterations in laboratory test results. Age-related responses coupled with possible drug interactions may make the difficult task of laboratory test interpretation almost impossible. For example, a host of drugs can alter thyroxine level tests (Lamy, 1986). The clinician must become aware of such possible instances of laboratory test perversion to avoid inaccuracies in diagnoses. The patient must be examined with respect to the complete clinical picture, not just an isolated disease state.

DRUG REGIMEN COMPLIANCE

Compliance is defined as the degree to which an individual adheres to instructions regarding a drug regimen (O'Brien and Kursch, 1987). Drug compliance is a problem for all age groups. Some researchers believe that it is a bigger problem in the elderly (Abrams and Andrews, 1984), but other research has not supported this contention (Darnell, Murray, Martz, and Weinberger, 1986).

Anywhere from 30 to 50 percent of elderly people do not adhere to their drug regimens (Morrow, Leirer, and Sheikh, 1988; Shimp, Ascione, Glazer, and Atwood, 1985). This noncompliance rate is consistent with that of the general population, but the consequences of noncompliance among the elderly may be more serious. Other authors suggest that noncompliance among the elderly does not always result in clinically significant problems (Simonson, 1984). Sometimes noncompliance is based on a patient's experience with a given drug (Quinn et al., 1983).

Types of Noncompliant Behavior

Individuals display a variety of noncompliant behaviors. Simonson (1984) lists those important in the elderly: omitting medications, taking too large a dose, discontinuing a medication, or taking medications with interfering agents or those that are self-prescribed. Additionally, some prescriptions are never filled or medications may be taken at incorrect times.

As much as 90 percent of noncompliance among the elderly may be attributed to taking less than a prescribed dose (Darnell et al., 1986; Montamat et al., 1989). Undercompliance may be related to inadequate finances, lack of transportation to the pharmacy, a rational decision not to take a prescribed dose, or forgetfulness. Excessive consumption or overcompliance does occur among the elderly, but this behavior is rare. In one study, only 7.5 percent of noncompliance was due to overcompliance (Darnell et al., 1986); another study reported only a 13 percent overcompliance rate (Shimp et al., 1985).

Intelligent Noncompliance

Not all noncompliant behaviors are detrimental to the elderly. In some instances, no adverse health consequences occur. Individuals may make dosage adjustments or discontinue a drug on the basis of a rational decision-making process. Individuals who practice rational noncompliance often do so to avoid adverse reactions associated with their prescribed drugs while still achieving the desired therapeutic effect (Weintraub, 1981). Some individuals are able to judge when there is no longer a physiologic need for medication. Upon clinical examination these individuals are often judged to be adequately treated; thus, they are correct in their assessment regarding their need for medications.

This rational noncompliance is called "intelligent noncompliance." Weintraub (1981) recommends that the concept of intelligent noncompliance be considered when prescribing drug regimens to elderly patients. They know their bodies and can offer a wealth of information to the prescriber regarding their response to particular drug treatments.

Risk Factors of Noncompliance

Various authors have researched reasons for noncompliant behavior among the elderly. Three broad categories have been identified: individual factors, those related to the disease process or therapeutic regimen, and prescriber factors (Simonson, 1984). One or more of these factors may contribute to either intentional or unintentional noncompliance (see Table 16.4).

TABLE 16.4 Factors affecting noncompliance

Individual Factors

Sensory deficits (decreased hearing and vision)
Cognitive impairment
Impairments of dexterity
Living alone, i.e., lack of supervision
Deficient knowledge regarding:
- Disease process
- Need for drug therapy
- Proper administration techniques

Lack of belief in the prescriber or the drug efficacy
Insufficient economic resources to buy drugs
Religious or cultural prohibitions against drug therapy
Loneliness or depression, causing a lack of motivation to live
Hesitation to clarify misunderstanding regarding therapeutic regimens
History of self-medication or self-help behaviors
Illiteracy or little formal education
Much education and independent thinking
Lack of transportation to get to pharmacy
English not the first language
Fear of becoming dependent on the drug
Too ill or weak to take medications

Disease Process/Therapeutic Regimen Factors

Complexity of therapeutic regime
- Many drugs
- Difficult dosing schedule
- Frequent dosing schedule

Polymedicine
Many diseases superimposed on one another

Chronic disease pattern with long-term therapy (medication compliance diminishes over time)
Undesirable side effects
Asymptomatic disease
Characteristics of the drug:
- Tablets difficult to swallow
- Undesirable taste, smell, or appearance

Exorbitant cost of drugs on limited budgets
Use of child-proof containers or other difficult receptacles for dispensing
Low benefit ratio; for example, drugs have little or no ability to alleviate symptoms or cure disease; may be coupled with adverse reactions

Prescriber Factors

Poor communication technique, which may include
- Use of medical jargon
- Rushed interaction
- Condescending attitude toward patients
- Cues that say, "I'm busy, don't ask me questions."
- Use of only one sense in instruction
- Lack of eye contact
- Use of vague language

Complex therapeutic regimens
Selection of medication *not* based on:
- Fewest potential side effects
- Lowest cost
- Medication history (prescription and nonprescription)

Lack of specific instructions on label
Little or no relationship with patient
Lack of scheduled follow-up visits for reevaluation

Methods to Enhance Drug Compliance

Some health care professionals believe that a good patient is an obedient and, therefore, a compliant patient. In contrast, some disagree with the idea that compliance should always be achieved, for this would imply that *all* clinicians are correct 100 percent of the time – and this is rarely the case (Weintraub, 1981). In the best of situations – that is, assuming the clinician's diagnosis and recommended prescription for drug therapy are correct – the goal of the health professional is to achieve compliance in therapeutic practices among his or her patients. Strategies for accomplishing such compliance have been proposed.

Simplification of the drug therapy can increase the probability of compliance (Carty and Everitt, 1989). An inverse relationship appears to exist between the number of drugs prescribed and compliance. Consideration of drug format, dosing schedule, and number of drugs must be a part of the effort to increase compliance. Tablets are not always the best format for those who experience dysphagia or other problems of the throat or mouth. Combined-effect drugs might be considered for individuals with multiple disease conditions (Wade and Bowling, 1986). Furthermore, vague or complex dosing schedules must be avoided. Schedules that coincide with an individual's daily routine have a better chance of being observed than do schedules without such considerations (Coe, Prendergast, and Psathas, 1984; Norell, 1985).

Choosing drugs with the fewest adverse effects can enhance compliance, as such effects cause individuals to discontinue a drug therapy prematurely (Lamy, 1980). The patient should be encouraged to play an active role in reporting any adverse drug reactions. However, this may be difficult if the patient does not know what to expect or if the clinician is unapproachable or difficult to reach. One study by Quinn et al. (1983) demonstrated that only 12 percent of their sample had knowledge of side effects associated with their prescribed drugs.

Promotion of patient understanding of the disease process, the reason for a particular drug therapy, and instruction are important means of improving compliance (Jernigan, 1984; Mathieson, 1986). Dialogue must be encouraged between clinicians and patients, and sufficient time must be allowed for elderly patients to absorb information and ask questions (Giannetti, 1983). Some elderly persons hesitate to ask questions of their health care providers for fear of taking too much valuable time or sounding unintelligent. Alleviating these fears and building an open and honest relationship with elderly patients, in fact all patients, may contribute to greater compliance or at least to a cooperative understanding of the need for certain drug therapies. Several studies have shown that educational programs and patient counseling increase the possibility of compliance among elderly patients (Edwards and Pathy, 1984; Hammarlund, Ostrom, and Kethley, 1985; Johnston, Clark, Mundy, Cromarty, and Ridout, 1986). It must be reiterated, however, that any professional providing drug information must follow the ideals of open, honest, and unrushed communication with elderly people.

Packaging and labeling techniques can help elderly patients in drug regimen compliance (Hurd and Butkovich, 1986). Large type should be used on prescription labels to help vision-impaired persons read instructions. Supplemental inserts highlighting the important instructions regarding drug therapy are helpful for the patient. However, inserts provided by the drug companies are usually written in highly technical language and in small type, offering nothing more than increased frustration for elderly persons.

Drug containers may significantly affect compliance. Child-proof containers and bubble packs may be difficult for elderly hands to open (Andrews, 1984; Swift, 1988). One group of researchers devised a procedure to assess functional abilities associated with drug compliance problems (Hurd and Butkovich, 1986). The test included measures of label-reading, color vision, handling of child-resistant containers, short-term memory, and label interpretation. This assessment kit can be made with materials found in any pharmacy or physician's office. Using it, the clinician can quickly discover useful information about the patient's ability to comply with a prescribed drug regimen.

One issue of compliance often overlooked by clinicians is the elderly patient's economic resources (Raffoul, 1986). In order to ensure compliance, the patient must first obtain the prescription. Clinicians must not shy away from assessing their patients' ability to bear the cost of prescription and nonprescription drugs. The use of generics or the suggestion to shop around for the least expensive pharmacy are two alternatives. However, the latter suggestion may be impossible if the elderly patient has limited or no transportation.

Finally, the use of compliance aids has been suggested by several authors (Ferrini and Ferrini, 1989; Pucino et al., 1985). These aids are generally employed to offset noncompliance resulting from forgetfulness or complicated multiple-drug regimens. Devices such as drug calendars and dosage cassettes may serve as reminders to take the appropriate dose of a drug at the appropriate time. However, many manufactured dosage cassettes may be small and awkward for stiff hands and difficult to read for vision-impaired persons. Homemade pill containers such as egg cartons or muffin pans may be easier for older hands to manage (Mathieson, 1986).

RECOMMENDATIONS FOR RATIONAL DRUG MANAGEMENT

In order to establish safe and effective drug therapy for the elderly, a number of factors must be considered. A delicate homeostatic balance can be easily upset with inappropriate recommendation of medicinal agents that can produce adverse reactions and interact with other drug products or foods in the body. The presence of multiple chronic conditions and various age-related changes in physiology also necessitates some tricky maneuvering when managing drug therapy in the elderly. Drug management among elderly patients is made still more difficult by the physiologic heterogeneity of the elderly. Therefore, it is difficult but not impossible to establish some criteria for drug prescribing and drug management in elderly patients (Carty and Everitt, 1989). The ultimate goal in drug therapy for the elderly is to maintain or enhance health. To accomplish this goal, various authors have formulated the following recommendations to assist health care providers in managing drug therapy in the elderly.

Accurate diagnosis.   A clearly defined diagnosis is of extreme importance when considering drug therapy for the elderly (Royal College of Physicians of London, 1984). Elderly people often report multiple vague symptoms that make accurate diagnosis a challenge (Kane et al., 1989). Atypical symptoms can lead the clinician on a "wild goose chase." Furthermore, clinicians must be aware that various symptoms may not be associated with a disease but may instead reflect a drug interaction. In such cases, prescribing yet another drug may exacerbate existing symptoms or create other problems.

Complete drug history.   Usually, neither the patient nor the clinician has a complete record of the total drug regimen (Carty and Everitt, 1989; Kleinfeld and Corcoran, 1988). Because elderly persons may see a number of health care professionals, there may not be a coordinated drug record available. The "brown bag" approach to office or clinic visits is recommended. The clinician should ask the patient to bring in all the drugs he or she takes for any reason, even those taken very rarely and those bought over the counter or recommended by family or friends. In addition, direct questions regarding the intake of alcohol, caffeine, and nicotine must be asked, because these substances may also interact with drugs.

Complete medical history. Like medication histories, medical histories are also fragmented. All diseases and their symptoms must be reviewed. As mentioned earlier, drug-disease interactions may occur. Certain disease processes, particularly those diseases affecting the liver or the kidneys, can interfere with drug action in the body.

Avoidance of unnecessary drug therapy. Frequently, the diseases elderly people suffer may not pose immediate harm and do not require drug therapy (Caird, 1990; Crooks, 1983). Sometimes doing nothing is the best prescription. Overenthusiastic prescribing can be the cause of iatrogenic diseases. However, essential drug therapy should not be withheld solely on the basis of age.

Knowledge of the pharmacology of drugs chosen. The diverse pharmacokinetics and pharmacodynamics of individual elderly patients must be considered (Kleinfeld and Corcoran, 1988). Although some trends for age-related physiological changes have been suggested, individualized assessments must be done by the clinician. This information, coupled with an intimate knowledge of the drug's activity, will aid in the selection of a suitable drug therapy.

Titration of appropriate doses. Because the elderly are such a heterogeneous group, clinicians must embark on a "start low and go slow" journey when initiating drug therapies for their patients (Ho and Triggs, 1984; Wieman, 1986). Possibilities of decreased physiologic function, disease states, and altered drug sensitivity must be considered when prescribing for the elderly. Evaluation of the clinical response must be made to determine the appropriate dosage. The clinician must be warned against assuming that *every* elderly person will need a low dose on the basis of age alone. Individualized therapeutic plans must be developed.

Anticipation of adverse drug effects. Potential adverse effects can be identified and monitored by health care professionals (O'Brien and Kursch, 1987). It is imperative that adverse drug reactions and drug interactions be recognized for what they are and not be seen as "inevitabilities of aging" or as another disease process.

Consideration of the route of administration and the dosage form. Some elderly persons have physiologic impairments that may preclude certain forms and administration routes of drugs (Ho and Triggs, 1984; Lamy, 1984). Elderly patients who have trouble swallowing or are predisposed to esophageal injury should not be prescribed tablets or capsules. Suppositories or liquid drug suspensions might alleviate some discomfort and improve compliance.

Establishment of a simple drug regimen. The greater the number of drugs and the more complex the drug regimen, the greater the risk of adverse drug reactions and compliance errors (Denham, 1990; Swift, 1988). The clinician should explore the individual's daily routine and try to match the dosage schedule with it. Not only does this provide a good memory cue to enhance compliance, but it may also help build a cooperative relationship between the patient and the clinician.

Exploration of socioeconomic factors. A person cannot take a drug he or she cannot afford (Kleinfeld and Corcoran, 1988). It is important to ask about a patient's financial resources in a nonthreatening manner. The clinician should investigate inexpensive generic drugs with consideration of variation in the bioequivalence between generics and trade name drugs. Another way to make drugs more affordable is to prescribe small quantities.

Assessment of social support. The clinician must determine whether the patient needs help administering his or her medications (Caird, 1990; O'Brien and Kursch, 1987). If the patient has some functional deficit, family, friends, or visiting health care professionals can help with drug regimens. They can also provide valuable information regarding adverse drug reactions or inadequate therapeutic response.

Allowance for patient education. Knowledge about the disease and its drug therapy may affect compliance (Ives, Bentz, and Gwyther, 1987). The clinician should provide clear, succinct instructions in both verbal and written form. The more senses involved in an educational experience, the better the recall. Time should be allowed for questions; in fact, questions should be invited by asking the patient to repeat the instructions. If possible, a family member or a friend should be involved in the process. Finally, the clinician should be sure to describe any side effects or effects of drug interactions to the patient and should encourage him or her to report immediately any problems thought to be associated with the drug therapy. In this way, treatment of symptoms, rather than legitimate disease conditions, may be reduced.

Reevaluation of the drug regimen. The drug regimen should be reconsidered every three to six months to decide whether it is still necessary (Harper et al., 1989; Wieman, 1986). The clinician should always ask himself or herself, "Is this drug necessary?" and "Are there any drugs that I can terminate?" In this way, polymedicine can be kept to a minimum, and so can the risk of the development of adverse drug reactions and drug interactions. This practice can also aid in compliance by reducing the number of drugs and thus the complexity of the drug regimen.

Encouragement of the use of medication aids. The clinician can ensure compliance and successful use of a drug by recommending the use of a medication calendar or labeled dose containers (O'Brien and Kursch, 1987). These may help patients to manage multiple daily drug doses. It does not take a memory deficit or confusional state to forget to take one dose in a multiple drug regimen – anyone can make a mistake.

Consideration of nondrug treatment alternatives. Although this recommendation is stated last, it is probably the most important. In the search for a quick fix, those of us in the health care field often neglect nondrug therapies (Lamy, 1984). However, nondrug therapies may prove to be effective in and of themselves or may serve as important adjuncts to drug therapy (O'Brien and Kursch, 1987). Dietary modifications, relaxation therapy, exercise and physical therapy, and counseling may alleviate the discomfort associated with some disease states in the elderly. At any rate, drug therapy should be initiated only if, after all possible alternatives have been examined, it still seems to be the best choice for treating the condition.

STUDY QUESTIONS

1. Name four pharmacokinetic factors that may contribute to altered drug activity in the elderly.
2. Why are alterations in pharmacodymanics difficult to identify?
3. How does the heterogeneous nature of physiologic changes in the elderly affect drug-prescribing practice for the elderly? Consider both age-related and disease-related changes.
4. Why is the use of creatinine clearance rates to estimate kidney function in the elderly subject to scrutiny?
5. Define adverse drug reaction and explain four or five common manifestations of these reactions in the elderly.
6. Drug interactions are common among the elderly. Identify four categories of drug interactions and provide recommendations to avoid these problems.
7. Explain the concept of intelligent noncompliance and state its significance in drug therapy for the elderly.
8. Identify major considerations associated with rational drug-prescribing practice for the elderly.

9. An elderly person complains of fatigue, disturbance of sleep pattern, loss of appetite, and other vague physical symptoms. What might be some factors to consider in identifying the problem?

BIBLIOGRAPHY

Abrams, J., and Andrews, K. 1984. The influence of hospital admission on long-term medication of elderly patients. *Journal of the Royal College of Physicians of London*, 18(4): 225-227.

Andrews, K. 1984. Drugs in the rehabilitation of the elderly. *International Rehabilitation Medicine*, 6(3): ix-xii.

Bauwens, E., and Clemmons, C. 1980. Foods that foil drugs. In Medical Economics Company (Eds.), *Practical guide to medications*. Oradell, NJ: Medical Economics Company.

Buechler, J. R., and Malloy, W. 1989. Drug therapy in the elderly: How to achieve optimum results. *Postgraduate Medicine*, 85(6): 87-94, 97-99.

Cadieux, R. J. 1989. Drug interactions in the elderly: How multiple drug use increases risk exponentially. *Postgraduate Medicine*, 86(8): 187-186.

Caird, F. I. 1985. Towards rational drug therapy in old age: The F. E. Williams Lecture 1985. *Journal of the Royal College of Physicians of London*, 19(4): 235-239.

Caird, F. I. 1990. Newer aspects of drug therapy in the elderly. *Klinische Wochenschrift*, 68(12): 623-626.

Carty, M. A., and Everitt, D. E. 1989. Basic principles of prescribing for geriatric outpatients. *Geriatrics*, 44(6): 85-88, 90-92, 97-98.

Cherry, K. E., and Morton, M. R. 1989. Drug sensitivity in older adults: The role of physiologic and pharmacokinetic factors. *International Journal of Aging and Human Development*, 23(3): 159-174.

Coe, R. M., Prendergast, C. G., and Psathas, G. 1984. Strategies for obtaining compliance with medications regimens. *Journal of the American Geriatrics Society*, 32(8): 589-594.

Crooks, J. 1983. Rational therapeutics in the elderly. *Journal of Chronic Disease*, 36(1): 59-65.

Darnell, J. C., Murray, M. D., Martz, B. L., and Weinberger, M. 1986. Medication use by ambulatory elderly: An in-home survey. *Journal of the American Geriatrics Society*, 34(1): 1-4.

Dawling, S., and Crome, P. 1989. Clinical pharmacokinetic considerations in the elderly: An update. *Clinical Pharmacokinetics*, 17(4): 236-263.

Denham, M. J. 1990. Adverse drug reactions. *British Medical Bulletin*, 46(1): 53-62.

Edwards, M., and Pathy, M. S. J. 1984. Drug counseling in the elderly and predicting compliance. *The Practitioner*, 228: 291-292, 294-300.

Ferrini, A. F., and Ferrini, R. L. 1989. *Health in the later years*. Dubuque, IA: William C. Brown.

Giannetti, V. J. 1983. Medication utilization problems among the elderly. *Health and Social Work*, 8(4): 262-270.

Gordon, M., and Preiksaitis, H. G. 1988. Drugs and the aging brain. *Geriatrics*, 43(5): 69-71, 75-76, 78.

Hammarlund, E. R., Ostrom, J. R., and Kethley, A. J. 1985. The effects of drug counseling and other educational strategies on drug utilization of the elderly. *Medical Care*, 23(2): 165-170.

Harper, C. M., Newton, P. A., and Walsh, J. R. 1989. Drug-induced illness in the elderly. *Postgraduate Medicine*, 86(2): 245-256.

Hershey, L. A. 1988. Avoiding adverse drug reactions in the elderly. *Mount Sinai Journal of Medicine*, 55(3): 244-250.

Ho, P. C., and Triggs, E. J. 1984. Drug therapy in the elderly. *Australian and New Zealand Journal of Medicine*, 14(2): 179-190.

Horwitz, D., Lovenby, W., Engelman, K., and Sjoerdsme, A. 1964. Monoamine-oxidase inhibitors, tyramine and cheese. *Journal of the American Medical Association*, 188: 1108-1110.

Hurd, P. D., and Butkovich, S. L. 1986. Compliance problems and the older patient: Assessing functional limitations. *Drug Intelligence and Clinical Pharmacy*, 20(3): 228-231.

Ives, T. J., Bentz, E. J., and Gwyther, R. E. 1987. Drug-related admissions to a family medicine inpatient service. *Archives of Internal Medicine*, 147(6): 1117-1120.

Jernigan, J. A. 1984. Update on drugs and the elderly. *American Family Physician*, 29(4): 238-247.

Johnston, M., Clarke, A., Mundy, K., Cromarty, E., and Ridout, K. 1986. Facilitating comprehension of discharge medication in elderly patients. *Age and Aging*, 15(5): 304-306.

Kane, R. L., Ouslander, J. G., and Abrass, I. B. 1989. *Essentials of clinical geriatrics*, 2nd ed. New York: McGraw-Hill.

Kleinfeld, M., and Corcoran, A. J. 1988. Medicating the elderly. *Comprehensive Therapy*, 14(6): 14-23.

Lamy, P. P. 1980. *Prescribing for the elderly*. Littleton, MA: PSG Publishing.

Lamy, P. P. 1984. Hazards of drug use in the elderly:

Commonsense measures to reduce them. *Postgraduate Medicine*, 76(1): 50-53, 56-57, 60-61.

Lamy, P. P. 1986. The elderly and drug interactions. *Journal of the American Geriatrics Society*, 34(8): 586-592.

Mathieson, A. 1986. Old people and drugs. *Nursing Times*, 82(2): 22-25.

Mead, R. A. 1985. Medication problems in elderly persons. *Comprehensive Therapy*, 11(1): 3-5.

Meyer, B. R., and Hirsch, B. E. 1990. Renal function and the care of the elderly. *Comprehensive Therapy*, 16(9): 30-37.

Montamat, S. C., Cusack, B. J., and Vestal, R. E. 1989. Management of drug therapy in the elderly. *Medical Intelligence*, 321(5): 303-309.

Morrow, D., Leirer, V., and Sheikh, J. 1988. Adherence and medication instructions: Review and recommendations. *Journal of the American Geriatrics Society*, 36: 1147-1160.

Nolan, L., and O'Malley, K. 1989. Adverse drug reactions in the elderly. *British Journal of Hospital Medicine*, 41(5): 452-457.

Norell, S. E. 1985. Memory and medication compliance. *Journal of Clinical and Hospital Pharmacy*, 10(1): 107-109.

O'Brien, J. G., and Kursch, J. E. 1987. "Healthy" prescribing for the elderly: How to minimize adverse drug effects and prevent "dementia in a bottle." *Postgraduate Medicine*, 82(6): 147-151, 154, 156-157.

Patton, L. L. 1985. Special considerations in drug therapy for elderly dental patients. *Special Care in Dentistry*, 5(1): 24-26.

Pucino, F., Beck, C. L., Seifert, R. L., Strommen, G. L., Sheldon, P. A., and Silbergleit, I. L. 1985. Pharmacogeriatrics. *Pharmacotherapy*, 5(6): 314-326.

Quinn, B. P., Applegate, W. B., Roberts, K., Collins, T., and Vanderzwaag, R. 1983. Knowledge and use of medications in a group of elderly individuals. *Journal of the Tennessee Medical Association*, 76(10): 647-649.

Raffoul, P. R. 1986. Drug misuse among older people: Focus for interdisciplinary efforts. *Health and Social Work, 11(3): 197-203.*

Roe, D. A. 1984. Therapeutic significance of drug-nutrient interactions in the elderly. *Pharmacological Reviews,* 36(2): 109S-122S.

Royal College of Physicians of London. 1984. Medication for the elderly: Recommendations of RCP working party. *Lancet*, 1(8371): 271-272.

Shimp, L. A., Ascione, F. J., Glazer, H. M., and Atwood, B. F. 1985. Potential medication-related problems in noninstitutionalized elderly. *Drug Intelligence and Clinical Pharmacology*, 19(10): 766-772.

Simonson, W. 1984. *Medications and the elderly: A guide for promoting proper use.* Rockville, MD: Aspen.

Swift, C. G. 1988. Prescribing in old age. *British Medical Journal*, 296(6626): 913-915.

Swift, C. J. 1990. Pharmacodynamics: Changes in homeostatic mechanisms, receptor and target organ sensitivity in the elderly. *British Medical Bulletin*, 46(1): 36-52.

Tregaskis, B. F., and Stevenson, I. H. 1990. Pharmacokinetics in old age. *British Medical Journal*, 46(1): 9-21.

Tsujimoto, G., Hashimoto, K., and Hoffman, B. B. 1989. Pharmacokinetic and pharmacodynamic principles of drug therapy in old age, Part 1. *International Journal of Clinical Pharmacology, Therapy, and Toxicology*, 27(1): 13-26.

Wade, B., and Bowling, A. 1986. Appropriate use of drugs by elderly people. *Journal of Advanced Nursing*, 11(1): 47-55.

Weintraub, M. 1981. Intelligent noncompliance with special emphasis on the elderly. *Contemporary Pharmacy Practice*, 4(1): 8-11.

Wieman, H. M. 1986. Avoiding common pitfalls of geriatric prescribing. *Geriatrics*, 41(6): 81-82, 85-86, 89.

Woodhouse, K. W., and James, O. F. W. 1990. Hepatic drug metabolism and ageing. *British Medical Bulletin*, 46(1): 22-35.

CHAPTER **17**

Exercise, Health, and Aging

$\mathbf{R}$ecently a number of research reports have indicated that moderate exercise can retard the effects of aging (Brown, Cundiff, and Thompson, 1989; Kaplan, 1987; Ostrow, 1984; Thomas, 1981; Shephard, 1978). There are also some indications that exercise may be able to reverse some age-related effects (Ostrow, 1984). The role of physical activity in the aging process has interested humans since as early as 3000 B.C. In the ancient Middle East and China, scholars attempted to explain how balanced physical and mental activity might influence longevity and life expectancy (Heyden and Fodor, 1988).

In ancient Greece, Hippocrates was the first to note that regular exercise might retard the aging process (Sager, 1983). Plato believed that moderate exercise could help preserve the body and mind by ordering "the particles and affections which are wandering about the body." Despite these early thoughts on the subject, throughout much of history the tendency has been to think that age-related changes were inevitable and uncontrollable.

In contemporary Western society, the relationship between aging and exercise is typically characterized as inverse. That is, with aging there is a tendency to do less exercise. This decline may be related to cultural values that urge us to "slow down," "act our age," and "take it easy." Until recently many people felt that this decline in activity was due to biological changes associated with aging that naturally limited our ability to exercise. Bortz (1982), however, has called attention to the similarities between the physiological changes that occur with aging and the response that occurs in people of any age when they are subjected to periods of prolonged inactivity.

Today, it is perhaps more important than ever to distinguish the activity limitations imposed by age from those that are the products of our individual and societal experiences. This approach may allow us to learn how to use fitness-promoting exercise to delay age-associated declines in body function (Rowe and Kahn, 1987). Yet, efforts to study exercise and aging are beset by difficulties in interpretation. Longitudinal studies are scarce. Most research has been cross-sectional in nature, comparing people of different ages at one point in time. Such studies may be flawed if they fail to take into account cohort and/or period effects on health status.

The improved status of older cohorts may be due to the elimination of weaker individuals by death and disease and to the fact that volunteers for fitness tests often are healthier older people. This situation produces a homogeneity in older subjects not often found in other groups (Ostrow, 1984).

AGE-RELATED CHANGES: EXERCISE, WORK, AND ACTIVITY PATTERNS

Cardiopulmonary Changes

The heart muscle decreases in mass and contractility with age. Cardiac mass, however, is directly related to heart strength. This reduction in strength influences three major processes: (1) the duration of systole, (2) the volume of blood expelled from the ventricles, and (3) the blood pressure generated.

Decreased contractility of the heart muscle is probably due to infiltration by connective tissue as well as the formation of small scars. Because of these changes it takes longer to expel blood from the heart while at the same time allowing less time for filling. This in turn contributes to a decline in maximum heart output.

The amount of blood expelled from the heart is known as stroke volume. *Stroke volume* declines with age, but in most individuals it is generally adequate for carrying out mild work. However, the maximum stroke volume, which is necessary for heavier work, declines by 15 to 20 percent from early adulthood to old age. At the same time that maximum stroke volume and maximum heart rate

are declining, the resistance to the flow of blood through the arteries and arterioles is increasing. This increase in resistance is due to plaque formation in the vessels and the calcification of the medial layer of arterial vessels. The plaque provides physical resistance, and the changes in arterial structure limit expansion of the vessels during systole. This increased resistance to blood flow can raise the blood pressure 10 to 40 mm Hg at systole and 5 to 10 mm Hg at diastole.

The *vital capacity* of the lungs declines 40 to 50 percent as we age. This may be due to (1) lung tissue becoming less elastic, (2) the thoracic cage becoming stiffer, (3) decreased lung surface, and (4) decline in alveolar function. The total surface area of the lung decreases from 80 to 60 square meters (Smith and Gilligan, 1984). Alveolar decline may be the result of loss of elasticity, which results in the closure of some air sacs and the reduction or cessation of capillary blood flow to some alveoli.

As a result of these pulmonary changes coupled with the decreasing strength and efficiency of heart muscle, maximum consumption of oxygen at the peak all-out effort declines with age. Bortz (1982) and Smith and Gilligan (1984) suggest a rate of decline of close to 10 percent a decade. Such a decline can lead to a dramatic change in the activity pattern of an older person.

Changes in Muscular Strength

Skeletal muscle mass also declines with age. Calloway and Zannie (1980) suggest that the rate of decline after age 25 is 2 to 3 percent per decade. Smith and Gilligan (1984) found a muscle mass decline of 20 to 25 percent with age that is accompanied by a parallel decline in strength. Muscle mass declines include a reduction in both the number and the size of muscle fibers.

Grip strength and grip strength endurance have been studied extensively and show a decline with age after peaking between 20 and 24 years. The decline is most dramatic after age 60. Harris (1977) found that the greatest loss of strength with age occurs in the leg and trunk muscles, an observation with significant implications for the mobility of elderly individuals.

Changes in Muscular Flexibility

A gradual loss in the range of joint motion has been observed with age. It may be due to shortening of muscles; calcification of cartilage, ligaments, and tendons; and the prevalence of arthritic conditions. Joint flexibility is important for the efficient performance of ordinary, everyday activities. A joint may lose a considerable range of motion through inactivity or degenerative disease, although Adrian (1981) suggests that there is no evidence to show that biological aging causes decreased flexibility.

Changes in Neuromuscular Integrity

Aging brings a lengthening of rapid muscular reaction time. Nerve conduction velocity declines between 10 and 15 percent as we age and leads to increased reaction time for muscle contraction. This situation may reflect (1) chemical and structural change at the synapse, (2) change in the nerve fiber itself, and (3) changes in muscle fiber. It is also probable that the central nervous system contributes to the change in neuromuscular efficiency. Fast-twitch muscle fibers needed for quick all-out contractions show greater changes with age than slow-twitch fibers. Slow-twitch fibers are significant for prolonged endurance activity. This differential change may be related to noticeable declines in quick reactions and to the more gradual declines observed for muscular endurance. Neuromuscular efficiency and weakness may be influenced more by disease than by age.

Bone Strength and Integrity

Loss of bone mass is a universal characteristic of aging. It starts earlier in women – around age 35 – and progresses at a more rapid rate of up to 2 percent per year. Men are also affected, but the process starts at age 50 and proceeds at a rate of only 0.5 percent per year. The impact of bone mass loss is far greater in women, and by age 75 fractures related to osteoporosis are widespread in this group.

Fractures related to osteoporosis are significant for the elderly population in general. It is estimated that osteoporosis is responsible for 1.3 million fractures a year and that the costs in health care are between $3 and $6 billion a year. For 15 to 30 percent of those affected, the condition is fatal; others suffer pain and deformity, as well as limitation of mobility with a possible loss of independence.

THE EFFECTS OF EXERCISE ON THE ELDERLY

Cardiopulmonary and Cardiovascular Changes

Most of the research on endurance-type training among the elderly suggests that regular participation improves cardiopulmonary efficiency (Sidney, 1981). The evidence for this generalization is based on epidemiological and experimental research. Devries (1970) found that regardless of prior habits of exercise the maximum oxygen consumption (VO_2) increases 10 to 30 percent with a program of aerobic exercise. It has also been noted that aerobic exercise lowers the blood pressure 5 to 10 mm Hg, although it has been suggested that this decrease is due to reduction in anxiety experienced by participants in programmed exercise (Buccola and Stone, 1975). Hagberg (1989) reports that endurance exercise training produces reductions in blood pressure in hypertensives 60 to 69 years old comparable to those it produces in younger individuals.

Muscle Strength and Endurance

Moritani (1981) did experiments with the elderly that showed increases in strength and significant improvement in muscle function through training after a one-year aerobic program. Sidney, Shepherd, and Hamson (1977) showed that there was a 10 percent increase in lean body mass and muscular strength. In another study, Sidney (1977) also observed that a one-year walking program led to a 17 percent decrease in skinfold fat.

With respect to muscular strength and endurance, the trainability of older people does not apparently differ from that of younger people, if the age groups are compared on a percentage-of-change basis (Moritani, 1981). In a study of 60- to 72-year-old males, Frontera and colleagues (1988) found sizable increases in both the size and the strength of muscles after a twelve-week program of strength training. Strength training has the potential to improve the quality of life of older people because a number of basic daily tasks, such as climbing stairs and shopping, depend on muscular strength. Serfass (1980) found that by the sixth decade, strength gains through training are independent of gender.

Flexibility Change

Joint flexibility is modifiable through training across age groups. Munns (1981) at the Biogerontology Laboratory of the University of Wisconsin studied 40 participants age 65 to 88 years who took part in an exercise dance program. She tested six body sites with a *Leighton flexometer* and noted a statistically significant change at all the sites.

In a study of 20 participants who averaged 72 years of age, Munns found an increased range of motion in all joints after a twelve-week flexibility program. The percentage increases for each joint were as follows: neck, 28 percent; wrists, 13 percent; shoulder, 8 percent; knees, 12 percent; ankles, 48 percent; and hips and back, 27 percent.

Neuromuscular Changes

After extensive studies on exercise and neuromuscular change, Spirduso (1980) makes the following propositions. Exercise:

1. helps greater synchronization of motor units and reduces random firing of neurons.
2. postpones structural changes in nerve cells and the loss of dendrites in the aging brain (enhances blood flow to various parts of the brain).
3. maintains hormonal regulator systems that control to some extent the integrity of the nervous system.
4. delays reductions with age of oxidative capacities of the brain and in neurotransmitter substances.
5. retards the age-related decline in fast-twitch muscle fiber.

Bone Loss and Exercise

When stress is placed on bone through weight-bearing exercise, calcium content and resistance to fracture are increased (Smith and Raab, 1984; Dalsky, 1988). In a three-year, low-intensity exercise program for the elderly, Smith and Redden (1976) noticed a 4.2 percent increase in bone mineral content among exercisers and a 2.5 percent decrease in the nonexercising members of the control group. Even in the very old, Smith, Redden, and Smith (1981) noticed some change. They studied 12 female nursing home residents, all in their eighties. Chair exercises were provided for 30 minutes, three times a week for a year. The bone mineral content of the group increased 2.29 percent, while members of the control group lost 3.28 percent.

Glucose Tolerance, Lipoproteins, and Exercise

Exercise can lead to an improvement in glucose tolerance in the elderly diet, fat reduction, and/or endurance training. Krotkiewski (1983) found that increased sensitivity to insulin after exercise was related to the enhanced capacity of muscles to take up and store glucose. Changes in diet and levels of physical activity also have a synergistic effect. Exercise combined with a hypocaloric or reduced-fat diet can improve both carbohydrate and fat metabolism (O'Dea, 1984; Wood, Stefancik, and Dreon, 1988). Physical exercise and body composition are both important contributors to age-related alterations in lipoproteins. Studies show that improvement in lipoprotein ratios did not occur until individuals lost body weight and improved physical training (Seals, 1984).

Psychological Effects

The psychological evaluation of test groups is difficult among the elderly because of the desire of many participants to please the investigator, which affects reported or perceived gains. Observed changes may also be due to increased personal and medical attention rather than to exercise itself (Thomas, 1979).

Some investigators have reported that exercise reduces anxiety and relieves tension (Ostrow, 1984). Relief of stress could result from the fact that exercise does at least one of the following:

1. Retards possibly harmful chemicals released as part of the stress response.
2. Speeds up the metabolism of chemicals released as a stress response.
3. Helps release chemicals that lift depression.

A recent Purdue study of men between 40 and 60 years of age indicates that those who jogged three times a week had less depression than a sedentary control group (Ostrow, 1984).

Regular exercise may lead to changes in body image as well as in attitude toward life. It is also possible that those who attempt an exercise program and fail may suffer negatively in terms of both body image and attitude. When exercise is done as part of a group, the social aspect of group activity may help overcome loneliness while also giving a sense of belonging and worth. Blumenthal, Schocken, Needles, and Hindle (1982) noted improved mood and greater feelings of satisfaction in 40 to 50 percent of the elderly participants in an eleven-week stationary bicycle study. Buccola and Stone (1975) reported greater feelings of self-sufficiency after a fourteen-week program of walking and jogging. Figure 17.1 provides a checklist of possible benefits resulting from exercise.

Physical Effects

_____ decreased heart rate

_____ strengthened heart muscle

_____ increased oxygen transport capacity

_____ lowered blood pressure

_____ improved pulmonary function

_____ improved systemic circulation

_____ increased collateral circulation

_____ increased cardiac reserve

_____ increased HDLs

_____ decreased triglycerides

_____ decreased cholesterol

_____ improved muscle tone

_____ improved muscle flexibility

_____ improved muscle coordination

_____ increased muscle mass

_____ increased muscle strength

_____ stimulation of bone growth

_____ increased bone mass

_____ retarded development of osteoporosis

_____ increased joint flexibility and range of motion

_____ altered body composition (more muscle and less fat)

_____ improved glucose tolerance

_____ improved insulin sensitivity

_____ improved gastrointestinal mobility

Psychological Effects

_____ increased sense of well-being

_____ better mental outlook

_____ increased competence and confidence

_____ improved psychomotor reaction time

_____ help in overcoming depression

_____ mood elevation

_____ decreased anxiety

_____ reduced fatigue

_____ alleviation of loneliness

FIGURE 17.1   Checklist of possible benefits of exercise

EXERCISE PROGRAMS FOR THE ELDERLY

It would appear from the research evidence that exercise programs for the elderly can be useful for improving physical and psychological health. However, the perceptions that older people have about the role of physical activity may affect implementa-tion of more widespread programs. Conrad (1976) found that older people held the following views about physical activity:

1. The need for physical activity decreases with age.
2. Exercise is dangerous for the elderly.
3. Light, sporadic exercise is beneficial to health.
4. Their own personal physical abilities are limited.

Those over age 60 tended to overestimate the time spent at heavy physical activity. Their perception at all levels of heart rate was two to three times higher than in younger people (Conrad, 1976). It also appears that physical training alters perceived exertion at any given workload. This perception phenomenon surely influences many older people attempting to maintain an appropriate level of physical activity (Weinstein, 1988).

Medical Evaluation Prior to Exercise

It is wise to consult a physician before starting an exercise program. Radeheffer (1984) has estimated that by age 70, more than one-half of men in the United States have some form of coronary artery disease, and the case for women is only a little less significant. It is estimated that about one-in-five of those screened for exercise programs are rejected for entry.

A medical evaluation should include a detailed medical history and a basic physical examination. Although a *stress test* is not mandatory, it is useful for detecting asymptomatic coronary artery disease. Studies indicate that the stress test is more valid in elderly groups than in younger ones (Morse and Smith, 1981). Even if the medical indication clears an individual for exercise, however, knowledge of coronary artery disease symptoms would be helpful. Fair, Rosenaur, and Thurston (1969) believe that the elderly should be made aware of such symptoms as a precautionary measure.

Aerobic Exercise

Aerobic exercise is exercise that strengthens the cardiopulmonary system. It includes jogging, cycling, skiing, swimming, brisk walking, dancing, and circuit training. Aerobic exercise aims to place a moderate stress on the heart in order to strengthen this muscle. As the heart becomes stronger, the rest of the system will operate more efficiently.

In order for the stress on the heart to be beneficial, it should result in a heart rate that equals 60 to 90 percent of the maximum heart rate. In order to calculate the maximum heart rate for a given age, the following formula is used:

$$220 - \text{Age} \times (60\% \text{ to } 90\%^*) = \text{target rate}$$
$$\text{(in heart beats/minute)}$$

*depending on what percentage of maximum heart rate it is desired to attain

For example, if one is 50 years of age, the target rate at the 60 percent level is 102 heart beats/minute (bpm) ($220 - 50 \times 0.60$) and at the 90 percent level is 153 heart beats/minute ($220 - 50 \times 0.90$). It is suggested that 100 beats per minute be the lowest level targeted because we have little research on the effects of a target rate under 100 bpm. It is important to remember that a 65-year-old requires less activity than a 40-year-old to reach a targeted maximum (see Table 17.1).

Sedentary individuals should move into an exercise program slowly. This will avoid physical injury to a muscle or joint and hopefully encourage continued participation. For a program to be helpful, it should consist of three sessions per week for 15 to 60 minutes. The duration of a session is determined by the intensity of the activity. If one is operating at 60 percent of maximum, the duration should be one hour, but if operation is 90 percent of maximum, 15 minutes would suffice. Warm-up and cool-down periods of five minutes each are also helpful in the avoidance of trauma. These sessions can consist of stretching, light calisthenics, or slow walking.

TABLE 17.1 Target heart rate zones (all heart rates are for 1 minute)

Age	Level I (50-60% MHR)	Level II (60-70% MHR)	Level III (70-85% MHR)
20-29	102-120	120-150	150-168
30-39	96-114	114-144	144-162
40-49	90-108	108-138	138-156
50-59	86-102	102-126	126-144
60-69	78-96	96-120	120-132
70 and older	72-90	90-108	108-126

Note: Beginners who have been inactive for some time can exercise at 50 to 60 percent of their maximum heart rate (MHR). Most people can tolerate this comfortably for 20 to 30 minutes. Beginners who have been active can exercise at 60 to 70 percent of their maximum heart rate. If you are reasonably fit, exercise at 70 to 85 percent of your maximum heart rate.

Circuit Training as Aerobic Exercise

Weight lifting does not qualify as aerobic exercise. Because of the longer rests between exercise and the smaller number of repetitions, it does not maintain the heart beat at targeted maximum long enough. However, circuit training, a modified form of light weight lifting, does qualify as aerobic exercise.

Circuit training consists of 20 to 40 minutes of lifting relatively light weights for 10 to 20 repetitions per station or exercise. The rest between exercises is about 15 seconds; thus, the heart beat does not fall below the targeted maximum. Circuit training, though certainly less aerobic than jogging, can result in a VO_2 increase of 5 to 8 percent (Gettman and Pollack, 1981). It can be used as a beneficial supplement to heavier aerobics or for those with locomotor problems. In addition to its aerobic benefits, circuit training helps with muscle strength and flexibility.

The Effects of Aerobics

Epidemiological and clinical evidence suggests that aerobics can inhibit the progression of coronary artery disease. Although the evidence for this is sub-stantial, it is not absolute (Thomas, 1979). Exercise itself is valuable physiologically (see Table 17.2), but it also affects other risk factors such as lipid level and weight. Aerobic exercise also has the following possible benefits:

1. Lowers blood pressure in hypertensives.
2. Reduces weight (see Table 17.3).
3. Improves glucose tolerance in diabetics.
4. Increases the high-density lipoproteins (HDLs).
5. Reduces the tendency of the blood to clot.
6. Encourages the development of a more health-conscious life-style (Thomas, 1981).

TABLE 17.2 Effects of heavy exercise

	Resting	Heavy exercise
Cardiac output	5 liters/min.	35 liters/min.
Heart rate	75 beats/min.	195 beats/min.
Ventilation	8 liters air/min.	16 liters air/min.
Oxygen utilization	0.25 liter/min.	5 liters/min.
Systolic pressure	120 mm	180 mm
Diastolic pressure	80 mm	85 mm

Note: Heavy exercise includes running, jogging, rowing, skiing, cycling, and brisk walking (4 mph).

TABLE 17.3 Approximate number of calories burned per minute

Activity	Weight		
	120 lb.	160 lb.	200 lb.
Canoeing	2.5	3	4
Cycling	5.5	7	9
Fishing	3.5	4.5	5.5
Hiking (no load)	6.5	8.5	11
Running (8 min./mi.)	11.5	15	18
Skiing, cross-country	7.5	10	12.5
Skiing, downhill	6	8	10
Snowshoeing	9	12.5	15
Swimming (crawl)	7	9	11.5
Walking	4	5.5	7
Weight training	10	13	16.5

Source: Adapted from F. I. Katch and W. D. McArdle, *Nutrition, Weight Control, and Exercise,* 1977, Appendix B.

Low-Intensity Exercise

Low-intensity exercises are those that have little effect on the cardiopulmonary system. They include light calisthenics, light walking, golfing, bowling, fishing, and weight lifting. These kinds of exercise, however, help in weight control and bone demineralization as well as muscle strength and flexibility.

Many myths surround the concepts of exercise and conditioning. Eight of them are listed in Table 17.4. For the elderly, these myths can be a source of anxiety and can prevent elderly persons from participating in an appropriate exercise program.

OBESITY AND WEIGHT CONTROL AMONG THE ELDERLY

Determining whether an individual is overweight or obese is more difficult than it would seem. By one definition, obesity is present when the accumulation of fat in body tissue is equal to or more than 20

TABLE 17.4 Myths about exercise and conditioning

Myth	Fact
Muscle will turn to fat if you stop exercising.	Muscle itself does not turn to fat, but if unused it atrophies. Many people who stop exercising gain weight.
Strenuous exercise is bad for your heart.	Exercised hearts grow more muscular and stronger, which makes them more efficient.
Avoid fluids when exercising.	Exercising causes sweating, and this lost water must be replaced to avoid dehydration.
Heavy sweating is a way to lose weight.	The loss is only temporary and should be replaced promptly to avoid harm.
The body needs extra protein to make muscle grow faster.	A normal, balanced diet is all that is needed for muscle growth and repair. The body does not store excess amino acids.
Women who exercise regularly lose femininity.	Women who exercise regularly may become slimmer and more graceful. Bulging, masculine muscles do not develop.
Eating a candy bar before exercising will give you extra energy.	The energy used in exercise is already stored in the muscles. The candy would not be digested, absorbed, and assimilated fast enough to be used for exercise.
Exercise is dangerous for older people.	In the absences of severe pathology, exercise can improve the strength, flexibility, and endurance of people at all ages.

percent of the body weight in males and 30 percent in females. However, one can be overweight without being fat, with the excess weight being muscle, as is seen, for example, in football players and weightlifters.

Diagnosing obesity poses at least as many problems as defining it. Appearance is often used, but does not differentiate between fat, muscle, and water accumulation. Weight and height tables are difficult to use with the elderly because of their lessened physical stature. These tables have recently come under criticism for persons of all ages because they tend to underestimate ideal weight by as much as 20 percent even when body build is controlled for (Kart and Metress, 1984). X-rays are hazardous and expensive, and flotation techniques are impractical for most people. An accurate approach in the determination of obesity involves the use of skinfold measurements, although the elderly present special problems for this technique because of age-related skin changes. Triceps skinfold thickness is a measure of subcutaneous fat and is considered an index of the body's energy stores. Precision in measurement is absolutely necessary. In addition, as with weight in general, measurements must be evaluated in terms of actual age, height, and even the theoretically correct weight for a given age.

Estimates of obesity in the general U.S. population vary from 25 to 45 percent. Data on older adults are available from the Ten-State Nutrition Survey (U.S. Department of Health, Education, and Welfare, 1975). Older black women had the highest prevalence of obesity – over 45 percent in the 45- to 60-year-old group. More than one-third of all white women aged 55 to 65 years in the survey were defined as obese. Among the elderly, the lowest prevalence of obesity was found in black males. Data from the Health and Nutrition Examination Survey (HANES) show a similar pattern (National Center for Health Statistics, 1974). In both studies, low income was associated with a higher incidence of obesity.

Some obesity is juvenile in onset. Overeating in childhood may give rise to fat tissue containing large numbers of fat cells. One hypothesis is that an excess of fat cells makes it difficult to keep weight off because these cells must be depleted before a normal weight can be reached. However, a number of researchers have challenged the methodological basis of this hypothesis (Salans, Cushman, and Weismann, 1973).

Adult-onset obesity appears in the middle years of adulthood and usually has its origin in overeat-ing, ignorance of proper nutrition, and reduced activity. Metabolic problems account for only a small proportion (perhaps 2 percent) of all obesity in adulthood.

Obesity is reported as adversely affecting almost every system of the body. Life expectancy is lower and morbidity rates are higher. High blood pressure, gallbladder problems, coronary heart disease, diabetes, and postsurgical complications are more prevalent among the obese. However, Mann (1971) is not sure that obesity in itself is bad. Becoming obese through diminished activity and increased consumption of refined sugar and fats is another matter. Mann states that the effect of obesity alone as a predictor of heart disease is very small and of borderline statistical significance. Recent research by Keys (1980a, 1980b) also tends to support a less negative assessment of the effects of being overweight.

The elderly have a special problem of weight control. Busse (1978) estimates that basic metabolism declines 16 percent between 20 and 70 years of age, necessitating a decrease in caloric intake of approximately one-third. Ahrens (1970) calculated a per-decade decline of 43 calories/day in the requirements for males from age 25 on and a per-decade decline of 27 calories/day for females from age 25 on. It is likely that this change is due to alterations in basal metabolism, body composition, and activities related to aging per se. In addition to basic metabolic decline, many of the elderly are subject to additional stresses that contribute to obesity, including grief, economic insecurity, and social isolation, to name a few. In such cases, social-psychological counseling, support, and contact with others may be more important in dealing with the problem of obesity than nutrition education or medical aid.

Advertising encourages eating in general and heavily emphasizes sugar and snack foods that can contribute to caloric imbalance. Affluence allows us to eat for entertainment and pleasure rather than just for subsistence. At the same time, we can afford labor-saving devices that let us reduce our exertion of energy. Modern processing allows us to eat low-bulk foods that are sweet and highly refined, simply for their greater palatability. Paradoxically, impoverished people may become obese because cost forces them to eat high-calorie foods, which are generally cheaper than nutritionally protective foods.

What available weight control methods are functional for the elderly? Logically, reduced intake of food along with increased activity goes a long way in controlling weight. The elderly (like everybody else) must be educated to moderation in these matters. Realistic goals should be established, meals should not be skipped, and plateaus in weight loss must be anticipated. It is also wise to avoid eating out because little control over food preparation can be exerted and the social atmosphere is conducive to overeating. A reduction of about 500 calories a day can result in the loss of one pound a week. Some people have found a pattern of one day on diet and one day off to be successful, especially for weight maintenance.

Crash diets, including fasting and novelty diets, can be harmful and should be avoided. Real medical problems may be aggravated or potentiated by such diets. Dietary regulation with drugs should be approached with caution and medical supervision. Even under supervision, the usefulness of so-called diet pills is limited, and tolerance can develop, necessitating an increased dose. Initial success in weight loss is often nullified by a rebound effect that finds the individual eating more than before to compensate for feelings of deprivation.

In the elderly, drugs present special problems for weight loss because of interaction with other medications and potential errors of dose and timing. Liquid protein formulations designed for the extremely obese (50 pounds overweight) should probably be avoided. Though reactions vary individually, these formulas can be extremely dangerous. Over 40 deaths, most often related to calcium and potassium imbalances, have been associated with their use (Lantigua, Amatruda, Biddle, Forbes, and Lockwood, 1980).

Increased activity, including exercise, should be a part of any dietary plan, though age and the existence of chronic disease or disability must be taken into account. Strenuous activity can burn calories, decrease appetite, raise resting metabolism, and increase muscular efficiency and tone (see Table 17.5). The psychological lift, sense of achievement, improved self-image, and confidence many of the elderly get from participation in activity and exercise programs cannot be overlooked. Positive aspects of exercise carry over into daily activities related to psychosocial well-being, eating habits, and overall health maintenance.

TABLE 17.5 Using calories

	Calorie content	Average time needed to burn calories by activity (minutes)				
		Recline	Walk	Bicycle	Run	Swim
Apple, 1 large	100	66	28	16	5	8
Bacon, 2 strips	96	64	27	16	5	8
Beer, 1 glass	115	76	32	19	6	9
Bread/butter	78	60	15	10	4	6
Cookie, plain	15	12	3	2	1	1
Doughnut, 1 medium	125	96	24	15	4	8
Hamburger/bun	350	233	100	58	19	30
Orange juice	120	92	23	15	6	9
Potato chips, 10	115	76	32	19	6	9

LIFELONG PHYSICAL ACTIVITY AND AGING

It is apparent that aerobic exercise can have both preventive and rehabilitative effects with respect to age associated and degenerative changes (Kaplan, 1987). We are entering an era of research and knowledge in which it behooves us to develop lifelong programs of physical activity. The development of such programs must start in our school years and continue throughout life.

Recently, Paffenbarger, Hyde, Wing, and Hsieh (1986) released the results of a large study of Harvard University alumni. Almost 17,000 males who graduated between 1916 and 1950 were followed up to 1978. The findings have interesting implications for programs of lifelong physical activity. These were:

1. Men who walked 9 miles per week had a 21 percent lower risk of mortality.
2. Men who exercised strenuously for 6 to 8 hours per week (cycling) had a 50 percent lower mortality risk.
3. Extremists – those who used more than 3,500 calories per week at such things as full-court basketball and squash – had a higher mortality risk.

Among athletes, he found that the risk was higher for those who either were too active or completely ceased activity. They also found that those men who had gained 15 pounds since graduation lived longer than those who had lost considerable weight. In Paffenberger's opinion, if we eliminated cancer, the years gained per person would be the same as those gained by lifelong exercise. He feels that a lifelong exercise program is comparable to a major medical breakthrough in preventing or curing disease.

STUDY QUESTIONS

1. Identify the major age-related changes associated with the following:
   a. cardiopulmonary function
   b. muscular strength and endurance
   c. muscular flexibility
   d. neuromuscular integrity
   e. bone strength and integrity
2. Identify the major biological and psychological effects that an exercise program can have on the elderly. How are individual perceptions of the role of exercise and exertion significant in the implementation of exercise programs for the elderly?
3. What are the nature and role of a medical examination consultation prior to embarking on an exercise program?
4. Differentiate aerobic and low-intensity exercise. What are some basic principles necessary to consider in the development of aerobic programs for the elderly? How do you calculate the maximum heart rate for reference in aerobic training programs?
5. What is circuit training and what is its significance for the elderly? What are some of the major effects of aerobic training on the individual?
6. In what ways is low-intensity exercise valuable to the individual?
7. Why is an accurate diagnosis of obesity so difficult? Differentiate juvenile and adult-onset obesity.
8. Why does Mann disagree with the idea that obesity in itself is bad? Is obesity a special problem for the elderly?
9. List some important principles of weight control for the elderly.
10. How does metabolism change with age? In what ways can strenuous activity affect metabolism?
11. What were some of the major results of Paffenbarger's work that are significant for exercise and longevity? According to Paffenbarger, what is the significance of a lifelong exercise program?

BIBLIOGRAPHY

Adrian, M. J. 1981. Flexibility in the aging adult. In E. L. Smith and R. C. Serfass (Eds.), *Exercise and aging.* Hillside, NJ: Enslow.

Ahrens, R. A. 1970. *Nutrition for health.* Belmont, CA: Wadsworth.

Blumenthal, J. A., Schocken, D. D., Needels, T. L., and Hindle, P. 1982. Psychological and physiological effects of physical conditioning in the elderly. *Journal of Psychosomatic Research*, 26: 505-510.

Bortz, W. M. 1982. Disuse and aging. *Journal of the American Medical Association*, 148: 1203-1208.

Brown, S. P., Cundiff, D. E., and Thompson, W. R. 1989. Implications for fitness programming: The geriatric population. *Journal of Physical Education Recreation and Dance*, 60: 18-23.

Buccola, V. A., and Stone, W. J. 1975. Effect of jogging and cycling programs on physiological and personality variables in aged men. *The Research Quarterly*, 46: 134-139.

Busse, E. W. 1978. How mind, body and environment influence nutrition in the elderly. *Postgraduate Nutrition*, 63(3): 118-122, 125.

Calloway, D. H., and Zannie, E. 1980. Energy requirements of elderly men. *American Journal of Clinical Nutrition*, 32: 2088-2092.

Conrad, C. C. 1976. When you're young at heart. In *Aging*. Washington, DC: U.S. Department of Health, Education and Welfare, Administration on Aging.

Dalsky, G. P. 1988. Weight-bearing exercise training and lumbar bone mineral content in post-menopausal women. *Annals of Internal Medicine*, 108: 824-828.

Devries, H. A. 1970. Physiological effects of an exercise training regimen upon men aged 52 to 88. *Journal of Gerontology*, 25: 325-336.

Fair, J., Rosenaur, J., and Thurston, E. 1969. Exercise management. *Nurse Practitioner*, 4: 13-15, 17-18.

Frontera, W. R., Meredith, C. N., O'Reilly, K. P., Knuttgen, H. G., and Evans, W. J. 1988. Strength conditioning in older men. *Journal of Applied Physiology*, 64: 1038-1044.

Gettman, L. R., and Pollack, M. 1981. Circuit weight training: A critical review of its physiological benefits. *The Physician and Sports Medicine*, 9: 44-60.

Hagberg, J. M. 1989. Exercise, fitness, hypertension. In *Proceedings of the International Congress of exercise, fitness and health*. Champaign, IL: Human Kinetics Press.

Harris, R. 1977. Fitness and the aging process. In R. Harris and L. J. Finkel (Eds.), *Guide to fitness after 50*. New York: Plenum Press.

Heyden, S., and Fodor, G. J. 1988. Does regular exercise prolong life expectancy? *Sports Medicine*, 6: 63-71.

Kaplan, G. A 1987. Mortality among the elderly in the Alameda County study. *American Journal of Public Health*, 7: 307-312.

Kart, C., and Metress, S. 1984. *Nutrition, the aged and society*. Englewood Cliffs, NJ: Prentice-Hall.

Keys, A. 1980a. Alpha lipoprotein. *Lancet*, 2: 603-606.

Keys, A. 1980b. Overweight, obesity, coronary heart disease, and mortality. *Nutrition Today*, 15(4): 16-22.

Krotkiewski, M. 1983. Physical training in the prophylaxis and the treatment of obesity, hypertension and diabetes. *Scandanavian Journal of Rehabilitation*, 9(Suppl.): 55-70.

Lantigua, R., Amatruda, J. M., Biddle, T. L., Forbes, G. B., and Lockwood, D. H. 1980. Cardiac arrythmias associated with a liquid protein diet for the treatment of obesity. *New England Journal of Medicine*, 303: 735-738.

Mann, G. V. 1971. The obesity spook. *American Journal of Public Health*, 61: 1491-1498.

Morey, M. C., et al. 1989. Evaluation of a supervised exercise program in a geriatric population. *Journal of the American Geriatrics Society*, 37: 348-354.

Moritani, T. 1981. Training adaptations in the muscles of older men. In E. L. Smith and R. S. Serfass (Eds.), *Exercise and aging*. Hillside, NJ: Enslow.

Morse, C. E., and Smith, E. L. 1981. Physical activity programming for the aged. In E. L. Smith and R. C. Serfass (Eds.), *Exercise and aging*, Hillside, NJ: Enslow.

Munns, K. 1981. Effects of exercise on the range of joint motion in elderly subjects. In E. L. Smith and R. C. Serfass (Eds.), *Exercise and aging*. Hillside, NJ: Enslow.

National Center for Health Statistics. 1974. *First health and nutrition survey, United States, 1971-1972*. Washington, DC: U.S. Department of Health, Education and Welfare.

O'Dea, K. 1984. Marked improvement in carbohydrate and lipid metabolism in diabetic Australian Aborigines after temporary reversion to traditional lifestyle. *Diabetes*, 33: 596-603.

Ostrow, A. C. 1984. *Physical activity and the older adult*. Princeton, NJ: Princeton Book Company.

Paffenbarger, R. S., Hyde, R. T., Wing, A. L., and Hsieh, C. 1986. Physical activity, all cause mortality and longevity of college alumni. *New England Journal of Medicine*, 314(10): 605-613.

Radeheffer, R. J. 1984. Exercise cardiac is maintained with advancing age in healthy human subjects. *Circulation*, 69: 203-213.

Rowe, J. W., and Kahn, R. L. 1987 Human aging: Usual and successful. *Science*, 237: 143-149.

Sager, K. 1983. Senior fitness – for the health of it. *The Physician and Sports Medicine*, 11: 3-36.

Salans, L. B., Cushman, S. W., and Weismann, R. E. 1973. Studies of human adipose tissue: Adipose cell life and number in nonobese and obese patients. *Journal of Clinical Investigation*, 52: 929-941.

Seals, D. R. 1984. Endurance training in older men and women II: Cardiovascular responses to exercise. *Journal of Applied Physiology*, 57: 1024-1029.

Serfass, R. C. 1980. Physical exercise and the elderly. In G. A. Still (Ed.), *Encyclopedia of physical education, fitness and sports*. Salt Lake City, UT: Brighton.

Shepherd, R. J. 1978. *Physical activity and aging*. Chicago: Yearbook Publishers.

Sidney, K. H. 1977. Activity patterns of elderly men and women. *Journal of Gerontology*, 32: 25-32.

Sidney, K. H. 1981. Cardiovascular benefits of physical activity in the exercising aged. In E. L. Smith and R. C. Serfass (Eds.), *Exercise and aging*. Hillside, NJ: Enslow.

Sidney, K. H., Shepherd, R. J., and Hamson, J. E. 1977. Endurance, training and body composition in the elderly. *American Journal of Clinical Nutrition*, 30: 326-333.

Smith, E. L., and Gilligan, G. 1984. Exercise sport and physical activity for the elderly: Principles and problems of programming. In B. McPherson (Ed.), *Sport and aging* (pp. 97-100). Champaign, IL: Human Kinetics Publications.

Smith, E., and Raab, D. 1984. Osteoporosis and physical activity. *Acta Medica Scandinavia*, 711: 149-156.

Smith, E., and Redden, W. 1976. Physical activity: A modality for bone accretion in the aged. *American Journal of Roentgenology*, 126: 1297.

Smith, E., Redden, W., and Smith, P. 1981. Physical activity and calcium modalities for bone mineral increases in aged women. *Medicine and Science in Sports and Exercise*, 13: 80-84.

Spirduso, W. W. 1980. Physical fitness, aging and psychomotor speed: A review. *Journal of Gerontology*, 35: 850-865.

Thomas, G. S. 1979. Physical activity and health: Epidemiologic and armed evidence and policy implications. *Preventive Medicine*, 8: 89-103.

Thomas, G. S. 1981. *Exercise and health: The evidence and the implications*. Cambridge, MA: Oelgeschlager, Gunn and Hain.

U.S. Department of Health, Education and Welfare. 1975. *Ten-state nutrition survey, 1968-70*. Washington, DC: Health Resources Administration.

Weinstein, L. B. 1988. Exercise: A beneficial activity for older adults. *Activities, adaptations, and aging*, 11 (1): 85-94.

Wood, P. D., Stefancik, M. L., and Dreon, D. L. 1988. Changes in plasma lipids and lipoproteins in overweight men during weight loss through dieting as compared with exercise. *New England Journal of Medicine*, 319: 1173-1179.

The Biologizing of Aging: Some Precautionary Notes

This book has sought to describe the biological bases of normal human aging and chronic disease for beginning students, undergraduate and graduate, of gerontology. In many respects, this is an encyclopedic task. To achieve this end, the book's focus has been single-minded – unidimensional, if you will. In many respects, we had no choice. The field of gerontology has seen such explosive growth in new knowledge and expertise in the last two decades that the idea of encompassing all of the biology, psychology, and sociology of aging and health in a single text has long since passed. Still, the intention of this book was *not* to take the view that the health status of older people could be understood through biological explanation and the biomedical model alone. Such a single-minded focus is antithetical to the field of gerontology and increases the danger that cultural, social structural, and psychological influences on the aging process

and the health status of older people will be ignored.

After all, gerontology, the systematic study of the aging process, is an interdisciplinary study. Its major elements are drawn from the natural and social sciences, but the humanities and arts, business, and education are also represented in the content of gerontology. Gerontology is both an academic discipline and a field of practice. In this regard gerontology is not a "disinterested science." For many gerontologists, understanding the aging process is not enough. They must also address the practical and immediate problems of old people. In 1909 a Vienna-born physician, I. L. Nascher, coined the term *geriatrics* to describe one subfield of gerontological practice, the medical care of the aging. In 1954 Clark Tibbitts, a pioneer in the modern scientific era of gerontology, introduced the term *social gerontology* to describe the study of the impact of social and sociocultural factors on the aging process. Tibbitts and others recognized that aging, even biological aging, does not occur in a vacuum. Rather, the aging process occurs in some social context – a social context that helps determine the meaning of aging as both an individual and a societal experience.

Some have characterized the single-minded focus represented in this text as reflecting a "biomedicalization of aging" (Estes and Binney, 1991). The biomedicalization of aging has been defined as describing both thinking about aging as a medical problem and the behavioral and policy consequences of thinking about aging in this way (Estes and Binney, 1991).

In this epilogue we refer more broadly to this single-minded focus as a "biologizing" of the aging process and offer some precautionary notes on this approach. Biomedicalization may be a component of the biologizing of aging. The fact is, however, that we biologize aging not just by thinking about aging as a medical problem but also by misattributing symptoms of medical and social problems to biological aging.

THE MEDICAL MODEL

As we have already indicated, a key contributor to this biologizing of aging is what is sometimes referred to as the medical or biomedical model. The concept of the medical model describes the basic paradigm that rules medical practice. Eliot Freidson (1988) employs the term "medical-intervention pattern" to describe what is meant here.

> The medical man is prone to see the patient's difficulty as a transitory technical problem that can be overcome by some physical or biochemical intervention which only the physician is qualified to perform. The assumption is that the patient can be cured and discharged. (pp. 132-133)

In this model, attention is aimed at obtaining a diagnosis of a condition and developing a treatment regimen for its cure. Efforts are almost always geared at identifying just one condition or dysfunction. Among the elderly in ill health, however, a single condition is unusual. More often, elderly patients have multiple conditions, including degenerative changes associated with biological aging and diseases associated with pathological aging. In addition, specific disease states may manifest themselves differently among the elderly than is the case among the young. These multiple changes along with age-based differences in symptom manifestation can lead to confusion in trying to diagnose accurately and to further difficulty in generating an appropriate treatment plan.

This confusion would occur even if the presence of disease, its diagnosis, and its treatment could be defined objectively. There is considerable evidence that such objectivity is a questionable assumption underlying the medical model, however (Wolinsky, 1988). Zola (1962, 1966) has demonstrated that the differing world views of patients and/or differences in their cultural backgrounds affected how they presented symptoms to attending physicians. For example, Irish patients tended to understate their symptoms, whereas Italians were more likely to generalize and even embellish theirs. Wolinsky (1988) summarizes the sociological principle in effect here:

> . . . the selection, salience, and presentation of symptoms are at least partially determined by sociocultural factors and conditioning. . . . If the symptoms of disease are socioculturally relative, then disease itself must be in part defined relative to sociocultural phenomena. (p. 77)

Even if symptoms of illness were presented in some objective fashion, there is a serious question about whether all physicians would or could identify the signs and/or presence of disease. As Wolinsky (1988) points out, although physicians are comparably trained, there is no uniform mechanical procedure for examining all patients or even all elderly patients. Some physicians routinely check blood pressure, pulse, and respiration during an examination or office visit; others do not. Also, diseases linked to sociocultural traits (obesity and hypertension among older black women or osteoporosis among elderly white women) may cue physician attention toward or away from particular diagnoses.

Kovar (1977) has addressed the fact that the medical model treats all older people as if they were representatives of a homogeneous grouping.

> The range in health status is just as great in this age group as in any other, even though the proportion of persons who have health problems increases with age and a minor health problem that might be quickly alleviated at younger ages tends to linger. Aging is a process that continues over the entire lifespan at differing rates among different persons. The rate of aging varies among populations and among individuals in the same population. It varies even within an individual because different body systems do not age at the same rate. (p. 9)

The World Health Organization defines *health* as "a state of complete physical, mental, and social well-being," not merely the absence of disease. This definition extends beyond biological considerations. To the extent that modern medicine has been concerned with "what went wrong" biologically, it has sacrificed recognition of the broader social and emotional elements that contribute to health. The case of 70-year-old Mr. Hernandez provides a useful example. After discharge from the hospital following cataract surgery, he went home to his inner-city project apartment, where he lived alone.

> When the public health nurse arrived a week later, she found him weak from hunger. The refrigerator was empty, and there were but a few cans of food in the cupboards. In addition, the apartment was dirty and cluttered with garbage and soiled clothes. The patient's limited eyesight and recent hospitalization had left him disoriented and unsure of himself in his own home. He was afraid to brave the stairs or elevator leading from his apartment to pick up his Social Security check in the mailbox, let alone to go shopping, do his laundry, or throw out the garbage. He could neither cook nor tend to his personal hygiene. And he had no friends or family near. (Luke, 1976, p. 26)

Although no one would challenge Mr. Hernandez's need for cataract surgery, many would debate whether he was healthier after medical intervention. Health care extends beyond the doors of the health care institution. Understanding the factors that contribute to or detract from health may be less dramatic than developing "miracle cures," but it is no less important. Until organized medicine shifts its focus and identifies those conditions that enable people to thrive rather than merely survive, older people like Mr. Hernandez will continue to be "doing better and feeling worse" (Daedulus, 1977).

In the United States there has been a general reduction in the incidence of infectious diseases and an increase in the importance of chronic conditions. Today, most health problems of middle-aged and older adults are not "transitory technical problems" (i.e., acute illnesses); rather, they are chronic conditions. In fact, when compared with younger age groups, middle-aged and older adults show lower rates of many acute conditions, including infective and parasitic conditions, respiratory conditions, conditions of the digestive system, and injuries (U.S. Bureau of the Census, 1985, Table 186).

The actual presence of a chronic condition is often less important to people than the impact the condition has on their ability to carry out usual activities. Chronic illness can be burdensome in terms of activity limitations, bed days, hospital days, and doctor visits. Arthritis and rheumatism are particularly interesting examples in this regard. Though accounting for relatively few hospital days, these conditions are responsible for about 16 percent of days spent in bed by older people, nearly as much as for heart disease, and about 6 percent of doctor visits, more than for cancer.

Still, as was pointed out earlier in this text, an indicator as important as actual medical status in predicting general emotional state and behavior in the elderly is self-assessment of health. This indicator is not prominent in the medical model, which defines health and illness almost solely in terms of physiological criteria. Nevertheless, data from the 1984 National Health Interview Survey, Supplement on Aging, show that the great majority of older people assess their health as either excellent, very good, or good. Further, among the aged, the more positive the self-report of health status, the greater the perceived control over health, and the more positive is a person's assessment of the job he or she is doing in taking care of his or her own health.

In this latter regard, it is important to remember that professional care constitutes the minority of health care provided to people today, regardless of age (see Kart and Dunkle, 1989, for some review of the self-health care literature). Self-evaluation of symptoms and self-treatment are the basic and predominant forms of primary health care. They represent efforts on the part of people to retain and/or take control of their health. As Cassedy (1977) has observed: ". . . wherever people have been able to obtain their own medicines, or have read books about hygiene, or have had relatives, neighbors, or travellers to suggest remedies, they have been ready in large numbers to rely on such sources and

on their own judgments rather than resort to physicians even with serious ailments."

Last (1963) has used the term "illness iceberg" to describe the fact that most symptoms do not lead to a medical consultation. This refers to individuals with severe symptoms that would likely respond to treatment as well as those with mild, unobtrusive symptoms not necessarily requiring medical intervention (Ingham and Miller, 1979; Morrell and Wale, 1976). Many who do have contact with medical care providers have treated their disorders themselves before seeking medical care from professionals (Williamson and Danaher, 1978). Even those who seek professional medical care and follow a prescribed treatment regimen often supplement this regimen with self-prescribed remedies (DeFriese and Woomert, 1983).

Nevertheless, the medical model does attempt to vest authority for health and illness in the physician. To the extent the model is successful, the patient gives up control over his or her own physical body to the physician. In addition, in many circumstances the physician is given the power to constrain or restrict the exercise of individual liberty through diagnosis and treatment that may require quarantine (e.g., for contagious diseases) and/or confinement (e.g., in cases of mental illness). Because the profession of medicine is autonomously regulated and licensed, there are often no higher authorities to appeal to in matters of medical decision making.

It is worth noting here that efforts to analyze health away from the medical model have a considerable history developed over the past forty years or so. For example, Parsons (1951, 1972, 1975) sought to define health in terms more consistent with American values and the organization of the U.S. social system. He defined health on the basis of a person's participation in the intricate social web of our society, as: "the state of optimum capacity of an individual for the performance of the roles and tasks for which he has been socialized" (1972). For

Parsons, illness becomes any reduction in an individual's capacity to perform the roles and tasks typically expected of him or her. Thus, Parsons was among the first to recognize that a key issue in health and aging is not the presence or absence of physiological malfunction but, rather, the retention or attrition of functional capacities.

ATTRIBUTION AND MISATTRIBUTION OF ILLNESS

Health is as much a subjective as an objective phenomenon. Individuals assess their health on the basis of various factors, including their own expectations about how people like themselves should feel. People experiencing changes in usual body functioning try to make sense of their experiences, often by hypothesizing about the possible causes of their symptoms. A central issue in most perceptions of causality is whether to attribute a given experience to internal or external states (Freedman, Sears, and Carlsmith, 1978). *External* attribution ascribes causality to anything external to the individual, such as the general environment, role constraints or role losses, stressful tasks being worked on, and so on. *Internal* causes include such factors as disease states, biological aging, personality, and mood and motivation (Freedman, Sears, and Carlsmith, 1978).

Potentially, the development of illness attribution and misattribution can be affected by many factors both internal and external to the individual. These include the perceived seriousness of symptoms, the extent of disruption of normal activities involved, the frequency and persistence of the symptoms, the amount of pain and discomfort to which a person is accustomed, the medical knowledge of the person, the need to deny the illness, the nature of competing needs, the availability of alternative explanations, and the accessibility of treatment (Mechanic,

1978). Sex (Nathanson, 1975), social class (Koos, 1954; Andersen, Anderson, and Smedby, 1968; Osborn, 1973), and the presence of a community referral system (Freidson, 1960, 1961) also affect how symptoms are evaluated and defined.

According to Jones and Nisbett (1971), *actors* and *observers* tend to make different causal attributions. Actors usually see their behavior as a response to an external situation in which they find themselves; typically, observers attribute the same response to factors internal to the actor. This difference between an actor's and an observer's attributions can lead to misunderstanding, perhaps especially so in a health care context. Patients and their physicians may see the same event from different perspectives. The patient attributes his or her response to environmental factors (for example, stress at home) that are out of the purview of the physician, but the physician attributes the patient's response to internal physical processes – disease states or biological aging. These internal processes are, for the most part, the only causal explanations available to the physician, who may be handicapped by a lack of information about those factors to which the patient is responding in the environment.

This is the basis for problems in the doctor–patient relationship. The physician may deem the noncompliant patient uncooperative or recalcitrant – "the patient has a personality problem" – whereas the patient may attribute noncompliance to situational factors – "the medication made me sick" (Janis and Rodin, 1979).

The elderly themselves seem overly ready to make attributions to internal physical processes rather than to the environment (Janis and Rodin, 1979). Their perceptions often include grossly exaggerated notions of what happens during normal aging. Too many associate pain and discomfort, debilitation, or decline in intellectual function with aging in itself. These are not normal accompaniments of aging. Unfortunately, such associations are supported by significant others ("What do you expect at your age?") as well as by physicians. In fact, the relationship between an aged patient and the doctor may be a *special case* of actor–observer interaction, when both agree that events are attributable to internal physical processes (for example, biological aging). This consensus may reinforce a set of consequences that are essentially negative. First, elderly individuals may assume that aging has had a greater impact on them than it really has. For example, Kahn and his associates (Kahn, Zarit, Hilbert, and Niderehe, 1975) found that only a small amount of memory loss was evident in an elderly sample; yet patients perceived a high degree of loss. These perceptions were highly correlated with depression. Second, the elderly may attribute all negative changes in health and mood to aging per se. Chest pain as a warning signal of heart disease may be considered another attack of heartburn; bone pain, which may herald a fracture or bone cancer, may be ascribed to age-related rheumatism. A change in bowel habits is a well-known danger signal of cancer, but such an alteration may easily be ignored by an older person who seems to be plagued by bowel problems. Even rectal bleeding may be attributed to hemorrhoids.

Attributing illness or biological changes to "normal aging" may incorrectly focus an elderly person (and his physician) away from situational and social factors that are stress-inducing and affect health. Much gerontological literature is concerned with the impact on health status of retirement, widowhood, and changing living environments, among other factors.

In general, no social science support has been found for the notion that retirement is detrimental to health. Yet, as Butler and Lewis (1982) point out, reconciling social science and clinical data may be difficult because individuals get lost in the mass of data. Butler (1975) has used the term "retirement syndrome" to describe the fact that retirement may be pathogenic to some individuals. Ellison (1968) suggests that some retirees become "ill" be-

cause they define illness as a more legitimate role than being retired. Simon and Cahan (1963) reported that patients with reversible (acute) brain syndromes were likely to have fewer family ties, and their retirement tended to occur before age 65.

It is well established that the mortality rate for many causes of death is much higher among widows and widowers than among married persons of the same age (Parkes, 1964). Kraus and Lilienfeld (1959) showed that the effects of widowhood (grief and accompanying environmental changes) are the most likely causes of this increased mortality. Informative studies having to do with widowhood and morbidity are scarce. One noteworthy report published nearly fifty years ago indicated that the physical reactions to grief experienced by older people included stomach distress, shortness of breath, lack of strength, and "subjective distress" (Lindemann, 1944). Another more recent study also showed increases in physician visits during the first year of bereavement, especially for psychological symptoms (Clayton, 1973).

The relationship of environmental change to mortality and morbidity has been investigated in mental hospitals, nursing homes, and homes for the aged. Moving the older person from a familiar setting into an institution, or even into surroundings similar to his or her own home, has been reported to cause psychological disorganization. Verwoerdt (1976) offers the case of the 74-year-old recluse who lived in an old shack in filth and in constant danger of being burned. After great effort, the old man was persuaded to move to a more modern facility. Shortly after the move, the social worker was called to the facility where he found the man in a disoriented state with evidence of incontinence all about. Mental health and continence had not been problems prior to the move. Although some researchers might emphasize the stress of relocation involved in this anecdote, others might focus on environmental discontinuity or the degree of change between the new and the old environment. Lawton (1974) believes the newly institutionalized elderly are in double jeopardy in this regard. He argues that individuals with health-related incapacities are less able than the healthy to adapt to new environmental situations.

Clearly, when individuals exaggerate the effects of normal aging and attribute all negative changes to inevitable aging processes, actions that might be beneficial are not undertaken. This is the case whether the misattribution ignores real disease processes or overlooks environmental factors. Sometimes misattribution can have tragic consequences. Unfortunately, reeducating aged individuals about the effects of normal aging may not be effective in correcting incorrect attributions. Data from studies by Ross, Lepper, and Hubbard (1975) show that incorrect attributions tend to persevere. Although this research was not carried out in a health context, it suggests the importance of early education about the effects of normal aging. This may be the only effective device for reducing misattribution of illness to aging among the elderly.

THE BIOMEDICALIZATION OF AGING

Estes and Binney (1991) identify two closely related aspects of the biomedicalization of aging: (1) the social construction of aging as a medical problem and (2) the practice of aging as a medical problem.

Social Construction of Aging as a Medical Problem

The social construction of aging as a medical problem equates aging with illness and disease. Thus, despite increasing evidence of the importance of social and behavioral factors in the relationship between health and aging, the elements of the medical model – with its emphasis on objectivity in diagnosis and treatment of disease, concern solely for matters of physiological functioning, and evaluation solely in the domain of physicians – define the basic processes and problems of aging. As a result, our thinking about aging emphasizes more sophisticated diagnosis, therapeutic intervention or prevention, and identification of modifiable biological markers of aging (Adelman, 1988).

From this perspective, aging is considered an undesirable pathological condition, rather than a phase or stage in the life cycle that brings new risks but also opportunities. Aging is equated with reduced activity, disengagement from social life, an exchange of independence for dependency, and a general loss of personal control and self-esteem (Rodin and Langer, 1980). As Estes, Gerard, Zones, and Swan (1984) have noted elsewhere, all this places social control of the elderly in the hands of physicians who medically define, manage, and treat them.

The Practice of Aging as a Medical Problem

According to Estes and Binney (1991), the practice of aging as a medical problem has four component parts that are inextricably woven together. We briefly identify these parts here to suggest the complexity of relationships involved in maintaining aging front and center as a medical problem and also to point up the pervasiveness of the process of the biomedicalization of aging in U.S. society.

1. *Equating the biomedical model with basic science.* The biomedical model is closely aligned with the scientific method. As a result, this model has achieved widespread acceptance and increasingly is employed in efforts to solve problems of everyday life (Schneider and Conrad, 1980). The biomedical model has defined old age in negative terms of decline and disability. So-called normal aging is seen as a relatively immutable set of biological and psychological processes. Individuals are

identified in terms of diagnosis, course of disease, and response to treatment plan, with emphasis on individual problems that have individual causes and individual solutions. This approach has at least two problems worthy of mention here.

First, the model focuses on a pattern of "usual aging," when in fact there is substantial heterogeneity in even the physiological changes associated with age (Rowe, 1991). "Successful aging" is more common than most believe and, more important, the effects of usual aging may be reversible and preventable (Rowe and Kahn, 1987; Rowe, 1991). Second, the model diverts attention from economic, political, and social-structural elements in society that have impact on the health status of the aged and more broadly define the position of older people in the United States.

2. *The biomedical model and professional training.* The content of professional medical education has affected and been affected by the biomedicalization of aging. The clinical orientation promoted by the biomedical model is one based on acute illness, an orientation in some conflict with the majority of chronic illnesses and conditions with which most elderly are afflicted (Estes and Binney, 1991). Geriatric training is low on the status hierarchy in medical and nursing schools. Also, the orientation of professional medical education is away from holistic approaches more appropriate to caring for clients with chronic illness.

3. *The biomedical model and governmental policy initiatives.* Major governmental initiatives to provide health and medical services to older people, including Medicare and Medicaid, are dominated by the biomedical model with its orientation toward acute illness and care. In almost all cases of service provision under these programs, physicians retain virtually sole authority for the management and control of the elderly.

Resources allocated by the federal government for research and education in aging have also been dominated by a biomedical or disease model of aging (Association for Gerontology in Higher Education, 1988). This contributes to the identification of aging almost solely in terms of illness and treatment. And, as Estes and Binney (1991) point out, it requires that social and behavioral science research on problems of the elderly such as income, housing, transportation, nutrition, and retirement be framed in terms of their links to illness and debilitation.

4. *The biomedical model and public perception of aging.* The biomedical model has contributed to the construction of a reality in which the public views aging and older people in negative terms. Myths of aging abound (Kart, 1990). Even the elderly buy into these myths, including the belief that problems of aging are often, if not primarily, biological and physiological. As a result, older people consume vast amounts of medical services and technology. In turn, as a group they are blamed for high taxes, the huge federal budget deficit (Binstock, 1983), the high cost of health insurance and services, and the overutilization of scarce health and technical resources (Callahan, 1987).

Binstock identifies three important consequences of this scapegoating of the aged for U.S. society. First, it diverts attention from other public policy issues, including unemployment and the deficit in the federal budget. Second, it produces conflict between generations as representatives of the young and the old battle for scarce resources. Third, it diverts attention from long-standing issues of equity and justice in public programs of support for people of all ages.

FINAL PRECAUTIONARY NOTES ON BIOLOGIZING AGING AND THE AGED

As we have sought to describe in this epilogue, the biologizing of aging and the aged is widespread in the society and, unfortunately, represents the dominant paradigm in the society for understanding the aging process and the aged. Still, there are dents in the armor of this paradigm that suggest widespread resistance to its implications.

1. The population of older people who are healthy and active is expanding rapidly. The chronological definition of old age is being redefined, and the age-specific life expectancy of older people in the United States is approaching 20 years on average.

2. Throughout the society there is increasing attention to life-style modifications that improve health and reduce risks for illness and debilitation. Areas for life-style modification include nutrition, exercise, and stress reduction, as well as widespread awareness of the risks associated with smoking tobacco and consuming alcohol.

3. As noted, there is increasing interest in self-health care and in the self-help movement in health, although we know too little about these fledgling social movements. Self-help and self-health care may be part of an increasing consumer movement in health care that has been identified as challenging to the authority of physicians (Haug and Lavin, 1983).

4. There is increasing understanding that, in general, medical interventions (both prophylactic and chemotherapeutic) have contributed very little to the overall decline in mortality in the United States in the twentieth century. As McKinlay and McKinlay (1977) have pointed out, medical measures have often been introduced decades after a marked decline in death rates from a specific disease have set in. For example, they estimate that only about 3.5 percent of all the decline in mortality since 1900 is attributable to medical intervention for influenza, pneumonia, diphtheria, whooping cough, and poliomyelitis.

Reduction in the death rate of the U.S. population reflects at least four factors, all of which involve attempts to control the environment begun in the nineteenth century: (1) increased food supply, (2) development of commerce and industry, (3) changes in technology and industry, and (4) increased control over infectious diseases (Dorn, 1959).

5. The medical model has not been able to show progress in addressing macrostructural problems implicated in the origins of illness. These include social, economic, and environmental causes of ill health such as cultural barriers to good health, the relationship between poverty and illness, and the effects of air and water pollution and other toxins in the environment on health status. There is increasing understanding that significant progress cannot be forthcoming given the focus of the medical model on individual health behaviors and life-styles.

BIBLIOGRAPHY

Adelman, R. 1988. The importance of basic biological science to gerontology. *Journal of Gerontology*, 43: 1, B1-2.

Andersen, R., Anderson, O., and Smedby, B. 1968. Perceptions of and response to symptoms of illness in Sweden and the U.S. *Medical Care*, 6: 18-30.

Association for Gerontology in Higher Education. 1988. *Public policy and the future of aging education*. Washington, DC: Author.

Binstock, R. H. 1983. The aged as scapegoat. *Gerontologist*, 23(2): 136-143.

Butler, R. 1975. *Why survive? Being old in America*. New York: Harper & Row.

Butler, R., and Lewis, M. 1982. *Aging and mental health*, 2nd ed. St. Louis: C. V. Mosby.

Callahan, D. 1987. *Setting limits: Medical goals in an aging society*. New York: Simon and Schuster.

Cassedy, J. H. 1977. Why self-help? Americans alone with their diseases, 1880-1950. In G. Risse, R. Numbers, and J. Leariff (Eds.), *Medicine without doctors*. New York: Science History Publications.

Clayton, P. 1973. The clinical morbidity of the first year of bereavement: A review. *Comprehensive Psychiatry*, 14: 151-157.

Daedalus. 1977. *Doing better and feeling worse: Health in the U.S.* (Vol. 106).

DeFriese, G. H., and Woomert, A. 1983. Self-care among U.S. elderly: Recent developments. *Research on Aging*, 5: 2-23.

Dorn, H. 1959. Mortality. In P. Hauser, and O. D. Duncan (Eds.), *The study of population*. Chicago: University of Chicago Press.

Ellison, D. 1968. Work, retirement, and the sick role. *Gerontologist*, 8: 189-192.

Estes, C. L., and Binney, A. A. 1991. The biomedicalization of aging: Dangers and dilemmas. In M. Minkler and C. L. Estes (Eds.), *Critical perspectives on aging*. Amityville, NY: Baywood Publishing.

Estes, C. L., Gerard, L., Zones, J. S., and Swan, J. H. 1984. *Political economy, health and aging*. Boston: Little, Brown.

Freedman, J., Sears, D., and Carlsmith, J. 1978. *Social psychology*, 3rd ed. Englewood Cliffs, NJ: Prentice-Hall.

Freidson, E. 1960. Client control and medical practice. *American Journal of Sociology*, 65: 374-382.

Freidson, E. 1961. *Patients' view of medical practice*. New York: Russell Sage Foundation.

Freidson, E. 1988. *Profession of medicine*. Chicago: University of Chicago Press.

Haug, M., and Lavin, B. 1983. *Consumerism in medicine: Challenging physician authority*. Beverly Hills, CA: Sage Publications.

Ingham, J., and Miller, P. 1979. Symptom prevalence and severity in a general practice. *Journal of Epidemiology and Community Health*, 33: 191-198.

Janis, I., and Rodin, J. 1979. Attribution, control and decision making: Social psychology and health care. In C. G. Stone, F. Cohen, and N. E. Adler (Eds.), *Health psychology – a handbook*. San Francisco: Jossey-Bass.

Jones, E., and Nisbett, R. 1971. *The actor and the observer: Divergent perceptions of the causes of behavior*. Morristown, NJ: General Learning Press.

Kahn, R., Zarit, S., Hilbert, N., and Niederehe, G. 1975. Memory complaint and impairment in the aged. *Archives of General Psychiatry*, 32: 1569-1573.

Kart, C. S. 1990. *The realities of aging*, 3rd ed. Boston: Allyn and Bacon.

Kart, C. S., and Dunkle, R. E. 1989. Assessing capacity for self-care among the aged. *Journal of Aging and Health*, 1(4): 430-450.

Koos, E. 1954. *The health of Regionville*. New York: Columbia University Press.

Kovar, M. G. 1977. Health of the elderly and use of health services. *Public Health Reports*, 92: 9-19.

Kraus, A., and Lilienfeld, A. 1959. Some epidemiologic aspects of the high mortality rate in the young widowed group. *Journal of Chronic Diseases*, 10: 207-217.

Last, J. 1963. The iceberg: Completing the clinical picture in general practice. *Lancet*, 2: 28-31.

Lawton, M. P. 1974. Social ecology and the health of older people. *American Journal of Sociology*, 64: 257-260.

Lindemann, E. 1944. Symptomatology and management of acute grief. *American Journal of Psychiatry*, 101: 141-148.

Luke, B. 1976. Good geriatric nutrition is a lifelong nursing matter. *RN* (July): 24-26.

McKinlay, J. B., and McKinlay, S. M. 1977. The questionable contribution of medical measures to the decline of mortality in the United States in the twentieth century. *Milbank Memorial Fund Quarterly/Health and Society*, 55(3): 405-428.

Mechanic, D. 1978. *Medical sociology*, 2nd ed. New York: Free Press.

Morrell, D., and Wale, C. 1976. Symptoms perceived and recorded by patients. *Journal of the Royal College of General Practitioners*, 26: 398-403.

Nathanson, C. 1975. Illness and the feminine role: A theoretical review. *Social Science and Medicine*, 9: 57-62.

Osborn, R. 1973. Social rank and self-health evaluation of older urban males. *Social Science and Medicine*, 7: 209-218.

Parkes, C. 1964. Effects of bereavement on physical and mental health – A study of the medical records of widows. *British Medical Journal*, 2: 274-279.

Parsons, T. 1951. *The social system*. New York: Free Press.

Parsons, T. 1972. Definitions of health and illness in light of American values and social structure. In E. G. Jaco (Ed.), *Patients, physicians and illness*, 2nd ed. New York: Free Press.

Parsons, T. 1975. The sick role and the role of the physician reconsidered. *Milbank Memorial Fund Quarterly*, 53: 257-278.

Rodin, J., and Langer, E. 1980. Aging labels: The decline of control and the fall of self-esteem. *Journal of Social Issues*, 36(2): 12-29.

Ross, L., Lepper, M., and Hubbard, M. 1975. Perseverance in self-perception and social perception: Biased attributional processes in the debriefing paradigm. *Journal of Personality and Social Psychology*, 32: 880-892.

Rowe, J. W. 1991. Reducing the risk of usual aging. *Generations*, 15(1): 25-28.

Rowe, J. W., and Kahn, R. 1987. Human aging: Usual and successful. *Science*, 237: 143-149.

Schneider, J., and Conrad, P. 1980. The medical control of deviance: Conquests and consequences. In J. A. Roth (Ed.), *Research in the sociology of health care: A research annual* (Vol. 1). Greenwich, CT: JAI Press.

Simon, A., and Cahan, R. 1963. The acute brain syndrome in geriatric patients. In W. Mendel and L. Epstein (Eds.), *Acute psychotic reaction*. Washington, DC: Psychiatric Research Reports.

U.S. Bureau of the Census. 1985. *Statistical abstract of the United States, 1986*. Washington, DC: U.S. Government Printing Office.

Verwoerdt, A. 1976. *Clinical geropsychiatry*. Baltimore: Williams and Wilkins.

Williamson, J. D., and Danaher, K. 1978. *Self care in health*. London: Croom Helm.

Wolinsky, F. D. 1988. *The sociology of health*. Belmont, CA: Wadsworth.

Zola, I. K. 1962. *Sociocultural factors in the seeking of medical care*. Unpublished Ph.D. dissertation, Harvard University.

Zola, I. K. 1966. Culture and symptoms: An analysis of patients presenting complaints. *American Sociological Review*, 31: 615-630.

Glossary

accommodation Method of processing incoming information by changing the knowledge base to make it a better approximation of the environment.

acetylcholine A neurotransmitter.

achalasia Failure to relax the smooth muscle of the GI tract at any juncture.

achlorhydria Absence of hydrochloric acid from the stomach juices.

acoustic trauma Noise-induced hearing loss.

actinic keratosis Horny growth of the skin due to exposure to the sun.

acute illness Condition, disease, or disorder that is temporary.

adaptation Process of adjusting to the environment through assimilation and accommodation.

adenomatous coli polyps Colon polyps that often become malignant.

adipose Referring to fat.

adverse drug reaction (ADR) Any unintended or undesired effect of a drug (intentional overdose is not included in this definition).

age-specific life expectancy Average duration of life expected for an individual of a given stated age.

alimentation Process of ingesting food.

aluminum hydroxide gel A substance used in antacids.

alveoli Air sacs of the lungs.

Alzheimer's disease A progressively deteriorating form of senile dementia of unknown etiology. It involves a diminution of intellectual capabilities, memory loss, impaired judgment, and personality change.

amino acids Organic acids that contain an amine group (NH_2) and are the hydrolysis products of proteins (e.g., lysine, tyrosine, glutamate).

amylase An enzyme that digests starch.

amyloid infiltration An abnormal material, probably a glycoprotein, resembling starch that invades tissues with age.

amyloidosis Accumulation of amyloid material in various body tissues.

analgesics Drugs used as pain-relieving remedies (aspirin, ibuprofen, acetaminophen).

ancestry group Defined by individuals in terms of the nation or nations of family origin.

anemia Disorder in the oxygen-carrying capacity of the blood.

angina pectoris Suffocative pain in the chest due to a reduction in oxygen to the heart muscle.

antediluvian theme Belief that people lived much longer in the distant past.

anticholinergic Drug that blocks the passage of impulses through autonomic nerves.

anticoagulants Agents that prevent coagulation of the blood (i.e., warfarin, heparin).

anticonvulsants Drugs that inhibit convulsions.

antidiuretic hormone Pituitary hormone that controls urine production.

antihistamine Drug that counteracts the action of histamine.

antioxidant Substance that reduces the rate of cellular oxidation.

antiperoxidative activities Activities that inhibit the oxidation of cell membranes.

antipsychotic agents Drugs that antagonize the symptoms of psychosis (hallucinations, delusions, and belligerent behavior); major tranquilizers.

antrum Cavity or chamber, especially within a bone.

apatite Series of minerals containing calcium.

aphasia Loss of the ability to express oneself by speech or writing or to comprehend spoken or written language resulting from injury or disease of the brain centers.

appendicitis Inflammation of the appendix.

argon laser photocoagulation therapy A type of laser treatment that seeks to seal off abnormal vascular growth.

arteriosclerosis Generic term indicating a hardening or loss of elasticity of the arteries.

arthritis Inflammation and/or degenerative joint change, often characterized by stiffness, swelling, and joint pain.

articular cartilage Cartilage that lines the joints.

aspiration pneumonia Pneumonia related to the aspiration of foreign material into the lungs.

assimilation Method of processing incoming information by fitting it into the existing knowledge base.

atheroma Lesion of atherosclerosis.

atherosclerosis Condition marked by lipid deposits and a thickening of the inner wall of an artery.

atherosclerotic plaque Lesion of atherosclerosis.

atrophic senile macular degeneration Slowly progressing form of senile macular degeneration.

atrophy Diminution of the size of a cell, tissue, or organ.

attrition Wearing away.

autoantibody Antibody that attacks host tissue.

autoimmunity State in which antibodies attack host tissue.

average life expectancy at birth Defined as the average number of years a person born today can expect to live under current mortality conditions.

bacterial deconjugation Process of breakdown by bacteria of bile salts.

bacteriodes A genus of bacteria.

bacteriostatic State of bacterial equilibrium.

bacteriuria Presence of bacteria in the urine.

basal cell The early keratinocyte present in the basal layer of the epidermis.

basal cell carcinoma Form of cancer found on the face below the eyebrow and above the ear lobe level; a pearly nodule that becomes encrusted and develops into a shallow ulcer.

basal membrane Demarcates the border between the skin's epidermal and dermal layers.

basal metabolism rate (BMR) Energy required to maintain the body at rest.

beta blockers Drugs used to counteract the effects of epinephrine (adrenaline) on the heart so as to treat symptoms of hypertension, angina, or arrhythmia (e.g., propranolol, nadolol).

biochemical individuality The concept that individual biochemical requirements are very variable.

biocultural Interaction between biological and cultural factors.

bone formation Addition of new bone.

bone remodeling Process by which bone material is built up and broken down.

bone resorption Dissolution of bone on the inside.

Bouchard's nodes Nodules on the second joints of the fingers.

calculi Stones that form internally in the kidney or gallbladder.

cardiovascular agents Drugs that have their action on the heart or peripheral blood vessels for the treatment of hypertension, angina, heart failure, or cardiac arrhythmia (e.g., beta blockers, nitroglycerin, digoxin).

carotid artery syndrome Condition marked by transient occlusion of the major arteries supplying the brain.

carpometacarpal joint Place where the wrist bones meet the hand.

cataract Opacity of the normally transparent lens of the eye, resulting in reduced visual acuity.

catheter Tube used to drain the bladder.

centenarians Those who have lived 100 years or more.

central vision Permits visual detection of detail via the function of cones within the macula or center of the retina.

cerebral hemorrhage Escape of blood from an artery into the cerebrum; a form of stroke.

cerumen Ear wax.

cholangitis Inflammation of the bile duct.

cholecystitis Inflammation of the gallbladder.

cholelithiasis Gallstones in the gallbladder.

chronic bronchitis Long-continued inflammation of the bronchial tubes characterized by a chronic cough and sputum production for a minimum of three consecutive months for at least two consecutive years.

chronic illness A condition, disease, or disorder that is permanent or that will incapacitate an individual for a long period of time.

cilia Hairlike cells.

circuit training Modified form of weight lifting, consisting of 20 to 40 minutes of lifting relatively light weights with only a short, 15-second rest between exercise sets.

claudication Limping or lameness brought on by physical activity.

clitoris A small sensitive projection at the front of the vulva that is sexually reactive.

Clostridia A genus of bacteria.

cochlea Auditory receptor organ located in the inner ear; houses the organ of Corti.

cochlear implant Electronic prosthetic device that utilizes a microsurgical implant to stimulate the auditory nerve.

coenzyme Small molecule that works with an enzyme to promote the enzyme's activity.

cognitive state theories Intellectual concern focused on the thought processes behind test performance.

cohort Term used for a group of persons born at approximately the same time. Though defined broadly, no two birth cohorts can be expected to age in the same way; each has a particular history and arrives at old age with unique experiences.

cohort effects Specific environmental events and circumstances experienced by most members of a particular generation, producing developmental differences from other generations.

coitus Sexual intercourse.

collagen Structural protein of skin and connective tissue.

collateral circulation Movement of blood by secondary vessels after obstruction of the principal vessel supplying an area.

colles fracture Fracture of the lower end of the radius.

colostomy Surgical removal of part of the colon.

combined systolic-diastolic hypertension Elevated blood pressure equal to or greater than 160 mm Hg/95 mm Hg.

complex carbohydrate Starch.

complicated lesion Advanced lesion of atherosclerosis associated with occlusive disease.

conductive hearing loss Hearing loss resulting from the interrupted conduction of sound waves.

congestive heart failure State of circulatory congestion produced by the impaired pumping action of the heart.

cor pulmonale   In pulmonary heart disease, the enlargement of the right side of the heart.

coronary artery disease   Occurs when arteries supplying the heart become narrowed, reducing blood flow to the heart.

coronary thrombosis   Heart attack due to a blood clot.

cortical bone   The compact bone that makes up the shaft of the long bones, giving them strength.

cross-linkage   Process whereby proteins in the body bind to one another.

cross-sectional research   Studies based on observations representing a single point in time. Studies employing this research design are useful for emphasizing differences.

crush fractures   Fractures, usually in the vertebrates, that are the result of osteoporosis.

crystallized intelligence   Intelligence obtained through experience and formal education.

cutaneous tumors   Tumorous growth of the skin.

cystitis   Bacterial infection of the urinary bladder.

decub   Lying down.

decubitus ulcers   Pressure or bed sores.

degenerative joint disease   Osteoarthritis.

dementia   Family of brain disorders, some of which are reversible but some of which are progressive and fatal.

dementing illness   Any disease that produces a decline in intellectual abilities of sufficient severity to interfere with social and/or occupational functioning (memory disorder is usually prominent).

demography   Study of the size, territorial distribution, and composition of population and the changes therein.

depression   The most common functional psychiatric disorder among older people; it can vary in duration and degree and can show psychological as well as physiological manifestations.

dermis   Inner layer of the skin.

detoxification process   Breakdown and neutralization of toxic substances.

diabetes insipidus   Metabolic disorder accompanied by excess urine output without an excess of sugar.

diabetes mellitus   Metabolic disorder of carbohydrate utilization.

diabetic retinopathy   Complication of diabetes affecting the capillaries and arterioles of the retina.

diastolic pressure   Denotes arterial pressure while the heart is resting between beats.

diuretics   Drugs used to promote the excretion of urine so as to treat symptoms of heart failure and hypertension (e.g., furosemide).

diverticula   Outpouchings of the wall of an organ, especially the large intestine.

dopamine   Intermediate product in synthesis of norepinephrine; a neurotransmitter.

dorsal kyphosis   Increased curvature of the thoracic spine leading to hunchback.

dorsal root ganglia   Groups of spinal nerve cell bodies located outside the central nervous system.

dowager's hump   Extreme kyphosis associated with osteoporosis.

drug–drug interaction   Adverse drug reaction produced when a second drug modifies the way the body handles or reacts to the first agent.

duodenum   First three inches of the small intestine.

dyspareunia   Painful sexual intercourse.

dysuria   Painful urination.

edema   Presence of excessive amounts of fluid in the intercellular tissue spaces.

edentulous   Lacking all teeth.

eighth cranial nerve   Auditory nerve.

embolus   Clot or other foreign plug carried by the blood and blocking a vessel.

emphysema   Overinflation of air sacs, resulting in destruction of capillary beds and shortness of breath.

emulsification   Breakup of fat molecules.

enculturation   Process of learning one's language and culture.

endarterectomy   Surgical removal of a thickened, atherosclerotic arterial lining.

endogenous   Produced internally.

epidermis   Outer layer of the skin.

epilepsy   Seizure disorder; chronic condition characterized by paroxysmal attacks of brain dysfunction, usually associated with alteration of consciousness.

erectile dysfunction   Inability to maintain an erection sufficient for desired sexual activity.

error catastrophe   Theory maintaining that aging results from mutations.

erythrocyte sedimentation rate   Test that measures abnormal concentrations of fibrinogen and serum globulins that may accompany pathology.

esophagitis   Inflammation of the esophagus.

essential hypertension   Elevated blood pressure, the cause of which is unknown.

estrogen-replacement therapy   Medical treatment for postmenopausal osteoporosis.

excessive effect   An adverse drug reaction that is dose-related and predictable because symptoms are an exaggeration of the desired therapeutic effect (diarrhea with certain laxatives, hypoglycemia with antidiabetic agents, hypotension with beta blockers).

exophthalmia   Condition in which the eyeballs protrude abnormally.

expertise   Development of knowledge in a specific domain.

expressive aphasia   Language deficit characterized by inability to express oneself via the spoken or written word as a result of damage to the brain centers controlling such activity.

exudative   Pertaining to exudation, whereby fluid and/or debris escape from blood vessels to be deposited in or on tissues.

family dependency ratio   Defined in simple demographic terms (e.g., population 65-79/population 45-49), this ratio crudely illustrates the shifts in the ratio of elderly parents to the children who would support them.

fat-soluble vitamins   Those vitamins that are soluble in fat, such as A, D, E, and K.

fatty streak   The earliest lesion of atherosclerosis.

fertility rate   Number of births that occur in a year per 1,000 women of childbearing age.

fibroma   Tumor consisting of connective tissue.

fistula   Abnormal canal, frequently in the anal region.

fluid intelligence   Innate information-processing skills independent of acquired experience and formal education.

food faddism   Extreme pursuit of food-related activity in hope of achieving some health benefit.

free radical   Unstable molecule produced in the course of cellular oxidation.

gallstones   Insoluble stones that form in the gallbladder.

gastric   Pertaining to the stomach.

gastritis   Inflammation or irritations of the stomach lining.

gelling or gel phenomenon   Stiffness associated with arthritis.

gingivitis   Inflammation of the gums.

glaucoma   Group of diseases characterized by increased intraocular pressure and optic nerve damage.

glomerulonephritis   Inflammation of the renal glomeruli.

glucose tolerance   Ability of the body to utilize sugar or carbohydrates.

glycosuria   Presence of sugar in the urine, often associated with diabetes.

gout   Painful condition associated with urate deposits in the joints.

Grave's disease   Diffuse hyperplasia with hypothyroidism.

gustatory   Related to the sense of smell.

hair cell   Hairlike cells, those within the inner ear, which are important in transmitting sound.

heart failure   Condition wherein the heart fails to pump blood efficiently so that fluid accumulates in peripheral tissues and lungs, producing edema and shortness of breath.

Heberden's nodes   Small hard nodules formed usually at the distal interphalangeal articulation of the fingers, in osteoarthritis.

hematuria   Presence of blood in the urine.

hemianopia   Defective vision or blindness in half of the visual field.

hemiparesis   Muscular weakness on one side of the body.

hemiplegia   Paralysis of one side of the body.

hemodialysis   The removal of waste products from the blood by mechanical means.

hepatitis   Inflammation of the liver.

hepatobiliary   Referring to the liver and gallbladder.

herpes zoster   Another name for the varicella-zoster virus.

high-density lipoprotein (HDL)   Transports cholesterol from cells to the liver; increased concentrations seem to protect against coronary heart disease.

homeostasis   State of balance; a stable internal environment of the organism.

housing inadequacy   Housing unit with a deficiency in its physical condition, a high degree of overcrowding, or an inability of the household to afford the unit.

hyperborean theme   Belief that people live much longer in remote, faraway places.

hypercalcemia   Increased levels of calcium in the blood.

hyperglycemia   Increased blood sugar levels.

hyperkinesis   Abnormally increased mobility or motor function.

hypertension   High arterial blood pressure.

hyperthermia   Abnormally high body temperature.

hyperthyroidism   Overactivity of the thyroid gland.

hypervitaminosis   Excess of one or more vitamins in the body.

hypocalcemia   Low levels of calcium in the blood.

hypocholesteremia   Low blood cholesterol levels.

hypochondriasis   Overconcern for one's health, usually accompanied by delusions about physical dysfunction or disease.

hypoglycemia   Abnormally low concentration of sugar in the blood.

hyponatremia   Salt depletion or deficiency of sodium in the blood.

hypotension   Diminished blood pressure, often related to postural changes from supine to erect posture.

hypothermia   Low state of body temperature due to dysfunction of thermoregulation.

hypothyroidism   Underactivity of the thyroid gland.

idiopathic   Of unknown origins.

idiopathic hypertension   Elevated blood pressure of unknown cause.

idiosyncratic reaction   An adverse drug reaction that is neither dose-related nor predictable (i.e., lowered white blood cell count with chloramphenicol, malignant hyperthermia with anaesthetic agents).

ileum   Distal portion of the small intestine.

iliac crests   Bony edge of the hips.

immunocompetence   Characterized by the ability to produce a proper immune response.

in vitro   Within a glass or test tube.

insulin shock   Acute hyperglycemia related to sudden lowering of blood glucose due to an overdose of insulin or oral hypoglycemics.

intercostal muscles   Group of muscles of the thoracic cavity involved with the inspiration and expiration of breathing.

interleukin-2   Substance important in the production and maintenance of an appropriate immune repose.

intermittent claudication   Characterized by pain, weakness, and fatigue of the legs due to occlusive atherosclerotic disease.

interphalangeal joints   Place where the finger bones meet each other.

intima   Innermost layer of an artery, specifically known as the tunica media.

intrinsic factor Factor present in the stomach that is necessary for the proper absorption of Vitamin B_{12}.

introitus Penile entry into the vagina.

islets of Langerhans Insulin-producing portion of the pancreas.

isolated systolic hypertension Systolic blood pressure of 160 mm Hg or above occurring in the presence of a diastolic pressure of less than 90 mm Hg.

jaundice Yellowing of the skin and eyes caused by too much bile in the blood.

keratin An insoluble protein that is the principle component of epidermis, nails, hair, bony tissues, and the organic part of tooth enamel.

ketonuria Excessive ketones in the urine.

labia Outer folds of skin surrounding the vulva.

lactose intolerance Inability to digest lactose due to absence of the enzyme lactase.

L-dopa Compound used to treat the symptoms of Parkinson's disease.

left ventricular hypertrophy Enlargement of the left pumping chamber of the heart.

Leighton flexometer Mechanical device for measuring flexibility.

lens Transparent structure of the eye through which light passes; its movement allows for visual focusing.

leukoplakias White thickened patches on the cheeks, gums, or tongue.

levodopa Drug used in the treatment of Parkinson's disease (also L-dopa).

life review Postulated by Robert Butler to describe an almost universal tendency of older people toward self-reflection and reminiscence.

life span The extreme limit of human longevity; the age beyond which no one can expect to live.

life-span construct A person's unified sense of the past, the present, and the future.

life story A personal narrative history that organizes autobiographical events into a coherent sequence.

life table Shows the probability of surviving from any age to any subsequent age based on the death rates at a particular time and place.

lipase Enzymes that digest fat.

lipids Fats.

lipofuscin A class of fatty pigments that accumulate with age.

lipoprotein Fat and protein complexes that transport cholesterol via the blood.

longitudinal research Studies designed to collect data at different points in time. This research design emphasizes the study of change.

low-density lipoprotein (LDL) Transports cholesterol from the bloodstream to cells; elevated levels have been associated with increased risk of coronary heart disease.

low-tension glaucoma Optic nerve damage occurring in the absence of elevated intraocular pressure.

L-thyroxine Drug used to treat hypothyroidism.

lumen An opening or channel.

lymphokine Substance important in activation and maintenance of the immune response.

lymphoma Tumor of lymphoid tissue.

macrocytic anemia Anemia characterized by abnormally large red cells.

macronutrients Essential nutrients needed by the body in large amounts.

macula Key focusing area of the retina.

mandible Lower jaw.

mandibular dentures Lower plate of dentures.

maximum life span Hereditary capability of a species for survival or length of life.

media Middle layer of an artery, specifically known as the tunica media.

megadoses Doses of a nutrient or chemical in great excess of the normal requirement.

melanin Pigment in the skin that determines darkness or lightness.

melanocyte A cell that is responsible for the synthesis of melanin.

melanoma Tumor made of melanin-pigmented cells, with a marked tendency to metastasis.

menopause Cessation of menstruation between ages 40 and 55.

mesenteric Referring to the fold of peritoneum that attaches the intestine to the posterior abdominal wall.

metacarpophalangeal joint Place where the bones of the hand meet the fingers.

metamemory Knowledge of one's own memory ability.

metatarsophalangeal joints Place where the bones of the foot meet the toes.

micronutrients Essential nutrients needed by the body in trace amounts.

micturition Urination.

migration Movement of populations from one geographical region to another.

minimum adequate diet Lowest cost food budget that could be devised to supply all essential nutrients using food readily purchasable in the U.S. market.

monialiasis Infection of the mucus membranes caused by fungus of the genus candida.

monoamine oxidase inhibitors Drugs that block the breakdown of monoamine neurotransmitters (dopamine and norepinephrine).

monoclonal hypothesis Theory maintaining that atherosclerotic plaque formation arises from a neoplastic transformation of arterial smooth muscle cells.

morbidity Condition of being ill; often used to refer to the rate of illness per some unit of population in a society.

mortality rate Total number of deaths in a year per 1,000 individuals in the society.

multiple myeloma Malignant tumor of the bone marrow.

multiple sclerosis A disease characterized by hardening of the brain and spinal cord as a result of hyperplasia.

mycobacterium tuberculosis   Bacterium that causes tuberculosis.

myocardium   Heart muscle.

myxedemia   Hypothyroidism in adults.

neovascular   Formation of new blood vessels.

nephosclerosis   Hardening and thickening of kidney tissues.

nephropathy   Kidney disease.

neurotoxin   Substance that is poisonous to nerve tissue.

neurotransmitters   Chemicals that promote the transmission of nerve impulses in the central and peripheral nervous systems by translating electrical to chemical energy, then back again.

nocturia   Need to get up during the night to urinate.

nodular hyperplasia   Benign enlargement of the prostate.

nonliquid assets   Assets that are not easily convertible into cash.

nucleic acids   DNA and RNA of the cell nucleus.

old-old   Those 75 years of age and older.

old-age dependency ratio   The ratio of the population of ages too old to work to the population of working age.

organ of Corti   Located within the inner ear, it consists of the hair cells or hearing receptors.

organic mental disorder   Designates a particular organic brain syndrome that has a known or presumed cause.

organic brain syndrome   Constellation of psychological or behavior signs and symptoms without reference to etiology.

organization   Concept in Piaget's theory describing how people's thinking is put together.

orgasmic phase   When muscle tension and engorgement of blood vessels peak during sexual activity.

orgasmic platform   Narrowing of the vaginal opening providing a tighter grip on the penis during sexual activity.

ossicles   Small bones.

osteoarthritis   Also known as degenerative joint disease, characterized by chronic breakdown of joint tissues.

osteoblast   Young bone-forming cell.

osteoclast   Cell that absorbs bone tissue.

osteophyte   Bony outgrowth.

otitis media   Inflammation or infection of the middle ear.

otosclerosis   Formation of spongy bone within the ear.

ototoxic drugs   Drugs that have a toxic effect on the eighth cranial nerve or on hearing.

over-the-counter-medication   Medication that can be purchased in a pharmacy without a prescription (analgesics, laxatives, cold remedies, etc.).

overdosage   Adverse drug reaction manifested by symptoms of an excessive dose, even if that dose may be routinely prescribed and well tolerated by many (tinnitus with aspirin, weakness with beta blockers).

oxalates   Salt of oxalic acid.

oxalic acid   Chemical that tends to combine with some nutrients to produce indigestible oxalates.

oxidation   Combination of substances with oxygen.

p.r.n.   Abbreviation of the Latin *pro re nata*, meaning to give a drug (or procedure) according to needs (e.g., "sleeping pills p.r.n. insomnia," "analgesics p.r.n. pain").

prolongevity   Significant extension of the length of life by human action.

Paget's disease   Chronic localized bone disease of unknown origin that causes skeletal deformity, usually in those over 50.

pancreatitis   Inflammation of the pancreas.

pancreozymin   Intestinal hormone that stimulates the secretory activity of the pancreas.

papillae   Small nipple-shaped projections on elevations.

paranoia   Form of psychopathology that involves delusions, usually of a persecutory nature.

parathyroid hormone   Substance produced by the parathyroid glands that regulates calcium metabolism.

parenteral   Generally refers to medications given through a route other than the mouth.

Parkinson's disease   Central nervous system disorder characterized by muscular rigidity and a rhythmic tremor.

pectin   Complex carbohydrate that is a component of dietary fiber.

penile detumescence   Subsiding of erection of penis after ejaculation.

pepsinogen   Substance in the stomach that is changed into pepsin by hydrochloric acid; acts in protein digestion.

peptic ulcer   Ulceration of a mucous membrane caused by the action of gastric juice.

periodontal disease   Pathology of the gum tissue.

periodontitis   Inflammation of the gums.

peripheral vision   Side vision.

peripheral vascular disease   Atherosclerotic disease of the extremities, especially the lower leg.

peritonitis   Inflammation of the peritoneal membranes lining the abdominal cavity.

pernicious anemia   Megablastic anemia related to vitamin B_{12} deficiency or its lack of absorption.

peroxidation   Process of the transfer of oxidation out of the cell.

pharmacodynamics   Biochemical and physiological effects of drugs and their mechanisms of action.

pharmacokinetics   Study of how long, how much, when, how, if, and where a drug will be absorbed, transported, and metabolized and excreted.

phenylbutazone   Chemical used as an analgesic and antipyretic.

phytic acid   Substance that tends to form insoluble products with nutrients.

platelet   Thrombocyte found in mammalian blood which is involved in the coagulation or clotting of blood.

Plummer's disease   Hyperthyroidism associated with simple adenoma.

political economy   Critical approach that allows for broadly viewing old age and the aging process within the economic and political context of society.

polyarticular   Affecting many joints.

polyps   Tiny fingerlike projections from a mucous surface.

polyunsaturated fats   Fats containing a high percentage of polyunsaturated acids, which tend to be liquid and includes corn, soybean, safflower, sunflower and fish oils; has been associated with decreased levels of serum cholesterol.

polyuria   An increase in urine production.

porphyria   Defect in porphyrin metabolism.

postcentral gyrus   Convolution of the parietal lobe located between the central and postcentral sulci.

postformal thought   Level of thinking characterized by increased tolerance of ambiguity, acceptance of more than one correct answer to problems, and the realization that reality constraints are important.

post-herpetic neuralgia   Pain along the course of one or more nerves associated with herpes zoster.

postmitotic cells   Cells that do not divide.

preparatory depression   Depression associated with impending death.

presbycusis   Hearing loss that occurs with age.

presbyopia   Impaired vision due to farsightedness associated with aging.

pressure sore   Ulcer caused by prolonged pressure on a spot in a patient confined to bed for a long time.

primary hypertension   Elevated blood pressure the cause of which is unknown.

primary mental ability   Type of ability in psychometric theories of intelligence representing relationships among performances on intelligence tests.

primary osteoarthritis   Osteoarthritis of idiopathic or unknown cause.

prostatitis   Inflammation of the prostate.

proteinuria   Presence of protein in the urine.

prothrombin   Glycoprotein present in the plasma that is converted to thromboplastin as part of the clotting process.

pruritus   Itching.

psychometric approach   Way of viewing intelligence as representing performance on standardized tests of intelligence.

ptyalin   Enzyme produced by the salivary glands that digests starch.

purine   Colorless, crystalline substance not found in nature and important part of some uric acid compounds.

pyelonephritis   Bacterial infection of the kidney.

pylorus   Sphincter that controls the opening between the stomach and the small intestine.

radioimmuneassays   Analysis of radioactivity.

radioiodine   Radioactivity of iodine.

reaction time   Measure of psychomotor performance affected by familiarity of task, practice at a task, task complexity, and other factors.

reactive depression   Depression associated with the various losses that accompany illness and dying – that is, loss of functional ability, employment, and so on.

receptive aphasia   Language deficit characterized by an inability to understand the spoken or written word due to damage within the brain's speech center.

refractory period   Period after orgasm while returning to an unstimulated deeply relaxed state.

renal calculi   Kidney stones.

renal excretion   Clearance of a drug via the kidneys.

residual urine   Urine retained in the bladder after urination.

resorption   Loss of substance through physiologic or pathologic means.

response to injury hypothesis   Theory that maintains that atherosclerosis is initiated as a result of injury to the inner layer of the artery.

rheumatoid arthritis   Arthritic inflammation associated with rheumatism.

rheumatoid factor   Autoantibody found in the blood that might be indicative of rheumatoid arthritis.

right ventricular hypertrophy   Enlargement of the right pumping chamber of the heart, characteristic of pulmonary heart disease.

rugae   Ridges, wrinkles or folds in mucous membranes.

saturated fat   Tends to be a hard fat at room temperature, found in butterfat, meat, coconut oil, and certain shortenings; diets high in this substance tend to increase serum cholesterol levels.

scenario   Person's expectations for his or her future.

schizophrenia   A chronic psychiatric disorder manifested by psychotic thinking, withdrawal, apathy, and impoverishment of human relationships.

sclera   The white of the eye.

seborrheic keratosis   Benign, noninvasive tumor of epidermal origin which appears as a thin, greasy scale.

sebum   Secretion of the sebaceous glands.

secondary hypertension   Elevated blood pressure related to a definable cause such as previously existing kidney disease.

secondary memory   Type of memory that holds information for reasonable periods of time.

secondary osteoarthritis   Osteoarthritis due to an injury or other stress.

secondary side effect   Adverse reaction that is an indirect consequence of a drug's action but nevertheless predictable (lowered potassium with diuretics, nausea with digoxin, dry mouth with antidepressants).

senescence   Process of aging; the term used by biological gerontologists to describe all the postmaturational changes in an individual.

senile macular degeneration   Visual impairment as a result of damage to the focusing area of the retina.

senile osteopenia   Loss of bone with age.

senile pruritus   Intense itching of the aged skin.

sensorineural hearing loss   Hearing loss related to disorders of the inner ear where conducted sound vibrations are transformed into electrical impulses.

sensory deprivation   State of limited sensory contact and experiences.

sex ratio   Number of males for every 100 females (× 100).

shingles   Illness caused by herpes zoster virus that presents itself with intense burning pain in the dermatomes of the affected nerve roots.

silent heart attack   Heart attack unaccompanied by chest pain.

skin cancer   Malignant growth of skin.

sociocultural matrix   Network of social and cultural factors.

squamous cell cancer   Warty nodules that ulcerate, forming an irregular ulcer with firm everted edges found usually on exposed skin.

squamous carcinoma   Scaly or platelike cancer cells.

stasis   Stagnation or stoppage.

status epilepticus   Condition seen in epileptic patients in which one seizure closely follows another without an intervening period of alertness.

streptococcus mutans   Species of bacteria that may be related to dental decay.

stress test   Test that examines physiological reaction to an individual.

stroke volume   Amount of blood expelled from the heart during contraction.

subcutaneous fat   Fat layer beneath the skin.

sublingual spider nevi   Blood vessel pattern on the underside of the tongue, weblike in appearance.

substantia nigra   Area of the brain that undergoes a loss of dopamine-producing cells in Parkinson's disease.

Sunbelt   Made up of those states in the southern and southeastern regions of the United States.

sundowner syndrome   Behavioral pattern often exhibited at night among those who have undergone a loss in sensory stimulation.

superoxide dismutase   Enzyme that can scavenge free radicals.

support system   System of relationships (friends, neighbors, and family) in which health and social services are provided to the aged.

synovial membrane   Lining of a joint cavity.

systolic pressure   Denotes the force exerted when the heart beats, sending blood into the arteries.

tardive dyskinesia   Abnormal involuntary movement disorder caused by chronic use of antipsychotic agents.

thalamus   Main relay center in the brain for sensory impulses to cerebral cortex.

thermoregulation   Heat regulation.

thymus gland   Endocrine gland located in the chest which plays an essential role in immunity, it produces a hormone which directs the maturation of special immune cells.

thyrotoxicosis   Hyperactivity of the thyroid gland.

tinnitus   Ringing in the ears.

trabecular bone   Spongy bone that makes up long bone heads and vertebral bodies.

trypsin   Enzyme that digests protein.

tympanic membrane   Ear drum separating the external and middle ear.

Type I osteoporosis   Earlier fractures characteristic of trabecular bone such as vertebrae.

Type II osteoporosis   Later fractures that affect cortical bone such as the hip.

tyramine   Organic acid contained in red wine, bleu cheese or pickled herring that can imitate the effects of monoamine neurotransmitters (dopamine and norepinephrine) in the brain (a "false neurotransmitter").

urea   Final product of the decomposition of protein in the body, and form in which nitrogen is given off.

uremia   Renal or kidney failure.

ureolytic   Pertaining to the decomposition of urea.

uric acid   One of the products of protein metabolism found in the urine.

urinalysis   Microscopic or chemical analysis of the urine.

vaginismus   Involuntary spasm of the muscles surrounding the vagina which makes penetration painful or impossible.

varicella-zoster virus   Herpes virus that causes chicken pox and shingles.

vasocongestive response   Occurs when more blood flows into an organ than flows out of it.

veillonella   Genus of bacteria.

very-old   Those 85 years of age and older.

vesical   Small saclike or bladderlike cavity filled with fluid.

vital capacity   Total inspiration capacity and expiration reserve of the lungs.

vulva   External structures of the female genitalia.

water-soluble vitamins   Those vitamins that can be dissolved in water, such as vitamin C and the B complex.

wisdom   Interpretive knowledge combining breadth and depth.

xerosis   Dry skin.

young-old   Those aged 55 to 74 years.

Index